P9-CRS-831

IMAGES OF DEVIANCE AND SOCIAL CONTROL

A SOCIOLOGICAL HISTORY

Stephen J. Pfohl

Professor of Sociology
Boston College

105480

McGRAW-HILL BOOK COMPANY

New York St. Louis San Francisco Auckland Bogotá
Hamburg Johannesburg London Madrid Mexico Montreal New Delhi
Panama Paris São Paulo Singapore Sydney Tokyo Toronto

To the many students with whom I've worked. Your questions and concerns have given form to words that follow.

This book was set in Times Roman by J. M. Post Graphics, Corp.
The editors were Christina Mediate, David V. Serbun, and Barry Benjamin;
The production supervisor was Diane Renda.
The cover was designed by Janice Noto.
The illustrations were done by Joseph LaMantia and Stephen Pfohl.
R. R. Donnelley & Sons Company was printer and binder.

IMAGES OF DEVIANCE AND SOCIAL CONTROL

A Sociological History

Copyright © 1985 by McGraw-Hill, Inc. All rights reserved. Printed in the United States of America. Except as permitted under the United States Copyright Act of 1976, no part of this publication may be reproduced or distributed in any form or by any means, or stored in a data base or retrieval system, without the prior written permission of the publisher.

1 2 3 4 5 6 7 8 9 0 DOCDOC 8 9 8 7 6 5 4

See Acknowledgments on page xiii.
Copyrights included on this page by reference.

Library of Congress Cataloging in Publication Data

Pfohl, Stephen J.
Images of deviance and social control.

Includes bibliographies and index.
1. Deviant behavior. 2. Social control. 3. Power (Social sciences) 4. Deviant behavior—History.
I. Title.
HM291.P4849 1985 302.5'42 84-12274
ISBN 0-07-049757-5

WESTMAR COLLEGE LIBRARY

IMAGES OF DEVIANCE AND SOCIAL CONTROL

CONTENTS

PREFACE

This is a text about other texts and their context. The texts it examines are those used to explain nonconformity and justify its control. Their context is a changing landscape of power within western history. As structured arrangements of power have changed, so have society's images of those whom it fears. These people, whether we call them "criminals," "witches," "rebels," or "lunatics," have deviated from the dominant order. They stand outside the common sense of society and its relations of power. Whether by anguish, accident, or desire, they resist falling in line with that power. For some, resistance may be primarily symbolic. This, however, may be no less threatening than the nonconformity of those who strike out with their fists or checkbooks. Think of the considerable fear generated by people who feel different sexually, think different politically, or wear skin of a different color. In a world constructed as much by symbolic action as physical behavior, this may be reason enough to call in the forces of control.

The forces of control—they sweep in upon us in three waves. The first consists of a host of everyday social rituals. By these, individuals are born and bound into the collective life of society. If such rituals are successful, individuals will feel at home, both with themselves and with the "natural," or commonsensical, character of a social order. They will be engulfed by what Émile Durkheim referred to as a sense of collective conscience. They will be surrounded both from within and from without. Such rituals come in many forms. E. A. Ross's 1901 text *Social Control* pioneered the study of these matters by surveying such order-producing rituals as parenting, religion, education, the mass mediation of public opinion, ceremonial-like expressions of style and fashion, and the social organization of music, art, and visual imagery. The power of such rituals to produce conformity is, however, circumscribed by the distribution of power in society at large. In a society in which power is unequally distributed, conformity is undermined by the resistance of those less blessed by the existing order. Such deviance ushers in a second wave of control. On its crest ride various agents of containment—priests, police, doctors, judges, therapists, and the like. Whether by prayer, punishment, counseling, or surgery, these control agents strive to wash clean the shores of the dominant social order.

Behind the first two waves there rolls a third. It is constituted by explanations as to why certain forms of control are necessary and how they can best be executed. It provides a justification for certain arrangements of power and for the controls which secure their reign. This third wave consists of theorists and the conceptual images they produce about nonconformity. This text is about them and the knowledge they claim about deviants. It is a text about knowledge and its relationships to power.

The story told within this text is a sociological story. It is the story of how powerful theoretical images of deviance and social control blossom in the historical soil of one social landscape and languish in another. It employs a social-historical perspective to describe and analyze the theory, methods, and control policies associated with nine major ways of conceiving deviant behavior. The theoretical images examined span a wide variety of religious, legal, medical, psychological, social, economic, and political concerns. By examining how theoretical perspectives are related to programs of empirical research and practical public policy and by considering the continued importance of each in today's world, it is hoped that theory will come alive in the imagination of the reader. Rather than look at theories as dry, abstract, or highly technical propositions, this text locates these "ways of seeing" deviance in the politically charged social contexts in which they arise.

The work involved in producing this text has spanned nearly a decade, and those to be thanked for their support, encouragement, and criticism are many. The questions it pursues were first raised for me by Simon Dinitz and a cohort of exceedingly capable and creative graduate students with whom I studied sociological criminology at the Ohio State University. There my interest in the historical study of social theory was also nurtured by Gisela and Roscoe Hinkle and Clyde Franklin. In more recent years I am indebted to feedback from Richard Quinney and Charles Sarno. Charles worked tirelessly as my research assistant throughout this project. Thanks also to my many other colleagues at Boston College, particularly Sandra Joshel, John Williamson, Andrew Herman, Avery Gordon, David Karp, Lynda Holmstrom, Benedict Alper, John Donovan, Diane Vaughan, Susan Guarino Ghezzi, Michael Rustad, Cheryl Boudreaux, Javier Trevino, Phyllis Meaghan, Maria Pavlaki, Mary Brady, Robert Lavizzo-Mourey, Michele Garvin, Jennifer Wilton, Steven Dolliver, Kate Stout, Delia Johnson, Tom Shamshack, Jeanne Chislom, Dick Batten, Nancy Frankel, Ann Marie Roucheleau, and Laura Carr (who assisted in the preparation of the footnotes). Also acknowledged is the periodic input of Ray Michalowski, Ron Kramer, Malcolm Spector, Jim Thomas, and Peter Conrad, and the substantive support for this project provided by a grant from the National Institute of Mental Health and by Yale University, where I spent the 1981–82 academic year as a postdoctoral fellow in the sociology of social control. In New Haven the regular comments of Albert J. Reiss, Harry Mika, Kirk Williams, and Robert Holden proved invaluable. In Boston my companionship and conversation with Theresa Burns has provided a continuous source of care and inspiration, while thanks also go to David Serbun, Christina Mediate, Barry Benjamin, Eric Munson, and Rhona Robbin, my editors at McGraw-Hill, and to Gary Jensen, John DeLamater, and James MacIntosh, whose thoughtful review comments have helped guide this book into final form. My gratitude extends as well to Alice Close, Shirley Urban, and Sara White for their ceaseless assistance in converting my scribbling into a completed manuscript.

A final note of gratitude to Joseph LaMantia. Joseph and I created the illustrations found at the beginning of each chapter. These visual images were constructed from a variety of original drawings, photographic materials, and paintings. Each collage represents key elements of the theoretical images considered in this book. The process of collaboratively designing and producing these images was a particularly rewarding way of completing this manuscript.

Stephen J. Pfohl

ACKNOWLEDGMENTS

For permission to include material from copyright works, I owe thanks to the following authors and publishers. Specific citations are included in footnotes.

Theresa Burns. "The Sociology Room" from *Seven Dreams,* copyright © 1981, Theresa Burns. Used by permission of author.

Michel Foucault. Excerpt from pp. 3–5, *Discipline and Punish: The Birth of the Prison,* translated by Alan Sheridan, translation copyright © 1977 by Alan Sheridan. Reprinted by permission of Pantheon Books, a division of Random House.

Michael Jones and John Miller. Excerpts from lyrics of "Clampdown," from album *London Calling* by the Clash, copyright © 1979, Riva Music Inc. Reprinted by permission of publisher.

Jon King and Andrew Gill. Excerpt from lyrics of "Why Theory," from album *Solid Gold* by Gang of Four, copyright © 1981, Gill-King Inc. Excerpt from lyrics of "Muscle for Brains," from album *Songs of the Free* by Gang of Four, copyright © 1982, Gill-King Inc. Reprinted by permission of publisher.

Joseph LaMantia and Stephen Pfohl. Chapter opening illustrations: *Shadow Control, Sword of Sanctity, Cool Man Calculated Normalizing Relations, Adrift Chicago, The Social Machine, It Turns Me On, Suicidal Walkman, Enforced Imitation, Lining Labels,* and *Make-Over,* copyright © 1984, Marty Martin Productions Inc. Used by permission of publisher.

Joseph Stephans, "They Absolved Hinkley Yesterday. I Saw It on Television," and "Regress toward the Mean," from Author's Notebooks, copyright © 1984, Marty Martin Productions Inc. Used by permission of publisher.

Sting. Excerpt from lyrics of "Every Breath You Take," from album *Synchronicity* by the Police, copyright © 1983, Regetta Music Ltd. Reprinted by permission of publisher.

Mark Twain. Excerpts from "The War Prayer," pp. 394–398, *Europe and Elsewhere,* copyright © 1923, 1951. Used by permission of Harper and Row, Publishers, Inc.

Lesley Woods, Paul Ford, Pete Hammond, and Jane Monroe. Excerpts from lyrics of "Headache for Michelle," from album *Playing With a Different Sex* by Au Pairs, copyright © 1981, CBS Songs Ltd. Reprinted by permission of publisher.

Shadow Control By Joseph LaMantia and Stephen Pfohl

CHAPTER 1

IMAGES OF DEVIANCE AND SOCIAL CONTROL: *An Introduction*

We equate sanity with a sense of justice, with humaneness, with prudence, with the capacity to love and understand other people. We rely on the sane people of the world to preserve it from barbarism, madness, destruction. And now it begins to dawn on us that it is precisely the sane ones who are the most dangerous.

It is the sane ones, the well-adapted ones, who can without qualms and without nausea aim the missiles and press the buttons that will initiate the great festival of destruction that they, the sane ones have prepared. . . . No one suspects the sane, and the sane ones will have perfectly good reasons, *logical, well-adjusted reasons for firing the shot. They will be obeying sane orders that have come sanely down the chain of command. And because of their sanity they will have no qualms at all. . . . The ones who cooly estimate how many millions of victims can be considered expendable in a nuclear war, I presume they do all right with the Rorshach ink blots too. On the other hand, you will probably find that the pacifists and the ban-the-bomb people are, quite seriously, just as we read in* Time, *a little crazy.*

Thomas Merton[1]

The scene is a crowded church during the American Civil War. "It was a time of great and exalting excitement. The country was up in arms, the war was on, in every breast burned the holy fire of patriotism." So says Mark Twain in his short and searing parable—*The War Prayer.*[2] Amidst the clamor of beating drums, marching bands, and toy pistols popping, Twain describes an emotional church service. A passionate minister stirs the gallant hearts of eager volunteers, bronzed returning heroes, their families, friends, and neighbors. The inspired congregation await their minister's every word.

> And with one impulse the house rose, with glowing eyes and beating hearts, and poured out that tremendous invocation—
>
> God the all-terrible!
> Thou who ordainest,
> Thunder thy clarion
> and lightning thy sword!
>
> Then came the "long" prayer. None could remember the like of it for passionate pleading and moving and beautiful language. The burden of its supplication was that an ever-merciful and benignant Father of us all would watch over our noble young soldiers and aid, comfort, and encourage them in their patriotic work; bless them, shield them in the day of battle and the hour of peril, bear them in His mighty hand, make them strong and confident, invincible in the bloody onset; help them to crush the foe, grant to them and to their flag and country imperishable honor and glory.

Wars come and go. Words vary. Nonetheless, the essential message of this "God is on our side" sermon remains alarmingly the same. What is unusual in Twain's story happens next. It is not only unusual but "deviant." After the minister completes his moving prayer an "unnaturally pale," aged stranger enters the church. He is adorned with long hair and dressed in a body-length robe. He moves to the front, motions the startled minister aside, and informs the shocked parishioners that he is a messenger from Almighty God. He tells the congregation that God has heard their prayer and will grant it, but only after they consider the full import of their request. In a penetrating rephrasing of the original sermon the old messenger reveals the darker side of the congregation's prayer. When they ask blessing for themselves in battle they are, at the same time, praying for the merciless, barbaric, and unmentionable destruction of other human beings (their enemies). In direct and graphic language the messenger portrays the unspoken implications of their request.

> help us to tear their soldiers to bloody shreds with our shells;
> help us to cover their smiling fields with the pale forms of their patriotic dead;
> help us to draw the thunder of the guns with shrieks of their wounded, writhing in pain;
> help us to lay waste their humble homes with a hurricane of fire;
> help us to wring the hearts of their unoffending widows to unavailing grief;
> help us to turn them out roofless with their little children to wander unbefriended the wastes of their desolated land.

The strange old man continues—blight their lives, bring tears, and stain the snow with blood. He completes his war prayer with a statement about the humble and contrite hearts of those who ask God's blessings. The congregation pauses in silence. He asks if they still desire what they have prayed for. "Ye have prayed it; if ye still desire it, speak! The messenger of the Most High waits." We are now at the final page of Twain's book. The congregation's response is simple and abrupt. As suggested previously the old stranger was clearly a social deviant. In Twain's words: "It was believed afterward that the man was a lunatic, because there was no sense in what he said."

The stranger in *The War Prayer* directly threatens the normal, healthy, patriotic, and blood-lusting beliefs of the embattled congregation. Yet it is with ease that they contain and control this threat. They do not have to take seriously the chilling implications of his sermon. Their religious and patriotic senses are protected from his disturbing assault. Why? The reason is as simple as their response. It was believed that he was a lunatic. It was believed that he was a deviant. By classifying the old man as a deviant they need not listen to him. The congregation's beliefs are protected, even strengthened. The old lunatic's beliefs are safely controlled. *The War Prayer* is thus a story of how some people imagine other people to be "deviant," and thereby protect or isolate themselves from those whom they fear and from that which challenges the way in which "normal" social life is organized. It is a story of how people convince themselves of what is normal by condemning those who disagree. It is a story of both deviance and social control. So is the book you are reading.

CONTROLLING NORMAL AND DEVIANT SOCIAL LIFE

The story of deviance and social control is a battle story. It is a story of the battle to control the ways people think, feel, and behave. It is a story of winners and losers and of the strategies people use in struggles with one another. Winners in the battle to control "deviant acts" are crowned with a halo of goodness, acceptability, normality. Losers are viewed as living outside the boundaries of social life as it ought to be, outside the "common sense" of society itself. They may be seen by others as evil, sleazy, dirty, dangerous, sick, immoral, crazy, or just plain deviant. They may even come to see themselves in such negative imagery, to see themselves as *deviants*.

Deviants are only one part of the story of deviance and social control. Deviants never exist except in relation to those who attempt to control them. Deviants exist only in opposition to those whom they threaten and those who have enough power to control against such threats. The outcome of the battle of deviance and social control is this. Winners obtain the privilege of organizing social life as they see fit. Losers are trapped within the vision of others. They are labeled deviant and subjected to an array of current social control practices. Depending upon the controlling wisdom at a particular moment in history, deviants may be executed, beaten brutally, fined, shamed, incarcerated, drugged, hospitalized, or even treated to heavy doses of tender loving care. But first and foremost they are prohibited from passing as normal women or men. They are branded with the image of being deviant.

When we think of losers in the battle to control acceptable images of social life, it may seem natural to think of such persons as the burglar, the rapist, the homosexual, the mentally ill individual, the religious heretic, the exhibitionist, or the prostitute. Indeed common sense tells most of us that such people really are deviant. But where do we get this common sense from? How do we come to know that the acts of some people are deviant, while the acts of others are accepted as normal? Is it that deviants behave in a more dangerous or destructive fashion than other people? Some people think so. Is this really the case?

Think of the kinds of deviants described above. Are their behaviors truly more harmful than those of people not labeled as deviants? In many cases the answer is no.

Consider the burglar. Late at night she may sneak into your house, rip off your stereo, and sell it for a fraction of its worth to a "fence" who deals in stolen merchandise. If caught the burglar runs the risk of being incarcerated as a hard-core criminal deviant. But what about the respectable corporate executive who participates in decisions to manipulate gasoline prices or build unsafe automobiles? The executive may cause society far more damage than any burglar. Yet, if caught, the executive is far less likely to be viewed or treated as a serious deviant. The same goes for the lawfully wedded husband whose physical and mental assaults may cost his battered wife as much or more than any convicted rapist. Similar things might be said of the sexist heterosexual whose mixture of sex with manipulative power may cost his or her partners far more than the caress of an affectionate homosexual lover; or of the sane general whose decision to defend national honor at any price may harm society in a much worse fashion than the actions of any so-called mentally ill person; or the religious zealot whose witch-hunts and inquisitions cost more than the doubts of any heretic; or the clothing manufacturer whose seductive advertising may encourage people to steal in order to dress well and look right, and thereby cause far greater damage than the momentary embarrassment created by any exhibitionist; or the business person whose sale of her or his blind ambition for a wage may cost much more than a prostitute's sale of her or his body.

From the preceding examples it should be evident that many forms of labeled deviance are not more costly to society than the behaviors of people who are less likely to be labeled deviant. Why? The answer proposed by this book is that labeled deviants are viewed as such because they threaten the control of those with enough power to shape the way society imagines the boundary between good and bad, normal and pathological, acceptable and deviant. This is the crux of the effort to understand the battle between deviance and social control. Deviance is always the flip side of the coin used to procure social control.

THEORETICAL PERSPECTIVES: IMAGES OF DEVIANCE AND SOCIAL CONTROL

The present book is the story of one important aspect of the battle between deviance and social control. It is the story of the formation of theoretical perspectives on deviance. Such perspectives are ways of looking at and acting toward deviance. Throughout history priests, philosophers, politicians, police, therapists, social scientists, and others have produced a variety of theoretical perspectives on these matters. In this book we shall examine the dominant theoretical imagery, research strategies, and practical control policies associated with nine perspectives which have, at various points in time, captured the theoretical imagination of western society. A central theme in our investigation is that perspectives on deviance and control reveal as much or more about those who invent or use them as they do about deviance itself. This is particularly true when we consider the disciplinary backgrounds of those who use certain theoretical perspectives and the diverse ways in which power relations shape and are shaped by the manner in which people imagine nonconformity.

iES

Disciplinary Images of Deviance: Toward an Interdisciplinary Perspective

There are today numerous specialists in the study and control of deviance, professionals who provide expert opinions regarding the causes, consequences, and cures of nonconformity. Not all such specialists view deviance in the same way. Indeed, specialists often divide their vision along disciplinary lines. Psychiatrists, sociologists, psychologists, criminologists, medical researchers, and other specialists frequently present divergent and even contradictory images of deviance. In this sense images of deviance are commonly organized according to the selective vision of the disciplines into which specialists are trained. The images of deviance which someone is trained to see in the police academy vary greatly from those learned in medical school, in the psychology lab, the historical archive, the anthropological field study, the seminary, or the sociology classroom. This point is well illustrated in the following poem.

The Sociology Room

by Theresa Burns

In the sociology room
the children learn
that even dreams are colored
by your perspective.

I toss and turn all night.

The overspecialized division of theoretical images between competing disciplines is unfortunate. Some of the most fertile insights about deviance are those born in the cracks between disciplinary perspectives. There we are forced to confront such things as the rich and complex relationships between material and spiritual forces, between the economy and culture, between life today and life yesterday, between the body, mind, and social environment, or between society as we know it and society as it is organized in other places and times. Because of these things I have tried in this book to draw upon the diverse viewpoints of numerous disciplines. This is true in terms of the topics selected for study and the materials used to examine these topics. The topics, nine distinct theoretical images of deviance and social control, span the concerns of several disciplines. These include theology, law, medicine, psychology, anthropology, social work, special education, psychiatry, and sociology.

The materials used to examine these diverse theoretical images are also drawn from numerous disciplines. I have been trained as a sociologist, but in reading this book you will learn that I place great value on insights gathered from other, related fields of study. Throughout I have attempted to combine the vision of sociology with that of history. Other perspectives are used as well, those listed above and some that are considered more as "arts" than "sciences." In referring to materials from poetry, films, music, novels, paintings, I mean to do more than provide cute "arty" examples. By pointing to parallels between the images of deviance produced by scientific experts and those portrayed by various sorts of artists, I mean to suggest that both types of imagery arise out of a pool of common experience—the experience of people in history attempting to make sense of the long human struggle for control over ways of thinking, feeling, and behaving.

Power-Related Images of Deviance: Toward a Power-Reflexive Perspective

In addition to the way that theoretical imagery may be shaped by one's disciplinary perspective, images of deviance and control are also shaped by one's political viewpoint. Deviants challenge the power of those who benefit most from the way that society, or a particular segment of society, is organized. When deviants are opposed by those in power, it is because they threaten to destroy or destabilize the way things are. Sometimes this threat is economic. It affects the social organization of material resources. At other times deviance may affect the organization of spiritual, cultural, or aesthetic resources. At all times it is political. By this I mean that it affects the way that power is socially organized and used. It affects who gets to think, feel, or behave in a certain fashion, even against the resistance of others.

Deviance and its control are essentially political events. When the burglar steals a stereo, she is challenging those who have the power to organize economic relations. When a gay person follows his heart's desire, he is challenging the power of militant heterosexuals to define acceptable sexual relations. When the madman or madwoman mumbles to voices that others don't hear, he or she is challenging the power of those who demand that conversations be carried on in a rational, mutually understandable fashion. Deviance and its control are always political events. To speak about them is to speak, at least implicitly, about the way that power relations are socially organized. Because this is true, professional visions of deviance are also always informed, in part, by the political commitments of those who do the looking. Thus it is not surprising that those scholars who see the present political order as good or desirable are likely to see deviance in quite a different fashion than those who believe it to be highly imperfect, unjust, or immoral.

Those who fit comfortably into the existing political order may seek to explain the causes of deviance in such a manner as to better control deviant people. Such scholars are often well rewarded for their work. They may receive lucrative research grants or be awarded prestigious chairs in elite universities. Those who are less comfortable with things as they are might have visions of deviance which are less profitable. They may view deviance as but a troubling symptom of the way that society is organized by those in power. Such scholars may find that their more critical visions are less easily funded by those toward whom their criticisms are directed—the government and elite private foundations. Some might even find their ideas less publishable than those of a more conventional variety and thereby be denied access to prestigious positions in teaching and research.

How do you view our society? How do your professors and fellow students view the current political orders? Their viewpoint will impact on the way they formulate images of deviance and social control. The study of deviance and social control is decidedly political. It is never neutral or value-free. This does not mean that those of us who study these things should give up our search for maximum clarity of vision, for maximum objectivity. We must not. Our search for clarity and objectivity must be continuous. This search must also include a willingness to expose, reflect upon, and even revise our political vision in accordance with what we learn and unlearn. Otherwise the end point of our scholarly journey will be no different than its beginning. We may see much, but we will miss seeing how power relations penetrate deeply all discussions of deviance, and how we ourselves may be penetrated by power. We must, in other words, carefully attend to the diverse ways in which our own political vision shapes and is shaped by what we understand about those who refuse or fail to conform.

The materials presented in this book are intended to aid our search for maximum clarity and objectivity. They do so, not by pretending that we can become fully detached from political commitments, but by systematically exploring the ways that certain political commitments become attached to our images of deviance and social control. In examining nine theoretical images we shall also be examining the political ties and ramifications of each of these ways of conceiving nonconformity. In this sense, we shall be using what might be described as a *power-reflexive perspective*. In examining the interweaving of theoretical and political visions we shall continuously reflect upon and perhaps clarify and become more objective about the political commitments which lie behind or in front of our own vision.

Which images fit our own vision of how things are and should be? Which attract us? Which are we repulsed by? By exploring these questions we come to a deeper and more comprehensive understanding of our own politics—of our own relationship to and responsibility for the past, present, and future organization of power in society. We will never be totally clear or totally objective. We are, after all, part of the world we are studying. As the Bible says, we in this world see, but as through a glass darkly. Yet we can shed as much light as possible upon matters which remain poorly illuminated. We will not discover any absolute truths about deviance and social control. There are none. I hope that we will discover some better ways of looking; ways which we did not have at the beginning of our journey; ways which provide a clearer and more objective vision of how we deviate from and exert control over one another; and ways which, if we so chose, may aid us in acting better toward one another, and in together organizing a better world.

UNEASY QUESTIONS: SUBSTANTIVE AND PERSONAL CONCERNS

There is little escape from the questions raised in the preceding pages. Whether dealing with a strange-acting roommate, an unfaithful lover, a frightening mugger, or a politician promising to reinstitute the death sentence, we are confronted daily with questions of deviance and the often harsh realities of social control. Nor are such questions easy. In fact, they are quite uneasy. They are uneasy in two senses. They are uneasy because questions about what causes deviance and its control are difficult to answer. In subsequent chapters we will examine a range of proposed answers. Some place the burden of deviance on the free choice of nonconformists. Others view deviance as biologically or psychologically determined. Another views it as something which is learned. Still another sees deviance as primarily a problem of overly repressive social control. Which, if any, are correct? By what standards is correctness measured? The task before us is an uneasy one. It requires that we dig deeply into the social, political, and economic landscapes out of which images of deviance are born and upon which they implant their vision of social control.

What are the major perspectives that humans have used to make sense of deviance and make sensible certain programs of social control? Where do these perspectives come from? Like acts of deviance and strategies of social control, theoretical images are produced at certain moments of history. Put into practice they create history as well. What are their consequences? How well have they stood the tests of time, experience, and systematic research? How exactly have they been translated into social control policy and practice? What are their social, political, or economic implications? What should we think of them? Are they sound or unproven, helpful or useless, good or bad? These are the central substantive questions which will occupy us during our journey through this book. They are not easy questions to answer. They require that we combine questions of theory with those of research and practice.

Questions about deviance and social control are uneasy at a second level as well. This is at the level of our own personal choices, feelings, and political commitments. At this level questions about deviance and social control challenge us to go beneath our surface thoughts and feelings to become reflective and critical about things we have come to take for granted as acceptable and things we oppose or are even repulsed by. How is it that we have come to accept or reject certain ways of thinking, feeling, and acting? How have we been influenced or shaped by the processes which promote social control and/or deviance? What are the consequences for others and for ourselves of living within the confines of our present social, economic, and political realities?

How do we benefit or lose by accepting or deviating from the dominant realities of our time? How are the lives of others directly or indirectly influenced by the way we presently endorse normality and oppose deviance? Could we do better? Should we seek to alter the images of deviance produced in the context of present social, political, and economic arrangements? Would we be deviants if we did? These are the second set of uneasy questions that confront us. They will not and should not make us feel comfortable. They ask us, not only about who we are, but about who we could become as well.

The uneasy nature of our questions about deviance and social control is quite real. It is not an uncommon experience for the serious student of such matters to experience an initial sense of dizziness, a sense of lost innocence about the "natural" character of things that were previously taken for granted as being simply deviant. If you are unwilling to risk this discomforting experience, stop reading now. If, on the other hand, you are willing to examine critically the simultaneous formation of deviant and normal realities, including the ways that our own personal realities have been shaped by the ever-present processes of social control, the end experience can be quite exhilarating.

Our worlds can become wider and deeper. This expansion will lead behind and below the ordinary surface of everyday social life; by taking a hard look both at deviants, who they are and what they do, and at control processes, at who or what gets controlled, how, and why. This expansion can provide us with the freedom of greater personal and social movement. Some of the old, "seemingly natural" binds, bonds, taboos, and rules may loosen up. This new awareness may permit us greater space within which to celebrate the dance that is human life. It may also present us with new senses of human responsibility for our actions and those of our fellow deviants and controllers alike. Having said all of this, it may be useful to provide a brief overview of the form and content of the present book. We begin with some additional thoughts on the meaning of theoretical perspectives and their relationship to the study and control of deviance.

THEORETICAL PERSPECTIVES: CONCEIVING AND CONTROLLING DEVIANCE

Any "theory" of deviance is much more than a set of abstract notions about its causes, nature, and consequences. . . . An image of deviance determines one's action in concrete instances. It underlies the individual's pronouncements and it even determines what he considers deviant.

J. L. Simmons[3]

I walk into the darkened room. It is late and I am weary. I click on the light. From the shadows leans a coiled shape. A snake poised to strike! I jump back, grabbing for something to ward off the attack. My eyes blink. I look again. My frozen posture yields a sigh of relief. I laugh. A snake? The coiled object is simply my garden hose. How could I have forgotten that I left it there? Its sight sent me into such a state of alarm. Only now do I recognize the tension that had gripped my whole body. The hammer that I had reflexively clenched in my fist. Why had I perceived the hose as a snake? Perhaps it was the mood I was in, the movie I just saw, or my apprehension about tomorrow. Whatever it was, once I defined the object as a snake, as a danger, I instantaneously mobilized my defenses against it.

The term *theoretical perspective* may sound rather abstract and boorishly academic. It is, however, no more abstract than the snake in the preceding narrative. Theoretical perspectives are ways of naming, ways of conceptually ordering our senses of the world. They are tools with which we decide what it is that we experience, why something is the way that it is, and how it is that we might act or react to it. Having defined the shape as a snake, I direct my action toward it in a particularly defensive manner. Why? Because coiled snakes are dangerous to one's health. The coiled shape was, from my perspective, a real danger that demanded defense. Cast into another perspective its meaning and my actions toward it change. This was the case when I redefined it as a hose. The shape didn't change. What changed was my perspective on it. That change made all the difference.

Theoretical perspectives provide us with an image of what something is and how we might best act toward it. They name something as this type of thing and not that. They provide us with the sense of being in a world of relatively fixed forms and content. Theoretical perspectives transform a mass of raw sensory data into understanding, explanations, and recipes for appropriate action. Without them we would be lost in space and time. Everything would be undefined, in flux, without order, chaotic. Without theoretical perspectives we would have no control over what we experience. Such chaos is the stuff of nightmares. In the nightmare, terrifying changes of perspective are beyond our control. Our kind mother becomes the vampire, our pet dog a hideous monster, our room a darkened void in space. Without the guidance of theoretical perspectives we are lost, unable to define, explain, or know how to act toward the objects of our experience.

The link between theoretical perspectives and the sense of having control over a world of ordered experience is important. To have a theoretical perspective on something, to name it in a certain fashion, is the first step in gaining control over it. To cast something into a theoretical perspective is to control it by restricting it to being a certain type of thing. By its being named a snake, the coiled object was trapped in the theoretical imagery in which I conceived it. For the moment it could be nothing else. It was caught in a web of names: frozen in a perspective. In the words of philosopher Jean-Paul Sartre, to cast something into a theoretical perspective is "to catch living things in the trap of phrases." Describing this naming process as one of "persistent illusion," Sartre suggested that by combining words ingeniously, "the object would get tangled up in the signs. I would have hold of it."[4]

Sartre may have correctly described the illusionary quality of theoretical perspectives. They are nonetheless powerful illusions. They exert control over that which they name. This, biblical scholars inform us, is the reason that the God of the Old Testament never revealed his name to his followers. He was known only as the unnameable Yahweh or "He who is." He refused to be cornered into a name by those who professed to be his servants.

Deviants have been less fortunate. Throughout history they have been the subject of numerous namings, numerous theoretical perspectives. Each provided explanatory images regarding why people deviate and images of control, images suggesting strategies for restoring conventionality. Some of these theoretical perspectives have been simple, relatively unreflected upon, and, for the most part, taken for granted. They may be called *commonsense theoretical perspectives*.

There are today a variety of competing commonsense perspectives on deviance. As J. L. Simmons points out, one may alternatively consider the deviant as sick, as a boat-rocker, as immoral, as statistically rare, as a hero, or as just another human being. Each perspective sheds light on some aspects of deviance, while casting a shadow on others. Moreover, most people think and act on the basis of different perspectives in different concrete situations. According to Simmons, "a person will usually have different attitudes toward different kinds of deviants; he sees the drug addict as sick, the promiscuous woman as depraved, the rowdy neighborhood youth as a disturber of the peace, his spiritualist friend as curiously different, the hobo he passes as semi-heroic, and his adulterous brother as understandably human and male."[5]

While recognizing the importance of commonsense theoretical perspectives, the present book is concerned with another type of theoretical imagery—the *formal theoretical perspective*. Formal theoretical perspectives are generally more elaborate, more explicitly stated, and subject to a continuous process of refinement and validation. It is upon formal theoretical perspectives that society erects its public policies for dealing with deviance. While this is true, one should not exaggerate the distinction between commonsense and formal theories. These two ways of theorizing are at all times interrelated. Formal theories grow out of and feed back upon theories grounded in the "common sense" of a particular period in history. The various spiritual, social, political, and economic forces affecting common sense influence and are influenced by the formal theories of a given age. As a result, in examining formal theories we must remain attentive to the various ways that such perspectives are grounded in the material and spiritual realities of everyday social existence.

FORMAL THEORIES OF DEVIANCE IN THE WEST

We all have opinions. Where do they come from? Each day seems like a natural fact and how we think changes how we act.

Jon King and Andrew Gill[6]

Any one human act can be conceptualized in terms of literally hundreds of formal theoretical perspectives. Each names the act in a particular way, directing attention to certain of its aspects, while selectively ignoring others. Consider the police officer blowing her whistle. This act could be conceptualized in terms of physical principles explaining the generation of whistle sound waves, biological principles of human breath exhalation, psychological principles associated with her need to assert her authority, anthropological principles suggesting the cultural meaning of whistle blowing among advanced primates in North America, or sociological principles related to the norms governing police-citizen encounters, etc., etc., etc. This list could go on and on. The same can be said of perspectives on deviance and social control.

Throughout the remainder of this book we shall take an in-depth look at what I believe to be nine of western society's more important theoretical perspectives on deviance and control. Each offers a distinctive theoretical image of what deviance is, how it can best be studied, and how it should be controlled. Why nine perspectives? There is nothing magical about the number. This is simply how I have categorized, or lumped together, the major strands of thought, study, and action directed regarding deviance and social control. Had I arranged these matters somewhat differently, perhaps we would be talking about four, twelve, or twenty perspectives. Several of the nine perspectives contain a variety of subthemes or subperspectives. Each is considered in somewhat chronological fashion. The first, the supernatural or demonic perspective, is certainly the oldest way of making sense out of nonconformity. The last, the conflict perspective, is perhaps the most controversial of perspectives today. Yet there is considerable overlap. They are ordered in terms of the general time periods in which each emerged as influential or dominant. Each, however, is still alive and important in today's world.

Why consider only western images of deviance? The choice is purely pragmatic.

I am writing primarily for an audience of American and western European students. As such I am writing about the perspectives that have been used to conceive and control deviance in the times and places that are closest to home. To include perspectives originating in the historical lives of Asian, African, and other nonwestern peoples would require a volume much larger than that which you see before you. If, by chance, this book should encourage some reader to explore comparative or cross-cultural theoretical developments, I trust that we all will be richer for the experience. On the other hand, there are good practical reasons why nonwestern readers might be interested in this story of western perspectives on deviance. In the hearts and minds of western colonizers, imperialists, and missionaries, these perspectives have frequently been used to control the behaviors of indigenous peoples the globe over.

HOW THIS BOOK IS ORGANIZED

The next nine chapters explore a number of competing images of the deviant and how she or he might be controlled. Each image is attached to a constellation of theoretical research and practical human concerns. Of what do these images consist? Where do they come from? To whom do they appeal? How do they get translated into research? How are they related to practical social control policy? How useful are they in terms of research, policy, and the promotion of a just human order? These are the central questions raised in each of the following chapters.

The nine perspectives on deviance and control cover a wide range of thought and action. Each is considered with three general objectives in mind. These include: (1) describing the basic theoretical imagery, research strategies, and social control policies associated with each perspective; (2) locating each within a general sociohistorical framework, and (3) developing a sense of critical evaluative thinking regarding a perspective's strengths and weaknesses.

Describing the Basic Theoretical Imagery, Research Strategies, and Control Policies An in-depth description of these issues is the primary objective of this book. Remember that the way we look at deviance shapes our reaction to it. This is true in terms of both public policy and personal response. Deviance is not one thing. It is as many things as there are ways of looking at it. The same is true for methodological strategies for identifying and studying deviance. The same is true for social control.

As suggested previously, how one conceives of deviance influences and is influenced by one's methods of research and one's ideas about appropriate strategies of social control. Each of the perspectives discussed in this book is aligned with a particular methodology for identifying and studying deviance. Each is also associated with a unique vision of social control. A detailed description of the theory, methods, and control policies related to each perspective is the first objective of each of the following chapters.

Theoretical Images and Their Sociohistorical Context Different perspectives have dominated different periods in history. What factors contribute to the popularity or predominance of one perspective over another? How is it that each perspective remains influential today? Perspectives do not live or die on their scientific merits alone. Some fit better into particular historical constellations of political, economic, cultural, and social forces. Others are rejected precisely because they do not. To adequately understand the development and acceptance of a given perspective we must locate its emergence and use within a particular social-historical landscape. Why does it blossom in the soils of one landscape and languish in another? This is a second objective of the following chapters—to provide a historical framework in which to view theoretical images of deviance and the research and control strategies with which they are connected.

Developing the "Conceptual Tools" of Critical Assessment Competing perspectives on deviance may be valued highly by those who advocate them. This does not mean that each is equally valuable as a tool for research, an instrument of public policy, or a contributor to a just human order. Each has its strengths and weaknesses, its theoretical, methodological, and practical advantages and disadvantages.

Which is best? I cannot answer this for you. Some perspectives you will like. Others you will not. The important thing is to develop an informed critical sense of your own. I will try to assist you by evaluating what I believe to be the merits and drawbacks of each perspective. My own preferences will undoubtedly shine through. I have attempted to ground these preferences in sound logic and an assessment of all the available evidence. It is my hope that you will do the same.

I will not tell you what to think about this or that approach to deviance. There are already too many people telling you that already. Day in and day out we are bombarded with their opinions. The television, radio, newspaper, classroom, dormitory, and workplace are full of messages about why people should act in a certain fashion and what happens to the deviants who don't. The campaigning politician, the concerned parent, teachers, landlords, bosses, and lovers all hit us with similar messages. They tell us who and what is considered deviant, and why deviance is to be controlled in some specific way.

How are we to think, feel, and act about such matters? As mentioned previously, there is no easy answer to this question. Yet, think, feel, and act we must. We must make decisions about deviance and its control. If we don't, others will make them for us. The third objective of the following chapters involves learning a critical approach to such decision-making. In adopting this approach, the task of evaluating various perspectives will become yours as well as mine. We may agree. We may not. If you believe my analysis is correct, it will be because you have thoughtfully arrived at the same conclusion. If you disagree, your dissent will be similarly grounded. As author and reader we will enter into a dialogue that is informed, responsible, and articulate.

With these things in mind, let us begin our journey into competing images of deviance and control. Our consideration of each perspective is divided into five sections: (1) basic theoretical image; (2) dominant strategies for identifying and/or studying deviance; (3) related strategies of social control; (4) the perspective today; and (5) an assessment of the perspective's adequacy. We will start with the "demonic perspective." This perspective envisions deviance as sin and social control as a matter of religious duty.

NOTES

1 Thomas Merton, "A Devout Meditation in Memory of Adolph Eichmann," as excerpted in *Edward Rice, The Man in the Sycamore Tree: The Good Times and Hard Life of Thomas Merton,* Doubleday, Garden City, N.Y., 1970, p. 89.
2 All the excerpts from Twain's poem are taken from Mark Twain, *The War Prayer,* Harper & Row, New York, 1970.
3 J. L. Simmons, *Deviants,* Glendessary, Berkeley, Calif., 1969, pp. 12–13.
4 Jean-Paul Sartre, *The Words,* Braziller, New York, 1964, p. 184.
5 Simmons, *Deviants,* p. 24.
6 Jon King and Andrew Gill, lyrics from "Why Theory?", from Gang of Four album, *Solid Gold.*

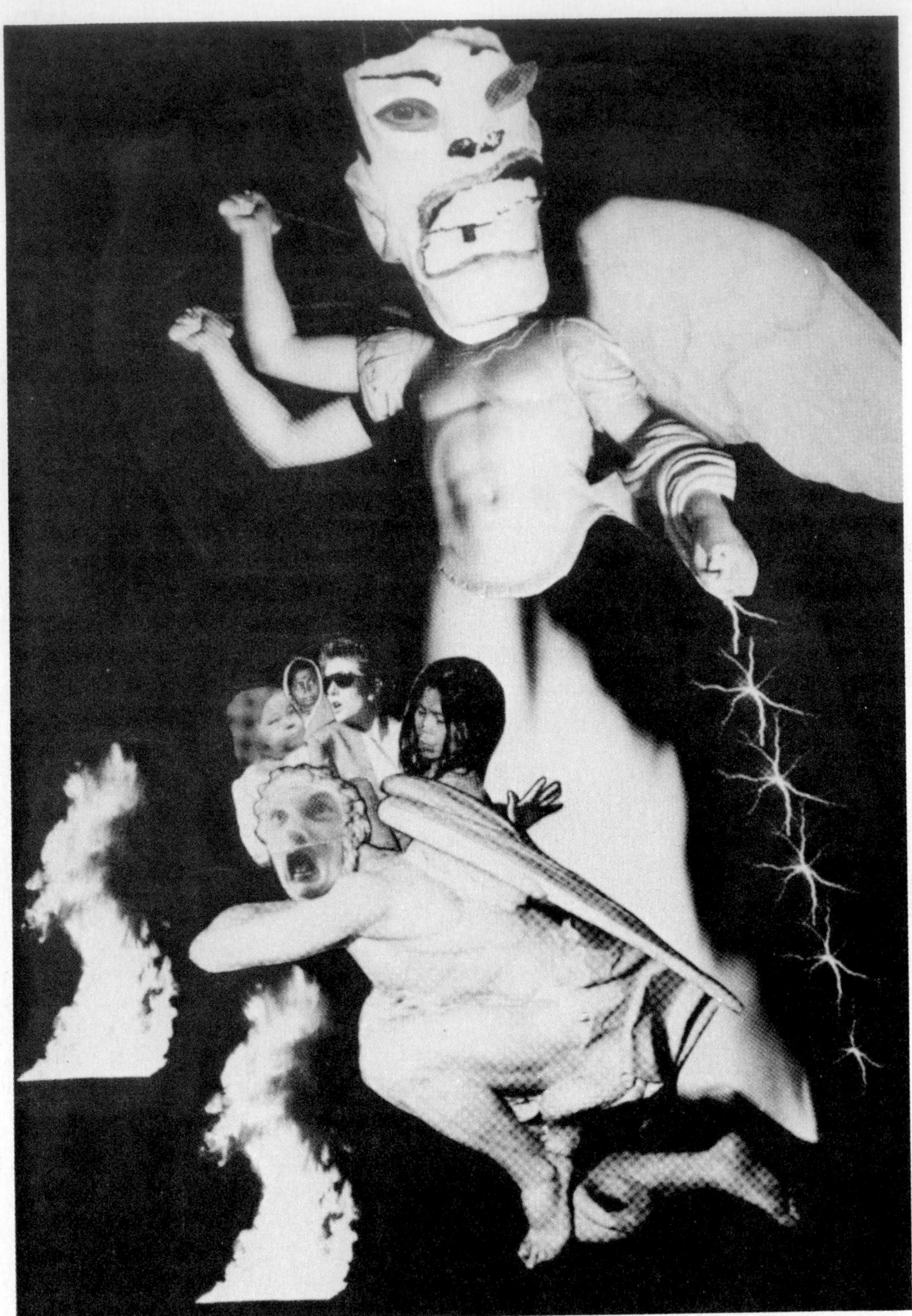

Sword of Sanctity By Joseph LaMantia and Stephen Pfohl

CHAPTER **2**

THE DEMONIC PERSPECTIVE: *Otherworldly Interpretations of Deviance*

I have seen the grim statistics on divorce, broken homes, abortion, juvenile delinquency, promiscuity and drug addiction. I have witnessed firsthand the human wreckage and the shattered lives that statistics can never reveal in their totality. I am convinced that we need a spiritual and moral revival in America if America is to survive the twentieth century.

Rev. Jerry Falwell[1]

Pilate went back into the palace and called Jesus to him. "Are you King of the Jews?" he asked. . . . "Indeed I am a King," Jesus replied; "the reason for my birth and the reason for my coming into the world is to witness to the truth. Every man who loves truth recognizes my voice.". . . To which Pilate retorted, "What is 'truth'? . . . Won't you speak to me? Don't you realize that I have the power to set you free, and the power to have you crucified?" "You have no power at all against me," replied Jesus, "except what was given to you from above."

John 18:33, 37–38; 19:10–11

INTRODUCTION

On February 16, 1980, a fight broke out between Arne Johnson and his best friend, Alan Bono. The 19-year-old Johnson had gone over to Bono's house to help repair a broken radio. With him were his two teenage sisters and his girl friend. Within a short time an event occurred which radically altered the course of Arne Johnson's life and ended that of his friend. Alan had been drinking. He started talking rudely to the young women. Arne took offense. A fight broke out. A knife flashed—a 5-inch folding knife. It belonged to Arne Johnson. Alan Bono died. In the fall of 1981 Arne Johnson stood trial for Bono's death.[2]

The trial of Arne Johnson was a puzzling and dramatic event. I suppose any trial of a shy, gentle small-town Connecticut boy who had delivered papers and captured Little League trophies would be somewhat puzzling and dramatic. But Arne's trial was more puzzling and more dramatic. This was not simply because he was known as "such a nice boy," an All-American boy, a boy who had once used his "Newsboy of the Year" prize money to buy his mother a much-needed second-hand car. Nor was it because he had been "such a religious boy," a boy who had been honored by his local minister for bringing in the most students to his Bible class. What made Arne Johnson's trial so puzzling and dramatic was the basis for his plea of not guilty. Without challenging the facts of the stabbing, Arne's attorney argued that he should not be held criminally responsible for Bono's death. Why? The reason, we are told, is because at the time of the stabbing Arne Johnson had been possessed by a demonic spirit.

A demonic spirit? This sounds like something out of a "made for TV" horror movie. So do the other "facts" of Arne's case. These involve what, in Connecticut, has become known as the strange case of the "Brookfield demons." The case begins in the home of the Glatzel family. Debbie Glatzel was Arne Johnson's girl friend. Arne was around when Debbie's younger brother began acting strangely. The 11-year-old Glatzel reported seeing frightening apparitions. He had been helping Debbie move into her new apartment when he suddenly felt shoved from behind. When he turned around he saw the shape of an elderly man pointing an ominous finger in his direction. He heard the voice of the old man warning him to beware. The old man disappeared as quickly as he had come. The frightened boy asked his mother to take him home. Later that evening he experienced a second vision, this one more terrifying than the first. It was the old man again. This time he had cloven feet and was accompanied by two hideous-looking "helpers." The first appeared to have a bullet hole in his forehead. His face dripped with blood from the open wound. The second was a dark figure—burned and blackened. This nightmarish trio would return several times to frighten and harass the young Glatzel boy. They would shortly be joined by some forty other "demons."

Several weeks after the initial apparitions Debbie Glatzel's younger brother was plagued by all the classic symptoms that experts associate with demonic possession. Two such experts, psychic researchers Lorraine and Ed Warren, were recommended to the Glatzel family by their parish priest. The Warrens were well known in psychic circles for their previous investigations of the so-called Amityville Horror. During the first ten minutes of the Warrens' visit to the Glatzel home they heard loud knocking and a banging beneath their feet. Within a short time they decided that the Brookfield case fit a known pattern of what they understood as demonic possession.

The Warrens joined with Catholic priests from the diocese of Bridgeport in trying to aid the afflicted 11-year-old boy. Arne Johnson also tried to help. He was there as the "possessed" child's symptoms multiplied. The child began to quote esoteric passages from Milton's *Paradise Lost*. The child had no prior knowledge of these texts. How is it that he recited them precisely? How was he able to report accurately on events that occurred in rooms beyond his sight and hearing? Was it the same way in which he foretold events that were yet to happen? He once told a young woman that the demons were going to "fix" her; that they were going to do something to her eye.

The next day her own child "accidentally" poked his thumb into her eye. She had to be taken to an emergency room for treatment. He told of an auto accident that subsequently occurred and accurately predicted that a neighborhood dog would be hit by a car. He also informed Arne Johnson that Arne was to die the next day. Arne fell out of a 70-foot tree. His fall was partly broken when his foot became ensnared in one of the branches. He was injured but did not die.

A team of Catholic priests performed four religious rituals aimed at freeing the boy from his possession. Arne Johnson was present at two of these ceremonies—a high mass celebrated at the Glatzel home and an all-night vigil conducted at a local convent. Johnson assisted in restraining the boy while his body shuddered under one or another of his strange "attacks." On one occasion he did more than that. He challenged the "demons" to substitute his body for that of the afflicted boy. According to Ed Warren, "He saw this little boy choking, strangling, being beaten and thrown across the room. He screamed out 'Don't do it to him. Do it to me. Take me on. I'm stronger.' Nobody, not the priests nor the nuns nor Lorraine nor myself would ever say anything like that, because we know the consequences."[3]

The consequences—? According to the Warrens and other observers, Arne Johnson also began to display symptoms of possession. At least four times between August and the following February Johnson exhibited signs of "being taken over." One time he fell into a seizure of violent shaking. In another instance he smashed his fist through a chest of drawers. The next day he recalled nothing of the incident. A third time he was presented with a vision of a figure which proceeded to slap and shake him. The fourth time was the night of Alan Bono's murder. When Arne Johnson's case went to court, Ed and Lorraine Warren were prepared to testify that, at the time of his argument with Bono, Arne was again seized by demons and that the demons directed his hand in the brutal stabbing of his friend.

The case of the "Brookfield demons" and the murder of Alan Bono is most extraordinary because it occurred in a time and place far from those in which demonic possession was viewed as a plausible interpretation of deviant behavior. Perhaps it would be less extraordinary if it had occurred during the Middle Ages or in bewitched Salem, Massachusetts, during the seventeenth century or in some tribal society which even today experiences the "reality" of the spirit world as a "reality" equal to or greater than the "reality" of the natural world. In such other contexts the "demonic perspective" functions as a powerful explanation of the causes, consequences, and control of deviant behavior. In our own western society such a perspective is apt to be viewed as little more than superstition.

It has been several centuries since western society has operated under a "sacred canopy" of supernatural understanding. Historians of religious thought trace our own "breakthrough" into essentially secular, naturalistic, or nonreligious explanations of the world to a constellation of events occurring between the fifteenth and nineteenth centuries. Such scholars point to the fracturing of a unitary Christianity under Protestantism, the spread of secular economic rationality under capitalism, the primacy of reason during the eighteenth-century Enlightenment, and the development of modern science and technology as forces of secularization.[4]

What does it mean to have a secularized as opposed to a supernatural or "demonic" view of the world? According to the sociologist Peter Berger, secularization refers to "the process by which sectors of society and culture are removed from the domination of religious institutions and symbols. . . . Put simply, this means that the modern West has produced an increasing number of individuals who look upon the world and their own lives without the benefit of religious interpretations."[5]

If western society has become increasingly secularized, why begin a consideration of theoretical perspectives on deviance with a perspective whose dominance is largely in the past? The answer is severalfold. First, as seen in the case of the Brookfield demons, our contemporary world is not entirely devoid of demonic or supernatural theories about what causes people to act deviantly. Additional evidence for this position is presented later in this chapter. Second, in order to fully appreciate the form and content of what are currently more acceptable or more plausible theories of deviance, it is important to understand that which went before and that against which these secular understandings do battle. Third, critics of certain modern secular perspectives have recently argued that some of these are little more than the same old demonic explanation under a new guise. In order to understand and evaluate such a critique we must first examine the nature of the demonic perspective in its original form.

THEORETICAL IMAGE

To go against the order of society as religiously legitimated . . . is to make a compact with the primeval forces of darkness.

Peter L. Berger[6]

The demonic perspective is the oldest of all known perspectives on deviance. It suggests that we look for the cause and cure of deviant behavior in the realm of the supernatural. Deviance is equated with sin. It is viewed as a transgression against the will of God (or the gods). According to the demonic perspective the human world is but a battleground for the forces of another, more powerful world—the world of the supernatural. We humans are pictured as constantly torn between the supernatural forces of good and those of evil. When we succumb to the influence of evil forces we are drawn into deviant behavior. This happens in one of two ways: through temptation or through possession.

The road of temptation is the first route to demonic deviance. Along this road we are reduced by the alluring temptations of that which is evil. The biblical story of Adam and Eve's fall from grace into the domain of Satan is the prototype of all such seductions into deviance. Lured on by the promise of God-like knowledge, our biblical parents eat the forbidden fruit and are thereafter weakened and forever susceptible to the dark forces of evil. As the story goes we inherit their weakness. Also seducible by the devil, we must fight a constant battle to stay on the straight and narrow path of the good.

The first road to demonic deviance, the road of temptation, is one in which we humans are afforded some measure of choice. We can, in principle, say no to Satan (or whichever demonic figure our particular religious tradition employs to symbolize the forces of evil). Yet, following our ancestral fall from grace, we are said to be weakened and seducible by the multiple forms taken by the devil—sloth, anger, lust, pride, envy, gluttony, greed, or however else one might catalogue the "deadly sins" of deviance.

The second road to demonic deviance is more determinant. This is the road of possession. A possessed person is believed to be literally taken over by the devil or by some evil spirit. Once possessed, a person may be viewed as no longer responsible—as no longer able to choose between good and evil, sin or conformity. But could an essentially good or innocent person ever become possessed? The demonic perspective is not entirely clear about this. It does suggest, however, that the possession of innocents may, on occasion, be possible. A case in point involves the outbreak of witchcraft in the Massachusetts Bay Colony in 1692. This case will be considered in greater detail later. For now it is sufficient to point out that the religious officials who attempted to control the manifestation of the devil in Salem made a clear distinction between a small cadre of possessed girls who had been "taken over" by Satan and the accused witches who were believed to have been seduced into acting as "mediums" or "hand maidens" for Satan's demonic mischief. The girls were to be given spiritual assistance. The witches were to be burned.

In summary, there are two roads to demonic deviance—temptation and possession. The first is less deterministic than the second. Yet, in neither does a deviant ever act entirely on his or her own. Behind every act of deviance lurks the devil. Viewed from this perspective, the deviant might quite literally employ the language of comedian Flip Wilson in proclaiming: "The devil made me do it."

One other thing should be considered when describing the theoretical image of deviance under the demonic perspective. This involves what might be called the "cosmic consequences" of any deviant act. From the demonic viewpoint deviant acts are believed to harm more than a particular or immediate victim. Each act of sin or deviance is also a transgression against God. Beyond that, it is also an act against the whole order of nature itself, against the entire cosmos. Every creature in the cosmos—all plants, rocks, animals, and fellow humans—is affected by the deviant behaviors of others. In this sense the vested interests of all are clearly linked to the control of deviance. This sense of deviance as "cosmic disruption" is found in numerous religious and literary depictions. Deviance brings the storm or the shadow over the whole of the earthly world and human community.

In performances of Shakespeare's *Macbeth,* theatrical imagery effects are often used to convey this sense of the cosmic consequences of deviance. Macbeth and Lady Macbeth tragically succumb to the temptations of ambition and greed. They set out to kill King Duncan in order to gain his throne. In doing so, they not only assume the bloody stains of their own deviance but radically upset the whole balance of nature itself. As the murderous knife strikes, so does the sound of thunder. In the background we hear the terrified sounds of screeching horses and baying dogs. All of creation feels the consequences of this deviance. Peace and order will not be restored until the guilty pay the price for their demonic acts.

Instigated by the devil and affecting the entirety of the cosmos—these are the essential features of the demonic perspective. How are the perpetrators of such deviance to be identified and controlled? In examining these issues the next two sections, after a brief side trip to present-day Africa, take a step backward into western history, back to a period in which the demonic perspective reigned supreme. The demonic perspective continues in the west today but nowhere to the extent it did during the Middle Ages. Thus, my description of the identification and control of demonic deviance is drawn largely from past history.

IDENTIFYING DEMONIC DEVIANCE

Anthropologist Raymond Verdier provides us with a fascinating account of what might be called the identification of demonic deviance among the Kabré tribe of northern Togo.[7] For the Kabré justice means two things: conformity to the plan of the creating God, and respect for the God-given ways of tribal custom. The "justice of men" must then always reflect the "justice of God" in a society organized around what are predominantly supernatural beliefs. But how exactly is this form of justice accomplished? The Kabré employ a form of public trial or a tribunal of "notable elders" who attempt to hear evidence and reconcile disputes between tribal members who cannot settle allegations of wrongdoing in private. Judicial decisions, however, may not always be so simple. How is guilt assessed when alleged acts of deviance involve matters where there are no visible witnesses? Of particular concern is the matter of witchcraft or the hurting of others by casting an evil spell.

When accusations of witchcraft are put forward the tribe consults a diviner. Such persons are believed to possess a God-given "second sight" such that they can trace the origins of evil spirits and spells. The expert testimony of a diviner is, however, open to challenge. In this sense the role of the diviner is much like that of a psychiatrist in a contemporary criminal trial within our own society. The opinion of the diviner may be very damaging. Yet, if it is denied by the accused, the tribal judges must seek a clearer reading on deviance by consulting God. This is done by subjecting the accused to a very painful trial by ordeal. An accused person who overcomes this ordeal is declared innocent. One such diagnostic ritual consists of having the accused plunge his or her hand into a pan of blazing oil in an effort to retrieve an iron ring without being burned. Of the person who succeeds, it is said *bi li sa i,* "it got him out"; of the one who fails, *bi kpa i,* "it took him."

The Kabré trial by ordeal closely resembles the inquisitional methods used to identify deviants during the medieval heyday of the demonic perspective within our own society. These pain-producing diagnostic techniques were once satirized on the popular television program *Saturday Night Live* by comedian Steve Martin. Dressed like a medieval monk and brandishing an array of weaponlike "tools" for discovering "evidence of the devil," Martin proceeded to inflict torture on a group of accused sinners. Laughable by today's standards, Martin's grotesque satire was not far from the "facts" of the trial by ordeal as once practiced in the name of God. Such ordeals relied upon the correct reading of supernatural signs provided by God to sort the good from the bad, deviants from the rest of the faithful. These identification strategies were often equivalent to or as painful as the punishment for deviance. This, however, was of little importance to a society immersed in otherworldly concerns.

Trial by ordeal quite frankly meant trial by torture. Such trials were presided over by priests or other ordained representatives of the divine will here on earth. Admissions of deviance were literally produced by the disembodiment of deviants from their present sinful state. The reactions of suspected deviants to the searing pain of inquisitorial torture were studied as a sign from above as to whether the accused was guilty of a particular act. While the guilty eventually cried out admissions, it was believed that God fortified the innocent to persevere during the ordeal of their diagnosis. Thus it was entirely possible that the innocent might ultimately be vindicated only by the steadfast endurance of pain until death.

While such torturous diagnostic practices may today seem horrific, during the demonic period there was nothing particularly sacred about the body. In a world which gave primacy to supernatural imagery there was little profit in preserving the body at the expense of the soul. The ordeal of subjecting the body to religious authority was symbolic of the true supernatural order of things. Thus, divinely ordained inquisitioners were carefully trained to "find the tenderest point through which to assail the conscience and the heart."[8] In the words of the historian H. C. Lea, they were "relentless in inflicting agony on body and brain; . . . using without scruple the most violent alternatives of hope and fear. . . . Yet through all this there shines the evident conviction that they were doing the work of God."[9]

Trial by battle was another method commonly used to identify demonic deviance during the Middle Ages. The image most associated with this strategy is that of two knights jousting. Since it was believed that the justice of God was mirrored in natural events, the good person would be victorious, while the deviant would fail. Strength in combat was thus a sign of innocence. Although trial by battle was reserved more for those of wealth than was trial by ordeal, both methods used natural means to achieve supernatural ends. Both served to diagnose the handiwork of the devil.

Discerning the Devil in Colonial America

While trial by ordeal was common in continental Europe, inquisitional techniques of extracting evidence of the devil were largely absent in England. There, and in the American colonies, a system of common law evolved which emphasized such things as trial by jury, separation of prosecution and judge, the rights to confront one's accusers and to appeal a verdict of guilt. How then, during the reign of a demonic world view, did the British system identify the "hand of the devil"? An answer is provided by the historical record of the Salem witch trials of 1692.

The "facts" of the Salem case are clear evidence of the continued dominance of demonic theorizing right up until the end of the seventeenth century. The story begins in the colonial home of Rev. Samuel Parris. There several young girls (ages 9 to 20) spent play time with Tituba, a mysterious "kitchen slave" from Barbados who was reputedly skilled in the art of magic. The story ends with the deaths of twenty-two convicted witches. What exactly happened may never be known. What was alleged to have happened involves the gradual possession, or "taking over," of the young girls by a demonic spirit. "They would scream unaccountably, fall into grotesque convulsions, and sometimes scamper along on their hands and knees making noises like the barking of a dog."[10] Who was it that had conspired with the devil to cause such an outrage? Colonial magistrates demanded an answer. They implored the possessed maidens to identify their assailants.

The names Tituba, Sara Good, and Sara Osburne were spewed from the mouths of the possessed. One could not have imagined a more likely and more vulnerable trio of defendants: Tituba, the strange dark foreigner; Sara Good, the pipe-smoking, leather-faced village hag; Sara Osburne, a woman of higher social standing but also a woman of scandalous reputation, a woman who had shocked the Puritan community of Salem by "living with a man" without being married to him. These three were brought to trial, convicted, sentenced to death, and executed. But the epidemic of witchcraft did not end there. More signs of the devil appeared. Animals died suddenly. Children were born dead. Good people, such as Ann Putham, lost several children at birth. The search for more witches continued. The possessed girls were asked to name more names and did. Soon the whole Salem community was caught up in a mania of witches. The devil and his disciples were everywhere. Such deviants were to be identified and put to death. But how, lacking a tradition of inquisitional torture, were Puritan magistrates to properly sort out evidence of the devil?

Five types of evidence were accepted to identify the Salem witches. The first was a trial by clever test, if not exactly by painful ordeal. It involved making accused witches say the Lord's Prayer in public. Since witches were believed to say this prayer backwards, it was believed that they would slip up when asked to say it in the correct God-fearing manner. Any slips of the tongue were then taken to mean that those tongues belonged to demonic deviants. A second form of evidence simply involved the testimony of those who attributed their own bad fortune to the demonic activities of the accused. A third directed examiners to search for "physical marks of the devil"; warts, moles, scars, or other bodily imperfections through which the devil might have penetrated the alleged deviant. The fourth was confession of guilt. Of the hundreds of persons tried *only* fifty confessed. Ironically they were among those who by their repentance were spared the gallows. Of the twenty-two put to death (nineteen by formal execution, one pressed to death after remaining mute before the inquiries of examiners, two dying in jail) none had publicly confessed. So much for this fourth form of "hard evidence." The fifth, the most commonly relied upon, entailed what has been described as "spectral evidence." This involved reports of persons who had supposedly seen "floating specters," or ghostly forms which had taken on the shape or appearance of one of the accused. The basis for this particular identification strategy was the belief that the devil cannot assume the shape of an innocent person.[11]

It is very unlikely that any of the five types of evidence mentioned above would be taken seriously in a court of law today. In fact, two of them (mistakes in saying the Lord's Prayer and contested accusations by afflicted parties) were precluded by Puritan officials themselves as the number of witch trials expanded into the hundreds. Two others (physical marks and confessions induced under a situation of great stress) also came to be viewed with suspicion. In actuality it seems that "spectral evidence" became the central tool used to diagnose witches as the trials dragged on to their deadly completion.[12] Imagine putting someone to death because of spectral evidence? In today's world someone who sees specters is likely to be put in a mental hospital. But this was far from the case during the reign of the demonic perspective. Spectral evidence was, after all, supernatural evidence, and this was the truest form of evidence available to God's community on earth.

SOCIAL CONTROL OF DEMONIC DEVIANCE

If your right eye leads you astray, pluck it out and throw it away; it is better for you to lose one of your members than that your whole body should be thrown on to the rubbish-heap.

Matthew 5:29

The demonic perspective differentiated little between various types of deviants. Insomuch as all were seen as demonically inspired, each (whether a murderer, adulterer, or heretic) was subject to the same general strategy of control—a religiously administered ritual of public punishment. The purpose of such punishment was to purge the body of a sinner of traces of the devil and thereby restore the body of the community as a whole to its proper relation to God. Rituals are highly patterned actions which, when performed correctly, connect people to a mythic or transcendental sense of what things are and should be, of what is real and how we should act in accord with that reality. Rituals of religious punishment remind participants of the supreme reality of God's will and, by purging evil, restore humans to their proper relationship as servants of the divine.

During the reign of medieval Christianity obedience to God meant obedience to the church. Priests acted as official mediators between God, the sinner, and a spiritual community afflicted with the devil. In presiding over the ritual sacrament of penance, priests granted God's forgiveness and prescribed punishments which cleansed an infested body of evil. Church officials also acted to prevent demonic temptations, particularly those associated with heresy and sins of the flesh. In the years following the Protestant Reformation, for instance, the Roman Catholic church unleashed its army of Jesuits to combat heretics by a fearsome preaching of the papal gospel. So, likewise, was the spread of unorthodox religious thought countered by church censorship. Of particular importance was the papal Index of Prohibited Books, which forbade believers from tempting their eyes with devilish reading matter. No control policies, however, were as feared or symbolically important as the supernatural sanctioning of physical punishment. Often intense, brutal, and searingly painful, the ritual execution of such punishments symbolized the supremacy of spirit over matter. Think of the imagery evoked by burning a demonically infested body. Burning was a form of punishment which reached its peak during the high point of demonically generated deviance—the Spanish Inquisition. Why? Burning evoked an image of hell as the ultimate resting place for unpurged sinners. The act of burning the heretic or infidel symbolized this aspect of the "true" nature of the supernatural world. Thus burning functioned as a "divine reflective punishment . . . to give the living a taste of hell before he passed on."[13]

Another symbolic aspect of religious punishment was found in the principle of *lex talionis,* or "an eye for an eye, a tooth for a tooth, stroke for stroke, burning for burning." This principle was used to justify the mutilation of sinners. Thus the thief had a hand cut off, while the penis of a rapist, the tongue of a liar, or the heart of a traitor might be ritually excised. Such punishments underscored the subordination of natural bodies to supernatural struggles between good and evil.

What would become of the demonic spirit which had previously lived within the body of the dead sinner? Fear of such spirits lead to a variety of apotropaic rituals—rituals which accompanied the use of the death penalty and which served as a means of warding off evil spirits. Such rituals provided "practical" protection against such spirits lingering in or around the body of the condemned. They also served as symbolic reminders of the primacy of the supernatural.

Consider the apotropaic function of that particularly brutal punishment known as "breaking on the wheel." This form of purging may be traced back to the practice of *apotympanismos* in ancient Greece. After the deviant was pegged to a board with irons, an executioner proceeded to break all his major bones with a heavy metal bar. Later variations of the "sacred punishment" included such things as tying someone to the broad side of a wheel and then rolling it down an incline, and pegging a person to the ground and running him over with a spiked wheel. Why such elaborate means of death? Because in breaking the bones of a sinner one breaks the hold that an evil spirit exercises over an earthly body. As Graeme Newman suggests, "The bones are seen as the most enduring, lasting part of the body, so by breaking the bones it is believed the culprit's spirit will be prevented from getting around too easily."[14]

A similar logic has been used to explain such other practices as casting the ashes of a burned sinner to the wind, drawing and quartering, sinking a drowned body into a bog, staking a body into a fixed position, beheading, and even hanging. For instance, it was not until comparatively modern times that the body of a hanged deviant was taken down and buried. In a world enchanted by all kinds of spirits there was fear that demons within the body of the executed might seep into the earth and thereby endanger its fertility. Hence during the earliest periods of known hangings the dead body would remain swinging between heaven and earth until it decayed and was safely "returned to dust."[15]

Another symbolic consequence of religious punishment was the way in which certain supernaturally ordained control rituals provided a divine blessing for hierarchical class distinctions between humans. Compare the ritual of beheading with death by hanging. Beheading was largely reserved for offenders of the highest status. William the Conqueror first introduced this type of "noble punishment" into England when, in 1076, he ordered the execution of the earl of Northumberland. Over the next six centuries the lives claimed by beheading generally included the God-ordained elite of deviants. In 1644 Archbishop Laud actually petitioned to be beheaded rather than hanged. To behead someone is to strike him or her dead with a sword or an axe to the throat, both symbols of valor since ancient times. On the other hand, "Hanging and other lesser forms of execution were appropriate to a class that was held in disdain. . . . In contrast to beheading, throughout history being hanged has been a disgrace, particularly if one were also stripped naked."[16]

Public Executions: "Rituals of a Thousand Deaths"

The purgative and symbolic dimensions of demonic punishment were nowhere more evident than in that spectacle of spectacles—the public execution. This elaborate ceremony of religiously sanctioned pain was neither swift nor efficient. Known as the "ritual of a thousand deaths" it involved the application of purifying pain inch by inch to the demonically infested body, with death but the last step in the restoration of supernatural order.

Michel Foucault describes the torturous detail of one such execution.

> Bouton, an officer of the watch, left us his account: "The sulphur was lit, but the flame was so poor that only the top of the hand was burnt, and that only slightly. Then the executioner, his sleeves rolled up, took the steel pincers, which had been especially made for the occasion, and which were about a foot and a half long, and pulled first at the calf of the right leg, then at the thigh, and from there at the two fleshy parts of the right arm; then at the breasts. Though a strong, sturdy fellow, this executioner found it so difficult to tear away the pieces of flesh that he set about the same spot two or three times, twisting the pincers as he did so. . . .
>
> "After these tearings with the pincers, Demiens, who cried out profusely, though without swearing, raised his head and looked at himself; the same executioner dipped an iron spoon in the pot containing the boiling potion, which he poured liberally over each wound. Then the ropes that were to be harnessed to the horses were attached with cords to the patient's body. . . .
>
> "Monsieur Le Breton, the clerk of the court, went up to the patient several times and asked him if he had anything to say. He said he had not; at each torment, he cried out, as the damned in hell are supposed to cry out, 'Pardon, my God! Pardon, Lord.'. . . Several confessors went up to him and spoke to him at length; he willingly kissed the crucifix that was held out to him; he opened his lips and repeated: 'Pardon, Lord.'
>
> "The horses tugged hard, each pulling straight on a limb, each horse held by an executioner. After a quarter of an hour, the same ceremony was repeated and finally, after several attempts, the direction of the horses had to be changed, thus: those at the arms were made to pull towards the head, those at the thighs toward the arms, which broke the arms at the joints. This was repeated several times without success. He raised his head and looked at himself. Two more horses had to be added to those harnessed to the thighs, which made six horses in all. Without success.
>
> ". . . After two or three attempts, the executioner Samson and he who had used the pincers each drew out a knife from his pocket and cut the body at the thighs instead of severing the legs at the joints; the four horses gave a tug and carried the two thighs after them . . . ; then the same was done to the arms, the shoulders, the arm-pits and the four limbs; the flesh had to be cut almost to the bone, the horses pulling hard carried off the right arm first and the other afterwards.
>
> "When the four limbs had been pulled away, the confessors came to speak to him; but his executioner told them that he was dead, though the truth was that I saw the man move, his lower jaw moving from side to side as if he were talking."[17]

Other Rituals of Religious Control: More Shame Than Pain

While the ritual application of physical pain remained a primary symbol of social control during the demonic period, other control rituals were more representational in nature. These punishments symbolized the supernatural subjugation of the body without taking pain to its human limits.[18] Thus, the baker who short-weighted his loaves was punished by having bread tied around his neck, while a fishmonger convicted of selling bad fish might be fitted with a collar of decayed smelts. In medieval Europe heretics accused of advocating Judaism were forced to feed on pork in public, while gossiping "scolds" in the American colonies had their tongues cooled by a good public dunking. At other times scolds and such "mouthy" sinners as drunkards, swearers, and noisy schoolchildren were treated to the "scold's bridle," an iron cage placed over the head, with a sharp frontal plate, frequently spiked, protruding into the mouth. A remnant of this religiously inspired ritual of ridicule continued in Providence, Rhode Island, until the eighteenth century. There a "cleft stick" or "whispering stick" was inserted into the mouths of children caught swearing or talking in school.[19]

Other symbolic rituals of religious penance were self-imposed. These included rituals of mild self-degradation in which a penitent sinner might parade barefoot, clad only in a white sheet, publicly begging God's forgiveness. Other rituals, such as the brutal self-whippings of medieval flagellants, were far more dramatic. Most rites of public humiliation were less voluntary. Like the shaved head or the "scarlet letter" imposed upon the body of the adulterous woman or the **T** branded upon the forehead of the English thief, the shameful stigma of demonic deviance was forced upon the sinner as she or he journeyed through this world to the next. Yet, regardless of whether punishment was more painful or shameful, two additional elements of religious control were invariantly present: a reliance upon centralized authority, and the local or community nature of control practice.

In the Name of Centralized Authority

The demonic perspective centralizes the control of deviance in the hands of religious authorities. Divinely ordained officials administer ritual punishments that purge offenders of demonic influence and restore God's blessing upon the entire community of the faithful. Most traditional histories of social control view this centralization of the authority to punish as a progressive development. Prior to the rule of religious authority, harm was said to beget more harm, as the kin of an offended party retaliated against a deviant clan in a direct and often brutal manner. This practice of blood revenge could lead to a spiraling cycle of ad hoc violence and prolonged periods of social instability. With the institution of centralized religious authority, the primitive practice of feuding came to an end, or so the story is usually told. Religious laws restricted the arbitrary nature of revenge, while religious officials tempered the horrors of private bloodshed by granting "asylum" to persecuted rule-breakers and declaring "the truce of god" (*treuga dei*), a temporary peace for fugitives from divine justice.

Today anthropologists recognize that these progressive consequences are only part of the story. Some things were lost as well as gained in the birth of centralized religious authority. Lost was a legacy of reconciliatory control rituals, used to solve problems in the "headless," or *acephalous,* societies which characterized the first 30,000 of our 40,000 years as the species Homo sapiens.[20] The rudimentary level of technology in these societies required the full-time work commitment of each member simply to secure the conditions of material survival for the group as a whole. In these collectively cooperative social units nobody was in charge; nobody was authorized to organize life for others. Power was reciprocally shared among group members in a manner which is hard for most of us to imagine today. While we typically imagine that centralized authority is a natural social condition, acephalous peoples imagined the opposite. There nobody legitimately commanded others. A cooperative sharing of power was seen as both necessary and natural.

A full discussion of acephalous societies is beyond the scope of our present project. Suffice it to say that the radical social and economic equality of such groups was complemented by a diffuse role structure (providing for a high degree of common experience), a kin-based social organization (creating familial blood-ties between all members), and a belief system emphasizing the collective nature of success and failure. Together these organizational characteristics produced a high level of cooperation and a significantly different style of social control. While blood revenge was one mechanism used to control wrongdoing between acephalous groups, it was neither as common as once imagined, nor was it typically used as a form of control within acephalous groups. The reasons are simple. Between groups revenge might engender a cycle of feuding dangerous to the survival of these highly interdependent, collectively organized social units. Within groups the idea of personal revenge made no sense, given the close identification of each member with the group itself. The group rather than the individual per se was perceived as both the true offender and the victim. Trouble within or between groups must be resolved. It was not sufficient for action to be taken against a troublemaker or individual deviant. As such, the most common control rituals of acephalous societies were directed at reconciling parties in troubling situations rather than exorcising trouble out of particular individuals. This later practice awaited the birth of centralized religious authority. In acephalous societies ceremonial mechanisms of group reconciliation were more creative.

Often the reconciliatory control practices of acephalous communities involved the mediative efforts of skilled negotiators, such as the "monkalun" among the acephalous Ifugao tribe of the Philippines[21] and the "leopard skin" mediator of the Nuer in southern Sudan.[22] Such mediators possessed no legal authority. Their only power was found in their ability to bring deviating parties back together.[23] Ordinarily this was accomplished by means of symbolic rituals designed to dissolve the trouble between deviating parties. One such ritual was observed among the Tiwi of Australia.[24] Tiwi society is composed of large polygamous households in which older men are surrounded by many younger wives. This leads to a scarcity of young unattached females. Imagine the trouble this presents for young heterosexual males. Older males commonly accuse the young of seducing their women. How are such accusations of deviance resolved? Troubling situations of this kind are defused by an elaborate and dramatic simulation of deadly duel. In this ritual of reconciliatory control, an agile young man (unarmed or armed only with a stick) dodges spears thrown by a less threatening elder. This continues for about five to ten minutes as the younger man retains his honor. The ritual reaches its climax when the younger man permits himself to be hit. The old man thus regains honor without dishonoring his younger "opponent." The ceremony ends. Reconciliation is complete. Both parties are symbolically satisfied. Neither totally wins or totally loses. Neither is advantaged by deviantizing the other. Neither is excluded from a return to honorable life within the group.

A similar reconciliatory outcome occurs in the "song duels" of troubled Eskimos.[25] A complaining victim and an accused deviant join in a sharp-tongued battle of song. In the course of exchanging derogatory verses about each other, both deviating parties are at once honored and humiliated. Trouble is dissolved. It is replaced by reconciliation. This is the most common product of diverse rituals of symbolic satisfaction. "Similar solutions can be reached through wrestling matches or other contests of strength in which no lasting damage is done."[26] In acephalous groups possessing a common medium of economic exchange, victim restitution, a ceremonial paying back of harm, was another common means of reconciliation. No matter the form, acephalous control rituals typically resulted in the reunion of members and the defusing of trouble within the community as a whole.

All of this changed as changes in technology permitted groups to create an economic surplus above and beyond that needed for simple material survival. This enabled some members of the group to become full-time managers of the labor and social activities of others. For the first time in history power was hierarchically arranged such that a few people were able to legitimately command the deference of everyone else. This marked the transition from acephalous to centralized state rule, and with it a whole new strategy of social control. No longer was the reconciliation of troubled parties a primary concern. Why? Because the institution of centralized authority was itself a source of trouble. It drove an institutional wedge through the equalitarian cooperation which was so prominent a feature of acephalous life. The benefits and liabilities of group life were now no longer equally distributed. Some people were in authorized positions of greater power than others. They could announce rules and enforce them. But why? Why some people instead of others? In its earliest forms, centralized authority was justified by divine precept. Just at that moment in history when technological changes made centralized rule a material possibility, God's voice was heard by "his" prophets. They were chosen, God said, set above others to rule in "his" name. This historical link between material and spiritual developments is well documented by students of acephalous society such as the anthropologist E. E. Evans-Pritchard.[27] His analysis of the end of acephalous rule among the Nuer of the Sudan suggests that the appearance of prophets was occasioned by an intrusion of Arabs and Europeans into the traditional life of the group. Threatened by the power of other state-organized societies, the Nuer suddenly found "sky spirits" gracing certain of their members (and eventually the offspring of these members) with the previously unknown mantle of divinely authorized leadership.

I am not here suggesting that material changes cause spiritual changes. I am suggesting that material changes are commonly accompanied by spiritual changes; that each impacts upon the other; that each provides a condition for the existence of the other. In the case of centralized religious authority, it is important to note that it is conditioned by the existence of an economic surplus which enables some people to gain an upper hand over others, just as it provides a condition for hierarchical rule by justifying this unequal power in the name of God. This, of course, is exactly what happens as the charismatic voice of a prophet becomes institutionally transformed into the lawful authority of priests. Soon an elaborate religious organization arises, complete with a table of authorized "organizational agents" and an official code specifying who can do what, when, where, and why. Such codes also specify what is to be done to those deviants who violate them. As such they legitimately defined the institutionalized social inequalities which are ushered into history with the advent of centralized authority. We shall further examine this troubling feature of centralized authority in Chapter 10. For now it is sufficient to recognize that the blessings of religious control rituals are mixed. On one hand, they reduce the arbitrary nature of revenge. On the other, they provide a justification for the authorized domination of some people by others.

Community Control of the Demonic

Although justified by the principle of centralized religious authority, supernaturally ordained control rituals were practically administered within local geographic communities. Thus, during the dominance of demonic thinking in the medieval west, there were no "out of sight and out of mind" institutions to remove deviants from the public eye. Those who violated the laws of God, as written into the ecumenical laws of the church, were to be dealt with locally, purged in public as visible reminders of the ever-present struggle between God and the devil.

Except for a handful of sixteenth- and seventeenth-century "workhouses" in several of Europe's early industrialized cities, the control of demonic deviance was largely the responsibility of local communities and their families. Each community had its mentally afflicted "lunatics" and feeble-minded "idiots" who wandered the streets. The care of such persons was, for the most part, a family or neighborhood matter. Although the proper recognition of deviance was viewed in terms of a centralized religious authority, the practical control of deviants was generally a matter of informal local initiative. Moreover, no clear distinctions were made regarding an undifferentiated assembly of deviants, most of whom we presently classify and control separately.

What "care," as distinct from punishment, was provided for the dependent (i.e., lunatic, sick, poor, etc.) members of the above-described deviant class was not the effort of any organized religious or secular response. It was provided by those who were intimately connected to the deviant and was generally guided by spiritual concern both for their fellows and for their own souls. It was only the exceptionally burdensome deviant or the person lacking any supportive ties to family or friends who would be housed under the same roof with others of his or her kind. Two kinds of roofs provided for the control of these exceptional cases—the small religious hospital and the jail. Both, however, were locally based and bear little resemblance to the centralized institutions which would later separate deviants from the local community.

While medieval religious hospitals sometimes provided a shelter for both the seriously sick and the honestly poor, jails housed a much wider range of deviant clientele. These early "prisons," however, should not be confused with the houses of correction and penitentiaries of a later age. It was not until the nineteenth century that imprisonment became a major form of punishment. As mentioned previously, demonic deviants were largely subject to physical punishment or fines. Nor were jails typically administered by the state or the church. In general, jails were small, privately administered places which housed deviants within the geographical and visual boundaries of the local community. According to Andrew Scull,

> Frequently housed in ramshackle buildings, gaols [jails] were private speculations run on behalf of municipalities, or ecclesiastical dignitaries. The inmates found themselves crammed together in a single heterogeneous assemblage. As well as lunatics and debtors, some were there "as a means of securing the payment into the Exchequer of debts due to the Crown," while others were held as punishment for various minor infractions. But most were in custody simply to ensure their appearance at their trials or their executions.[28]

The public administration of punishment was likewise a manifestation of the commitment to community control during the "demonic" period. All were invited and frequently required to witness the ceremonies of bodily penance by which the entire community was restored to grace. The exception to this was with deviants who had come from other communities. They were to be controlled properly in the community of their origin. Such outside deviants were generally punished and sent packing. Ceremonial punishments, such as tar and feathering, were reserved as warnings for those who broke local rules but who were themselves not "local folks."

The sentence of death would, of course, remove the body of the deviant from its earthly ties to the local "community of the faithful." Bodily removal from the community was, in this sense, the ultimate in punitive sanctions. Interestingly enough, a form of symbolic bodily removal, "outlawry," was considered almost as severe. This form of punishment emerged during a time in the late Middle Ages in which epidemic plagues reduced vast proportions of the laboring population, thus making the extensive use of mutilations and executions a severe hardship on the bodily needs of an agrarian workforce. Fines or some form of economic compensation to victims of deviants' acts were instituted as punishment substitutes. These economic punishments exacted from convicted lawbreakers the fruits of the body's work, if not the agony of the body's pain. Fines were calculated, moreover, on the believed social-community value of a victim. Thus, even in communities guided by demonic visions of deviance, not all members were equally valued in the "eyes of the Lord." Greater compensation was demanded if one offended a person of higher social standing. Thus it was safer then, as it is today, to victimize the poor than to disturb the rich.

In any event, if a fined deviant was unable to pay the demanded compensation, he or she fell under the sentence of outlawry. Bodily present within the community, outlaws were condemned to be outside the protected lawful body of "those faithful gathered together." It was as if one were legally dead. Unguarded and unprotected, outlaws were literally outside the law which bound others together.[29] Should harm be committed against them, the community of "insiders" would no longer respond. A feared punishment, outlawry symbolized the importance of the local community in its immediate and direct responsibility for its own body of deviants; punishing most, while physically or symbolically removing the bodies of the worst.

THE DEMONIC PERSPECTIVE TODAY

Originating in antiquity and continuing as the predominant interpretation of deviance until the time of the eighteenth-century Enlightenment, the demonic perspective may seem far removed from our modern, secular, and scientific world. Yet, for many people demonic explanations remain the only true explanations. Evangelical preachers fill football stadiums and amass large radio and television audiences with sermons suggesting that behind rising crime rates and the spread of sexual immorality lies the malicious hand of the devil. One need not attend a religious revival to be confronted with this message. Few of us who own a TV, listen to the radio, open our mail, or attempt to walk the streets have not confronted the "word" of those who tell us that deviance is sin and that its only control is conversion, prayer, and perhaps the donation of money to a particularly holy cause.

Recent advocates of the demonic perspective have made particular forms of deviance the specific targets of highly organized crusades for morality. Many such crusades are generally aligned with the new conservative politics of the so-called radical right. In the United States well-funded moral campaigns have been directed toward the prohibition of abortion, the elimination of liberal social welfare programs, a retreat from advances in the areas of civil rights, particularly the rights of women, gays, and peoples of color, and the advocacy of a foreign policy dedicated to opposing communism (a political philosophy which, if one believes the words of President Ronald Reagan, seems inspired as much by Satan as by Karl Marx). Some contemporary instances of demonic theorizing are even more extreme. In 1982, for instance, one California state legislator actually introduced a bill aimed at the prohibition of rock music on the grounds that this form of popular entertainment was both satanically inspired and morally degenerate.[30]

One group particularly targeted for "moral control" is gays. For instance, in the early 1970s in Columbus, Ohio, when a gay rights bill was presented to the mayor, a group calling itself the Full Gospel Christian Businessmen's Association immediately parked itself outside City Hall. This group of wealthy fundamentalist Christians, headed by a Bible-quoting car dealer, cited passages from Scripture "proving" that homosexuality was sinful and demanded that the mayor veto this effort to secure a legal place for Satan in society. The bill was vetoed. The same issue rose to national prominence several years later when popular singer and orange juice promoter Anita Bryant led a "Christian" campaign against a similar gay rights referendum in Dade County, Florida. Bryant also believed that homosexuality was of the devil's doing. During the course of her highly publicized campaign she claimed that her own prayers had turned numerous "sinful gays" away from their demonically inspired deviance.

In several state legislatures debates over the Equal Rights Amendment have also had an "otherworldly" religious tone. Arguments opposing guarantees of legal equality for women have suggested that the ERA would lead to a deviant state of affairs, out of keeping with the will of God. Yet, perhaps the most focused religious or supernatural opposition to a particular type of deviance has been in the the "right to life" campaign against abortion. Clearly the abortion issue has been challenged on otherworldly grounds. Abortion is, for many, not merely an earthly wrong, but a sinful or demonic form of deviance as well. The religious nature of organized political efforts to prohibit abortion has been nowhere more apparent than in Massachusetts, where in 1979 the Catholic archbishop of Boston wrote a letter to all parishioners urging them to vote against political candidates favoring legalized abortion. The letter was read publicly in Catholic churches on the Sunday preceding elections.

The 1980s and the Power of the Moral Majority

If anyone is still unconvinced of the contemporary political clout of groups organizing around a demonic perspective on deviance, consider the recent impact of the so-called Moral Majority. In the late 1970s and early 1980s this group, spearheaded by Rev. Jerry Falwell, was instrumental in the political defeat of numerous liberal-leaning legislators and in the election of conservative President Ronald Reagan. For the extremely well financed Moral Majority such things as homosexuality, abortion, and sexual permissiveness and even the rights of women are viewed as demonically inspired deviance. In the words of Falwell, a Baptist minister from Lynchburg, Virginia, whose TV program *The Old Time Gospel Hour* reaches millions of Americans on a weekly basis:

> It is now time to take a stand on certain moral issues. . . . We must stand against the Equal Rights Amendment, the feminist revolution, the homosexual revolution. We must have a revival in this country. It will come if we will realize the danger and heed the admonition of God found in II Chronicles 7:14, "If my people which are called by my name, shall humble themselves and pray, and seek my face and turn from their wicked ways; then will I hear them from heaven, and will I forgive their sin, and will heal their land. . . .[31]

The extent and influence of groups like the Moral Majority as new voices for the demonic perspective is today enormous. In 1980 this resurgence in demonic thinking was being broadcast nationwide by thirty-six separate "religious" television stations, 1,300 "religious" radio stations, and dozens of programs buying time on mainstream commerical airwaves. Moreover, during that same year an assembly of 18,000 fundamentalist pastors gathered in Dallas, Texas, for a "Religious Roundtable Conference" were urged to turn their parishes into political precincts in order to bring America back to God.[32] The political objectives of this curious blend of "old-time religion" and new-time electoral politics are described by critics as a "New Prohibitionism."[33] Much of its theological base is rooted in a selective use of the Scriptures. According to the editors of the periodical *Christian Century,* while using the Bible to attack gays and women and to defend the free enterprise system, the new religious right conveniently overlooks scriptural references to matters such as social justice. "They are not accurate and they are not fair. But they are effective."[34]

Progressive Uses of Religious Imagery

To see Reality in our time is to see the world as crucifixion. . . . The revolutionary is the man of conscience in today's world.

James W. Douglas[35]

Much of what has been said may leave the reader with the impression that contemporary political uses of the demonic perspective have been conservative in nature. This is not always the case. In recent years we have also witnessed the change-oriented, or progressive, use of religious imagery to "deviantize" certain forms of social oppression, domination, or injustice.

Think, for instance, of the role played by black ministers and other religious leaders in combating racism during the American civil rights movement. Rev. Martin Luther King, Jr. and others were clear in viewing racism as a form of spiritual malaise and as a social blot covering this nation's soul. During the height of the civil rights movement the National Council of Churches denounced segregation and racism as a violation of the Gospel and called upon the church "to confess her sin of omission and delay, and to move forward to witness to her essential belief that every child of God is a brother of every other."[36] Through such tactics as prayer, fasting, and other forms of nonviolent protest, King and other religiously informed dissidents hoped to eradicate the national sin of racism.

Religious imagery was also a vital part of certain persuasive sectors in the antiwar movement of the Vietnam era. Consider the religious motivations of the "Plowshares Eight" and people like Daniel Berrigan and William Sloane Coffin, who violated draft headquarters and destroyed draft records in an attempt to end American participation in the war. The dissenting voices of Catholic priests, brothers, and nuns, Protestant clergy, Jewish rabbis, and Buddhist disciples all rendered spiritual as well as political judgment on what may have been described as the demonic nature of United States foreign policy.

Even with the alleged ascendancy of the "New Religious Right" in the 1980s, progressive uses of what might be considered a demonic perspective are still having a significant impact in the world today. The Protestant and Catholic churches, for example, are a major force in the nuclear weapons freeze movement sweeping both the United States and Europe. Leaders of all the major religious groupings have taken strong stands against the "idolatry" of the arms race.

Perhaps most innovative and radical of all is the work currently being done in the area of "liberation theology," particularly by the Catholic church in Latin America. Theologians such as Gustavo Gutiérrez and José Miranda have combined Marxian social analysis with traditional Catholic social teaching in order to help realize the "Kingdom of God" for the poor, oppressed, and dispossessed of Latin America and the entire third world.[37] Meeting at Medellin in 1968, Latin American bishops declared that "God has sent his Son so that in the flesh he may come to liberate all men from slavery which holds them subject, from sin, ignorance, hunger, misery, oppression—

in a word, from the injustice and hate which stem from human egoism."[38] In the words of Camilo Torres, a revolutionary priest from Colombia: "If the good of all mankind cannot be achieved except by changing the temporal structures of society, it would be sinful for Christians to oppose change."[39] The progressive use of the demonic perspective is nearly always combined with the more naturalistic and rationalistic modes of social analysis which will be described in the folowing chapters, and in this respect differs from the way it is used by conservative counterparts such as the Moral Majority, who rely on "the fruits of the Spirit" rather than reason. At the same time the concept of sin and a notion of personal (and social) evil remain a concrete reality even for those who employ the perspective for progressive, change-oriented purposes.

THE ADEQUACY OF THE DEMONIC PERSPECTIVE

How adequate is the demonic explanation of social deviance? How are we to assess its adequacy? Judged by the naturalistic standards of the secularized modern world, the demonic perspective is very inadequate. It relies on belief rather than observable fact and is thus said to be totally untestable. Stated more correctly, one might say that the demonic perspective relies on beliefs that are no longer believed as much as other beliefs. That is to say that a belief in the primacy of the supernatural explanation has been superseded by a belief in the primacy of naturalistic explanations. This has not happened worldwide. Indeed there are numerous places in the world where supernatural or demonic explanations still prevail. Spokespersons of our modern western perspective often refer to the "primitive" character of such beliefs. Yet, when viewed from the opposite direction the western world may appear little more than a wasteland of Godless paganism. Indeed, the Ayatollah Khomeini, revolutionary and spiritual leader of Iran, has often used such supernatural imagery when referring to the United States as "the Great Satan."

Nor is the use of naturalistic explanations entirely dominant even within a largely modernized nation like the United States. Recall our previous discussion of the rise of the Moral Majority. Consider as well the current controversy over what has come to be referred to as creationism or "creation science." Even as I write these words a legal battle swells over a recent Arkansas law which requires a balanced treatment for creationism and evolution theory in public schools.

Creationism involves belief that the universe and human life were brought into being in a sudden instance of creation, that humans and apes are of distinctly separate ancestry, that there once was a worldwide flood, and that the earth is of relatively recent origin (e.g., that it was created several thousand years ago, at a time corresponding to biblical estimates, and not several million years ago, as suggested by the most modern techniques of carbon-dating). All of this, of course, is contradicted by the evolutionary tenets of conventional science. Creationism attempts to reconstruct the "facts" of science to fit the "facts" of the Bible.

The Arkansas law which requires that creationism be taught in a balanced manner alongside teaching about evolution has been challenged by the American Civil Liberties Union on the grounds that it is religion and not science, and that the U.S. Constitution guarantees a separation of church and state. ACLU attorneys argued that creationism is not a science because science requires a commitment to materialistic causation which is at once tentative and testable. Scientific theory, in other words, is always open to the possibility of being proved wrong or revised. This is not the case with creationism. It is based upon unchangeable beliefs rather than verifiable naturalistic observations. In the words of one scientific expert called to testify, "It's religion, it doesn't invoke natural laws. It invokes miracles."[40]

Both sides in the debate over creationism raise issues that are as important as they are disturbing. While it may be true that creationism and other forms of supernaturalist or demonic interpretations of the world are essentially untestable, it is also true that natural science implies a certain commitment to looking at the world in a particular way. Without challenging anyone's religious faith or trying to come to a final resolution of this issue, I belive that there are distinct analytic advantages to suspending a supernatural view of the world in order to take a rigorous naturalistic look at the study of deviance and social control. The advantages of this approach are straightforward and simple. By suspending belief in the primacy of the supernatural interpretation, we are able to critically examine the way that things in this world impact on one another. By taking a naturalistic approach to the study of deviance and social control, we can consider such things as whether or not certain characteristics of the body make it more likely that a person will engage in certain acts of deviance, or whether a particular form of social organization is related to a specific type of social control strategy. These things are valuable to find out regardless of the nature of our religious beliefs. We cannot, however, truly discover much about them until we suspend our commitment to a demonic perspective. Otherwise we are forever stuck with saying that God or the devil caused our bodies or our forms of social organization to be this or that way. We learn nothing beyond the beliefs we start out with. For these reasons the remainder of this book employs what is essentially a naturalistic focus on deviance and social control.

Some Naturalistic Observations about the Supernaturalistic Perspective

Some naturalistic accounts of the demonic perspective have tried to explain away events which the perspective itself attributes to supernatural causes. The Salem witchcraft epidemic is a case in point. In a 1949 book, *The Devil in Massachusetts,* M. L. Starkey substitutes a psychoanalytic interpretation for a demonic one. According to Starkey, the young colonial girls were not possessed by the devil but by "hysteria." Their suffering was caused not by Satan but by sexual repression and boredom.[41]

Starkey's interpretation of the events in Salem attempts to explain away invisible things which most people no longer believe in (e.g., demonic possession) but substitutes an account based upon a new order of invisible things (e.g., psychologically induced hysteria) that are more acceptable to the modern mind. How is it that the invisible things of psychology or psychiatry are today more believable than the invisible things of demonology? This question is raised by contemporary critics of psychiatric explanations of deviance, such as the psychiatrist Thomas Szasz. According to Szasz there are numerous parallels between the untestable belief systems of religious explanation and those of medicine or psychiatry.

> For millennia, men and women escaped responsibility by theologizing morals. Now they escape from responsibility by medicalizing morals. Then, if God approved a particular conduct, it was good; and if he disapproved it, it was bad. How did people know what God approved or disapproved? The Bible—that is to say, the Bible experts, called priests—told them so. Today, if medicine approves a particular conduct, it is good; and if it disapproves it, it is bad. And how do people know what medicine approves or disapproves? Medicine—that is to say, the medical experts, called physicians—tells them so.[42]

Not all naturalistic accounts of demonic deviance attempt to explain away the supernatural world view. Hansen's analysis of the events at Salem contrasts sharply with that of Starkey. Hansen assumes that, since witches were a part of the belief system of people in the seventeenth century, and since witchcraft was known to have been practiced in New England, the 1692 outbreak of demonic possession was a serious social reality which both fit within and threatened the spiritual life of the Salem community as a whole.[43]

But why did the devil make his appearance in 1692? This question is examined by sociologist Kai Erikson in his book *Wayward Puritans*. Erikson relates the appearance of the witches to social disruptions within the Puritan community. According to Erikson, "No other form of crime in history has been a better index to social disruption and change, for outbreaks of witchcraft mania have generally taken place in societies which are experiencing a shift of religious focus—societies . . . confronting a relocation of boundaries."[44]

Erikson's contention that witchcraft appears at times of social and religious disruption is well illustrated in his own analysis of the witchcraft in Salem. In 1692 a new British government had revoked the once-secure charter of the Puritans in Massachusetts Bay. The entire community was enveloped in doubt and confusion. The once-proud leaders of a rigorous experiment in religious orthodoxy were becoming isolated from a new wave of religious tolerance sweeping through Europe and their mother country. Moreover, the internal religious beliefs of the community had been undergoing a radical shift. The original Puritan settlers believed that their destiny was totally in the hands of a God who personally supervised their every action on earth. Yet, after decades of fighting for survival on the fierce frontiers of America, there was born a new breed of Puritans. The sense of mystique which had accompanied the piety of a previous generation was being transformed into a sense of mastery which accompanied the power of their descendants.

The changes described above were compounded by the onset of extensive internal dissension. The once-unified followers of the "New England Way" had become divided by quarreling factions, land disputes, personal feuds, greed, jealousy, and a mass of litigation and counterlitigation. According to Erikson, "At the time of the Salem witchcraft mania, most of the familiar landmarks of the New England Way had become blurred by changes in the historical climate, like signposts obscured in a storm."[45]

The onslaught of the changes described by Erikson produced what he refers to as a "new wilderness" of religious turmoil and confusion. The old wilderness of thick forests and frightful storms gave way to a new wilderness of mythical beasts and flying spirits. As this happened, so too did the devil change his shape. He was no longer embodied in the form of the Indians, who, for the moment, had been defeated and driven westward. Nor was he experienced in the new waves of unorthodox "heretics." Greeted by previously unknown tolerance, such persons were permitted to live in peace. Nor did the devil present himself in the shape of the attacking armies of the Counter-Reformation. Such armies remained far from the distant shores of Massachusetts Bay. The devil came instead out of the new wilderness of spiritual malaise. He came in the form of demonic spirits. He came in the form of the witch.

Erikson's analysis suggests that even in a world dominated by demonic thinking the specific shape of the devil is dependent upon how religious communities are organized or disorganized at a given point in time. But why did the devil so often come in the form of a woman? Some estimate that of the nearly 1 million persons executed for witchcraft throughout history, 85 percent were women. Indeed beginning with the scriptural tale of Eve seducing Adam women have been blamed for luring men into evil. The religious traditions which have made such charges were, of course, dominated by men; men who theorized about their own role as instrumental providers, masters of nature, and about the role of women as expressive receptacles of nature, sensuous earth mothers and the like. Given this imprisonment of gender within the stereotypical confines of male language, it is hardly surprising that during times in which the great male mastery over nature seemed least secure, times of economic hardship and political instability, the priestly finger of men often found bewitching women to blame. Indeed, the 1484 *Malleus Maleficarum,* the authorative theological guide to witch-hunting in the west, makes reference to "normal female witch behavior" which "spirits away" male sex organs "resulting in impotence or castration."[46] Such projections of male inadequacy onto allegedly evil women are today the stuff of many a popular song. During the reign of the demonic perspective the classification of women as witches led to such ritual punishments as baths in boiling water, crushing by heavy weights, tearing the flesh from the breasts with searing-hot pincers, and torture of the female sex organs. Historians even recount incidents where the entire female populations of peasant villages were put to death in order to drive away the devil.[47]

The hunting of witches also distracted people from noticing the contributions of church officials to the perpetuation of medieval poverty. Convicted "witches were mainly peasant and lower-class women who opposed the existing authority structure and thus represented a political, religious, and sexual threat to the dominant class, particularly to men."[48] In the ritual of the witch-hunt, religious leaders diverted attention from themselves while pitting the lower rungs of the social order in fear and suspicion of each other. Thus the shape of the devil may be seen as influenced by social stratification as well as social disorganization.

Elliot Currie's analytic comparison between witchcraft in England and on the European continent suggests that it is "shaped" by the organization of social control machinery as well. For years continental Europe experienced huge outbreaks of witchcraft while in England rates were considerably lower. Why? According to Currie, the answer is found in contrasting the continent's "repressive control" machinery with the more "restrained control" mechanisms available in England.[49]

On the continent control was organized according to an inquisitional approach wherein "accusation, detection, prosecution and judgment" were concentrated in the hands of the same officials. The trial, rather than being a matter of accusation and defense, was more of an attack exerted toward obtaining a confession. It usually involved a trial by ordeal. It included something else as well—the prerogative of the court to confiscate the property of an accused witch. The processing of witches was, then, not only efficient but profitable. It resulted in what Currie describes as a "witchcraft industry." Control agents were paid well for their work. Moreover, the more witches they "discovered," the bigger the problem appeared. As a result, the unique organization of "repressive control" machinery guaranteed that both the "problem" and the "solution" would continue at high levels in somewhat of a self-fulfilling manner.

England's "restrained control" apparatus was much different. Witches, like all other demonic deviants, were assured some form of accusatorial rather than inquisitorial trial. This we mentioned when discussing the witch trials in Salem. Moreover, England never developed a system for confiscating the property of the accused. As a result, control agents in England, as contrasted with those on the continent, "had no continuous vested interest in the discovery and conviction of witches. . . . They had neither the power nor the motive for large scale persecution."[50]

Currie's analysis, like Erikson's, indicates that without explaining away demonic beliefs, it is possible to understand them in a different way by situating these beliefs within the social and historical context in which they are used. This is done by suspending judgment as to the truth of the demonic perspective and by naturalistically considering it as something which is both influenced by and influences a wide range of other cultural, political, and economic "things" by which our social world is organized. Once we apply a naturalistic perspective to the study of demonic theorizing, a number of new and exciting questions present themselves. We may ask, for instance, why at this point in time America is experiencing such a revival in demonic imagery. Why have groups such as the Moral Majority risen to such importance in recent years? Such groups see modern-day demons and witches behind nearly all forms of secular humanism. One wonders whether Erikson's analysis of the explosive appearance of witches in seventeeth-century Massachusetts can provide clues to the widespread belief in a new wave of demons in our own age. Erikson posited a relationship between the disrupted society and the society which sees demons. Is this what is going on in America today? Is it possible that the cultural disruptions of the late 1960s and early 1970s, the political disruptions of the post-Vietnam and post-Watergate era, and the economic disruptions of recession and never-ending inflation are producing a spiritual malaise not unlike that experienced by the Puritans in the late seventeenth century? A naturalistic view of the demonic perspective directs our attention to questions such as this.

Some Supernaturalistic Observations about the Naturalistic Perspective

I hope that what has been said above has convinced you of the advantages of taking a naturalistic perspective on supernaturalistic issues. In closing, however, I think it is important to mention that in the last few years there have been several calls by noteworthy scholars of deviance and social control to do the opposite—to reexamine naturalistic analysis in terms of its supernaturalistic dimensions. These scholars, at least the ones I have in mind, are in no way suggesting that we return to the primacy of the demonic or supernatural viewpoint. They are asking instead that we "transcend" or expand the confines of a purely naturalistic perspective, a perspective which often becomes so preoccupied with testable explanations of the "things" in this world that it forgets to consider their moral, spiritual, or cosmic dimensions. This call for transcendence of a purely naturalistic perspective is raised in a variety of recent works of critical sociological scholarship.

In his book *The Seven Deadly Sins* Stanford Lyman argues that a major deficit in most sociological studies of deviance is the lack of any perspective by which to judge the evils of the modern world. According to Lyman,

> Evil is a term that is rarely found in a modern sociology text. . . . To the extent that sociological thought embraces the study of evil today, it does so under the embarrassing, neutered morality of "deviance." Adopting for the most part an uncritical stance toward the normative structure of any given society, the . . . sociologist of deviance takes his cue from whatever the forces of law and restriction define as evil. Hence, the concerns of the vocal and powerful elements of a society become the resources for a sociological investigation of evil.[51]

Guided toward their fields of study by the "forces of law and restriction," most students of deviance have been content to examine what Alex Liazos once referred to as "the sociology of nuts, sluts and perverts."[52] Lyman calls upon sociologists to transcend the limits of a research diet prepared for them by the most vocal and powerful chefs of our modern day. The most important evils, suggests Lyman, are to be found at a deeper level, evils entrenched in the foundational bedrock of our society itself, evils rooted in "the corporate structure of modern society."[53]

One sociologist of deviance whom Lyman need not remind to look for the deeper structures of evil in society is Richard Quinney. Quinney's early critical analysis of crime, deviance, and social control linked the impersonal forces of corporate dominance to the political and economic structures of modern capitalist society. More recently Quinney suggests that the material problems of capitalism are multiplied by its "sacred" (i.e., spiritual) void. In Quinney's words:

> The contemporary world is caught in . . . a sacred void, the human predicament on both a spiritual and sociopolitical level. Among the characteristics that contribute to this void are a mode of production that enslaves workers, an analytic rationalism which dissipates the vital forces of life and transforms everything (including human beings) into an object of calculation and control, the loss of feeling for the bond with nature and the sense of history, the demotion of our world to a mere environment, a secularized humanism that cuts us off from our creative sources, the demonic quality of the political state, and the hopelessness of the future. . . . The void is historical, beginning with the emergence of capitalism and the breakdown of religious tradition under the . . . enlightenment.[54]

How is this sacred void to be overcome? Quinney urges us to move away from a purely naturalistic critique of society to one that incorporates the concerns of "prophetic theology." He argues for a form of "religious socialism" which will both promote social justice and heal the void found in contemporary existence. "By integrating into a Marxist materialist analysis a critical and prophetic theology of culture," Quinney believes, we will "develop an understanding of the world and a way of transcending the contemporary historical condition."[55] This cannot be done by a purely naturalistic critique or secular socialism. According to Quinney: "A socialism without the sacred would become a system as materialist and alienating as that of capitalism. What is emerging in the transition to socialism is a new religious concern, a concern which not only repudiates the essential secularity of capitalism, but one that makes socialism whole by integration of the sacred void.[56]

A third call for a type of spiritual transcendence of the purely naturalistic approach to deviance and social control is found in Larry Tifft and Dennis Sullivan's book *The Struggle to Be Human*. Tifft and Sullivan articulate an "anarchist" approach in which the rule of law or "external authority" is viewed as a villain which separates us from direct responsibility for the good and bad we create for one another. Once this happens we are said to "become the historical ghosts from whom we are struggling to free ourselves."[57] We forget that the world which seems to rule us is "in reality" a world of our own making. According to Tifft and Sullivan, "We deny ourselves our spiritual homes and our ability to become part of the process we create."[58]

Tifft and Sullivan reject an approach to social control which permits the state to act on our behalf in containing the legally defined deviant. When this happens, as it does in our own modern society, we lose the "cosmic sense" of ourselves as humans struggling together.[59] Approaches to the study of crime or deviance which accept the existence of state authority as something natural, as something given, are said to be guilty of a "warped spirituality." Just as impersonal control by state institutions should be replaced by strategies of mutual aid, direct personal resistance, and communal reconciliation, so also do Tifft and Sullivan urge that we "turn scientific inquiry over to the community" and that our research be guided by a sensitivity "to the mystery of life, the mystery of human experience, the mystery of a world of mutual aid."[60]

In different ways the writings of Lyman, Quinney, and Tifft and Sullivan remind us to temper the naturalistic analysis of deviance and social control with an awareness of the moral, spiritual, or cosmic nature of our subject matter. This reminder is a fitting way to close the chapter on the demonic perspective. After all, the demonic perspective informs us that deviance and its control is first and foremost a battle between good and evil. It is a battle over who gets to name the good and control the bad. This is often overlooked (or perhaps covered up) by the neutral-sounding language of some of our more "modern" perspectives. Let us not be fooled by this "devilishness." Deviance is and always has been a moral battle, the winners being declared saints and the losers sinners.

NOTES

1 Jerry Falwell, *Listen America!* Bantam, New York, 1980, from back cover.
2 My account of the "facts" of this case is drawn from Tom Killen, "By Demons Possessed," *Connecticut Magazine*, September 1981, pp. 47 ff.

3 Ibid., p. 50.
4 For a systematic review of the different processes contributing to secularization, see N. J. Demerath III and Phillip E. Hammand, *Religion in Social Context: Tradition and Transition*, Random House, New York, 1969, esp. pp. 103–114.
5 Peter L. Berger, *The Sacred Canopy: Elements of a Sociological Theory of Religion*, Anchor Books, Garden City, N.Y., 1969, pp. 107–108.
6 Ibid., p. 39.
7 Raymond Verdier, "Ontology of the Judicial Thought of the Kabré of Northern Togo," in Laura Nader (ed.), *Law in Culture and Society*, Aldine, Chicago, 1969, pp. 145–146.
8 H. C. Lea, *The Inquisition of the Middle Ages*, Harper & Row, New York, 1969, p. 168.
9 Ibid.
10 Kai T. Erikson, *Wayward Puritans*, Wiley, New York, 1966, p. 142.
11 Ibid., p. 151.
12 Ibid.
13 Graeme Newman, *The Punishment Response*, Lippincott, Philadelphia, 1978, p. 46.
14 Ibid., pp. 38–39.
15 Ibid., p. 37.
16 Ibid., pp. 33–35.
17 Michel Foucault, *Discipline and Punishment: The Origins of the Prison*, Alan Sheridan (trans.), Pantheon, New York, 1978, pp. 3–5.
18 John Lewis Gillin, *Criminology and Penology*, rev. ed., Appleton-Century, New York, 1926, pp. 203–205.
19 Newman, *The Punishment Response*, pp. 98–99.
20 The following discussion of social control in acephalous societies is based upon the analysis of Raymond J. Michalowski in *Order, Law and Crime: Introduction to Critical Criminology*, Scott, Foresman, Glenview, Ill., 1984. See also Michael Taylor, *Community, Anarchy and Liberty*, Cambridge, London, 1982, and Stephen J. Pfohl, "Labeling Criminals," in H. Laurence Ross (ed.), *Law and Deviance*, Sage, Beverly Hills, Calif., 1981, pp. 65–97.
21 R. F. Barton, *Ifugao Law*, University of California Press, Berkeley, 1919.
22 E. E. Evans-Pritchard, *The Nuer: A Description of the Modes of Livelihood and Political Institutions of a Nilotic People*, Oxford University Press, New York, 1940.
23 Donald Black, *The Behavior of Law*, Academic, New York, 1976, p. 129.
24 C. W. M. Hart and A. R. Pilling, *The Tiwi of North Australia*, Holt, New York, 1962.
25 J. Friedl and J. E. Pfeiffer, *Anthropology: The Study of People*, Harper & Row, New York, 1977, p. 476.
26 Ibid.
27 Evans-Pritchard, *The Nuer*, pp. 184–191.
28 Andrew Scull, *Decarceration: Community Treatment and the Deviant—A Radical View*, Prentice-Hall, Englewood Cliffs, N.J., 1977, p. 17.
29 Gillin, *Criminology and Penology*, p. 203.
30 The demonic interpretation of rock and roll is not new. For a review of conservative Christian criticism of rock see Benjamin R. Epstein and Arnold Foster, *The Radical Right: Report on the John Birch Society and Its Allies*, Vintage, New York, 1967.
31 Quoted in "The New Right Comes of Age," *Christian Century*, October 29, 1980, pp. 995–996. For an extended presentation of Falwell's views, see Falwell, *Listen America!*, p. 17.
32 See also Peggy L. Shriver, *The Bible Vote*, Pilgrim, New York, 1981.
33 Allan J. Lichtman, "The New Prohibitionism," *Christian Century*, October 29, 1981, p. 1029.

34 "The New Right Comes of Age," p. 996.

35 James W. Douglas, *The Non-Violent Cross: A Theology of Revolution and Peace,* Macmillan, London, 1966, p. 3.

36 Quoted in Benjamin Muse, *The American Negro Revolution,* Citadel, New York, 1970, p. 49.

37 For examples of the work which has been done by liberation theologians, see Gustavo Gutiérrez, *A Theology of Liberation,* Orbis, Maryknoll, N.Y., 1973; José (Bonino) Miguez, *Doing Theology in a Revolutionary Situation,* Fortrees, Philadelphia, 1976; and José P. Miranda, *Marx and the Bible: A Critique of the Philosophy of Oppression,* Orbis, Maryknoll, N.Y., 1974. For a general overview of the movement, see Arthur F. McGovern, *Marxism: An American Christian Perspective,* Orbis, Maryknoll, N.Y., 1980, esp. chap. 5.

38 Quoted in Peter Hebblethwaite, *The Christian-Marxist Dialogue,* Paulist, New York, 1977, p. 43.

39 Ibid., p. 41.

40 Daniel McShea, "The Nature of Science Is on Trial in Scopes II Case," *Boston Globe,* December 14, 1981, p. 3.

41 M. L. Starkey, *The Devil in Massachusetts,* Knopf, New York, 1949.

42 Thomas Szasz, *The Theology of Medicine: The Political and Philosophical Foundations of Medical Ethics,* Louisiana State University Press, Baton Rouge, pp. viv–xv.

43 C. Hansen, *Witchcraft at Salem,* Braziller, New York, 1969.

44 Erikson, *Wayward Puritans,* p. 153.

45 Ibid., pp. 139–140.

46 Barbara Yoshika, "Whoring After Strange Gods: A Narrative of Women and Witches," *Radical Religion,* vol. 1, no. 2, Spring 1974, p. 7. Publication of Radical Religion Collective, excerpted in Sheila Balken, Ronald J. Berger, and Janet Schmidt, *Crime and Deviance in America: A Critical Approach,* Wadsworth, Belmont, Calif., 1980, p. 232. See also Nancy van Vuuren, *The Subversion of Women,* Westminster, Philadelphia, 1973.

47 Barbara Ehrenreich and Deidre English, *For Her Own Good: 150 Years of the Experts' Advice to Women,* Anchor, Garden City, N.Y., 1978, pp. 35–39. See also Jules Michelet, *Satanism and Witchcraft,* Citadel, Secaucus, N.J., 1939, and Margaret Alice Murray, *The Witch-Cult in Western Europe,* Oxford University Press, New York, 1921.

48 Balken, Berger, and Schmidt, *Crime and Deviance in America,* p. 231. See also Marvin Harris, *Cows, Pigs, Wars and Witches,* Random House, New York, 1974, p. 237.

49 Elliot P. Currie, "Crime Without Criminals: Witchcraft and Its Control in Renaissance Europe," *Law and Society Review,* vol. 3, August 1968, pp. 7–32.

50 Elliot P. Currie, "Crimes without Criminals," as excerpted in Edwin M. Schuer, *Interpreting Deviance,* Harper & Row, New York, 1979, p. 173.

51 Stanford M. Lyman, *The Seven Deadly Sins: Society and Evil,* St. Martin's, New York, 1978, p. 1.

52 Alex Liazos, "The Sociology of Deviances: Nuts, Sluts and Perverts," *Social Problems,* vol. 20, Summer 1972, pp. 103–120.

53 Lyman, *The Seven Deadly Sins,* p. 4.

54 Richard Quinney, *Providence: The Reconstruction of Social and Moral Order,* Longman, New York, 1980, pp. 8–9.

55 Ibid., p. x.

56 Richard Quinney, *Capitalist Society,* Irwin, Homewood, Ill., 1979, p. 127.

57 Larry L. Tifft and Dennis Sullivan, *The Struggle to be Human: Crime, Criminology and Anarchism,* Cienfuegos Press, Orkney, Scotland, 1980, p. 39.
58 Ibid.
59 Ibid., p. 2.
60 Ibid., p. 20.

Cool Man Calculated By Joseph LaMantia and Stephen Pfohl

CHAPTER **3**

THE CLASSICAL PERSPECTIVE: *Deviance as Rational Hedonism*

Laws are the conditions, under which men, naturally independent, united themselves in a society. Weary of living in a continual state of war, and of enjoying a liberty which became of little value, from the uncertainty of its duration, they sacrificed one part of it, to enjoy the rest in peace and security. . . . But it was not sufficient only to establish this deposit; it was also necessary to defend it from the usurpation of each individual, who would always endeavor not only to take away from the mass his own portion, but to encroach on that of others.

Cesare Beccaria[1]

If the expected cost of crime goes up without a corresponding increase in the expected benefits, then the would-be criminal—unless he or she is among that small fraction of criminals who are utterly irrational—engages in less crime.

James Q. Wilson[2]

INTRODUCTION

Several years ago I had the privilege of accompanying a criminal court judge from the Netherlands on a tour of a large, newly constructed maximum-security prison in Ohio. The Dutch jurist was flabbergasted by the cold, impersonal magnitude of the huge steel cage. This penitentiary closed its cell doors upon approximately 1,300 inmates. Within were housed a number equal to about one-third of the entire prison population of Holland.

We had been given special permission from the governor's office for a "no holds barred" view of the entire facility. We observed its central video control room. Each main corridor was constantly "on the air," being watched by guards who manned electronic gate-release switches controlling movement between each cell block and subdivision of the mammoth "correctional center." We were shown its isolation units (these barren cells used to be called "the hole"), its underground intervention tunnels (designed for a speedy militarylike restoration of order in the event of a possible riot), and its ominous-looking electric chair. Its purpose needed no explaining. We spent hours examining the institution and talking with those sentenced to "do time" within its walls.

Our tour guide was the captain of the guards. He is now referred to as chief correctional officer. At numerous points along the tour the Dutch judge appeared to be amazed, even disturbed, by what he saw. The Netherlands incarcerates a far smaller percentage of its criminal population in much smaller facilities for a considerably shorter time. In broken English the judge would exclaim, "This is, how do you say, fantastic." I translated his message to mean, "I can't quite believe this." The guard captain must have interpreted him differently. He responded by saying, "Yeh, if you think that's somethin', judge, wait'l you see this next thing."

Upon completing our tour the judge, the captain, and I sat down over coffee in the staff cafeteria. The judge had many questions. Why do you build such large prisons? Why do you incarcerate people for such a long time? Don't inmates get angry and disillusioned locked up for such a long time like so many head of cattle; idle with little to do but pass time talking, sitting, playing cards, playing games of power and intimidation just as games of power and intimidation are played on them? The captain was surprised by the judge's questions. "You're a judge. You must see these kind of people in your court. Don't you do the same thing with them in your country?" The judge explained that he did not. He explained that in the Netherlands few convicted criminals were locked up. He explained that most offenders there, as in the States, were property offenders. His country relied much more on a system of costly fines and community-based approaches designed to make such offenders pay back their victims and society. Prison terms were reserved for hard-core and violent offenders. Even for these sentences were short. Most served under a year. Three years was viewed as an extraordinarily long period of time. After that, said the judge, incarceration worked against itself. It hardened rather than softened deviants. How else could a human being survive such a place?

All of this amazed the captain. "I can't believe it. You don't mean it. Say I come to your country. Say I plan this bank robbery. Say I get a gun; shoot somebody; the whole works. Then I get caught, but before I do I stash the loot. Say half a million dollars or whatever you call them over there."

"Guilders," replied the judge.

"Yeh, OK. Guilders. Say I stashed all those guilders so that when I got out I'd get my hands on them. How long would you give me if I came before your court?"

"Well, since you say you shot somebody, probably two years."

The captain shook his head in amazement. "You gotta be kiddin'"! Two years. Two years ain't nothin'. Do you know how much I make in two years? Man, two years—that's worth it. You're kiddin' me aren't you? No! Hey I'm comin'. I mean it. Just figure it out. Two years. It's like an investment. I'll take the two years, then I'll be rich. Just tell me how to get there, Judge."

Not wanting to get in the middle, I tried to wiggle diplomatically out of the conversation. I mumbled something about the Netherlands being a very different place. What I really thought was that in an odd way both the captain and the judge were voicing ideas that could be pulled directly from the pages of a treatise on the classical perspective on deviance and social control. At the heart of this perspective lies the notion that deviance involves a process of rationally calculated choice to achieve maximum pleasure at the cost of minimum pain. Clearly this is what the captain had in mind in fantasizing his criminal excursion to the Netherlands. In terms of social control the perspective emphasizes an equally rationally calculated approach to punishment. The judge appeared concerned with the same. What would really happen if the calculating captain got caught within the judge's rationalized system of social control? In this chapter we shall explore, at least in principle, the classical perspective's answer to this question.

THEORETICAL IMAGES

The classical perspective represented a radical departure from the long tradition of demonic or supernaturalistic explanation. It may be thought of as the first "modern" perspective on deviance and social control. It appeared first in the eighteenth-century writings of scholars such as Cesare Beccaria and Jeremy Bentham. These theorists viewed themselves as enlightened reformers, guiding society away from a dark age of superstitious and arbitrary social control toward a new order based upon the rational, fair, and consistent application of human reason.

Whereas demonic thinking emphasized the influence of supernatural forces, classical theorists conceived of humans as uninfluenced by anything but the calculative rationality of human reason. Deviance, like any other human act, was viewed as a freely calculated choice to maximize pleasure and minimize pain. Classical thought also departed from the idea of "cosmic-connectedness" which lay behind the demonic perspective's understanding of the supernaturally ordained character of human society. Gone was the notion that people were in some mysterious way bound to each other in spirit. This was replaced with a view of society as a contract, a legalistic agreement between people regarding how each should or should not act toward others.

The classical perspective's vision of human nature as a free and rationally calculated choice for pleasure and of society as a consensual social contract permeates everything it has to say about deviance and social control. Where does this particular vision come from? The answer is found in the intimate historical connection between classical thought and a host of major social, economic, political, and intellectual developments.

Sociohistorical Background of Classical Theorizing

It is no accident that classical thought emerged when it did. For historical purposes we mark its birth with the 1764 publication of Cesare Beccaria's important *Essay on*

Crimes and Punishments. In reality this new, highly rational way of seeing deviance was the offspring of massive transformations in the social landscape of Europe over the preceding several centuries. Several interconnected developments were particularly important in sowing the seeds of classical theorizing. These included major shifts in the size and shape of Europe's population, the transformation of the feudal economy into early forms of capitalism, the emergence of the modern nation-state, and the intellectual impetus of scholasticism and the Enlightenment. Together these changes broke the back of the local community structures which had contained deviance during the demonic period. Gone were the cosmic connections between saints and sinners and the collective social, economic, and political ties between those sharing a common supernatural destiny. These were replaced by the naturalistic principles of classical reasoning with its stress upon individual responsibility, free choice, and hedonistic calculation.

The story of how major demographic, economic, political, religious, and intellectual changes altered European society's conception of deviant behavior is a complex one. Its outline is briefly sketched in the following pages. With regard to demographic shifts it is important to note that from the sixteenth through the eighteenth century there was a great growth in the size, density, and heterogeneity of Europe's population.[3]

England, for instance, had grown from a population of 2.8 million in 1500 to 8.9 million in 1800. During that same time France grew from 16 million to 27 million, while the population of Italy expanded from 6 million to 17.2 million. More importantly, the shape and distribution of the European population was becoming more dense and heterogeneous than previous generations of people living within small, well-defined feudal kingdoms. The gradual redistribution of Europe's population followed new paths of social and economic development, opened initially by the armies of crusaders and subsequently by the merchants of a new commercial order of international trade. Cities began to rise in size and with them an anonymity of people unknown to the small local communities of the Middle Ages. Over several centuries London had mushroomed to a population of 750,000, while Paris had grown to 600,000 inhabitants.

Changes in the structure of the European population disrupted the community-based strategies of social control that were associated with the demonic period. Increases in population size increased the scope of the kinds of problems that during the Middle Ages had been dealt with swiftly and directly by small communities of people who knew each other as kin or neighbors. As density increases it becomes more likely that people who meet one another will be anonymous strangers. This anonymity increases the potential for deviance in that it loosens bonds of informal control which people experience when in the presence of well-known others.

The same happens as populations increase in heterogeneity. Heterogeneous populations lack a common history, a common juncture of beliefs, perceptions, and values. As such they are more prone to disagreement and less able to invoke the weight of collectively experienced tradition as a device for controlling deviance.

Similar problems arose in the economic and political spheres, where centuries of collective communal responsibility were exchanged for an individualist ethic of atomized citizenry. In the economic sphere this happened as the complex interdependent obligations of feudal reciprocity were replaced by the simple cash-for-labor contract of the capitalist marketplace. This is not to romanticize the structures of feudalism and the unequal system of economic exchange in which feudal lords and vassals dominated the material lives of serfs and their families. During feudalism vassals, by birth and divine precept, were the rightful controllers of the feudal manor, or estate, a collection of lands inhabited and tilled by serfs. Vassals were landlords to whom serfs paid a portion of their crops or agricultural labor. In exchange serfs were guaranteed protection by the vassal's army. By these traditional arrangements families of vassals and serfs were bound across generations. The ties of fealty, however, were more than economic. Vassals and serfs were also linked by "companionage," a set of mutually binding social obligations rooted in the idea of collective responsibility and the principle that "harm falling upon one fell upon all."[4]

The interdependent controls of companionage were dissipated first by the trade economy of mercantilism and subsequently by the full development of capitalism. These new economic forms stressed private rather than collective ownership of property and the exchange of labor for a fixed, impersonal wage rather than out of personal loyalty to a vassal. This significant and drastic departure from communal control gave rise to an ethic of *individualism*. The new merchant classes were committed to the business of making a profit and called unsympathetically for the rejection of anyone who might lose heavily in trade relations. Individuals, in other words, must go it alone in the new economic marketplace. In the words of Karl Marx, the new capitalist economy "left no other nexus between man and man than naked self-interest, than callous cash payment."[5]

Economic individualization was accompanied by political individualization. In part this was because the rise of the capitalist economic mode was historically interconnected with the rise of the modern nation-state. Indeed the birth of centralized state power in the west may be told as the story of a "squeeze play" in which an early capitalist-merchant class linked itself to the armed forces of national monarchs in an effort to secure fertile, safe, and consistent conditions for large-scale production and international trade. Squeezed out of power were legions of vassals, many of whom had forfeited mortgages on their feudal manors to merchants who had bankrolled ill-fated military adventures. Thus just as this new economic class triumphed over the old class of vassals, so did it become the monetary backbone of the emerging nation-state.

The political consequences of this triumphant coalition were enormous. Just as the emergence of a market economy destroyed the complex web of mutually binding feudal economic ties, the rise of the nation-state meant a dismantling of a host of collectively oriented medieval political institutions, in particular political power residing in kin, the church, and the local guild. Each of these was an intermediary institution, a link between individuals and the local community, another manifestation of community-oriented social control. With the growth of centralized state power these were replaced by the concept of the "citizen," an atomized individual owing political allegiance to none but the state and its laws. Like the anonymity generated by population changes, and the isolated individualism induced by wage-labor relations, this atomization contributed further to a breakdown in old control structures and to the necessity for a new way of envisioning the problem of deviance.

The Protestant Reformation contributed to the atomization of individuals in a similar manner.[6] This "spiritual" revolt against the authority of Roman Catholic religious rule was intimately connected to the more "material" changes described above. Although formally a division in theological understanding, this fracturing of western Christianity during the sixteenth century was buttressed by such other historical developments as the growing dissatisfaction of the laboring poor, serfs and local priests, with the ostentatious lifestyle of the bishops and abbots who occupied privileged seats of influence in the courts of powerful lords and monarchs. Also important were the religious desires of the successful merchant classes whose growth in such places as Germany, Switzerland, and the Netherlands fostered an increased autonomy from the economic and political structures of the old feudal order. These precursors of capitalism were inclined to administer their spiritual affairs as they did their businesses, as unmediated relations between individuals, in this case between God and the solitary believer. So, likewise, was the Reformation fostered by conflict between the secular kings and princes of the emerging nation-states and the centralized religious power of the pope in Rome. For years many of the new monarchs had quarreled with the Roman church over matters related to property, taxation, and legal jurisdiction. With the Reformation the rule of papal authority was dealt a deadly blow. Secular monarchs gained the power to determine which of several Christian churches would become the official religion of their land. Thus, the Church of England was nationally separated not only from the Church of Rome but from the Lutheran and Calvinist churches, which were allied with the secular state authority of other monarchs.

Once under way the Reformation had significant consequences for social control in western Europe. It tore asunder the appearance of a unitary set of religious standards by which to judge deviance. In countries won over by Protestantism it did far more. It stripped believers of a host of intermediary channels of salvation. Gone was the mediation of Catholic church officials, saints, guardian angels, and the Blessed Virgin. In their place was "faith alone," the naked individual's personal relation to the grace of God the Almighty. This was most evident in the Protestant denial of the efficacy of the sacrament of penance. When Martin Luther hammered his ninety-five theses onto the door of the castle church at Wittenberg in 1517, chief among his contentions was that a sinner was cleansed, not by the power of priestly absolution, but *sola gratia*, by the grace of God alone. This emphasis on the total dependence of individuals on the will of the divine was taken to the extreme by the Calvinists, who argued that people were predestined from birth for either salvation or damnation. But how could someone know if he or she was saved? Within a short time Protestants answered this question by coming to view worldly success and self-disciplined rationality as exterior signs of the interior working of God's grace. Thus, those who adhered to the highly constrained "work ethic" of Protestantism revealed in this world their status as God's chosen in the world which is to come. In this fashion Protestantism not only fostered, an individualistic approach to the problem of sin, but, by its emphasis on disciplined rationality, nurtured the development of capitalism, a force productive of individualization on its own.

Along with demographic, economic, political, and religious changes, two intellectual developments also contributed to the new rationalist perspective on nonconformity. The first was theological. Its most dramatic form was the way in which Protestant theology encouraged the equation of goodness with disciplined rationality. For Catholics an emphasis on the goodness of the rational was provided by scholastic theology. Given the Catholic educational background of Cesare Beccaria this is of particular interest. Scholasticism provided a conceptual bridge for the transition between the supernaturalistic and naturalistic viewpoints. Exposure to scholasticism provided Beccaria and others with theological teachings which emphasized human rationality, free choice, and a logically deducible natural law that justified obedience to secular state authority.

Scholasticism represented somewhat of a fusion between Christian doctrine and the philosophies of Plato and Aristotle.[7] At its core was a deep conviction of the power of reason. Scholastic theologians believed that humans could use reason to deductively arrive both at a proof for the existence of God and at the "natural laws" governing correct Christian morality. Natural laws, the benign product of God's infinite wisdom, were discovered by reason rather than miraculous supernatural signs. This belief in the beneficence of reason was a key part of the teaching of scholastic church fathers such as Thomas Aquinas. Aquinas believed that humans freely choose to do good when they allow their will to be guided by reason, or the "rational intellect." Free choice, moreover, "is possible only where there is knowledge of alternatives and the power of will to make choices."

Aquinas and other scholastic thinkers agreed with Aristotle that the virtues of "natural man" are fully realized only when appetites for such things as riches, pleasure, power, and knowledge are tempered, or controlled, by will and reason. But why should "natural" men temper their immediate appetites? The answer is found in the "reasonable" deduction that all good human action must direct itself toward the common good. This principle of common good paved the way for a scholastic justification of the state. The state arises naturally to secure a lawful order which would be agreed to by any reasonable person.

Scholastic theology equated sin with a failure to make free and calculably reasonable choices for the common good. This is a long step from a strictly supernatural interpretation of deviance. The will of God and the calculated choice of the reasonable "natural man" become one and the same. The task for morality is thus to establish a rule of reason, a rule of calculated rationality. This was the task chosen by Beccaria and other classical theorists. Schooled in scholastic theology, they borrowed heavily from its emphasis on the goodness of rational choice and obedience to the natural laws of the state. Although first developed in the Middle Ages, scholastic theology rose in preeminence during the same time in which the previously described forces of demographic, economic, and political change were altering the social and material life of European society. How interesting it is that we find a theological justification for such things as the importance of free individual choice, calculated rationality, and the naturalness of state authority at precisely those moments in which dramatic population shifts, the emergence of the capitalist marketplace, and the development of the modern state were also occurring. This is not to suggest that these changes "caused" a shift in theological thought. It does suggest that ideas never exist in an historical vacuum. They are influenced by and in turn influence the events in the social and material world in which they are located. The same is true of the philosophy of the Enlightenment.

The Enlightenment: Rationality and "Social Contract"

Scholastic theology prepared religiously educated thinkers such as Beccaria to break with previous supernaturally dominated accounts of deviance and evil doing. In the philosophy of the Enlightenment classical theorists discovered a related set of secular intellectual assumptions. Enlightenment philosophy also emphasized the primacy of reason and the role of calculated rational choice in realizing a state of natural human order. Yet, the most distinctive contribution of the Enlightenment to the classical perspective is found in the notion of the "social contract." Enlightenment thinkers viewed society as a legalistic contract between freely consenting human individuals. Whether individuals were motivated by that Montesquieu conceived of as the four innate desires of peace, hunger, sex, and sociability, or by Rousseau's posited need for companionship, or by Hobbes's conceptualized need to avoid perpetual conflict, the origin of society was commonly conceived of in terms of a freely entered upon contract of individuals.

Of all the enlightened social contract theorists Hobbes appears to have had the most influence in the development of the classical perspective. Hobbes believed that without the lawlike restraints of the sovereign state, social life would collapse into an ongoing war between people with conflicting self-interests. Any reasonable person could recognize this. Hobbes's arguments regarding the naturalness of the state are laid out in his renowned treatise *Leviathan*. The influence of this manuscript is felt on nearly every page of Cesare Beccaria's own major life work, *Essay on Crimes and Punishments*. *Leviathan* spells out what Hobbes considers to be the essential elements of the natural political community: monopoly of force by the state, the naturalness of centralized sovereignty, the supremacy of national values, and the atomlike character of the individual citizen. How did Hobbes arrive at these natural principles? Like other Enlightenment scholars, Hobbes argued that his "discoveries" were the logical deductions of disciplined reason. Maybe. Yet, as Robert Nisbet points out, the natural law which Hobbes articulated in the seventeenth century was, in actuality, little more than an updated transmutation of the principles of law of the ancient Roman state.[8] Both justified central state authority. Both rose at precisely those points in history in which the practical rule of the state demanded a kind of corresponding intellectual defense. Again we find an affinity between theoretical thought and practical social context. As Nisbet points out, Hobbes wrote at a time in which the emerging British nation-state was facing a political crisis of tremendous importance. The followers of the Stuarts were locked in a treacherous civil war with Cromwell and his army of Puritans. The countryside was being ravaged by more conflict than England had seen in centuries. Looting, pillaging, burning, and robbing had become daily occurrences. The monarch Charles I had been beheaded in public. The fate of the modern state appeared in doubt. In the midst of this widespread conflict Hobbes sought to provide firm intellectual footing for the strict imposition of centralized state authority.

Beccaria and Bentham inherited from theorists such as Hobbes a conviction as to the naturalness of "social contract" and the rational rule of state law. Combined with a belief in free will and the goodness of calculable rationality, these doctrines were a major impetus for classical thought. How did all of these things express themselves in classical theorizing? Let us answer this by first turning to the work of Beccaria.

Cesare Beccaria: Controlling the Rational Calculation of Deviant Pleasure

Born to noble parentage in Milan in 1738, Beccaria inherited the title marchese di Beccaria. His upper-class Italian background provided him with the advantages of a rigorous education at the Jesuit College at Parma. Although he was an undistinguished student in his early years, this exposure to the dogmatic demands of Jesuit thought may have influenced Beccaria's later rebellion. In any event, his most influential education occurred after college. Only then did Beccaria became seriously interested in the critical thought of the Enlightenment. He read Montesquieu's *Lettres persanes* and the writings of the Encyclopedists. Convinced of the power of disciplined reason he turned to the study of law at Pavia.

In 1761 Beccaria married Teresa di Blasco, the daughter of a relatively impoverished military officer. About the same time he entered into another marriage—this one to the "Academy of Fists," a talented, articulate, and radical group of Milanese youth. Its members were disenchanted with the archaic nature of European society. Their strident push for far-reaching social reform earned them the nickname of "punch-hards."

The young members of the Academy of Fists saw themselves as "Northern Encyclopedists," so many Voltaires and Diderots joined in opposition to the antiquated abuses of the current regime. Each was expected to study, master, and report on some specialized subject calling for inquiry and reform. Within this group Beccaria was most influenced by two brothers, Pietro and Alessandro Verri. Pietro, an abstract and dispassionate thinker, was an intellectual inspiration. Alessandro, a man of action, provided Becarria with a practical vision. Through Alessandro, who held a government post as the protector of prisons, Beccaria was exposed to the brutal and undifferentiated remnants of demonic social control. Beccaria witnessed a penal system ridden with corruption and dependent on the idiosyncratic discretion of individual judges. The irrationality and injustice of this system moved Beccaria into the stance of a reformer. In a short time he became a spokesperson for a new vision of social control. It was Pietro, however, who urged him to write down his thoughts and to develop a systematic plan for making legal social control more humane and more rational. Encouraged by Pietro, Beccaria began to scribble his ideas onto scraps of paper. The result was the major treatise of the classical perspective—*Essay on Crimes and Punishments*.

Fearful of condemnation by those who wielded control over Italy's antiquated system of law and criminal justice, Beccaria first published his work anonymously in 1764. Not only was Beccaria's name omitted but the first edition of *Essay on Crimes and Punishments* was distributed without even listing the name of the printer. Such caution proved unnecessary. The book was an explosive success, and almost immediately became a landmark of reform. Beccaria was invited to France to "commune" with such revolutionary thinkers as D'Alembert, Diderot, Helvetius, and D'Holbach. He was publicly praised by Catherine the Great of Russia and Maria Theresa of Austria-Hungary and quoted with admiration by such luminaries as the philosopher Voltaire, the legal theorist Blackstone, and those architects of the new American republic, Thomas Jefferson and John Adams.

Why was *Essay on Crimes and Punishments* such an immediate success? The book appealed almost instantaneously to a curious mix of conservatives who defended the continuance of monarchy and radicals, such as D'Alembert and Diderot, who were setting in motion forces that would topple it. Both sides had a common stake in preserving the power of the absolute state. Their differences lay more with how the state should be organized and who should control it. Both abhorred the continuation of antiquated demonic control policies, harsh and arbitrary reminders of the previous days of Inquisition and holy terror. Beccaria's book represented a masterful stroke of timing, an opportunity to bring dark, medieval penal practice into the age of Enlightenment. According to historian Mary Peter Mack, "It was Beccaria's genius . . . to gather up all those poignant cries and shape them into a simple, rational, elegant and passionately human theory, moving and persuasive to all men of good will."[9] This theory is summarized in the following six principles.

The Necessity of Rational Punishment in Preserving the Social Contract Beccaria followed the lead of Hobbes and other Enlightenment thinkers in arguing for a naturalistic theory of social contract. But what happens when someone steps outside the terms of this contract? What happens when someone breaks the law of the sovereign state? Beccaria argued that a system of rational punishment was necessary in order to remind individuals of their common interest in preserving social order. Such punishments "were necessary to prevent the despotism of each individual from plunging society into its former chaos."[10] In defending the prerogative of the state to punish, Beccaria was careful to distinguish between tyrannical punishments, involving arbitrary efforts by individuals to gain positions of advantage, and rational punishments aimed at "defending the public liberty . . . from the usurpation of individuals."[11]

Legislative Determination of Law; Judicial Determiniation of Guilt During the demonic period punishment was largely controlled by judges. Judges held enormous discretion both in discerning whether someone was guilty and in deciding the fate of convicted offenders. Little had changed by the eighteenth century. "Secret accusations, *lettres de cachet,* 'confessions' extracted by brutal tortures, mere charges considered prima-facie evidence of guilt, convictions without appeal, arbitrary pardons, and tyrannical punishments were all commonplace."[12]

This dark side of demonic justice was revealed to Beccaria by his friend Alessandro Verri, an administrator of prisons. Outraged by the irrational and often abusive nature of judicially administered punishments, Beccaria, in his classical reforms, called for a strict differentiation between the punishment-setting responsibilities of the legislature and the lesser role of judges. As sovereign representatives of the entire social contract, legislators were to determine which acts endangered the common good and assign to each a particular punishment. Judges were to have no role in deciding upon punishment. Once a person was found guilty of breaking the law, a fixed legislatively determined punishment was to be assigned automatically. In the words of Beccaria, "Judges have no right to interpret the penal law . . . When the code of laws is . . . fixed (by the legislature), it should be observed in the literal sense, and nothing more is left to the judge than to determine whether an action be, or be not, conformable to the written law."[13]

The Hedonistic Psychology of Deviance: Maximizing Pleasure and Minimizing Pain A third principle of the classical perspective concerns the utilitarian calculus that was believed to govern human motivation. Humans were described as rational hedonists whose actions were based on a rational assessment of the available alternatives for maximizing pleasure and minimizing pain. Deviant action was no exception. It was calculatively chosen over conformity because it would most likely yield the greatest amount of pleasure at the least cost. Thus, for theorists such as Beccaria, who viewed "pain and pleasure [as] the only springs of [human] action," deviance was essentially no different than any other form of human conduct.[14] One deviated for the same reasons that one made other reasonable investments—to reap the profits of maximum pleasure.

Social Control as Rationally Calculated Punishment If humans were indeed rational hedonists, then the control of deviance would require the certain administration of punishment that was slightly more painful than the pleasure of nonconformity. This meant that the irrational cruelty of demonic retribution must be replaced by a rational system of measured punishment, each calculated to exceed the pleasure expected from a specific act of deviance. This system, moreover, must be known to all and administered evenly and without exception. Thus, if burglary produces six units of pleasure, its punishment should involve seven units of pain. In this fashion Beccaria proposed a precise "political arithmetic" of rational sanctions. He argued that specific types of punishment should be rationally fixed by "a calculation of [pleasure-pain] probabilities to mathematical exactness."[15]

Deterrence as the Object of Social Control The purpose of the calculated punishment was to deter future acts of deviance. Deterrence would at once be specific and general, affecting both those who were caught and sanctioned as well as those who witnessed the certain application of rational punishment. Yet, for rational deterrence to operate effectively several conditions must be met. According to Beccaria punishment must be certain, swift, and slightly more severe than the fruits of deviation would be pleasurable. Most important were the criteria of certainty and swiftness (or celerity). If these conditions were not met, there was no reason to expect that people would reasonably be deterred from seeking the pleasures of lawbreaking. The same might be true if punishments were too severe. Overly severe punishments were said to "outdistance" the calculable frameworks which reasonable people use in weighing advantages and costs of action. For this reason Beccaria opposed the death penalty and other forms of extreme penal cruelty.

Control of Acts, Not Actors This final principle of classical thinking is extremely important. It is also that which offered most of the practical problems. The entire classical system was directed toward reducing deviant acts but paid little attention to deviant actors. According to Beccaria, "They err who imagine that a crime is greater or less according to the intention of the person by whom it is committed."[16] All actors were assumed to be endowed with free will and with a similar rational calculus. Thus, for classical theorists, it was important to know only whether a deviant act had occurred.

Once this was ascertained, it was believed that the pleasure of similar acts could be deterred by a simple application of slightly more painful punishment. Accordingly, classical theory showed a total disregard for other aspects of an actor's life and for the circumstances surrounding a particular deviant occurrence. Treat no deviant as an exception. Forget about whether an offender had a bad home, a bad night, or a bad self-concept. If the act occurred, deliver the punishment.

Jeremy Bentham: Extending the Utilitarian Calculus of Rational Punishment

Jeremy Bentham (1748–1832) was, like Beccaria, both a thinker and reformer. Whereas Beccaria was repulsed by the continuance of harsh demonic control strategies in Europe, Bentham was repelled by the archaic state of eighteenth-century British common law.[17] In his books *Fragment on Government* (1776) and *An Introduction to the Principles of Morals and Legislation* (1789) Bentham laid out a scheme for rational legal reform which closely parallels that of Beccaria. He too believed that human actions were motivated by a utilitarian or hedonistic calculus of pleasure and pain. Bentham's personal passion for quantitative method led him to formulate a mathematics of rational punishments aimed at deterring offenses against the "common good." The common good was, moreover, said to be calculable in terms of acts which ensured the greatest happiness for the greatest number of people.

Because Bentham's ideas so closely resemble those of Beccaria we shall not examine his classical theories in greater detail. It is sufficient to conclude that Beccaria and Bentham shared a common vision regarding a new, rational approach to deviance. Their proposals for legal reform and calculable punishment assumed that deviants were rational actors, responsive to enlightened state policies directed toward the deterrence of lawbreaking and the preservation of the social contract.

IDENTIFYING CLASSICAL DEVIANCE

The classical perspective has shown very little concern with the study of deviant behavior or deviant people. It assumes that deviants are no different than anyone else, that their actions are reflective of efforts to maximize pleasure while minimizing pain. The reason for this is simple. The system of lawful social controls is not rational enough to deter people from choosing pleasure beyond the prescribed boundaries of the social contract. Nothing more. Nothing less. The problem of deviance is thus not a problem of bad or inadequate people but of bad or inadequate laws. In consequence, the highly legalistic classical perspective directs our attention not so much toward the study of deviation as toward the study of law.

What little the classical perspective does tell us about the identification of deviance has already been described in the preceding section. In summary, classical theorists such as Beccaria and Bentham contend that the proper identification of deviant acts is the sole responsibility of the legislature. Judges are to ascertain only whether someone actually committed an illegal act. Neither legislators nor judges are to be concerned with deviants as people. Classical theory is concerned exclusively with deviant acts and with the punitive strategies of rational punishment which are believed to deter such acts.

One question remains. How are legislators to decide which acts are deviant and which acts are acceptable? Beccaria provides guidance on this matter. Like the scholastic theologians who preceded him, he appears to trust the wisdom of the sovereign state to regulate social life in the interest of the common good. But what will state officials perceive as the "common good"? In reviewing the background of the classical perspective, we noted the interdependent connectedness of the early capitalist economy and the modern centralized state as both emerge together in history. Does this mean that the state would be likely to equate the market values of capitalism with the good of society as a whole? A growing number of critical theorists suggest that this was the case. As Mark Kennedy points out, "the State created new crimes and punishments directly as the institutions of capitalism advanced."[18] This contention will be examined in greater detail in the final chapter of this book. For the present, it is enough to note that Beccaria's relative silence regarding exactly how state legislators will "naturally" and "reasonably" discern the common good is a silence that rings loudly and disturbingly in the ears of those concerned with the role of powerful economic, political, and social interest groups in shaping the style and context of law.

Bentham was not as silent on this issue. His principle of social utility presented a simple ethical command for those who ruled. Act always to ensure the greatest happiness for the greatest number! His inclinations toward rationally quantifying social and legislative policies provided him with a hopeful vision that this principle of the "greatest happiness" would someday be converted into a computable mathematical formula. But even if this could be done, what would happen to minorities, to those whose pleasurable desires fell outside the statistical boundaries of the greatest numbers?

While not resolving this question entirely, Bentham argued that a principle of "demonstrable social harm" was a necessary condition for legislatively prescribed sanctions. If there were no demonstrable victims there should be no punishment. Thus, homosexuality, even if it offends the moral vision of a large segment of people, should not be subject to penal sanction simply because it presents no demonstrable harm to those involved. This principle of demonstable harm differentiates the classical approach from the demonic. The demonic perspective recognizes no difference between immorality and deviance. The classical perspective offers somewhat of a tougher test—does observable harm result? This, perhaps, is the major contribution of classical thought to the methods for discerning deviance.

THE SOCIAL CONTROL OF CLASSICAL DEVIANCE

On March 9, 1762, Jean Calas, a 60-year-old French Huguenot merchant, was tried, convicted, and executed for the murder of his son. During two hours of "legal torture" the old man repeatedly protested his innocence. The prosecutor meanwhile alleged that Calas, a Protestant, had killed his son because the boy had converted to Catholicism. Calas refused to confess. The judge, convinced more by the prosecutor's emotional arguments than by Calas's cries, sentenced him to death. He was "broken on the wheel." His family was arrested. All his property was confiscated by the state. A short time later the real facts of the case became public. The son had committed suicide. His father had been falsely and mercilessly and savagely tried and executed under a demonic social control system that had dominated Europe for centuries. Critics and reformers called for an end to such antiquated control practices. The reform-minded philosopher Voltaire joined with other critics in obtaining a postmortem reversal of Calas's conviction. Although Calas was not able to be given a proper Christian burial, in the natural order of things the reversal represented a victory that was more symbolic than real.

Two years after Calas's death Cesare Beccaria published his famous *Essay on Crimes and Punishments*. The publication of the manuscript signified that the dominance of demonic control strategies was nearing an end. Beccaria's treatise quickly resulted in major changes in European social control policy. Its consequences were as practically real as they were symbolically important. Three of the more important practical control policies resulting from classical thinking include: (1) the highly rationalistic French Penal Code of 1791; (2) neoclassical modifications, and (3) the centralized control of deviants in state institutions.

The French Penal Code of 1791

The French Penal Code of 1791 was perhaps the most celebrated instance of applied classical thinking. French progressives were still fuming over the Calas case when Beccaria's book hit the intellectual marketplace. The French edition of *Essay on Crimes and Punishments* contained a laudatory introduction prepared by Voltaire. Its influence was enormous. French legislators soon came to accept many of Beccaria's ideas as their own. These were incorporated into the famous French Criminal Code of 1791.

The new French code read much like the rational control policy Beccaria had dreamed of. It made strict use of the doctrine of uniform punishment for specific crimes. It provided a scale of crimes arranged by seriousness, with punishments proportioned accordingly. It specified that all penal sanctions must be determined legislatively and that the role of judges be limited to determination of guilt. As John L. Gillin has suggested, "In this code there was an attempt not only to legislate on every crime, but to fix by statute the penalty for each degree of each kind. Nothing was left to the judgment of the court, except the question of guilt. There could be no abatement for extenuating circumstances, no added penalty for the heinousness of the way in which a particular crime was committed."[19]

The French code of 1791 came as close as any in history to incorporating a pure classical viewpoint. It was both extremely legalistic and administratively simple. If someone was found guilty, he or she was given the legislatively prescribed punishment no matter what. This was its greatest advantage. It represented "an exact scale of punishments for equal acts without reference to the individual involved or the special circumstances in which the crime was committed."[20] This was also its greatest disadvantage.

The 1791 code engendered enormous practical problems for which it had no legal answer. It was soon criticized for providing no just recourse for persons committing the same act under very different social circumstances. Shouldn't the law look differently upon someone who plans a crime with calculated premeditation than upon someone who acts criminally in the heat of passion? Was it fair to assign the same punishment to the passionately violent spouse reacting to marital infidelity as to the well-rehearsed murderer executing a prearranged killing for profit? Critics demanded that exceptions should be made. Yet no exceptions were available in the purely classical code of 1791. Similar questions were raised regarding the identical handling of first-time and repeat offenders. Both were assigned the same "rational" punishment. Nor did the code make exceptions for children, the insane, the retarded, or other persons whose capacity for rational choice might be impaired or underdeveloped. Critics demanded reasonable changes. This resulted in a host of neoclassical modifications of an otherwise highly rationalistic control policy.

Neoclassical Modification

In response to criticisms regarding its overly rigid rationality, the 1791 French Penal Code underwent a series of step-by-step revisions. In 1810 a certain discretion was returned to judges in order to deal with hardened repeat criminals. In 1819 exceptions were provided for certain "objective" circumstances affecting the seriousness of a particular act. These ambiguous revisions, while they reopened the door for a certain measure of judicial discretion, did not satisfy critics whose primary objections concerned the classical perspective's inability to consider the unequal "subjective" circumstances or mental state of deviant actors. These critics included the philosopher Feuerbach and that pioneer of modern law enforcement, Sir Robert Peel. They pushed for and achieved a wider set of modifications, which included attention to (a) the premeditation of the deviant act, (b) the possibility of extenuating or mitigating circumstances, and (c) the suggestion that some deviant actors should not be held accountable for their acts by virtue of their insanity.

The neoclassical modifications were intended to strengthen rather than replace the central tenets of classical theory. Like other classical theorists, the advocates of neoclassical reform believed that social control policy should, on the whole, be based upon the certain, swift, and proportionate application of rational punishment. Yet, in the following areas classical control strategies were said to need more flexibility.

Premeditation This refers to the prior planning of the act and was considered to be an indicator of the free will. The introduction of this concept during the neoclassical period, however, raised more questions than it answered. Consider the neoclassical assertion that first-time offenders were "freer in will" because their actions lacked the force of "habit." Should then they be treated more severely? This matter remained a theory issue in neoclassical scholastic.

Mitigating Circumstances This concept implies that both physical and social-environmental factors needed to be assessed in determining a deviant's responsibility. Such physical factors as the weather might impact upon the freedom of deviant choice. Unencumbered free will could hypothetically be eroded by heat and humidity. Socially, such factors as stress, pressure, and situational passion were allowed to be considered as well. This kind of reasoning was viewed as an exception to, and not a replacement of, the classical assumption of rationally based free choice as the basis for deviance. It began, however, to soften the shell of the free will doctrine. Conceptions of deviance moved closer to the determinism that would characterize the later pathological perspective.

Insanity The institution of the insanity defense, heralded by the 1843 trial of Daniel M'Naughten, is a third example of the neoclassical modifications. M'Naughten was brought to trial for the highly publicized murder of Mr. Drummond, the secretary to London police commissioner, Sir Robert Peel. Upon investigation it appeared that M'Naughten hardly fit the classical stereotype of the rational, calculating deviant. M'Naughten was a character who (in his own mind) experienced direct communication with God. In the course of their conversations, God had apparently informed M'Naughten that a demonic plot was afoot by which agents of the devil, masked as members of Britain's Tory (Conservative) party, were conspiring to establish a reign of Satan on earth. God further informed M'Naughten that this conspiracy could only be stopped by killing Sir Robert Peel, a noted leader of the Tories. What choice did the God-fearing M'Naughten have? He procured a weapon and tried to act in God's name by assassinating the demonic figurehead. The one problem was that M'Naughten did not know what Peel looked like. He staked out Peel's office and mistakenly gunned down Peel's secretary, Drummond. A saintly hero in his own mind, M'Naughten was quickly arrested and charged with murder. But was he guilty? Had he really intended wrong? Wasn't he guided (if admittedly a bit crazily) by what he believed to be the lawful and holy orders of the Most High?

M'Naughten's lawyers felt that whatever he was, he was not guilty of the crime of murder as traditionally defined. He had not intended murder as such. He had intended only to carry out what he (by virtue of some rather nonordinary mental processes) had honestly perceived as the orders of God. He was insane and should not be subject to the same punitive social controls as "rational" criminals. A panel of noted judges commissioned to rule on the controversial case agreed. M'Naughten was declared not guilty by reason of insanity because it was established that "at the time of the committing of the act, the party accused (in this case M'Naughten) was laboring under such a defect of reason, from disease of the mind, as to not know the nature and quality of the act he was doing; or if he did know it, that he did not know what he was doing was wrong.[21] This highly rational, highly cognitive test became, and, with modifications, continues to be, the basic standard for judging criminal insanity. As with the other modifications introduced in the neoclassical era, it suggests that there may be more to some deviance than rationally calculated free choice. Insanely calculated choices were of a different order and should be controlled differently.

As a result of the precedent set by the M'Naughten case, those declared "criminally insane," while not convicted of a crime, have been traditionally committed involuntarily and for "indefinite periods of time" to mental institutions (hospitals for the criminally insane) until "restored to reason." The insane were, in principle, to be "treated" rather than punished. This revision of classical thinking foreshadows what would become the predominant mode of social control under the subsequent pathological perspectives—belief in the "corrective treatment" of deviants.

Centralized Control of Deviants in State Penitentiaries

The primary objective of classical social control was to deter future deviance by the application of rationally calculated punishment. How practically was such punishment carried out? The answer is found in the invention and use of the large, centralized state prison. These first appeared in history just as the classical viewpoint was capturing the intellectual fancy of western society. From a contemporary vantage point this may seem odd. Large state prisons are today criticized as irrational and dehumanizing environments, as schools for crime. During the late eighteenth and early nineteenth century the promise of such institutions was different. Since deviant actors were seen as essentially rational, it was believed that by "doing time" in such places they would learn to "correct" their characters to fit with the calculatively rational demands of life in the modern world dominated by the complementary powers of the capitalist marketplace and the laws of the centralized state.

How did supporters of the classical control model arrive at such an optimistic view of the state penitentiary? The best answer is that institutional confinement originally had more to do with practical circumstances than with intellectual conviction. According to the historian Michel Foucault, there was something contradictory about this from the beginnning. The calculative principles behind rational punishment should have meant that each specific crime would be met by some other specific measure of proportionate deterrence. The nearly exclusive reliance on prison as punishment meant that different crimes received essentially the same punishment. The only thing which differed was the time spent within a penitentiary's walls. As Foucault points out, classical theorists envisaged imprisonment "but as one among other penalties."[22] The problem, however, was that "within a short space of time, detention became the essential form of punishment. . . . The theatre of punishment of which the eighteenth century dreamed and which would have acted essentially [as a deterrent] on the minds of the general public was replaced by the great uniform machinery of the prisons. . . . The diversity, so solemnly promised, is reduced in the end to this grey, uniform penalty."[23]

Why this shift from the diverse, public nature of classical punishment to the uniform and secluded mechanics of incarceration? Although there is no easy answer to this question, Foucault suggests an intriguing possibility—that the "total control" potential of prison technology resonated so well with the power structures of a society dominated by the capitalist marketplace and the centralized state that prison soon usurped all other forms of punishment. As a total institution prison captures not only the body but the "soul," or personality, of the inmate. The penitentiary enables the state to isolate, observe, and then, based upon observation, manipulate and change the offender into a person whose calculated rationality and improved "self-control" would fit better with the inner discipline demanded by the mass marketplace of modern society. In this sense, Foucault suggests that prisons were initially filled up with persons sentenced for rational punishment, but that the raw power of prison technology soon produced a new theory of social control, one based upon strategies of manipulative change, one suggesting that deviance results not from free rational choice but from observable and changeable defects or pathologies.

Is Foucault correct about this? Did the control technology of prison have such a great affinity with the diciplinary demands of capitalist and centralized state power that it "took in" classically sentenced rational deviants and "turned out" a new breed of nonconformer—the pathological deviant? Much of Foucault's argument rests on his examination of Jeremy Bentham's plans for constructing the "Panopticon"—the total prison, the ultimate in enforced penal control. Bentham anticipated that convicted offenders would be rationally sentenced to do time in this huge, rounded, glass-roofed "inspection house." At its center would be a central guard tower. There the watchful eyes of state authority could gaze at incarcerated inmates twenty-four hours a day. Each prisoner would pass time by being subject daily to the same monotonous routine of compulsive, dreary work and rigid discipline. The Panopticon was more than a planner's dream. Bentham drafted architectural specifications and obtained a government permit to build this model prison in Tothill Fields, England. Only when the British government defaulted on its agreement to finance the venture were plans for the Panopticon finally laid to rest.

Although the formal purpose of the Panopticon was simply to rationally punish, Foucault reads much more into its environmental design. He sees wider appeal in its possibility for constant surveillance and manipulative transformation. This was its greatest attraction to capitalist society and to the centralized rational state that secured the conditions for its survival. Bentham's own description of the Panopticon seems to suggest that Foucault may be correct about this matter. In describing the ideal prison Bentham appears to have gone well beyond the notion that prison would be strictly a place for rational punishment. In Bentham's own words, the Panopticon would be "a mill to grind rogues honest and idle men industrious."[24]

David Rothman's detailed history of the origins of the American prison system suggests essentially the same thing as Foucault's—that the implementation of classical control philosophy resulted in widespread reliance upon incarceration. Rothman's interpretation of this matter is nowhere as bold or suggestive as Foucault's. He argues simply that American reformers, caught up in the "immediate and widespread appeal" of Beccaria's classical proposals, thought little of the contradictions entailed in relying upon prison as punishment. In many ways prison seemed like a practical way to implement the classical schema. "Prisons matched punishment to crime precisely: the more heinous the offense, the longer the sentence."[25] According to Rothman, it was the "fact of imprisonment, not its internal routine," that was important to the early American reformers.[26] Convinced of the rational strength of their proposals and of the advantages of classical thought over the remnants of demonic control, advocates of the classical perspective in America were said to have paid little attention to what prison really was or what incarceration really meant. The results, however, were the same as those described by Foucault. The late-eighteenth-century experimentation with classical control strategies promoted the construction and use of state penal institutions. These same buildings would later be justified as laboratories for the rehabilitative strategies of pathological theory. The historical origins, however, are rooted in the blind enthusiasm of early classical thought.

THE CLASSICAL PERSPECTIVE TODAY

In many ways classical theorizing may seem nearly as outdated as the demonic perspective. Ideas about things which cause or determine deviance have, for over a century, replaced the emphasis on free will and rational hedonism. Efforts to treat or rehabilitate deviants have generally superseded an emphasis on rational punishment and its deterrent characteristics. Yet, today we are witnessing a resurgence of classical thinking, a return to the rationalistic and punishment-oriented thinking of the late eighteenth century. Even more than the demonic perspective, the classical perspective is alive and very well in the modern world.

My first exposure to a strong dose of contemporary classical thought came when I was a graduate student. I was attending a lecture by the well-known University of Pennsylvania criminologist, Marvin Wolfgang. Wolfgang was reporting on the results of his recently completed study, *Delinquency in a Birth Cohort.*[27] In that study Wolfgang and his colleagues, Robert Figlio and Thorsten Sellin, tracked the "criminal careers" of nearly 10,000 boys who were born in 1945 and were living in Philadelphia between their tenth and eighteenth birthdays. Using records of official police contacts, school reports, and Selective Service registration information these researchers sought to determine the percentage of boys apprehended for some violation of the criminal law. The boys they studied came from all walks of Philadelphia society.

The extent of the delinquency uncovered by Wolfgang and his associates was striking. By age 18, 35 percent of their Philadelphia birth cohort had been apprehended for a criminal offense. By age 26 this figure grew to 50 percent. This was the percentage who had committed at least one offense. What about repeaters? After the first recorded offense 47 percent of the boys had no subsequent record. This was the case no matter what was done with or to them. It mattered little, in other words, whether they were dealt with leniently or severely. They simply ceased committing delinquent acts. Or at least they ceased getting caught. Another large percentage, 35 percent, dropped from the cohort after the second offense. An additional 29 percent stopped after the third. Thereafter the percentage who stopped repeating leveled out to a very small figure, less than approximately 5 percent for each subsequent apprehension.

What are the policy implications of Wolfgang's findings? In addressing himself to this question Wolfgang made reference to the classical control ideas espoused by Beccaria and Bentham. Wolfgang used a baseball metaphor in speculating about what might be called a "three-strike" model of rational deterrence. Let us assume, suggested Wolfgang, that the vast majority of all potential criminals are rationally calculative actors. Let us also assume that people do make mistakes and slip up sometimes. Wolfgang thus aligned himself with what might best be described as a tradition of neoclassical thought. Since the data show that most offenders fall out of the pool of delinquents after one or two offenses, why not devise a crime control policy in which very little is done with people until they arrive at a third offense? This would both save costs and target scarce resources toward that small group of offenders who would repeat acts of delinquency again and again. According to Wolfgang, out of the initial cohort of nearly 10,000 only 627, or 6 percent, committed five or more offenses. Yet this small group of "chronic offenders" was responsible for over half of the total number of all offenses recorded for the cohort as a whole and for about two-thirds of all violent offenses. Given this fact, Wolfgang speculated whether a truly rational crime control policy should not provide swift, certain, but not very severe admonishments for those caught a first or second time and reserve the full force of its sanctions for offenders who strike out a third time. This latter group, he reasoned, was on a course toward becoming chronic offenders. In order to deter people from this course why not announce publicly that not much will happen for initial offenses, but once offenders cross over into their "third strike" they will automatically be dealt with in a severe fashion, with severity escalating heavily for each subsequent offense. And perhaps, suggested the noted criminologist, if people commit as many as five offenses they should be locked up forever. Moreover, since everyone would know this would happen without exception, such a policy would maximize the potential deterrence of the criminal law.

Wolfgang paused at this point in his presentation. He said that he was unsure whether his speculative proposal was liberal or conservative. His proposal for the permanent removal of chronic offenders from society sounded very tough. It reminded one of Beccaria, who had once advocated long-term penal slavery as a rational deterrent far superior to that of the death penalty.[28] On the other hand, the suggestion for relative leniency for first- and second-time offenders might appeal to liberals who believe that delinquents should be given a chance to reform themselves. What was not unsure about Wolfgang's reflections was the manner in which they drew upon the central tenent of the classical perspective.

Wolfgang's comments were, during the course of the 1970s, joined by an ever-widening chorus of criminal justice thinkers with renewed interest in classical thought. The reason for this involves the perceived failure of subsequent "more scientific" perspectives to produce workable solutions to the problem of crime. This issue will be dealt with in greater detail later. For now, it is enough to say that the recent swing backward toward classical thought is often justified by descriptions of the alleged practical inadequacies of the theories that had once replaced it. As Leon Sheleff points out, "As disillusionment sets in about the capacity to fully understand the etiology [causes] of crime, as reservations are increasingly being expressed about the rehabilitative goals of penal philosophy and correctional practices . . . so the basic framework . . . of Beccaria's and Bentham's ideas is slowly infiltrating back into criminological studies."[29]

One need only peruse the professional journals or attend a single criminal justice conference to learn that Sheleff is correct; faith in rehabilitative treatment is dead, or nearly so, and a concern with certain nondiscretionary and uniform systems of rational punishments is at the top of criminal justice priorities. Forget about trying to explain and treat the causes of crime. Deal with criminal deviance as a rational choice. Devise a fixed and certain system of punishments. Warn everyone that, if caught, offenders will be punished without exception. Eliminate the widely disparate discretion of judges in handing out sentences. Emphasize sentences that are fixed and mandatory. Do away with indeterminate minimum and maximum sentences, enabling judges to gear punishment to the correctional needs of the individual actor. Return to the act. Treat all actors alike. Get rid of parole. Release prisoners when the time of punishment is complete, not when it is estimated that they are cured or rehabilitated. Eliminate the insanity plea. Deal with serious juvenile offenders in the same fashion as adults. Punish and punish rationally. These are all current slogans and issues being debated in criminal justice circles. Each sounds remarkably similar to arguments made by Beccaria and the other proponents of the early classical perspective. Consider, for instance, the recent findings of the well-financed, four-year interdisciplinary investigation by the Committee for the Study of Incarceration. These are reported by Andrew von Hirsch in the book *Doing Justice*. According to von Hirsch:

> Some of our conclusions may seem old-fashioned. To our surpise, we found ourselves returning to the ideas of such Enlightenment thinkers as . . . Beccaria—ideas that antedated notions of rehabilitation that emerged in the nineteenth century. . . . We argue, as . . . Beccaria did, that severity of punishment should depend chiefly on the seriousness of the crime. We share Beccaria's interest in placing limits on sentencing discretion.[30]

Perhaps the foremost representative of the revival of classical thinking about deviance is James Q. Wilson, Harvard professor and President Gerald Ford's personal adviser on crime and criminal justice. In his book *Thinking About Crime,* Wilson totally denies the value of searching for the causes of crime.[31] Criminal justice policies should, instead, be based upon what Wilson calls a "new realism," a platform of rationality by which criminals will know simply that they will be punished if caught. According to Wilson, "The radical individualism of Bentham and Beccaria may be scientifically questionable but prudentially necessary.[32] Thus Wilson argues that criminals ought to be viewed as rational actors who will get the message if it is made known that their crimes will be met by a swift and certain punitive response. For every conviction for a nontrial offense, penalties should be assigned which "fit the crime" and which permit only a small amount of judicial discretion regarding such matters as mitigating and exacerbating circumstances. According to Wilson, penalties need not be long and severe as long as they are swift and certain. This will maximize their potential for deterrence.

On the surface Wilson's position sounds much like an update of Beccaria's. Yet, his arguments also betray a fundamental political conservatism which undermines the full rationality of his neoclassical platform. A major inconsistency with Wilson's proposals involves what he has to say or what he fails to say about corporate, organizational, or white-collar crime. Such crime is generally committed by highly calculating individuals in the rational pursuit of illegal profit. It is, moreover, among the most costly forms of lawbreaking to society as a whole. The annual economic toll of corporate crime totals billions of dollars, far exceeding that from any form of conventional or street crime. Yet the punishments for such crime remain among the lowest and most lenient. As criminologists Marshal Clinard and Robert Meir point out, "It is ironic that the penalties for white-collar crime are the least severe, while they are given to the very persons who might be the most affected by them. . . . In other words, if these offenders are potentially the most deterred, an increase in punishments and the intensity of enforcement might result in the greatest benefit to society."[33] Surely then the white-collar offender would be a logical target for the revived classical control strategies of Wilson and others. Wilson, however, dismisses this topic. His book, he argues, does not deal with white-collar crimes because it reflects his "conviction" and "the conviction of most citizens, that predatory street crime is a far more serious matter than consumer fraud, antitrust violations," and other varieties of corporate theft.[34] As a result, the "new realism" of Wilson appears more conservative than consistent, more selective than uniform in its return to classical thought.

While the above-described reemphasis of classical thinking sounds quite conservative, it is shared, to some degree, by liberal reformers. These persons are concerned with the rights of those under the sanctions of the law. Today, they argue, treating the causes of crime has meant, in practice if not on paper, more time spent under the control of the state. Waiting for the parole board to decide on one's rehabilitative status creates enormous uncertainty, anxiety, and the omnipresent possibility of the discriminatory use of discretionary powers. Most prisoner-rights and ex-offender groups share the desire of conservative "law-and-order" factions to eliminate the open-endedness of indeterminate sentencing and to establish a more fixed set of uniformly applied sanctions. Moreover, such groups have increased their opposition to the "noble lie" of nonvoluntary treatment and in recognizing punishment as the primary object of the penal system. By viewing the offender as responsible for his or her actions, as a bearer of punishment rather than the subject of treatment, it is argued that dignity is restored to those convicted. This is the dignity of the rational actor that was an essential component of the classical perspective.

The return to classical thinking is signaled by the replacement of rehabilitation with deterrence and rationally administered punishment as the primary goals of social control over criminality. Yet, even among the continued advocates of treatment, a renewed rationality has shown itself. "Reality therapy," one of the most popular of the contemporary modes of rehabilitation, places an extraordinary emphasis on the individual's acceptance of the consequences of his or her own freely chosen actions.[35] Clients are denied acceptance of "excuses" for their behaviors. It is demanded that they own up to their actions and accept the outcomes accordingly. Indeed, the assumptions of the classical perspective, while shelved for some time in favor of perspectives which replaced the concept of choice with that of cause, have reentered and reclaimed their place in the contemporary marketplace of social control.

ASSESSING THE ADEQUACY OF THE CLASSICAL PERSPECTIVE

At the core of the classical perspective lies the claim that rational punishment deters deviant behavior. In this closing section we will sort through a variety of evidence that has recently been gathered to test the adequacy of this claim. The chapter concludes with a short comment on another question of adequacy—the adequacy of the perspective to realize the rational justice it upholds as a goal.

Does Punishment Deter?

According to classical theorists, rationally calculated punishment reduces future deviance by instilling a fear of sanctions in both the punished offender (e.g., specific deterrence) and in the public at large (e.g., general deterrence). To fully realize this effect, it is argued, punishment must be swift and certain, and the severity of its calculated pain must outweigh the perceived pleasure associated with a given act of deviance.

Are classical theorists correct in their assessment of the deterrent effect of punishment? At a commonsensical level the principle of deterrence has a great deal of appeal. Don't we encounter situations each day in which we might have acted differently if we believed our actions would be met by a swift, certain, and severe stroke of social sanction? Think about something as simple as a parking violation. I pull up to the meter. I plan to run into the store for one item I forgot while shopping for tonight's dinner. I know I'll be gone only a minute. Yet, I know also that the likelihood of my dropping the required coins in the meter is dependent upon whether I think that I might have to pay a costly fine if I don't. I'm sure that seeing the police officer ticketing the car ahead of me will make a difference.

Aside from its commonsensical appeal, is there any substantive evidence that deterrence is an effective principle for social control policy as a whole? Until recent years there has been very little research on this important question. Why? The reason involves the short-lived dominance of the classical perspective as a tool for interpreting deviance and constructing control policy. As will be pointed out in our next chapter, the popular appeal of classical theorizing lasted less than a full century. It was soon replaced by the pathological perspective, with its promise to scientifically explain the cause of deviance and clinically produce the cure. As the precepts of pathological theorizing and other deterministic perspectives gained ascendency over the free-will tenets of classical thought, such ideas as the belief in the deterrent power of punishment were dismissed without ever being fully tested.

In *The Criminological Enterprise* Don Gibbons documents this lack of concern with testing the principle of deterrence by examining what is said about punishment by some of the leading texts in the field of crime, deviance, and social control.[36] According to Gibbons the subject of deterrence is a virtually ignored topic for inquiry. The value of punishment was dismissed as a matter of "emotional" rather than "scientific" procedure,[37] as being a "relatively inefficient method" of dealing with criminals and other deviants,[38] as representing a "child-like faith"[39] in something which was believed to have little causal relationship to deviant behavior.[40] Such criticisms were strong. Yet, they were not based on "hard scientific tests" of the evidence. In Gibbons's words: "The idea of punishment went against the grain, so that criminologists either expressed great hostility toward it or were uninterested in research on deterrence, opting instead for 'scientific' efforts to treat and rehabilitate offenders."[41]

Today things are different. As mentioned previously, the classical perspective has been "born again" in recent years. With the rebirth of classical thinking the study of deterrence has become a veritable "growth industry" within the field of criminology.[42] In the last decade we have witnessed dozens of published reports assessing the deterrent effect of punishment. Many have attempted to refine the meaning of deterrence so that policy-makers can better estimate the practical benefits of various strategies of punitive social control. Distinctions arise, for instance, between such notions as "partial" and "marginal" deterrence.[43] Measures of partial deterrence assess reductions in the level of deviance threatened by this or that rationally calculated form of punishment. Measures of marginal deterrence seek to compare such reduction rates with those achieved by other forms of punishment or social control.

The rapidly expanding body of research on deterrence is filled with technical distinctions of this kind. Without burdening the introductory reader with an array of specialized terminology, I would like to provide a simple overview of three of the most important topics emerging from the new literature on deterrence. These include studies of (1) specific deterrence, (2) general deterrence, and (3) the role of perception in mediating the effect of punitive sanctions. I shall conclude with some general reservations about the nature and findings of the research on this topic.

Specific Deterrence Does punishment reduce the likelihood of future offenses for offenders so sanctioned? This is a difficult question to answer. Its ideal test would seemingly involve a comparison between offenders who are punished and those who break similar laws in a similar fashion but whose deviant acts go unpunished. This, however, is a comparison that is not practically possible. Records of subsequent offenses are highly imperfect for punished offenders. The only known offenses are those for which a person actually gets caught. Such records are virtually nonexistent for the unpunished offender. Hence, studies of specific deterrence tend to compare subsequent offenses of persons assigned to various levels or degrees of punishment. Those who are imprisoned for a long time are compared with those imprisoned for a short time. Incarcerated offenders are compared with those placed on probation. Such comparisons are methodologically flawed. People sentenced with the most severe punishments are generally those with the longest records or those who have committed the most severe crimes. They may also be persons who systematically suffer social discrimination due to race and class, and who, once released with a "record," are more susceptible to police surveillance and future arrest. A comparison of such persons with those in lesser punishment conditions is thus made problematic from the outset. The findings of such studies are problematic as well. They appear to contradict the notion of specific deterrence. According to Jack Gibbs, a noted deterrence researcher, as the severity of punishment increases so does the likelihood that a specific offender will commit an offense again.[44] This, of course, is the opposite of what would be predicted by those convinced of the practical utility of punishment.

In order to get around some of the methodological problems encountered in many specific deterrence studies, some researchers have opted for self-report measures of deviation. The work of Martin Gold and Jay R. Williams is a case in point.[45] Using a self-report questionnaire Gold and Williams were able to develop two matched groups of thirty-five pairs of adolescent delinquents. Each group was similar to the other in terms of past offense histories between matched pairs (measured by the seriousness and frequency of self-reported offenses). What made them different was that the members of one group had been apprehended and sanctioned, while the members of the other had remained "uncaught." By constructing such comparison groups Gold and Williams hoped to control for the impact of prior offenses and the possibility that being apprehended increases the likelihood of being caught again in the future. The results of this study contradict what might be expected from a specific deterrence standpoint. In twenty matched pairs the apprehended delinquent had a higher level of subsequent offending than the nonapprehended delinquent. In five other pairs the levels were nearly identical. Apprehended offenders showed lower levels of subsequent offenses in only ten of the thirty-five pairs.

The negative findings of most specific deterrence studies have led some researchers to entertain quite different hypotheses. Liska suggests, for instance, that "an equally good case may be made for the opposite conclusion: punishment increases future law violations."[46] Liska directs our attention to what may be referred to as the "socialization" and "stigmatization" effects of certain forms of punishment. By "socialization" Liska refers to the possibility that sentenced offenders may learn "prodeviant" values, attitudes, and behaviors from persons with whom they associate in prison. By "stigmatization" he considers the possiblity that the postprison social environment is one in which an ex-con is denied entrance into certain acceptable or conventional social groups or avenues of economic opportunity. Blocked in nondeviant opportunity, the stigmatized deviant may fall back into a social group in which deviant options are both permitted and rewarded. In other words, it is possible for punishment to have the opposite effect from that envisioned by advocates of specific deterrence. This possibility has recently been acknowledged by deterrence researchers such as Charles Tittle. Tittle and others have suggested that future research efforts attempt to include measures of inprison and postprison social environments in better assessing the deterrent effect of punitive sanctions.[47]

General Deterrence Studies of specific deterrence, although methodologically flawed, have generally resulted in negative findings. The results of general deterrence research are more mixed. Measures of general deterrence seek to assess the impact of certain forms of punishment on the level of offenses committed by the public at large. One of the pioneer studies in this area was Jack Gibbs's comparative examination of homicide rates among states with different levels of punitive sanctions for the years 1959–61.[48] Gibbs's index of the level of punishment involved measures of the certainty and severity with which punishment was delivered. His findings support the thesis of general deterrence. As the certainty and severity of sanctions increased, the rate of homicide was found to decrease.

Gibbs's research was extended by Tittle to include the seven forms of major crime indexed in the FBI's *Uniform Crime Reports*. In addition to homicide these include rape, aggravated assault, robbery, larceny, or theft or over $50, burglary, and auto theft. Tittle's findings both support and modify the conclusions drawn by Gibbs.[49] Tittle discovered that certainty of punishment, as estimated by the percentage of convicted offenders sentenced to state prisons, was negatively related to offense rates in various states. As certainty increased, offense rates decreased. Such was not the case with severity of punishment. This variable was measured by the median of months served in prison for a given offense. Except in the case of homicide, increases in severity were not related to decreases in crime rate. The same general results have been confirmed in a number of subsequent studies.[50]

Certainty appears to count more heavily than severity. Research by Charles Logan goes so far as to suggest that the predominant influence of certainty may, in certain cases, obscure the potential influence of severity.[51] Logan discovered the states whose punishments were the highest in severity were also those which were the lowest in certainty. He interprets this finding to suggest that, when the available punishments are most severe, judges and juries may be more reluctant to find persons guilty and thus incarcerate them for lengthy periods of time. Severity may thus work against certainty in states where severity is highest. Because certainty is reduced in high-severity states, and because the impact of severity may depend upon a high level of certainty, a true test of the independent impact of severity is thus said to be missing. Logan attempted to correct for this by assessing the influence of severity only after controlling for levels of certainty. Controlling for certainty Logan discovered that severity had a consistent, if admittedly small, relationship to lowered rates of crime. Even then, however, the relationship between severity and lower crime rate was nowhere as high as that between certainty and lower crime rate. Indeed of the twelve major studies of general deterrence conducted since Gibbs's 1968 research, eight have reported very strong negative correlations between rates of crime and certainty of punitive sanction. That is, as certainty increases, the crime rate decreases.

Why has certainty of punishment been found to be so consistently related to lower rates of crime? The most obvious answer is that how one is punished may not be as important as whether one is punished. Several recent studies suggest that the issue may be more complicated. Research by Logan indicates that the impact of certainty is to some degree mediated by the level of severity. He concludes that just as certainty influences the rate of severity, the impact of certainty is itself greatest when the level of severity is highest.[52] Other studies have attended to the role of the so-called tipping effect and to the "overload hypothesis" in interpreting the observed negative relationship between certainty and crime rate. The tipping effect suggests that certainty must reach a certain level before it has a significant impact on crime rate. This effect is reported in Charles Tittle and Allan Rowe's study of municipal and county crime rates in Florida.[53] According to Tittle and Rowe, certainty has a measurable negative impact on crime rate only after the certainty of arrest for crime rises past a cutoff point of 30 percent.[54]

The tipping effect qualifies the suggested impact of certainty on crime rate. The overload hypothesis, however, questions the interpretation of the negative correlation between certainty and crime as one of deterrence. It asks, instead, about the way that the crime rate affects certainty of sanctioning. The overload hypothesis assumes that the general level of policing remains constant during periods of high and low crime. The difference is that police resources will be scattered during periods of high crime, thereby reducing the certainty of arrest and sanction. During periods of low crime the opposite happens. The police may have more time to investigate each case, and this increases the probability that offenders will be sanctioned. Which is the case? Does increased certainty reduce the crime rate, or does a reduction in the crime rate increase certainty? The answer to this question, as to so many others in the burgeoning field of deterrence research, awaits further, more careful and controlled investigation.

Perceptions of Punishment We have to this point been concerned with objective measures concerning such things as the severity and certainty of punishment. But what about the subjective perception of punishment? This would seemingly be at the heart of the classical perspective on deterrence. Beccaria's and Bentham's notion of a utilitarian calculus of pleasure and pain suggests that individuals size up the magnitude and likelihood of possible punishment before freely deciding to engage in deviant behavior. How, then, does the perception of possible punishment impact on the likelihood of acting deviantly?

There have to date been few studies of perception of punishment as it relates to deterrence. This is unfortunate, since according to the principles of the classical perspective, punishment will deter deviance only to the extent that individuals are aware of the price they may pay for straying from the straight and narrow path of conformity. This deficiency in deterrence research has recently been recognized, and new work is under way to explore the relationship between perceptions of possible punishment and the decision to deviate. Two things emerge, however, from the studies that have been completed to this point. The first is a consistent finding that perceptions of punishment are indeed negatively related to the likelihood of committing an act of crime or deviance. That is, as individuals' estimates of the likelihood of being sanctioned increase, the likelihood that they will deviate decreases.[55]

The second finding is more problematic and also less certain. It emerges in two recent self-report studies and is disputed by a third. It suggests that the observed negative relationship between perceived punishment and likelihood to deviate may be mediated by or explained away by the presence of a third variable—perceived level of social condemnation. Perceived social condemnation concerns what somebody thinks others think or feel about a certain action. This factor appears in the research of Matthew Silberman.[56] Silberman examined self-reported crime among a sample of college students. He concluded that reports of criminality were related not only to the perceptions of certainty and severity of punishment (in the negative way suggested by the deterrence thesis), but also to measures of a person's moral commitment to certain legal norms and to his or her associational ties to others who share a similar moral orientation. Hence, while perceptions of punishment may serve as deterrents, Silberman concluded that they are only part of a larger package of social factors affecting the likelihood to deviate.

Similar findings were reported by Maynard Erickson, Jack Gibbs, and Gary Jensen in 1977. These researchers collected self-report and perceptual data on 1,700 Arizona high school students.[57] They found that the perceived certainty of punishment and the perceived seriousness of certain acts (a measure they equate with perceptions of social condemnation) were so interwoven that it was impossible to say whether perceived punishment operates as a deterrent factor in its own right. Supporters of the so-called deterrence doctrine could, of course, argue that perceived punishment causes people to view acts as serious or as socially condemned. If they were not so serious, why would they be severely and certainly punished? Erickson, Gibbs, and Jensen argue that their "findings clearly cast doubts on the deterrence doctrine," and that until proponents of the doctrine demonstrate that "the relations between properties of legal punishments and the crime rate holds independently of the social condemnation of crime, then all purported evidence of general deterrence is suspect."[58]

Jensen, Erickson, and Gibbs answered their own call for more refined research in a publication a year later.[59] There they report on an expanded sample of self-reports for 5,000 Tucson, Arizona, high school students. Using more rigorous measures of social condemnation, indexes of both personal disapproval and involvement with others who deviate, they find no support for the position that perceived certainty of punishment is a derivative of social condemnation. Both factors appear to operate independently, although the strength with which perceived punishment relates to likelihood of deviation is bolstered by the perceived seriousness of the act in question. Thus the deterrence relationship is strongest for such offenses as grand theft, robbery, and burglary, and weakest for perceivably more minor offenses, such as drinking, truancy, and marijuana use. This later piece of research both preserves and modifies the deterrence perspective. The perceived anticipation of punishment is seen as an important but not an exclusive factor in an individual's choice to deviate or conform.

Deterrence: Some Concluding Comments and Reservations

What have we learned in examining research related to specific and general deterrence and to the role of perception in mediating the effect of punitive sanctions? We have learned that a better case can currently be made for the value of general than for specific deterrence, that certainty of punishment appears to weigh more heavily than severity, that perceptions of the certainty and severity of punishment appear related to whether or not someone will deviate, and that perceptions of punishment do not operate in a vacuum, but are modified, if not directly mediated, by such factors as the perceived seriousness, moral meaning, and peer assessment associated with particular acts of deviance. We have also learned that further research needs to be done on each of these topics before the scorecard on deterrence can be fully tallied.

Given the tentative nature of much current knowledge of deterrence, one should view this central precept of the classical perspective with a certain reserve. Several things prompt this reserve. These include (1) the real-world conditions of punishment, (2) the lack of public awareness about actual punishments, (3) the differential effects of punishments on certain types of people, and (4) the differential effects of punishments in different social contexts.

Real-World Conditions of Punishment Even if the deterrence thesis were totally confirmed in principle, it still would stumble in practice. Why? The reason is simple. For deterrence to function effectively as a means of social control, there must be some guarantee that a high percentage of offenders either really will be punished or at least believe that they will be punished. Law enforcement today is very different from this ideal situation of deterrence. Most criminal lawbreakers are never caught. Consider the crime of robbery. Of all robberies known to the police and voluntarily reported by the police for the FBI's *Uniform Crime Reports* in 1977, only 27 percent ever resulted in arrests. Moreover of every 100 persons arrested, one can expect that only about 36 will go to court and 20 will serve time in prison. The small percentage of offenders punished becomes even smaller when one considers that recent surveys of persons victimized indicate that only 53 percent of all robberies are reported to the police in the first place. For various crimes against property the chance of being caught and punished is even less. Only 16 percent of all known burglaries, 20 percent of all known larceny-thefts, and 15 percent of all known motor vehicle thefts result in arrest. Hence, whether one measures punishment by its certainty or by its severity or by its swiftness (a factor not yet incorporated into the investigations of contemporary deterrence researchers), the "real-world" conditions of punishment are not very conducive to a workable control policy based upon the principle of deterrence.

Lack of Public Awareness About Actual Punishments One of the central themes in the writings of Beccaria and Bentham was that the public should be duly informed about the specific nature of the sanctions that will be delivered for those convicted of lawbreaking. By any standard of measurement the contemporary American public is ignorant of all but the most general features of possible criminal punishment. Recent surveys in the states of Nebraska and California confirm this fact.[60] In California only 16 percent of the surveyed public had accurate knowledge of punishments related to rape and burglary with bodily injury. Thirty-nine percent knew the punitive cost of being convicted for drunken driving, but even in this area more than half were ignorant of possible sanctions. Perhaps it is enough to know simply that something bad could happen to you if apprehended for such an offense. Surely most people would know that. Maybe, but such a general level of awareness would seemingly undermine the specific, precise, and calculative nature of sanctioning which underlies the classical perspective's advocacy of deterrence.

Differential Effects of Punishment on Different Types of People Punishment may work differently for different people. Why should one assume that the same punishment will be equally effective for a person who is very future-oriented and for someone who lives for the moment? We shouldn't. And yet the classical perspective on deterrence asks us to do just that—to eliminate a concern with individual differences so as to devise punishments which deter the greatest mass of the public at large. Sociologists Marshall Clinard and Robert Meir identify certain types of offenders whom one can reasonably expect not to be as deterred by the threat of formal punishment as others.[61] These include persons who commit emotionally charged acts of violence, those who commit offenses (such as traffic offenses) which are commonly known to be committed by broad and respectable segments of the public, those with strong motives or heavy personal investment in illegal activity (whether such persons be drug addicts who need to "score" in order to survive or political revolutionaries whose value commitments lead them beyond the law), and young people who may be more worried about positive peer-group assessment than about the outcomes of getting caught. The suggestion that some persons are better deterred by punishment than others does not mean that the deterrence principle should be abandoned. It does mean, however, that the classical perspective's conception of deterrence needs to be expanded or made more flexible.

Differential Effects of Punishment in Different Social Contexts In 1970 Richard Salem and William Bowers sought to test the effectiveness of various levels of punitive sanctions among students at 100 colleges for such campus-related offenses as violating alcohol-use rules, getting drunk, stealing library books, marking up books, and cheating.[62] They initially discovered a negative relationship between the severity of a college's punishments and the rate of such offenses on campus. Yet, upon closer examination Salem and Bowers discovered that, after controlling for the effect of peer disapproval, much of the original relationship posited between tough sanctions and conformity simply disappeared. It appeared that student attitudes and various aspects of the immediate social environment (e.g., whether or not the school had an honor-system approach to the problem of possible cheating) were more important determinants of rates of deviance than were types of sanction per se. The work of Salem and Bowers directs our attention to various nonpunitive aspects of deterrence. It suggests that unlike the pleasure-pain calculations involved in classical thinking, such things as moral values and the influence of one's family, friends, or associates in defining acceptable social reality may be key factors in deterring one's move into deviance. Think about college students who choose not to "get high." Is this because they fear getting punished? Maybe. But it may also be because "smoking dope" is no longer valued by their preppie friends. This fourth area of reservation about the deterrence doctrine asks us to thoroughly consider the situational context in which the threat of punishment is experienced before making inferences about the independent impact of punitive sanctioning.

REALIZING RATIONAL JUSTICE: ANOTHER PROBLEM OF ADEQUACY FOR THE CLASSICAL PERSPECTIVE

In the preceding pages we have reviewed what is currently known and what remains to be discovered about the adequacy of classical ideas about deterrence. In closing this chapter I would like to raise a few additional questions about another aspect of the classical perspective—its commitment to the goal of realizing rational justice. The early classical theorists, it should be remembered, were reformists as well as thinkers. As Leon Sheleff points out, "The classical school represents an attempt to ensure the maximum expression of a rational system of justice. . . . Both Beccaria and Bentham were . . . humanists and liberals. . . . Theirs was a humanism that sought to do away with the influences and the inequities of earlier times; it was a humanism that sought to put all people on an equal basis, at least in terms of their intrinsic worth, their basic rights, and, specifically, their treatment in the courts of law.[63]

There is certainly much to be said for the rational dignity afforded the deviant by the classical perspective. As we shall see in our following examination of the pathological perspective, most contemporary understandings of deviants have portrayed them as "creatures subject to causation," as "abnormal human beings, unlike ourselves," as "persons in need of involuntary treatment because they are unable to help themselves." The classical perspective avoids such debasing imagery. It also attempts to avoid the inequalities inherent in a highly discretionary system of social control. If an act is done, its doer, regardless of social position, regardless of the positive or negative "feelings" of some judicial agent, will be punished in accordance with the set prescriptions of the law. Nobody, in principle, will escape the sanctions of rational punishment. As such, the classical perspective holds some appeal for those concerned with fairness and individual equality before the law.

Despite its emphasis on rational dignity and individual fairness, the classical perspective has been criticized for reinforcing socially structured inequities in our system of social control.[64] In principle, everyone stands an equal chance of avoiding or being subject to punishment. In practice, some social groups have always been subject to the scrutiny of closer social control than others. Poor thieves have always been more carefully policed than rich thieves. But even if this were not the case, would the classical perspective be fair? Abstractly, all citizens have an equal chance not to steal. But concretely, are the chances of the poor citizen, in a society that equates human worth with the possession of property, really equal to those of the rich citizen? Are the chances of a relatively powerless citizen, in a society that places an exaggerated emphasis on being powerful, really equal to those of a powerful citizen? I think not.

The abstract equality of the classical school breaks down when confronted with the concrete inequality of everyday living. In an unequal society, isn't an exclusive commitment to an equally punitive system of rational social control an avoidance of basic social contradictions? How free is "free choice" in an unfree world? These questions are simply not addressed by a strictly classical approach to deviance. Without some commitment to equalizing the human conditions in which choices for or against deviance are actually made, the classical perspective will favor a very specialized form of rationality, the rationality of the advantaged, the rich, the powerful. The rationality of the disadvantaged, the poor, the powerless, will either be denied or classified as deviant.

NOTES

1 Cesare Beccaria, *An Essay on Crimes and Punishments,* Philip H. Nicklin, Philadelphia, 1819, as excerpted in Sawyer F. Sylvester Jr. (ed.), *The Heritage of Modern Criminology,* Schenkman, Cambridge, Mass., 1972, p. 12.

2 James Q. Wilson, *Thinking About Crime,* Vintage, New York, 1975, p. 197.

3 Demographic data here cited are drawn from R. R. Palmer and Joel Cotton, *A History of the Modern World to 1815,* 5th ed., Alfred A. Knopf, New York, 1978, pp. 433–437.

4 Mark Kennedy, "Beyond Incrimination," in C. E. Reasons (ed.), *The Criminologist: Crime and the Criminal,* Goodyear, Pacific Palisades, Calif., 1974, pp. 106–135. For a related analysis, see Joan Smith, *Social Issues and the Social Order: The Contradictions of Capitalism,* pp. 3–52.

5 Karl Marx and Frederick Engels. "The Communist Manifesto," in *Selected Works,* International Publishers, New York, 1968, p. 37.

6 See, for instance, R. R. Palmer and Joel Cotton, *A History of the Modern World to 1815,* Alfred A. Knopf, New York, 1978, pp. 70–88.

7 See, for instance, Samuel Enoch Stumpf, "The Apex of Medieval Philosophy: The Scholastic System of St. Thomas Aquinas," in *Socrates to Sartre: A History of Philosophy,* McGraw-Hill, New York, 1966, pp. 185–211.

8 Robert Nisbet, *The Social Philosophers: Community and Conflict in Western Thought,* Crowell, New York, 1973, p. 139.

9 Mary Peter Mack, "Cesare Beccaria," in *International Encyclopedia of the Social Sciences,* Macmillan, New York, 1968, vol. 2, pp. 37–38.

10 Cesare Beccaria, *An Essay on Crimes and Punishments,* Henry Paolucci (trans.), Bobbs-Merrill, Indianapolis, 1963, pp. 5–6.

11 Ibid., p. 12.

12 Mack, "Cesare Beccaria," pp. 37–38.

13 Beccaria, *Essay on Crimes and Punishments* (Paolucci trans.), pp. 13, 17.

14 Ibid., p. 31.

15 Ibid., p. 29.

16 Ibid., p. 26.

17 Mary Peter Mack, "Jeremy Bentham," in *International Encyclopedia of the Social Sciences,* Macmillan, New York, 1968, vol. 2, pp. 55–58.

18 Kennedy, "Beyond Incrimination," p. 116.

19 John L. Gillin, *Crimonology and Penology,* 3d ed., Appleton-Century-Crofts, 1945, p. 229.

20 George B. Vold, *Theoretical Criminology,* 2d ed., prepared by Thomas S. Bernard, Oxford University Press, New York, 1979, p. 26.

21 As cited in Paul W. Tappan, *Crime, Justice and Correction,* McGraw-Hill, New York, 1960, pp. 403–404.

22 Michel Foucault, *Discipline and Punish: The Birth of the Prison,* A. Sheridan (trans.), Vintage Books, New York, 1979, p. 115.

23 Ibid., pp. 116–117.

24 Jeremy Bentham, *Works,* J. Bowering (ed.), Tait, Edinburgh, 1843, vol. X p. 226.

25 David Rothman, *The Discovery of the Asylum: Social Order and Disorder in the New Republic,* Little, Brown, Boston, 1971, p. 62.

26 Ibid.

27 Marvin E. Wolfgang, Robert Figlio, and Thorsten Sellin, *Delinquency in a Birth Cohort,* University of Chicago Press, Chicago, 1972.

28 For a critical discussion of Beccaria's opinions on this matter, see Ysabel Rennie, *The Search for Criminal Man,* Lexington Books, Heath, Lexington, Mass., 1978.

29 Leon Shaskolsky Sheleff, "The Relevance of Classical Criminology Today," in Israel L. Barak-Glantz and C. Ronald Huff (eds.), *The Mad, the Bad, and the Different: Essays in Honor of Simon Dinitz,* Lexington Books, Heath, Lexington, Mass., 1981, pp. 3, 6.

30 Andrew von Hirsch, *Doing Justice: The Choice of Punishments,* Hill & Wang, New York, 1976, p. 6.

31 Wilson, *Thinking About Crime.*

32 Ibid., p. 62.

33 Marshall Clinard and Robert F. Meir, *Sociology of Deviant Behavior,* 5th ed., Holt, New York, 1979, p. 252.

34 Wilson, *Thinking About Crime,* p. xx.

35 William Glasser, *Reality Therapy,* Harper & Row, New York, 1965.

36 Don Gibbons, *The Criminological Enterprise: Theories and Perspectives,* Prentice-Hall, Englewood Cliffs, N.J., 1979, pp. 121–126.

37 Edwin H. Sutherland, *Criminology,* Lippincott, Philadelphia, 1924, p. 360.
38 Ibid.
39 Harry Elmer Barnes and Negley K. Teeters, *New Horizons in Criminology,* 3d ed., Prentice-Hall, Englewood Cliffs, N.J., 1959, p. 286.
40 Walter C. Reckless, *The Crime Problem,* 4th ed., Prentice-Hall, Englewood Cliffs, N.J., 1967, p. 504.
41 Gibbons, *The Criminological Enterprise,* p. 122.
42 Ibid.
43 Franklin E. Zimring, *Perspectives on Deterrence,* National Institute of Mental Health, Washington, D.C., 1971.
44 Jack P. Gibbs, *Crime, Punishment, and Deterrence,* Elsevier, New York, 1975. In the studies reviewed by Gibbs, punishment severity was most commonly measured by length of sentence.
45 Martin Gold and Jay R. Williams, "National Study of the Aftermath of Apprehension," *Prospectus,* vol. 3, 1969.
46 Alan Liska, *Perspectives on Deviance,* Prentice-Hall, Englewood Cliffs, N.J., 1981, p. 98.
47 Charles R. Tittle, "Deterrents or Labeling?"
48 Jack Gibbs, "Crime, Punishment, and Deterrence," *Social Science Quarterly,* vol. 48, March 1968, pp. 515–530.
49 Charles R. Tittle, "Crime Rates and Legal Sanctions," *Social Problems,* vol. 16, Spring 1969, pp. 408–423.
50 See Louis N. Gray and T. David Martin, "Punishment and Deterrence: Another Analysis," *Social Science Quarterly,* vol. 50, September 1969, pp. 389–395, and William Bailey, T. David Martin, and Louis Gray, "Crime and Deterrence: A Correlation of Analysis," *Journal of Research in Crime and Delinquency,* vol. 11, July 1974, pp. 124–143.
51 Charles H. Logan, "General Deterrence, Effects of Imprisonment," *Social Forces,* vol. 51, September 1972, pp. 63–72.
52 Ibid.
53 Charles R. Tittle and A. Rowe, "Certainty of Arrest and Crime Rates: A Further Test of the Deterrence Hypothesis," *Social Forces,* vol. 52, June 1974, pp. 455–462.
54 A related study by Don Brown of California counties and towns suggests that the tipping effect may be applicable only to small cities. See Don W. Brown, "Arrest Rates and Crime Rates: When Does a Tipping Effect Occur?", *Social Forces,* vol. 57, December 1978, pp. 671–682.
55 Among the first studies to report this negative relationship were Gary F. Jensen, "Crime Doesn't Pay: Correlates of Shared Misunderstanding," *Social Problems,* vol. 17, Fall 1969, pp. 189–201, and Gordon P. Waldo and Theodore G. Chiricos, "Perceived Penal Sanction and Self-Reported Criminality: A Neglected Approach to Deterrence Research," *Social Problems,* vol. 19, Spring 1972, pp. 522–540. See also Charles R. Tittle, "Sanction, Fear and the Maintenance of Social Order," *Social Forces,* vol. 55, March 1977, pp. 579–596.
56 Matthew Silberman, "Toward a Theory of Criminal Deterrence," *American Sociological Review,* vol. 41, June 1976, pp. 442–461.
57 Maynard L. Erickson, Jack P. Gibbs, and Gary F. Jensen, "The Deterrence Doctrine and the Perceived Certainty of Legal Punishments," *American Sociological Review,* vol. 42, April 1977, pp. 305–317.
58 Ibid., p. 317.
59 Gary F. Jensen, Maynard Erikson, and Jack Gibbs, "Perceived Risk of Punishment and Self Reported Delinquency," *Social Forces,* vol. 57, September 1978, pp. 37–38.

60 For the results of the California survey, see Social Psychiatry Research Associates, *Public Knowledge of Criminal Penalties? A Research Report,* State of California Assembly Research Office, Sacramento, 1968. For the results of the Nebraska poll conducted for the Center for Studies in Criminal Justice at the University of Chicago, see Zimring, *Perspectives on Deterrence,* p. 57.

61 Clinard and Meir, *Sociology of Deviant Behavior,* pp. 248–249.

62 Richard G. Salem and William J. Bowers, "Severity of Formal Sanctions as a Deterrent to Deviant Behavior," *Law and Society Review,* vol. 5, August 1970, pp. 21–40.

63 Sheleff, "The Relevance of Classical Criminology Today," p. 5.

64 See, for instance, Ian Taylor, Paul Walton, and Jock Young, *The New Criminology,* Harper & Row, New York, 1973, pp. 1–10.

Normalizing Relations By Joseph LaMantia and Stephen Pfohl

CHAPTER **4**

THE PATHOLOGICAL PERSPECTIVE: *Deviance as Sickness*

A slow but steady transformation of deviance has taken place in American society. . . . Deviant behaviors that were once defined as immoral, sinful, or criminal have been given medical meanings. Some say that rehabilitation has replaced punishment, but in many cases medical treatments have become a new form of punishment and social control.

Peter Conrad and Joseph Schneider[1]

They absolved Hinckley yesterday. I saw it on television.

And today on The Guiding Light *Justin explained to*
Ross Marler that Carrie had no control over her
pathological behavior, no more than over some physical
sickness.

Sure, his wife had acted deviantly.
Last night in Josh Lewis's bed and
this morning, a finger on the trigger,
gun ready for Sara. Sick and out of
control, she was as crazy as Heather
on ABC, or as Hinckley.
"Which way to the Washington Hilton?" he asked Jodie.

"Tell a vision," commanded the jury.
Their inquiries led to General
Hospital, *where cures came in capsules or*
in counseling; positive prescriptions for

control. An alchemy of explanatory images,
changing badness into sickness and operating upon it.

Joseph Stephens[2]

INTRODUCTION

Alchemists are persons who attempt to transform one type of substance into another. The term *alchemy* was used by a secretive group of medieval chemists to describe their efforts to transform base metals into gold. In the preceding poem the term *alchemy* is used to describe the way in which pathological theories transform images of deviance from badness to sickness. Pathological theorists succeeded where medieval alchemists failed. Nobody has convincingly demonstrated that a variety of cheap metals can be transformed into gold. Indeed most historians regard medieval alchemists as little more than magicians in scientists' clothing. Pathological theorists, however, have convinced much of the modern world that deviants are no longer to be considered bad but sick; and that deviant behavior may be explained as the product of "irrational defectives," persons who have little or no control over their thoughts, feelings, or actions.

The successful alchemy of pathological theorists is a major theme in Stephens's poem. The image of deviants as sick people has deeply penetrated our everyday perceptions and formal policies of social control. How common it is to describe that which disturbs, offends, or disgusts us as "sick." We are today surrounded by such medical imagery—whether in the fantasy conversations of soap-opera characters or in the real-life decisions of jurors, such as those who voted John Hinckley, Jr., "not guilty by reason of insanity." There was no doubt that Hinckley shot President Reagan and several companions outside the Washington Hilton Hotel. This was never disputed by Hinckley's defense attorneys. They argued, instead, that he could not have acted differently, that he was the helpless victim of an insane and frustrated obsession to win the love of teenage actress Jodie Foster, that he was driven to crime by a pathological condition over which he had no control. The jury was convinced. They ruled that Hinckley was not responsible for his actions. Rather than being sentenced for punishment John Hinckley was hospitalized for treatment.

Pathological theorizing transforms the classical emphasis on free choice into an image of deterministic causation. Why do people deviate? They do so as the result of a disease or defect of the body or mind. Unlike medieval alchemists pathological theorists have successsfully dressed their transformation in the garb of science. This is not to say that their work is all science and no magic. Indeed, critics argue that, despite its elaborate scientific costume, pathological theorizing is little more than a powerful and convincing form of magic. According to such critics most pathological theories are no more scientific than the theories of medieval alchemy. Pathological theories are successful not because they are correct but because they are attractive to a particular historical audience—an audience thirsty for simple solutions to complex problems. They succeed in much the same way as *General Hospital* succeeded in capturing an audience once enthralled by other soap operas, in attracting attention to life dominated by medical explanations of what is and what might be. These are strong criticisms, but no less strong than the medicine offered by the pathological perspective itself. What is the truth of this perspective? Is it found in the vision of its theorists or in that of its critics? These questions are pursued in the following pages.

THEORETICAL IMAGE

The pathological perspective rose to prominence in the late nineteenth century. It represented a dramatic break with both the demonic and the classical traditions. Deviance was pictured as sickness, not sin, and as caused rather than chosen. It was the product of a disease which infected the body or mind. Its control demands a medical-like cure rather than either penance or punishment.

Early Instances of Pathological Theorizing

Most historians date the origins of pathological theorizing to the 1876 publication of Cesare Lombroso's *The Criminal Man.*[3] Lombroso, an Italian physician, was performing an autopsy on the body of the dreaded brigand Vilella when he was struck by what he perceived as the apelike structure of the criminal's skull. Vilella's skull had two unusual depressions, the *median occipital fossa,* a condition observable in certain lower primates. This led Lombroso to hypothesize that Vilella was an evolutionary throwback—an *atavist,* a born criminal.

Lombroso reasoned that the premodern bodies of atavists were ill-suited for the civilized demands of contemporary life and were thus prone to crime and deviation. He sought to test this thesis by comparing the bodies of some 400 Italian prisoners with those of a group of soldiers. Each was measured for evidence of such physical anomalies as unusual head size, eye defects, receding forehead, large ears, excessive jaws, fleshy and swollen lips, wooly hair, and long arms. According to Lombroso's measurements, 43 percent of the prisoners had five or more "atavistic" anomalies. None of the soldiers had five. Only 11 percent had more than three. This was taken as evidence that at least for some criminals, biology was destiny; that inferior or pathological bodies produced pathological behavior.

Lombroso's ideas about the pathological origins of crime and deviance were extremely influential. Together with his students Raffaele Garafalo and Enrico Ferri, Lombroso founded the important *Archives of Psychiatric and Anthropological Criminology,* a journal dedicated to the scientific study of the causes of deviance. Yet, despite the seminal nature of Lombroso's contributions, there are those who trace the origins of pathological theorizing to the *humoral theory* of ancient Greece.[4] Humoral theory suggested that human behavior was affected by the balance of the body's four essential fluids: blood, phlegm, black bile, and yellow bile. According to the physician Hippocrates, imbalanced humors may produce madness. Melancholia, or depression, resulted from the liver's excess production of black bile. Similar explanations were used to explain other forms of pathological deviance. One unruly or "choleric" temperament was, for instance, believed to be caused by a sudden influx of yellow (liver) bile into the brain.

Other historians credit the origins of pathological theorizing to the writings of Giovanni Battista Della Porta (1535–1615). In his 1586 work *The Human Physiognomy* Della Porta posited a relationship between human facial characteristics and criminal behavior. He argued that criminal types such as the thief could be diagnosed by the presence of small ears, bushy eyebrows, small nose, mobile eyes, sharp vision, and large, open lips.[5] Similar observations were elaborated in 1775 in the four volumes of Johann Casper Lavater's *Physiognomical Fragments*.[6] For Lavater, a Swiss scholar of theology and physiology, shifty eyes, weak chins, and arrogant noses betrayed the criminal type. Other deviance-prone traits included beardlessness in men and beardedness in women.

Of related concern were the *phrenology* theories of the Austrian anatomist Franz Joseph Gall (1758–1828)[7] and his student collaborator, Johann Casper Spurzheim (1776–1853). Spurzheim, a talented lecturer, was extremely influential in persuading European and American audiences that human behavior was explainable by the shape of the skull. According to the principles of phrenology the exterior of the human skull was said to conform to the shape of the brain. The brain (equated with the mind) consisted of a set of faculties, each governing a particular aspect of human behavior. The faculties of the normal person were dynamically balanced. The faculty for openness was balanced by a faculty for secretiveness, acquisitiveness with generosity. Problems arose when certain faculties were disproportionately developed. The individual would be unbalanced, driven perhaps toward deviance. The overdevelopment of the propensity for "amativeness" (the erotic faculty) was said to lead to rape and crimes of sex. An overdevelopment of acquisitiveness produced thievery and robbery. Too much secretiveness fostered things like treason. Murder was said to be related to an overexpanded faculty for combativeness. Such overdeveloped faculties produced protrusions of the brain, bumps and lumps shaping the exterior portion of the skull. By studying such bumps on the head trained phrenologists believed they could distinguish normal people from deviants.

Still others trace the beginning of the pathological perspective to the writings of the American physician-reformer Benjamin Rush.[8] In 1812 Rush, a signer of the Declaration of Independence, authored the first American text on psychiatry. Rush suggested that severe mental disorders were caused by an arterial disease of the brain. As a cure he prescribed a regime of hot and cold showers, purgatives, dietary changes, and bloodletting. Rush's definition of pathologically caused and medically curable deviance was extremely broad. His list of behavioral diseases included lying, crime, drunkenness, and "revolutiona," a sickness characteristic of opponents of the American Revolution.[9]

The Essential Components of Pathological Theorizing

All of the theories mentioned above viewed nonconformity as resulting from some physical or mental defect. For analytic purposes, however, we shall date the full development of the pathological perspective to the late-nineteenth-century work of

Lombroso. Lombroso's work combines the three essential components of pathological theorizing: (1) determinism, (2) positivism, and (3) an image of organismic infection.

Determinism Pathological theorists see deviance as the product of natural causes. This reflects a thorough acceptance of a scientific viewpoint on human life. In the late nineteenth and early twentieth centuries this was a matter of great controversy. Scientific determinism likened the life of humans to that of other species. The origins and organization of each were to be explained by the forces of nature.

The spread of deterministic, or causal, thinking was spurred by popularizations of the thought of Charles Darwin. Darwin's 1859 *The Origin of Species* suggested the evolutionary development of the plant kingdom in accordance with deterministic laws of natural selection. In his 1871 *Descent of Man,* Darwin suggested that natural laws governed the development of the human species as well.[10] Within a short time, applications of Darwinism were made to nearly all aspects of human life. Some applications were more careful than others. Some, linked to Darwin only by popular inference, were haphazard, erroneous, and racist. Certain forms of human behavior (generally those close to the conventions of white Anglo-European society) were said to be naturally superior. Other types of behavior were viewed as less developed and inferior. All, however, were determined or caused. Each was allegedly ordered or determined by some natural law. Evolutionary theorist Herbert Spencer, for instance, argued that human life was governed by the law of "survival of the fittest." Superior forms were believed to naturally prevail over those less in harmony with the laws of evolution.

Much pathological theorizing carries the shadow of evolutionary thinking. All pathological theorizing is deterministic. Deviance is transformed from a moral choice into a dependent variable. Pathological theorizing replaces classical concern with deviant acts with a preoccupation with the deviant actor and those factors (independent variables) which cause deviant behavior.

Positivism The pathological perspective contends that the causes of deviance can be known only through the canons of positivistic science. For positivists, valid knowledge is obtainable only through controlled observation and scientific experimentation. The causes of deviance will be known only when nonconformists are placed under the microscope of modern physiological or behavioral science. This, of course, is a radical break from previous ways of studying deviance. As Gideon Fishman points out, the positivist approach represented an "antithetical critique of classical attempts to explain crime as the willful, premeditated and controllable act of a rational human being."[11]

Organismic Infection Pathological theorists view society as an "organism" composed of interrelated parts. Society is likened to the human body. Deviance is likened to a diseased or sick part of that body. It weakens the whole body. Like the cancerous cell, untreated deviance is said to spread its sickness to other cells and dissipate the strength of the organism as a whole.

The History of Pathological Theorizing: Cycles of Optimism and Failure

The history of the pathological perspective is cyclical. From Lombroso to the present it has followed a course marked by optimism, then failure, then optimism again. In its optimistic phase the perspective is confident about scientific advance and humanitarian progress. In its phase of failure, previously promising images of pathology are undercut by an awareness of the faulty research methods which produced them. Humanitarian hopes fade. Little difference is seen between therapeutically tested cures and therapeutically justified controls. Yet, within a short time a new optimism is born, and the cycle of pathological investigations renews itself.

Subsequent sections on research methods and social-control indication account for this cyclical optimism by linking modern pathological theorizing to the dominant social forces which have transformed the material and cultural landscape of contemporary western society. The remainder of this section reads like a short history of the rise and fall of major physiological and psychological pathology theories from Lombroso's day until our own. Its purpose is to provide a familiarity with most important variations on the pathological theme, and to underscore the fact that pathological theorists have studied much but proven little.

The Physiological Pathology Tradition: From Body Types to Chromosomes

The enthusiasm for Lombroso's theory of the "born criminal" was dampened by the 1913 publication of research by the English physician Charles Goring.[12] Goring, a medical officer in the British penal system, compared the bodies of approximately 3,000 repeat offenders with a large control group of university students, hospital patients, and soldiers. His rigorous examination of thirty-seven types of physical anomalies failed to support Lombroso's thesis. For a short time the idea that deviance was caused by physiological inferiority was put to rest.

Hooton: The Ghost of Lombroso Lombroso's ideas did not lie dormant long. Within a few years American researchers were to revive the physical-inferiority thesis. Leading this revival was Harvard University anthropologist Earnest Hooton. In 1939, Hooton published *The American Criminal,* a twelve-year study comparing a sample of 13,873 incarcerated criminals with 3,203 controls from ten different states.[13] Each had been subject to no fewer than 107 separate physical measurements. Hooton concluded that criminals were "organically inferior," marked by such things as low foreheads, high, pinched nasal nerves, excessive nasal deflections, and compressed faces. These "organic weaknesses" were said to make people unable to cope with their environment and thereby produced deviant behavior. Hooton offered a bold classification of criminals by their body types. Tall, thin men were said to be predisposed to murder and robbery; tall, heavy men to forgery and fraud; undersized men to thievery and burglary; short, heavy types to assault and sex crimes. As a strategy of control Hooton advocated the elimination, or at least the "complete separation," of the "physically, mentally and morally unfit."

Hooton's findings were only slightly more reputable than Lombroso's. His methods were soon the subject of numerous critiques. Many of these are applicable to research within the pathological tradition in general.[14] In the first place, Hooton's sample of prisoners cannot be equated with criminals. Prisoners are criminals who have been caught. They are unsuccessful criminals. How representative are they of criminals in general? This cannot be answered without studying uncaught criminals as well. Hooton, like most pathological researchers, was content to erroneously equate prisoners with criminals.

A second critique was directed at Hooton's control groups. The attempt to compare criminals with controls was a good idea. Yet, Hooton's controls were hardly representative of the population at large. They were a strange conglomeration of Nashville firemen, Boston hospital outpatients, members of a state militia, patrons of a bathing beach, college students, mental patients, and others. Furthermore, Hooton's comparisons between criminals and controls were highly problematic. His data suggests greater differences between his Nashville and Boston samples than between prisoners and controls. No explanation was provided by Hooton, who glossed over such glaring contradictions.

Hooton's work is also suspect regarding the meaning of physical inferiority. Why is a compressed face inferior to a rounded face or a high forehead superior to a low one? These are value judgments. Hooton disguised them as a scientific fact. Even if they were signs of inferiority, Hooton did not prove that they were biologically inherited. Unhealthy bodies can result from poor nutrition, stress, lack of medical resources, and even prenatal trauma. Such things are social in origin. Preoccupied with individual pathology, Hooton failed to see the importance of a more complex analysis. Nor did Hooton realize that many repeat offenders had been previously incarcerated for some other type of crime. People classified as robbers may have been previously incarcerated for assault. This undermined Hooton's claim that certain body types were indicative of particular criminal types. Despite the excitement it generated, Hooton's work was soon thoroughly discredited. The only thing it reliably demonstrated was that prisoners had slightly smaller helixes and longer necks than controls.

Sheldon and the Study of Deviant Somotypes It was only a few years between the controversy surrounding Hooton's research and the reintroduction of physiological pathology in the writings of William Sheldon. Sheldon did not equate a particular body type with inferiority. He suggested instead that certain body types predispose people to certain types of deviant behavior.

Sheldon's book *Varieties of Delinquent Youth: An Introduction to Constitutional Psychiatry*[15] drew upon the earlier work of the German scholar Ernst Kretschmer.[16] Kretschmer coined the term *constitutional personality* to refer to a relationship between behavioral disposition and body type. While Kretschmer's constitutional-personality types were vague and imprecisely measured, Sheldon's "somo-types" were more defined. According to Sheldon, the adult body structure corresponds to the differential development of the three layers of embryonic tissue: the endoderm, which develops into digestive viscera; the ectoderm, which produces the skin and nervous system; and the mesoderm, which converts into bones, muscles, and tendons. Early embryonic structures mature at different rates or in different proportions. Hence one person's body may represent the disproportionate growth of the endoderm, and another's, of the ectoderm or mesoderm. More importantly, Sheldon believed that each resultant body type was accompanied by a particular personality type.

A disproportionate development of endodermic tissue produced the endomorphic body. This Sheldon characterized in terms of a relatively great development of digestive viscera, a tendency to put on fat, a soft roundness of the body, short tapering limbs, small bones, and a soft, smooth, velvety skin. The plump, rounded body of the "endomorph" was accompanied by a "viscerotonic" personality, a craving for the soft things in life, luxury, and relaxation. In a similar fashion, Sheldon described disproportionate maturation of the ectoderm and mesoderm as resulting in "ectomorphs" and "mesomorphs." The latter were dominated by muscle and bone development, by large trunks, chests, and wrists. Their bodies were hard and rectangular. As "somotonic" personalities they were active, dynamic, and assertive. They walked and talked aggressively. On the other hand, ectomorphs were frail, skinny persons. Their delicate bodies were characterized by the prominence of skin and appendages and by relatively little body mass spread over a great surface area. Their introverted personalities were "cerebrotonic," oversensitive, and plagued by chronic fatigue, skin trouble, and bodily complaints.

Sheldon's categories emerged out of his measurements of the bodies and temperaments of 200 boys housed in the Hayden Goodwill Institute in Boston. Each was scored on a seven-point scale measuring relative endomorphic, mesomorphic, and ectomorphic development, and examined in terms of 650 temperament or psychological attributes. Sheldon concluded that boys who were disproportionately mesomorphic were characterized by the aggressive somotonic personality and more prone to a life of delinquency.

Sheldon's findings gave new life to the idea that body structures produce deviance. His research methods and analytic techniques were, however, full of holes.[17] His definition of delinquency was extremely vague. Rather than characterize delinquents by what they did (i.e., break the law), Sheldon relied on psychological measurements of failure, or "disappointedness." Drug use, "insufficient" IQs, homosexuality, psychosis, and psychoneurotic tendencies were lumped together as measures of who was delinquent. This approach led Sheldon to categorize one "really healthy looking tom cat" as a nondelinquent. The individual in question scored well on mental and physical indices and was said to be a strong young man from "good physical stock." Ignored was the fact that the boy had committed several violent sexual assaults.

Sheldon's poor measurements of delinquency undermined his claims to have scientifically linked body type to deviant behavior. The same cannot be said of the more careful work of Sheldon and Eleanor Glueck.[18] The Gluecks used Sheldon's measurement techniques to compare the bodies of 500 adjudicated delinquents with a matched sample of nondelinquents. They concluded that delinquents were more likely to be mesomorphic.

Without arguing with the Gluecks' research methods, it is easy to think of several sociological reasons that explain why adjudicated delinquents have stronger-looking bodies. In the first place, maybe one needs a tough body to be a tough delinquent. A weak-looking, soft, or fat kid is less likely to be accepted as a delinquent than the tough, ready-to-fight street kid. Recall that the Gluecks' delinquents had been officially judged so by the juvenile court. How large a factor is perception of threat in such determination? It is commonly known that physical appearance plays a prominent role in interpersonal assessments. Does this happen in the juvenile court? The Gluecks' data raise more questions than they answer. Why interpret the findings in terms of physiological pathology? It seems that if you look for physical explanations, you'll find them everywhere.

Searching for the Feebleminded Deviant

The English physician Goring is credited with the critique of Lombroso's theory of atavistic criminality.[19] While his measurement of convict bodies suggested no patterns of physical anomaly, Goring nonetheless claimed that heredity was a central cause of deviance. Using the recently developed methods of modern statistics, he compared criminality between brothers and between fathers and sons. Using imprisonment as a measure of criminality, he suggested that correlations for criminality between male siblings and between fathers and male children were as high as those for ordinary physical traits. Goring employed two controls for environmental impact. He compared boys living in their father's home with those living elsewhere. One group was as criminal as the other. He attempted comparisons between highly visible crimes, which might bc imitated, with relatively invisible crimes, which fathers may conceal from sons. Stealing was an example of a visible crime. Invisible crimes were things like sex crimes. Once again, correlations were as high for one as the other. To Goring, this meant that hereditary factors outweighed environmental factors.

Goring's work led to speculation as to just what hereditary mechanisms controlled the relationship between heredity and crime. He hypothesized that an inheritance of poor mental ability might predispose one to a life of deviance. Goring, however, offered no evidence either that intelligence was inherited or that it was specifically related to deviance. Nor were Goring's environmental controls adequately constructed. No information was obtained regarding the environment of boys not living with their fathers. This was unfortunate in that separation from one's parents may have caused increased deviance among controls in Goring's study. Also problematic was the assumption about the invisibility of sex crimes. Such acts attract much public attention. It is hard to imagine them as less visible than crimes such as stealing. Despite such inadequacies, Goring's research opened a new Pandora's box of pathological research aimed at showing the link between heredity and deviance.

The Jukes The work of Goring was pale compared to the excitement generated by two sensational studies of degenerate families appearing in the late nineteenth and early twentieth centuries. The first, *The Jukes: A Study in Crime, Pauperism, and Heredity,* was published in 1877 by Robert L. Dugdale, a prison investigator in New York.[20] Dugdale was struck by the number of blood relatives he observed behind bars. In order to examine links between heredity and crime he gathered 150 years of information on a family he considered to be particularly degenerate—the Jukes. Beginning with Mas, "a hard drinker" who was "averse to steady toil," Dugdale allegedly found evidence of hereditary poverty and crime. One hundred and eighty of 709 family members studied had received welfare, while 140 were convicted criminals, including 7 murderers, 60 thieves, and 50 prostitutes, 40 of whom were said to have passed venereal disease to some 440 customers. Thirty others had been charged with bastardy, the bearing of illegitimate offspring. Without comparing such lurid data with any control group, Dugdale drew inferences as to the hereditary nature of deviancy. It was not until a critical-minded journalist compared the degenerate Jukes with the respectable Jonathan Edwards family that the "scientificity" of Dugdale's research was undermined. Both families had about the same proportion of deviants.[21]

Goddard: The Kallikaks and the IQ Test A second famous degenerate-family study was produced by Henry H. Goddard.[22] Goddard's history begins during the American Revolution when Martin Kallikak, a respectable young soldier in the colonial army, developed a sexual liaison with a feebleminded barmaid. The affair resulted in a child, whom Martin soon abandoned along with its mother. He returned home and married a "good girl" with "normal" intelligence and proper upbringing. By digging through family, town, and court records, Goddard sought to trace the comparative lineages of these two couplings: Martin and the feebleminded barmaid vs. Martin and the good girl. The result was predictable. The feebleminded side was filled with deviant offspring—progeny classified as feebleminded, illegitimate, sexually unmoral, alcoholic, and the like. Only forty-six were rated as normal. On the good-girl side there was only respectability. For Goddard this pointed in the direction of heredity.

The Kallikak study, despite its feebleminded bad girl vs. normal good girl comparison, is hardly a model of objective research. Goddard admitted difficulty in obtaining full and unbiased family records. Furthermore, one doesn't have to be Dick Tracy to realize that the dice were loaded against the offspring of the poor, abandoned barmaid. Goddard applied other family-history techniques in tracing the lineages of 327 residents of the Vineland School for the Feebleminded in New Jersey. The results again pointed toward heredity.[23] Goddard, however, recognized the limits of research such as his own. Previous ratings of intellectual capacity were too subjective to be considered scientifically valid. In searching for more objective measurements, Goddard pioneered the American use of the Binet-Simon IQ test. Developed in France in 1905, this "intelligence quotient" exam converted answers to a set of pencil-and-paper questions into an alleged measure of "native intelligence."

Was feeblemindedness (or what we today call "mental retardation") related to criminal behavior? Goddard tried to find out by administering IQ tests to the residents of the Vineland school and comparing their scores with those of inmates in several New Jersey jails and prisons. Ignoring the possibility that many residents of the Vineland school might have been previously misclassified, he found that nobody tested higher than a mental age of 13 and thereby set a mental age of 12 as the cutoff point for feeblemindedness. A median of 70 percent of the prisoners scored below this point. For Goddard this meant that low intelligence was a key factor in determining crime. Feebleminded persons were said to be unable to handle complex social conditions, and he suggested that hereditary feeblemindedness might account for as much as 50 percent of all criminal activity.

Goddard's findings were interpreted as support for the pathological perspective. The strength of this support was broken in 1926 by the publication of Carl Murchinson's *Criminal Intelligence,* the first large-scale assessment of IQ scores for noninstitutionalized populations.[24] Murchinson compared IQ data for all World War I recruits with scores from a composite of prison samples. Over 47 percent of the recruits fell below the mental age of 13, over 30 percent were below the mental age of 12. By comparison only 20 percent of the prison samples were so low. Something had to be wrong. Either Goddard's findings had been falsely interpreted or over a third of the army was feebleminded. In a gesture of intellectual honesty, Goddard admitted his error and reduced the upper mental age of feeblemindedness from 12 to 9. With this new yardstick, significant differences between prisoners, soldiers, and anyone else disappeared.

Intelligence and Deviance: A Critical Evaluation Although Murchinson's research put a damper on the equation between low IQ and deviance, there is today a resurgence of interest in this topic. Comparisons between prison samples and the population at large again point to a relationship between being incarcerated and having a low IQ score. What are we to make of such reports? While it is true that prisoners test lower, there are important methodological reasons to distrust causal inferences based upon such findings. These include such matters as the wide variation in IQ scores among both criminals and noncriminals, evidence that good schooling (something uncommon for most prisoners) is related to high IQ test scoring, while low motivation (a characteristic typical of in-prison test takers) is associated with low scoring, and information suggesting that the gap between prisoner scores and those of the general population is greatly reduced when comparisons are made with people of similar economic, linguistic, and educational backgrounds.

This last point is of particular importance. The vast majority of prisoners come from the lower class or from families discriminated against by virtue of color, ethnicity, or language. On the other hand, it is well known that standardized IQ tests contain questions and linguistic constructs which favor middle-class, suburban, white test-takers. Given this awareness it is senseless to suggest that lower prisoner IQ scores reflect the primacy of biological factors. The absurdity of this position is underscored by the poor IQ scores of middle-class children who took the so-called "chitling" test developed by black sociologist Adrian Dove. Dove's counterbalance intelligence test was modeled closely after other IQ tests with one exception. It was written in the street language of the urban ghetto. The results (blacks did much better than whites) reversed the ordinary patterning of IQ testing. One suspects that a similar thing would happen if such tests were administered within prisons. This provides an additional reason to question the validity of the posited relationship between low IQ and deviance.[25]

Other Hereditary Theories: Studies of Twins and Adoptees

Studies of intelligence fail to isolate genetic factors which are independent of environmental influence. Studies of twins and adoptees have tried to overcome this limitation. Beginning in 1929 with the research of German geneticist Johannes Lange,[26] a series of studies have claimed significant differences between the criminality of identical twins when compared to that of fraternal twins, born into the same families but without the same genetic make-up. While Lange's twin samples were too small to generate reliable generalization, subsequent research by Legras in 1932 and Kranz in 1936 was cited as evidence of the same general pattern.[27] In 1968 the most extensive twin study was compiled by Christiansen, who compared 7,000 identical and fraternal twins born in Denmark between 1880 and 1910.[28] Like previous researchers, he discovered higher levels of concordance in criminality among identicals than among fraternals. That is, when one identical twin was found to be criminal, it was more likely that his or her sibling would also be criminal than was the case for fraternals. While suggestive of a pattern, Christiansen's findings were hardly proof of a truly deterministic thesis. Identical males had the highest criminal concordance rate, 35.8 percent. This meant that persons with exactly the same genetic composition varied together in a little more than a third of the cases. While higher than the 21.3 percent concordance for fraternals, the difference between these two groups was in no way overwhelming. The difference was slightly greater for female identicals, whose concordance outdistanced fraternals by a rate of 21.4 to 4.3 percent.

What can be said of such small but consistent differences? If heredity really caused crime, we would expect 100 percent concordance. Perhaps the social environment simply affects identical twins more harshly than fraternals. Identical twins are often mistaken for each other. Attempts are made to blur their identities. Parents may dress them in similar clothes and hair-styles. This may breed resentment. Many identical twins find it difficult to establish an independent identity and complain about the unfairness of being constantly compared.[29] For such people experimentation with deviance may offer a social way out of this trip of forced identification. This, unfortunately, is rarely discussed by genetic researchers committed to the discovery of physiological pathology.

Other pathologically oriented researchers have compared the deviance of biological and adoptive parents to that of adoptees. Schulsinger, for instance, analyzed the psychiatric records of the biological parents of adoptees diagnosed as psychopaths.[30] A small but higher percentage of disturbance was discovered in biological as opposed to adoptive relatives. Since the adoptive family was assumed to exert the greatest environmental impact, the greater proportion of disturbed biological relatives was taken as support for the idea that deviance is genetically transmitted.

Crowe approached this topic from another perspective.[31] He compared fifty-two adopted children whose natural mothers were female offenders with a matched sample of adoptees from noncriminal biological mothers. While adoptees from criminal mothers had slightly more arrests, convictions, and incarcerations, the actual differences between the two groups were quite small. Only eight children of criminal mothers and two of noncriminal mothers became criminals. In a study of over 1,000 Danish male adoptees, Hutchings and Mednick found only a 6 percent difference between the offspring of criminal vs. noncriminal parents.[32] Moreover, the percentage of criminal adoptees whose adoptive fathers were criminal was higher than that of those whose biological fathers were criminals. These results deflate the notion that genetic predisposition is a primary determinant of future deviance.

In summary, while adoptee studies find a small but consistent trend suggesting that some adopted children reproduce the criminality of their biological parents, this finding may be more indicative of flawed research methods than actual genetic disposition. Consider Schulsinger's discovery that biological parents of psychopathic adoptees were more disturbed than adoptive parents. Think about why people give children over for adoption. Often this is done because parents lack the physical or emotional resources to raise children. It is thus hardly surprising that a slightly higher percentage of such parents may be more disturbed than those screened by adoptive agencies as good placements. Other methodological problems include a general lack of data as to (1) whether the adoptive parents knew of the criminality of the biological parents and whether this influenced their childraising, (2) the amount of time children spent with their biological parents before adoption, and (3) on the criminal records of both fathers and mothers. These problems undermine confidence in such pathological research efforts and represent yet another line of scientifically unconvincing inquiry.

XYY Chromosomes: Continuing the Search for Hereditary Pathology

Each cell in the human body normally contains within its nucleus 46 chromosomes. These microscopic filaments are found in pairs. One chromosome from each pair is transmitted from each parent at the time of conception. Through these pairs hereditary traits are passed from parents to child. Chromosomes governing sex-linked characteristics are labeled XX for females and XY for males. On rare occasions individuals are born with three of these sex-linked chromosomes.

The earliest discovery of such a chromosomal abnormality was the so-called Klinefelter's syndrome. The XXY syndrome refers to males with an extra "female" chromosome. Such persons are late in developing sexual characteristics and may have small testes and enlarged, "femalelike" breasts. Although a disproportionate number of XXY people are labeled mentally retarded, this may not be a purely biological phenomenon. What looks like retarded behavior may be a reaction to the negative reactions of others to one's unusual sexual characteristics. Moreover, there is no evidence linking Klinefelter's syndrome to criminality.

In 1961 evidence of another chromosomal abnormality was splashed from medical journals to the crime columns of newspapers worldwide. Scottish researcher Patricia Jacobs and her colleagues had isolated an extra male chromosome in 1 of 550 individuals tested.[33] This XYY pattern was soon labeled the "supermale syndrome" and hypothetically associated with an abnormal propensity for violence. The evidence for this was meager. Comparisons between the chromosomal structure of infants and a sample of maximum-security male patients in a Scottish hospital for the criminally insane revealed that 3 percent of the patient prisoners but only 0.15 percent of the newborns were XYY's. Early studies of XYY were extremely expensive and were generally limited to small, highly biased prison samples, such as very tall maximum-security inmates.

Despite a paucity of solid research, this new form of pathological theorizing quickly captured the public and legal imagination.[34] In 1968 the XYY syndrome was introduced as mitigating evidence in the highly publicized French murder case of Daniel Hugon.

Hugon had brutally murdered a 65-year-old Paris prostitute. A court-appointed panel of experts recommended that his sentence be reduced as a result of his being XYY. Shortly thereafter an Australian court allowed the syndrome to be used as the basis for a plea of not guilty by reason of insanity.

In the United States the XYY defense fared less well. In 1969 a Los Angeles judge ruled that there was no clear scientific link between this abnormality and criminal behavior. Nonetheless, the most publicized court case involving the XYY concerned Richard Speck, the convicted murderer of eight student nurses in a Chicago apartment. Speck's attorney hinted that his client may have been an XYY. Headlines depicting Speck as a "supermale" appeared everywhere. Had the XYY made him do it? This question was debated in the popular media for several weeks. When actually analyzed, however, Speck's chromosomes appeared normal.

Following the rash of publicity surrounding the XYY syndrome, the National Institute of Mental Health commissioned a costly program of research and a survey of all known studies.[35] Was the XYY linked with higher levels of deviance? Apparently not! After examining thousands of people worldwide it was found that 1 in every 1,500 to 3,000 males is an XYY. Although rates were highest among maximum-security prisoners, no evidence was found to link the XYY with higher rates of violence. The only characteristic with which the XYY syndrome was consistently paired was tallness. Once again we witness the rise and fall of a costly search for pathological deviance.[36]

Psychological Pathology: The Abnormal Mind of Nonconformity

The second major pathological tradition emphasizes sick minds rather than sick bodies. Its root may be traced to the early Italian school of positivistic criminology founded by Lombroso. Law professor Raffaele Garofalo, a student and colleague of Lombroso's, extended the idea of physiological atavism into the psychological realm. Garofalo hypothesized that certain criminals were "psychological degenerates [who] lacked the natural sentiments of probity and pity [altruism and sympathy] that were normally present in their civilized brethren."[37] Although Garofalo claimed that degenerate persons could be diagnosed by the trained clinical eye, his ideas were never validated by the canons of positivistic science. In recent years, however, several other interpretations of psychological pathology have risen to prominence. Three of the most influential include psychoanalysis, psychometric assessment, and the theory of psychopathy.

Psychoanalysis and Deviance: Unconscious Resistance to Social Control

From a psychoanalytic perspective, deviance is a matter of unconscious wishes, fears, or conflicts operating beneath the surface of everyday human life. For that matter, so is everything else. Life is not what it appears to be on the rational, conscious surface. It is guided, instead, by irrational or unconscious forces. Conformity and deviation are both explained by reference to unconscious components of personality or critical stages in the development of personality. By exposing such unconscious forces, psychoanalysis promises rational control over that which would otherwise remain irrational; conscious control over the unconscious.

Psychoanalytic theory originated in the research and clinical practice of the Austrian physician Sigmund Freud.[38] Freud's writings opened the doors of science for a serious study of the unconscious. Freud's clinical experience with emotionally disturbed patients convinced him of the importance of early childhood experiences, much of which may be lost to or repressed from the conscious mind. Psychoanalysis was intended as a science of recovery, a tool by which to rediscover subconscious thoughts and feelings.

As a clinical technique, psychoanalysis is laborious and time-consuming. The patient is encouraged to describe and reflect upon a wide range of troubling events, and often to recount dreams or to "free-associate" with whatever comes to mind. Therapists then offer interpretations of the meaning of a variety of otherwise unconscious symbolism. By gaining insight into the vast prison of the unconscious, the patient is offered a means for rectifying psychological imbalances and regaining freedom of thought and action.

The social practice and importance of psychoanalysis goes beyond the clinical couch of the therapist. By the mid-1950s psychoanalysis had become a perspective on life in general. Sociologist Peter Berger likened it to a new religious movement. Its impact was evident everywhere. Films, literature, paintings, and newspapers bristled with psychoanalytic imagery. Yet, its impact was nowhere greater than in the study of social deviance.

The application of psychoanalytic thinking to deviance generally takes one of two forms. The first views deviance as an imbalance in key components of the human personality—the id, ego, and superego. Freud's observations of repressed sexuality in many of his Victorian patients led him to picture the id as a warehouse of instinctual energies dominated by sexual drives and desires. These were part of a larger package of life energies called the libido. After witnessing the massive carnage of the First World War, Freud suggested the possibility of another set of energies within the id—the dark forces of thanatos. Whereas libido pushed toward the fertile celebration of life, thanatos pulled toward the grave. Together they compose the unconscious tug between life and death that characterizes the id.

The superego, a second psychoanalytic component of personality, arises in childhood socialization as a control over the chaotic forces of the id. Through the superego, id energy is subordinated to the authority of social rules, contained by an internalized checklist of dos and don'ts. Popularly equated with conscience, the working of the superego sometimes involves conscious moral choice or acts of self-restraint. Other times it operates unconsciously through guilt, fear, or involuntary physiological reactions. The uneasy stomach I feel just before stealing the candy is an example of the superego at work.

Between the id and the superego is the ego, or reality principle. In wide-awake, conscious action, a strong ego mediates between the internal desires of the id and the external demands of the superego, balancing the instinctual drives of the individual with the normative dictates of society.

A lack of balance between the key personality components is said to cause deviance. Of particular psychoanalytic concern are the overly developed id and the underdeveloped superego. In both cases the ego is weak, unable to mediate between drives and restraints. In the case of the uncontrolled id, individual desires take precedence over societal responsibility. Repeated episodes of antisocial behavior may result. On the other hand, someone dominated by an overexaggerated superego may one day explode in an outburst of overly constrained deviant impulses.

A second application of psychoanalytic thinking is concerned with problems incurred in major stages of personality development. Freud posited three such stages: *oral, anal,* and *phallic*. Each revolved symbolically around a critical life experience associated with a particular area of the body. The oral stage involved adjustments associated with weaning, the breakaway from feeding at the mother's breast. The anal was associated with control over one's bowel movements, with toilet training. The phallic involved the genitals and the management of sexual feelings. Freud's famous description of the Oedipus complex is at the core of the genital stage. Primitive sexual desire for the opposite-sex parent is censured by the strong assertive presence of the same-sex parent. A boy's lust for his mother is buried by the victorious assertion of the father's adult male power. Although less clearly described in Freud's own writings, the opposite is generally said to happen for the young female.

For Freud a successful passage through the three developmental stages was a prerequisite for the healthy adult personality. If someone fails to adequately pass through one or more stages, the likelihood of deviance increases. In such cases deviance assumes a symbolic relationship to some aspect of the unresolved developmental crisis. Hence, fast-talking con-artists are seen as fixated at the oral stage, symbolically unable to let go of maternal nurturement. Unless they are lucky enough to become radio announcers or college professors, their inadequately weaned mouths will lead them to deviance. Thieves, on the other hand, are psychoanalytically associated with poor anal control. Unable to smoothly let go of their own feces, the thieves become endlessly involved in the deviant acquisition and retention of property. The same is true for those who fail the tests of the genital stage. Inappropriately formed relations to sexual desire and parental power are said to produce acts of sexual deviance and/or violence. The rapist and the murderer are so cataloged psychoanalytically.

Applications of Psychoanalysis There have been numerous applications of psychoanalytic thought to the study of deviance. One classic example is *Roots of Crime*, a 1935 work by Franz Alexander and William Healy.[39] Following Freud, Alexander and Healy described how unconscious guilt may drive people to violate the law in order to get caught and punished. According to Freud, "In many criminals . . . it is possible to detect a very powerful sense of guilt which existed before the crime, and it is therefore not its result but its motive."[40] Alexander and Healy agree that efforts to alleviate Oedipal guilt are important unconscious determinants of crime. As evidence they cite the case of a 20-year-old man whose stealing was allegedly a substitute for the "forbidden sexual act." Other unconscious criminal motives were said to include overcompensation for a sense of inferiority, spite reactions toward a rejecting mother, and a desire for dependency. Psychoanalytic knowledge of these matters was drawn from clinical sessions with a small number of convicted criminals. By analyzing dreams, slips of the tongue, and free verbal associations, psychoanalytic theorists created a continuing story of the unconscious dimension of deviance. Manifest motives (such as stealing to obtain money) were supported by latent motives, such as acting out a legacy of repressed childhood trauma.

Psychoanalytic themes are also found in the work of August Aichhorn, a Viennese educator and friend of Freud.[41] Aichhorn suggested that juvenile delinquents bore the unconscious scars of too little parental love. As a corrective, he instituted a permissive therapeutic milieu where wayward youths could act out their troubles while being observed by staff trained in psychoanalytic interpretation. Of related concern is Bowlby's deprivation theory, which argues that parental rejection accounts for most cases of intractable delinquency,[42] and the work of Johnson and Szurek, which blames delinquency on the permissiveness of parents seeking unconscious gratification of their own id impulses in the deviance of their children.[43]

The psychoanalytic perspective appears to account for nearly everything. If one probes deep enough, unconscious motives can be found beneath any form of misbehavior. How adequate is this explanation of deviance? Although psychoanalytic reasoning has sparked the imagination of many, there are serious problems with this type of theorizing. The person who exposes his genitals to old ladies with green eyes and red dresses may be acting out some hidden trauma of his childhood. Perhaps he is subtly reminded of sexual feelings aroused by once seeing his mother and father making love under a green Christmas tree with red lights. But such cases are few and far between. Despite the apparent willingness of much of the public to equate deviance with psychological disturbance, there is simply no sound evidence that most deviance is rooted in the unconscious. When considering the psychoanalytic perspective one must remember several important criticisms:

The Circularity of Many Psychoanalytic Interpretations How do psychoanalysts know that unconscious impulses lie behind deviance? Such impulses are inferred from behavior. Since people are said to deviate because they are driven by unconscious forces, evidence of deviance is read by most psychoanalysts as a symptom of deep unconscious disturbance. There is, unfortunately, much circularity in this logic. To the degree that psychoanalytic insight rests on speculative inference it is nearly impossible to prove or disprove. A good example occurred several years ago when a group of Muslim activists seized several buildings in Washington, D.C., and refused to release their hostages until the U.S. government met a series of political demands. When asked to explain the actions of these political deviants, one noted American criminologist resorted to the crudest form of circular psychoanalytic conjecture. Without even meeting the Muslim protesters this expert announced to newspapers across the nation that their activities represented a subconscious male reaction to the growing power of women in Muslim society. The seizure of phallic-looking buildings was explained as a symbolic assertion of displaced masculinity. In a single stroke of psychoanalytic reasoning the political meaning of the Muslim protest was rewritten as a story of psychopathology. Recall, however, that the only evidence of inner psychological disturbance was an external display of deviant action. Inferences about sexual anxiety and displaced masculinity are based on nothing but the circular logic of psychoanalysis. Such circularity undermines the usefulness of psychoanalytic explanations. But then my objections might be explained as nothing more than my own unconscious fears. The circular nature of psychoanalytic thought goes round and round.

A Biased Sample of Disturbed Deviants Most psychoanalytic work is based upon clinical profiles of persons troubled by their own deviance. This represents a highly untypical sample of deviants, many of whom not only accept but enjoy their nonconformity. Untroubled deviants, in other words, may never bring their stories to the clinician's couch. This challenges the sweeping generalizations about deviance made by psychoanalytic theory. No wonder that critics have questioned the religiouslike belief structure of many of its unverifiable insights.

Exaggerated Importance of Childhood Experience Significant childhood experiences undoubtedly shape later thoughts, feelings, and actions. But so do a wide range of other social, political, and economic experiences. Why is a bad relationship to one's parents more important than a bad relationship to one's employer, peers, or government? Traumatic psychological experiences are not evenly divided between those of different racial, class, gender, age, or ethnic categories.

Unfortunately, few psychoanalytic theorists address the conscious or unconscious consequences of socially engendered adult trauma. For the most part, psychoanalytic theory has been confined to an analysis of the psychic scars of childhood. According to a recent survey of professional psychiatric articles on crime appearing between 1966 and 1971, only three of thirty-nine examined social factors other than those directly related to the events of childhood.[44] Once again we note a severe limitation of psychoanalytic theorizing as a general explanation of deviant behavior.

Measuring Deviant Personality Traits

Psychological tests are designed to measure aspects of the human personality. Clinicians who use such assessment instruments to diagnose deviance assume that certain personality traits dispose people toward deviant action. There is, however, little evidence to support this assumption. Extensive reviews of the clinical literature on this matter fail to provide evidence that psychological testing successfully distinguishes deviants from those who conform.[45] Two notable exceptions involve studies using either the Minnesota Multiphasic Personality Inventory (MMPI) or the California Personality Inventory (CPI). The MMPI contains over 500 questions, clusters of which are broken into scales measuring various dimensions of personality. One of these, the Pd scale, measuring "psychopathic deviation," consistently differentiates criminals from nonoffenders. The socialization scale of the CPI claims similar results. Is it possible that these scientific measurements of personality have at last isolated the pathological determinants of deviance? A closer look at each deflates faith in this possibility. The Pd scale solicits information about how someone views deviant activity. People convicted of criminal acts are found to respond in a more positive manner than noncriminals. This is hardly surprising. It is more surprising that pathological theorists interpret this as evidence of a crime-prone personality. In actuality such responses may result from the fact that someone has acted criminally and was caught. On the CPI criminals score as more hostile to authority. Again, this is hardly surprising. Convicted criminals, after all, are subject to the long and often harsh arm of the law. Authority is not on their side. No wonder they are more negative. Thus, despite predictive claims, neither the MMPI nor CPI gives us much hard scientific information about alleged personality characteristics which cause deviance.

Despite past failures there have been numerous recent efforts to nail down a measurable deviant personality. Two of the most notable include Eysenck's theory of genetic personality deficiency and Yochelson and Samenow's idea of the criminal personality.

Eysenck: Genetic Personality Deficiencies For British psychologist Hans Eysenck, criminals are persons who have neither learned to be deterred by punishment nor acquired the internal controls of "conscience."[46] According to Eysenck criminals possess certain personality deficiencies whereby they resist the control of others while having no internal controls of their own. This is evidenced by the fact that convicted criminals score higher on psychological measures of "extroversion" and "neuroticism." Eysenck speculates that this is the result of neurobiological weaknesses, such as a low level of cortical arousal and an autonomic nervous system that is highly susceptible to pain. From this Eysenck goes beyond the available evidence to suggest that the criminal personality may be genetically disposed toward deviance.

There are serious problems with Eysenck's theory. The first concerns his assumption regarding a neurobiological relationship between extroversion, neuroticism, and criminal behavior. There need be nothing genetic about this relationship. It is a well-known fact that body chemistry may be conditioned by how someone behaves. People who behave extrovertedly or neurotically may have a different biochemistry than people who don't. We know about such matters from studying the behavior of people who develop ulcers or have early heart attacks. This means that neurobiological differences can be social rather than biological in origin. To forget this is to fall prey to sloppy circular reasoning about the pathological origins of all physical differences.

A second trouble with Eysenck's theory concerns the way he conceives of the relationship between extroversion, neuroticism, and actual criminal behavior. According to critics such as Feldman, the relationship between reported criminality and neuroticism may reflect less about an alleged personality deficiency than about the tendency for anxious people to admit more deviant behavior.[47] On the other hand, extremely extroverted people may place themselves in situations where the opportunity for nonconformity is greater. The assumption that this is the result of a deficient personality is empirically unsupported. Both crime and certain personality traits may be the result of other, more complex patterns of social learning. This challenges the core of Eysenck's theory. As Michael Nietzel points out, "Eysenck has not been able to separate a differential predisposition to be conditioned from the different quality of conditioning opportunities which children will experience."[48] Consider learning that takes place in the lower-class urban ghetto. A high percentage of children may learn crime, extroversion, and neuroticism as normal aspects of everyday life. No genetic or pathological deficiencies are needed to explain how such children may learn deviant adaptations to a harsh and often conflictual social environment.

Yochelson and Samenow: The Criminal Personality According to psychologists Samuel Yochelson and Stanton Samenow, authors of *The Criminal Personality,* a decision to break the law is the result of abnormal thought patterns characteristic of the "criminal mind."[49] In place since early childhood, this abnormal mode of thinking remains fixed unless confronted with Yochelson and Samenow's unique brand of psychotherapy (a disciplined mix of group therapy, sexual abstinence, and unquestioned acceptance of the therapist's "objective" description of one's own criminal profile). Little is said about how such patterns originate, only that once operative they make criminals a manipulative and self-serving lot.

For the authors of *The Criminal Personality,* criminality is defined, not by unlawful behavior, but by one's state of mind. Thus, "the consequences of a lie told by a criminal and of a lie told by a non-criminal are very different."[50] But if two people act similarly, how can we say that one set of actions results from a criminal mind and the other does not? For Yochelson and Samenow, one needs only to know whether the people in question have a criminal record. If so, the criminal mind must be at work. The circularity of this reasoning is alarming. So is the praise heaped upon *The Criminal Personality* by a variety of law enforcement and criminal justice practitioners. Why such praise for a book which is little more than its authors' clinical assessments of offenders institutionalized in a federal mental hospital? It blurs distinctions between types of criminals and fails to employ control groups or measures of rate reliability. As proof for their theory Yochelson and Samenow demand that patients admit that they have the criminal personality. This may not sound like a very objective approach to scientific research. It isn't. Although *The Criminal Personality* is presented in the jargon and technical terms of scientific research, its real appeal is to those who intuitively "know" that criminals are pathological people.

The Elusive Search for the Psychopath

A final theme in the literature of psychological pathology involves the recurrent search for people who are devoid of conscience and, thereby, detached from the moral fiber of society. At various times such people have been labeled as morally insane, psychopathic, or sociopathic. Current diagnostic manuals use the term *antisocial personality*. Estimates vary as to the number of people afflicted with the antisocial personality. Some suggest as high as 3 percent of the entire adult population; others only 20 percent of the adult prison population.[51]

Belief in the existence of psychopathic people is as old as psychiatry itself.[52] French reformer Philippe Pinel used the term *manie sans délire* ("mania without delusions") to challenge the notion that intellectual impairment is always a feature of mental disorders. People could be rational and clear-thinking but still mentally ill. Their illness could be of a moral rather than an intellectual nature. American psychiatrist Benjamin Rush employed the term *moral alienation,* and English physician J. S. Prichard the term *moral insanity,* to connote a similar "disorder of affections and feelings." The term *psychopath* was first applied clinically in 1936 by Dr. Samuel Woodward, superintendent of the Massachusetts State Lunatic Hospital. Two years later Isaac Ray published a landmark treatise in which the psychopath was pictured as someone with no signs of mental disorder other than a history of wrongful acts for which he or she denied responsibility. In the twentieth century Freudian theorist Partridge suggested that sociopaths were "orally fixated," while other theorists located the origins of psychopathic impulsivity in early childhood trauma.

The publication of Hervey Cleckley's *The Mask of Sanity* marks the most comprehensive listing of the symptoms of the psychopathic, or sociopathic, disorder.[53] According to Cleckley, the antisocial sociopath is recognizable by the following checklist of symptoms:

1 Superficial charm and good intelligence.
2 Absence of delusions and other signs of irrational thinking.
3 Absence of nervousness and other psychoneurotic manifestations.
4 Unreliability.
5 Untruthfulness and insincerity.
6 Lack of remorse or shame.
7 Inadequately motivated anti social behavior.
8 Poor judgment and failure to learn by experience.
9 Pathologic egocentricity and incapacity for love.
10 General poverty of major affective reactions.
11 Specific loss of insight.
12 Unresponsiveness in interpersonal behavior.
13 Fantastic and uninviting behavior, with drink and sometimes without.
14 Suicide rarely carried out.
15 Sex life impersonal, trivial, and poorly integrated.
16 Failure to follow any life plan.

Examine these symptoms carefully. They are not very precise. How does one diagnose superficial charm (symptom no. 1) as distinguished from nonsuperficial charm? Even if this is possible, don't the codes of normal politeness instruct us all in the daily exercise of superficial charm? What about symptoms no. 2, 3, and 14? Under most conditions the absence of delusions, the absence of nervousness, and the failure to carry out suicide are not seen as negative. Why include them in this cluster of sociopathic symptoms? What exactly is fantastic and uninviting behavior (no. 13)? How can one adequately measure insincerity (no. 5) in a culture that promotes high-pressure salesmanship as a desirable business trait? What is an impersonal or trivial sex life (no. 15)? Couldn't this categorize all of those "hot and heavy" singles waiting in line for a "one-night stand"? The categories are simply too vague, too imprecise.

The empirical research on psychopathy is not much more precise. It generally fails to adequately distinguish the disease from the behaviors it is said to produce. Harrison Gough theorized that sociopaths never learned to empathize with the perspective of others.[54] Baker tested this idea by examining whether sociopathic inmates were less empathetic than their nonsociopathic cellmates.[55] The participating inmates were each asked to complete a questionnaire measuring their perceptions of themselves, their cellmates, and their cellmate's assessment of themselves and others. Sociopaths were found to be less able to see this through another's eyes. This may be true, but isn't it a criterion for classifying a person as a sociopath in the first place?

Such circular reasoning is unfortunately characteristic of other studies as well.

Albrecht and Sarbin found sociopaths to be "poor tension binders,"[56] while McCord and McCord documented them as remorseless, guiltless, and loveless.[57] Robins followed a group of ninety-four patients diagnosed as childhood sociopaths to discover that thirty years later they rated high on measures of financial dependency, poor work history, multiple arrests, unsuccessful marriage, impulsiveness, vagrancy, and use of aliases.[58] This tells us little about sociopathy as a disease. All that Robins's data really say is that people who acted antisocially as children were likely to act that way as adults. With no additional evidence, why equate such actions with a sickness?

Contemporary Studies of Sociopathy

Recent studies have suggested that biological abnormality may lie behind the psychological abnormality of the sociopath. These studies are intriguing but also plagued by serious methodological drawbacks. Funkenstein opened the door to physiological studies of sociopathy in 1944 when he injected fifteen sociopathic prisoners with the drug epinephrine.[59] The diagnosed sociopaths (thirteen men and two women) were all violent offenders, referred for court examination to the Boston Psychopathic Hospital. When compared to a comparison group of psychotics and neurotics, they sustained a much higher (75 mm Hg) rise in systolic blood pressure without experienced discomfort.

What does this mean? In 1955 D. T. Lykken suggested the answer when he reported that "primary sociopaths" revealed a diminished galvanic skin response (GSR) when lying and a reduced capacity for learning when stressed.[60] The galvanic skin response was measured by attaching sensitive wires to the subject's skin. Learning was measured by the time it took a subject confronted with aversive stimuli (electric shocks) to solve a mazelike task. This suggested that sociopaths are "hypoaroused." This meant that sociopaths have a body chemistry that is understimulated. With higher than normal sensory intake thresholds, sociopaths were said to be less sensitive to environmental stimuli. In order to experience their environment, they would have to act out, or make things happen. This is to suggest that sociopathic behavior is explainable by biological abnormality.

Lykken's work was followed by Schachtner and Latane's study of fifteen sociopaths.[61] Sociopaths were shown to have marked learning improvement (when given electric shocks) after having been injected with the stimulant epinephrine. Controls did not. Nor did sociopaths when given a placebo. Later studies by Lippert and Hare suggested that sociopaths manifested less galvanic skin response when exposed to threats and reacted more quickly than normals to situations of artificially generated stress.[62] At Ohio State University an interdisciplinary team of researchers replicated elements of previous studies, discovering a difference between "simple" and "hostile" sociopaths.[63] Simple sociopaths (defined as nonaggressive) manifested the hypoarousal syndrome; hostile or violent sociopaths did not.

The psychobiological research described above promises a breakthrough in the chemical control of antisocial behavior. It is nonetheless plagued by a basic methodological flaw. How are subjects defined as sociopaths in these hypoarousal experiments? While use is made of the Cleckley scale and the Minnesota Multiphasic

Personality Inventory, the single most important indicator is an anxiety scale developed by Lykken. Sociopaths are determined by extremely low levels of anxiety when confronted with so-called high-anxiety situations. They are then confronted with laboratory-generated anxiety arousers (electric shocks, etc.) and are found to behave more anxiously. Low-anxiety people are found to act with low anxiety. This is what differentiates them from "normals." Once again we are confronted with a disturbing circularity in pathological research methods. There is no doubt that low anxiety has a measurable biological correlate. Nor is there doubt that if you inject anxiety-producing drugs into low-anxiety people, you can make them more anxious. None of this proves that low-anxiety persons are carriers of a disease.

Two things stand out about psychobiological studies of sociopathy. The first concerns sampling procedure. Nonanxious or underaroused prisoners are classified as remorseless sociopaths. This is said to distinguish them from other sociopathic inmates. But what about the remorseless politician, police officer, or general who, with little anxiety, makes an unfulfillable promise, fires a deadly bullet, or releases a nuclear warhead? Although such people are not ordinarily labeled psychopathic, if measured by a Lykken scale or epinephrine experiments they may reveal a similar psychobiological profile. Such tests have not been performed. Thus it seems that the elusive search for the psychopath is, at least implicitly, a matter of political perception. Some people are subjects for psychobiological examinations. Others are not.

Another methodological problem with psychobiological studies involves the issue of causality. Sociopathic behavior may be correlated with underarousal. This does not mean that it is biologically caused. Maybe it is behavior which causes biochemical differences. This happens with ulcers or with high blood pressure. Few would argue that ulcers or high blood pressure cause people to lead a fast-paced, high-stress life. Why leap into such reasoning in the case of sociopathy? The answer has much to do with the simplistic social and political attractiveness of pathological theorizing.

IDENTIFYING PATHOLOGICAL DEVIANCE

Every breath you take
Every move you make
Every bond you break
Every step you take

I'll be watching you.

Sting[64]

The search for the causes and cures of pathological deviance is fueled by a faith in the power of positivistic science. Pathological theorists believe that valid knowledge is obtainable only through rigorous and quantifiable measurements of cause and effect. The true test of positivism lies in the scientist's ability to predict and control the way things occur in nature. Rational mastery over nature is its ultimate goal. This way of seeing the world is so deeply ingrained in modern consciousness that it is difficult to envision a time when positivist explanations were not applied to all that is human.

Today the human sciences offer causal theories about almost everything we think, feel, and do. When The Police sing the lyrics of "Every Breath You Take" they could well be referring to the omnipresent explanatory eye of positivism. When paired with an image of deviance as sickness, the positivistic human sciences promise a medical-like explanation and a therapeutic cure for the disease of nonconformity.

In the preceding pages we have reviewed many positivistic studies of pathological deviance. Most of these research projects were flawed by serious conceptual and methodological problems. Studies of physiological pathology have traditionally been hampered by imprecise definitions of abnormality, poor sampling procedures, and inadequate control-group comparisons. Psychological studies have fared no better. According to a recent review of the clinical literature, assessments of psychological pathology are typically biased by such factors as the professional socialization of diagnostic experts, contextual variations in diagnostic practice, problems of class and cultural stereotyping, and definitional ambiguity in the formulation of psychiatric classifications.

Given the inadequacy of so much pathological research, it is important to ask why this perspective has for so long been blessed by the halo of positivist respectability. The answer is found in the complex historical conjuncture between the masterful promise of positivistic human science and that offered by a medicalized vision of nonconformity. By examining the historical dynamics of this conjuncture we may better appreciate how it is that pathological research strategies have carried so much power.

The Positivistic Study of Deviance as Disease: Some Historical Considerations

It was no accident that from the beginning positivist explanations of human behavior were linked to pathological images of deviance. Both were linked historically to another phenomenon—the development of western capitalism. To understand these linkages, let us begin with capitalism and its relationship to human labor. Productive efficiency is a cornerstone of the capitalist economy. The more efficient that capitalists are in exercising rational control over both material and human resources, the greater will be their profit. This demand for efficiency precludes the possibility that capitalists will maintain direct physical control over the work of each wage laborer. This would be too costly. Under capitalism the centralized management of labor cannot be secured efficiently by the threatening hand of the boss. This is replaced by the "invisible hand" of a more subtle and omnipresent form of control—the technology of inner discipline. According to Michel Foucault this new internal technology of human subjugation produces the rationally self-controlled worker needed by capitalism.[65] It permits the capitalist system to accumulate a self-disciplined workforce in much the same way that individual capitalists accumulate a mass of raw materials or natural resources.

It is here that we discover an affinity between the disciplinary demands of capitalism and the promise of positivist human science. According to Jurgen Habermas, positivist human science has been wed, from the beginning, to a promise of technical control. Its aim is to make "possible the control of the social life processes . . . in a manner not unlike that in which material science becomes the power of technical control."[66]

Foucault goes a step further in tracing the origins of the positivist approach to the disciplinary laboratories of the early nineteenth century—the state penitentiary and other institutions of "total control." Although classical control agents sentenced criminals to such places for rational punishment, within a century they were transformed into institutions for corrective treatment or rehabilitation. Why? According to Foucault this transformation is rooted in the technical control possibilities of prison itself.

Prisons capture the bodies and minds of those they incarcerate. Day and night inmates are surrounded by the ever-watchful, yet often invisible, eye of those who stand guard. For control purposes inmates are classified into various types, each reducing concrete people into abstract categories suggestive of different ways of thinking, feeling, or acting. This classification was a first step toward what Foucault refers to as "capturing the soul," or *persona,* of the deviant. Out of this classificatory project grows the explanatory focus of positivist behavioral science. Early prison classification programs, with their detailed case histories and institutional logs on each inmate, are interpreted as a major impetus for the predictive-control promise of the human sciences. It is a short step from comparative classificatory typologies to explanatory causal accounts. Foucault concludes that "the sciences of man . . . which have so delighted our 'humanity for over a century, have their technical matrix in the petty, malicious minutiae of the [penal] disciplines.' "[67]

The impetus for human science arose simultaneously in other classificatory projects of the nineteenth century—the endless examination procedures by which educational institutions categorize students, weeding out the less able and the troublesome, and the clinical "gaze" of modern medicine, which analytically freezes the humanity of its subject into a machinelike arrangement of anatomical parts. Such projects herald a new vision of what humans are and how they might best be controlled. Not only were humans classifiable into a variety of different types, but the types themselves were arranged along a graded continuum of normality. Some were pictured as better adapted to the competitive demands of modern capitalist society; others were abnormal and did not fit into what was viewed as the natural order of things.

It may be hard for us to appreciate the newness of this today. Since birth we have been so classified. From the moment we leave our mother's womb (and often long before) we are subject to a host of medical, psychological, and intellectual measurements: eye tests, teeth tests, blood tests, IQ tests, achievement tests, entrance and exit exams. Throughout our lives we are measured and remeasured, classified and reclassified. In the early nineteenth century, such naturalistic classification was as new as its effect was profound. Out of this classification grew the human sciences, an array of disciplined positivistic examinations of factors believed to differentiate normal types from people who were pathological.

Just as the great classificatory project of the nineteenth century gave birth to the human sciences, so did it provide an intellectual justification for new strategies of disciplinary control, strategies aimed at correcting, rehabilitating, or curing abnormal types and thereby converting them into an internally motivated supply of human labor. In other words, in searching for scientific accounts and cures for abnormality, the human sciences legitimize the power of the capitalist enterprise out of which they are born. This is because the positivistic human sciences are a means of exercising instrumental or disciplinary control over people. This is not to say that the human sciences remain exclusively within the domain of the capitalist economy. They do not. They manifest an affinity with other modern "control at the top" political economies as well. The repressive use of the human sciences in the Soviet Union is a case in point. Behavioral scientists in the U.S.S.R. have contributed significantly to the development of techniques to modify, alter, or otherwise "normalize" nonconforming behavior. It is an unfortunate fact that many state-socialist regimes have been more successful in shedding the market structure of capitalism than the technologies of rational human control which were nurtured during its development.

SOCIAL CONTROL OF PATHOLOGICAL DEVIANCE

The pathological perspective is associated with a medical model of social control. Whether administered by physicians or other "helping professionals," such as psychologists, nurses, and social workers, treatment is prescribed as a cure for virtually all types of nonconformity.[68] Since the late nineteenth century, therapeutic controls have been devised for everything from violent crime to alcoholism, drug addiction, homosexuality, and even obesity. This proliferation of control in the name of treatment is described by Nicholas Kittrie as the rise of the "therapeutic state."[69] In such a state medical solutions are mandated for nearly all human problems, while the legal principle of *parens patriae* (the duty of the state to help those who cannot help themselves) is used to justify and often force treatment upon nonconformists.

While many people view the therapeutic state as a progressive historical development, there are several antihumanitarian features in its program of professional helping. Chief among these is the unwarranted assumption that deviants have no real choice in behaving the way they do. Also of concern is the way in which therapeutic control agents pretend to separate moral judgments from scientifically informed treatment. Conrad and Schneider cite several examples: treatments proposed by Dr. Samuel Cartwright, a respected southern physician who coined the term *drapetomania* to describe a disease affecting only slaves, the symptoms of which involved attempts to escape the plantations of "lawful" white masters; the use of mechanical or surgical controls by Victorian physicians to cure masturbation; and the work of Soviet physicians who diagnose political dissidents as mentally ill, as helpless victims of "paranoia with counterrevolutionary delusions."[70] Although these appear to be extreme examples, "they highlight the fact that all medical designations of deviance are influenced significantly by the moral order of society and thus cannot be considered morally neutral."[71]

Caught within the humanitarian dream of creating a healthy society, pathological theorists have rarely heeded such criticism. Most have lived to see their ideas translated into practical policies. Consider the therapeutic response to such crude theories as phrenology and atavism. As George Vold points out, "phrenologists were the *medicine men* of their day, lecturing for fees to an eager public, counseling and advising on public and private welfare."[72] Phrenology was also used as a control mechanism in public institutions. Between 1831 and 1904, all inmates at the Eastern State Penitentiary in Philadelphia were classified phrenologically according to the bumps on their criminal heads. Lombroso's ideas about atavism were put to similar use. Under the direction of Dr. Hamilton Wey, an American disciple of Lombroso's, delinquents at the New

York State Reformatory at Elmira were classified according to the presence or absence of atavistic anomalies. Wey believed that such measurements would aid in the diagnosis and treatment of the "criminal class." As a corrective, Wey advocated a rigorous program of physical therapy and exercise. By such control strategies, Wey hoped, inferior bodies would be strengthened and biological propensities toward deviance overcome.

More drastic were control strategies derived from the early theories of feeblemindness and heredity. During the early twentieth century these provided a "scientific" rationale for the repressive biological control efforts of the eugenics movement.

The Eugenics Movement: Putting Theories of Hereditary Pathology into Practice

What theories of hereditary deviance lacked in scientific rigor they made up in popular appeal.[73] A good example is T. W. Shannon's 1916 handbook *Eugenics*.[74] Within its pages one finds allegedly scientific rules of proper etiquette, social ethics for unmarried persons, techniques of hygienic bathing, and warnings about the dangerous effects of "self-pollution" (masturbation) and overindulgence in the sexual act. Violations of these rules were said to alter the normal course of heredity and breed deviance. Masturbation and overindulgence were particularly troublesome. "Touching oneself" was said to produce glassy eyes which permanently recede deep into their sockets. Too much sex "lowered the whole moral and physical tone of the race," destroyed human vitality, and led to "puny" or "scrawny" offspring, "many of whom in early life pass to untimely graves."[75]

Texts such as Shannon's may today seem outdated and humorous. These books, however, often contained humorless recommendations for "constructive" eugenic action. For instance, Charles R. Henderson's 1901 *Dependent, Defective and Delinquent Classes: And of Their Social Treatment* proposes that all so-called defective criminals be placed in air-tight chambers to be eliminated with poisonous (but not unpleasant) gas.[76] Such medical solutions to deviance were taken seriously by the Nazi architects of the Holocaust. Indeed the Nazis rationalized their atrocities with positivistically framed arguments about racial purity and the necessity of genetic control.

In the United States, one of the most repressive consequences of eugenic thinking came in the form of laws permitting the involuntary sterilization or castration of deviants. According to Charles McCaghy, between 1907 and 1937 thirty-one states passed laws allowing sterilization without consent for the mentally ill, the mentally deficient, and epileptics.[77] As late as 1976 twenty-six states still permitted involuntary sterilization of the mentally ill. Twenty-four allowed sterilization of the retarded, while fourteen permitted the operation for epileptics. Eleven other states allowed the sterilization of "hereditary criminals." Seven others permitted such procedures to be involuntarily used to control sex offenders, degenerates, and "moral degenerates." The vague terminology of such laws is troubling. Consider an Oregon statute allowing sterilization for "all persons who are feebleminded, insane, epileptic, habitual criminals, incurable syphilitics, moral degenerates or sex perverts, and who are . . . or will likely become, a menace to society."

The laws mentioned above are based upon the unproven assumptions of pathological theorizing. They have sanctioned over 70,000 involuntary sterilizations in the United States alone.[78] In the last few years many of these statutes have been challenged by advocates for those whose deviance has placed them under the scalpel of the eugenic surgeon. Most may soon be declared unconstitutional violations of individual rights. Yet, sterilization efforts have recently spread to new areas of control. McCaghy describes a 1973 incident in which two children of a welfare mother were involuntarily sterilized in a Montgomery, Alabama, family-planning clinic.[79] The mother of two girls, one diagnosed as retarded, the other normal, yielded to a case worker's insistence that she sign a form of parental consent. The woman did not understand that the operations were permanent. She had been told that welfare payments would be cut off if she refused consent. An investigation of this incident revealed eleven other instances in which involuntary sterilizations had been forced upon clinic clients during the same year. Similar incidents have been documented in states in every region in the country. Rooted in faulty logic and shoddy science, such operations are the lurid and repressive offspring of pathological theorizing.

The Mental Hospital: A Short History of Institutional Treatment

Advocates of eugenic control hope to prevent the birth of future generations of deviants. Other medicalized control practices seek to rehabilitate or change the behaviors of existing deviants. Perhaps the most important of these has been the use of hospitalization as a mode of "curative control" for those afflicted by some form of mental disorder.

Beginning with the great confinement of the late seventeenth and eighteenth centuries, large numbers of psychologically disturbed people have been treated behind the locked doors of the mental hospital or lunatic asylum.[80] As late as the early nineteenth century, medical treatments for madness differed little from those which had been practiced by nonmedical specialists for centuries: dunking, bloodletting, purgation, starvation, restraint. From that time to the present the history of the mental hospital reads like the cyclic history of other pathological control strategies; periods of optimism are followed by periods of devastating disillusionment. By the mid-nineteenth century the antiquated cures listed above had been replaced by a regime of disciplined routine known as the "asylum cure." Overseen by so-called moral physicians, this therapeutic program of enforced orderliness promoted a "cult of curability" which was overturned by the shocking investigative reports of reformers such as Dorothea Dix later in the century. Not only were cures not taking place, but the alleged disciplinary routines of the asylum were little more than a cover for what in actuality were practices of harsh custodial control.

By the mid-twentieth century little had changed. Despite increased medical involvement and the exhortations of progressive reformers, the hospitals were still essentially warehouses for the mentally impaired. Physical terror at the hands of an overworked, undertrained, and poorly paid staff was a common, if guarded, secret of life within the state hospital. A few new technologies of control had become popular—electroconvulsive, or "shock," therapy and psychosurgery—but talk or insight therapies, such as psychoanalysis, were seldom used. These forms of psychotherapy were reserved for patients from the higher social classes and for those in private or outpatient care.[81] Even then there is virtually no evidence that medically supervised psychotherapy is an effective cure for madness. After a comprehensive review of the treatment literature, Schwitzgebel concludes that "the results of controlled follow-up studies . . . have been consistently negative . . . traditional forms of therapy have been living for many years on public faith . . . treatment can in fact change behavior."[82]

The Psychopharmaceutical Revolution

In 1952 the mental hospital entered a new phase of optimism. In that year French researchers synthesized chlorpromazine, the first of the so-called psychotropic drugs. Two years later a giant pharmaceutical company, Smith, Kline and French, began an aggressive campaign to market this drug for psychiatric use in the United States. Sold under the name Thorazine, the drug was billed as an antipsychotic or major tranquilizer. A special task force of fifty high-powered salespersons promised that the new chemical agent would soon revolutionize the treatment of mental illness. It did. By medicating patients the drug could be used to quell severe symptoms, restore order to unruly hospital wards, and permit medical personnel to get on with the business of serious psychotherapy.

Proponents of the pharmaceutical revolution could not speak highly enough of the benefits of the new medications. Fueled by the advertising and promotional activities of the multi-billion-dollar pharmaceutical industry, hospital administrators praised the tranquilizing affects of Thorazine and heralded the day when chemotherapy would permit outpatient care for severely disturbed patients. Critics pointed to the fact that drugs were used more to control and manage patients than to cure and ameliorate the causes of mental disturbance. Dangerous side-effects were also noted. The heavy and long-term use of Thorazine frequently results in tardive dyskinesia, a disfiguring and disabling disorder of the central nervous system. This physician-induced condition has caused irreversible damage to thousands of medically tranquilized patients. Its symptoms include involuntary lip, tongue, hand, and finger movements, general bodily shaking, and distortions of speech, facial expression, and body posture.[83]

This might seem like a big price for patients to pay in order to be treated more professionally. It was and continues to be, and thus the optimism surrounding the pharmaceutical revolution was short-lived. Rather than preparing patients for treatment, the widespread use of psychotropic drugs soon became a form of treatment. Chemotherapy became a substitute for psychotherapy. Within a decade medication was the only demonstrable form of treatment offered to the vast majority of publicly institutionalized mental patients.

Depopulating Mental Hospitals: The Impact of Litigation and Fiscal Crises

The number of persons hospitalized in public mental institutions grew steadily until 1955, when the patient count nationwide reached 558,000. Thereafter, there occurred a steady decline in the use of involuntary hospitalization as a mode of social control. By 1977 the inpatient count dropped to 174,000.[84] Why this sudden decrease? The use of psychotropic drugs is commonly cited as the major reason. While this was undoubtedly a factor, the issue is considerably more complex. Two other factors were also of importance: a nationwide movement of right-to-treatment litigation on behalf of involuntarily hospitalized patients and the growing fiscal crisis of state government.

Right-to-treatment litigation contends that involuntarily confined mental patients have a constitutional right to be adequately treated in the least restrictive environment or to be released. By 1974 the principle was given constitutional standing in the landmark Alabama case of *Wyatt v. Stickney*. Following a hearing on conditions at Alabama's 5,000-patient Bryce Hospital, Federal District Court Judge Frank Johnson ruled, "There can be no legal (or moral) justification for the State of Alabama's failure to afford treatment . . . and adequate treatment from a medical standpoint . . . to the several thousand patients who have been civilly committed to Bryce for treatment purposes."[85] Johnson subsequently delineated three conditions for adequate treatment: (1) a humane psychological and physical environment, (2) qualified staff in adequate numbers, and (3) individualized treatment plans. These general conditions had to be accompanied by specific standards detailing everything from the required components of a treatment plan and a formula for determining adequate staff-patient ratios to the size and number of toilets and showers required for a humane environment.

The *Wyatt* decision and other patients'-rights rulings were the result of over a decade of hard-fought legal struggles on behalf of persons involuntarily committed to the dark wards and hallways of the nation's public mental hospitals.[86] Prompted by journalistic exposes, critical sociological research, and a series of successful patients'-rights litigations, the right-to-treatment movement represented a new optimism for those concerned with the medical cure of madness. Its effects include a dramatic reduction in the number of patients subject to involuntary hospitalization and the issuance of more stringent criteria for involuntary commitment. Psychiatric judgments that someone is dangerous are replacing previous criteria which permitted commitment for serious illness alone. Many states are also urging formerly involuntarily committed patients to switch their status to that of voluntary patient. By such strategies, states hope to reduce the incredible costs required to reshape outdated custodial institutions into humane and modern treatment centers.

The issue of costliness is an important one. According to sociologist Andrew Scull, it has been a prime mover for the depopulation of mental hospitals from the onset.[87] Scull presents evidence suggesting that the timing of depopulation closely parallels the growing fiscal crisis of state government. Burdened with expensive union contracts, old and costly-to-maintain state buildings and property, and inflation-struck decreases in actual tax revenues, state governments are said to be confronted by strong economic pressures to save money by deinstitutionalizing their control of deviant populations such as the "mentally ill." Such fiscal pressure rather than high-minded reform is, for Scull, the prime mover of hospital depopulation. Without denying the influence of right-to-treatment reformers, Scull's analysis reminds us of a more general affinity between principled reform and practical material circumstances. As mutually determinant historical events, each breaks ground for the influence of the other. Ideas about the need to depopulate mental hospitals coincide with material circumstances which promote fiscal savings and institutional cutbacks.

Public Mental Hospitals in the 1980s: An Uncertain Future

Changes produced by the right-to-treatment movement and the practical realities of fiscal cutbacks present uncertainties for the continued reliance on public mental institutions of treatment and control. States are seriously considering the possibility of getting out of the mental hospital "business" altogether. Proposals exist to contract for beds in private hospitals for the most severely disturbed of the state's patients. Others would have to seek medical assistance through normal, noninstitutional channels. The future of such proposals is unclear. What is not unclear is one highly negative consequence of hospital depopulation—the "dumping" of deinstitutionalized patients into communities that are ill-prepared to receive them.

Where do previously institutionalized patients go after release? This question is of the utmost importance for the thousands of old and long-term patients pushed out of hospitals by new policies resulting from twin forces of litigation and fiscal crisis. One place they generally do not go is the wide assortment of community health facilities opened nationwide during the 1960s. Although these federally funded centers were originally designed to care for the seriously mentally ill in locations closer to home, this goal was never realized. The new community mental health centers soon found themselves busy counseling family problems, school troubles, alcoholism, predelinquency, bad marriages, job losses, and even the problems of aging. Community mental health centers greatly expanded the reach of medical controls without significantly affecting the care of those who were already institutionalized.

If not to community-based mental health facilities, where do the large mass of formerly hospitalized mental patients turn? Too often, the answer is nowhere. This is particularly a problem for the many deinstitutionalized patients, especially elderly patients, who have spent their entire adult lives within a hospital. Unable to properly care for themselves they are released into communities ill prepared to handle them. This problem has been overlooked by many otherwise zealous reformers and buried beneath the budget of state bureaucracies. States which have undertaken extensive depopulation have experienced enormous difficulties. The city of San Jose, for instance, had to deal with an unanticipated influx of nearly 2,000 ex-patients when nearby Agnews State Hospital emptied its wards. Many released patients became the welfare tenants of area business entrepreneurs who purchased abandoned houses and filled them with ex-patients.

The situation may be even more dramatic in New York, where the population of patients hospitalized decreased from 78,000 to 34,000 during the mid-1970s. Private nursing homes, welfare hotels, and old-age homes were overburdened with the new releasees. In New York City alone, about 25 percent of the estimated 100,000 residents of welfare homes are considered to be "severely mentally dysfunctional." Most of these persons are ex-patients of state hospitals. The assembly of newly released patients in places like Long Beach, a town on the south shore of Long Island, is even more critical. Long Beach has 34,000 residents, thirty-one hotels, and 712 so-called walkers (a name given by townspeople to ex–mental patients). According to one report, "The walkers . . . get their name because they are often seen wandering aimlessly on the city's two-mile boardwalk. Most of them are old, most are schizophrenic, most are on phenothiazines or other medication, and all of them are on welfare."[88] The situation at Long Beach is not unique. To rectify such problems some legal advocates have asked courts to consider the right to proper posthospital care as an element of the right to treatment. Without such a remedy the future lives of former patients may be worse than their years of confinement. With this in mind we close our short history of mental hospitals, a history in which optimism about cures has recurrently been upstaged by the harsh reality of custodial control, a history in which effective treatment has rarely been realized.

THE PATHOLOGICAL PERSPECTIVE TODAY

Despite its long legacy of failure the pathological perspective is still very much alive. Indeed, reborn pathological theorizing often commands the favor of government agencies committed to fighting crime and nonconformity. This became particularly evident during the late 1970s and early 1980s, as economic turmoil and international instability prompted a new birth of conservative thought and action. Programs of social reform, many of which were poorly administered or inadequately funded, were shelved in favor of new strategies of physiological or psychological control. This has resulted in a new wave of sociobiological publications and in renewed governmental sponsorship of "basic" causal research on deviance.

This trend was presaged at the 1978 meetings of the prestigious American Society of Criminology when approximately half of the papers presented concerned biological approaches to criminal behavior. This "pathological" tone was set by ASC president C. Ray Jeffery. Known previously for his studies of environmental factors related to crime, Jeffery had become a born-again pathologist. In addressing the convention he stated:

> We must move beyond . . . measurements of environmental impact . . . We must develop the capacity for tracing painful stimulus into the organism to the associational and motivational areas of the brain and then to the motor centers and to behavior. Between the stimulus and the response is the great big black box. . . . It is here that we will find the questions we should be asking.[89]

Jeffery's allusion to "the great big black box" places him in the company of Lombroso and a long line of pathological theorists who locate deviance within the physiology of nonconformists. In his book *Biology and Crime,* Jeffery laments the "historical misfortune" by which sociology "captured" the study of crime, deviance, and social control during the 1920s.[90] Arguing that social science is rooted in biology, Jeffery beseeches students of deviance to attend to such allegedly urgent issues as the relationship between low intelligence and delinquency. He speculates about the possibility that protein deficiency may be the true biological culprit behind much nonconformity.

Jeffery is not alone in reviving interest in the pathological perspective. At the 1977 meetings of the American Sociological Association Donald Cressey urged researchers to return to solid "hard-science" research, such as that exemplified by Max G. Schlapp and Edward H. Smith's 1928 book *The New Criminology*.[91] This supposedly model study claims that criminality is caused by glandular disturbances resulting from chemical imbalances in the blood and lymph nodes of a criminal's mother during pregnancy. It advocates an assortment of pathological controls, including compulsive treatment for all defectives, euthanasia for uncurables, sterilization, and the mandatory registration of delinquents.

Other theorists advocate a synthesis of pathological and social factors. In their 1977 *Biosocial Bases of Criminal Behavior,* Mednick and Christiansen present data suggesting that, while lower-class crime may be overwhelmingly determined by socioeconomic conditions, genetic factors are relatively great in the middle classes.[92] This conclusion is drawn from a variety of supposedly environmentally controlled studies of Danish twins and adoptees. Unfortunately, environmental pressures were measured largely in socioeconomic deprivation. Neglected were factors more likely to affect middle-class persons, such as intrafamily conflict, adolescent alienation, boredom, and socially nurtured meaninglessness. Had such variables been included, researchers would probably have discovered strong but different environmental pressures.

In a 1979 essay entitled "Biosociology and Crime" Harold Kelly also calls for a pooling of biochemical and social research.[93] He suggests that hypoglycemia (an insufficiency in blood glucose levels) may aggravate and perpetuate criminal behavior, while cerebral allergies (the existence of which is disputed by most reputable medical authorities) may cause fatigue, nervousness, irritability, or even perceptual distortions and thus lead to deviant behavior. The proposed cure for such conditions is "biochemical change." Kelly urges sociologists to take an unbiased look at some of the newer findings of biochemical research. The political implications of such a position are thinly veiled. In Kelly's words, "As the biochemical causes are found and treated most all citizens would see the goals and means and rewards and punishments provided by advanced capitalist societies to be sufficient for them to conform."[94]

Lest one think that Kelly's words are more science-fictional than real, it is important to note that many new forms of biomedical control are already in place. Several years ago the probation department of Cuyahoga Falls, Ohio, began to routinely screen offenders for hypoglycemia. Moreover, as Stuart Hills points out, the use of drugs as a means of control in American prisons is now commonplace. "Inmates who show 'disrespect for authority' or highly politicalized inmates who harbor 'subversive beliefs' are considered particularly dangerous and sometimes become the research subjects of powerful psychopharmaceutical technology."[95] As further evidence of the far-reaching influence of pathological theorizing, let us consider two of its more prominent contemporary applications: the medical control of hyperkinetic behavior in children and the use of psychosurgery.

Pathologizing Unruly Children: The Case of Hyperkinesis

Hyperkinesis is today perhaps the number-one childhood problem. Thousands of special clinics, special diagnostic measures, and special school programs have been established, and millions of federal, state, and local dollars are earmarked for its cure. Once a young child is found to have hyperkinesis, the treatment of choice is generally pharmaceutical intervention. The drug Ritalen (methylphenidate) is prescribed to alter the child's behavior. Yet, although categorized as a disease, hyperkinesis is primarily a form of social deviance. It is recognized not by its physiological properties but by the unruly behavior of children.

The behavioral manifestations of hyperkinesis are several: hyperactivity (excessive motor activity), short attention span, and restless or fidgety behavior. Also included are fluctuations in mood, clumsiness, impulsive and/or aggressive behavior, low tolerance for frustration, trouble with sleeping at the proper time or talking at the proper age, and the inability to sit still and obey the rules of the schoolhouse. Such things make for an unruly child. Children who behave or misbehave in such ways present obvious control problems for parents, teachers, and other guardians. From an adult perspective such behaviors are clearly unacceptable. But why is it that such unacceptable behaviors have come to be seen in terms of sickness? Once they were signs of the bad child. Now they are symptoms of a disease. Why? This question was posed by sociologist Peter Conrad.[96] The answers he discovered are disturbing. They cast doubt on the physiological origins of a behavior problem that is commonly treated (or controlled) by drugs.

Conrad suggests that the equation of unruly child behavior with the disease of hyperkinesis may be more social than clinical in origin. Medical researchers never actually discovered an organic defect which causes hyperactive behavior. What was discovered was that certain drugs could change or reduce unruly behavior. Inferences regarding organic deficiency as the cause of unruliness were arrived at retrospectively. In other words, since chemicals were capable of changing unruly behavior, it was reasoned that chemical deficiencies must have caused the behavior in the first place. By such logic theorists converted what would otherwise be a social problem into a problem for medical control.

The diagnosis of hyperkinesis is a relatively recent phenomenon. Thirty years ago it was unknown. Troublesome children were simply troublesome children. In the last decade knowledge of the disease has caught on. How did this change come about? According to Conrad, the period of time from the mid-1950s to the early 1970s was ripe for such a discovery. Socially there had emerged within organized medicine a burgeoning interest in child mental health. The pediatric subspecialties within organized medicine were looking for new childhood diseases to combat. Many traditional organic diseases had already come under medical control. Pediatric know-how, particularly the administration of various drugs as preventatives for such diseases as smallpox, diphtheria, and polio, had made youth a more medically secure time of life. This presented mixed blessings for pediatric specialists. While successful they were aware that prestige within the medical profession was awarded commensurate with the dangerousness of the diseases being fought. Pediatric specialists were thus on the lookout for new dangerous diseases. The psychiatric problems of children was one area which attracted their attention.

Two developments in pharmacology commanded the interest of childhood-disease investigators. The first derived from Charles Bradly's 1937 observation that amphetamines altered the behavior of children with behavioral or learning problems. Amphetamines increased conformity and achievement scores. A related development involved the synthesis of the drug Ritalen in the mid-1950s. Ritalen had many of the same stimulant qualities as amphetamines but was said to have fewer negative side-effects. In 1961 the Federal Drug Administration approved the use of Ritalen for children. This paved the way for the medicalized control of unruly childhood behavior through drugs. But the fact that drugs alter behavior does not mean that such behavior is essentially chemical in origin. Marijuana may make someone laugh. Cocaine may enhance exhilarated action. Few, however, would argue that the lack of laughter or exhilaration is the result of a pathological deficiency of the chemicals in marijuana or cocaine. Such logic would be viewed as highly suspect. Yet a very similar logic is employed in calling hyperkinesis a disease or pathology. What gives legitimacy to such a retrospective logic within medicine?

According to Conrad, the second major factor contributing to the discovery of hyperkinesis was the pharmaceutical revolution in the mental health field. By the early 1960s the treatment of mental patients with drugs had become an established fact. In the 1950s a variety of psychoactive drugs were discovered to alter the symptoms of psychotic and other severely disturbed patients. The success of drugs in controlling such persons was cited as evidence that mental disorders may be physiological in origin. At least the use of such drugs reinforced the notion that the proper treatment of mental disorders was medical. Since pediatric specialists were scrutinizing the psychiatric problems of children for new diseases to combat, the fact that drugs had become available which controlled such problems reinforced the movement toward seeing nonacute childhood behavior problems as a disease. In discovering hyperkinesis this is exactly what happened.

The social factors mentioned above were not the only variables contributing to the discovery of hyperkinesis. Conrad also mentions political factors, such as the lobbying efforts of such influential groups as the Association for Children with Learning Disabilities, and the dominance of medical interests on a government committee established to investigate the use of drugs to treat childhood behavior problems. The most important factor, however, may have been economic. Major drug companies instituted a massive, high-intensity, and highly financed advertising campaign aimed at convincing physicians that hyperkinesis was a real disease and that it was treatable by drugs. As Conrad and his colleague Joseph Schneider point out:

> The pharmaceutical companies spent a great amount of time and money promoting stimulant medications for this new disorder. After the middle 1960s it is nearly impossible to read a medical journal or the free "throw away" magazines without seeing some elaborate advertising for either Ritalen or Dexedrine. These advertisements explain the utility of treating hyperkinesis . . . and urge the physician to diagnose and treat hyperkinetic children. . . . They often advise physicians that "the hyperkinetic syndrome exists" as a "distinct medical entity" and that the "syndrome is readily diagnosed through patient histories and psychometric testing." . . . These same firms also supply sophisticated packets of "diagnostic and treatment" information, . . . pay for professional conferences on the subject, and support research in the identification and treatment of the disorder.[97]

The drug companies were well rewarded for their high-pressure advertising. Reports suggest that one company, CIBA, reaped $13 million in profits on Ritalen in 1971 alone. Sales of Ritalen represented 15 percent of its total gross profits during that twelve-month period. While drug companies lined their pockets, medical professionals expanded their interests in the domain of social controls. Hyperkinesis emerged as yet another speculative category of pathological deviance.

The Surgical Control of Human Behavior

Psychosurgery is brain surgery aimed at changing human behavior. The first known psychosurgeries were performed by Dr. Gottlieb Burckhardt on six patients at an insane asylum in Prefargier, Switzerland, in 1890.[98] The patients involved were described as both dangerous and psychotic. Burckhardt removed a small section of each patient's brain. Despite his alleged success in rendering the patients harmless to themselves and others, Burckhardt's operations were soon halted by the ethical criticisms of his fellow medical practitioners.

In 1935 psychosurgery was reborn under the scalpel of António Moniz.[99] Moniz, a Portuguese physician, is credited with performing the first prefrontal lobotomy. With his associate Almeida Lima, he cut away portions of the frontal lobes of twenty long-term mental patients unaffected by a battery of other psychiatric treatments. Moniz claimed success in fifteen of his twenty operations. Unfortunately one of his "successful" patients would later pump five bullets into the renowned physician.

Moniz's efforts did not go unnoticed. In 1949 he was awarded the Nobel Prize. In the year following, his surgical techniques were carried to America by Walter Freeman and James Watts. These surgeons modified Moniz's approach by inserting an ice-pick-like tool through the eye socket. Freeman, working at George Washington University in the District of Columbia, conducted 4,000 such surgeries. By the early 1950s, 50,000 lobotomies had been performed in the United States alone, many upon military personnel returning from World War II with allegedly severe mental problems.[100] All were conducted to control disruptive human behaviors.

Advocates of psychosurgery make strong claims about the desirability of the operation for individual patients and for society. Negative outcomes are downplayed or pictured as the exception. The Freeman and Watts lobotomy technique was heralded as relatively safe in that its mortality rate was a mere 1.7 percent.[101] But don't lobotomies turn people into vegetables? Some did. The specter of an empty-eyed Jack Nicholson playing the part of the lobotomized McMurphy in *One Flew Over the Cuckoo's Nest* is hard to forget. A more common side-effect is for patients to lose the imaginative dimensions of human consciousness. Lobotomies are consistently followed by a dramatic reduction in the ability to fantasize, abstract, or think creatively. While not a total vegetable, the typical lobotomized patient loses some of the more distinctive features of human cognition.

During the 1950s a number of journalistic exposes revealed something of the darker side of psychosurgery. Stories of failure and of horrible side-effects came to the public's attention. Questions about the kinds of people selected for the operation were raised. The official position was that the operation was reserved for last-ditch cases, particularly those with a potential for violence. Critics remained unconvinced. Consider one of Walter Freeman's most well-known success stories. The person operated upon was a "peeping tom."[102] His crime was spying on the private lives of others. Such behavior is surely a social nuisance. It may even be frightening. But is its prevention worth the risks of psychosurgery? Freeman thought so. His operation was termed a success. After surgery the man never peeped around the backs of houses again. Unrestrained by previous inhibitions, he would confidently approach houses and peer through their front windows.

During the mid-1950s the use of lobotomies dropped drastically. Most observers believe that the introduction of psychotropic drugs made it easier to control difficult inmates without the use of a surgeon's scalpel. Nonetheless, testimony presented before Senator Edward Kennedy's U.S. Senate Subcommittee on Health revealed that nearly 600 lobotomies were being performed annually as late as 1973. Of greater significance is the "new wave" of psychosurgical techniques introduced in the late 1960s and early 1970s. Using ultrasonic beams and electrodes, proponents of these new behavior-modifying operations attempt to distinguish themselves from those who performed lobotomies. These new anatomical interventions are said to be more effective, more precise, and less dangerous.

The New Wave of Psychosurgery

The new wave of psychosurgical techniques is generally directed at several subcortical structures of the "old" paleomammalian brain or the limbic system. The limbic lobe forms a ring around the human brain stem and is believed to play a key role in the regulation of emotions, aggression, and sexual behavior. Of particular concern is the hypothalamus, a connector between the brain stem and the surrounding limbic system and the amygdala, a limbic structure related to the hypothalamus's functioning. Also important is the thalamus or cingulate portions of the cerebral cortex. Abnormal functioning in these interconnected structures is believed to be associated with displays of emotional rage and physical aggression.

This conclusion is drawn from a variety of experiments on nonhuman animals. In such experiments sham rage can be induced in otherwise quiet animals and attack behavior can be stimulated or reduced by interfering with the hypothalamus or related structures. The new wave of psychosurgery is modeled upon such experiments.

New psychosurgical techniques are said to be less messy and less "hit or miss" than lobotomies. Neurosurgeon H. Thomas Ballentine, one of a small number of surgeons currently performing such operations in Massachusetts, recently described the procedures involved in a cingulotomy.[103] Two small holes are drilled just above the hairline on either side of the head. Hollow needles about $2\frac{1}{2}$ inches long are inserted. Through these a current of air is followed by intense heat. This destroys about a forefinger of nerve tissue on either side. Ballentine has performed over 250 such operations during some fifteen years of psychosurgery.

How successful and how safe are such procedures? Advocates present them as relatively sure and safe mechanisms for normalizing some of society's most intractable and fearful deviants. Critics, including some prominent physicians, have strong reservations. They contend that psychosurgical operations are nothing but experiments. It is known that changing brain tissue changes brain functioning. It is not known whether the behavioral problems originate in the brain tissues which are operated upon. According to George J. Amos, director of the Boston University Center for Law and Health Science, psychosurgeons operate without really knowing what they are doing.[104] Another critic, psychiatrist Peter Breggin, points to dangers in the surgical procedure. According to Breggin, "the procedure is not even experimental, it's simply dangerous and mutilative. We know enough about . . . the brain to know that any mutilation or destruction of the normal tissue will lead to brain damage and dysfunction."[105]

Two of the strongest proponents of psychosurgery are Dr. Vernon H. Mark and Dr. Frank R. Ervin, authors of *Violence and the Brain*.[106] In 1973 Mark and Ervin's federally funded research project at Harvard University was halted by negative publicity and public protest. Mark and Ervin attempt to justify psychosurgery by citing evidence from studies of the brain chemistry of nonhuman animals suggesting a link between aggressive behavior and abnormalities in the structure and/or functioning of the brain. Regarding humans, they argue that psychosurgery constrains aggression and should thus be applied to a violence-prone population suffering from the so-called dyscontrol syndrome. How valid are these contentions?

Regarding animal studies, it is true that repeated research has shown that emotional rage and aggressive behavior can be modulated by altering the electrical activity of regions of the brain, particularly the hypothalamus.[107] The most famous of such studies was conducted at Yale University in the laboratories of Jose Delgado. Delgado and his associates implanted sensitive radio receivers in the brains of cats, monkeys, and other species. By artificially activating parts of the hypothalamus and other parts of the limbic system, Delgado was able to create variations in what he observed to be aggressive behavior. In one of his more dramatic experiments, the behavior of a charging bull was halted in the process of attack. In research with rhesus monkeys, however, electrical stimulation could not get animals to violate fixed hierarchies of social deference. Low-ranking monkeys, even if electronically stimulated, would not attack those of a higher dominance. Thus it appears that, even under controlled conditions, aggressive acts are as dependent upon environmental stimuli as upon electrobrain stimulation.

Other researchers implanted chemical tubes in the hypothalamus to produce behavioral changes.[108] Experimental animals were divided into two groups. Naturally aggressive rats were, for instance, separated from their passive counterparts. Chemicals which either activated or deactivated the hypothalamus were then injected into each group. Passive rats were converted into aggressive rats. "Killer rats" became docile. The chemical effects wore off after several hours, and the animals returned to their previous patterns of behavior.

What can one reasonably conclude about human behavior from such animal studies? There is little doubt that altering the electrical chemistry of the nonhuman brain is associated with changes in aggressive behavior.[109] This does not mean that aggressive behavior is caused by electrical or chemical changes per se. Aggression may be triggered by physiological change, but what triggers physiological change itself? It is reasonable to suggest that environmental cues ordinarily trigger the physiological changes which are associated with displays of aggression. Animals, after all, normally act aggressive only in relation to certain environmental stimuli. There is no pathology involved. The monkeys and rats in most experiments, even those which acted naturally aggressive prior to experimental intervention, were normal and not sick or pathological. Despite this fact, biomedical researchers make reference to such things as "yet undetected lesions" of "present, but not yet observed pathologies." This is strange language for supposedly hard-nosed positivistic scientists. Why speculate about undetected lesions? It seems as if researchers are convinced that pathology must be present if aggression is observed. Using similar logic, surgeons such as Mark and Ervin make giant leaps from data derived in animal studies to arguments about the physiological basis of human violence.

There are no studies of the biology of human violence comparable to the experiments performed on nonhuman animals. Nonetheless, Mark and Ervin point to known similarities between nonhuman primate and human brains and to instances where observable brain pathology is associated with altered behaviors. A clear example is epilepsy. Lesions in the brains of epileptics produce periodic fits in which persons may temporarily lose control of their psychomotor functioning. Yet, despite the dramatic appearance of some severe epileptic fits, there is no evidence that epileptics act more aggressively toward others before, during, or after a seizure. Popular mythology aside, epileptics are no more violence-prone than anyone else. On the other hand, there have been a few rare instances where episodic explosions of ragelike human behavior have been linked to documented damage to key areas of the limbic system. Such documented instances are rare and hardly a typical profile of human violence. Nonetheless, Mark and Ervin boldly leap beyond the evidence. They follow the inferential logic of some animal researchers in suggesting that brain pathology may lie behind a wide range of human violence.

Mark and Ervin offer a profile of potentially violent people as targets for psychosurgery. The people described by this profile are hypothetically carriers of a severely damaged limbic system, ready to erupt into violence at the slightest provocation. They are said to be victims of the dyscontrol syndrome, the combined symptoms of which make them candidates for neurological social control. These symptoms include: (1) a history of physical assaults, especially against women and children; (2) intoxication (even with small amounts of alcohol) which is frequently associated with displays of aggression; (3) impulsive sexual behavior, often leading to sexual assault; and (4) a history of accidents, particularly automobile accidents.

Implicit in the above profile is an image of pathology or sickness. Is there another interpretation? The history of assaults, intoxication, impulsive or aggressive sexuality, and accidents may also bring to mind an image of the angry, frustrated lower-class male. Indeed, contemporary profiles of criminal violence suggest that lower-class males are by far disproportionately overrepresented in the ranks of those who commit acts of overt physical harm. Such persons are constantly bombarded with the "All-American" message that to be male is to be powerful. At the same time they are daily denied equal access to legitimate nonviolent channels of social power. Their search for power is deflected from the public to the private realms of social life. In physical violence, drinking, and sexual aggression, lower-class males play out a masculine "power game." Others, with greater economic, political, or social resources, might play out this game at the office, the convention, or the country club. The constricted power of lower-class males is steeped in danger. Anger is present on the surface of many private social encounters. The line between deliberate action and fatalistic accident may be frequently blurred. Conditions such as these increase the probability that lower-class males will use violence as a means to power. They suggest a social link between violence and power. Isn't this a reasonable nonpathological interpretation of the so-called dyscontrol syndrome? Why leap to ambiguous inferences of brain pathology based upon "as yet unobserved" abnormalities?

In a paper published in the prestigious *Journal of the American Medical Association*, Mark, Ervin, and a colleague, W. H. Sweet, respond to the "social conditions" objection to the dyscontrol profile. Yet, as clever pathological theorists, they transform questions about slum conditions into hypotheses for neurological investigation. On the trail of a physiological basis for urban violence, they reduce the political implications of urban rioting to speculation about the pathological brains of the rioters. Their mission is to "pinpoint, diagnose and treat those with low violence thresholds." Thus they argue that "if slum conditions alone determined and initiated riots, why are the vast majority of slum dwellers able to resist the temptations of unrestrained violence?" Is there something peculiar, ask these psychosurgeons, about the violent slum dweller that differentiates him from his peaceful neighbor?[110]

As pathological theorists, Mark and Ervin view violence as a public health problem. They propose "early warning tests" to detect citizens with low thresholds for impulsive violence. But how effective is their program of surgical control? Mark and Ervin report on a number of successful cases. The most well known is now recognized as a major failure. The case involved Leonard A. Kille, an engineer in his thirties. Following a head injury Kille developed a form of psychomotor epilepsy and would occasionally exhibit outbursts of violent rage. Kille became a patient of Mark and Ervin and consented to undergo a bilateral amygdalotomy. Six years later Kille had become permanently incapacitated. His psychomotor coordination was reduced to vegetablelike status. His memory was severely impaired, and he suffered repeated hospitalizations and delusions. His violent explosions had increased. Acting on his behalf, Kille's mother brought suit against Mark and Ervin for $2 million in damages. In the spring of 1979, the surgeons were absolved of legal responsibility, not because they had refuted the sad facts of Kille's impairment but because the patient had given his prior consent to the dangerous operation.

Not all psychosurgery cases end so badly. Two recent studies on Boston-area psychosurgery patients did not find the same record of long-term impairment. Nor did they find significantly positive behavioral changes.[111] Yet both discovered that patients' intelligence, as measured by IQ tests and such things as card-sorting tasks, sank for about a four-month period after surgery, but returned to its previous level thereafter. Boston University researchers compared twenty-seven surgical patients with a small control group of persons with relatively similar symptoms who were not operated upon. The surgical patients demonstrating the greatest improvement were those whose initial complaints were more physical than behavioral, people experiencing severe head pain. Once this physical-pain-only group was removed from the sample, surgical patients showed no more improvement than controls. Thirty percent of both groups showed some improvement.[112] Such evidence does little to convince us that surgery is an effective therapeutic tool. Its appeal is, if anything, more politically attractive than scientifically proven.

The Future of Psychosurgery

The future of psychosurgery remains uncertain. Its controversial and often dangerous record has created a climate of relative caution among government officials charged with its regulation. A National Commission for the Protection of Human Subjects of Biomedical and Behavioral Research recently issued a set of standards by which such operations may be permitted. According to the commission, psychosurgery would be allowed (1) if it is effective, (2) if it serves the advancement of science, (3) if the patient has been chosen for the right reasons (i.e., for his own good), and (4) if there is informed consent.[113] Several of these criteria are themselves quite controversial. What determines effectiveness? Can the operation ever really be considered effective if those who perform it don't even know why it does what it does? The issue of informed consent has been equally problematic. In the landmark case of *Kaimowitz v. the Department of Mental Health,* a Michigan court ruled that the operation could not be performed upon patients involuntarily hospitalized. Involuntary commitment was seen as limiting a person's ability to make a free and fully consenting choice.

While legal restrictions have limited the spread of psychosurgery, they have not limited the imagination of pathological theorists. Some propose bold new biotechnical controls which take us beyond the frontiers of current surgical practice. In *Physical Control of the Mind: Toward a Psychocivilized Society,* a pioneer psychosurgical researcher, Jose Delgado, calls for the formation of powerful national agencies (following the model of the National Aeronautics and Space Administration) and a full-scale media campaign to promote a program of neurobiological control.[114] Garage doors and television sets are already activated by remote-control radio transmitters. Why not regions of the brain? Two-way radio systems could be implanted in the brain. These would permit society to monitor and control the neurological activity of deviants. According to Delgado, "Neuronal activity related to behavioral disturbances . . . could be recognized in order to trigger stimulation of specific inhibitory structures."[115] The possibilities are both limitless and horrifying. Who will make what decisions to "inhibit" which kinds of behaviors? At the far extremes of the pathological perspective we are confronted with the total-control potential of positivistic science. This potential is not far from being realized. Our readiness for it is another matter.

ASSESSING THE PATHOLOGICAL PERSPECTIVE: Reducing Social Trouble to Individual Sickness

Only in the most limited sense is any historical event or problem like an illness. It is invariably an encouragement to simplify what is complex.

Susan Sontag[116]

Much of what has been written about the pathological perspective in this chapter has not been positive. The pathological perspective promises much but has delivered little. It claims to be rigorously scientific but has been wrought with poor methodological procedures. It hails the principles of curative treatment but often practices the politics of repressive intervention. Nonetheless, the perspective is not without its positive side. Its emphasis on the naturalistic causes of deviance represents an important break from a world dominated by battles between those who damn devils and those who see deviance as a freely calculated choice.

Other positive aspects of this perspective are outlined by Conrad and Schneider in their book *Deviance and Medicalization*.[117] These "brighter" dimensions of the pathological approach include its humanitarian intent, its seemingly eternal optimism, and its flexibility. Also important are the social advantages of the sick role for deviants who comply with the therapeutic prescriptions of rehabilitative specialists. Pathologically defined rule-breakers are able to avoid blame and shun responsibility as long as they behave as good patients, desirous of being cured of their nonconformity.

Despite such advantages, the liabilities of empirically unsupported pathological theorizing far outweigh its strengths. These weaknesses are also noted by Conrad and Schneider, who point to the way in which the highly individualistic and overly deterministic imagery of the medical model denigrates the roles of both human choice and structured social influence. Life is rarely a matter of free choice, but neither is it usually totally determined.[118] Somewhere between freedom and determination we assert our being. The assertion of deviance is no different. Pathological theorizing misses this point. Pathological theorizing gives the false impression that the lives of "deviants" are more determined than those of so-called normal people.

This major failing of the pathological perspective is compounded when its adherents cloak themselves in the false garb of moral neutrality. There is nothing neutral about viewing deviants as sick. Prior to drawing head measurements, conducting chromosome tests, or administering psychological exams, the pathological researcher has made a moral judgment that deviant subjects have acted wrongly. While, in principle, the pathological perspective concerns itself with neutral-sounding references to "syndromes" and "disease types," in practice these are little more than code words for moral judgments about the undesirability of certain forms of behavior. Moreover, once troublesome behaviors are defined as sick, their resolution is taken from the hands of ordinary people and turned over to experts, whose professional careers are staked on the premise that deviance is a problem of aberrant or abnormal individuals. No wonder the game of pursuing pathological traces is played from one losing season to the next. The expert control of deviance is a multi-billion-dollar business. Those who have cornered the medical control market have little interest in depathologizing the ballgame.

Pathological theorizing also errs by individualizing complex social problems. Nothing would be deviant if nobody was bothered by certain types of nonconformity. This obvious sociological fact is usually ignored by the pathological perspective. It sidesteps the complex network of social forces which push or pull people toward certain types of behavior. The rich and often troubling complexity of life is reduced to biochemical or psychological formulations. We are, of course, biochemical and psychological beings. But we are never just that. Our biochemistry and psychology are always in interaction with those of our fellow social animals. By reducing theoretical explanations to psychophysiology the pathological perspective is untrue to the complexity of human life itself.

So also does pathological thinking ignore the essential politicality of all nonconformity. Deviance and its control are always matters of power and politics. Blinded by its narrow vision and its commitment to positivist rationality, pathological theorizing ignores this concern. Dissidents are chemically controlled, not because they are politically troublesome, but because they are mentally disturbed. Illegal drug users are forced into treatment, not because their escape into pleasure threatens an instrumental, or achievement-oriented, society, but because they are sick. Murderers are treated psychiatrically, not because their actions tell a story of distorted social power, but because they may be psychopathic.

I do not intend to romanticize the deviant as a self-conscious political rebel. Most deviants cannot be accurately described in this manner. Nonetheless the story of deviance is always a story of resistance to power, regardless of whether the resistance is deliberate or inadvertent. This is true whether the deviant be an alcoholic struggling with the fermented demons of unobtainable power, an angry teenager who finds power in random violence, or a trained terrorist who takes up a rifle in order to change the world. To fully confront the problem of deviance we must be open to the political dimensions of nonconformity. The pathological perspective is not. It denies that deviance is shaped by anything but abnormal body or mind.

A final problem with the pathological perspective is the way in which it systematically obscures questions about what is evil and what is good. The good and bad intentions and consequences of human action are blurred within a technocratic framework devoid of reference to right or wrong. As Conrad and Schneider point out, "there is little to be gained by deploying such a medical vocabulary of motives. It only hinders us from comprehending the human element in the decisions we make, the social structures we create, and the actions we take."[119] As an example, they point to medicalized explanations which reduce the violent actions of persons such as Hitler to clinical profiles of pathological disturbance. Imagine portraying the horrors of the Holocaust, the pain of slavery, or even the abuses of Watergate in such a fashion. By pathologizing "bad actors" we are all spared the responsibility of having created social contexts which nurture wrongdoing. If this is not evil, what is?

In summary, pathological theorizing has multiple weaknesses. It has not proved itself in the laboratories of rigorous positivistic science, nor does it adequately address matters of human responsibility. Furthermore, while cloaking itself in the false neutrality of expert medical control, it reduces complex social and political problems to a simplistic pursuit of technocratic solutions. Moreover, insomuch as the image of pathology impairs our ability to confront questions of good and evil, one wonders whether there is something evil about this perspective itself.

In spite of all these problems, the pathological perspective remains perhaps the single most-accepted theory of deviance. About this we can say for certain that as long as our image of deviance remains hospitalized within the positivist asylum of medicalized theorizing, we shall forever be denied a full vision of deviance and social control as aspects of the practical struggle of people together in history. In order to escape the institutional confines of this individualistic perspective, we now turn to a variety of sociological interpretations.

NOTES

1 Peter Conrad and Joseph Schneider, *Deviance and Medicalization,* Mosby, St. Louis, 1980, p. 1.
2 Joseph Stephens, "They Absolved Hinckley Yesterday. I saw it on Television." Previously unpublished poem, included here with permission of author, June 22, 1982.
3 Cesare Lombroso, *L'Uomo Delinquente,* Hoepli, Milan, 1876. See also Cesare Lombroso, *The Female Offender,* Unwin, London, 1895.
4 Conrad and Schneider, *Deviance and Medicalization,* pp. 39–40.
5 Stephen Schafer, *Theories in Criminology,* Random House, New York, 1969, p. 113.
6 George B. Vold, *Theoretical Criminology,* 2d ed., prepared by Thomas J. Bernard, Oxford University Press, New York, 1979, pp. 52–53.
7 Sybil Leek, *Phrenology,* Macmillan, New York, 1970.
8 Conrad and Schneider, *Deviance and Medicalization,* p. 49.
9 Ibid.
10 Charles Darwin, *Descent of Man,* John Murray, London, 1871.
11 Gideon Fishman, "Positivism and NeoLombrosianism," in C. Ronald Huff and Israel Barak (eds.), *The Mad, the Bad and the Different,* Lexington Books, Heath, Lexington, Mass., 1981, p. 15.
12 Charles Goring, *The English Convict,* H. M. Stationery Office, London, 1913.
13 Ernest A. Hooton, *The American Criminal: An Anthropological Study,* Harvard, Cambridge, Mass., 1939.
14 Robert K. Merton and M. F. Ashley Montague, "Crime and the Anthropologist," *American Anthropologist,* vol. 42, August 1940, pp. 384–408.
15 William H. Sheldon, *Varieties of Delinquent Youth: An Introduction to Constitutional Psychiatry,* Harper, New York, 1949.
16 Ernst Kretschmer, *Physique and Character,* W. J. H. Sprott (trans.), Kegan Paul, Trench, Trubner, London, 1925.
17 Edwin H. Sutherland, "Critique of Sheldon's *Varieties of Delinquent Youth,*" *American Sociological Review,* vol. 18, 1951, pp. 142–148.
18 Sheldon Glueck and Eleanor Glueck, *Physique and Delinquency,* Harper, New York, 1956.
19 Goring, *The English Convict.*
20 Robert L. Dugdale, *The Jukes: A Study in Crime, Pauperism, and Heredity,* Putnam, New York, 1877.
21 Samuel Hopkins Adams "The Jukes Myth," *Saturday Review,* vol.14, April 2, 1955.
22 Henry H. Goddard, *The Kallikak Family: A Study in the Heredity of Feeble-Mindedness,* Macmillan, New York, 1912.
23 Henry H. Goddard, *Feeble-Mindedness: Its Causes and Consequences,* Macmillan, New York, 1914. See also Henry H. Goddard, "Feeblemindedness and Delinquency," *Journal of Psycho-Asthenics,* vol. 25, 1921, pp. 168–176.
24 Carl Murchinson, *Criminal Intelligence,* Clark University Press, Worcester, Mass., 1926.
25 For a summary critique of the posited relationship between intelligence and criminality, see Daniel Glaser, *Crime in Our Changing Society,* Holt, Rinehart & Winston, New York, 1978, pp. 136–137.
26 Johannes Lange, *Verbrechen als Schicksal,* George Thieme, Leipzig, 1929. English translation by Charlotte Haldane, as *Crime and Destiny,* Boni, New York, 1930.

27 A. M. Legras, *Psychose en Criminaliteit bei Tweelingen,* Kremink, Utrecht, 1932; Heinrich Kranz, *Lebensschicksale Kriminelle Zwillinge,* Springer, Berlin, 1936.

28 Karl O. Christiansen, "Threshold of Tolerance in Various Population Groups Illustrated by Results from Danish Criminologic Twin Study," in A. V. S. deReuck and R. Porter (eds.), *The Mentally Abnormal Offender,* Little, Brown, Boston, 1968, pp. 107–116; Karl O. Christiansen, "Seriousness of Criminality and Concordance Among Danish Twins," in Roger Hood (ed.), *Crime, Criminology and Public Policy,* Free Press, New York, 1974.

29 Ernest R. Mowrer, "Some Factors in the Affectional Adjustment of Twins," *American Sociological Review,* vol. 16, August 1954, pp. 468–471.

30 Fini Schulsinger, "Psychopathy: Heredity and Environment," *International Journal of Mental Health,* vol. 1, 1972, pp. 190–206.

31 Raymond R. Crowe, "The Adopted Offspring of Women Criminal Offenders," *Archives of General Psychiatry,* vol. 27, November 1972, pp. 600–603.

32 Barry Hutchings and Sarnoff A. Mednick, "Criminality in Adoptees and Their Adoptive and Biological Parents," in Sarnoff Mednick and Karl O. Christiansen (eds.), *Biosocial Bases of Criminal Behavior,* Gardner Press, New York, 1977, pp. 127–241.

33 P. A. Jacobs, M. Bruton, M. M. Melville, et al., "Aggressive Behavior, Mental Subnormality and the XYY Male," *Nature,* vol. 208, December 1965, pp. 1351–1352.

34 See Richard S. Fox, "The XYY Offender: A Modern Myth?" *Journal of Criminal Law, Criminology and Police Science,* vol. 62, March 1971, pp. 59–73.

35 National Institute of Mental Health, *Report on the XYY Chromosomal Abnormality,* PHS Publication no. 2103, NIMH, Rockville, Md., 1920.

36 Theodore R. Sarvin and Jeffery E. Miller, "Demonism Revisited: The XYY Chromosomal Anomaly," *Issues in Criminology,* vol. 5, no. 2, Summer 1970 pp. 199–207.

37 Raffaele Garofalo, *Criminology,* Little, Brown, Boston, 1914.

38 Sigmund Freud, *A General Introduction to Psychonalysis,* Boni & Liveright, New York, 1920.

39 Franz Alexander and William Healy, *Roots of Crime,* Knopf, New York, 1935.

40 Sigmund Freud, *The Standard Edition of the Complete Psychological Works of Sigmund Freud,* Hogarth, London, 1963, vol. 19, p. 51. See also David Abrahamson, *The Psychology of Crime,* Columbia, New York, 1960, and Walter Bromberg, *Crime and the Mind: A Psychiatric Analysis of Crime and Punishment,* Macmillan, New York, 1965.

41 August Aichhorn, *Wayward Youth,* Viking, New York, 1963.

42 T. Bowlby, *Child Care and the Growth of Love,* Penguin, Baltimore, 1953.

43 A. M. Johnson and S. A. Szurek, "The Genesis of Antisocial Acting Out in Children and Adults," *Psychoanalytic Quarterly,* vol. 21, 1952, pp. 674–683.

44 Jan Hankin, "A Sociological Critique of Psychiatric Theories of Crime," unpublished paper cited in Marshall B. Clinard and Robert F. Meir (eds.), *Sociology of Deviant Behavior,* 5th ed., Holt, Rinehart & Winston, 1979, p. 98.

45 See Karl F. Scheussler and Donald R. Cressey, "Personality Characteristics of Criminals," *American Journal of Sociology,* vol. 55, March 1950, pp. 483–484; Gordon Waldo and Simon Dinity, "Personality Attributes of the Criminal: An Analysis of Research Studies," *Journal of Research in Crime and Delinquency,* vol. 4, July 1967, pp. 185–202.

46 Hans J. Eysenck, *Crime and Personality,* Houghton Mifflin, Boston, 1964.

47 M. P. Feldman, *Criminal Behavior: A Psychological Analysis,* Wiley, New York, 1977.

48 Michael T. Nietzel, *Crime and Its Modification: A Social Learning Perspective,* Pergamon, New York, 1979, p. 89.

49 Samuel Yochelson and Stanton Samenow, *The Criminal Personality,* Aronson, New York, 1976.

50 Ibid., p. viii.
51 Simon Dinitz, "Chronically Abnormal Offenders," in John Conrad and Simon Dinitz (eds.), *For Fear of Each Other,* Heath, Lexington Books, Lexington, Mass., 1977, p. 22.
52 Sydney Maughs, "A Concept of Psychopathy and Psychopathic Personality: Its Evaluation and Historical Development," *Journal of Criminal Psychopathology,* vol. 2, April 1940, pp. 465–499.
53 Hervey Cleckley, *The Mask of Sanity,* 4th ed., Mosby, St. Lewis, 1964.
54 Harrison Gough, "A Sociological Theory of Psychopathy," *American Journal of Sociology,* vol. 53, March 1948, pp. 359–366.
55 B. Baker's unpublished work is summarized in Theodore R. Sarbin, "Role Theory," in Gardner Lindzey (ed.), *Handbook of Social Psychology,* Addison-Wesley, Cambridge, Mass., 1954, p. 246.
56 R. Albrecht and T. R. Sarbin's unpublished work is summarized in Theodore R. Sarbin, "Role Theory," p. 246.
57 William McCord and Joan McCord, *Psychopathy and Delinquency,* Grune & Stratton, New York, 1956.
58 Lee Robins, *Deviant Children Grow Up,* Williams & Williams, Baltimore, 1966.
59 D. H. Funkenstein, M. Greenblatt, and H. C. Solomon, "Psychophysiological Study of Mentally Ill Patients," *American Journal of Psychiatry,* vol. 106, 1949, pp. 359–366.
60 D. T. Lykken, "A Study of Anxiety in the Sociopathic Personality," Ph.D. dissertation, University of Minnesota, Minneapolis, 1955 (University Microfilms, Ann Arbor, no. 55–944).
61 Stanley Schachter and Bibb Latane, "Crime, Cognition and the Autonomic Nervous System," in David Levine (ed.), *Nebraska Symposium of Motivation,* University of Nebraska Press, Lincoln, 1964, pp. 271–274.
62 W. W. Lippert, "The Electrodermal System of the Sociopath," (Ph.D. dissertation, University of Cincinnati, 1965 (University Microfilms, Ann Arbor, no. 65-12,921); R. D. Hare, "Psychopathy, Autonomic Functioning, and the Orienting Response," *Journal of Abnormal Psychology,* vol. 73, suppl. 1968, pp. 1–24.
63 H. E. Allen, L. A. Lindner, H. Goldman, and S. Dinitz, "The Social and Biomedical Correlates of Sociopathy," *Criminologica,* vol. 6, 1969, pp. 68–75, and "Hostile and Simple Sociopaths: An Empirical Typology, *Criminology,* vol 9, 1971, pp. 27–47; H. Goldman, L. A. Linder, S. Dinitz, and H. E. Allen, "The Simple Sociopath: Physiologic and Sociologic Characteristics," *Biological Psychiatry,* vol. 3, 1971, pp. 77–83.
64 Sting, "Every Breath You Take," from the album *Synchronicity* by The Police. A&M Records Inc., Hollywood, Calif., 1983.
65 Michel Foucault, *Discipline and Punish,* Alan Sheridan (trans.), Pantheon, New York, pp. 220–221.
66 Jurgen Habermas, "Knowledge and Interest," in D. Emmet and A. MacIntyre (eds.), *Sociological Theory and Philosophical Analysis,* Macmillan, New York, 1970, J. Shapiro (trans.), Beacon Press, Boston, 1971.
67 Foucault, *Discipline and Punish,* p. 226.
68 Malcolm Spector, "Beyond Crime: Seven Methods to Control Troublesome Rascals," in H. Lawrence Ross (ed.), *Law and Deviance,* Sage, Beverly Hills, Calif., 1981, p. 138.
69 Nicholas Kittrie, *The Right to Be Different: Deviance and Enforced Therapy,* Johns Hopkins, Baltimore, Md., 1971.
70 Conrad and Schneider, *Deviance and Medicalization,* p. 35.
71 Ibid.
72 Vold, *Theoretical Criminology,* p. 54.

73 This description of the eugenics movement is indebted to the excellent overview of this pathological control strategy in Charles H. McCaghy, *Deviant Behavior: Crime, Conflict and Interest Groups,* Macmillan, New York, 1976, pp. 19–21.

74 T. W. Shannon, *Eugenics,* Mullikin, Marietta, Ohio, 1916.

75 Ibid., p. 160.

76 Charles R. Henderson, *Dependent, Defective, and Delinquent Classes: And of Their Social Treatment,* Heath, Boston, 1901, as discussed in McCaghy, *Deviant Behavior,* p. 20.

77 McCaghy, *Deviant Behavior,* p. 21.

78 Ibid.

79 Ibid.

80 Michel Foucault, *Madness and Civilization,* Pantheon, New York, 1965.

81 August B. Hollingshead and Frederick C. Redlich, *Social Class and Mental Illness,* Wiley, New York, 1958.

82 Ralph K. Schwitzgebel, "The Right to Effective Mental Treatment," *California Law Review,* vol. 3, May 1974, pp. 943, 948.

83 Stuart L. Hills, *Demystifying Social Deviance,* McGraw-Hill, New York, 1980, p. 125.

84 Conrad and Schneider, *Deviance and Medicalization,* pp. 62–63. Data on inpatients, state and county mental hospitals by courtesy U.S. Department of Health, Education and Welfare, National Institute of Mental Health.

85 *Wyatt v. Stickney,* 325 F. Supp. 781–785 (1974)

86 See Stephen J. Pfohl, *Right to Treatment Litigation: Judicial Intervention into Mental Health Policy,* Ohio Division of Mental Health, Columbus, 1975.

87 Andrew T. Scull, *Decarceration: Community Treatment and the Deviant—A Radical View,* Prentice-Hall, Englewood Cliffs, N.J., 1977.

88 *Medical World News,* April 11, 1974, p. 47.

89 C. Ray Jeffery, "Punishment and Deterrence: A Psychobiological Statement," paper presented to annual meeting of American Society of Criminology, Dallas, November 1978, p. 19.

90 C. Ray Jeffery (ed.), *Biology and Crime,* Sage, Beverly Hills, Calif., 1979, p. 7.

91 Max G. Schlapp and Edward H. Smith, *The New Criminology: A Consideration of the Chemical Causation of Abnormal Behavior,* Boni & Liveright, New York, 1928.

92 Sarnoff Mednick and Karl O. Christiansen, *Biosocial Bases of Criminal Behavior,* Gardner Press, New York, 1977.

93 Harold E. Kelly, "Biosociology and Crime," in C. Ray Jeffery (ed.), *Biology and Crime,* Sage, Beverly Hills, Calif., 1979, pp. 93–94.

94 Ibid., p. 98.

95 Hills, *Demystifying Social Deviance,* pp. 126–127.

96 Peter Conrad, *Identifying Hyperactive Children: The Medicalization of Deviant Behavior,* Heath, Lexington, Mass., 1976.

97 Conrad and Schneider, *Deviance and Medicalization,* pp. 159–160.

98 Richard Moran, "Medicine and Crime: The Search for the Born Criminal and the Medical Control of Criminality," in Peter Conrad and Joseph Schneider, *Deviance and Medicalization,* Mosby, St. Louis, 1980, pp. 224–226.

99 S. Chorover, "Big Brother and Psychotechnology," *Psychology Today,* vol. 7, October 1973, pp. 43–54; S. Chorover, "Psychosurgery: A Neuropsychological Perspective," *Boston University Law Review,* vol. 74, March 1974, pp. 231–248.

100 Moran, "Medicine and Crime," p. 224; see also McCaghy, *Deviant Behavior,* pp. 27–31.

101 Moran, "Medicine and Crime," p. 224.

102 Lee Edson, "The Psyche and the Surgeon," *New York Times Magazine,* Sept. 30, 1973, p. 79.

103 Ballentine's description is found in Joel Greenberg, "Altering Behavior with Brain Surgery," *New England Magazine, Boston Sunday Globe,* January 1, 1978, pp. 6–12.

104 George J. Amos, as quoted in Greenberg, "Altering Behavior . . . ," p. 8.

105 Peter R. Breggin, as quoted in Greenberg, "Altering Behavior . . . ," p. 8.

106 Vernon Mark and Frank Ervin, *Violence and the Brain,* Harper & Row, New York, 1970.

107 For an overview of this research, see Harold Goldman, "The Limits of Clockwork: The Neurobiology of Violent Behavior," in J. Conrad and S. Dinitz (eds.), *In Fear of Each Other,* Heath, Lexington, Mass., 1977, pp. 43–76; and Saleem-Shah and Loren H. Roth, "Biological and Psychophysiological Factors in Criminality," in Daniel Glaser (ed.), *Handbook of Criminology,* Rand McNally, Chicago, 1974, pp. 101–173.

108 D. E. Smith, M. B. King, and B. G. Hoebel, "Lateral Hypothalamic Control of Killing: Evidence for a Cholinoceptive Mechanism," *Science,* vol. 167, 1970, pp. 900 ff.

109 W. W. Roberts and H. O. Kiess, "Motivational Properties of Hypothalamic Aggression in Cats," *Journal of Comparative and Physiological Psychology,* vol. 58, 1964, pp. 187 ff.; C. H. Woodworth, "Attack Elicited in Rats by Electrical Stimulation of the Lateral Hypothalamus," *Physiology and Behavior,* vol. 6, 1971, pp. 6 ff; B. H. Turner, "Sensorimotor Syndrome Produced by Lesions of the Amygdala and Lateral Hypothalamus, *Journal of Comparative and Physiological Psychology,* vol. 82, 1973, pp. 82 ff.

110 V. H. Mark, W. H. Sweet, and F. R. Ervin, "Role of Brain Disease in Riots and Urban Violence," *Journal of the American Medical Association,* vol. 201, 1967, p. 895.

111 These two studies conducted by researchers Corkin at Massachusetts Institute of Technology and Mirsky and Orzack at Boston University are summarized in Greenberg, "Altering Behavior . . . ," pp. 6–12.

112 Greenberg, "Altering Behavior . . . ," pp. 6–12.

113 Samuel I. Shuman, Psychosurgery and the Medical Control of Violence, Wayne State University Press, Detroit, 1977.

114 Jose Delgado, *Physical Control of the Mind: Toward a Psychocivilized Society,* p. 259.

115 Ibid., p. 200.

116 Susan Sontag, *Illness as a Metaphor,* Farrar, Straus, & Giroux, New York, 1978, p. 85.

117 Conrad and Schneider, *Deviance and Medicalization,* pp. 246–248.

118 Ibid., pp. 248–252.

119 Ibid., p. 252.

Adrift Chicago By Joseph LaMantia and Stephen Pfohl

CHAPTER **5**

THE SOCIAL DISORGANIZATION PERSPECTIVE: *Rapid Change and Normative Breakdown in the Slums of Chicago*

With the growth of great cities, with the vast division of labor which has come in with machine industry, and with movement and change that have come about with the multiplication of the means of transportation and communication, the old forms of social control represented by the family, the neighborhood, and the local community have been undermined and their influence greatly diminished. The process by which the authority and influence of an earlier culture and system of social control is undermined and eventually destroyed is . . . social disorganization.

Robert E. Park[1]

INTRODUCTION

Over the Edge is a movie about middle-class teenagers who are literally out of control. Its fictitious setting is a half-completed "condo community" named New Granada, Colorado. Don't be surprised if you have never seen or heard of this movie. Although it was completed in 1979, its distributor (Warner Brothers) has largely withheld this explosive motion picture from a national viewing audience. It didn't play in New York until January of 1982, and then only to a limited audience at two midtown theaters. Why this select and confining distribution? It is not because *Over the Edge* is a film that fails. Where it has been viewed, the film has drawn good crowds and sensational critical reviews. This perhaps is its problem. It succeeds in engaging viewers in a story that somebody is scared to let teenagers see—a story of teenagers cut loose from the moral norms and internalized social controls of conventional society.

In the movie's final scenes, the teenagers of New Granada go on a rampage; terrorizing their parents and trashing their school. Worried that the film may ignite similar episodes of teenage violence, distributors have kept a heavy lid on *Over the Edge*. According to director Jonathan Kaplan, the film was "delivered . . . at the time

Boulevard Nights and *The Warriors* [which caused a few disturbances] were in general release. The theater owners in the suburbs were scared. They said, 'We don't want a picture where kids are going to tear up the sixplexes.' "[2]

The teenagers in *Over the Edge* are the offspring of a fast-paced, rapidly changing society. They are all new immigrants to an instantaneously erected "hi-tech" community, a community of flat, tasteful dwellings with manicured lawns, sliding glass patio doors, wood-beamed ceilings. The teenagers of New Granada have been moved there by parents who hope to escape the dirt, pressures, and tensions of city living. Inadvertently, however, the adults of New Granada recreate the alienating atmosphere of the world from which they sought refuge. The moral gulf which separates them from their children is dug deep by the rush of rapid social change. In one of the film's most telling scenes, a prospective business investor, horror-stricken by the deviant antics of the town's young people, tells the town's mayor, "You have turned your kids into what you were trying to get away from."

The neatly packaged world which New Granada's parents have arranged for their children produces a generation of lost souls. It is one change too many. Raised on color TV and stereophonic rock music, the kids retreat into a set of headphones and smoke dope while their parents mix drinks with complaints and worry about what has gone wrong. The parents don't understand. How could they? They have moved, the kids were moved. They have produced and procured technologies for a better world. The kids have become technological junkies, dependent on the electricity of ever more sensational stimulation. They have sought to protect their young from what they perceived as the cold anonymity of urban living. The kids have once again been subject to massive changes beyond their control; now transplanted into a barren and boring array of backyards and bedrooms.

The kids of New Granada are the victims of socially institutionalized rootlessness. Like their real-life counterparts, the teenagers of Foster City, California, upon whom screenwriters Tim Hunter and Charlie Haas constructed their story, they react deviantly to the onset of rootlessness. In the words of film critic David Denby, they are "privileged nihilists, often stoned or smashed, growing up in a vacuum; their friendship for one another and a shared loathing for New Granada are the only values they've got. . . . [T]he kids are cut off, sequestered in their instant 'community.'"[3]

The parents had hoped that New Granada would be a comfortable, organized place in which their children could grow into respectable adults. For the kids, New Granada is experienced as a disorganized nightmare. Everything has changed too fast. Everything is new. There is little continuity between life today and life yesterday, and virtually no continuity between the aspirations and expectations of their parents and those of their peers. As Denby points out, "Even a big city slum neighborhood has its traditions, its places to hang out, but the elders of New Granada are so eager to protect their investments that they send the cops to hassle the kids wherever they gather."[4] In the film this idea is painted in the recurrent visual imagery of kids wandering along the side of the road, kids passed by the speeding cars of their parents racing off to complete plans for a brighter future, kids by the side of a road going nowhere.

The rapid and uncontrolled changes to which New Granada's teenagers are exposed pushes them in the direction of deviance. Their lives seem disorganized and disorderly until they come together in a climactic celebration of rebellion. They vandalize. They riot. They strike out at the symbols of their parents' mortality. In so doing, the deviant teenagers appear, at least for an instant, to regain control over a world which ordinarily races ahead of them. How accurate is this cinematic portrayal of teenagers going over the edge? Is deviance actually associated with socially produced disorganization and lack of control? Are such events necessarily triggered by the forces of rapid change? In order to answer these questions let us consider the writings of theorists associated with the social disorganization perspective.

THEORETICAL IMAGE

The social disorganization perspective emerged in the writings and research of sociologists at the University of Chicago during the 1920s. The early proponents of this perspective are often referred to as the "Chicago school." By emphasizing social causation, as opposed to rational choice or illness, the Chicago school departed from the individualistic focus of classical and pathological theorizing. Moreover, in demanding that sociological theory be tied to a rigorous scientific investigation of social life, Chicago's disorganizational theorists separated themselves from a previous generation of speculative, sentimental, and reform-oriented social pathologists.

Disorganizational theorists developed a model of naturalistic social causation. Deviance was viewed as a natural by-product of rapid social change. High rates of nonconformity occurred when too much change in too short a time disrupted the normative order of society. The disorganization perspective views society as a collectivity of people bound together by a set of interrelated rules or norms. Norms are guidelines for action. They inform us how we are to act, toward whom, where, and when. Norms are accompanied by values. Values justify norms and provide believable reasons as to why we should conform.

The Chicago theorists ask us to image the well-organized society. In such a society we find people who have internalized the norms which surround them: people who paradoxically have surrounded themselves from the inside out; people who act as their own watchtowers of control; people like gyroscopes; people whose internal mechanisms of self-balance are first set in motion and then continuously affected by the push and pull of forces external to their spin down the straight and narrow path of conformity. In this well-organized society the actions of people would be well coordinated because each person is bound within the same web of social norms. Having internalized these norms, people value the rules which control them.

This description of the well-organized society might imply that the Chicago theorists longed for the good old days of small-town America. This was not the case. The members of the Chicago school were not sentimental about the days of yesteryear. They were a breed of hard-nosed social scientists who refused to view social change in moralistic terms. Change was pictured as a natural social phenomenon. Change was as natural as normative social organization itself. While rapid change may temporarily fracture the normative organization of society, the Chicago theorists viewed this as but one phase in an ongoing process of social reorganization. Disorganization was a step toward reorganization.

The Chicago theorists thus viewed reorganization as the sociological stepchild of disorganization. Prior to reorganization, society would experience an interim period of competition; competition between different and perhaps conflicting normative frameworks. Normative competition, conflict, or dissensus is a key characteristic of social disorganization. One of its by-products is an increase in the incidence of deviant behavior. The reason is simple. The normative web of society has been stripped of its power to control people. People are set free of normative constraints. Like the off-centered gyroscope they tilt and turn into a dizzy path of unpredictability and nonconformity. Anything goes. An increasing number of people drift from conformity into deviance.

This is the kernel of the so-called Chicago perspective. Rapid changes damage the organized society's web of normative controls. This results in social disorganization. Normative consensus is replaced by normative dissensus. Disorganization has multiple by-products. One is long-term. It involves movement in the direction of normative reorganization. The second is more immediate or short-term. It involves movement in the direction of deviance.

What kinds of rapid change produce a shift from normative organization to disorganization and back again? Early disorganization theory focused on changes that were apparent in American society during the 1920s: changes in the areas of technological development, organization, and immigration. Its study of these matters involved two interrelated developments: (1) outlining the conceptual dynamics of social disorganization, and (2) studying the ecological or social-spatial dimensions of disorganization. The first development is best exemplified in the writings of W. I. Thomas and Florian Znaniecki; the second in the work of Robert Park, Ernest Burgess, and their students. Before considering the specific writings of these Chicago theorists, let us step back and view the origins of the Chicago school within its particular sociohistorical context.

The 1920s and the University of Chicago: A Time and Place for the Study of Social Disorganization

To appreciate the theoretical image of social disorganization it is helpful to locate its development within a particular time—the 1920s—and a particular place—the University of Chicago. The 1920s were particularly important for the development of sociology in America. In the aftermath of the tragic events of World War I, sociologists were confronted with the task of rethinking optimistic assumptions about the inevitability of progress and the increasing rationality of the human social world. They were also challenged by the omnipresent manifestations of unprecedented social change and by demands from the emerging middle class of managerial professionals for factual knowledge with which to technically and efficiently direct the course of change. These challenges came to be concentrated at the University of Chicago, where sociologists found themselves visibly surrounded by the most pronounced changes in America's social landscape and by financial and political support from business elite of the nation and the city. In responding to these challenges, the Chicago sociologists produced a new theoretical image related to the nature and control of social problems: the image of social disorganization.

A Time for Social Disorganization: The Aftermath of World War I and the Professional Management of Rapid Social Change

Before World War I American sociology had not differentiated itself from speculative social philosophy. Although claiming the cloak of science, most early American sociologists remained dressed in the ethical armor of progressive social reform. Their commitment to the scientific character of sociology was largely a commitment to a form of evolutionary theorizing in which the rational development of society was speculatively deduced as a kind of natural law. Science was viewed as a progressive feature of this natural human evolution, a guide for the rational human conquest of nature.

According to Albian Small, one of the "founding fathers" of American sociology, the pre–World War I generation of sociologists was characterized by four general assumptions: (1) a belief that the purpose of sociology was to deduce "natural laws" of social existence; (2) a commitment to evolutionary theorizing, accompanied by faith in the inevitability of progress; (3) advocacy of social reform as a means of accelerating progressive social evolution; and (4) an emphasis on the individual and upon motivated individual behavior as the core building block of social theory.[5] These assumptions provided great optimism. By speculatively deducing natural laws of social evolution, sociologists believed they would hasten the inevitable bandwagon of rational reform and social betterment.

The dark shadows of World War I dimmed this optimistic viewpoint. The bloody trenches of Europe stood in stark contrast to the sociological images of rational progress. Faith in the benign promise of scientific guidance was shattered by the awareness that the technological offspring of science had become the tools of ruthless and irrational destruction. For many European social theorists, the horrific spectacle of the "Great War" gave birth to a spirit of pessimism and to philosophies such as existentialism, which stressed the profound irrationality of life and the absurdity of the human condition.

American sociologists were also shaken by the events of the war. As Roscoe and Gisela Hinkle point out:

> The war severely shook the intellectuals' faith in progress. Many sociologists concurred with other intellectuals in concluding that man is not essentially rational. . . . Sociologists thus became pessimistic about progressive improvements which had heretofore been regarded as the inevitable products of man's rationality.[6]

For American sociology, the chilling disillusionment of World War I was short-lived. For decades many European social theorists would continue to question the objectivity and value of social science. In America, momentary pessimism was followed by efforts to reformulate the scientific character of the sociological enterprise. American sociology was soon characterized by a new optimism, an optimism which contrasted sharply with the previous faith in the inevitability of progress, but an optimism nonetheless.

In reformulating the basis of its scientific identity, postwar American sociology came to view faith in the inevitability of progress as incorrect. The events of the war had proved this position untenable. Irrationality loomed large as a feature of life itself. This, however, was no reason to abandon the scientific study of social life. For postwar sociologists, the naive theories of the preceding generation were viewed as lacking scientific rigor. For "natural laws" deduced before the war were now seen as more speculative than factual. Postwar sociologists proposed a different starting point for sociological theorizing. Sociology was to begin, not with speculation, but with the careful observation and measurement of social life—with inductive inquiry or rigorous empirical study. This was the basis for American sociology's postwar optimism. It assumed that a precise empirical investigation of social life would yield both an explanation and a pragmatic program by which to control social chaos and irrationality.

The postwar transformation of American sociology was far-reaching. Speculative assumptions about natural social laws were replaced by rigorous empirical inquiry. Belief in the progressive character of evolution was abandoned. Where once sociology was equated with partisan progressive reform, now sociologists pledged allegiance to the principles of scientific neutrality. An analytic focus on individuals receded in favor of increased attention to society as a force in its own right. Each of these changes contributed greatly to the emergence of the social disorganization perspective.

Why the optimism of postwar sociology in America? Part of the answer lies in the fact that America emerged victorious from an awful war fought at a great distance. Unlike Europe, the heartland of America remained unravaged by the deadly tools of twentieth-century war. America's political power and economic influence multiplied without blood being spilt upon its own soil. Yet this answer is partial at best. The old optimism about the inevitability of progress was put to rest in America as well as in Europe. The new optimism of American sociology was rooted in something different. It is better understood by a conjuncture of two factors: a decade of unprecedented social change and the managerial response of an emerging professional class of technical problem-solvers to problems brought about by such change. At the center of this conjuncture were the University of Chicago sociologists, themselves members of this new professional class, who aimed to battle social change with the conceptual weapons of a new theoretical perspective—the theory of social disorganization.

A Decade of Rapid Change

Rapid social change was a central feature of the American landscape in the 1920s. The American economy was thrown into full gear by the war. This resulted in several developments which drastically altered the life and work styles of Americans. Long strides were made toward the increased mechanization or technologicalization of both industrial and agricultural production. Demands for large-scale and efficient production were bolstered by major technological advances in the fields of communication and transportation. These developments propelled business organizations toward greater centralization, combination, and control of industrial effort. By 1923, for instance, the heyday of the small independent producer was largely past. Although only 4 percent of all American businesses hired more than 250 workers, these companies had become the employers of well over half of the entire industrial labor force.[7] This movement toward centralized control is described by James T. Carey as a "trend toward national integrative structures."[8] This trend was accompanied by a similar growth in centralized governmental regulatory agencies.

Changes such as these produced additional changes as well. Change, as the Chicago theorists would note, led to further change. The increased mechanization of agriculture produced technological unemployment. This resulted in a drift of farm workers to cities. There they joined large populations of foreign-born workers, an increasing number of women workers who had entered the industrial labor force during the war, and black workers who had migrated from the south to the urban industrial centers of the north and west. By 1930, the black urban population in northern and western states was 2,228,000, nearly twice what it had been a decade earlier.[9] During the same decade, as the number of people living in rural areas shrank by 12 million, the nation's urban population increased by more than 14 million. Cities of more than 1 million persons had approximately 5 million more residents.[10] Many were immigrants. By 1930, one-third of all American whites were foreign-born. Most of them were located in urban areas.[11]

The changes associated with increased technologicalization, immigration, and urbanization were compounded by massive occupational and organizational changes in American industry. The increased centralization of industrial effort resulted in expansion of the administrative, managerial, and clerical sectors. The aggregate number of professional, technical, and managerial employees doubled between 1910 and 1930, increasing from 6,599,000 to 12,546,000. This proportional increase far outdistanced the more modest expansion of the working-class, or direct-production, occupational sector, which grew from 19,730,000 to 25,813,000 during the same period.[12]

Such changes did not affect all Americans equally. This was particularly the case for the American working class, persons described as blue-collar or wage laborers. The working class was affected negatively by significant increases in mechanized production and growth in the middle class of white-collar professionals and salaried employees. This "unevenness of prosperity" is documented by James Carey, who points to ground lost by the growing number of urban, immigrant, and blue-collar workers and by small farmers and farm laborers affected by massive mechanization and technological unemployment. Accordingly, while "increasing shares went to receivers at the top . . . working men and women could not purchase what they produced."[13]

The Tension of Change: Social Reactions to Technologicalization, Immigration, and Urbanization

The differential impact of change in the 1920s was accompanied by considerable tension, fear, and anxiety. There was, however, little visible protest by those affected most adversely by change—the displaced rural laborers, immigrants, and minorities concentrated in urban areas, each competing against the other for wage positions, and each affected negatively by postwar overproducing, mechanization, and the growing dominance of salaried white-collar workers. In contrast to the decades which went before, the 1920s was marked by a relative absence of organized labor strikes and violent collective outbursts, such as riots.[14]

Why so little collective expression of rapid change? Perhaps, dissent was fragmented by the disruptive influence of mass society. Displaced persons, thrown together in the anonymity of the expanding urban scene, were further disadvantaged by the social context in which they found themselves. Although people were crowded together in physical proximity, the anonymity of urban life created a social distance between them, inhibiting them from identifying with each other and perceiving social troubles in collective rather than individualistic terms.

In summary, those whose material destinies were most directly and negatively affected by the rapid changes of the 1920s (displaced agricultural and industrial laborers, immigrants, and the urban poor) were involved in little collective social protest against the new mass society which engulfed them. This was not the case for another large segment of the American population, those who clung to the cultural ideals of white, Protestant, small-town America. This group was also threatened by the increased centralization and technologicalization of social and economic life, by urbanization, and by what its members perceived as the strange and alien influx of immigrants.[15] This group reacted to the tensions of change with what may be described as the politics of nativism. Nativism is a term used to describe several strands of collective social action, each directed toward returning America to the good old days in which white, Protestant, small-town interests reigned supreme. The nativist reaction involved "hostility toward particular minority groups, especially radicals and recent immigrants, fanatical patriotism, and conviction that internal enemies who seriously threaten national security must be eliminated."[16]

The appeal of nativism has not vanished from the American landscape. In recent years groups such as the Ku Klux Klan and certain of the far-right supporters of President Ronald Reagan emphasize similar themes. During the 1920s nativism manifested itself in a number of collective social movements. Notable among these were successful campaigns to restrict immigration and prohibit the manufacture and distribution of alcohol. Although prohibition proved impossible to strictly enforce and was later repealed, the research of sociologist Joseph Gusfield suggests that it was first and foremost a symbolic victory for those who favored the old, conservative, and small-town ideals of an America that was rapidly changing.[17] Other examples of nativism include the so-called Red Scare of 1920, a wave of fear and repression directed against those suspected of being Communists, the ban on the teaching of evolution in the public schools,[18] and the rapid growth and terrorist actions of the Ku Klux Klan.[19]

The Professional Management of Change: The Liberal Response

Nativism represented the reaction of groups whose previous dominance was eroded by the changing economic, political, and social landscape of America in the 1920s. What was the reaction of groups whose power was enhanced by these changes? Two groups are particularly important in this regard: those emerging at the top and those ascending to powerful professional positions in the managerial middle.

By those at the top, I am referring to the small number of individuals, families, or business associates who came to control and dominate the ownership of America's corporate economy following its period of centralization and consolidated combination during the 1920s. According to data recently reviewed by sociologist Maurice Zeitlin, "if we count up what the richest 1 percent of the population own, we find that they have a seventh of all the real estate in the country, more than half the corporate stock, and almost all the trust assets."[20] Moreover, when considering only the richest of the corporate rich, one discovers that this "tiny owning class at the tip of the top, barely more than 1/20th of 1 percent of American adults, has a fifth of all the corporate stock."[21] But what about the other four-fifths? Because stock ownership is widely dispersed among members of both the middle and upper classes, it is sometimes argued that the real ownership of the American economy resides with the millions of people who possess small shares of huge corporations. In practical terms, the opposite is the case. As Zeitlin points out: "Precisely because the number of shareholders is so large and their holdings typically so minute compared to the few biggest shareholders in a large corporation, it may not take more than 1 or 2 percent of a company's stock to control it."[22]

In addition to those who disproportionately controlled economic ownership, a second group emerged from the 1920s with increased power and influence—professionals occupying positions in the managerial middle. As suggested previously, increases in technological complexity and the centralized bureaucratic expansion of the workforce demanded a new form of specialized managerial expertise. Professional managers of all sorts came to fill positions in the middle and upper echelons of corporate life. This has prompted some students of economic organization to posit the advent of a managerial revolution. By this they mean that the ownership of corporations became separated from the day-to-day control over operations. This appears to be both true and untrue.

It is untrue insomuch as the upper echelons of management are continuously hired and fired by corporate boards or directorates which remain controlled by a small number of elite stockholders. On the other hand, professional managers bring to the economic organization a distinctive approach to the problems of human labor coordination. This approach involves a rational plan for the "scientific management" of human labor and a plan calculated to maximize both efficiency and profit." Since the 1920s, the day-to-day control of corporate business operations has increasingly been characterized by such professionally planned coordination. Yet, the fate of any particular managerial strategy remains dependent on whether or not it advances the profit margin of corporate owners. In this sense, the interests of managers and owners are relatively indistinguishable. According to Zeitlin: "Whatever their so-called professional motivations or power urges, their technocratic teamwork and bureaucratic mentality, managers' decisions on how to organize production and sales have to be measured against the bottom line: They dare not imperil corporate profit."[23]

Joined in the common pursuit of efficiently coordinated profit-making, corporate owners and managerial professionals came to share a common view regarding solutions to the problems of rapid change. Each was desirous of a stable social climate in which to conduct business. Although they too saw rapid change as a threat to stability, the owners and managers, unlike the nativists, had no romantic dreams of going backwards in time. How could they? The rapid social change that had led to the developments feared by the nativists had created their own positions of power in the first place. They were the true beneficiaries of rapid technologicalization, urbanization, and immigration.

Technologicalization permitted work to be more efficient and centrally controlled. Urbanization permitted industry to draw upon a concentrated workforce and to expedite systems of transportation, communication, and mass marketing. Immigration assured a large pool of laborers competing against each other for relatively low wages. But these were short-term gains. Over the long haul, such immediate advantages were likely to produce future liabilities. In urban America this is exactly what was happening. Cities became characterized by high rates of personal and property crime, mental illness, alcoholism, divorce, and prostitution. For corporate owners and managers, such matters were omens of impending instability which demanded a new form of professional-technical problem-solving. This they would obtain from the theoretical labor of the University of Chicago sociologists.

The Birth of Chicago Sociology: The Concept of Disorganization as a Liberal Tool for the Professional Management of Change

Having rejected the call of nativism, those who controlled the centralized corporate economy became advocates of a new form of problem-solving. Social problems should be managed with the same professional detachment and technical efficiency as the business organization itself. During the 1920s this viewpoint resulted in a powerful coalition of business, governmental, and professional problem-solving and the birth of a new American political philosophy—liberalism. Unlike the reactionary nativists and the morally exultant progressivists of an earlier era, liberals accepted both the naturalness of social problems and their professionally managed resolution. Social problems were stripped of their moral and political character. Liberals did not view social problems as the bad deeds of people, but as the manageable by-products of such natural occurrences as rapid social change. While the management of programs of social adjustment might be carried out by public servants and government officials, a central tenet of liberalism was that the diagnosis and planned solution of social problems were the responsibilities of specialized professional problem-solvers. With this in mind, let us return to our consideration of the sociologists at the University of Chicago in the 1920s.

The Chicago school and its theory of deviance as social disorganization is a classic example of the early liberal imagination. Chicago theorists produced a professional sociological diagnosis and solution for the instability resulting from social change. Their work found support among the business elite, in particular the philanthropic concerns of the Rockefellers. The Rockefellers were, after all, instrumental in the founding and ongoing funding of the University of Chicago. The work of the Chicago sociologists was also connected to the public policy initiatives of the Chicago business community and to the intervention strategies of a new generation of salaried governmental problem-solvers (welfare workers, youth workers, urban problem specialists, etc.). As James Carey suggests, "The Chicago sociologists responded 'both' to the concerns of this new salaried professional class" and "to the business-dominated urban society taking shape in the 1920's. . . .They did this by cooperating with certain elements within the business and welfare communities in an effort to alter the more undesirable features of urban institutional life."[24]

The theory of social disorganization helped propel the University of Chicago's department of sociology to a position of dominance within the discipline. As Roscoe and Gisela Hinkle point out, "during the period between the end of World War I and the Depression. . .the research, theorization, and graduate instruction at the University of Chicago gave its Department of Sociology an unprecedented preeminence."[25] In part, this was because disorganization theory was highly responsive to the post–World War I demands that sociology be grounded in the concreteness of inductive empirical research. Disorganizational theorizing was from its onset a theory built upon the bedrock of empirical data—first-hand observations and detailed statistical analyses. No less important was the theory's responsiveness to America's new managerial style of social problem-solving. By viewing change as a natural social phenomenon, sociologists undermined the political positions of those both to the conservative right and to the radical left of the new liberal managerial middle class.

In one grand sweep of sociological imagery, the Chicago theorists dismissed both the sentimental longings of the nativists and the structural critique of the radicals. By conceiving the negative consequences of rapid change as a deviant reaction of the naturally disorganized, rather than as a discontented reaction of the structurally or historically disadvantaged, the Chicago school contributed to a depoliticalized image of social problems. This depoliticalization was viewed favorably both by the business community and by governmental problem-solving professionals. These groups had a clear stake in distinguishing between what they saw as social problems and as political problems. Social problems were viewed as naturally caused and technically correctable. Political problems were seen as the result of competing ideologies and resulted in little more than bitter partisan dispute. Yet, beneath this effort to distinguish the social from the political, there lay a deeper commitment to the fundamental structures of the existing social order.

The close and compatible relationship between the theorical perspective of the Chicago school and demands for an apolitical scientific analysis of social problems during the rapidly changing 1920s is better understood by considering certain characteristics of Chicago as a city, of the University of Chicago as an institution, and of the Chicago sociologists as a social group. As a city, Chicago surrounded its sociologists with everpresent reminders of the massive changes that were occurring within American society. The importance of this environmental inducement to study change was observed by Chicago sociologist Robert E. L. Faris, who describes the "vigorous city" of Chicago as a "supporting atmosphere" in which "the sociologists. . .were to find encouragement to dig and discover in amounts not customary in the gentler academic atmospheres where ivy sometimes grew faster than knowledge."[26]

As for the University of Chicago itself, a number of factors contributed to the early formulation of its unique brand of sociology. Foremost among these was the philanthropic backing which provided a stable financial base for its theoretical work, its research, and its application of knowledge to public problem-solving. And foremost among its philanthropic supporters was John D. Rockefeller, whose corporate fortunes provided a total of $35 million to the university's funding. So too was the university supported by substantial gifts from Chicago-area donors who provided generous matches for the huge Rockefeller bequests.

There are numerous interpretations regarding the motives of wealthy philanthropists for donating to an institution of higher education. Some emphasize the idea of stewardship—the belief by wealthy persons that they have a moral obligation to further the betterment of society. Others stress the lucrative tax breaks afforded by such donations. Still others emphasize the symbolic advantages of legitimating the equation of being wealthy with being good or the desire to direct the course and content of intellectual activity. All of these things may have been a factor. Of greatest significance, however, may have been the simple fact that corporate giants like Rockefeller perceived the development of first-rate educational institutions as an essential element in producing the professional specialties and technical know-how needed to solve problems and provide the social stability necessary for the continued advance of profitable business. Nonetheless, corporate donations were often accompanied by directives as to how certain funds were to be spent. In the area of sociology this meant support for research aimed at the administrative or managerial control of the by-products of rapid change. Here one discovers a powerful coincidence between the theoretical concerns of the Chicago sociologists and the financial support of the business elite. In the words of James Carey, "The major impact of philanthropical support seems to have been. . .a more specific focus on urban problems which could be solved administratively."[27]

In addition to the financial backing of the wealthy philanthropists, the openness of university administrators to innovative ideas and approaches to research, the university's commitment to providing professional contributions to the management of public life, and the exposure of key members of the sociology department's senior faculty to the disciplined research model characteristic of German universities were important factors favoring the emergence of a new perspective on theory and research. Also important were the stable links with members of Chicago's local business and governmental elite. All of these things operated as institutional supporters for the development of a theoretical vision emphasizing both the naturalness and the solvability of problems related to rapid technologicalization, urbanization, and immigration.

A final factor contributing to the formulation of the kind of theory that was produced at the University of Chicago involves the social backgrounds of the Chicago sociologists themselves. Carey's recent study of this matter suggests that Chicago sociologists in the period from 1918 to the depression came from considerably different backgrounds than the founding generation of previous social scientists in the years before World War I.[28] The Chicagoans were far more heterogeneous, less religiously oriented, more urban, and more politically liberal. This means that the Chicago sociologists were similar to members of the emergent American middle class of managers and professionals. No wonder they found congeniality with the problem-solving strategies of this class. They were part of it.

In short, the Chicago sociologists were much like the other new liberals. They were part of the emerging class of managerial and professional problem-solvers attempting to guide social change toward stability. When professionals sought to manage and control such social problems as crime, mental disorders, family breakdown, and alcoholism, Chicago sociologists "stood by to help; they came from the same stratum as the new professionals and gave qualified acceptance to their views of what constituted problems." What kind of help did the Chicago sociologists offer? It came in the theoretical form and control possibilities associated with their perspective on social disorganization. With this in mind, let us examine how the Chicago theorists first conceptualized the dynamics of disorganization and later employed social-ecological models to study its differential impact.

The Dynamics of Disorganization: The Legacy of W. I. Thomas and Florian Znaniecki

The basic theoretical image of social disorganization was initially formulated by University of Chicago sociologist W. I. Thomas. Thomas was a dedicated liberal reformer as well as an important and influential scholar. His advanced political ideas, flamboyant appearance, and bohemian lifestyle made him a controversial figure at the university. Thomas's intellectual accomplishments were many. They ranged from detailed ethnographic research to general social-psychological theory and study of social disorganization. Yet, in 1918, Thomas was expelled from his faculty position in what sociologist Lewis Coser describes as "one of the shameful chapters in the history of American universities."[29] The impetus for Thomas's dramatic expulsion involved allegations by the FBI and the conservative *Chicago Tribune* that Thomas had violated the Mann Act, a federal statute outlawing the transportation of young women across state lines for "immoral purposes."

After examining the facts of the case, it appears that Thomas's real crime involved inferences that he had had an affair with the wife of an American army officer away on duty in France. Formal legal charges, dubious as they were, were dropped. Professor Thomas was nonetheless dismissed by the university's president, Henry Pratt. Why? Given the University of Chicago's general reputation as a center for liberal or progressive thought, one wonders about the real issues behind the Thomas case. Why had the FBI been involved in the first place? This question remains unanswered even today. There are, however, clues regarding the overreaching arm of federal law-enforcement officials. As Lewis Coser remarks, "it has been suggested that Thomas's wife was under surveillance for her pacifist activities and that the F.B.I. might have thought it expedient to discredit the husband so as to humiliate the wife."[30]

Although Thomas was forced to leave the University of Chicago, his ideas remained. His initial conceptualization of the problem of disorganization was a seed which germinated into a full-blown sociological perspective during the 1920s. The most succinct statement of this perspective is found in the classic study conducted by Thomas and his colleague Florian Znaniecki, *The Polish Peasant in Europe and America*.[31] According to Thomas and Znaniecki, social disorganization was to be defined "as a decrease of the influence of existing social rules of behavior upon individual members of the group."[32] Thomas and Znaniecki discovered just such a decrease in the lives of rural Polish peasants who had migrated to large U.S. cities in the early twentieth century. By analyzing the thematic content of letters, diaries, and other personal documents of Polish immigrants, Thomas and Znaniecki produced a detailed sociological story regarding the manner in which rapid social change dissipates the impact of social norms.

The Polish Peasant in Europe and America is a story of the disruptive forces accompanying immigration, of the disorientation of life caused by the rapid transportation of rural people with a different cultural tradition into the midst of the industrializing American city. It is a story of social disorganization. In document after document, Thomas and Znaniecki discover evidence of the inability of immigrant families to exert social control over their members. The ways of the "old world" do not work in the "new world." Nor is it easy for immigrants to quickly assimilate the norms and standards of their new social environment. Immigrants are described as living in a world devoid of secure normative standards, as dwelling in a world of social disorganization. Without strong normative standards, immigrants develop an attitude that can best be described as a belief that "anything goes." This attitude facilitates a drift into deviance, a drift into delinquency, divorce, mental disorder, and the other forms of unruly behavior studied by the Chicago school.

Thomas and Znaniecki's depiction of social disorganization had a great influence on other sociologists working at the University of Chicago at the time. This is particularly evident in the writings of Robert Park. Park, a journalist and a humanitarian activist, had studied social philosophy and social science in Germany. His efforts to improve race relations in the United States attracted the attention of W. I. Thomas, who, in 1914, was instrumental in bringing Park into the sociology department at Chicago. While at Chicago, Park embarked upon a detailed study of changes in the American social landscape, particularly changes associated with urbanization. In making sociological sense of these changes, Park drew heavily on the disorganizational framework introduced by Thomas. As Park stated: "The process by which the authority and influence of an earlier culture and system of social control is undermined and eventually destroyed is described by Thomas. . . . We are living in such a period of . . . social disorganization."[33]

The Ecology of Disorganization: The Legacy of Park and Burgess

Robert Park did more than simply adopt the basic conception of social disorganization proposed by W. I. Thomas. With his colleague Ernest Burgess, Park introduced an ecological model for the study of disorganization that is today the hallmark of the Chicago school's perspective on deviance. Ecology refers to the study of spatial relations between various species of living organisms. In attempting an ecological analysis of human society, Park and Burgess borrowed concepts from the field of plant ecology. Plant ecologists use the term *symbiosis* to denote the interdependent character of plants within a natural community of other plants and organisms. The life of each affects and is affected by all others within the superorganic community as a whole.

The image of symbiotic relationships between organisms within a superorganism had a certain attraction for Park. As an urban journalist, Park had observed the complex network of interrelated human parts that make up the life of the city. Viewing human social life in this fashion, Park made direct use of the terminology of plant ecologists. In *Human Communities,* he states that "the urban community turns out to be something more than a mere congeries of peoples and institutions. . . . Its component elements, institutions, and persons are so intimately bound up that the whole tends to assume the character of . . . a superorganism."[34]

Ecologists assume a symbiotic interdependence of organisms within a given geographical community. They describe dangers in the activity of an ecological community in terms of a fourfold process involving (1) invasion by a competing species, (2) conflict for dominance between species, (3) the accommodation of weaker species to those that demonstrate their dominance, and (4) assimilation of a new order of symbiosis based upon the accommodative outcomes of the previous three stages. Think, for instance, of the invasion of a pine forest by a competing species of oak trees. Conflict will occur. For a while the symbiotic organization of the forest will be in disarray. Eventually, the more powerful oaks will emerge as dominant. Pine trees will literally be uprooted. They will accommodate the oaks by replanting themselves in the soil of some adjacent area of the forest, where their own invasion must be accommodated by another, less deeply rooted, foliage, such as broom sedge. The new and old members of the previous pine forest will now be assimilated into a new symbiotic order based upon the dominance of oaks. The ecological community of the forest has thus been transformed.

Park and Burgess viewed change in human communities in a similar fashion. This had a particular importance for the study of deviance. The normative order of the well-organized community was viewed as a kind of social symbiosis which was disrupted by the invasion of some competing basis for social order. The forces of change that swept the American landscape of the twenties—rapid technologicalization, urbanization, immigration, and the like—were conceptualized as forces of invasion. Each was said to produce conflict for dominance within symbiotically interdependent human communities. This was another way of visualizing the process of social disorganization described by Thomas and Znaniecki. Throughout the stage of conflict for dominance, symbiotic coordination was lacking. The community lost its superorganic control over component parts. In human terms, the breakdown of normative structure represented a breakdown in social control. Deviance was widespread. It would remain at high levels until the process of accommodation and assimilation were complete, until society became symbiotically reorganized around a new dominant form of normative order.

Using the ecological imagery of invasion, conflict, accommodation, and assimilation, Chicago sociologists attempted to identify "natural areas" of high or low deviance. High-deviance areas were spatially the most susceptible to the competitive invasion of the forces of rapid change. Low-deviance areas were least susceptible. In order to test this notion, social ecologists mapped out the "natural" physical spaces of the city into a ring of five concentric zones. Each zone possessed a unique population with a unique organizational style. The inhabitants of each zone possessed qualities, interests, and cultural characteristics that were similar to each other, but different from

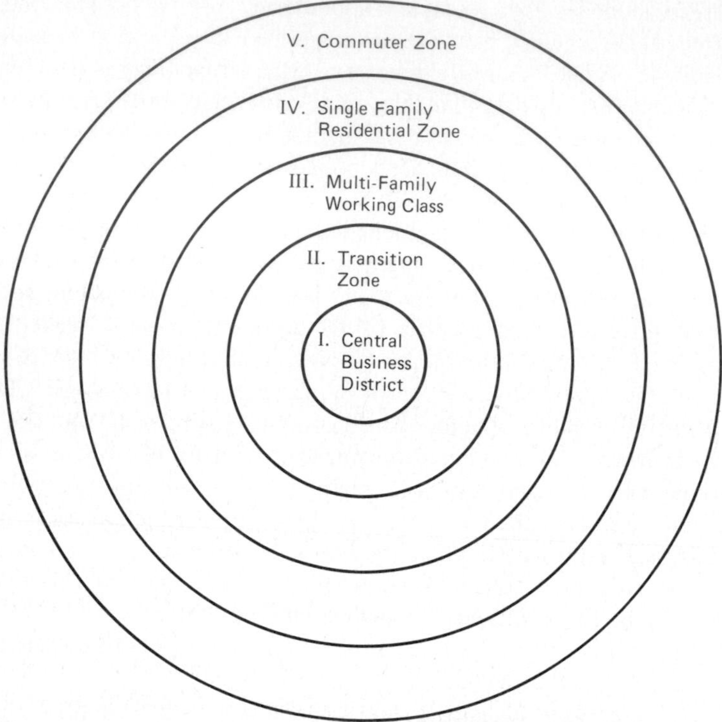

FIGURE 5-1
Concentric zones of deviance: The Parks-Burgess model of natural urban areas. Ecological maps resembling that depicted above often accompany Chicago researchers' analysis of deviance. Rates of officially recorded deviance were typically highest in Zone II (transition zone) where forces of social change originating in Zone I (the central business district) were said to have the greatest impact. Rates decreased progressively through Zones III, IV, and V.

those of the inhabitants of other zones. Each zone, in other words, was organized or disorganized by virtue of a varying symbiotic relationship between its component parts and its organic whole.

The concentric zones mapped by Chicago theorists are displayed in Figure 5-1. At the center of the five urban zones was the central business district. This was literally the heart of the city, its center of organic power, the core of business, technology, and industry. This powerful zone was conceived as the dynamic force behind city life, as the focus of the primary energies of urbanization, as the source of urban social change. At the outer reaches of the city was the commuter zone. Here lived the wealthy commuters, whose spatial, social, and economic resources provided them with some buffer of stability against the forces of urbanization located in the central business district (Zone I). Zone III (a working-class neighborhood, characterized by the omnipresent arrangement of two- and three-family flats) and Zone IV (the old city neighborhood of one-family houses) were more affected, but spatially somewhat removed from the forces of social change located in the outwardly expanding central business district.

The zone most affected by change was that into which the growing central business district constantly pushed. This was Zone II, the transition zone of most social disorganization and resultant deviance. At the very edge of the constantly expanding central business district, ecological theorists observed light industry, warehouses, and "hobohemia," a place of rootless people, vagabonds, street bums. Immediately beyond lay the interstitial, or transition, zone. In plain language—a slum. In this natural area, the battle of competition-dominance was being fought. Its residents were the losers. Disorganized by rapid change, they were said to experience the highest rates of such measured deviance as delinquency, school truancy, adult crime, serious mental illness, prostitution, gambling, suicide, and taxi dance halls (barlike establishments for the isolated and lonely). Each of these types of deviance was statistically measured by Chicago researchers. The prevalence of each decreased with increased ecological distance from the urban center of rapid change.

The Natural Areas of Deviance: Social-Ecological Studies of Disorganizational Deviance

The Chicago school emphasized the importance of maintaining a close connection between theory and empirical research. Let us briefly examine two areas in which their social-ecological model was applied to the study of deviance—studies relating to the disorganizational causes of juvenile delinquency and mental disorders.

The Social Ecology of Delinquency: The Shaw and McKay Tradition Clifford Shaw and Henry McKay were sociological researchers employed by a state-supported child-guidance clinic in Chicago—the Institute for Juvenile Research.[35] Although not formally affiliated with the University of Chicago, Shaw and McKay were greatly influenced by their close association with Ernest Burgess, who, with several students and other university faculty, maintained ongoing ties to a program of delinquency-prevention projects sponsored by the institute.

In 1929, Shaw and McKay and several colleagues published *Delinquency Areas,* a classic work in the social disorganization study of delinquency. This report was based on the analysis of 55,998 juvenile court records compiled in the city of Chicago over a period of approximately thirty years.[36] In subsequent years, Shaw and McKay extended their analysis of the ecological distribution of delinquency to cities in other parts of the nation.[37] The findings of their research are supportive of the central tenets of disorganizational theorizing. In mapping delinquency rates throughout the various zones of a city, Shaw and McKay discovered (1) an uneven spatial distribution of the incidence of delinquency; (2) that the highest rates of delinquency occurred in the natural areas closest to the expanding central business district, and that rates decreased proportionately with distance from the center; (3) that certain ecological areas (slums or transition zones) were consistently characterized by the highest rates of delinquency, regardless of the changing ethnic composition of residents; and (4) that areas highest in delinquency were also highest in a number of assumed indicators of social disorganization, e.g., demographic instability, high percentage of foreign-born residents, high percentage of nonwhites, low percentage of home ownership, high percentage of families on relief, low median income, etc.

Shaw and McKay interpreted their findings in accordance with the basic imagery of disorganization theory. The uneven spatial distribution of delinquency was explained by the fact that "in the areas of low rates of delinquents there is . . . uniformity, consistency, and universality of conventional values. . . . Whereas, in the high-rate areas, systems of competing and conflicting moral values have developed."[38] Similar logic explained the increased rates of delinquency for persons living in natural areas closest to the city's changing center. There "change involves the introduction of a new population with different institutions and practices" such that "institutional disruption and role discontinuity are to be expected."[39] For transition-zone adolescents, the problem may be doubly acute. They are in both a time (adolescence) and a space (the slum) where "disorganization accompanying rapid change may be virtually complete."[40] Thus, "children living in such communities are exposed to a variety of contradictory standards and forms of behavior rather than to a relatively consistent and conventional pattern."[41]

The pioneering research of Shaw and McKay prompted several subsequent studies of the social ecology of delinquency. In 1954, Bernard Lander examined the spatial distribution of 8,464 delinquency petitions filed in Baltimore, Maryland.[42] After analyzing rates of delinquency across 155 Baltimore census tracts, he concluded that high delinquency was associated with measures related to both lower class standing and high social disorganization.

Shaw and McKay had also discovered that class was related to the delinquency distribution. As early as 1942, they reported that high delinquency areas were also "low income areas, where there is the greatest deprivation and frustration." Why was this the case? Shaw and McKay proposed an answer that departs from the normative-breakdown focus of most disorganizational theorizing. "Crime," they suggested, "may be regarded as one of the means employed by people to acquire . . . the economic and social values generally idealized in our culture, which persons in other circumstances acquire by conventional means."[43] In general, however, Shaw and McKay placed a greater emphasis on the role of disorganization factors. Although the deprivations of class might increase a person's motives for committing a crime, the causal factors with which they were most concerned were the disorganizational forces which freed the individual from the scrutiny and control of conventional society.

Like Shaw and McKay, Lander emphasizes social disorganization rather than social class. Lander discovered that high-delinquency areas were characterized by overcrowding, low rents, low levels of owner occupancy, and low levels of education. The crux of his theory, however, is related to the racial composition of high-delinquency areas. If status deprivation increases delinquency, then one might reason that areas with the highest percentage of nonwhite residents would also be those highest in delinquency. To be nonwhite in America is, after all, to be in a position of status deprivation. Given the long history of racial discrimination, one can at least make a reasonable sociological argument along these lines. Lander's data do not support this interpretation. The rate of delinquency increases as the percentage of nonwhites increases from 0 to 50 percent.

It decreases as the nonwhite percentage increases from 50 to 100 percent. To Lander this means that disorganization, as indicated by the "invasion" of communities by new culture groups (the 0 to 50 percent nonwhite condition), is what causes high delinquency. The 50 to 100 percent condition is associated with lower rates of delinquency because the changing ecological community has entered into a process of normative reorganization, or accommodation-assimilation. Lander attempts to buttress this controversial interpretation by suggesting that such factors as low percentage of owner-occupants and high percentage of renters are also indicators of disorganization—that they are better indicators of transience than disadvantage.

In 1959, David Bordua published the results of research which attempted to replicate Lander's study in Detroit, Michigan.[44] The results were less favorable to a disorganization perspective. Bordua found the same relationships between lower class, or status-deprivation, factors and high delinquency, but no evidence for the mixed racial area–disorganization interpretation. Bordua's study included an additional measure of social disorganization—the ratio of unattached individuals to intact families. This he found related to delinquency. Areas that had the highest ratios of unattached persons were also those with the highest rates of delinquency.

In 1964, Roland Chilton published a study which attempted to resolve the inconsistencies between the findings of Lander and Bordua.[45] After reanalyzing the earlier findings and presenting new data from Indianapolis, Chilton found no clear evidence favoring a disorganizational interpretation. The only consistent data favoring the disorganization thesis involve percentage of home ownership. The percentage of nonwhite was not a significant factor. Nor are there consistent findings regarding such factors as proportion of unmarried men, high levels of residential mobility, or high numbers of persons per household (each of which had been used as an indicator of disorganization). Research in this area has advanced little beyond the conclusions drawn by Chilton. Inferences about the disorganizational causes of delinquency remain ambiguous.

Psychoses in the Transition Zone: Social Disorganization and Mental Disorders Chicago sociologists H. Warren Dunham and Robert E. L. Faris mapped the ecological distribution of public hospitalization for serious mental disorders.[46] In general, their findings supported a social disorganization interpretation. Rates of hospitalization were highest for residents of the transition zone and decreased proportionately to distance from the central business district. This pattern was applicable, however, only for schizophrenia, the diagnosed disorder which represented most of the cases. Schizophrenia is characteristically described as one of two disorders which comprise the psychoses, the most serious category of mental illness. Schizophrenia is generally diagnosed as a severe distortion of reality accompanied by aural and/or visual hallucinations, and/or delusions (illusionary thoughts or self-perceptions not shared by others). According to Dunham and Faris, the ecological distribution of schizophrenia resembles that of social disorganization. Their research was heralded as an important breakthrough in the study of the social causation of psychiatric problems. According to Faris and Dunham, "The highest rates for schizophrenia are in hobohemia, the rooming-house, and foreign-born communities close to the center of the city . . . as these communities represent areas of some disorganization due to their close proximity to the steel factories."[47]

Manic-depressive psychosis did not fit the classic pattern of social disorganization. Manic-depressive psychosis is characterized by severe and uncontrollable mood swings, from giddy excitation to a deep and apathetic state of dejection. The Chicago data discovered that this form of mental disorder was distributed somewhat randomly throughout all zones of the city. Dunham speculated that this finding might be the result of a systematic error or bias on the part of psychiatric diagnosticians—i.e., that psychiatrists do not "see" this disorder when diagnosing persons from disorganized areas because they perceived them as more likely to be schizophrenic. He was also open to the possibility that, unlike schizophrenia, social factors may play less of a causative role in the generation of manic-depressiveness; that "there is a certain justification for asserting the priority of hereditary and constitutional factors."[48]

The research by Dunham and Faris was a landmark in the sociological study of mental disorders. Yet, within a short time medically oriented critics raised an important question about their disorganizational thesis. Why assume that disorganization caused schizophrenia? Wasn't it equally possible that seriously disturbed schizophrenics drifted into disorganized areas because they could not cope with life in the city's more organized zones?

Faris and Dunham sought to answer this criticism (the so-called downward-drift hypothesis) by obtaining data on the residential patterns of the fathers of hospitalized schizophrenics. They found no evidence of downward drift. The parents of schizophrenics lived basically in the same ecological areas as their offspring. The downward-drift hypothesis was examined again in other studies in New Haven, Connecticut, Hagerstown, Maryland, and Buffalo, New York, and was found lacking there as well.[49]

A more damaging critique is not as easily dismissed. This criticism applies not only to Dunham and Faris but to social disorganization research in general. The point is that studies in this tradition typically fail to separate social disorganization from organized social disadvantage, social stratification, or lower-class status. We shall return to this critique in the closing section of this chapter.

The Theoretical Imagery of Disorganization: A Summary Comment

The social disorganization perspective departs from the individualistic focus of previous theorizing by emphasizing factors associated with the social causation of deviance—rapid social change resulting in a breakdown in normative social control. The social-ecological approach permitted disorganizational researchers to study natural areas of the city in which these causative factors were most powerful. Chicago theorists also obtained first-hand accounts of people most affected by the forces of change and disorganization. We conclude our discussion of the theoretical imagery of disorganization with an excerpt from one such account: Clifford Shaw's *The Jack Roller*.[50] Shaw presents a detailed life history of a young man lured into delinquency by the forces of disorganization. In the following passage, Shaw describes the causal impact of the disorganized transition zone. The concluding reference to West Madison Street's exclusive "Four Hundred" is an allusion to the corporate offices located in Chicago's central business district, the nucleus of change and primary source of social disorganization.

> The lures and the irresistible call drew me on like a magnet and I was always helpless before them. I was like a canoe on a storm-swept sea, buffeted here and there, helpless and frail. I had about as much chance of controlling my desires as of braving the storm. But here I mingled with bums and derelicts like myself, and people did not stare at my rags and misery. Here I felt at home, for "misery loves company." So, I drifted on with the rest of the human driftwood carried on by the current of W. Madison Street's exclusive "Four Hundred" or more.[51]

IDENTIFYING DISORGANIZATIONAL DEVIANCE

The study of social disorganization by University of Chicago sociologists combined two different traditions of social research. The first tradition emphasized efforts to objectively measure external factors and conditions which were believed to affect the organization or disorganization of society. Chicago researchers employed this tradition to develop statistical maps of natural areas within the city. These maps were said to reveal the spatial or ecological origins and consequences of social disorganization. The second Chicago research tradition emphasized the subjective side of social life. It sought to explore the meaning of social life as experienced by people themselves. It involved such things as in-depth interviews, first-hand observations, and the recording of life histories.

The willingness to combine external-objective and internal-subjective approaches to the study of social life was a definite strength of the early Chicago studies. Today these two different research traditions often represent points of unreconcilable division between sociologists. Some researchers adhere almost dogmatically to the external-objective tradition. They argue that social research must be quantitative or statistical if it is to be scientific. Zealous adherents to the internal-subjective tradition argue the opposite. Sociologists committed to qualitative or field methods often contend that it is necessary to first understand the meaning of human action before attempting to explain patterns or structures of action.

This division over the proper methods of social research is as old as the discipline of sociology itself. Since the early part of the nineteenth century students of society have debated whether sociology should aspire to the status of a natural science or whether its distinctive subject matter (reflective human beings who create, maintain, and change social institutions in history) requires a special form of investigation. In nineteenth-century Europe this question prompted social theorists like Wilhelm Dilthey to argue for the formation of a distinctively human science *(Geisteswissenschaften)* based on the principles of subjective understanding, as opposed to natural science *(Naturwissenschaften)*, which stressed the formulation of objective causal laws.[52]

In America this methodological debate surfaced dramatically in the period following the First World War. Although sociologists of both methodological persuasions stressed the need for rigorous empirical research, lines were drawn between those who advocated quantitative approaches and those who advocated qualitative approaches.[53]

These antagonisms were dissolved by the early Chicago researchers, who combined both traditions. The result was a detailed body of empirical literature that is broad in its quantitative scope and deep in qualitative description.

The methodological eclecticism of the early Chicago researchers was nurtured by the complementary theoretical insights of W. I. Thomas and Robert Park. Thomas reminded students of the importance of considering the way that people define their own social situations. Park stressed the importance of external societal constraints in shaping the situations in which people found themselves. For Park spatial or ecological factors were of greatest importance. Yet, despite the difference in theoretical emphasis, Thomas and Park were close and mutually respectful colleagues who, in Thomas's words, "enjoyed a very long and profitable association."[54] Exposure to Thomas and Park provided members of the Chicago school with a sense that a full scientific study of social disorganization required a look at both its external-objective and its internal-subjective dimensions. As such, the empirical investigation of deviance by the Chicago sociologists represented a pioneer effort in the areas of both sociological statistics and field research.

Sociological Statistics on Disorganization

Social disorganization researchers charted the distribution of many types of deviance across the landscape of urban America. Using statistics drawn from the official records of the police, the criminal courts, hospitals, mental institutions, and other public agencies, they methodically plotted the known presence of deviant populations throughout the various zones of the city. This data provided empirical support for theoretical claims regarding the impact of "naturally" disorganized areas in producing high rates of deviance.

An excellent illustration of the Chicago researchers' use of sociological statistics is found in the quantitative studies of delinquency conducted by Clifford Shaw and Henry McKay.[55] Shaw and McKay employed three different types of statistical mapping techniques: spot maps, rate maps, and zone maps. Spot maps pinpointed the residential patterns of juvenile offenders in accordance with their level of involvement in the criminal justice system. Hence maps depicting the residential concentration of arrested offenders could be compared with maps for convicted offenders, and so forth. Rate maps were used to show the percentage of the entire juvenile population involved in this or that stage of the criminal justice system. This second form of map was constructed for 140 separate square-mile areas. When compared to spot maps, rate maps suggested that the areas with the highest percentage of delinquency were not necessarily those with the highest numbers of delinquents. The reason for this involved the fact that certain high-rate areas had a smaller absolute number of juvenile residents. Yet, when converted to a third form of map—the zone map—the pattern most distinctively associated with the disorganization perspective was revealed. Zone maps depicted distance from the central city, i.e., distance from the believed nucleus of urban change. Spot and rate maps suggested considerable variation in the distribution and rate of delinquency from one specific area to the next. Nonetheless, zone maps depicted a general concentration of youth crimes in zones closest to the central business district.

Field Research into Social Disorganization

The field studies of the early Chicago researchers complemented their statistical investigations. Some researchers, such as Clifford Shaw, contributed as much to the qualitative exploration of deviant life as to the quantitative mapping of rates of deviation. Notable among the early field studies were Shaw's *The Jack Roller* and his collaborative contributions to *The Natural History of a Delinquent Career* and *Brothers in Crime*.[56] Other field-research portraits of deviant life under the sway of social disorganization include *The Unadjusted Girl,* W. I. Thomas's intimate examination of the life of a prostitute, *The Hobo: The Sociology of the Homeless Man* by Nels Anderson, *The Ghetto* by Louis Wirth, *Gold Coast and Slum* by Harvey W. Zorbaugh, and *The Taxi-Dance Hall: A Sociological Study of Commercialized Recreation and City Life* by Paul G. Cressey.[57]

Howard Becker compares the scientific enterprise to a mosaic.[58] Each piece adds a little to the understanding of the whole. This is a good metaphor for describing the way in which statistical and field reports on disorganization fed into and illuminated one another. As Clifford Shaw suggested, field data were used "not only as a means of making preliminary explorations" but as the basis of "hypotheses . . . tested by the comparative study of other detailed case histories and by the formal methods of statistical analysis."[59]

SOCIAL CONTROL OF DISORGANIZATIONAL DEVIANCE

Social control was a key concept in the early writings of the Chicago school. According to Robert Park, "social control was the central fact and the central problem of society." Yet, because of their self-defined mission of creating an objective social science, the Chicago theorists disclaimed interest in advocating a particular strategy of social control. The Chicago sociologists were, in other words, eager to dissociate themselves from the image of sociology as social reform. In the words of Park, "It is probably not the business of the universities to agitate reforms nor to attempt directly to influence public opinion in regard to current issues. To do this is to relax its critical attitude, lessen its authority in matters of fact."[60]

Despite this posture of scientific neutrality the social disorganization perspective spawned a distinctive approach to the problem of social control. What distinguishes its program of control from those discussed previously, is its goal of treating society rather than treating individuals. This control strategy is intimately associated with the perspective's vision of the disorganized society as the principal cause of the deviance of its members. Disorganization theorists believed that it would be a major mistake to treat the individual in isolation from the societal roots of his or her disorganizational malaise. Consider the following remarks by Clifford Shaw and Henry McKay:

> Successful treatment of the problem of delinquency in large cities will entail the development of programs which seek to effect changes in the conditions of life in specific local communities and in whole sections of the city. Diagnosis and supervision of the individual offender will probably not be sufficient to achieve this end.[61]

Shaw and McKay suggest that effective control programs must restore normative stability within disorganized communities. In 1932 this strategy of social reorganization was put into practice with the founding of the Chicago Area Project. This public experiment in neighborhood reorganization was coordinated by the Institute for Juvenile Research, where Shaw and McKay worked as researchers. Utilizing twenty-two different neighborhood centers in six areas of the city, the Chicago Area Project operated continuously for twenty-five years until the death of Shaw in 1957.

The Chicago Area Project represented an effort to translate disorganizational theorizing into a practical program of delinquency prevention. Local residents were placed in positions of key organizational decision-making. Moreover, most staff were recruited from among the ranks of those residing in so-called disorganized neighborhoods. In this sense, the organizational structure of the program was itself a vehicle for planned social reorganization. Under the leadership of neighborhood representatives the program sought to prevent delinquency by two broad strategies. The first involved coordinating the community resources of a wide variety of otherwise fragmented and even competing groups. Efforts were made to solicit the joint efforts of schools, churches, labor unions, industrial and business interests, clubs, and other local groups in organizing to collectively combat community problems. The second project strategy involved sponsoring a host of specific youth-activity programs. By organized participation in such programs it was hoped that currents of social disorganization would be reduced and that potentially deviant youths would be given a lifeline back to the normative shores of the well-organized society.

Three types of youth-activity programs operated under the auspices of the Chicago Area Project. The first was specifically geared toward the reduction of criminal or delinquent behavior. It included such things as sending field workers out to become involved with and to counsel members of neighborhood youth groups, aiding youths placed in training schools for delinquents and those on or preparing for parole, and assisting police officers and court personnel in developing special youth-oriented programming. Two other types of project activities related more indirectly to the prevention of delinquency. The first involved a host of general neighborhood-improvement programs. These involved such things as upgrading health and sanitation conditions and strengthening education, law enforcement, environmental conservation, and traffic safety. The second focused on expanding recreational resources. Summer camps were opened. Church basements, storefronts, and unused spaces within police stations were employed to provide youths with constructive recreational alternatives to life on the street. When considered as a whole, the central objectives of these diverse programs were, as Terrence Morris points out, "to develop a positive interest by the inhabitants in their own welfare, to establish democratic bodies of local citizens who would enable the whole community to become aware of its problems and to attempt their solution by common action."[62]

How successful were the activities of the Chicago Area Project in realizing its goals of community reorganization and delinquency prevention? Sympathetic commentators such as Martin Haskell and Lewis Yablonsky have praised its organizational efforts and have suggested that "in all probability delinquency was reduced."[63] Such praise may be based more on faith than on concrete data. The practical accomplishments of the Chicago Area Project were, unfortunately, never thoroughly and systematically evaluated.[64] As Allen Liska points out, "The Chicagoans were more concerned with implementing the policy implications of their theory and research than in evaluating the success of their programs."[65]

A somewhat similar project in Boston was evaluated by Walter Miller. Miller's analysis of Boston's "total-community delinquency control project" provides clues to the strengths and weaknesses of control strategies based upon the disorganizational perspective.[66] Miller examined the impact of the Boston reorganization project over a three-year period. His findings were mixed. On one hand, he discovered that the project succeeded in promoting close ties between community organizers and local youth gangs and in organizing many gang members into more conventional, clublike associations. The Boston total-community project also increased recreational outlets and access to educational and occupational opportunities, fostered greater citizen involvement in local community programs, and stimulated higher levels of interagency cooperation. Regarding the prevention of delinquency the project was much less successful. It had only a "negligible impact."[67] Miller's assessment draws heavily upon the field reports recorded daily by the project's outreach workers. Workers were asked to classify the behavior of youths with whom they had contact. Behavior was classified as moral or immoral (as judged by the conventional moral standards of society) and as legal or illegal. Miller assumed that success in reducing delinquency would be reflected in trends recorded by the outreach workers. As the community became more organized, the behavior of youths should hypothetically become more moral and more legal.

This failed to happen. The ratio of moral to immoral conduct remained constant throughout the project's duration. There was, however, a slight decrease in the classification of known illegal acts. This improvement was, unfortunately, counterbalanced by an increase in the number of major or serious illegal acts committed. Thus the project as a whole appeared to do little to reduce the general level of delinquency, particularly serious delinquency. This finding was corroborated by another type of data—statistics on court appearances recorded before, during, and after the term of the project. Miller compared the court appearances of boys with project contact with a control group of similar boys not involved in the project. No measurable differences were found.

Miller's evaluation of the Boston project does not speak well for the practical utility of the preventive social control program suggested by disorganization theory. Gains were made in general community reorganization but not in the reduction of delinquency prevention. Does this mean that the Chicago theorists were incorrect? This is the conclusion of critic Terrence Morris, who declares that disorganization and deviance may both be products of yet another factor—structured social inequality.[68] From Morris's point of view, efforts at neighborhood reorganization that do not address this deeper structural factor are doomed to fail. At best they treat symptoms of the deeper problem of inequality while "leaving the malady untouched." We will return to this issue later. For now it is sufficient to note the general nature of control efforts derived from disorganizational theorizing. Following the lead of the Chicago sociologists, programs such as the Chicago Area Project and Boston's total-community project sought to put into practice what the perspective preached—that deviance can best be controlled by controlling the disorganizational impact of rapid social change. Although its practical efficacy has not been confirmed by sound evaluation data, this strategy of control represents a major departure from the individualistically oriented redemptive, the punitive, and the therapeutic control models suggested, respectively, by demonic, classical, and pathological theorizing.

THE SOCIAL DISORGANIZATION PERSPECTIVE TODAY

The social disorganization perspective arose during the 1920s in the scholarly writings and empirical research of the Chicago school. In subsequent decades this perspective exerted an enormous influence on the study and control of deviant behavior in America. For a period of time social disorganization become the dominant theoretical imagery for thinking about such matters. As Don Gibbons points out, "During the 1950's, a generation of undergraduate students was introduced to formulations that attributed a variety of socially undesirable behavior . . . to social disorganization."[69]

A short time later the social disorganization perspective began to lose its powerful grip on the sociological imagination. In part this was because of the criticisms discussed in the closing pages of this chapter. In part it was because of the emergence of alternative formulations of the deviance problem: the functionalist, anomie, and learning perspectives discussed in subsequent chapters. In part it was because of the waning influence of the University of Chicago as "the" center for American sociology. Following the death of several of its key founding figures in the late 1930s, the unprecedented dominance of the Chicago school passed eastward to the elite universities of the Atlantic seaboard.[70] Thus, the gradual decrease in use of disorganizational imagery to explain deviance is due, in part, to intellectual and organizational changes within the field of sociology itself.

While this is undoubtedly true it may also be the case that the decline in disorganizational thinking reflects a change in American social life in general. The decline in disorganizational theorizing was paralleled by a decline in the rate of uncontrolled industrialization, urbanization, and immigration. Laws have greatly reduced the levels of immigration, while for many, urbanization and industrialization have become routine features of everyday life. As a result, "social disorganization theory may be less applicable to contemporary America than to a bygone era."[71]

Disorganizational Deviance in Developing Countries

Despite its decline in dominance the social disorganization perspective continues to influence contemporary studies of deviance. One area of research where disorganizational imagery has shown a particular vitality involves the study of deviance in developing countries. In such settings one might suspect the metaphor of disorganization to still be applicable because within developing nations the processes of industrialization and urbanization are still in their early and potentially most disruptive stages. Recent work by S. Kirson Weinberg on the problem of juvenile delinquency in Accra, Ghana,[72] and by Marshall Clinard and Daniel Abbott on property crime in

Kampala, Uganda,[73] illustrates the use of the disorganizational framework in the cross-cultural study of deviance in developing nations.

Weinberg's research tests Shaw and McKay's theories about the ecological distribution of disorganizational deviance. Although Weinberg's work lacks the rigor of the statistical mapping techniques used by the Chicago researchers, his descriptive ethnographic data point toward similar conclusions. Areas with high delinquency were high in social disorganization. Delinquent youths were concentrated in areas where families had migrated from northern rural settings into urban slums characterized by physical deterioration, high rates of adult crime, alcoholism, poverty, unskilled labor, poor education, disintegration of traditional family structures, and a decline of social control. In such places as contemporary Accra youths are said to be exposed to "processes of susceptibility to delinquency" similar to those previously discovered in Chicago.[74] Traditional mechanisms of tribal social control were broken by the rapid process of urbanization and industrial change. The tight web of tribal values and norms was torn asunder. Integrated tribes were transformed into disintegrated ethnic groups. The bonds of social control were loosened, and with this loosening, Weinberg notes there was an increase in delinquent behavior.[75]

Clinard and Abbott were concerned with similar questions of social disintegration. They gathered perceptual and official-indicator data on the extent of property crime in two slum areas of Kampala, Uganda. Both slums were similar when considered in terms of their deteriorated physical condition. Yet, in terms of property crime the two communities were radically different. The first, Kiseruji, was high in property crime. The second, Namuwongo, was low. Why? The answer, according to Clinard and Abbott, is found in differences in the degree of normative social organization between the two communities. Clinard and Abbott employed the Liberson technique, a means of estimating the tribal homogeneity or heterogeneity of each community, and a series of interviews with community members to document and explore the nature of such differences. Following the logic of social disorganization, Clinard and Meir sought to discover whether the higher crime rates of the Kiseruji slum were associated with such indicators of normative breakdown as lesser degrees of tribal homogeneity, lower levels of communicative integration, lesser family stability, and higher residential mobility.

Clinard and Abbott's findings reflect positively on the social disorganization perspective. Both communities were very poor and living under conditions of social disadvantage. For this reason Clinard and Abbott ruled out differences in economic conditions as a factor accounting for differences in the level of property crime. Significant differences were found, however, in areas of normative social organization. The low-crime Namuwongo slum was discovered to be more homogeneous, in terms of both population mix and shared tribal customs. When compared to the high-crime Kiseruji community, Namuwongo was also characterized by a lesser rate of residential change and higher rates of intimate communication and visiting between nonfamilial residents, greater family stability, and more participation in community organizations, including religious organizations. Clinard and Abbott reasoned that the low-crime community was thus better organized to exercise normative control over its members. Higher property crime in the less-organized slum was thus seen as a function of its weaker web of normative social control.

Other Contemporary Uses of Disorganizational Imagery

In addition to studies of deviance in developing countries the disorganizational perspective continues to influence research conducted within modern western societies. One important example is found in Marshall Clinard's *Cities with Little Crime: The Case of Switzerland.*[76]

Switzerland represents an exception to the observation that high rates of crime follow high rates of industrialization and urbanization. Clinard measured Swiss crime by a variety of indicators: studies of public concern over crime, official crime rates, crime victimization surveys, insurance rates for burglary, theft, and auto theft, and the extent of crime as reported in the newspapers.[77] When controlling for a high level of affluence, a characteristic which Swiss society shares with such countries as Sweden, the United States, and the Federal Republic of Germany, the problem of crime was seen as far lower in Switzerland. The contrast with Sweden is most instructive. Switzerland and Sweden rank numbers one and two respectively in terms of per capita affluence. Both are also high in industrialization and urbanization. Nonetheless, the Swiss have far lower crime rates. Why? Clinard suggests an explanation which falls, in large part, within the theoretical scope of the social disorganization perspective.

The Swiss, a people with multiple language and ethnic communities, appear far more heterogeneous than the Swedes. According to Clinard, "In sharp contrast to the Swiss diversity, Swedes are remarkably homogeneous." Swedes possess a unitary language, a state religion (on paper if not in practice), and a common cultural heritage. If heterogeneity were equated with disorganization one would expect the Swiss to rank higher in crime. Yet the opposite is true. The Swiss, for all their diversity, have lower crime rates than the homogeneous Swedes.[78] This Clinard explains by reference to three general social factors which promote the tight normative organization of Swiss society: (1) the slow development of urbanization, (2) a tradition of political decentralization and local responsibility, and (3) a tradition of age integration.

Switzerland is today highly urbanized. A great percentage of its citizenry lives in metropolitan areas. Nonetheless, as a process urbanization has been gradual rather than sudden and disruptive. Its spread had been dispersed across several moderate-sized cities (Zurich, Basel, Geneva) rather than concentrated, as in the case of Sweden, in one superurban area (Stockholm). Although Switzerland is heterogeneous as a nation, migration to particular Swiss cities has been relatively homogeneous. Different waves of linguistically and ethnically similar migrants have gradually followed one another into the same urban areas. This buffered the disruptive impact of rapid rural-to-urban population change. As a result, Switzerland was spared the radical disjuncture between the rural and the urban, a disjuncture characteristic of urbanization in other western nations, including Sweden. From a social disorganization point of view this is significant. Switzerland became urbanized but not normatively disrupted. According to Clinard, "even after years of residence in large cities, most persons still think of 'home' as their traditional canton. . . . A large proportion of urban inhabitants have never broken in spirit with the soil or the rugged mountain lands of their ancestors."[79]

The gradual urbanization of Switzerland may have minimized disorganization. Also important may be the long Swiss tradition of political decentralization. Clinard points out that the Swiss distrust the delegation of much responsibility to the national, or federal, level of government. Swiss society is characterized by its high levels of citizen participation in localized democratic rule and by an almost "ingrained faith in mutual help and solidarity."[80] Its nearly 6 million people are politically subdivided into twenty-five semiautonomous cantons and half-cantons. Each canton is largely governed by its own legislature and controls its own educational institutions, its courts, and its police. Cantons are, in turn, divided into some 3,000 communes, smaller political units which handle the collection of taxes, the maintenance of public buildings, the selection of teachers, and the administration of elections and relief funds. This decentralization contrasts sharply with Sweden and its large, centralized, impersonal federal bureaucracies. Sweden's bureaucracies ensure material welfare but contribute little to a feeling of direct, interpersonal social control. Individuals may feel, instead, that their lives are governed by vast, impersonal forces beyond their immediate and direct experience.

The opposite is said about Switzerland. High levels of direct participation in decentralized government are said to instill a widespread feeling among the Swiss "that they are their own masters."[81] Such widespread political participation nurtures a deep sense of involvement in the affairs of others. When combined with observations about high levels of age integration within Swiss society, Clinard's analysis suggests that reciprocal involvement and mutual responsibility strengthen the normative web of Switzerland—closing the door upon disruptive social disorganization and resultant high levels of deviance. As Clinard points out, "in Switzerland everyone is his own policeman."[82]

Clinard's account of the low Swiss crime rate is by no means the only recent study to apply social disorganization imagery to the study of deviance in western society. Michalowski's study of vehicular homicide can also be interpreted within the general boundaries of the disorganizational framework.[83] Michalowski discovered that people held responsible for automobile fatalities tend to come from ecological zones traditionally associated with disorganization. Such people were also bombarded with such disorganizing experiences as recent marital trouble, loss of employment, emotional turmoil, and/or alcohol abuse. Sollenberger has also invoked disorganizational imagery to account for the traditionally low incidence of violent crime in tightly knit, family-oriented Chinese-American communities.[84] Extremely low divorce rates, positive attitudes toward spouses, strong beliefs in the moral authority of the family, high aspirations for children, and clear normative prohibitions against aggressiveness were said to combine in producing organized social controls against fighting and physical assault.

Contemporary Control Theory: A Social-Psychological Extension of the Disorganizational Model

According to the basic logic of the disorganizational perspective, social disorganization is likely to be followed by personal disorganization. A breakdown in normative controls increases the likelihood that individuals will experience a similar breakdown in moral constraints in their everyday behavior. Why? Disorganizational theorists point, at least implicitly, in the direction of socialization. Socialization, the process through which one generation of people passes its beliefs, values, and normative constraints to another, is disrupted by social disorganization. The power of traditional beliefs, values, and norms is dissipated by a disorganized moral climate in which "anything goes." At the individual level this means that many people will fail to develop the self-censoring consciences which are said to regulate behavior in the well-organized society. Simply stated, disorganizational theorists assume that (1) the presence of normative chaos results in disrupted socialization, and (2) disrupted socialization results in weakened internal normative constraint.

The first part of the chain linking disorganization, disrupted socialization, and deviance was documented in such early disorganizational research efforts as Thomas and Znaniecki's *The Polish Peasant in Europe and America*. There an analysis of the letters and autobiographical reflections of recent immigrants revealed a stark picture of the inability of one generation to successfully socialize its young. A more precise formulation of the second part of the chain, the part linking disrupted socialization with the actual occurrence of deviant behavior, awaited the development of contemporary control theory. Control theory, as prefigured in the work of Walter Reckless, another member of the Chicago school, and refined in recent years by Travis Hirschi, examines factors associated with the production of social conformity. Control theory and disorganization theory are commonly concerned with processes which lessen the likelihood that people will be normatively constrained. For this reason control theory may be read as a social-psychological extension of the concerns of the Chicago school.[85] While early Chicagoans examined the deterioration of normative constraints, control theorists have focused on the manner in which this deterioration results in nonconformity or deviance. Control theorists make explicit something left implicit in most disorganizational theorizing—the link between disrupted or inadequately constraining socialization and the likelihood of acting deviantly.

Reckless's Version of Control Theory: The Principle of Containment

Walter Reckless was one of the first generation of graduate students to study sociology at the University of Chicago. A student of Park, Reckless was also a skilled first-hand observer of life in a city beset by the forces of social disorganization. He defrayed some of the cost of his education by playing the fiddle in a cafe reputedly controlled by the mobster Al Capone. In such settings Reckless noted that while the general processes of social disorganization may have unhinged the normative constraints of many persons, many others were never drawn into a life of deviance. To Reckless this meant that social-structural factors, such as social disorganization, were mediated by social-psychological factors surrounding the process of socialization. Reckless conceived of these factors as those of *inner containment* and *outer containment*.

For Reckless inner containment consists largely of such factors as "self-control, good self-concept, ego strength, well-developed superego, high frustration tolerance, high resistance to diversions, high sense of responsibility, goal orientation, ability to find substitute satisfactions, tension-reducing rationalizations, and so on."[86] Such inner constraints or containments, once produced in the process of socialization, were said to isolate an individual from pushes or pulls in the direction of deviance or nonconformity. Such inner containment factors existed, however, in a kind of dynamic tension with the relative presence or absence of a host of outer containment factors. According to Reckless the forces of outer containment represent a "structural buffer in the person's immediate social world."[87] When strong this buffer reinforces the control power of inner containment. When weak it chips away at the forces of inner containment. According to Reckless, the buffer of outer containment includes such things as a consistent presentation of moral values, institutional support for belief in and realization of internalized norms, goals, and expectations, clear social delineation of roles, rules, and responsibilities, the effective operation of supervision and discipline, the availability of safety valves for letting off steam in a nondeviant fashion, and the opportunity for acceptance, identity, and belongingness.

During periods of high social disorganization a variety of external containment factors would, by definition, be lacking. Thus Reckless's theory of containment accounts, at least in principle, for resultant social-psychological strains in the direction of nonconformity. Nonetheless, Reckless contends that strong inner containment factors may still shield people from the lure of deviance.[88] According to containment theory the study of deviance must always consider the relative strengths and dynamic interplay between two generic forces of control—inner and outer supports for conformity.

Hirschi's Control Theory: Failure of the Social Bond

Reckless's containment theory examines the ways people become insulated from pressures to deviate. Travis Hirschi's control theory addresses this topic from a slightly different perspective. Hirschi's theory is presented in his 1969 book, *Causes of Delinquency*.[89] It focuses on the social bonds which tie people to the normative web of conventional society. Like the disorganizational perspective as a whole, Hirschi's theory locates the cause of delinquency or deviance in those processes which set people free from the bonds of normative constraint. According to Hirschi, "delinquent acts result when an individual's bond to society is weak or broken."[90] Unlike most disorganizational theorists, Hirschi attempts to specify several dimensions of the social bonding process which, when underdeveloped or disrupted, increase the likelihood of deviant behavior.

For Hirschi, social bonding has both inner and outer dimensions. Its inner dimension is characterized by socialization into a set of conventional beliefs about how one should act, toward whom, where, and when. A similarity in beliefs is said to induce a similarity in behavior. Thus, socialization into a society's conventional belief system is a central feature of bonding or social control. Conventional beliefs, however, are not always followed by conventional action. Sometimes, the push or pull of external forces may lead individuals to act in a manner inconsistent with or in contradiction to their internalized beliefs. Imagine yourself a teenager who honestly believes that shoplifting is wrong. In most instances, this might mean that you would not even consider shoplifting. Yet, on a particular evening, surrounded by the exhortation of peers to prove that you are one of the gang, angry at your parents for treating you like a child, bolstered by the intoxication of comradery and booze, feeling that you have nothing to lose, isn't it possible that your beliefs will take a backseat to the immediacy of your desires for acceptance and adventure? This possibility prompts Hirschi to consider several outer dimensions of social bonding which, like the internalization of conventional beliefs, operate as social-psychological controls against the likelihood of deviant behavior.

The outer dimensions of social bonding are described in terms of attachment, commitment, and involvement. *Attachment* refers to the strength of a person's ties to others, particularly to other persons who conform to society's normative standards. For Hirschi, relational ties to one's parents and conventional peers are the most emphasized sources of attachment. Strongly attached people are pictured as very sensitive to the opinions of others. They have a great investment in achieving or maintaining the respect of those with whom they associate. If someone's associates are conventionally oriented, then the greater the attachment to them, the less likely is a person to deviate from conventionality.

Commitment refers to the degree that a person is tied to conventional ways of behaving by virtue of the social rewards one obtains from acting in accordance with the prevailing norms. The logic of commitment is this: the more that one gains by acting conventionally, the more that one stands to lose by deviating, and thus the less likely that one will break from the prevailing norms. Consider the professor who is also a homosexual. In which situation is the professor more likely to be public about her or his personal sexual preferences: a situation in which she or he is currently being reviewed for tenure at a small, rural, conservative Southern Baptist college or a situation in which she or he already has the guarantee of tenure at a large, urban, liberally oriented university in the San Francisco Bay area? According to the logic of commitment, the answer is obvious. The professor would have much more to lose in the first situation than the second. Hence, she or he is more likely to play it straight in the first situation, and more likely to come straightforwardly out of the closet in the second.[91]

Involvement, the third of Hirschi's outer dimensions of social bonding, refers to the proportion of a person's time engaged in the pursuit of conventionality. The logic here is that if a great percentage of someone's time (and perhaps energy as well) is taken up by "appointments, deadlines, working hours," etc., then there is little time left over for potential deviance. This, perhaps, is what those who direct seminaries or administer boarding schools mean by the old saying, "A busy mind is a pure mind." By totally scheduling the lives of their young residents, by filling even periods of "free time" with mandatory participation in supervised athletics, rectors and headmasters have long sought to curb thoughts of sex and other supposed lures toward deviance.

Taken as a whole, Hirschi's fourfold analysis of inner and outer bonding mechanisms represents a social-psychological consideration of forces which control or constrain persons to stay within the straight and narrow boundaries of the established normative order. According to disorganizational theorizing, rapid social change destroys the control power of the normative order. Hirschi's depiction of the bonding process permits us to imagine more concretely how this happens. Change disrupts one or more of the components of bonding; weakening or suspending the power of internalized beliefs and/or external attachments, commitments, and involvements.

In order to obtain a systematic measure of the adequacy of his theory, Hirschi presented self-administered questionnaires to a sample of approximately 1,300 Richmond, California, boys in grades 6 through 12. He asked them to report on delinquent activities which they had committed and sought to determine their levels of social bonding. To determine the degree that a person was attached to conventional associations, he asked about a youth's attraction to parents, peers, and school officials. Students were presented with such questions as "Would you like to be the kind of person your father is?" To determine commitment to a system rewarding conformity, he asked about the importance students placed upon getting good grades. To determine involvement in conventional, or deviance-precluding, activities, he obtained information on time spent in various school-oriented projects. The conventionality of internalized beliefs was measured by questions assessing such things as respect for the law or the police.

In general, Hirschi's research findings support the central positions of his control theory. Although most of the delinquency reported by youths was of a minor nature, Hirschi's data suggest that high levels of attachment, commitment, involvement, and belief are related to a low level of delinquency. Consider the question regarding a youth's desire to be like his father. For boys who "would like to be like their father in every way," 64 percent reported a low level of delinquency. This was the case for only 41 percent of those who did not want to be like their fathers. Hirschi's analysis of other measures of social bonding reveals a similar pattern. These findings were, with one notable exception, confirmed in research conducted by Michael Hindelang a few years later.[92] Hindelang's measures of delinquency and bonding were similar to Hirschi's. His sample was composed of boys and girls in a rural east coast location. His results were consistent with Hirschi's except with regard to attachment. Hirschi's data suggest that as parental, peer, and school attachments increase, levels of delinquency decrease. Hindelang did not find evidence of this pattern. Perhaps the reason lies in the fact that neither researcher had reliable data about the actual conventionality of the persons with whom the youths had the most attachment. If people are greatly attached to unconventional persons, they may be influenced in the direction of deviance rather than conventionality. This is suggested in Hirschi's data and in other studies that examine the impact of delinquent peers on the likelihood of one's becoming delinquent.[93]

In summary, Hirschi's control theory may be viewed as a promising social-psychological extension of basic themes involved in the disorganizational perspective. The disorganizational perspective locates the causes of deviant behavior in the disruption of society's normative order. Hirschi's control theory locates the realms of immediate social and psychological experience where norms actually come into play. If the disorganizational perspective is correct in asserting that disrupted norms increase the likelihood of deviant behavior, then this societal-level increase should be mirrored at the level of individual social-psychological experience. Empirical support for Hirschi's theory suggests that this is the case. Thus, control theory represents further evidence of the continued importance of disorganizational theorizing.

ASSESSING THE DISORGANIZATION PERSPECTIVE

The disorganization perspective is a thoroughly social viewpoint on the study of deviance and social control. It transcends many of the individualistic limitations and biases of previous perspectives. This is its primary strength. In the period of rapid social changes following World War I, the disorganizational perspective permitted American sociologists to shed previous illusions about the inevitability of rational progress without pessimistic disillusionment about the usefulness of social science. The disorganizational perspective rejected both speculative evolutionary theorizing and romantic attachment to the ideals of white, Protestant, small-town America. It did so, moreover, without abandoning faith in the belief that the careful study of social life is helpful in constructing a more humane and knowledgeable approach to the problems of living. These conclusions are reflected in the Chicago school's twin commitments to disciplined empirical research and liberal social policy formation. As James Carey points out:

> The disorganization perspective had a broad . . . appeal to . . . sociologists, because it was more complex than the evolutionary view. It did not automatically assume the superiority of American ways and it allowed for a more penetrating analysis of probable outcomes of meetings between diverse peoples. It seemed better suited to the realities of a complex, differential society.[94]

Another strength of the disorganization perspective is that it asks us to imagine that deviants are people like ourselves. They are in no way spiritually cursed, rationally miscalculative, or pathologically defective. The factor that separates deviants from anyone else is an unfortunate spatial location in the natural ecology of a changing society. Deviants, argues the perspective, are disproportionately exposed to the disruptive forces of rapid social change. Nondeviants suddenly confronted with the same disruptive forces would find themselves pulled similarly toward nonconformity.

Despite its strengths, there are serious weaknesses in the formulation and application of disorganized theorizing. Five important criticisms are noted below. A consideration of each reminds us that this perspective has serious blind spots as well as interesting areas of illumination.

Inadequate Operationalization of the Concept of Disorganization

In testing the key components of a theoretical perspective, researchers must be careful to precisely and consistently operationalize their concepts so that measurements adequately reflect ideas suggested by the theory itself. Despite a consistent emphasis on relating theory to research, disorganizational researchers were not always careful in operationalizing conceptual measurements. Problems in this area assumed one of two forms. Sometimes, researchers failed to justify why a particular indicator of disorganization was taken as a measure of normative breakdown. Consider several of the indicators of disorganization used in studies of delinquency. Measures such as a high proportion of working women, a high proportion of unmarried men, and a high number of persons per household have all been used to indicate the presence of disorganization.

Why? Why should we assume that working women are more disorganized than nonworking women, or that unmarried men or large households are overtaken by normative breakdown? Such things have been used as indirect measurements of normative disorganization, and yet we are not told exactly how or why. Perhaps, they do reflect normative chaos. On the other hand, they may indicate little more than a researcher's own prejudice or bias.

A second problem in the measurement of disorganization was that statistics on deviance were themselves occasionally used as indicators of disorganization. This is troublesome because disorganization is then said to cause deviance. Can something be both an indicator and a cause of the same thing? Logically, the answer is no. Unfortunately, disorganizational researchers were not always logically consistent. Consider the following statement by Chicago researchers Robert E. L. Faris and H. Warren Dunham. In explaining high rates of deviance among second- and third-generation immigrants, Faris and Dunham offer the following analysis:

> A type of disorganizing factor operates among the members of the second and third generations. The very high delinquency rate among the second-generation children has been shown by Shaw. This disorganization can be shown to develop from the nature of the child's social situation.[95]

In the passage excerpted above, Faris and Dunham appear to see the high delinquency rate as something which was both an example of disorganization and something caused by disorganization. Such confusion was unfortunately all too common in social disorganization research.

Confusion of Disorganization and Differential Organization

Disorganizational theorists (like most scientists) come from backgrounds which are disproportionately male, middle class, and white. Often their sociological journeys do not take them beyond the constraints of this background. They may fail to appreciate the ways that people from other class, cultural, or ethnic backgrounds organize their world. Differences in organization may thus be perceived as examples of disorganizations.

An important instance of such confusion involved the so-called Moynihan Report.[96] This report *(The Negro Family: The Case for National Action)* was prepared for President Lyndon Johnson in 1965 by Daniel Patrick Moynihan, then assistant secretary of labor and White House adviser. The basis for a compassionate stance on race relations by Johnson, the report was nonetheless mired in the biases of disorganizational theorizing. High rates of black crime, delinquency, and other forms of deviance were explained by the social disorganization of the black family. Originating in slavery and reinforced by the latter-day forces of rapid urbanization and unemployment, the family structure of blacks was said to be the opposite of that of whites. Higher rates of fatherless homes, divorce, separation, and marital desertion, the reverse of traditional (white) husband-wife roles, and greater vulnerability to economic and criminal victimization were said to have disrupted the organization of lower-class black family life. The resulting lack of normative controls fostered deviance and made the problem cyclical, passed on from generation to generation.

Since the time that the Moynihan Report was first issued, it has become the subject of considerable debate and criticism.[97] One wave of criticism questioned the equation of female-headed households with disorganization.[98] Wasn't this historical development within the black family an organized, highly adaptive response to the systematic removal of black males, initially through slavery and later through a socially discriminatory economy, the welfare rules of which penalized families with low-income male household heads?

A later wave of criticism questioned the empirical accuracy of the lack of adult male presence.[99] Subsequent research suggested that males were more involved, even if not officially married into the family, than previously estimated. The lower-class black family was differently organized rather than disorganized. Bound by a singular ethnocentric view of what constitutes proper organization, researchers were blind to this important distinction. Confusion of this kind is a liability of much disorganizational theorizing.

The Neglect of Organized, Respectable Deviance

The types of deviance discovered in the transition zone (street crime, delinquency, mental illness, drug addiction, etc.) were generally "disrespectable" in character. But what of such acts as embezzlement, deceitful advertising, the abuse of governmental power, and corporate price fixing? These kinds of deviance are typically performed by "respectable" persons. Those who commit such acts are more likely to reside in the protected commuter zone than the troubled transition zone. How has disorganization theory dealt with these forms of deviance? The answer is simple. It hasn't. The disorganization perspective has been biased in its consideration of disrespectable over respectable deviance. This bias limits its utility as a general explanation of deviance.

Relative Inattention to Social Stratification

The emphasis on deviance as a natural by-product of rapid social change has led critics to suggest that the disorganization perspective fails to consider the potential causative influence of structured differences in social power and social class. Such structured differences are referred to by sociologists as social stratification. Research by the Chicago school discovered the highest rates of officially recorded deviance in the so-called transition zone. This ecological region was said to be most disorganized by social change. Deviance was its unfortunate by-product. Its residents were conceived of as victims of change. Perhaps. But isn't it just as plausible to suggest that its residents were victims of a highly unequal system of social stratification?

By describing slum dwellers as disorganized, the disorganizational perspective neglects the fact that they are also poor. Slums are the product of an unequal distribution of material resources. Yet, disorganizational theorists talk about slums as if they were somehow natural, rather than socially created. The central business zone is talked about as the natural center of change. It is also the socially structured location of powerful and privileged economic forces which exploit as well as disorganize. People are said to engage in deviance because social disorganization has robbed them of norms and constraints. Neglected is the possibility that people deviate because social stratification has robbed them of human resources and a sense of dignity.

Isn't it possible that poor people may experience higher rates of what the society officially defines as deviant, not because they lack organized normative constraints, but because they are frustrated, angry, or seeking escape from the oppression of a stratified social existence? The social disorganization perspective is relatively inattentive to such matters. Disturbing political questions about the unequal organization of our whole society are bypassed in favor of questions about the disproportionate disorganization of specific ecological sectors.

Whatever the benefits of the disorganizational metaphor, its disadvantages for the socially and economically powerless are significant. What the Chicago theorists describe as natural ecological conflict is really an unequal human struggle over the control of urban space. This is documented by John Rex and Robert Moore, whose study of ecological conflict in a British city modifies the disorganizational format by including differences in political power as a central determinant of the outcomes of competition for spatial dominance.[100] This is also a central theme in David Downes's *The Delinquent Solution*[101] and Terrence Morris's *The Criminal Area*.[102] These British researchers do not counter the Chicago school's observation that common crimes and deviance are concentrated in slums and zones of ecological transition. What differs is the interpretation of such findings. Whereas the Chicago tradition blurred the natural forces of disorganization, critical British researchers have defined disorganization as a historical by-product of social domination by the powerful.

Not all of the Chicago researchers ignored the issue of social stratification. The later work of Clifford Shaw and Henry McKay, for instance, gave increasing emphasis to structural factors related to unequal social position. As Harold Firestone observes, Shaw and McKay shifted from "an emphasis upon the 'push' factors . . . represented by . . . social disorganization" toward "the 'pull' factors represented by access to an illegitimate opportunity structure."[103] A similar observation is made by Albert J. Reiss, who suggests that "one of the great contributions of Shaw and McKay is . . . that delinquency is endemic in certain neighborhoods and that the problem of becoming delinquent is greater for persons in lower than higher income status groups."[104]

Firestone and Reiss are correct. The later work of Shaw and McKay moves beyond the confines of disorganizational theorizing by recognizing that "the struggle for space in the city is not independent of the struggle for power, prestige and material well-being in society as a whole."[105] With this in mind, we too shall move beyond the disorganizational perspective and examine several other sociological viewpoints on deviance and its control.

NOTES

1 Robert E. Park, Ernest V. Burgess, and Roderick D. McKenzie, *The City*, University of Chicago Press, Chicago, 1967, pp. 106–107.

2 Jonathan Kaplan, as quoted in David Denby, "Mondo Condo," *New York*, January 18, 1982, p. 62.

3 Ibid.
4 Ibid.
5 Albian Small, "Points of Agreement among Sociologists," *Publications of the American Sociological Society,* Vol. I, 1907, pp. 55–71.
6 Roscoe C. Hinkle, Jr., and Gisela J. Hinkle, *The Development of Modern Sociology: Its Nature and Growth in the United States,* Random House, New York, 1954, p. 21.
7 James T. Carey, *Sociology and Public Affairs: The Chicago School,* Sage, Beverly Hills, Calif., 1975, p. 29; See also E. F. Gay and L. Wolman, "Trends in Economic Organizations," *Social Trends, Recent Social Trends,* McGraw-Hill, New York, 1933, pp. 218–267.
8 Carey, *Sociology and Public Affairs,* p. 29.
9 Ibid., p. 19.
10 Ibid., pp. 19–20. See also R. D. McKenzie, "The Rise of Metropolitan Communities," in *President's Research Committee on Social Trends,* McGraw-Hill, New York, 1933, pp. 443–496.
11 Carey, *Sociology and Public Affairs,* p. 20.
12 R. G. Hurlin and M. B. Givens, "Shifting Occupational Patterns," in *President's Research Committee on Social Trends,* McGraw-Hill, New York, 1933, p. 299.
13 Carey, *Sociology and Public Affairs,* p. 16.
14 Ibid., pp. 23–27. One notable exception involves the Wall Street bombing of 1920. Yet, as Carey (p. 26) suggests, this act of protest "was apparently the work of a small group of anarchists." See also S. Cohen, "A Study in Nativism: The American Red Scare of 1919–1920," *Political Science Quarterly,* Vol. 79, March 1964, pp. 52–75. For analysis of labor during this period, see I. Berstein, *The Lean Years: Workers in an Unbalanced Society,* Houghton Mifflin, Boston, 1960.
15 W. E. Leuchtenberg, *The Perils of Prosperity, 1914–1932,* University of Chicago Press, Chicago, 1958.
16 Carey, *Sociology and Public Affairs,* p. 24.
17 Joseph Gusfield, *Symbolic Crusade: Status Politics and the American Temperance Movement,* University of Illinois Press, Urbana, 1963.
18 M. Gordon, *Assimilation in American Life,* Oxford University Press, New York, 1964.
19 R. D. Brown, "The American Vigilante Tradition," in H. D. Graham and T. R. Gurr (eds.), *Violence in America: Historical and Comparative Perspectives,* Washington, D.C., 1969; see also D. M. Chalmers, *Hooded Americanism,* Doubleday, Garden City, N.Y., 1965.
20 Maurice Zeitlin, "Who Owns America?" in Richard Quinney (ed.), *Capitalist Society,* Dorsey, Homewood, Ill., 1979, p. 60.
21 Ibid.
22 Ibid., p. 65.
23 Ibid., p. 66.
24 Carey, *Sociology and Public Affairs,* pp. 41, 34.
25 Hinkle and Hinkle, *The Development of Modern Sociology,* p. 18.
26 Robert E. L. Faris, *Chicago Sociology: 1920–1932,* Chandler, San Francisco, 1967, p. 7.
27 Carey, *Sociology and Public Affairs,* p. 64.
28 Ibid., p. 49.
29 Lewis A. Coser, *Masters of Sociological Thought: Ideas in Historical and Social Context* 2d ed., Harcourt, Brace, & Jovanovich, New York, 1977, p. 535.
30 Ibid.
31 W. I. Thomas and Florian Znaniecki, *The Polish Peasant in Europe and America,* Gorham Press, Boston, 1920.

32 W. I. Thomas and Florian Znaniecki, "The Concept of Social Disorganization," in S. H. Traub and C. B. Little (eds.), *Theories of Deviance,* Peacock, Itasca, Ill., 1975, p. 35.
33 Park, *The City,* p. 107.
34 Robert E. Park, *Human Communities,* Free Press, Glencoe, Ill., 1952, p. 118.
35 For a summary description of the work of Shaw and McKay, see Don C. Gibbons, *The Criminological Enterprise,* Prentice-Hall, Englewood Cliffs, N.J., 1979, pp. 40–46.
36 Clifford R. Shaw, Frederick M. Forgaugh, Henry D. McKay, and Leonard S. Cottreel, *Delinquency Areas,* University of Chicago Press, Chicago, 1929.
37 Clifford R. Shaw and Henry D. McKay, *Juvenile Delinquency and Urban Areas: A Study of Rates of Delinquency in Relation to Differential Characteristics of Local Communities in American Cities,* University of Chicago Press, Chicago, 1969.
38 Clifford R. Shaw and Henry D. McKay, "Juvenile Delinquency and Urban Areas," in Leon Radzinowitz and Marvin E. Wolfgang (eds.), *Crime and Justice,* Basic Books, New York, 1971, vol. I, p. 411.
39 Shaw and McKay, *Juvenile Delinquency and Urban Areas,* p. 382.
40 Ibid.
41 Ibid., p. 412.
42 Bernard Lander, *Towards an Understanding of Juvenile Delinquency,* Columbia, New York, 1954.
43 Shaw and McKay, "Juvenile Delinquency and Urban Areas," p. 418.
44 David J. Burdua "Juvenile Delinquency and Anomie: An Attempt at Replication," *Social Problems,* vol. 6, Winter 1959, pp. 230–238.
45 Roland J. Chilton, "Continuity in Delinquency Area Research: A Comparison of Studies for Baltimore, Detroit and Indianapolis," *American Sociological Review,* vol. 29, February 1964, pp. 11–83.
46 Robert E. L. Faris and H. Warren Dunham, *Mental Disorders in Urban Areas,* University of Chicago Press, Chicago, 1939.
47 Ibid., p. 95.
48 Ibid., p. 101.
49 See, for instance, August B. Hollingshead and Frederick C. Redlich, "Social Stratification and Schizophrenia," *American Sociological Review,* vol. 19, 1954, pp. 302–306; R. Lapouse et al., "The Drift Hypothesis and Socioeconomic Differentials in Schizophrenia," *American Journal of Public Health,* vol. 46, 1956, pp. 978–986; John A. Clausen and Melvin L. Kahn, "Relation of Schizophrenia to the Social Structure of a Small City," in Benjamin Pasomanick (ed.), *Epidemiology of Mental Disorder,* American Association for the Advancement of Science Publication 60, Washington, D.C., 1959, pp. 69–85.
50 Clifford R. Shaw, *The Jack Roller: A Delinquent Boy's Own Story,* University of Chicago Press, Chicago, 1930.
51 Ibid., p. 93.
52 H. A. Hodge, *Wilhelm Dilthey: An Introduction,* Routledge & Kegan Paul, London, 1944; See also Wilhelm Dilthey, "On the Special Character of the Human Sciences," in Marcello Truzzi (ed.), *Verstehen: Subjective Understanding in the Social Sciences,* Addison-Wesley, Reading, Mass., 1974, pp. 8–17.
53 Hinkle and Hinkle, *The Development of Modern Sociology,* p. 24.
54 Coser, *Masters of Sociological Thought,* p. 554.
55 Shaw and McKay, *Juvenile Delinquency and Urban Areas.*
56 Shaw, *The Jack Roller;* Clifford Shaw and Maurice Moore, *The Natural History of a Delinquent Career,* University of Chicago Press, Chicago, 1931; Clifford Shaw and James F. McDonald, *Brothers in Crime,* University of Chicago Press, Chicago, 1938.

57 W. I. Thomas, *The Unadjusted Girl,* Little, Brown, Boston, 1923; Nels Anderson, *The Hobo: The Sociology of the Homeless Man,* University of Chicago Press, Chicago, 1923; Harvey W. Zorbaugh, *Gold Coast and Slum,* University of Chicago Press, Chicago, 1929; Louis Wirth, *The Ghetto,* University of Chicago Press, Chicago, 1928; Paul G. Cressey, *The Taxi-Dance Hall: A Sociological Study of Commercialized Recreation and City Life,* University of Chicago Press, Chicago, 1932.

58 Howard Becker, "Introduction," in Shaw, *The Jack Roller,* p. viii.

59 Shaw, *The Jack Roller,* p. 19.

60 Robert E. Park, *Selected Papers,* Ralph E. Turner (ed.), University of Chicago Press, Chicago, 1967, p. xi.

61 Shaw and McKay, *Juvenile Delinquency and Urban Areas,* p. 4.

62 Terrence Morris, *The Criminal Area,* Humanities Press, New York, 1966, p. 83.

63 Martin R. Haskell and Lewis Yablonsky, *Juvenile Delinquency,* Rand McNally, Chicago, 1974, p. 423.

64 George Volk, *Theoretical Criminology,* 2d ed., prepared by Thomas J. Bernard, Oxford, New York, 1979, p. 197.

65 Allen E. Liska, *Perspectives on Deviance,* Prentice-Hall, Englewood Cliffs, N.J., 1981, p. 80.

66 Walter B. Miller, "The Impact of a 'Total-Community' Delinquency Control Project," *Social Problems,* vol. 10, Fall 1962, pp. 168–191.

67 Ibid., p. 187.

68 Morris, *The Criminal Area,* p. 84.

69 Don C. Gibbons, *The Criminological Enterprise: Theories and Perspectives,* Prentice-Hall, Englewood Cliffs, N.J., 1979, p. 45.

70 Hinkle and Hinkle, *The Development of Modern Sociology,* pp. 44–70; Carey, *Sociology and Public Affairs,* p. 119.

71 Liska, *Perspectives on Deviance,* p. 83.

72 S. Kirson Weinberg, "Shaw-McKay Theories of Delinquency in Cross-Cultural Context," in James F. Short (ed.), *Delinquency, Crime and Society,* University of Chicago Press, Chicago, 1976, pp. 167–185.

73 Marshall B. Clinard and Daniel J. Abbott, "Community Organization and Property Crime: A Comparative Study of Social Control in the Slums of an African City," in James F. Short (ed.), *Delinquency, Crime and Society,* University of Chicago Press, Chicago, 1976, pp. 186–206.

74 Weinberg, "Shaw-McKay Theories of Delinquency in Cross-Cultural Context," pp. 173, 169, 177.

75 Ibid., p. 173.

76 Marshall B. Clinard, *Cities with Little Crime: The Case of Switzerland,* Cambridge University Press, Cambridge, 1978.

77 Ibid., pp. 12–82.

78 Ibid., p. 10.

79 Ibid., p. 106.

80 Ibid., p. 111.

81 Ibid, p. 81.

82 Ibid., pp. 112–113.

83 Raymond Michalowski, "The Social and Criminal Patterns of Urban Traffic Fatalities," *British Journal of Criminology,* vol. 17, no. 2, April 1977, pp. 126–140.

84 R. T. Sollenberger, "Why Chinatown's Children Are Not Delinquent," *Transaction,* vol. 5, September 1968, p. 3.

85 The link between control theory and disorganization was first suggested by Gary Jensen, in a thoughtful review of an earlier version of this book.

86 Walter C. Reckless, *The Crime Problem,* 5th ed., Prentice-Hall, Englewood Cliffs, N.J., 1973, pp. 55–56.

87 Ibid.

88 A partial test of Reckless's idea is found in the good self-concept as containment research of Reckless and his associates at Ohio State University. See, for instance, Walter C. Reckless, Simon Dinitz, and Ellen Murray, "Self Concept as an Insulator Against Delinquency," *American Sociological Review,* vol. 21, December 1956, pp. 744–756; Walter Reckless, Simon Dinitz, and Barbara Kay, "The Self-Component in Potential Delinquency and Potential Non-Delinquency," *American Sociological Review,* vol. 22, October 1957, pp. 566–570; Frank R. Scarpitti, Ellen Murray, Simon Dinitz, and Walter C. Reckless, "The 'Good Boy' in a High Delinquency Area: Four Years Later," *American Sociological Review,* vol. 25, August 1960, pp. 555–558; and Walter C. Reckless and Simon Dinitz, "Pioneering with Self-Concept as a Vulnerability Factor in Delinquency," *Journal of Criminal Law, Criminology and Police Science,* vol. 58, December 1967, p. 517.

For criticism of this research, see Clarence Schrag, *Crime and Justice: American Style,* National Institute of Mental Health, Rockville, Md., 1971, p. 88; Michael Schwartz and Sandra S. Tangri, "A Note on Self-Concept as an Insulator Against Delinquency," *American Sociological Review,* vol. 30, December 1965, pp. 922–926; Sandra S. Tangri and Michael Schwartz, "Delinquency Research and the Self Concept Variable," *Journal of Criminal Law, Criminology and Police Science,* vol. 58, June 1967, pp. 182–190; James Orcutt, "Self Concept and Insulation Against Delinquency: Some Critical Notes," *Sociological Quarterly,* vol. 2, Summer 1970, pp. 381–390.

89 Travis Hirschi, *Causes of Delinquency,* University of California Press, Berkeley, 1969.

90 Ibid., p. 16.

91 Ibid., p. 22. An edited composite of excerpts from several confidential biographical essays written for a course in deviant behavior at a large midwestern university during the mid - 1970s.

92 Michael T. Hindelang, "Causes of Delinquency: A Partial Replication and Extension," *Social Problems,* vol. 20, Spring 1973, pp. 471–487.

93 Eric Linden and James C. Hackler, "Affective Tie and Delinquency," *Pacific Sociological Review,* vol. 16, January 1973, pp. 27–46; Rand Conger, "Social Control and Social Learning Models of Delinquency: A Synthesis," *Criminology,* vol. 14, May 1976, pp. 17–40.

94 Carey, *Sociology and Public Affairs,* p. 119.

95 Robert E. L. Faris and H. Warren Dunham, *Mental Disorders in Urban Areas,* University of Chicago Press, Chicago, 1939, pp. 8–9.

96 For an overview of this issue, see Ritchie P. Lowry, *Social Problems: A Critical Analysis of Theories and Public Policy,* Heath, Lexington, Mass., 1974, pp. 164–167.

97 Lee Rainwater and William L. Yancey, *The Moynihan Report and the Politics of Controversy,* M.I.T. Press, Cambridge, Mass., 1967.

98 Lawrence Rosen, "Matriarchy and Lower Class Negro Male Delinquency," *Social Problems,* vol. 17, Fall 1969, pp. 175–189; Lee Rainwater and William L. Yancey, "Black Families and the White House," *Transaction,* vol. 3, July/August 1966, pp. 6–11, 48–53.

99 Reynolds Farley and Albert I. Hermalin, "Family Stability: A Comparison of Trends Between Blacks and Whites," *American Sociological Review,* vol. 36, February 1971, pp. 1–17.

100 John Rex and Robert Moore, *Race, Community and Conflict: A Study in Sparkbrook,* Oxford University Press, London, 1967.
101 David Downes, *The Delinquent Solution,* Routledge & Kegan Paul, London, 1966.
102 Terrence Morris, *The Criminal Area,* Humanities Press, New York, 1966.
103 Harold Firestone, "The Delinquent and Society: The Shaw and McKay Tradition," in James F. Short (ed.), *Delinquency, Crime and Society,* University of Chicago Press, Chicago, 1976, p. 33.
104 Albert J. Reiss, Jr., "Settling the Frontiers of a Pioneer in American Criminology: Henry McKay," in James F. Short (ed.), *Delinquency, Crime and Society,* University of Chicago Press, Chicago, 1976, p. 71.
105 Ian Taylor, Paul Walton, and Jock Young, *The New Criminology: For a Social Theory of Deviance,* Harper & Row, New York, 1973, p. 119.

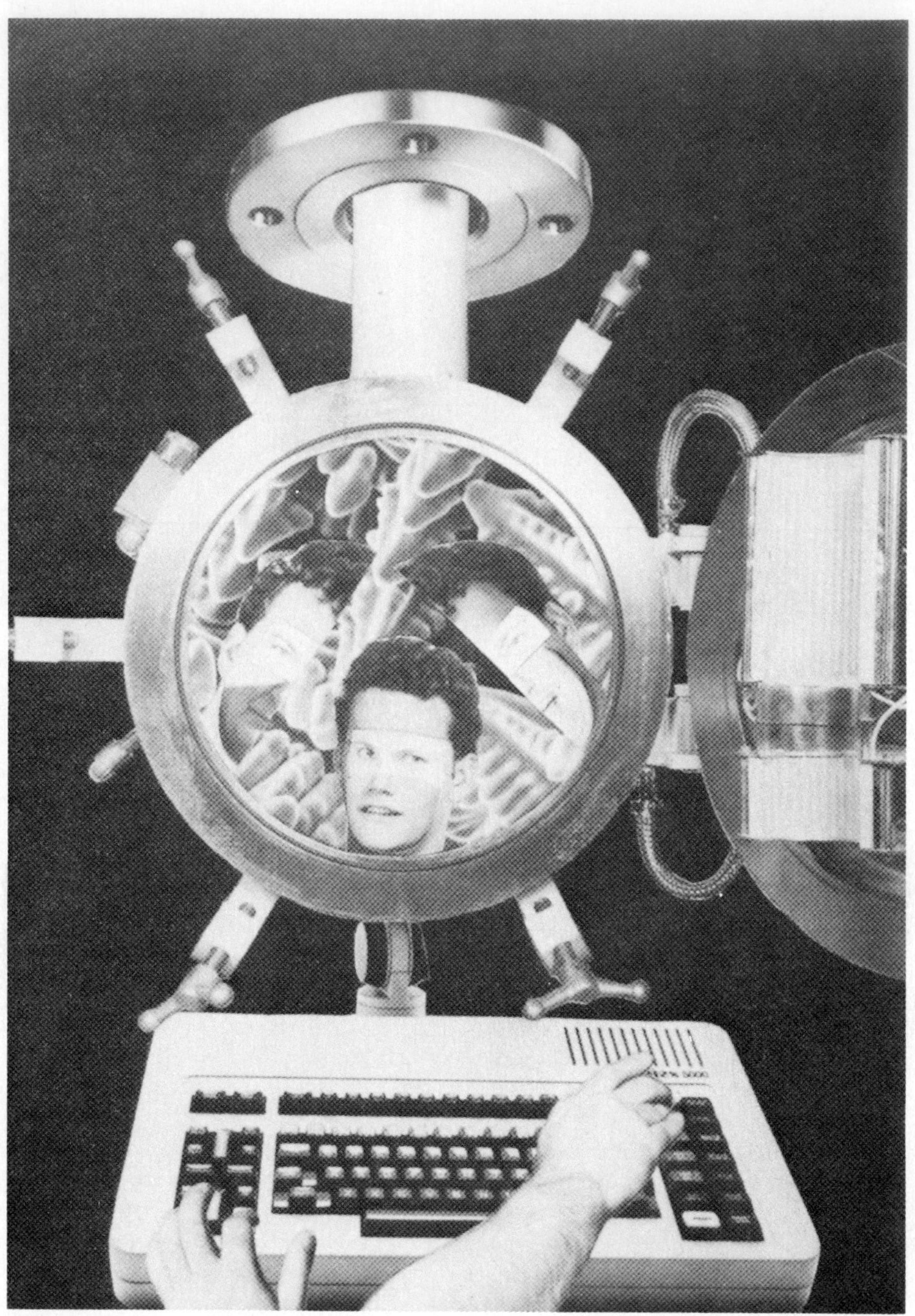

The Social Machine. It turns me on. By Joseph LaMantia and Stephen Pfohl

CHAPTER **6**

THE FUNCTIONALIST PERSPECTIVE: *Order and Disorder; The Functions and Dysfunctions of Deviance*

Crime is . . . necessary; it is bound up with the fundamental conditions of all social life, and by that very fact it is useful.

Émile Durkheim[1]

Societies somehow "need" their quotas of deviants and function in such a way as to keep them intact.

Kai T. Erikson[2]

INTRODUCTION

In 1978 photographer Inge Morath and author Arthur Miller traveled extensively throughout China. Everywhere they were confronted with a singular theme—that nearly all of China's current troubles had been caused by a small band of deviants, the Gang of Four. Indeed, this quartet of former political officials, whose number include Jiang Qing, Mao's wife, was said to be responsible for everything from inefficient work practices to generalized moral decay, governmental corruption, and a rash of personal and political violence. According to Miller:

> From our first hour in China my wife and I were regaled—pelted, bathed, swabbed would be better words—with accounts of the depredations of the Gang of Four. After the initial shock it almost began to seem funny to be blaming the ills of a country of perhaps one billion on three men and one woman, and it was difficult at first to take absolutely seriously.[3]

Blaming the ills of 1 billion on four people! What was the real meaning of the massive Chinese attack on the evildoing of the Gang of Four? It seems that China was scapegoating all its tensions on a few sacrificial political victims. In 1978 China was in the process of reorganizing its political, economic, and cultural institutions in the wake of the death of its long-time leader, Mao Zedong. Following Mao's death a new group of less radical leaders rose to power. These more bureaucratically minded Chinese officials sought to erase a legacy of mass collective action and ongoing cultural revolution. One means by which to accomplish this goal was to attack the Gang of Four, close allies of Mao identified with the "popular justice" practices of his regime. According to sociologist Jim Brady the trial of the Gang of Four was a spectacular attempt to showcase the values of the new revisionist Chinese regime.[4] Nobody could literally believe that the gang was personally responsible for the 34,000 deaths and multitudinous acts of deviance with which it was charged. The issue was more symbolic. By dramatically condemning all that was bad about the Gang of Four, the new regime was simultaneously underscoring all that it believed was good. Would this reverse itself someday? At some later time would the goodness of the Gang of Four be resurrected? Would the deviants of 1978 become the saints of a decade later?

Such questions were asked by journalists and political analysts during the several years in which Chinese society ritualistically decried the deviance of the Gang of Four. These questions could be asked about other forms of deviance as well. Behind these questions is another, deeper question—does deviance contribute something positive to society? We are almost conditioned to say no. We have been informed since childhood that deviance is something negative. Nonetheless, the benefits derived by Chinese society from having the Gang of Four around as objects of public scorn and condemnation suggest that the consequences of deviance may sometimes be positive (at least for those who benefit most from current social arrangements). What about our society? Do we also derive a certain benefit from having juvenile delinquents, political dissidents, homosexuals, and welfare recipients around to condemn and symbolize "what is really wrong with society today"? It is this question that the functionalist perspective asks us to consider.

THE THEORETICAL IMAGES OF FUNCTIONAL DEVIANCE

The functionalist perspective on deviance is unique in that it emphasizes the positive contributions of deviance. Something is defined as functional if it has positive consequences for the organization of society as a whole. If its consequences are negative it is dysfunctional. Deviance is said to be functional because it strengthens the bonds of an existing social order. This view of deviance as constructive originates in the late-nineteenth-century writings of the French social theorist Émile Durkheim.

Durkheim: Searching for the Moral Integration of the Social Organisms

Durkheim, who in 1887 taught the first French university course in sociology, was preoccupied with the problems of social modernity, with the normative disintegration generated by the transition from a simple to a complex society.

Durkheim's concern with the moral crisis of his age led him to view sociology as a scientific solution for social disruption. Religious belief and philosophical speculation were seen as no longer capable of providing a sense of collective social order. The basis of a new modern order would await the lawlike findings of scientific sociology. For Durkheim sociology was first and foremost a science of morals. As Lewis Coser points out:

> Durkheim . . . wanted to devote himself to a discipline that would contribute to the clarification of the great moral questions that agitate the age, as well as to practical guidance of the affairs of contemporary society. . . . What he considered imperative was to construct a scientific sociological system, not as an end in itself, but as a means for the moral direction of society.[5]

As a "moral scientist" Durkheim attempted to identify the necessary or normal features of any healthily functioning society. He also sought to analyze the conditions under which the normative could be restored in societies endangered by the pathology of disintegration. According to Durkheim a pathological society was one in which norms were paradoxically either too strong or too weak. When they were too strong, society would be overly conformist, unable to flexibly adapt to changing environmental circumstances. When they were too weak, it would be too loosely defined and its members too weakly joined to accomplish basic tasks needed to assure its own survival. Durkheim's analysis of the pathological "looseness" of modern society is examined in the discussion of the anomie perspective in Chapter 7. In this chapter we explore Durkheim's view of deviance as normal.

Deviance as Normal: Contributions to Moral Integration

In *The Rules of the Sociological Method* Durkheim argued that a social phenomenon was normal if it was both universal and necessary. By universal, Durkheim meant that something must be present in all, or the majority of all, societies of the same type. By necessary he meant that it represented a determining condition, i.e., that it was needed for the continued existence of society. If both criteria were met, something could be deemed normal. Such was the case with crime or deviance, an aspect of social life that Durkheim viewed as universally present and as the product of certain determining conditions which necessitated its existence. This is the essence of Durkheim's view of deviance as functional. It was an omnipresent feature of social life necessary for the existence of a stable social order. In Durkheim's own words:

> Crime is present not only in the majority of societies of one particular species but in all societies of all types. There is no society that is not confronted with the problem of criminality. . . . [This] is not to say merely that it is an inevitable, although regrettable phenomenon, due to the incorrigible wickedness of men; it is to affirm that it is a factor in public health, an integral part of all healthy societies.[6]

According to Durkheim and other functionalists, deviance contributes to social order in several ways: by setting moral boundaries, strengthening in group solidarity, allowing for adaptive innovation, and reducing internal societal tensions.

Boundary-Setting Function The boundary-setting function of deviance was first discussed by Durkheim in *The Rules of the Sociological Method*. Deviance was said to help define the moral boundaries which distinguish between right and wrong. In sanctioning the deviant, society informs its members of the type of person they cannot become and still live "normally" within its boundaries. It symbolizes what we are to avoid and reminds us of the sanctions we face if we stray beyond established normative conventions. Such boundary marking enables us to know what is expected of us. We are provided with a kind or moral map to guide us in the dos and don'ts of everyday social life.

For Durkheim the boundary-setting functions of deviance had a certain elasticity. Even if a society was extremely conformist, deviance would not disappear. It would merely be redefined in narrower terms. What had previously been acceptable may not be condemned. The boundaries would be drawn more tightly. As an example, Durkheim asks us to "image a society of saints, a perfect cloister of exemplary individuals. Crimes, properly so called, will be there unknown: but faults which appear venial to the layman will create there the same scandal that the ordinary offense does in ordinary consciousness."[7] Thus while specific forms of deviance may vary, some forms must exist in every society. Without deviance there will be no moral boundaries, and without such boundaries there can be no society.

Group Solidarity Function In addition to setting boundaries, deviance may also bring society together against a common enemy. It may increase group solidarity for those united in collective opposition to the normative threats of nonconformity. To wage war against deviant "outsiders" may thus strengthen the social bonds of non-deviant "insiders."

Although noted by Durkheim, the group function of deviance is nowhere better expressed than in the writings of the early American sociologist and philosopher George Herbert Mead. In "The Psychology of Punitive Justice," Mead states that "the revulsions against criminality reveal themselves in a sense of solidarity within the group . . . [which] inhibits tendencies to criminal acts in the citizen himself."[8]

Innovation Functions The functionalist perspective also recognizes that overly rigid boundaries may limit a society's adaptability. Imagine that a particular society had become extremely successful in controlling and creating conformity. On one hand such a society may appear to be very strong. On the other hand, it may be weakened in its capacity to flexibly adapt to an ever-changing external environment. It might become locked into outdated traditions, unable to adjust to the new, and thereby would stagnate or wither away. Innovative deviance encourages society to revise its rules in response to new environmental problems. In Durkheim's words:

> Where crime exists, collective sentiments are sufficiently flexible to take on a new form, and crime sometimes helps to determine the form they will take. How many times, indeed, it is only an anticipation of future morality—a step toward what will be.[9]

Deviance may help society to adapt by challenging the foundation of old and outdated rules. The deviant rule-breaker of today may be an innovator of new rules tomorrow. Durkheim cites the example of Socrates. Although Socrates was condemned as a deviant thinker in his own day, his ideas later came to constitute a new basis for conformity. More recently, Martin Luther King exemplifies the deviant as an innovator. King clearly deviated from the social boundaries established by a racist and segregated society. He deliberately broke laws which he considered to be morally objectionable, laws that subordinated blacks to whites. In doing so he paid the price of being deviant. He was harassed, arrested, and beaten by "normal" citizens and by those empowered to guard the "acceptable" social boundaries. Yet, through the deviance of Martin Luther King and his followers the boundaries of race relations in the United States came to be partially altered. The acceptable social rules he once opposed are now themselves illegal. His deviant actions paved the way for a subsequent redefinition of normative social boundaries.

Tension-Reduction Function Deviance may also be useful by functioning as a safety valve for strains within society itself. Society sometimes projects its own problems onto the shoulders of some deviant group. Minorities, for instance, may be blamed for tensions produced by society as a whole. By scapegoating its own problems on witches, hippies, Jews, Communists, welfare recipients, or homosexuals, society may temporarily drain off some of its own self-produced contradictions and tensions.

The tension-reduction idea also recognizes that a bit of deviance may drain off some of the tensions that people accumulate in their day-to-day attempts to conform to the announced rules of society's game. In previous times a socially sanctioned "feast of fools" was a common part of the calendar year. On such a day people were permitted to deviate from the routine restraints of conformist living, to let off steam.[10] One wonders if "getting crazy" on weekends and "fooling around" at the annual professional convention are not modern-day counterparts to such ritualistically scheduled times for letting off steam.

Latent Functions of Deviance Besides identifying the positive consequences of deviance, functionalist theorists distinguish those consequences which are recognized and intended from those which are not. Recognized and intended consequences are referred to as manifest functions. Unrecognized and unintended contributions are called latent functions. Deviance is usually seen as manifestly dysfunctional. It is controlled against because society recognizes its disintegrating consequences. Nonetheless it may at the same time have latent functions. For this reason certain acts may be manifestly condemned but latently permitted.

The distinction between manifest and latent functions is attributed to the sociologist Robert K. Merton.[11] Merton applied this distinction in analyzing the corrupt big-city political machine. Manifestly the lawless practices of the machine were dysfunctional to a society ordered by the rule of law. Latently, the machine helps create order by integrating people who were integrative and by meeting the needs of marginal urban subgroups, such as immigrant or ethnic minorities. As an efficient provider of extralegal services, it maximized the political privileges of "underdogs" and "topdogs" alike. As an intermediary in the plight of the urban needy, the machine was functionally superior to the slow and impersonal workings of the official government bureaucracy.

Another example of the latent functions of deviance is found in Kingsley Davis's study of prostitution.[12] Although Davis makes certain assumptions which today we would probably recognize as sexist, his work illustrates the ease with which functionalist theorists can find positive consequences for just about anything. Prostitution is said to have manifest dysfunctions for a society which normatively confines legitimate sexual relationships to married heterosexual couples. The married couple is said to express the combined sexual goals of reproduction and sentimental attachment. The prostitute, who exchanges sex for money, defies both of these goals and is thus manifestly condemned and subject to criminal sanctioning.

Although prostitution is manifestly condemned it is rarely shut off entirely. Prostitutes (and only recently their customers) are periodically rounded up and cycled through short periods of imprisonment. They are not once and for all eliminated. In fact, observes Davis, this oldest of professions has existed throughout most of human history. Why? Latently it must be playing some important function, contributing some needed social service. Davis locates its contribution by examining what he assumes is a higher male need for sexual adventure or experimentation. Although today most sexually knowledgeable men and women would regard this premise as absurd, at the time Davis did his work the assumption was probably culturally widespread. Following this premise one could reasonably foresee certain structural tensions arising within the marriage dyad. Higher sexual needs would constantly push the male outside the coupled unit. If he directed his sexual energies toward another "eligible" female, sex might soon be infused with love and the male would be caught between loves (the eternal triangle and all that). This division of affections would inevitably produce high rates of marital conflict, divorce, and assumed societal instability. But what if a male's excessive sexual need was to be met by a "noneligible" female, one who exchanged sex not for love but for money. Sentimental attachments would not be formed. Male sexual drives could be expressed without getting connected with love. Sex with a prostitute would thus provide a useful contribution to social order. Latently prostitution would protect the emotional bonds which preserved marriages and at the same time would permit men to realize their supposedly higher sexual needs. By such functionalist logic, Davis "discovered" the latent functions of prostitution.

In the 1960s and 1970s major changes in sexual attitudes, behaviors, and understandings have occurred, such that we are increasingly aware that males and females display equal degrees of sexual interest. Given this new awareness, let us speculatively extend the functionalist narrative outlined above. It is possible that a recognition of equalitarian needs for sexual adventure or experimentation accounted for an increase in "swinging," another manifestly deviant sexual activity, while at the same time promoting a decrease in the need for prostitution? Swinging, or "mate swapping," gained much attention in the late sixties and early seventies.[13] These terms refer to the highly organized way that some modern spouses permit their mates to pursue sexual relations outside of marriage without threatening the marriage. What distinguishes swinging from other forms of extramarital sexual involvement is that husbands and wives who swing generally agree to have sexual relations with other persons, couples, or groups at the same time and place. Swingers might, for instance, go together to a private club or party where it is understood that at some point in the evening they will be permitted and encouraged to have free and impersonal sex with others.

Couples typically find out about or are recruited into swinging in one of several ways. Some may be attracted to experimenting with mate swapping by learning about swinging clubs or bars. Others may learn about swinging from experienced couples who pass the word or invite friends to join them in the pursuit of carefully controlled nonmonogynous and nonmonandrous sexual pleasure. Still others may read of this deviance in one of a variety of swinger magazines, or by simply perusing the personal ad sections of many "respectable" publications.

Is it possible that the impersonal sexual exchanges engaged in through swinging are a functional equivalent of the latent consequences of prostitution outlined by Davis? Those who have studied swinging contend that it permits participants to release sexual fantasies for an evening or a weekend without damaging the sentimental bond of marriage. In an article subtitled "The Family That Swings Together Clings Together," Diane Denfield and Michael Gordon report that swinging may actually prolong marriage.[14] Romantic involvements are taboo among most swingers in much the same manner as between prostitutes and their customers. According to the suggestive logic of functionalist analysis, both types of deviance may be viewed as latently positive for society as a whole.

IDENTIFYING FUNCTIONAL DEVIANCE

There is no one research strategy that is the exclusive property of functionalist theory. Nonetheless, most functionalist interpretations of deviance are based upon a relatively common set of analytic assumptions. These constrain researchers to see nonconformity in a particular way. Functional analysis begins with the assumption that deviance must be studied in terms of its relationship to society as a whole. Functionalist theorists view society as a system of interrelated parts or structures. Each part is to be examined for its relationship to others and to the operation of the entire system. Each part is to be analyzed for the way it contributes to or detracts from the integrated survival of the system. This image of social life as a system of interrelated parts is present in Durkheim's choice of an organic metaphor to describe the workings of society.

In contemporary sociological theory the functional interrelationship of systemic parts is a central concern in the highly influential writings of sociologist Talcott Parsons. For Parsons functionalist analysis involves "relating all problems explicitly and systematically to the total system."[15] His book *The Social System* includes a detailed catalog of the functional contributions of all major parts of the system to the system.[16] Parsons's work is considered in greater detail in our subsequent discussion of the social control of functional deviance. At present it is sufficient for us to ask how Durkheim, Parsons, and other functionalist theorists sought to document claims regarding the positive contributions of deviance.

According to Durkheim, for functional analysis to be properly scientific, it must separate the study of what causes a particular social phenomenon from an examination of its consequences. For the study of deviance this meant that observations regarding its universal presence were to be analytically distinct from those considering its cause or determining conditions. For Durkheim this rule was stronger in principle than in practice. Durkheim's "analyses of actual phenomena . . . lapsed into assertions that the need for integration caused a particular event."[17] This resulted in the twin problems of *tautology* (circular reasoning) and *false teleology* (the assertion that things like deviance happen in order to realize the goals of the system, without specifying how exactly the system causes these functional activities to arise in the first place).

The problems of tautology and false teleology sound very abstract. They nonetheless create very concrete and practical problems for the truth claims of functional analysis. Consider tautology. To suggest that deviance is functional for society because it can be found (universally) in every society represents a kind of circular logic. Because it exists it must be functional! If it were not functional it would not exist! Such reasoning catches us in a circle of word games. It tells us very little about the specific reasons that deviance is found in all societies. Durkheim was aware of this problem. He argued that the functionality of deviance cannot be determined solely by the criteria of universality. In order to know whether deviance is truly functional we are asked to consider a second criterion—the criterion of determining conditions.

What exactly are these determining conditions? What exactly causes deviance to come into being and be sustained as a continuing phenomenon within all societies? On this issue Durkheim is unfortunately vague. His answer seems to slip into the region of false teleology. In *The Rules of the Sociological Method,* Durkheim cautions functionalist researchers to avoid this problem. False teleology, he argues, arises when researchers assume that social phenomena come into being because society needs them to survive. This assumption confuses the study of cause with that of function. Society may need deviance. Yet, as Durkheim points out, "The need we have of things cannot give them existence."[18] This is not to say that once some needed thing comes into being it will not be reciprocally supported by the very society which needed it in the first place. As Anthony Giddens remarks, Durkheim's attempt to avoid false teleology by separating the study of cause from the study of functional consequences did not prevent him from positing a reciprocal relation between these two things.[19] According to Durkheim, "The effect can doubtless not exist without its cause; but the latter, in turn, needs its effect. It is from the cause that the effect draws its energy; but it also restores it to the cause on occasion, and consequently it cannot disappear without the cause showing the effects of its disappearance."[20]

For Durkheim the effects of deviance are to secure integrated social stability while allowing for flexible adaptive change. These are its primary functional contributions. These effects are what makes deviance normal. But what actually causes deviance, and how do its effects "on occasion" restore energy to its cause? If you as a reader think such matters to be vague and highly abstract you are not incorrect. Durkheim provides us with very little concrete information about the actual causes of normal deviance or about the ways its effects reinforce these causes. We are left, instead, with a series of statements which pair the existence of deviance with its functional contributions. Crime or deviance, states Durkheim, "is a factor in public health, an integral part of all healthy societies. . . . [I]t is bound up with the fundamental conditions of all social life, and by that very fact it is useful, because these conditions of which it is a part are themselves indispensable to . . . normal evolution."[21]

Durkheim warns us not to equate the functions of deviance with goal-like end-states which are said to cause their own realization. Yet by pairing the existence of deviance with its functional contributions Durkheim provides just such an equation. At other points Durkheim moves even closer to suggesting that functional needs operate (teleologically) as goals which set in motion certain processes which guarantee goal fulfillment. In discussing the possibility that society could curb all crime or deviance, Durkheim suggests that "the very cause which would thus dry up the sources of criminality would immediately open up new ones. Indeed, for the collective sentiments which are protected by the penal law . . . to take hold of the public conscience . . . they must acquire an intensity greater than that which they had hitherto had."[22] Here Durkheim comes dangerously close to false teleology. What causes greater intensity in the penal sanctioning of deviance? Its cause becomes equated with its functional consequence—the collective sentiments it produces. Why? We are left, at least implicitly, with the idea that a need for social integration operates as a goal or end-state which paradoxically produces the deviance which produces it. Here Durkheim tilts heavily in the direction of false teleology. He tells us virtually nothing about the original causes of deviance or about the process of reciprocal causation in which functional effects feed back upon that which caused them. Despite intentions to the contrary, Durkheim's functional analysis remains trapped in a mire of confusing tautologies and unwarranted teleological reasoning. After reading what Durkheim has to say about the functional contributions of deviance one is left with the distinct sense that deviance exists because it is brought into being to fulfill the purposes or goals of society as an organic system.

Few theorists have fared better than Durkheim in overcoming the problems of tautology and false teleology. These problems seem endemic to functional analysis. Nonetheless, one recent theorist, Robert K. Merton, has provided a methodological guide designed to eliminate many of the shortcomings of previous functionalist theorizing.[23] According to Merton functionalist researchers must avoid all assumptions regarding (1) the harmonious integration of all parts of a social system, (2) the relationship between the existence of a social phenomenon and the belief that it must contribute to the maintenance of the social whole, and (3) the idea that genuine societal needs can only be served by the structural unit which appears to positively or functionally contribute to the fulfillment of such needs in the present. There can, in other words, be various alternative structural paths for fulfilling even the most basic of society's needs.

Merton's suggestions have important implications for the study of deviance. By not assuming the harmonious integration of all parts of the system, Merton paves the way for functionalists to consider the possibility that deviance may be functional for some people (i.e., those who benefit the most from the way that social life is organized at the present time) but dysfunctional for others (i.e., those who benefit least from the existing system, particularly those who are condemned, punished, or ostracized as deviants). By not assuming that because a particular pattern of social interaction exists it must be functional, Merton directs attention to the "net balance" of positive and negative consequences. This provides a corrective for an otherwise one-sided emphasis on positive contributions. Also to be considered is the possibility of both manifest (recognized and intended) and latent (unrecognized and unintended) functions. Recall the previous discussion of the manifest and latent consequences of prostitution and the corrupt political machine. Moreover, by not assuming that there is only one structural alternative for fulfilling a particular social need, Merton asks us to explicitly compare alternative means for fulfilling that same need.

Why, for instance, does our society rely so heavily on correcting the deviant rather than on changing the societal conditions out of which deviance grows or generating efforts to reconcile offenders and those offended? These strategies represent divergent alternatives to the problem of nonconformity. A more traditional (and more tautological and falsely teleological) functionalism might simply assume that the present state of things exists because it contributes positively to the entire society. Merton's functional analysis is more careful. Once it has identified the dominant alternative employed to control deviance, it seeks to locate its causal origins. It does this, not by identifying its contributions to society as a whole, but by examining its relationship to a host of other socially structured economic, political, and cultural alternatives. Merton's program of functional analysis is designed for researchers who wish to explain the causes of particular forms of deviance and social control and to assess the net balance of their positive and negative consequences. According to Merton a proper functionalist analysis must follow five steps.

1 *Provide a specific description of the form of deviance or social control being studied.* (How are activities structured or patterned between specific actors or groups or organizations under investigation? The research is instructed to describe as precisely as possible the dominant pattern of interaction followed by the social units under analysis.)

2 *Indicate the range and type of alternatives excluded by the dominant pattern of deviance or social control.* (This methodological prescription is aimed at directing researchers' attention to what Merton calls the "structural context" in which a particular pattern of deviance or social control emerged. Consider the topic of child abuse. Why, for instance, are more lower-class parents officially discovered as abusers than middle- and upper-class parents? Why is it so common for abusers to report that they too had been abused as children? Why when laws were passed to control child abuse was preference given to control strategies based upon therapeutic treatment rather than corrective punishment? By exploring such questions Merton hoped that researchers would derive clues as to both the causes and functional [or dysfunctional] consequences of observed interaction patterns.)

3 *Assess the meaning of the deviant or social control activity for those involved.* (What does deviance or control work mean subjectively to those who engage in it? By asking this question Merton hoped that functional analysts would arrive at some insights into the manifest or intended consequences of a particular activity. Once again, consider the matter of child abuse. Why is it that so many abusive parents state that they did nothing to "really" hurt their child. What does the administration of brutal punishment actually mean to a parent who beats his or her child? On the social control side of the problem, how is it that child abuse means so much to the large army of medical practitioners who today fight against it, while before the 1960s, when child abuse was first discovered as a major social problem, most doctors saw some unexplained physical trauma as the cause of mysterious childhood bruises, broken bones, and lacerations?)

4 *Discern the motives for conforming to or deviating from a particular dominant interaction pattern.* (Here Merton refers the research to the social-psychological needs served or not served by conforming to or deviating from a particular action pattern. In this search Merton hoped to further uncover clues to the consequences which certain deviant or control practices create for actors in a given society. What does acting in a certain fashion do for people? By asking this question Merton's functionalism seeks to connect the individual deviant or controller to structured patterns in society at large.)

5 *Describe patterns not recognized by participants but which appear to have consequences for either the particular individuals involved and/or other patterns or regularities in the wider social context.* (The aim here is to examine potentially latent consequences of deviance or control work which, even if they escape the attention of actors involved, may affect the activities being studied by affecting other activities in related sectors of society.)

The five principles for functional analysis outlined by Merton are today considered to be the most comprehensive guidelines for this approach to social research and theory building. In principle they avoid the circular and falsely teleological problems encountered by Durkheim and other early functionalists. In practice the application of these principles may be considerably elusive. This is particularly true regarding the notion of latent consequences. Consider Merton's analysis of the latent positive functions of the corrupt big-city political machine. Merton states:

> Proceeding from the functional view . . . we should ordinarily (not invariably) expect persistent social patterns and social structures to perform positive functions which are at the time not fulfilled by other patterns and structures, the thought occurs that perhaps this publicly maligned organization is, under present conditions, satisfying basic latent functions.[24]

Despite his warnings against assuming a relationship between persisting patterns and contributing functions, Merton starts out with (almost) just such an assumption. The phrase "not invariably" may spare Merton the charge of being technically tautological. Yet, the "thought" which occurs to him that the "maligned organization" may be "satisfying latent functions" appears to represent a serious lapse into false teleological reasoning. Does the machine really operate to fulfill societal needs? Was this happening even if nobody intended it to happen? Was this happening even if nobody, until Merton, recognized that it was happening? How easy it is for even the most careful of functional theorists to see systemic needs behind every act of deviance. Perhaps functional deviance can never fully escape the dual trap of tautology and false teleology.

SOCIAL CONTROL OF FUNCTIONAL DEVIANCE

Following Durkheim the functionalist perspective recognizes the positive, or functional, contributions of deviance. Some deviance is good for the system. But what about a lot of deviance? Isn't deviance dysfunctional as well? Durkheim thought so. His statements about the usefulness of deviance were prefaced by the qualification that it must not exceed a certain level. Excess deviance was seen as pathological rather than normal. According to Durkheim, "This excess is . . . undoubtedly morbid in nature. What is normal . . . is the existence of criminality, provided that it attains and does not exceed . . . a certain level."[25]

The problems of excess deviance are of great concern to modern functionalists such as Talcott Parsons. Until his death in 1979, Parsons was the foremost functionalist theorist in sociology. Like Durkheim, Parsons considered society as a "thing in itself." The healthy society was equated with the stable society. The social activities of its members would be highly coordinated as interrelated parts of an organic system. By such coordination the social system fulfilled its basic needs.

What are the basic needs of society? According to Parsons there are four functional prerequisites for the survival of any social system.[26] These include: (1) *adaptation* to the external environment; (2) *integration* of all of the system's parts, such that the values, roles, interests, and motives of its members contribute to the orderly operation of society as a whole; (3) *goal attainment,* or the coordinated, cooperative achievement of collective social objectives; and (4) *pattern-maintenance tension reduction* (also referred to as "latency"), the ongoing recruitment of individuals into the patterned social roles needed to keep the system functioning and mechanisms to reduce the systemic strains of conformity.

Parsons suggests that basic social institutions arise to fulfill the needs outlined above. Social institutions are defined as relatively stable patterns of interaction between actors whose roles in the system are governed by an internalized set of norms or expectations. Basic institutions rise up to meet each of the basic societal needs or functional requisites. Economic institutions develop relatively stable ways of adapting to society's external physical and human environment, to natural resources and the demands of other social systems. By providing a system of commonly shared beliefs and values the institution of religion was said to play a central role in integration. Political institutions contribute to setting and realizing societywide goals. Educational institutions teach people necessary social roles. Education thus functions as an institution of pattern maintenance. The family, in both teaching and supporting its members in doing their part, also serves a pattern-maintenance function. So too can it act as an institution of tension reduction. After a hard day's work family members return home, where they are often permitted to blow off the steam accumulated in conforming to prescribed institutional norms. When tensions become too great, people may deviate. When this happens other tension-reduction institutions are mobilized to back up the family. Such social control institutions range from those which use therapy to return actors to their expected roles to those which use coercion to enforce conformity.

Parsons's vision of social life as an equilibrium-producing system is highly mechanistic. It likens the exchange between individual parts of the system to the cybernetic exchange between parts of a self-regulating machine. Strains or tensions in one part, between parts, or between one system and another are said to produce adjustive reactions by which the system restabilizes itself. This description of the self-adjusting system is pictured as society's response to deviance. The onset of deviance sets into motion control mechanisms to dissolve tension and return the system to equilibrium. For Parsons deviance was like the overheating of a part within a machine containing a built-in "cool-out component." When the temperature rises above a certain safety point an automatic sprinkler is activated to reduce the heat. Deviance is like the heat. Social control is like the automatic sprinkling component.

For Parsons and other modern functionalists, the heat of excessive deviance was cooled by four mechanisms of social control: socialization, profit, persuasion, and (when all else fails) coercion.[27] If socialization was totally successful, no other mechanism would be needed. Socialization teaches people to internalize the patterned roles necessary for achieving ordered social equilibrium. When socialization is imperfect, profit and persuasion arise as additional mechanisms to secure conformity. Profit reinforces equilibrium-producing behaviors. It teaches us that we get payoffs when we conform and punishment when we don't. Payoffs can range from such things as obtaining a good grade or a top salary to getting the desired smile from a person we value. Punishment can run the same wide gamut.

In singling out persuasion as the third mechanism of control, Parsons suggests that people organize their lives as much by symbols as by practical rewards. Sometimes persuasion attempts to correct an existing pattern of deviance. The minister delivering a sermon to sinners and the psychiatrist who exhorts patients to gain insight into their psychological deviance are using persuasion as a corrective. Other forms of persuasion aim at preventing deviance. Think of television advertising. This form of persuasion may induce us to adopt a certain look, feel, or way of acting that is compatible with the dominant economic (adaptive), political (goal attainment), religious (integrative), and family-educational (pattern maintenance–tension reduction) institutions of our day.

Socialization, profit, and persuasion are together said to contribute to social control by providing, reinforcing, and legitimizing lines of conformity. When socialization is imperfect, when profit is lacking, when persuasion is weak, the likelihood of deviance increases. Members become alienated from society. They become lost within the machine—dysfunctional parts which endanger the system's equilibrium. Such alienation may be active or passive and could involve either a direct rejection of conformity or an indirect avoidance of doing the "responsible" thing. Active rejection is associated with hostile or aggressive deviance. Passive rejection involves withdrawal, perhaps into a world of "madness." An active and compulsive avoidance of responsibility is illustrated by the career of the hobo. On the other hand, the alcoholic and the drug abuser may represent a more passive form of responsibility avoidance. Modern functionalism views all of these types of deviance as examples of the failure of socialization, profit, and persuasion. If unchecked they pave a destructive path of disequilibrium. To limit this disequilibrium, society must institute a fourth mechanism of control—coercion.

For functionalists, coercion is society's trump card in the game of social control. Its concern with curtailing the forces of disorder underscores the need and legitimacy of coercive state power. According to functionalists the state must exercise its prerogative to constrain nonconformists, even if by violence.

THE FUNCTIONALIST PERSPECTIVE TODAY

Although the origins of functionalist theory are commonly traced to Durkheim, it was under the guidance of Talcott Parsons that functionalism emerged as the dominant perspective in American sociology during the 1950s. Its preeminence continued until the mid-1960s, when a variety of competing perspectives arose, challenging its grip on the sociological imagination. Before considering examples of the empirical application of functionalist imagery, we shall locate the rise of functionalism within its contemporary historical context.

The Great Depression: A Crisis in American Social Order and the Rise of Functionalist Imagery

The dominance of functionalism during the 1950s has led commentators to associate this perspective with a time of economic prosperity and perceived political stability. Parsons's image of society as a self-adjusting system of interdependent parts is seen as but an abstraction of the naive optimism of that decade. This depiction of functionalism misses an important point—that Parsons's theoretical project was largely accomplished in the decade preceding the 1950s. To miss this point is to overlook the relationship between functionalism and what Alvin Gouldner has referred to as "the general crisis of the American middle-class."[28]

According to Gouldner, this crisis was occasioned by the great depression of the 1930s. To fully appreciate Gouldner's thesis, it is necessary to recall the sociological optimism of the Chicago school a decade earlier. As suggested in the preceding chapter, its optimism was based on several interrelated assumptions: (1) that disruptive social disorganization was a temporary by-product of rapid social change, (2) that temporary disorganization was but a phase in the natural course of social reorganization, and (3) that reorganization could be efficiently facilitated by empirically informed professional problem-solving.

Each of these assumptions as upended by the depression. The depression, in other words, undermined sociologists' confidence in their ability to rationally control social problems.

The depression triggered problems which could not be explained as the by-products of rapid change, problems which presented deeper images of disorder, problems which challenged the fundamental structure of the American economy. During the 1920s, sociologists, like other members of the expanding American middle class, viewed the economy as strong, resilient, and adaptive. This view was proved wrong by the economic collapse of the next decade. As Gouldner points out: "In the 1930's, the economic system had broken down. It could no longer produce the massive daily gratification that helped hold middle-class society together and foster commitment to its values."[29] Moreover, it rendered "the previous American tradition of the study of isolated social problems" as "manifestly incompetent to deal with social strains that obviously ramified through all institutions and social strata."[30]

The depression crystalized a general mood of unease which had hung like an ominous storm cloud over the European and American middle classes since the end of the First World War. Other events contributing to this mood included the war itself, with its irrational images of the dark side of human nature, the Russian Revolution and the resulting political struggle between east and west, and the rise of fascism in Italy and Germany, which "signaled that the European middle class's anxieties had become a panic that undermined social and political stability."[31] For a time, America's geographic isolation may have spared its middle class the acute anxiety experienced by Europeans. During the depression this changed. Americans were drawn into an international crisis that simultaneously threatened the middle class in capitalist countries worldwide.

Existing American sociological theory was unable to fully comprehend the international crisis described by Gouldner. Its emphasis on piecemeal technical problem-solving rendered it unable to deal with the more fundamental structural problems posed by the international collapse of the capitalist economy. What other theoretical alternatives presented themselves? Marxism was one alternative debated in European intellectual circles. In the United States, however, Marxism had not yet emerged as a serious intellectual tradition within the American university.[32] Its proposals for overturning the capitalist economic system were alien to most of the middle-class sociologists whose investment in that system had increased so dramatically in the years following World War I. Where then would American sociology turn? The answer is found in the theoretical appeal of Parsonian functionalism.

Parsons's description of society as a self-maintaining homeostatic system offered an image of social order that was relatively independent of questions related to economic order. Economic institutions were seen as counterbalanced by other institutions—the state, the family, the church, etc. Parsons described the stabilizing exchanges between the various parts of the system in a highly abstract language removed from the everyday realities of concrete economic crisis. For many critics this has meant that Parsons's abstract functionalism was devoid of relevance for American life. Gouldner disagrees. Although Parsons wrote little about practical social problems—delinquency, family instability, poverty, etc.—his extremely abstract notion of a self-preserving social system is interpreted as the basis of the essential relevancy of functionalism for the crisis-embattled American middle class. Parsons's emphasis on orderly equilibrium provided a conceptual escape from a world engulfed by economic and social disorder. It allowed sociologists to make peace with the existing order on the assumption that society would work things out in time. It offered a new optimism based, not upon anything observable, but upon abstract generalities. As Gouldner points out, "He one-sidedly emphasized the adaptability of the status quo, considering the ways in which it was open to change rather the manner in which its own characteristics were inducing the disorder and resisting adaptation to it."[33]

Gouldner provides a biographical account for Parsons's conservative optimism. Born in 1902, the son of a Congregational minister in central Ohio, Parsons was too young to have directly experienced the horrors of World War I. Completing his graduate education during the prosperous 1920s, Parsons had settled into marriage and a comfortable faculty position at Harvard University two years before the stock market crash in 1929. Financially secure, Harvard was little affected by the economic crisis of the thirties. Moreover, unlike the University of Chicago during the 1920s, Harvard was an elite institution with a long tradition of detachment from the problems of its surrounding community. Within Harvard's ivy-coated classrooms, Parsons's optimistic view of the self-adjusting social system was transmitted to an entire generation of influential sociologists. Under Parsons's influence the dominant center for American sociology shifted from Chicago to the Atlantic coast.

By the 1950s American sociologists had come to embrace functionalist thought as their dominant theoretical perspective. Just as the birth of functionalism's conservative optimism was occasioned by the crisis of the great depression, its widespread acceptance was prompted by America's triumphant emergence from the depression during and after the Second World War. The American system's adjustment was linked to the New Deal economic policies of the Roosevelt administration. In purely functionalist terminology, political institutions had provided an adjustive balance for the strains arising within economic institutions. In point of fact, they restored the American economy. As Gouldner points out, "During the war and after it, prosperity returned; at least for the middle-class, American society was reknit by affluence and by war-induced solidarity. The working class and its unions became increasingly integrated into the society; the sense of an imminent threat to public order disappeared."[34] Given functionalism's deceptive emphasis on mechanisms of systemic equilibrium, it is at once ironic and revealing that the popularity of this perspective was conditioned not by smooth societal self-regulation but by violent conflict.

Sociology After World War II: Temporary Images of Prosperity and the Reign of Functionalism

During World War II, many sociologists worked for the federal government, conducting research on such matters as the social organization of command, the training of recruits, and the origins of combat fatigue. The American triumph in the war was, moreover, accompanied by the triumph of professional sociology as a science. In the years following the war the abstract generality of functionalism provided sociology with an identity as a science of high-level conceptualization, and even predictive ability. After all, hadn't functionalist theorizing prefigured the return to economic prosperity which manifested itself in America during the postwar years? This apparent functionalist strength was more illusionary than real. It disguised as much as it revealed. In describing American society as a system of interdependent parts, it ignored (or was incapable of seeing) deeper cleavages in the economic, racial, and sexual organization of America itself. The rose-colored glasses of functionalist optimism were seemingly tinted by the conservativism of those who benefited most from the way in which stability was currently arranged, those at the top of the social, political, and economic order, those whom critical sociologist C. Wright Mills designated as the "power elite." For more than a decade the rose-colored glasses of functionalism belonged to the power elite, and so, perhaps, did most sociologists of the time.[35]

The surfacing of suppressed racial and political tensions during the 1960s destroyed the dominance of functionalist theory. Arguing that society was better described as a coordination of conflictual interest, many sociologists abandoned ideas about self-regulating systemic equilibrium. Yet, despite its limitations, the functionalist approach has shed light on certain aspects of deviance previously shadowed by darkness. The following is an overview of two of the more influential studies derived from the functionalist framework. The thoughtful questions raised by these projects remind those of us who are critical of functionalism of the age-old maxim "don't throw the baby out with the bathwater."

Dentler and Erikson's Analysis of the Functions of Deviance in Groups In their study, Dentler and Erikson depict the positive consequences of deviance for the organization of ten Quaker work projects and for basic trainees in the U.S. Army.[36] They employ a variety of field-research techniques to examine the consequences of deviance in each case. The specific goals of the two groups were, of course, different. While the army sought to train competent combatants, the Quakers hoped to induce "conformity with norms of tolerance, pacificism, democratic group relations and related social attitudes."[37] Nonetheless, data gathered on both groups were said to illustrate three functionalist propositions:

1 Groups tend to induce, sustain, and permit deviant behavior.

2 Deviant behavior functions in inducing groups to maintain group equilibrium.

3 Groups will resist any trend toward alienation of a member whose behavior is deviant.

In each Quaker group a deviant recurrently emerged who acted, dressed, and talked differently than other members. The existence of such deviants provided the group with someone whose irritable oddness became the target of other members' tolerance and care. Groups went out of their way to adjust to and not alienate or exclude such functional deviants. This process of adjustment symbolized dominant group values, such as tolerance, and enhanced members' solidarity. According to Dentler and Erikson, groups with "more extremely deviant members" were actually those which achieved the highest equilibrium or intensity in social relationships.[38]

Similar things happened in the basic-trainee situation. Each high-stress boot-camp group produced a clumsy, bumbling deviant. This "helpless," "soft," and "off-beat" person contributed to group unity in an interesting way. Remember that army life, particularly in basic training, is tightly structured, authoritarian, hard, and traditionally "masculine." The soft helplessness of deviant trainees "introduced emotional qualities which the population—lacking women and younger persons—could not otherwise afford." As such, the deviant was seen as functional in reducing tensions and maintaining group equilibrium. Although manifestly a low producer and a potential handicap, latently the deviant contributes something that nondeviant members cannot. Thus, according to Dentler and Erikson, "the group neither exerts strong pressures on him to conform nor attempts to expel him from the squad. Instead, he is typically given a wide license to deviate."[39]

Such research on the functions of deviance in groups opens our eyes to another side of nonconformity. Do groups really produce deviants to meet their own needs? The description of the bumbling boot-camp deviant may seem familiar to those who have shared a house, a dormitory floor, or a long-term work situation with a small group of people. Isn't it often true that someone in such groups becomes singled out as deviant? Arlene Kaplan Daniels and Richard Daniels have written of this in a fascinating article on the social role of the "career fool." Such deviants were said to "appear in small, rather tightly knit social worlds" and provide others with "a feeling of comfortable superiority and confidence," and "vicarious satisfaction . . . that not everyone is broken or 'processed' by the system."[40] This unorthodox way of seeing deviance is a good illustration of the functionalist perspective. For a wider, society-level view, we shall examine Kai Erikson's historical study of deviance in seventeenth-century Massachusetts.

The Wayward Puritans: Moral Boundaries and the Constancy of Social Control By examining court records and other historical documents, Erikson attempted to reconstruct the role of deviance among the Puritans of the Massachusetts Bay Colony.[41] He draws three conclusions supportive of the functionalist perspective. The first concerns the establishment of moral boundaries. In keeping with Durkheim, Erikson observes that "each time the community moves to censure some act of deviation, it sharpens the authority of the violated norm and restates where the boundaries of the group are located."[42]

In addition to establishing moral boundaries, the nature of the acts declared to be deviant is reflective of the dominant values of society at a particular time. For the Puritans, a constant concern with heresy and witchcraft revealed not only the "shape of the devil," but the shape of the community's focal values. Erikson documents this point by noting that the specific content of Puritan crimes varied with changes in the nature of the threats to the community's religious purity. Accordingly, "it is not surprising that deviant behavior should appear in a community at exactly those points where it is most feared. Men who fear witches soon find themselves surrounded by them; men who become jealous of private property soon encounter eager thieves."[43]

Does the fear of deviance create deviance, or does deviance create fear? Erikson never really answers this question, although he admits that the affinity between these two things "has been a continuous source of wonder in human affairs."[44] He observes, however, that over a period of thirty years the volume of persons charged with deviance remained remarkably constant. This suggests that deviance may be produced by society in proportion to its capacity for social control. Nonetheless, while the volume of criminals remained relatively constant, the number of action convictions changed during difficult time periods. Conviction rates increased in times when the dominant religious values of the Puritans came under threat. During such "crime waves" the community was called upon to reaffirm its moral boundaries.

Despite periodic fluctuations of conviction rates, the observed constancy of an offender population is taken as evidence that society generates something like "quotas" of functionally needed deviants.[45] The so-called Quaker invasion, which may have induced higher levels of general religious conformity, is suggestive of this point. Even at the height of this moral revival, the "pool" of deviants remained constant. As such, Erikson offers a general functionalist observation that *society channels certain of its members into relatively fixed careers in deviance*.[46]

Erikson's analysis may raise more questions than it answers. Historians have questioned the adequacy of his use of official documents.[47] Sociologists have asked questions about the comparability of the small, tightly knit, authoritarian Puritan society and the large, amorphous, and multivalued world of today. Others have wondered whether the volume of deviance isn't better explained by the self-serving organizational activities of control agents themselves. Nonetheless, *Wayward Puritans* stands as an imaginative and provocative piece of research that raises significant questions about a society's functional need for deviance.

THE ADEQUACY OF THE FUNCTIONALIST PERSPECTIVE

The genius of the functional perspective is that it transports the concept of deviance away from its nearly exclusive identification with the dark and shadowy. In "lightening up" the study of deviance the functionalist perspective sensitizes us to its more positive consequences. In contributing to social boundaries, group solidarity, and tension reduction, deviance helps order rather than disorder the social system. In its innovative dimensions deviance may contribute to social vitality by challenging outdated ways of doing things.

Despite its advantages, there are decided disadvantages built into the logic of the functionalist thinking. These include (1) an overly mechanistic view of social life as a social system, (2) the circularity of functional analysis, and (3) the conservative bias of functional analysis.

An Overly Mechanistic Image of Society: The Specter of False Teleology

From a functionalist perspective the social system creates and modulates deviance for its own needs. This is very neat on paper, but where in everyday life do we find such a system? It is people who create and control deviance, not some impersonal machinelike "system."

As a poetic metaphor the idea of a social system is quite interesting. When you are stuck on the freeway at eight on a weekday morning, in line at the supermarket, or in a hospital bed, life may seem to be controlled by some giant computer which regulates our needs and modulates our tensions. In actuality, things are less "rational." Freeways, weekday mornings, supermarkets, and sterile hospital rooms were not created by some system. They are the fortunate or unfortunate products and by-products of the way that humans have created history. If social life seems more systemlike than spontaneous, more impersonal than personal, more imposed than chosen, more constraining than creative, it is because we (or those of us who have had the power to do so) have made it that way. Like Dr. Frankenstein, we have allowed our creations to become more masterful than ourselves. We should be wary of the oversimplification and overmechanization of human life inherent in the functionalist perspective.

We have previously noted the relationship between functionalist analysis and the problem of false teleology. With regard to the study of deviance a proposition is falsely teleological if it asserts that nonconformity comes about in order to realize the goals of the system, without specifying how exactly the system causes this to happen. The reason that functionalists find it so difficult to escape the specter of false teleology involves their reliance on the overly mechanistic metaphor of the social system. This metaphor suggests that deviance exists because it fulfills the goals of the system. The system metaphor traps functionalists into describing society in these terms. Once within this conceptual trap functionalists fail to distinguish between a society of real people struggling in history and a "social machine" which stabilizes itself by molding people into well-oiled parts. Life may be like a system with nearly everything feeding into and affecting everything else. That is not to say that life is a system. It is not. The functionalistic perspective is set up to miss this point. As such it "systematically" overlooks the element of human variability, irrationality, creativity, and struggle that is part of every story of deviance and social control.[48]

The Circularity of Functional Analysis: The Specter of Tautology

Following Durkheim the functionalists note the universal presence of crime and deviance and describe the ways that they contribute to social order. As suggested previously, there is a kind of circular reasoning at work here. If something exists, then, by the typical logic of functionalist analysis, it must be contributing to the health of the whole society. With enough imagination one can find a positive function for anything. Child abuse may contribute to population control. Bank robberies may promote a more rational system of computerized monetary allocations. Arson can rid the society of old buildings which occupy valuable space and waste energy.

The circular nature of much functionalist analysis is nowhere more evident than in Herbert Gans's analysis of the functions of poverty.[49] Gans suggests that poverty, despite all the bad press it gets from "bleeding-heart" liberals, can be viewed as a positive and necessary feature of social life. Gans offers us a laundry list of the fifteen "latent functions" of poverty. Among other things, it provides a constant market for spoiled or defective commodities, and it ensures that there will be needy people available to do the distasteful but necessary social "dirty work," a guaranteed surplus of people ready to assume jobs with low wages and poor working conditions. Gans also observes that poverty provides needed employment opportunities for helping professionals and those trained in the control of social disorder, and offers the opportunity for the nonpoor to vicariously participate in the poor's stereotypically uninhibited sexuality. The crux of Gans's satirical analysis involves a description of the contribution of poverty to political stability. Poverty is associated with a fatalistic view of life and with low interest in voting. Since poor people vote less, the political system is free to ignore them. Imagine what would happen if this were not the case. Thank heavens for poverty! If the poor participated fully in the political process, they would almost certainly demand a basic redistribution of jobs and incomes, "and would thus generate further political conflict between the haves and have-nots."

When stretched to its imaginative limits the circular logic of functionalism can identify the positive consequences of virtually any aspect of social life. Gans's list of the useful contributions of poverty is a clear illustration. Yet, this analysis tells us nothing about the historical conditions that bring about or perpetuate poverty or about the concrete experiences of those subject to impoverishment. The same is true regarding the supposed positive functions of deviance. The circular logic of functionalism has a self-fulfilling character. By emphasizing benefits to the system as a whole, functionalism generally ignores the importance of historical circumstances and personal meanings.

The Conservative Bias of Functional Analysis

In addition to its mechanistic and circular features the functionalist perspective is also plagued by a certain conservative bias. In documenting positive contributions, the perspective fails to ask whether deviance might be more positive for some than for others. The arrested criminal might serve as a moral boundary marker or as a scored target for solidarity, but is being arrested functional for the deviant? Martin Luther King's acts of courageous political deviance may have been innovative from the viewpoint of the 1980s, but were his long nights in jail during the 1960s functional for him and his family?

Some people benefit more from deviance and/or its control than others. Who gains the most, and who loses the most? This question is alien to the conservative logic of functionalism. From the functionalist point of view the whole system benefits. Assuming the functionalists are correct, shouldn't we then ask who within the system benefits most? As a social system Nazi Germany may have benefited from the mass deviantizing of Jews. It would be absurd, however, to argue that all German citizens, including Jews, benefited equally from the Holocaust. When confronted with such issues the functionalist perspective reveals its fundamental conservatism. The system's benfits are recited without exploring who controls the system. Deviance may be functional. Yet in an unequal society its functions will not be equally distributed.

NOTES

1 Émile Durkheim, *The Rules of the Sociological Method,* trans. Sarah A. Solovay and John H. Muller and edited by Sir George E. G. Carlin, Macmillan, New York, p. 70.
2 Kai T. Erikson, *Wayward Puritans: A Study in the Sociology of Deviance,* Wiley, New York, 1966, p. 181.
3 Inge Morath and Arthur Miller, *Chinese Encounters,* Farrar, Straus, Giroux, New York, 1979, as excerpted in *Book Digest Magazine,* vol. 7, no. 2, February 1980, p. 36.
4 James Brady, *Justice and Politics in the People's Republic of China: Legal Order or Continuing Revolution,* Academic, New York, 1982.
5 Lewis A. Coser, "Some Functions of Deviant Behavior and Normative Flexibility," *American Journal of Sociology,* vol. 69, September 1962, pp. 172–182, reprinted in M. Lefton, L. K. Skipper, Jr., and C. H. McCaghy (eds.), *Approaches to Deviance,* Appleton-Century-Crofts, New York, 1968, p. 286.
6 Durkheim, *The Rules of the Sociological Method,* p. 67.
7 Ibid., p. 71.
8 George Herbert Mead, "The Psychology of Punitive Justice," *American Journal of Sociology,* vol. 23, 1918, p. 586.
9 Durkheim, *The Rules of the Sociological Method,* p. 71.
10 See, for instance, Roger Caillois, *Man and the Sacred,* Meyer Barash (trans.), Free Press, New York, 1959; and Richard Stivers, *Evil in Modern Myth and Ritual,* University of Georgia Press, Athens, 1982, pp. 37–44.
11 Robert K. Merton, *Social Theory and Social Structure,* Free Press, New York, 1957, 1968.
12 Kingsley Davis "Prostitution," in R. K. Merton and R. Nisbet (eds.), *Contemporary Social Problems,* 3d ed., Harcourt, Brace & Jovanovich, New York, 1971.
13 For research on swinging, see Gilbert D. Bartell, *Group Sex,* Wyden, New York, 1971; Gilbert D. Bartell, "Group Sex Among the Mid-Americans," *Journal of Sex Research,* vol. 6, 1970, pp. 113–130; James R. Smith and Lynn G. Smith, "Co-Marital Sex and the Sexual Freedom Movement," *Journal of Sex Research,* vol. 6, 1970, pp. 131–142; Charles and Rebecca Palson, "Swinging Wedlock," *Society,* vol. 9, 1972, pp. 28–37; and Mary Lin-

denstein Walshak, "The Emergence of Middle-Class Deviant Subcultures: The Case of Swingers," *Social Problems,* vol. 18, 1971, pp. 488–495.

14 Diane Denfield and Michael Gordon, "The Sociology of Mate Swapping: On the Family That Swings Together Clings Together," *Journal of Sex Research,* vol. 6, 1970, pp. 85–100.

15 Talcott Parsons, *Essays in Sociological Theory,* Free Press, New York, 1949, p. 217.

16 Talcott Parsons, *The Social System,* Free Press, New York, 1951.

17 Jonathan Turner, *The Structure of Sociological Theory,* 2d ed., Dorsey, Homewood, Ill., 1978, p. 19.

18 Durkheim, *The Rules of the Sociological Method,* p. 90.

19 Anthony Giddens, *Capitalism and Modern Social Theory: An Analysis of the Writings of Marx, Durkheim and Max Weber,* Cambridge University Press, Cambridge, 1971, p. 91.

20 Durkheim, *The Rules of the Sociological Method,* pp. 95–96.

21 Ibid., p. 67, 70.

22 Ibid., p. 67.

23 Robert K. Merton, *Social Theory and Social Structure.*

24 Ibid., p. 127.

25 Durkheim, *The Rules of the Sociological Method,* p. 66.

26 See Talcott Parsons, Robert F. Bales, and Edward A. Shils, *Working Papers in the Theory of Action,* Free Press, Glencoe, Ill., 1953, and Talcott Parsons and Neil L. Smelser, *Economy and Society,* Free Press, New York, 1956.

27 Parsons, *The Social System.* For a summary analysis of Parsons's conception of social control, see Nanette J. Davis, *Sociological Constructions of Deviance,* 2d ed., Brown, Dubuque, Iowa, 1980, pp. 91–97; S. N. Eisenstadt, "Societal Goals, Systemic Needs, Social Interaction and Individual Behavior: Some Tentative Explanations," in H. Turk and R. L. Simpson (eds.), *Institutions and Social Exchange: The Sociologies of Talcott Parsons and George C. Homans,* Bobbs-Merrill, Indianapolis, 1971, pp. 36–55; Jonathan Turner, *The Structure of Sociological Theory,* 3rd ed., Dorsey, Homewood, Ill., 1982, pp. 48–49.

28 Alvin W. Gouldner, *The Coming Crisis of Western Sociology,* Basic Books, New York, 1970, pp. 144–148.

29 Ibid., p. 141.

30 Ibid., p. 177.

31 Ibid., p. 25.

32 Patrick J. Gurney, "Historical Origins of Ideological Denial: The Case of Marx in American Sociology," *American Sociologist,* vol. 16, 1981, pp. 196–201.

33 Gouldner, *The Coming Crisis,* p. 147.

34 Ibid., p. 142.

35 C. Wright Mills, *The Power Elite,* Oxford University Press, New York, 1956.

36 Robert A. Dentler and Kai T. Erikson, "The Function of Deviance in Groups," *Social Problems,* vol. 7, Fall 1959, pp. 98–107.

37 Ibid., p. 102.

38 Ibid., p. 104.

39 Ibid., p. 105.

40 Arlene K. Daniels and Richard R. Daniels, "The Social Role of the Career Fool," *Psychiatry,* vol. 27, August 1964, pp. 219–229, reprinted in M. Lefton, J. F. Skipper, Jr., and C. H. McCaghy, *Approaches to Deviance,* Appleton-Century-Crofts, New York, 1968, pp. 308, 309.

41 Erikson, *Wayward Puritans.*

42 Ibid., p. 13.

43 Ibid., p. 22.

44 Ibid.

45 Ibid., pp. 163–181.

46 Ibid., p. 181.

47 See, for instance, Ann Nelson and Hart Nelson, "Problems in the Application of a Sociological Method to Historical Data: A Case Example," *American Sociologist,* May 1969, pp. 149–151. See also John B. Williamson, David A. Karp, John R. Dalphin, and Paul S. Gray, *The Research Craft,* 2d ed., Little, Brown, Boston, 1982, pp. 239–259.

48 Nanette J. Davis, *Sociological Constructions of Deviance,* 2nd ed., W. C. Brown Publishers, Dubuque, Iowa, 1980, pp. 110–111.

49 Herbert Gans, "The Positive Function of Poverty," *American Journal of Sociology,* vol. 78, September 1972, pp. 275–289.

50 Ibid., p. 283.

Suicidal Walkman By Joseph LaMantia and Stephen Pfohl

CHAPTER **7**

THE ANOMIE PERSPECTIVE: *Normlessness, Inequality, and Deviant Aspirations*

To pursue a goal which is by definition unattainable is to condemn oneself to a state of perpetual unhappiness.

Émile Durkheim[1]

Frustration and thwarted aspiration lead to the search for avenues of escape from a culturally induced intolerable situation.

Robert K. Merton[2]

INTRODUCTION

During the spring of 1977 I experienced my worst day as a college teacher. I discovered a mass outbreak of cheating on the midterm for my course in criminology. As a young lecturer I was teaching without the help of teaching assistants. This meant that I'd have to grade nearly 200 midterms on my own. The thought was staggering. I had always distrusted multiple-choice tests. Although easy to grade, I thought them better indicators of test-taking ability than sociological reasoning. Despite what I am about to tell you, I still believe this.

Another problem with multiple-choice tests is that they systematically discriminate against many lower class, minority students and others denied the advantages of "college prep" curriculums and resourceful educational environments. These facts present no great sociological mystery. They are well known to even the most casual observer. And since they were well known to me also, I experienced a dilemma that was both practical and ethical. Practically, I couldn't imagine how I could grade 200 non-multiple-choice exams. Ethically I was worried about penalizing students who didn't read as well or quickly, those less adept at coping with in-class exam pressure, or who simply required more time to do their best. My solution was to offer an out-of-class multiple-choice exam. This provided students with an extended period of time and was to be completed according to the honor system. Students were to pick up the exam from the department secretary, go to a quiet setting, answer all questions without using notes (just like an in-class exam), and return the exam before the day's end. With this solution, my troubles began.

It didn't take long for me to realize that things had gone wrong. The exams were available to students at 9:00 a.m. At 9:30 a student appeared at my door in tears. Everybody was cheating, the student reported. The student was correct. I soon learned that cheating was occurring everywhere—from private dorm rooms to the public corridors of the library. Students were apparently even cheating while gulping down "Big Macs" at the campus McDonald's. But why? How could I have been so naive, the frustrated student complained. Nobody gives an honor-system exam these days. Nobody knew what to do. Nobody knew what the rules were. If you didn't cheat and others did, then you'd be penalized. Everyone knows that teachers mark on a curve, and so, no matter how hard you studied, if others cheated harder, you'd be penalized. Hence, you'd better cheat too, if you wanted to come out of this chaotic situation with a decent grade. All of this made good sociological sense, at least from the anomie perspective on deviance.

There are two related versions of the anomie perspective. The first, developed by Émile Durkheim, sees deviance as the result of a state of normlessness in which nobody knows the rules. The second version of anomie theory is more complicated. It defines anomie as a discrepancy between socially engendered goals and the availability of legitimate means to achieve such goals. Both versions apply to the cheating incident. By offering an honor-system exam, I had introduced a type of normlessness into an otherwise orderly academic world. Ordinarily exams were tightly proctored. Teachers even had multiple versions of the same exam printed with the questions in different sequences so as to penalize those who copied from other students' computerized answer sheets. Given the routine nature of such drastic control policies, my use of the honor system may have generated a situation in which few knew what was expected. The honor system may also have produced a strain between established goals (i.e., getting a good grade) and legitimate means to achieve goals (i.e., not cheating when one knows that others are cheating).

This brings us to the conclusion of this disconcerting tale of "anomic cheating." Since I had no means of knowing who cheated, I announced that everyone would be assigned an A, but that course grades would be determined by a curve combining the midterm and final exam grades. This meant that in actuality the grades would be determined by the final. An exception was made for students who had studied, done well without cheating, and were willing to defend their knowledge in a short oral exam. On the final, students were asked to write an essay using theoretical perspectives to explain the high rate of cheating on the midterm. A great number of students drew upon the imagery of the anomie perspective to explain this deviant episode. In examining this perspective, perhaps we shall learn why.

THEORETICAL IMAGE

At the heart of the anomie perspective is the notion that deviance arises as a result of unfulfilled human aspirations. There are two distinct traditions within this perspective. Each conceives of aspirations and their lack of fulfillment in slightly different terms. The first tradition is rooted in the work of Émile Durkheim; the second in the writings of Robert K. Merton. While the two traditions are related, they are each sufficiently distinct as to merit our separate consideration.

Durkheim: Anomie as Normlessness

Durkheim used the term *anomie* to describe a state of normlessness. A society beset by anomie was said to lack the regulatory constraints necessary for the adequate social control of its members. As such, the concept of anomie resembles the idea of social disorganization envisioned by the theorists of the Chicago school. Anomie and social disorganization are both seen as consequences of social change. Both are also characterized by a kind of normative chaos.

There are, however, several important differences between the concept of social disorganization and that of anomie. Social disorganization was typically presented as a spatial or social-ecological problem affecting the particular parts or zones of a society most exposed to the forces of rapid change. On the other hand, anomie was conceived more as a temporal problem affecting the entirety of a given society. Anomie was a discrete problem, a historically specific problem of societies in transition from the traditional to the modern world. Social disorganization, however, was a problem for all societies at all periods of time, an ongoing problem characterized by change, disruption, and reorganization. Thus the consequences and control implications of anomie and disorganization were conceived differently. In terms of consequences, Durkheim suggested that anomie unleashed an instinctually based form of human greed, the pursuit of unlimited aspirations. Social disorganization produced a search for reorganization, sometimes through involvement in deviance. Regarding social control strategies, while disorganizational theorists supported efforts to "patch up" or restore the normative organization of particular zones or sectors of society, Durkheim saw the need for a massive, societywide reorganization of the normative structure.

Durkheim's View of Human Nature: Normatively Controlled Greed

In attempting to understand the origins and consequences of Durkheim's conception of anomie, it is necessary to consider two things: Durkheim's view of human nature and his perceptions of the social context in which he lived. Durkheim's conception of human nature was extremely ambivalent, even contradictory. Durkheim asserted that there is no human nature (as he knew it) without society. Individuals had no existence apart from society. What people thought, how they perceived the world, how they conceived of their relationship to the world—all of these things were shaped by participation in society. This commitment to the primacy of society over the individual is found in many of Durkheim's writings but is nowhere stronger than in his book *The Elementary Forms of the Religious Life.*[3]

Elsewhere Durkheim seems to allow for a set of human propensities, a kind of human nature that exists prior to society. These propensities, or natural tendencies, could not, however, be realized outside of society. They are almost described as the reason or basis for society. In his work *Suicide,* for instance, Durkheim suggests that our human nature is characterized by an "inextinguishable thirst"; that our capacity for desire and feeling is in itself an insatiable and bottomless abyss. For this reason human nature can never be simply "in itself." It would demand too much. By themselves our needs or desires (seemingly rooted in our psychobiological capabilities) would be too great. Somehow, our inextinguishable thirst, our unlimited capacity for desire, must be curbed or regulated. It is to provide this proportion, to regulate our otherwise insatiable aspirations, that society apparently comes into being. According to Durkheim:

> Human nature is substantially the same among all men. . . . It is not human nature which can assign the variable limits necessary to our needs. They are thus unlimited so far as they depend on the individual alone. Irrespective of any external regulatory force, our capacity for feeling is in itself an insatiable and bottomless abyss. . . . [S]ociety alone can play this moderating role; for it is the only moral power superior to the individual, the authority of which he accepts. It alone has the power necessary to stipulate laws and to set the point beyond which the passions must not go.[4]

I will not here try to reconcile Durkheim's ambivalence as to the existence of a human nature independent of society. Perhaps it is enough to say that while Durkheim believed that humans possess an unlimited appetite of aspirations or desire, he also argued that it is society which arouses specific aspirations. What is clear in both instances is that aspirations cannot be infinitely filled. Desired social resources are finite. Everyone cannot have everything. There must be limits. These limits, since not internally generated, must come from society. They must be perceived as fair. They must be perceived as moral. When they aren't, there will be trouble. Too much unregulated desire! Too few resources with which to fulfill limitless desires! The lack of moral norms constraining human aspirations! Anomie! This was what Durkheim saw around him; the crisis of modern society and the basis for his understanding of anomic deviance. In *Suicide* Durkheim described this crisis in the following manner:

> Religion has lost most of its power. And government, instead of regulating economic life, has become its tool and servant. . . . [I]ndustry, instead of being still regarded as a means to an end transcending itself, has become the supreme end of individuals and societies alike. Thereupon the appetites thus excited have become freed of any limiting authority.[5]

The Transition from Traditional to Modern Society: The Social Context of Durkheim's Analysis

We have already considered Durkheim's contribution to the functionalist theory of deviance. It was Durkheim who argued that deviance was a normal and necessary social phenomenon which contributed to the order of a given society. That functionalist viewpoint was in keeping with Durkheim's analysis of the interrelationships of the parts or structures of society at any given point in time. Durkheim, however, was not exclusively concerned with society at any given point in time. He was also concerned with society at a particular point in time—his own time, a time characterized by the transition from the traditional to the modern world. Durkheim described this transition as a shift in the basic normative patterns around which societies are organized. In his own terms this involved a shift from the patterns of *mechanical solidarity* to those of *organic solidarity*. The specific meaning of these terms will be spelled out later. For now it is enough to note that the problems presented by the transition from simple, traditional forms of society to complex, modern forms were problems which occupied the entirety of Durkheim's career as a social theorist. They were problems which were filled with danger. They were problems which shaped Durkheim's conception of anomie and its relationship to deviant behavior.

Durkheim's analysis of the dangers involved in the transition from traditional society to modern society was undoubtedly related to his own biographical location within history.[6] He was born into a highly traditional society. He spent his adult life in an intellectual wrestling match with a society undergoing the pains of modernization. He was born in 1858, the son of a rabbi in the eastern French province of Lorraine. The Jews who lived in that region of France belonged to the Ashkenazic branch of Judaism. The Ashkenazim had remained relatively isolated from the whole of French society since their migration from Germany into the eastern French provinces of Alsace and Lorraine during the sixteenth century. For years most members of the community spoke entirely in Yiddish and Hebrew, maintaining a traditional Jewish cultural identity which insulated them from the forces of modernization sweeping the French nation as a whole. In this sense the Ashkenazim differed greatly from the Sephardic Jews of southwestern France. Although living in France for about the same length of time as their Ashkenazic brethren, the Sephardic Jews (who had fled religious persecution in Spain and Portugal) had taken far greater steps toward assimilation into the modernizing mainstream of the nation. The Ashkenazim, however, retained their traditional forms of social organization long after the revolution had emancipated Jews and granted them French citizenship in the early nineteenth century.

Although reared within the traditional world of the Ashkenazic community, Durkheim was also exposed to the rigors of a demanding secular French education. Attending the school of his hometown, the Collège d'Épinal, Durkheim was soon recognized as a brilliant student and was the recipient of numerous honors and awards. In the process Durkheim developed what Coser describes metaphorically as an intense romance with the principles and politics of the secular French republic.[7] In pursuit of this romance he left Épinal to attend one of France's outstanding secondary schools, the Lycée Louis-le-Grand in Paris. From there he proceeded to the prestigious École Normale

Supérieure and entered into deep intercourse with the intellectual elite of French society. In other words, within the course of a lifetime Durkheim made the transition which French society as a whole took several centuries to make—the transition from traditional to modern social life. Hence, through the journey which was his own life, Durkheim became acutely aware of the consequences of massive social transformation. His description of these consequences is concentrated in his analysis of anomie.

Anomie, Deviance, and the Study of Suicide

Durkheim's analysis of the relationship between anomie and deviance is concentrated in his analysis of suicide. His book *Suicide* was first published in Paris in 1897. The culmination of nearly ten years of research and reflection, *Suicide* is a classic example of the use of a sociological perspective to explain human problems. In many ways *Suicide* provided Durkheim with a concrete example by which to demonstrate the explanatory potential of sociology. Although suicide is commonly thought of as a very private act, Durkheim persuasively argued that changes in the rate of suicide could not be explained adequately by the individualistic sciences of psychology and biology. Fluctuations in the rates of suicide within and between societies were explained, instead, by the way that societies are structured.

Durkheim's work on suicide represents what might be considered as the intellectual "culmination of the moral statistics tradition" begun in Europe during the eighteenth century.[8] This tradition involved the collection of different kinds of statistics on such things as economic, geographic, racial, and even climatic factors and their relationship to a wide variety of such contemporary "moral" problems as insanity, crime, and suicide. Durkheim carefully examined the available statistical data on patterns of suicide and produced a thoroughly sociological account by which to explain variations in the suicide rate. In 1889 he published his first article on the topic. His thoughts on the matter were expanded during the course of a full year's lecture course on suicide which he taught during the 1889–90 academic year. During the next seven years he collected statistics and with the assistance of his nephew Marcel Mauss developed the theoretical groundwork for his 1897 book.

Despite the intellectual challenge presented by using available statistics to demonstrate the utility of the perspective and methods of the new science of sociology, Durkheim's analysis of suicide was prompted by concerns that were as deeply personal as they were professional. Once again we see the intersection of historical biography and explanatory vision in the formulation of social theory. For Durkheim suicide was but a symptom of the growing social malaise of a society in transition, of his own suicide. By wrestling with the problem of suicide Durkheim was in actuality wrestling with what he perceived as the dissolution of normative constraints in European society as a whole. Thus, as Steven Lukes suggests in his intellectual biography of Durkheim, "the study of suicide offered a means of approaching 'the causes of the general malaise currently being undergone by European societies,' since it was 'one of the forms through which the collective malady . . . is transmitted.'"[9] For Durkheim the matter was even more personal. Durkheim was affected greatly by the suicide of Victor Hommay, a close friend and colleague at the École. Convinced that more than psychological factors were involved in Hommay's death, Durkheim was moved to explore the sociological grounds for suicide. As Lukes points out, Hommay's death "influenced not only his [Durkheim's] interest in suicide but also his explanation of it."[10]

Durkheim's primary explanation of the comparatively high rates of suicide in the modernizing industrial nations of western Europe involves his conception of the deviance-producing potential of anomie. In addition to anomie, however, Durkheim outlined three other forms of social organization which induced high rates of suicide: *egoism, altruism,* and *fatalism.* In contrast to the normlessness of anomie, these other social forms represented instances where the normative or moral order encourages its members to take their own lives. For Durkheim, "moral order" was described as an external force which constrained human passion and desire. The moral order is symbolized in ritualistic expressions of what Durkheim referred to as the collective conscience. By this Durkheim meant that individual morality is first shaped by ritualized participation in the collective morality or conscience of the society as a whole. In egoistic, altruistic, and fatalistic societies, rituals of collective moral order are said to increase the likelihood of suicide. Before turning to a specific analysis of anomie, we shall briefly consider the way that social structures produce suicide in the three other suicide-prone moral orders discussed by Durkheim.

Suicide in Egoistic, Altruistic, and Fatalistic Societies

The first form of morally induced suicide was labelled as "egoistic." Here the collective conscience of a given society paradoxically contains the seeds of its own destruction. The moral order contains ideas which encourage a radical separation between individuals and the social group. Durkheim viewed the moral orders of Protestantism and of western intellectual society as constraining individuals in such a paradoxical fashion. Each gives birth to a type of dangerous individualism by socially providing a moral vision of people as responsible for their own actions; Protestantism by stressing the individual's direct, unmediated relationship to God, and intellectualism by stressing the rule of individual reason over the traditions of the social group.

Durkheim noted a similar focus on egoistic individualism in the normative order surrounding unattached or single persons as opposed to that governing the married couple. Married people are bound by normative rules which tie them into a system of regulated interaction. Single persons were said to lack such ties and the socially controlling constraints which come with them. Such exaggerated individualism raises the probability of suicide. The person constrained by this morality of individual responsibility was seen to be especially vulnerable to suicide. In times of trouble or error the moral individualist has no community to turn to for support. The problem of egoistic suicide is generated not by the lack of authoritative moral norms but by the presence of norms oddly encouraging individual freedom from norms.

Durkheim's second form of morally induced suicide is less complicated. It is found in societies in which the collective conscience is so binding that there is virtually no distinction between the individual and the group. The individual literally lives for the group. His or her own personality is but a reflection of the collective personality of the group. All members are as one. As such the individual is willing to give his or her life for the life of the group. Examples of such "altruistic suicide" are typically found in extremely close-knit societies. For years the Japanese rite of *hara-kiri* has been used by sociology teachers as an example of what Durkheim meant by altruistic suicide. A dramatic illustration is the 17th-century story of the forty-seven Ronin. When their master was insulted, these legendary Samurai warriors followed his example by collectively taking their own lives after assassinating the palace official who had offended their leader's honor. Following their collective moral code, the forty-seven warriors killed themselves out of closeness to, rather than distance from, society.

A more contemporary example of *hara-kiri* is found during the Second World War. Bound by a code of collective identification with the life of their nation, Japanese pilots willingly crashed their planes into the decks of American carriers. Although they would die as individuals, they valued their individual lives less than the collective life of the nation. An even more current example is that of Jonestown. In that bizarre community in Guyana, hundreds of followers of Rev. Jim Jones apparently took their own lives so that they might journey together to the promised land. Mesmerized by Jones's hypnotic preaching, the Jonestown faithful drank poison and went to their deaths in a classic instance of what Durkheim referred to as altruistic suicide.

In addition to egoistic and altruistic suicide Durkheim made brief reference to "fatalistic suicide." Although relatively unelaborated in his own writings, this type of suicide was socially induced by the hopelessness structured into the regulatory frameworks of slave societies. Durkheim offered it as a sociological account of high suicide rates among enslaved populations. Under slavery, Durkheim apparently believed, human aspirations may be totally crushed rather than channeled into the pursuit of individual responsibility (as in the egoistic society) or into sacrifices for the collective good (as in the altruistic society). Those who live in slavery are devoid of aspirations and dominated by a sense of fatalism—a sense that their actions cannot change their state in life—and thus slavery, according to Durkheim, is yet another socially structured route toward high rates of suicide.

Anomic Suicide: The Rise and Fall of Economic Aspirations

The egoistic, altruistic, and fatalistic forms of suicide were each encouraged by the normative structures of certain societies. But what happens when the normative structure of a society is weak or disrupted? This is what Durkheim meant by anomie, a social condition which also produces high rates of suicide and, by implication, other forms of deviant behavior as well. Why? To understand the full meaning of anomie we must return to Durkheim's notion of the collective conscience. Recall that it is the collective conscience, the normative force of society, which shields individuals from the "inextinguishable thirst," from the "bottomless abyss" of unlimited aspiration. When something disrupts the normative structure, the thirst of aspirations emerges as again insatiable. This is said to happen during periods of severe economic crisis or sudden prosperity and growth. During economic crisis "something like a declassification occurs which suddenly casts certain individuals into a lower state than their previous one."[1] The rewards that people have come to expect as the just deserts of their positions in society are no longer forthcoming. A new and unaccustomed order of morality, of readjusted expectations, must be learned. This is difficult and cannot be achieved overnight. In the meantime, people continue to cling to old aspirations, nurtured by the now irrelevant norms of precrisis society. This only makes things more painful. The old norms do not fit the new situation. According to Durkheim, people "are not adjusted to the condition forced on them, and its very prospect is intolerable."[12] Such a state of anomie increases the likelihood of suicide by heightening "the suffering which detaches [people] from a reduced state of existence even before they have made a trial of it."[13]

Anomie resulting from economic disaster might be used to explain increases in the suicide rate during depressions. The image of people leaping out of Wall Street windows was a familiar accompaniment of the onslaught of economic collapse during the 1930s. Durkheim claims that sudden turns toward prosperity also create anomie and result in high rates of suicide. The "unknown limits" of economic growth disrupt norms which had kept aspirations in check. "Appetites, not being controlled by a public opinion, become disoriented, no longer recognizing the limits proper to them."[14] Sudden prosperity destroys the authority of traditional norms. Passionate desires escalate without constraint. The sky appears to be the limit. But it is not. Social and economic resources are always finite in character. It is the illusion of anomie which prevents people from realizing this.

Everyone cannot have everything. Unchecked by a regulative morality, the awareness is lacking. Competition and aspirations spiral together; spiral until they crash into the empty abyss of unfulfillment. The race for unlimited aspirations is described as a race for an unobtainable goal, a race offering "no other pleasure but that of the race itself."[15] Competition becomes both more violent and more painful. In Durkheim's words: "Effort grows, just when it becomes less productive. How could the desire to live not be weakened under such conditions?"[16]

Long-Term Anomie: A Problem of Modern Times

Anomie would be destructive enough if limited to short periods of economic crisis or rapid prosperity. In Durkheim's opinion the problem was much greater. Anomie was becoming a chronic, if tragic, condition in the modern world. Durkheim viewed society's turn into the twentieth century as the passage of an entire century in which economic progress consisted largely in the freeing of industrial relations from all social-moral constraint.

In previous times the normative powers of religion, of the state, and of occupational groups had imposed constraints on the economic order. The force of religion impacted on both workers and masters, the poor and the rich. The poor had been provided with an otherworldly vision of compensation in the next world for suffering in this. The rich had been constrained by a belief that worldly interests are but a part of the human lot, a part not to be pursued without rule or restraint. Moreover, the subordination of the economy to the temporal power of the state and the regulation of the salary structure by occupational guilds were seen as additional constraints on the rise of human economic aspirations.

These restraints were losing their force. Here Durkheim made his important distinction between restraints governing simple, relatively undifferentiated traditional societies and those needed to restrain complex, highly specialized, modern societies.

Members of simple societies generally approach each other as whole persons and engage in very similar social and economic activities. Simple societies were constituted by a group of people whose whole lives were relatively visible to one another and who were tightly joined by what Durkheim calls the repressive norms of *mechanical solidarity*. Individual uniqueness was repressed in favor of collective oneness. One set of diffuse norms mechanically governed society as a whole. Think of the small tribe or town, bound together in face-to-face interaction under the constraining rituals of commonly held religious beliefs. Think also of the mechanical solidarity of the Ashkenazic Jews of eastern France. It was in this community that Durkheim spent his early years. Undoubtedly his experiences with the traditional bonds of the Ashkenazim provided the great French sociologist with a vivid image of a traditional society under attack by the forces of modernization.

Simple societies were on the decline. Massive increases in the volume and density of human populations had made social life more complex. The personalness of simple society was being replaced by anonymity; the similarity by a highly specialized division of labor roles. The common religious beliefs and rituals which promoted solidarity were losing their power. New rules and regulations were needed. These were to be based, not on the mechanical repression of difference, but on the rational "restitutive" regulation of variety. Science, not religion, would guide the construction of this new order of morality. Yet the rules of the new order, the rules of what Durkheim called *organic solidarity,* were slow in coming. What was visible to the classical French sociologist was the lack of order, the lack of morality! The old, normative "mechanical" order was disappearing more quickly than the new "organic" order was emerging. As a result society was thrown into a state of anomic deregulation. Suicide and, by implication, other forms of deviance, was on the rise.

The decline of commonly held religious constraints on the economic activity of complex societies hastened a state of anomie. So did the ascendance of the unfettered pursuit of economic prosperity over the previous constraints of governmental and occupational-group regulation. These developments combined to sanctify economic and industrial success at the expense of all other aspects of human life. In Durkheim's mind, economic achievement had "become the supreme end of individuals and societies alike. Thereupon the appetites thus excited have become freed of any limiting authority. By sanctifying them, so to speak, this apotheosis of well-being has placed them above all human law. Their restraint seems like a sort of sacrilege."[17] Anomie had become the unholy fruit of unrestrained economic activity. People were unable to fulfill unrealistic economic goals, yet the lack of constraining norms failed to prevent them from trying; failed to prevent them from jumping into the abyss of disillusionment; failed to prevent them from becoming subject to those social forces which promote suicide and other forms of self-destructive deviance.

Robert K. Merton: Inequality in Opportunities to Conform

Durkheim's theory of anomic suicide grew out of the influential French sociologist's interpretation of the crisis of early-twentieth-century European society. Robert K. Merton's extension of the anomie perspective into a formal theory of deviance grew out of Merton's interpretation of the crisis of mid-twentieth-century America. For Merton the American crisis was conceived of as a structured disparity between promises of achievable prosperity and real-life opportunities to realize those promises. Unfulfilled aspirations were still a central concern. Normlessness was not. In his 1938 essay "Social Structure and Anomie" Merton pictured anomie as a socially structured contradiction between normative aspirations and the lack of available means for legitimately attaining valued cultural goals.

Robert Merton was born on July 5, 1910, in the slums of South Philadelphia, the child of immigrants from eastern Europe. According to his own recollections the slum was a lively, noisy place where he joined in the zesty, if largely ceremonial, gang warfare between groups of streetcorner boys.[18] Much as Durkheim's early life in the traditional Jewish community of eastern France may have contributed to his vision of anomie, so was Merton's reformulation of this concept probably influenced by his childhood in the slum. Gifted in intellectual activity Merton achieved a way out of the slum by obtaining a scholarship to Temple University. Four years later he was awarded a fellowship to pursue graduate studies at Harvard. Such opportunities are, however, far rarer than is implied by the American promise of prosperity for anyone who tries hard. Most of Merton's slum neighbors did not fare so well. The reason had little to do with their motives and a lot to do with their lack of socially structured opportunities for successfully pursuing the American dream. In spite of his own success, this was a lesson of slum life which Merton never forgot.

Merton's theory examines the relationship between two aspects of social life: cultural goals and socially available means of goal attainment. Unlike Durkheim, Merton makes no assumptions regarding the unlimited nature of human aspirations for individuals unrestrained by societal norms. The reverse is more the case. Norms induce certain aspirations. Aspirations are cultural artifacts. They are learned in the family, in the school, in the church, in listening to and watching the media, in the whole cultural life of society. American culture teaches people the aspirations of success. Become rich! Become powerful! Become prestigious! Everybody can do it. Any child can become president. Everyone should try. These aspects of the great American dream are seen by Merton as the aspirations or culturally induced goals of American society. The probability of deviance increases when the "anybody can do it" aspirations of American society are confronted with the "not everybody has an equal chance" opportunity structure of the same society. Durkheim argued that desired resources are finite. Merton expanded this argument by suggesting that they are unequally obtainable as well. Everyone is exposed to the goals of success. Only a few are provided with the legitimate means needed to be successful. Imagine a society in which everyone learned and accepted the same goals and was provided with an equal opportunity to achieve those goals. There would be far less deviance. Everyone would desire and could achieve the same social aspirations. Conformity would be the normal product of such an equal society. Merton did not view American society in such ideal terms. Merton saw the obvious disjuncture between American goals and means. Not everyone could achieve the widely accepted goals of wealth, power, and prestige. For many the American dream was a lie. Deviance was the normal product of such an unequal society.

Table 7-1
MERTON'S TYPOLOGY OF INDIVIDUAL ADAPTATION TO ANOMIE*

	Culturally given goals or aspirations	**Institutionally available means of goal attainment**
I. Conformity	+	+
II. Innovation	+	−
III. Ritualism	−	+
IV. Retreatism	−	−
V. Rebellion	±	±

*This modified representation of Merton's typology is based upon the depiction of these modes of adaptation in Robert K. Merton, "Social Structure and Anomie," *American Sociological Review*, 3(Oct.1938), pp. 672–682.

Merton's analysis of deviance reveals a set of adaptations to the socially structured contradiction between cultural goals and available means of goal attainment (see Table 7-1). Each adaptation contrasts with the path of conformity. The conformist is one whose experience in society leads to the acceptance of both culturally prescribed goals and the socially legitimate means for reaching those goals. He or she accepts the goals and plays by the rules because they work. The "right" family background, attendance at the "right" schools, placement in the "right" firm, promotion at the "right" times, etc., convinces the conformist that the rules of society are "right." There is no need to deviate. According to Merton the path of conformity is the most common adaptation to socially structured goals and means. If this were not so, "the stability and continuity of society could not be maintained."[19]

While Merton believed conformity to be the most common type of goal-means adaptation, it was not the only path. The inequality of American life was said to produce structural pressures toward deviations along four other paths. The first of these was the path of *innovation*. This was the path of persons who accepted the dominant cultural goal of success, but whose experience in a stratified society led them to reject legitimate avenues of goal attainment. The legitimate channels (e.g., hard work, patience, waiting one's turn, etc.) simply proved unsuccessful. Think of youngsters in the ghetto or of the slum gangs that were part of Merton's youth. The door of success is not as open for these persons as it is for the "ivy league" sons of the wealthy. The call to success may, however, be just as strong. One has only to watch a half-hour of television to be "turned on" to the get-ahead, be-successful, look-good, "drive-a-good-car" goals of American society. What happens when people accept goals but later discover that they are unreachable by the lawful rules of the society's game? Put simply, washing dishes provides little access to major channels of wealth, power, and prestige. How is the contradiction to be resolved?

One way to resolve the contradiction presented above is through *innovation*. Merton uses this term to refer to the "creative" use of illegitimate means to obtain valued legitimate ends. He states that, "Given the American stigmatization of manual labor . . . , and the absence of realistic opportunities for advancement beyond this level, the result is a marked tendency toward deviant behavior."[20] For persons systematically deprived of access to avenues of success, how can the "honest" job of dishwashing compete with the easy money obtained through dishonest behavior? For persons systematically denied access to other, more promising avenues of legitimate success, it is not hard to understand why the prospect of years of washing dishes often pales in comparison to the easy money, quick power, and instant status promised by a life of crime. This is the logic of Merton's analysis. Innovative deviance is a normal outgrowth of having accepted cultural goals without having been provided with the opportunity to legitimately achieve those goals. Relatively ineffectual legitimate means are rejected. Promising illegitimate means are explored. Innovation occurs. Deviance occurs. The criminal career of former Chicago gang boss Al Capone is cited by Merton as the prototype of this important deviant adaptation. According to Merton: "Capone represents the triumph of amoral intelligence over morally proscribed 'failure,' when channels of vertical mobility are closed or narrowed in *a society which places a high premium on economic affluence and social ascent for all its members*."[21]

A second, less frequently discussed, deviant adaptation is what Merton calls *ritualism*. Here goals are rejected but legitimate means are accepted. One does not really believe in the goals, does not really care about becoming number one, has little desire to get to the top. Yet, one plays by the rules anyway. Think of the middle-level corporate bureaucrat, government worker, or tenured college professor who really doesn't care about getting further ahead. Such a person may play the game, put in the appropriate time, work the nine-to-five shift. Yet he or she cares little for advancement, and perhaps desires only to get through the day without making waves and then to go home and get stoned. We all know someone who plays the part without really believing in it. Although difficult to spot from a distance, ritualists are the second type of deviants identified by Merton's analysis.

One recent and important example of ritualism involves what corporate executives refer to as the negligent sabotage of the assembly line by careless or uncommitted workers. Indeed the American economy abounds with reports of workers who put in their time but care little for the products of the companies they work for. Why? Merton's conception of ritualism provides a sociological answer. Workers may get what they can from an economic system upon which they must depend for survival, but have little structural incentive for truly committing themselves to the goals of a company whose success shows little evidence of trickling down to the employees who actually operate it. Put in your time. Check in on time. Punch out when the hour comes. A relatively unstudied form of ritualistic deviance, negligent sabotage looms large within the American economy. It affects companies and affects all of us who, like the driver of an unsafely made automobile, experience the anomic impact of a systemic disparity between nurtured goals and offered means.

Retreatism is the third of Merton's deviant adaptations. This involves a lack of attachment to either goals or means. One neither accepts the success values nor acts in conformity with the acceptable way of doing things. One retreats from both the conventional goals and the conventional means. In this category Merton lumps the "adaptive activities of psychotics, artists, pariahs, outcasts, vagrants, tramps, chronic drunkards and drug addicts."[22] The social experience of such persons has led them to be the "true aliens." They have excluded themselves from both shared values and shared activities. They are the drop-outs, according to Merton. They "can be included as members of society . . . only in a fictional sense. . . . People . . . in the society but not of it."[23]

Retreatists escape, or drop out of, major societal goals and normative activities. Merton's final category of adaptation is reserved for those who not only drop out but actively seek to replace old goals and normative activities with new ones. This is the adaptation of *rebellion*. The terrorist or revolutionary best exemplifies this category. These rebels may use illegitimate means (e.g., civil disobedience, sabotage, assassination, kidnapping, hijacking, etc.). Their goal cannot be defined in the terms of the present culture. It is their intention to replace one set of cultural standards with another. The illegitimate activities of the rebel should not be confused with those of the innovator. The gangster who kidnaps for money and the Red Brigade member who kidnaps to destroy the system are quite different. The first uses illegitimate means to obtain the dominant get-rich goals of society. The latter seeks to *replace* the dominant goals and means with "something better." He or she rejects established goals and means in order to hasten the birth of a new set of norms, a new standard for aspirations and acceptable action.

This last of Merton's adaptations is directed toward what might be called the political deviant. Like the other adaptations, rebellion is viewed as the normal product of a contradictory and stratified structuring of society's goals and means. Deviance is explained by the manner in which society strains people, rather than by the way people strain society.

Extending Merton's Theory of Anomie: The Contributions of Parsons and Dubin

Merton's provocative thesis has generated a number of extensions, reformulations, and modifications. In 1951 Talcott Parsons extended Merton's notion of strain between culturally nurtured goals and institutionally available means to include strains at the interpersonal and individual level.[24] Parsons argued that, in addition to the anomic structural strains described by Merton, deviance can also be generated by strains involving such things as the inability to reconcile one's own expectations with the expectations of others, or strains produced by the failure to make institutionally prescribed object-attachments, such as socially appropriate romantic involvements with members of the opposite sex. Another extension of Merton's ideas was proposed by Robert Dubin in 1959.[25] Dubin attempted to reformulate Merton's original five categories of deviant adaptation by subdividing the notion of institutionally available means of goal attainment into norms about how one should act and behavioral descriptions about how people actually act. While this distinction permitted a more specific analysis of a variety of adaptational options, Merton himself believed that Dubin's complex formulation shifted attention away from the core theoretical imagery of anomie theory—that a systemic disjuncture between goals and the means necessary to achieve those goals produces a strain in the direction of deviant behavior.[26]

Richard Cloward: Differential Opportunity for Illegitimate Means

Two other modifications of Merton's work have been heralded as significantly advancing the anomie perspective. These involve the contributions by Richard Cloward and Albert Cohen. Cloward accepted Merton's basic assumptions about the deviance-producing strain generated by differential access to systemically nurtured societal goals. Indeed, Cloward's study of deviance produced by blocked access to culturally encouraged aspirations within a military prison is among the earliest empirical applications of Merton's perspective.[27] Yet, for Cloward, opportunities to deviate successfully were also seen as differentially available. In other words, blocked access to the legitimate means of goal attainment should not be equated with open access to the means of deviation. In his 1959 article "Illegitimate Means, Anomie, and Deviant Behavior," Cloward asserts that access to illegitimate means can be blocked as well.[28] In so arguing Cloward provides a sociological dynamic missing in Merton's category of retreatism. Why should persons retreat rather than innovate in their deviant adaptations? The answer, according to Cloward, is found in the idea of "double failure." According to Cloward, retreatists may be persons who fail or are denied access to both legitimate and illegitimate channels of goal attainment. In Cloward's words, "If illegitimate means are unavailable, if efforts at innovation fail, then retreatist adaptations may be the consequence, and the 'escape' mechanism chosen by the defeated individual may perhaps be all the more deviant because of his 'double failure.'"[29]

Cloward and Ohlin: Subculture Opportunities for Deviance Attention to the differential availability of illegitimate means of goal attainment is elaborated by Cloward and his colleague Lloyd Ohlin in their 1960 book *Delinquency and Opportunity*.[30] This book is dedicated to Robert Merton and to Edwin Sutherland, whose learning perspective on deviance is discussed in the following chapter. Cloward and Ohlin's work attempts to synthesize key elements of Merton's anomie thesis with Sutherland's theory that deviance is learned in everyday social interaction with others. One need not describe Sutherland's theory in detail to outline the basic tenets of Cloward and Ohlin's position. In the first place, Cloward and Ohlin firmly adopt Merton's position in locating the fundamental sociological cause of strains toward deviance in blocked opportunities to achieve socially valued goals. Cloward and Ohlin are concerned with the "position discontent" of persons faced "with limitations on legitimate avenues of access to conventional goals."[31] While they argue that such position discontent produces frustration and a search for alternative means of fulfilling one's aspirations, Cloward and Ohlin maintain that "pressures that lead to deviant patterns do not necessarily determine the particular pattern of deviance that results."[32] At this point they turn to Sutherland's proposition that deviance is learned in interaction with others in order to explain the particular dynamics by which one form of adjustment to frustration is selected instead of others.

In exploring the formation of delinquent subculture, Cloward and Ohlin introduce an analytic approach that can be applied to other forms of deviance as well. They view subcultures as collective social adjustments to the strains of blocked opportunity. Within subcultures people learn to adjust to the frustrations of position discontent in a particular fashion. The manner in which this occurs is, however, not evenly distributed throughout society. Cloward and Ohlin argue that, like channels of legitimate opportunity, the opportunities for particular kinds of subcultural adjustments, and hence particular types of deviant behavior, are unequally distributed. Their study of juvenile delinquency identifies these general forms of subcultural involvement: the *criminal* subculture, the *conflict* subculture, and the *retreatist* subculture. The general source of societal strain is the same for all three—anomie produced by blocked legitimate opportunities. What varies is the specific channel for deviant adaptation.

Criminal subcultures are available to youths raised in specialized social environments—environments which integrate offenders at various age levels and connect conventional and illegitimate values. Youths who reside in such environments and who experience blocked legitimate opportunity channels are nonetheless offered the illegitimate opportunity of an orderly introduction into a world of profitable deviant adaptations. Their delinquency will be organized, disciplined, rational, and respectful of the deviant or organized criminal authority structure. Think of alienated youths who learn their delinquency within an environment dominated by professional or organized criminals. This is the kind of environment envisioned by Cloward and Ohlin in discussing the differential opportunities to deviate offered by criminal subcultures. In such environments youths may adjust to the strains of anomie by becoming apprentices in highly organized deviant activities.

The second type of adaptation environment discussed by Cloward and Ohlin is that of the conflict subculture. There is little age integration between alienated persons and a minimum of convergence between conventional and deviant values. In such environments one is less apt to learn deviance as an instrumentally successful means of obtaining socially valued rewards and more likely to see it as "a way of expressing pent-up angers and frustrations."[33] In such environments there is little opportunity for an orderly apprenticeship into crime as a successful form of business. Adult criminals in such environments are largely unskilled, unsuccessful, and disorganized. Youths within such environments "are deprived not only of conventional opportunity but also of criminal routes to 'big money.' "[34] The collective conflict-subculture adjustment most typical of such neighborhoods is the expressively violent juvenile gang.

The third of Cloward and Ohlin's collective adaptations to position discontent on the part of juveniles is the *retreatist* subculture. Here they reformulate Merton's notion concerning the meaning of retreatism. Merton describes this adaptation in terms of persons who, unable to reach culturally valued goals through legitimate channels, were unable to employ illegitimate means because of internalized prohibitions. This may be the case for some retreatists. Yet, in commenting on youthful drug addicts, Cloward and Ohlin are quick to point out that "the great majority" of such retreatists "had a history of delinquency before becoming addicted."[35] At this point they introject Cloward's thesis regarding the link between retreatism and double failure. What they describe as the retreatist subculture is really more of a collection of drop-outs from the two previously described subcultural adaptations. It is a collectivity of persons who have doubly failed in both legitimate and illegitimate channels. In summary, Cloward and Ohlin state:

> Whether the sequence of adaptations is from criminal to retreatist or from conflict to retreatist, we suggest that limitations on legitimate and illegitimate opportunity combine to produce intense pressures toward retreatist behavior. When both systems of means are simultaneously restricted, it is not strange that some persons become detached from the social structure, abandoning cultural goals and efforts to achieve them by any means.[36]

Albert Cohen: Subculture Adjustments to Frustration

Albert Cohen has been viewed as simultaneously a critic and an advocate of Merton's anomie perspective. As a critic he argued that while Merton's theory was a "sociologically sophisticated and highly plausible . . . explanation" of utilitarian, or instrumentality-oriented, forms of deviance, it failed to account for nonutilitarian or expressive, forms, such as that described by Cohen in his book *Delinquent Boys: The Culture of the Gang*.[37] Moreover, in a 1965 article subtitled "Anomie Theory and Beyond" Cohen argues that Merton's formulation is "too atomistic" and that it places undue emphasis on the discontinuity of the deviant act.[38]

In using the term *atomistic* Cohen means that Merton's discussion of deviant adaptations is too individualistic. It presents an image of the isolated person confronted by the strain of blocked opportunity. In contrast, Cohen argues that the way a person experiences strain and selects one or another mode of deviant adaptation is highly dependent upon his or her interpersonal associations, upon his or her social reference group.[39] In stating that Merton's theory reflects a false discontinuity between acts of conformity and deviance Cohen is suggesting something similar. According to Cohen, Merton "treats the deviant act as though it were an abrupt change of state, a leap from a state of strain or anomie to a state of deviance."[40] Is involvement in deviance really such a discontinuous jump? For Cohen the answer is no. Cohen views the entrance into modes of deviant adaptation as a more gradual, step-by-step process; a process in which people constantly define and redefine their situations in relation to the actions and responses of others.[41]

Two things are particularly important about Cohen's criticisms of Merton's theory. First, Cohen's ideas represent concrete suggestions for improving and strengthening the anomie perspective. Second, Merton acknowledged the insightfulness of Cohen's suggestions and incorporated a discussion of the mediating role of group interactional process into subsequent revisions of anomie theory. In 1964 Merton pointed out that, except for his first formulation, in which preoccupation with structural variables "usurped" a discussion of interaction process, all of his subsequent presentations of anomie theory have included an emphasis upon reference groups and the importance of social interaction in shaping the adaptational alternatives selected by persons confronted with the strains of anomie.[42] Merton argues that his revised theoretical presentations actually consolidate the anomie perspective with the interactional learning model presented by Edwin Sutherland, one of Cohen's teachers.[43] Thus Merton asserts that there is nothing "integral to the theory of SS and A [social structure and anomie] . . . which requires it to be atomistic and individualistic" in the manner suggested by Cohen.[44]

In responding to Cohen's constructive critique Merton actually advances upon previous formulations of the anomie perspective and incorporates several of Cohen's concerns as his own. He argues that a key concept in Cohen's analysis of delinquent subcultures implicitly contains an important connection to anomie theory. The bulk of Cohen's analysis involves a depiction of the "short-run hedonism" of the delinquent subculture as a collective reaction-formation against the unreachable yet valued status of middle-class culture. For Cohen the irrational, malicious and unaccountable delinquent subculture offers lower-class boys a means of solving the status-frustration problem generated by the denial of access to the world of the middle class. Merton does not take issue with Cohen on these points. Nor does he contest Cohen's account of the self-perpetuating character of existing delinquent subcultures. Indeed, once operative, delinquent subcultures may well provide the frustration-relieving rewards needed to sustain members' involvement, as well as recruit and instruct new members into nonutilitarian, malicious, and negativistic ways of delinquency.

But what of the origins of delinquent subcultures in the first place? Here Merton (and most other readers) sees great similarity between Cohen's analysis and his own. While much of Cohen's work is concerned with the interactional dynamics by which youths collectively recognize the delinquent subculture as a solution to their status-frustration problems, he is quite explicit about the structural contradictions or strains which generate status-frustration in the first place. In Cohen's own words, "The delinquent subculture . . . is a way of adjustment [to] status problems: certain children are denied status in respectable society because they cannot meet the criteria of the respectable status system."[45] Why can't they meet these criteria? Cohen proceeds at length to outline the structurally generated blocks to lower-class youths' ability to realize culturally desired goals. These include class differentials in the organization of child-rearing and parental aspirations which make it more likely that lower-class youths will fail in school and the world of work and thereby experience an exaggerated sense of status-frustration, making them particularly vulnerable to the solution offered by the delinquent subculture: a collective rejection of middle-class aspirations that they were structurally unable to obtain in the first place.[46] Without formally using the term *anomie,* Cohen thus appears to make an argument that is highly compatible with Merton's use of this concept. In this sense, Cohen's work, like that of Cloward and Ohlin, represents a valuable extension of the line of sociological reasoning introduced by Émile Durkheim and reformulated by Robert K. Merton.

IDENTIFYING ANOMIC DEVIANCE

In the period following the Second World War, America was alive with a renewed faith in the positive power of science. American scientific know-how had, after all, ended the war. In the postwar years it was up to science to likewise conquer the natural and social problems of a more peaceable time and to preserve the world for the American way of life. This naive revival of faith in the scientific enterprise is somewhat bizarre, given that America's greatest scientific achievement during the war was the nuclear holocaust of thousands of people in Hiroshima and Nagasaki. Perhaps the horrific nature of this scientific accomplishment was simply too staggering for Americans to grasp. In any event, the postwar years were filled with a new scientific commitment to the ever more destructive technologies of defense, as well as the conquest of outer space, bodily disease, and such diverse social problems as poverty, crime, drug addiction, and mental disorders.

The research methods used by social scientists associated with the anomie perspective have generally reflected the professional-technical interests of the post–World War II liberal welfare state. For the most part, anomie researchers used the quantifiable tools of survey research (fixed questionnaires and coded interviews) or data drawn from official statistics. These tools produced statistical measures of anomie and its relationship to deviance. By adopting such quantifiable research instruments sociologists dressed themselves in the authoritative garb of "hard science" and thereby managed to obtain a piece of the profitable pie of scientific problem-solving.

Unfortunately, this commitment to a hard-science method of social research distracted most anomie researchers from the insights which were potentially available from other, less quantifiable forms of investigation. In particular, most anomie research was lacking in a historical perspective on the origins of the social structures being studied and in the rich experiential viewpoint provided by field studies. Indeed, a comprehensive inventory of eighty-six studies of anomie published between 1941 and 1964 indicates that only four included the use of historical methods, while only nine employed field-observation or participatory techniques. On the other hand, sixty studies used the quantitative tools of the survey (questionnaire and interview methods), and another fifteen involved the analysis of official statistics.[47] This is not to suggest that anomie research failed to provide a variety of useful insights into the contradictory relationship between social structure and deviant behavior. It is simply to point out that the vast percentage of such studies operated within the narrow confines of the professional-technical research model which came to dominate American sociology in the mid-twentieth century. For the most part, this model systematically neglected the historical development of specific social-structural arrangements and the concrete human experiences of persons said to be caught up in such structures.

Specific Measures of Anomie

Within the general confines of the professional-technical research tradition described above, investigators developed several well-known measures of anomie. In the following paragraphs, I will describe three of the most commonly discussed measurement techniques. The first presents itself as an objective measure of normlessness within a given community. The second and third represent attempts to quantitatively assess the subjective experience of anomie at the individual level.

One of the best-known and most commonly cited objective indicators of anomie was developed by Bernard Lander in his study of 8,464 cases of delinquency in Baltimore, Maryland, between 1939 and 1942.[48] The substantive results in Lander's work have been discussed previously, as they provide data related to certain themes of the social disorganization perspective. With regard to anomie, Lander devised a three-factor cluster index which included official data on the rate of delinquency, a measurement of the percentage of nonwhite population within a particular geographical area, and the percentage of homes which were owner-occupied. According to Lander, these things were indicative of normlessness within a given community insomuch as they were believed to reflect "the breakdown or weakening of the regulatory structure of society."[49] While delinquency was taken as direct evidence of the lack of normative regulation, a large percentage of nonwhites in a previously white area was considered to be an indicator of the transitory or unstable nature of a particular neighborhood. Lack of home ownership was taken as a measure of family instability, another indicator of normlessness.

In analyzing these factors, Lander found high rates of delinquency to be related both to low percentage of home ownership and to high rates of nonwhite population (until this measure reached 50 percent, after which the rate decreased in proportion to an increasing percentage of nonwhites). Lander's findings have been challenged by researchers such as Roland Chilton, who has underscored the importance of economic as well as anomic factors in relationship to delinquency.[50] Nonetheless, Lander's methods have been commented upon positively by Merton, who characterized them as "a symptomatic advance" toward "a measure of anomie, as an objective condition of life."[51]

Subjective measures of anomie have generally taken one of two directions—the use of the five-item scale developed by Leo Srole in 1956[52] or some variation of what might best be described as a measure of position discontent. The Srole scale attempts to identify the experience of anomia, or an individual's sense of being dislocated within the world of social structure. It does so by posing five questions. These seek to tap a person's sense regarding whether (1) community leaders are indifferent to his or her needs; (2) little can be accomplished in a society which is basically unpredictable and lacking order; (3) life goals are receding rather than being realized; (4) life holds little meaning and small prospect for one's children; and (5) one cannot count on associates for social and psychological support.

Do the questions posed by Srole really tap into the concept of anomie as developed by Durkheim and/or modified by Merton? According to Dorothy Meier and Wendell Bell, Srole's scale can be better described as an index of such things as despair, hopelessness, and discouragement.[53] Other researchers point to a certain imprecision in differentiating anomie from the more generic concept of alienation. As Gwynn Nettler points out, although "alienation and anomie are undoubtedly correlated; at least it is difficult to conceive of any notable degree of anomie that would not result in alienation . . . this seems poor reason for confusing the two."[54] Robert Merton, however, viewed Srole's scale of anomia in somewhat different terms.[55] Merton recognized that Srole's instrument measured anomia as a subjective condition of individuals (a concept closer to the psychological meaning of alienation than Merton's own formulation of anomie as a structural disjuncture between socially promoted goals and socially approved means of goal attainment). Nonetheless, Merton argued that when aggregated, the Srole scale could provide an effective measure of the means-ends discrepancy within the society at large. In other words, by combining individual measures of anomia into an aggregate measure, one "would then constitute an index of anomie for the given social unit under investigation."[56] For Merton, this procedure offered the distinct advantage of "combining indices of anomie (of social systems) with indices of (individual) anomia" and thereby of testing the hypothesis that individuals with like degrees of anomia "are more apt to engage in deviant behavior, the higher the degree of anomie in the social system."[57]

A second subjective measure of anomie, a measure of position discontent, attempts to obtain an index of the degree of pressure toward deviant behavior that is exerted by one's aspirations. Following the lead of Merton and the subsequent extension of his theory by Cloward and Ohlin, and by Cohen, the position-discontent measure seeks to identify discrepancies between a person's socially nurtured aspirations and his or her socially positioned expectancy to fulfill those aspirations. Such a measure was used by James Short and his associates in a series of studies of delinquency in Chicago.[58] Through the use of interviews, Short obtained measures of discrepancies between occupational aspirations and expectations, as well as information on discrepancies between a father's actual occupation (a somewhat more objective measure) and the aspirations and expectations of boys studied. Using these measures of anomie, Short compared gang boys with nongang boys from the same neighborhoods as well as with middle-class boys from other neighborhoods. Black and white subsamples were also obtained for each category so as to assess the differences between the socially positioned aspirations and expectations of youths in a society where race makes a difference.

A Concluding Comment on Anomie Research: The Use of Official Statistics on Deviance

While anomie has commonly been measured by one of the objective or subjective measures discussed above, the measurement of deviance by anomie researchers has generally involved the use of official government statistics. This introduces a certain bias into the research process. Official data cannot be equated with valid and reliable scientific data. They are collected by and for the use of public agencies. At one end of the reporting process they include commonsense stereotypical perceptions by police and various diagnostic agents as to who is likely to be seen as deviant. Such things as location of residence, appearance, demeanor, race, gender, social class, and the timing and context of the official judgment all play a part. In the middle of the record-keeping process are organizational factors affecting the quantity and style of official data production. These include such things as pressure from above or below, the style of management, the availability of clerical help, and the reward structure within the social control agency. On the other hand, a number of overtly political factors also contribute to official reports. What will the public think? How will the presentation of data affect future funding? All of these factors make the exclusive use of official data a poor vehicle for assessing deviance.

Dependence upon official statistics to define deviants is not limited to the anomie perspective. Indeed most researchers associated with the social disorganization and functionalist perspectives chart the distribution of deviance in a similar fashion. Yet, because of the critical potential of anomie theory, its nearly exclusive reliance on official data by anomie theorists is particularly disturbing. Why? Given their awareness of the systemic nature of structured social inequality, why should Merton and his students be satisfied with the inequality of the data on deviance that find their way into the public record? Perhaps the answer is to be found in what we have referred to as the professional-technical posture of post–World War II government-sponsored social science research. While Merton himself opposed the abandonment of social science problem formulation to the demands or needs of state bureaucracies, it is today evident that the bulk of social science research accepted official definitions of what and who was deviant. Definitions of problems followed the money. The question for most liberal social scientists was to explain the troublesome deviance of the lower class. Research in the anomie tradition generally followed suit.

SOCIAL CONTROL OF ANOMIC DEVIANCE

Control strategies associated with the anomie perspective aim at changing the structures of society as a whole. Different structural changes are recommended by each of the perspective's two dominant theoretical strands. For the Durkheimian strand social control is said to begin with the reconstruction of the normative, or moral, structure of society. There is a certain contemporary ring to this call for moral reconstruction. America during the 1980s is experiencing a widescale return to traditional moral and religious values. Recall our discussion in Chapter 3 of the rise of the Moral Majority and other groups preaching a revival of morality. When I presented an early draft of that chapter to a postdoctoral seminar on the sociology of social control at Yale University, one of the participants commented upon what he perceived to be a great similarity between the chapter's opening quotation by Rev. Jerry Falwell and Durkheim's descriptions of anomie and the need for moral reconstruction. Indeed, Falwell and Durkheim offer related diagnoses of the moral malaise affecting the modern world. They part ways, however, regarding what to do about this malaise. Falwell wants us to return to the fundamentalist religious values of yesteryear. Durkheim beckons us toward the establishment of a new civic or secular moral order. For Durkheim, religion was viewed as the basis for moral order in the previous days of traditional *mechanical* society. Modern *organic* society must construct a new secular base for civic morality.

Durkheim: Constructing a Secular Moral Order for Modern Society

Durkheim's call for establishing a new secular moral order took two general forms. The first involved his proposal for the formation of occupational associations which would provide experiential ties for increasingly specialized workers in the highly rational modern economy. In traditional or mechanical society workers performed more similar economic tasks and were in this sense linked together in the rituals of everyday labor. In modern organic society a highly specialized division of the labor force separated workers from each other and thereby inhibited the development of common moral perspectives on life and its organization. By proposing the development of modern occupational associations Durkheim envisioned the development of socially organized "modal points" where workers in varying occupational positions could come together and forge a common perspective.[59]

Durkheim was, unfortunately, never very specific about the exact nature of his proposed occupational associations. They would not be equated with trade unions, which Durkheim saw as creating a permanent conflict between workers and employers. Nor were they a revival of the medieval guild, an organization regulating the economic activities of a particular craft or trade. They would be wide in scope and more interested in the general social structure than either of these forms. They would mediate political relations between individuals and the centralized state and resolve conflicts within and between local groups. Such occupational associations would also be involved in a wide range of educational and recreational activities. They would be "close enough to the individual for him to be able to rely directly upon [them], and durable enough to be able to give him a perspective."[60]

The second general area for moral reconstruction was education. Durkheim was an active adviser to the Ministry of Education in France during the period of the Third Republic. In that capacity Durkheim argued that it was the moral duty of social scientists to use their knowledge to guide public affairs along an enlightened course.[61] The course Durkheim had in mind was one informed by the scientific findings of sociology. In this sense, sociology was for Durkheim the functional equivalent of what religion had been in the past—a means of making sense of the world and of morally orienting oneself toward future action.

In his book *The Rules of the Sociological Method* Durkheim stated that "the future is already written for him who knows how to read it."[62] And how better can one read the future than by the disciplined study of sociology? Durkheim believed that sociology would foster a new form of secular morality based upon a rational comprehension of social facts. In France, where Durkheim's influence was enormous, sociology was introduced as a key element in the curriculum of the *écoles normales,* institutions which prepared future generations of primary and secondary school teachers. By 1914, the Durkheimian perspective had become a standard feature of elementary school courses in civic morality throughout France.[63]

Merton: Reducing Aspirations or Increasing Opportunities

For Merton the social control of anomic deviance took a different form. It was directed at efforts to eliminate the strain between societal goals and differentially available means. In principle this could be achieved in one of two ways. First, society could be resocialized to accept the "reality" that all persons were not meant to achieve the same goals. This would reinforce, rather than eliminate, the present class system. It would introduce the ideology of caste, eradicating any sentiments favoring the "myth" that all people were to have equal access to societal resources. The poor were meant to be indigent and the rich wealthy! Without aspirations which could not be met there would be little tension between goals and means, no structural inducement toward deviance.

The classic sociological example of a society organized without structured conflict over unmet aspirations is that of traditional India. Guided by religious principles, traditional Indian society was organized into distinct castes. Some castes were highly privileged. Others were less advantaged. At the bottom was a caste of "untouchables," truly the lowest of the low. According to traditional Indian beliefs all of this inequality was supernaturally ordained. Nobody aspired to more. One's caste was one's fate for life. It could not be changed. Mobility between caste groupings was unthinkable. In such a fatalistic system one would expect few of the structural strains toward deviance suggested by Merton's analysis.

As attractive as it may be for those at the top of society, it would be difficult to effectively establish a caste-system ideology within American society. For too many years too many people have spent too much time trying to convert the "noble lie" about equality in America into some semblance of truth.

The second control strategy flowing from Merton's formulation demands far more of the same. Smash the lie about equality of means and replace it with a genuine system of equal access for all! The realization of current affirmative-action, equal-opportunity, antiracism, and antisexism strategies would be in keeping with this aspect of the anomie perspective. By removing barriers to equal access to societal goals, one might hope to eliminate contradictions with the American social structure. Deviance would thus be reduced because people had been given an equal opportunity to conform.

In the early 1960s Merton's ideas about anomie were translated into an applied program of social reform. This was particularly the case for the portions of Merton's work embodied in Richard Cloward and Lloyd Ohlin's thesis regarding the relationship between delinquency and the opportunity structures of society. At the time that they were completing their book *Delinquency and Opportunity,* Cloward and Ohlin worked closely with staff members of the Henry Street Settlement in New York City's Lower East Side. The result was a sociologically informed program of "action research" referred to as Mobilization for Youth. Plans for this program called for a massive assault on the socially structured obstacles to success for youths in a predominantly nonwhite sixty-seven-block area of Manhattan. In essence, Mobilization for Youth was directed at the following objectives:

1 to increase the employment ability of youths from low-income families,
2 to improve and make more accessible training and work preparation facilities,
3 to help young people achieve employment goals equal to their capacities,
4 to increase employment opportunities for the area's youth, and
5 to help minority-group youngsters overcome discrimination in hiring.[64]

To meet the above-stated objectives, Mobilization for Youth proposed a series of programmatic interventions designed, not only to deliver specialized educational, vocational, and youth-worker services, but also to assist residents of lower-income neighborhoods in developing effective strategies of community organization. These things, it was hoped, would in turn reduce delinquency and other, related forms of deviance (alcoholism, drug addiction, etc.). Mobilization for Youth was a far-reaching program of theoretically based social experimentation, an attempt to systematically blend sociology with social reform.[65] In the early 1960s this blend resonated well with the liberal domestic politics of President John F. Kennedy. Soon after his 1961 inauguration, Kennedy voiced a long-standing family commitment to the problems of youth by appointing a high-level presidential commission on juvenile delinquency. David

Hackett, the executive director of this group (the President's Committee on Juvenile Delinquency and Youth Crime), was briefed on the central tenets of anomie theory by officers of the philanthropic Ford Foundation. Cloward and Ohlin were consultants to the Ford Foundation. Hackett soon recognized an affinity between their ideas and the Kennedy administration's promise of a New Frontier of equal opportunity.

Ohlin, a professor at Harvard, was invited to join the committee in devising a new battle plan to combat delinquency. Fresh with ideas about the proposed Mobilization for Youth, Ohlin helped shape the course of federal legislation authorizing the expenditure of $10 million over the course of three years. This legislation called for coordinated community action to alter the opportunity structures constraining the integration of low-income youths in the mainstream of American society. Its preamble reads like a passage from Cloward and Ohlin's book on this topic.[66]

New York City's Mobilization for Youth was among the first programs to receive federal funds under the new legislation. This program was, after all, something of a blueprint for the legislative package as a whole. On May 31, 1962, Mobilization for Youth was blessed by a formal White House garden ceremony and awarded a three-year grant of $12.5 million. Additional funds were provided by the Ford Foundation and by New York City. Ideas originating in the sociological writings of a former street-gang member from South Philadelphia (Merton) were now officially sanctioned as those of the U.S. government. These ideas had been well received in academic circles. How well did they fare when put into practice on New York's Lower East Side?

Mobilization for Youth was a precursor of seventeen similar programs established during the early 1960s.[67] How successful were such programs? If measured by a specific reduction in delinquency, they generated few positive outcomes. Why? The general consensus among thoughtful observers is that such programs were doomed to failure because they were at once too radical and not radical enough.

Programs based on the Mobilization blueprint were generally too radical for those who had originally commissioned them. This was especially the case for their community-organization components. Recall that a key aspect of Mobilization for Youth involved efforts to "organize the afflicted—to overturn the status quo and replace it with a higher level of stability, without delinquents, alcoholism or drug addiction."[68] Some participants may have become too serious in realizing this goal. Lower-income citizens actually began using federal funds to strategically oppose a wide range of systemic blocks to equal opportunity. Mobilization efforts supported rent strikes, public demonstrations, and legal action on behalf of welfare clients. Participants began to collect data on patterns of discrimination and housing code violations by landlords.

Theoretically these political developments should be judged as evidence of the project's success. Poor people were using the tools of the system to make the system more responsive to their goals and aspirations. This was not how those who were already part of the system saw it. Within a short time participants in Mobilization for Youth were being described by the *New York Daily News* as "Commies and Commie sympathizers."

It was not long before Mobilization, a child of the government, became harassed and thereafter abandoned by its fearful parent. The Federal Bureau of Investigation conducted investigations of key community organizers. Project files were confiscated. The use of federal and local funds was questioned and eventually denied.[69] A similar dismantling was occurring in Washington. The presidential committee which had promoted the Mobilization concept was allowed to wither away. This committee had always encountered resistance from entrenched bureaucratic interests within the federal government. Yet, as LaMar Empey points out, when complaints and charges of radicalism reached the legislative halls of the Capitol, "influential members of Congress made it clear that the mandate of the President's Committee was to reduce delinquency, not to reform urban society or try out sociological theories on American youths."[70] But what was it that was so radical about Mobilization for Youth? What could be more American than trying to incorporate all people into the opportunity structure of the society as a whole? The answer is provided by Richard Quinney, who suggests that what was most fearful about Mobilization for Youth was its potential for becoming a "widespread movement among the poor."[71] According to Quinney, "to provide the poor with services and assistance from above has been the traditional way of doing things; it is regarded as subversive when the poor attempt to change the social pattern of their poverty."[72]

Rife with controversy, Mobilization for Youth soon dissolved into the unequal American opportunity structure which it had been designed to challenge. Its challenge was short-lived. Its last days were full of conflict, not only between participants and opponents, but also between staff and those who were to benefit from staff efforts.[73] Within a few years the program has become little more than a reminder of the turbulent 1960s in which it was conceived. There has been little in the way of serious assessment of its actual effect on the rate of delinquency. Perhaps its vision was simply never radical enough. The practical power of the sociological reformers proved no match for the strong political and economic interests of those threatened by a fundamental restructuring of the American opportunity system. With this in mind it is easy to understand why Mobilization for Youth was sentenced to death before attempting its crime. The reason is simple. In the words of Alan Liska, "changing social conditions means changing the lives of those in power, and they resist."[74]

THE ANOMIE PERSPECTIVE TODAY

The anomie perspective has had enormous influence on contemporary thinking about deviance and social control. In his book *Sociology Since Mid-Century* Randall Collins observes that anomie "was the dominant theory in the area of deviance from the early 1950s until about 1970."[75] According to Collins, Merton's essay "Social Structure and Anomie" is the "most cited paper in all of sociology."[76] A similar point was made by Albert Cohen. Writing in 1965, Cohen noted that "'anomie theory' . . . has been the most influential single formulation in the sociology of deviance in the last 25 years."[77] No small credit for this should go to Cohen himself. In considering the fact that Merton's essay sat dormant for about fifteen years after its first publication in 1938, Collins suggests the possibility that its importance became widely recognized only after Cohen's critique. Collins asks that we consider the possibility that "it was really Albert K. Cohen who made Merton famous in this area, and not vice versa."[78] In this regard, one should also note the role of Richard Cloward and Lloyd Ohlin in attracting attention to the anomie framework. A recent survey of literature on crime and delinquency discovered that Cloward and Ohlin's book *Delinquency and Opportunity* was one of the two most cited publications in the field of criminology.[79]

The writings of Cohen and of Cloward and Ohlin undoubtedly contributed to the widespread recognition of Merton's anomie formulation, but they do not account for its general acceptance by sociologists of deviance through most of the 1950s and 1960s. Was the available empirical evidence so convincing that the theory could not be denied? Hardly! Although a fairly large number of studies drew upon the conceptual imagery of anomie, few provided a direct test of Merton's position. According to Don Gibbons and Joseph Jones, "anomie propositions have been employed most commonly as a high-level explanatory metaphor, with no real attempt to assess their theoretical utility."[80] Relatively few of the papers citing Merton provide a test of his theory. Even fewer present contradictory evidence. Most simply reference Merton's formulation as part of a review of the literature or as support for their own theoretical positions.

Why was the anomie perspective so widely accepted despite a lack of clear empirical support for its central concepts? According to Marshall Clinard, the widespread endorsement of anomie theory reflects "a common tendency in sociology to accept intriguing and well-formulated theories in advance of adequate empirical support."[81] What accounts for this tendency? The most plausible sociological answer is that the vision offered by an untested but commonly accepted theory shares an affinity with the more general, commonsensical vision of scholars at the time. Indeed this was clearly the case with anomie theorizing. This becomes evident when one considers the historical situation of American sociology in the years following World War II. During the postwar years nearly all walks of American society were affected by what is today commonly known as the rise of the modern welfare state. This term refers to the spiderlike involvement of government bureaucracies in the organization of everyday life. Most historians mark the New Deal, or the massive entrance of the federal government into the social and economic life of the nation during the 1930s depression, as a significant step in the direction of the modern welfare state. During World War II the influence of government grew larger, and it stayed large after the war's completion. In the years following the war millions of Americans came to believe in the necessity and efficacy of the the government's involvement in, and regulation of matters related to, nearly all human social problems. Put into practice this belief led to an enormous expansion of governmental agencies. This expansion was so great that by the early 1970s opposition to the long reach of governmental bureaucracy had become a major political battle cry.

In what ways did the rise of the welfare state affect the discipline of sociology? The answer to this question provides significant clues as to why the anomie perspective was adopted so readily by sociologists during the 1950s. The growth of the welfare state led to a growth in professional sociology. As Alvin Gouldner points out, "The social sciences increasingly became a well financed technological basis for the Welfare State's effort to solve the problems of its industrial society."[82] In one three-year period in the early 1960s federal spending on social science research rose approximately 70 percent. In 1962 the federal government invested $118 million in such research. By

1964 it spent $200 million.[83] This large-scale government financing of sociological research was accompanied by a demand for applied, or useful, programs of research. It also altered what was demanded from sociological theory. Theory must be made to fit the practical needs of bureaucratic problem-solvers because along with government money comes the expectation "that the social sciences will help administrators to design and operate national policies, welfare apparatus, urban settlements, and even industrial establishments."[84]

The demand for usable, applied sociological theory presented certain dilemmas for sociologists of the 1950s and early 1960s. In the first place, American sociology remained generally within the conceptual grip of functionalist theorizing. As suggested in the preceding chapter, functionalism provided sociology with an optimistic viewpoint on how problems such as deviance could be viewed as actually contributing to the vitality of the social system as a whole. Yet, since functionalism could easily identify a manifest or latently positive consequence of almost anything, it offered little of the "system-fixing" utility demanded by government funding agencies.

Sociologists could, of course, abandon their theoretical concerns when turning their eyes toward applied matters. Many did. This led to a kind of schizoid division between sociological theory and research, to the gulf between what sociological critic C. Wright Mills described as the vacuous realm of "grand theory" and the administratively oriented practice of "abstracted empiricism."[85] It also led to the danger that sociologists would be co-opted by those who paid them, or as Nanette Davis states, that they would be "drafted as common intellectual laborers, capable of fulfilling technical tasks, but unable to understand . . . the direction and form of dominant institutions."[86]

How could sociologists escape the dilemmas outlined above? How could they respond to demands for applied theorizing while retaining the intellectual heritage of sociology? The work of Robert K. Merton provided a solution. Merton argued for a theory of the "middle range." Such a theory would retain functionalism's concern for the interrelationship of parts within the structure of the system as a whole. At the same time it would be pitched at a low enough level of abstraction so as to be translated into empirical research and concrete policy analysis. Middle-range theory was an ideal solution for sociologists at work in the welfare state. It would be theoretically abstract enough for them to maintain their identity as detached scholars. It would be practically concrete enough for them to maintain attachments to the business of problem-solving and to reap the financial and political benefits associated with government-sponsored research.

One area of sociological specialization to particularly benefit from Merton's concept of middle-range theory was that involving the study of deviance. Merton's theory of social structure and anomie was the middle-range theory par excellence. It was commonly viewed as both theoretically sophisticated and practically useful. It excited both the sociological imagination and that of the bureaucratic welfare-state reformer. It had another advantage as well. It could be viewed as critical of certain elements in the existing social structure without being read as critical of the system as a whole. In this sense Merton's theory of anomie was basically an "All-American" theory. As Randall Collins suggests, "the great American creed of social mobility occupies the center of the stage, and lack of mobility opportunities (not the more fundamental structure of inequalities of distribution) is the villain of this structural drama."[87] It was this quality more than any other which may have enhanced the marketability of the anomie perspective during the 1950s. Having said this, let us examine the legacy of anomie as it was translated into a practical program of sociological research.

Empirical Studies of Anomic Deviance

Numerous empirical studies have employed concepts related to anomie. Studies of mental disorders have sought to document the relationship between rising rates of schizophrenia and "breakdown in [the] controlling and regularity functions" of the social system as a whole.[88] Studies of drug use and addiction have also drawn upon the anomie framework. Of particular importance are studies clarifying the applicability of Merton's category of retreatism. Are drug users actually persons who are blocked in the use of both legitimate and illegitimate means? Merton argued that such persons were externally constrained in the use of legitimate means. At the same time, they were said to be denied illegitimate means by the tight internal moral constraints of conscience. Cloward and Ohlin disagreed. They viewed drug users not as doubly blocked escapists but as double failures. They were persons who had unsuccessfully explored both illegitimate and legitimate avenues of goal attainment before dropping out into a retreatist subculture. This interpretation is challenged by data presented by reseachers Daniel Glaser[89] and Michael Lewis.[90] In separate studies Glaser and Lewis conclude that lower-class drug addicts do not really drop out of the innovative-means or illegitimate-means category. To support their expensive habits addicts commonly work hard within the employment structure of the criminal world. Nor is the initial choice of drugs an exclusively retreatist endeavor. As Alfred Lindesmith and John Simon suggest, the differential availability of drugs within different neighborhoods may be as much or more of a factor in determining drug use than strains toward retreatism.[91]

In addition to studies of mental disorders and drug use, a considerable body of anomie-related research has accumulated on the topic of suicide.

Indeed some of the most significant studies of the problem have been guided by the theoretical imagery of anomie. Of particular importance are the 1954 work of Henry and Short,[92] the 1969 research of Ronald Maris,[93] and the more recent investigations of Jack Gibbs and Walter Martin.[94] In varying ways each of these studies attempts to document the relationship between the absence of normative constraint or social integration and the presence of high rates of suicide.

Also important is the large of body of delinquency research which draws upon the analytic framework of anomie. For a comprehensive review of this research see LaMar Empey's *American Delinquency*.[95] Of particular relevance is Empey's consideration of the relationship between socially structured strain and juvenile lawbreaking. This crucial area of anomie reseach may also be the most confusing. It is crucial because strain is typically viewed as the causal link between a contradictory social structure and concrete instances of deviance. It is confusing because this concept has rarely been measured in precise terms. Most delinquency research simply assumes that strain must be present when youth report such things as the low likelihood that they will graduate from school. Unfortunately there have been few direct measures of strain itself. Thus, according to Empey, "we do not really know whether . . . assumptions [regarding the presence of strain] are true."[96] This lack of knowledge has yielded the center stage of delinquency research to studies of aspiration levels, such as that conducted by Travis Hirschi. Hirschi found that juveniles with high aspirations were less likely to be deviant than those with lower aspirations. From this he concluded that "frustrated occupational ambitions . . . cannot be an important cause of delinquency."[97]

Empey entertains the possibility that Hirschi might be correct. He also explores the suggestion that youthful frustration may arise from something other than a failure to realize long-term occupational aspirations. Reference is made to a variety of studies suggesting that for many students, particularly those who do not present themselves in terms of a set of preformulated aspirational goals, school itself may be a frustrating experience.[98] Anomie strain, in other words, may be "created not by frustration of deeply held conventional goals, but by the interaction of students who lack such goals with teachers and principals who think they ought to have them."[99] Hirschi argues somewhat differently. Seemingly determined to turn the anomie argument inside out, Hirschi contends that those who get in trouble in school are neither disproportionately lower-class nor teacher-frustrated. They are simply those with a minimal commitment to the legitimate means of success, those who are little motivated toward hard work, deferral of gratification, and long-range planning. Hirschi views such troublesome youths as poorly or inadequately controlled.

Maybe, but what is the root cause of this out-of-controlness? In Chapter 6 we considered the specifics of Hirschi's own control theory. This focuses upon the immediate interactional context in which people acquire internal constraints and come under the normative control of others. The anomie perspective asks that we relocate individuals, and their internal and interactional constraints, within the wider world of social structure. Failing to find a relationship between class position and strains toward delinquency, Hirschi retreats to the level of individual and interactional analysis. This retreat should not be taken as evidence of the insufficiency of the anomie perspective. Perhaps it is a structured denial of a sense of control over one's own destiny that frustrates youth and not class position or school experience alone. In our society self-control is an aspiration for nearly all males. Nonetheless in the mundane and often boring routines of everyday life, few of us find that we are actually in control of our own social, political, or economic destinies. What a horrific awareness—anomie in its most extreme form. Perhaps most nondelinquents have simply been protected from this awareness by a variety of things which distract them from this fundamental lack of control—concern with interpersonal relations, looking good, having a car that works, getting to the job on time—things which Hirschi might view as elements of control, but which a more radical version of anomie theory might see as illusions of control. Delinquents, on the other hand, through some combination of structural position and life experience, might more clearly see and act toward the social world as it "really" is—as out of control. I do not in any way mean to romanticize the delinquent. My point is simply to suggest one of the many as yet unexplored possibilities for the study of anomie strain.

THE ADEQUACY OF THE ANOMIE PERSPECTIVE

Aspirations to deviate are rooted in the structural contradictions of society. This is the essential message of the anomie perspective. It is an important message, one that has had an enormous impact on the sociological study of deviance in the mid-twentieth century. It is also the message of two enormously important sociologists, Durkheim and Merton, scholars who have oriented and reoriented social science inquiry toward the analysis of the systemic interrelationship between parts within the structure of society as a whole.

This is not to say that most sociologists have come to agree upon the specifics of Durkheim's or Merton's analysis. Each has been the subject of major and sustained criticism. Yet, despite a variety of specific critiques, the general theoretical thrust of both Durkheim's and Merton's formulation has endured.

Specific Criticisms of Durkheim and Merton

Durkheim's work on anomic suicide has been the subject of numerous critical essays. Whitney Pope, for instance, points to several specific weaknesses in Durkheim's formulation.[100] According to Pope, Durkheim's conception of the causal link between normative deregulation and suicide is vague and occasionally contradictory. In developing his explanation Durkheim refers to such diverse matters as a structurally induced discrepancy between aspirations and means, stress created by the collapse of external standards, meaninglessness resulting from a breakdown in social constraints, and even social irresponsibility generated by moral deregulation. Pope argues that this inconsistency prevented Durkheim from developing a coherent explanation of the dynamics of anomic suicide. Pope also quarrels with Durkheim's interpretation of his statistical data. After reanalyzing many of the statistics used by Durkheim, Pope argues that empirical support for Durkheim's thesis is less conclusive than once believed. Instances are noted where cases that don't fit are either ignored or inadequately explained.[101]

Merton's work has also been criticized on numerous grounds. Marshall Clinard lists eleven areas in which Merton's thesis has been faulted by contemporary sociologists.[102] Many of these criticisms have been discussed earlier in this chapter. Some have been incorporated into subsequent revisions of Merton's theory. This is the case, for instance, with Cohen's criticisms regarding the overly atomistic and falsely discontinuous aspects of the theory of social structure and anomie. Others have taken issue with the implication that the highest rates of deviance occur among the lower classes. The structural position of lower-class persons might make them more susceptible to the opportunities offered by certain deviant adaptations. The same, however, might be said of middle-class managers and upper-class owners of highly competitive corporations. Aren't such persons also exposed to powerful strains to use any available means to achieve the great American dream of being number one? The failure of Merton and his students to systematically consider anomic deviation by the more privileged social classes may be associated with what we have previously referred to as the theory's responsiveness to the prepackaged problem-solving demands of the

American welfare state, and with its users' unfortunate reliance upon the analysis of official statistics. Other criticisms are directed toward what is left out of Merton's theory—attention to the intervening impact of being labeled deviant and the failure to consider anomie in societies where social position is fixed or ascribed, as opposed to those societies in which aspirations for upward mobility are culturally reinforced.

Enduring Theoretical Concerns: The General Importance of Durkheim and Merton

The general theoretical message of the anomie perspective has weathered the storm of numerous specific criticisms. The ideas presented by Durkheim and Merton have become part of the theoretical core of the contemporary sociological imagination. In this sense, both sociologists realized their own theoretical goals. Each was concerned more with presenting a general conceptual orientation than with laying out a series of precisely testable propositions. This, for Durkheim, was the proper role of sociological theory for a science "still in the stage of system building." In his preface to *Suicide* Durkheim notes a preference for "brilliant generalities," as opposed to casting a more focused "light upon a limited portion of the . . . field."[103] Merton viewed his own theoretical project in similar terms. According to Merton the goal of sociological theory is to provide "general orientations toward data, suggesting types of variables which theorists must . . . take into account, rather than clearly formulated, verifiable statements of relationships."[104] This is a good description of what Durkheim's and Merton's theories accomplished. On these terms their work can only be judged as a success.

Durkheim's and Merton's conceptual concerns converge at a general point of theoretical orientation. High rates of deviance are said to be structurally encouraged by contradictory developments in the organization of society. If you ask a sociologist how to deal with the problem of deviant people, don't be surprised if the answer suggests that you must first deal with the problem of social structure. This is the basic point made by most sociologists today. According to theoretical commentator Robert Bierstadt, the point is simply this: "It is not wayward personalities but ordinary social structure that motivate behavior that is labeled deviant."[105]

Concluding Comments: Limitations of the Anomie Perspective

The attempt to link deviant behavior to the contradictory organization of social structure is clearly a strength of the anomie perspective. Nonetheless, in closing our discussion of anomie I will point to two general problems with the use of social-structure concepts by anomie theorists. The first involves an overly exaggerated sense of the unity of social structure. The second suggests an area where structural analysis is not extended far enough.

Overly Exaggerated Structural Unity Anomie theory overly exaggerates, or reifies, the idea of a unitary structure for society as a whole. Merton paints a picture of a unitary U.S. society bound together in a common cultural commitment to the goals of the great American dream. But is American culture really as homogeneous as Merton suggests? Merton's position is challenged by those who view society as a collection of interrelated but frequently competitive subgroups or subcultures, each with a relatively distinct set of cultural goals. Merton is undoubtedly correct that the entirety of American society is bombarded by the mass mediation of cultural values. Indeed the American household without a television or two is a rarity. Nonetheless, the specific impact of mass mediation may itself be mediated by a plurality of diverse ethnic, regional, gender, class, age, and neighborhood reference groups.

Critics of the unitary-culture thesis, such as Edwin Lemert, contend that American society might better be described in terms of value pluralism.[106] Lemert suggests that what appears as unitary in American culture is, in actuality, the result of the efforts of dominant groups to extend their own values in such a way as "to become a basis for normative regulation of ethnic or religious populations having divergent values."[107] Lemert envisions society as a collective of subgroups competing with unequal resources for the prize of cultural dominance. Other critics view subcultures as arising out of or in reaction to the cultural categories of dominant groups. This is the way Cohen explained what he perceived to be the anti-middle-class values of the delinquent culture. The subculture of delinquent boys was described as a collective reaction formation against the values and goals of a parent culture which systematically denied access to those with lower-class backgrounds. In somewhat different fashion Walter Miller described the entirety of lower-class culture as founded upon values differentiating it from other groups in society. Miller viewed the lower-class subculture as providing a basis by which disadvantaged groups might adjust to the realities of class society. At the same time, focal concerns of lower-class culture (trouble, toughness, smartness, excitement, fate, and autonomy) constantly pitted the lower class against the dominant institutions of the wider society. This contradictory and somewhat paradoxical characteristic of subcultures has led sociologist Milton Yinger to the development of the idea of *contracultures*. Of related interest is the recent use of the term *subculture* by Dick Hebdige and other British scholars.[108] In studying the coded meaning of the contemporary punk subculture, Hebdige suggests that subcultural styles represent a forceful, if often unrecognized, rejection of the cultural dominance, or *hegemony,* of those in structured positions of power.

Each of the above-mentioned subcultural approaches rejects assumptions regarding the cultural unity of society as a whole. So do recent studies of the deviance and criminality of women. Theorists like Eileen Leonard point out that women in America have been presented with goals quite dissimilar from those presented to men.[109] In contrast to the success-oriented male version of the American dream, "The goal that women are traditionally socialized to desire . . . is marriage and a family; the accepted means is to secure the romantic love of a man through courtship."[110] Leonard criticizes Merton's formulation for failing to recognize this basic division of American culture in terms of gender. But what if Merton's theory was reformulated so as to apply to the deviance of women culturally indoctrinated into the goals of wifehood and family raising? Leonard reformulates anomie theory in such a way. Her revision of Merton's theory offers a partial explanation for traditional differences between the crime rates of men and women. Women, argues Leonard, have had relatively easy access to the goals of marriage and the family. For this reason, she suggests, they may not have been subject to the same anomic strains toward crime as men, exposed to the less achievable goals of economic dominance. In Leonard's words, "Women have very low aspirations and their goals are extremely accessible."[111]

The same logic may be used to explain the notable rise in women's crime rates in recent years. According to Leonard, "Emancipation has increased somewhat, and certain women are now aiming to achieve financial success. . . . Challenging traditional restrictions and expectations can lead to anomie and, hence, to an increase in female crime."[112] All of this appears to support the general utility of Merton's theory, once it is reformulated to account for the differential organization of aspirations by gender. Nonetheless the specific value of the theory diminishes when it comes to analyzing the criminal adaptations available to marriage-oriented women in traditional society. Once again we have a case where anomie theory is useful as a general orientation but inadequate as a specific theory.

Extending Anomie to a Critique of the Political-Economic Structure Anomie theory is frequently read as a critique of the structural organization of contemporary society. Alvin Gouldner, for instance, notes an affinity between Merton's theory and Marxist analysis. Both, at least implicitly, point to contradictions inherent in the social structure of capitalist societies. Capitalism presents a contradictory message to those who labor under its economic constraints. On one hand, it promises a free market of opportunity in which those who work hard can rise as far as their abilities permit. At the same time, capitalism systematically limits access to decisions affecting the allocation and distribution of economic resources to those who control what Marx referred to as *the means of production* in society.[113] Thus a fundamental contradiction is built into the political-economic structure of capitalism. Capitalism promises something for all which can be achieved only by some. According to Gouldner, a tacit recognition of this contradiction of capitalism is a major element of Merton's theory.[114]

British criminologists Ian Taylor, Paul Walton, and Jock Young agree with Gouldner's assessment. They describe Merton as a "cautious rebel" who "stand[s] outside the system and make[s] criticisms, which, if taken to their logical conclusion, would necessitate radical social change."[115] Having made this point, they criticize Merton for never fully realizing the logic of his own position. Merton settled for a critique of the lack of equal opportunity and for a reformist strategy aimed at expanding access to the American dream. Merton failed to recognize that full and equal access to the political and economic resources of society is prohibited by the structural organization of capitalism itself. This point is made somewhat poetically by Laurie Taylor, who likens Merton's model of society to that of individuals playing an electronic game rigged so that only some players are consistently rewarded. "But in the analysis nobody appeared to ask who put the game there in the first place. Criticism . . . is confined to changing the pay-out sequences so that the deprived can get a better deal."[116]

How might Merton's analysis better realize its full critical potential? What remains tacit or implicit in Merton's work must be made explicit. The political-economic structure of capitalism must be seen as a basic source of the contradictions which produce high rates of deviance. To resolve these contradictions, and thereby structurally curtail deviance, capitalism must be replaced by a system of economic relations by which everyone would be guaranteed, not simply access to wage labor, but equal access to the means by which production is organized and its benefits distributed. In practical terms this means some form of participatory economic democracy or democratic socialism. According to certain of Merton's critics, this is the logical implication of anomie theory. Partial reforms within the system are not enough. The system is itself the problem. Workers may obtain greater access to employment or procure higher wages for their labor, yet they will still be systematically denied access to the means by which economic activities and economic payoffs are socially structured. Those who control the production process will continue to reap unequal benefits at the expense of those whom they employ. As such, unequal access to culturally desired goals and high rates of deviance will continue as well. Efforts to structurally reduce the systemic character of anomic deviance must go beyond the liberal orientation of the perspective as traditionally formulated. With this in mind let us turn from the structural questions of anomie theory to the more concrete interpersonal concerns of the social-learning perspective.

NOTES

1 Émile Durkheim, *Suicide,* John A. Spaulding and George Simpson (trans.), Free Press, New York, 1952, p. 248.

2 Robert K. Merton, "Social Structure and Anomie," *American Sociological Review,* vol. 3, 1938, p. 680.

3 Émile Durkheim, *The Elementary Forms of the Religious Life,* Joseph W. Swain (trans.), Free Press, New York, 1965.

4 Durkheim, *Suicide,* p. 247.

5 Ibid., p. 255.

6 For greater detail on Durkheim's biography and on the social context in which he wrote, see Lewis Coser, *Masters of Sociological Thought,* Harcourt, Brace, Jovanovich, New York, 1971, pp. 129–174.

7 Ibid., p. 162.

8 For a discussion of Durkheim's relationship to the moral statisticians of France, Belgium, Germany, and Italy, see Steven Lukes, *Emile Durkheim, His Life and Work: A Historical and Critical Study,* Penguin, Middlesex, England, 1971, pp. 191–192.

9 Ibid., p. 193.

10 Ibid., p. 190.

11 Durkheim, *Suicide,* p. 252.

12 Ibid.

13 Ibid.

14 Ibid., p. 253.

15 Ibid.

16 Ibid.

17 Ibid., p. 255.

18 For additional biographical information on Merton, see Morton Hunt, "A Biographical Profile of Robert K. Merton," *New Yorker,* January 28, 1961.

19 Robert K. Merton, *Social Theory and Social Structure,* Free Press, New York, 1957, p. 141.

20 Ibid., p. 145.

21 Ibid., p. 146.
22 Ibid., p. 153.
23 Ibid.
24 Talcott Parsons, *The Social System,* Free Press, New York, 1951. For a discussion of Parsons's work as it applies to the theory of anomie, see Marshall B. Clinard, "The Theoretical Implications of Anomie and Deviant Behavior," in Marshall B. Clinard (ed.) *Anomie and Deviant Behavior,* Free Press, New York, 1964, pp. 23–24.
25 Robert Dubin, "Deviant Behavior and Social Structure: Continuities in Social Theory," *American Sociological Review,* vol. 24, April 1959, pp. 147–164.
26 Robert K. Merton, "Social Conformity, Deviation and Opportunity Structures: A Comment on the Contributions of Dubin and Cloward," *American Sociological Review,* vol. 24, April 1959. Merton also criticizes Dubin for confusing the notion of normative constraint with attitudes toward norms, and for producing a theory related more to options for conformity than strains toward deviation.
27 Richard A. Cloward, "Social Control in the Prison," *Theoretical Studies of the Social Organization of the Prison,* Bulletin no. 15, Social Science Research Council, New York, March 1960, pp. 20–48, esp. 28–35.
28 Richard A. Cloward, "Illegitimate Means, Anomie, and Deviant Behavior," *American Sociological Review,* vol. 24, April 1959, pp. 164–176.
29 Ibid., p. 168.
30 Richard A. Cloward and Lloyd E. Ohlin, *Delinquency and Opportunity: A Theory of Delinquent Gangs,* Free Press, New York, 1960.
31 Ibid., pp. 82, 86.
32 Ibid., p. 40.
33 Ibid., p. 175.
34 Ibid., p. 180.
35 Ibid., p. 186.
36 Ibid.
37 Albert J. Cohen, *Delinquent Boys: The Culture of the Gang,* Free Press, New York, 1955.
38 Albert J. Cohen, "The Sociology of the Deviant Act: Anomie Theory and Beyond," *American Sociological Review,* vol. 30, February 1965, pp. 5–14.
39 Ibid., p. 6.
40 Ibid., p. 8.
41 In stressing the importance of the interaction process in the development of deviance, Cohen reflects the influence of learning-perspective theorist Edwin Sutherland. Cohen was one of Sutherland's students. Sutherland's work is discussed in detail in Chapter 8.
42 Robert K. Merton, "Anomie, Anomia and Social Interaction," in Marshall Clinard (ed.), *Anomie and Deviant Behavior,* Free Press, New York, 1964, pp. 213–242.
43 Ibid., p. 231. In this article Merton cites his statements at a May 1955 conference on the sociology and psychiatry of delinquency, published verbatim as part of the conference record, as evidence that he was concerned with interaction long before Cohen's published criticisms. See Robert K. Merton in *New Perspectives for Research on Juvenile Delinquency,* Helen L. Widmer and Ruth Kotinsky (eds.), GPO, Washington, D.C., 1956, pp. 37–38.
44 Ibid., p. 234. Merton was here responding to an earlier version of Cohen's criticism included in Cohen's paper "Towards a Theory of Deviant Behavior: Continuities Considered," presented at the annual meeting of the American Sociological Association in 1963.
45 Cohen, *Delinquent Boys,* p. 121.
46 See particularly ibid., pp. 73–119.

46 See particularly ibid., pp. 73–119.
47 Stephen Cole and Harriet Zuckerman, "Inventory of Empirical and Theoretical Studies of Anomie," in Marshall B. Clinard (ed.), *Anomie and Deviant Behavior,* Free Press, New York, 1964, pp. 243–289.
48 Bernard Lander, *Towards an Understanding of Juvenile Delinquency,* Columbia, New York, 1954.
49 Ibid., p. 65.
50 Roland J. Chilton, "Continuity in Delinquency Area Research: A Comparison of Studies for Baltimore, Detroit, and Indianapolis," *American Sociological Review,* vol. 29, February 1964, pp. 71–83.
51 Robert K. Merton, *Social Theory and Social Structure,* rev. ed., Free Press, New York, 1957, p. 165.
52 Leo Srole, "Social Integration and Certain Corollaries: An Exploratory Study," *American Sociological Review,* vol. 21, December 1956, pp. 709–716.
53 Dorothy L. Meier and Wendell Bell, "Anomia and Differential Access to the Achievement of Life Goals," *American Sociological Review,* vol. 24, April 1959, pp. 189–208.
54 Gwynn Nettler, "A Measure of Alienation," *American Sociological Review,* vol. 22, December 1957, p. 672. For a related discussion, see also Melvin Seeman, "On the Meaning of Alienation," *American Sociological Review,* vol. 24, December 1959, pp. 783–791.
55 Merton, "Anomie, Anomia, and Social Interaction," pp. 212–242.
56 Ibid., p. 229.
57 Ibid.
58 James F. Short, "Gang Delinquency and Anomie," in Marshall B. Clinard (ed.), *Anomie and Deviant Behavior,* Free Press, New York, 1964, pp. 98–127.
59 Anthony Giddens, *Capitalism and Modern Social Theory: An Analysis of the Writings of Marx, Durkheim and Max Weber,* Cambridge University Press, Cambridge, 1971, p. 103.
60 Émile Durkheim, "La famille conjugale," as excerpted and translated in Giddens, *Capitalism and Modern Social Theory,* p. 103.
61 Émile Durkheim, *Education and Society,* Free Press, New York, 1956.
62 Émile Durkheim, *The Rules of the Sociological Method,* London, 1964, p. 368.
63 Coser, *Masters of Sociological Thought,* p. 168. LaMar T. Empey, *American Delinquency: Its Meaning and Construction,* rev. ed., Dorsey, Homewood, Ill., 1982, p. 24.
64 *Action on the Lower East Side,* Program Report: July 1962–January 1964, Mobilization for Youth, New York, 1964, as excerpted in Richard Quinney, *Criminology: Analysis and Critique of Crime in America,* Little, Brown, Boston, 1975, p. 246.
65 For detailed discussion of Mobilization for Youth, see James F. Short, Jr., "The Natural History of an Applied Theory: Differential Opportunity and Mobilization for Youth," in N. J. Demerath, III et al. (eds.), *Social Policy and Sociology,* Academic Press, New York, 1975, pp. 193–210. See also LaMar T. Empey, *American Delinquency,* rev. ed., Dorsey, Homewood, Ill., 1982, pp. 193–210.
66 Peter Marris and Martin Reen, *Dilemmas of Social Reform,* 2d ed., Aldine, Chicago, 1973, p. 22.
67 Frances Fox Piven and Richard Cloward, *Regulating the Poor: The Functions of Public Welfare,* Vintage, New York, 1971, p. 290.
68 Murray Kempton, "When You Mobilize the Poor," *New Republic,* December 5, 1964, p. 12, excerpted in Richard Quinney *Criminology,* 2nd ed., Little, Brown, Boston, 1979, p. 368.
69 Ibid.
70 Empey, *American Delinquency,* p. 209.

71 Quinney, Ibid., p. 369.
72 Ibid., p. 368.
73 Robert Arnold, "Mobilization for Youth: Patchwork or Solution?", *Dissertation,* vol. 11, Summer 1964, pp. 347–354.
74 Allen E. Liska, *Perspectives on Deviance,* Prentice-Hall, Englewood Cliffs, N.J., 1981, p. 52.
75 Randall Collins, *Sociology Since Mid-Century: Essays in Theory Cumulation,* Academic Press, New York, 1981, p. 299. Collins credits (without citation) the work of Stephen Cole as the basis for his remarks about the dominance of Merton's contribution.
76 Ibid.
77 Cohen, "The Sociology of the Deviant Act," p. 5.
78 Collins, *Sociology Since Mid-Century,* p. 299.
79 James Q. Wilson, *Thinking about Crime,* Vintage Books, New York, 1975, p. 48.
80 Don C. Gibbons and Joseph F. Jones, *The Study of Deviance: Perspectives and Problems,* Prentice-Hall, Englewood Cliffs, N.J., 1975, p. 92.
81 Clinard, "The Theoretical Implications of Anomie and Deviant Behavior," p. 55.
82 Alvin W. Gouldner, *The Coming Crisis of Western Sociology,* Basic Books, New York, 1970, p. 345.
83 Ibid.
84 Ibid., p. 343.
85 C. Wright Mills, *The Sociological Imagination,* Oxford University Press, New York, 1959.
86 Nanette J. Davis, *Sociological Constructions of Deviance,* Brown, Dubuque, 1980, p. 148.
87 Collins, *Sociology Since Mid-Century,* p. 299.
88 H. Warren Dunham, "Anomie and Mental Disorder," in Marshall B. Clinard (ed.), *Anomie and Deviant Behavior,* Free Press, New York, 1964, p. 149.
89 Daniel Glaser, Bernard Lander and William Abbott, "Opiate Addiction and Non-Addicted Siblings in a Slum Area," *Social Problems,* 18 (Spring 1971), pp. 510–521.
90 Michael Lewis, "Structural Deviance and Normative Conformity–the 'Hustle' and the 'Gang,' in Daniel Glaser, (ed.), *Crime in the City,* Harper and Row, New York, 1970.
91 Alfred R. Lindesmith and John H. Simon, "Anomie and Drug Addiction," in Marshall B. Clinard (ed.), *Anomie and Deviant Behavior,* Free Press, New York, 1964, pp. 158–188.
92 Andrew Henry and James F. Short, *Suicide and Homicide,* Free Press, Glencoe, Illinois, 1954.
93 Ronald W. Maris, *Social Forces in Urban Suicide,* Dorsey, Homewood, Ill., 1969.
94 Jack P. Gibbs and Walter T. Martin, "A Theory of Status Integration and Its Relationship to Suicide," *American Sociological Review,* vol. 23, April 1958, pp. 140–147. See also Gibbs and Martin, *Status Integration and Suicide,* University of Oregon Press, Eugene, 1964.
95 Empey, *American Delinquency,* pp. 245–254.
96 Ibid., p. 247.
97 Travis Hirschi, *Causes of Delinquency,* University of California Press, Los Angeles, 1969, pp. 182–183.
98 Delbert S. Elliot and Harwin Voss, *Delinquent and Dropout,* Heath, Lexington, Mass., 1974; Dean E. Freese, "Delinquency, Social Class and the Schools," *Sociology and Social Research,* vol. 57, July 1973, pp. 443–459; Kenneth Polk and Walter E. Schaefer (eds.), *School and Delinquency,* Prentice-Hall, Englewood Cliffs, N.J., 1972.
99 Empey, *American Delinquency,* p. 248.
100 Whitney Pope, *Durkheim's "Suicide": A Classic Reanalyzed,* University of Chicago Press, Chicago, 1976.

101 Liska, *Perspectives on Deviance,* pp. 42–47.
102 Clinard, "The Theoretical Implications of Anomie and Deviant Behavior," pp. 55–56.
103 Durkheim, *Suicide,* p. 35.
104 Merton, *Social Theory and Social Structure,* p. 47.
105 Robert Bierstadt, *American Sociological Theory: A Critical History,* Academic Press, New York, 1981, p. 461.
106 Edwin M. Lemert, "Social Structure, Social Control and Deviation," in Marshall B. Clinard (ed.), *Anomie and Deviant Behavior,* Free Press, New York, 1964, pp. 57–97.
107 Ibid., p. 64.
108 For some fascinating studies on the rise of British youth subcultures, see Dick Hebdige, *Subculture: The Meaning of Style,* Methuen, London, 1979; Stuart Hall and Tony Jefferson, *Resistance Through Rituals,* Hutchinson, London, 1975; and Paul E. Willis, *Profane Culture,* Routledge & Kegan Paul, London, 1978.
109 Eileen B. Leonard, *Women, Crime and Society: A Critique of Criminology Theory,* Kongman, New York, 1982.
110 Ibid., p. 58.
111 Ibid., p. 59.
112 Ibid., p. 60.
113 Karl Marx, *Capital,* Lawrence & Wishart, London, 1970.
114 Gouldner, *The Coming Crisis of Western Sociology,* p. 426.
115 Ian Taylor, Paul Walton, and Jock Young, *The New Criminology: For a Social Theory of Deviance,* Harper & Row, New York, 1973, p. 101.
116 Laurie Taylor, *Deviance and Society,* Michael Joseph, London, 1971, p. 148.

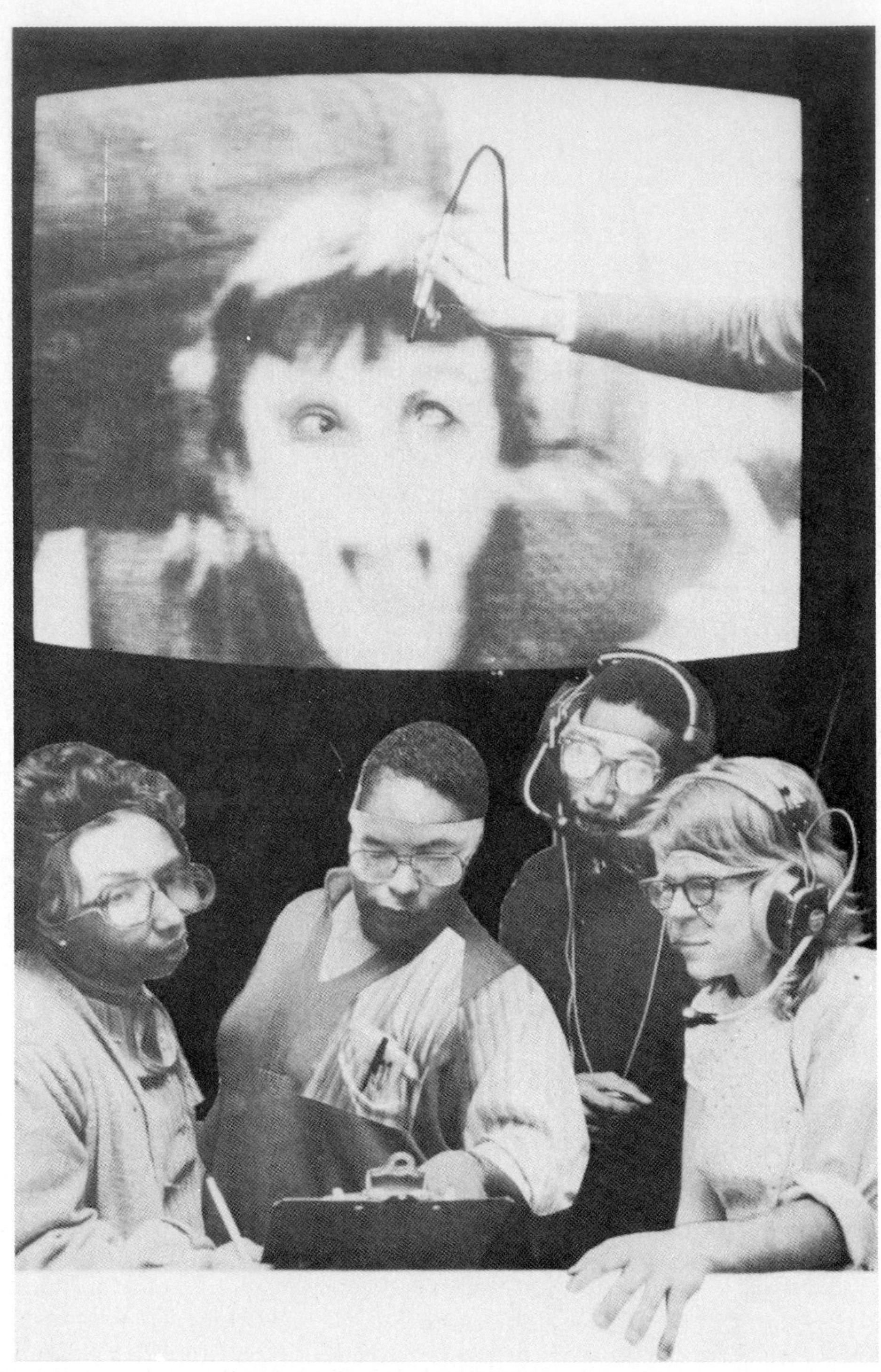

Enforced Imitation By Joseph LaMantia and Stephen Pfohl

CHAPTER **8**

THE LEARNING PERSPECTIVE: *Acquiring Deviance in Association with Others*

All the important acts of social life are carried out under the domination of example. . . . One kills or does not kill, because of imitation.

Gabriel Tarde[1]

When persons become criminal they do so because of contacts with criminal patterns and also because of isolation from anti-criminal patterns.

Edwin Sutherland and Donald R. Cressey[2]

INTRODUCTION

Jack Henry Abbott was in prison when he wrote *In the Belly of the Beast*.[3] This book depicts the brutal manner in which prison teaches people who they are—criminals deserving the torturous experience that is incarceration. This book helped Jack Henry Abbott get out of prison. Its convincing narration and penetrating insight gained Abbott a reputation as a skilled author and a rehabilitated inmate. Abbott was praised in the high circles of New York's literary elite and was soon granted an early parole by state officials.

Months after being rehabilitated and released, Abbott became engaged in a verbal dispute with a New York City waiter. It was late at night. Abbott wanted to use the restaurant's men's room. The waiter informed him there was none. The two stepped outside. Accounts vary about what happened next. Some witnesses say that the waiter was escorting Abbott outside so that he could urinate in the alley. According to Abbott, it seemed as if the waiter was going to attack him. Abbott reacted as one might in prison; he had a knife and used it. Charged with the waiter's death, Abbott did not so much dispute the facts of the case as their interpretation. He claimed that he acted as he did because he had learned to act that way. Most of Jack Henry Abbott's learning occurred throughout a lifetime of imprisonment in an assortment of juvenile and adult institutions. Because of this Abbott claimed that the State of New York, rather than himself as an individual, should be held responsible for his act of violence. Abbott's claim was a sociological one. He argued that a process of social learning, a process over which he had little personal control, was the real culprit in his act of deviance. His claim is echoed in the theoretical imagery of the learning perspective.

THEORETICAL IMAGE

The central theme in this perspective is simply that deviance is a form of learned behavior. In this regard learning deviance is essentially no different than learning to tie one's shoes, learning to like modern art, or learning to become a sociologist. The learning perspective is a sociological perspective. Yet, unlike the disorganization, functionalist, and anomie perspectives, the learning perspective does not view society as a whole as the cause of deviance. Society is considered as an abstraction. What really counts is the collective activity of its members. What is society aside from people? The learning perspective answers this question by turning its attention to people and what they do together. Rather than look at the social system as a whole, the learning perspective views deviance as arising in the diverse ways in which people learn through interacting with each other in everyday life.

Gabriel Tarde and the Imitation of Deviance

One of the earliest formulations of a learning perspective on deviance is discovered in the writings of the French social theorist Gabriel Tarde (1843–1904). Tarde, a critic of Durkheim's conception of society as a "thing in itself," directed attention to the social processes whereby forms of behavior and ways of thinking and feeling are passed on from group to group and person to person. His was a theory of "imitation and suggestion." The origins of deviance were pictured as very similar to the origins of fads and fashions. Each was a socially learned acquisition, governed by what Tarde referred to as the "three laws of imitation." These included: (1) the law of close contact, (2) the law of imitation of superiors by inferiors, and (3) the law of insertion.

By the law of close contact, Tarde meant simply that people have a greater tendency to imitate the fashions and customs of those with whom they have the most contact. Thus, if I were regularly surrounded by people involved in a world of deviant behaviors, ideas, and/or lifestyles, I would be more likely to imitate those people than I would others with whom I had little association. Direct contact with deviance was believed to foster more deviance.

What about indirect contact? Think of a world (such as our own) in which many of our contacts with people, their actions and beliefs, are mediated by mass communications. Tarde's writing anticipated such a world of indirect imitation. He believed that the media played a central role in the proliferation of such nineteenth-century "epidemics of deviance" as the rise in mutilations of women, the practice of women disfiguring the faces of male lovers, and the rash of "Jack the Ripper" type murders. In Tarde's own words, "infectious epidemics spread with air or wind; epidemics of crime follow the telegraph."[4] If only Tarde had known of television. Surely his law of close contact is relevant to the current debate over whether violence and other forms of deviance are learned from models displayed by the mass media.

Tarde's second law suggests that superiors, or persons of higher social status, are more commonly imitated than imitators. Perhaps people follow the model of high-status people in hopes that their imitative behavior will procure some of the rewards associated with being of a "superior" class. In any event, Tarde's ideas have a particular relevance in our own age of visibly "high-class" deviance. Does post-Watergate knowledge of the deviance of "superior" persons, such as high governmental officials and corporate executives, increase the likelihood of deviance by us all? Tarde's law of imitation of superiors suggests that possibility.

The law of insertion, Tarde's third law, refers to the power inherent in newness or novelty. New "fashions" were said to replace old "customs." When two mutually exclusive ways of doing something come into conflict, Tarde believed that the newer one would ordinarily win out. The replacement of the knife by the gun as a weapon of deviant destruction was cited as an example of this process.

Tarde's three laws are rather loose and have been criticized for being overly simplistic and for neglecting a host of other physical, psychological, social, political, and economic factors related to deviance. Some of the dynamics of these laws were never specifically laid out. Why, for instance, was newness more attractive than established custom? Is the disruption of routine itself alluring? Are we more likely to accept new forms of doing things if they do old things better? Tarde was not clear about such issues. Nonetheless, his ideas about the imitative origins of deviance opened the door for an interpretation of deviance as learned behavior. Tarde rejected biological explanations and those which viewed society as independent of the activities of its members. He planted the theoretical seeds of a perspective which would later come to fruition in Edwin Sutherland's theory of differential association. Note the importance placed upon associative imitation in the following excerpt from Tarde's *Penal Philosophy*.

> The majority of murderers and notorious thieves began as children who have been abandoned, and the true seminary of crime must be sought for upon each public square and/or each crossroad of our towns, whether they be small or large, in those flocks of pillaging street urchins, who like bands of sparrows, associate together, at first for marauding, and then for theft, because of a lack of education and food in their homes.[5]

Sutherland's Theory of Differential Association

Edwin H. Sutherland's theory of differential association was first formally presented in the third edition of his textbook *Principles of Criminology* in 1939. Key concepts of this learning theory of crime or deviance were present in the 1934 version of the same text. There, Sutherland hypothesized that "any person can be trained to adopt and follow" a pattern of criminal behavior.[6] At that time, however, Sutherland was more interested in explaining variations in the rate of crime between different groups in society than in articulating a general thesis regarding the sociobiographical or sociogenetic origins of criminal behavior. Sutherland had been trained in the tradition of the Chicago school and spent much of his early sociological career modifying central aspects of the social disorganization perspective. For Sutherland, differences in the rates of crime between groups in the same society could better be explained by the principle of differential social organization than by the idea that crime-prone groups were disorganized.

By "differential social organization," Sutherland referred to the fact that modern society, at least since the time of the industrial revolution, had become divided into a variety of ethnic and normative subcultures. Guided by a common belief in individualism, the pursuit of monetary wealth, and ever greater social mobility, subcultures competed with each other for a slice of society's pie. Access to this pie was not, however, distributed equally. Some culture groups had greater access than others. These groups possessed not only differential access to valued social resources but the ability to define norms and cultural standards and to impose them upon others. For Sutherland this differential access to social resources and dominant social norms offered an explanation of differential rates of deviant behavior.

Sutherland's idea of differential social organization made extensive use of the concept of culture conflict, a concept that was elaborated by his colleague Thorsten Sellin.[7] Indeed, Sutherland went so far as to argue that in the differentially organized society, the criminal law operates as "a device of one party in conflict with another."[8] Sutherland's ideas also foreshadowed the theoretical imagery of opportunity conflict contained in Robert K. Merton's theory of anomie. The work of Sellin and Merton is discussed elsewhere in this book. At present let us turn to the manner in which Sutherland's focus on differential social organization was later dwarfed by his concern with differential association.

Sutherland's initial concerns were with expanding the conceptual boundaries of the Chicago school. He did this by relating the differential organization of society to differential rates of crime between subgroups or subcultures within society. Sutherland recalls his own surprise when, in 1935, Henry D. McKay made reference to his distinctive "theory of criminal behavior."[9] What was this theory? McKay pointed to a section of his 1934 text in which Sutherland had paired the concept of culture conflict with the suggestion that a lack of harmonious social influences may lead individuals to be trained into a pattern of criminal behavior. McKay's comments alerted Sutherland to his own implicit social-psychological emphasis on the process of learning. Indeed, according to Sutherland's own recollections, he would shortly conclude "that learning, interaction, and communication were the processes around which a theory of criminal behavior should be developed."[10]

By 1937, Sutherland had explicitly incorporated the systematic learning of crime as a central theme in his case study *The Professional Thief.*[11] In tracing the criminal career of "Chic Conwell," Sutherland outlined the social-learning process that was said to be essential to a professional thief's acquisition of the proper norms, values, and techniques of the criminal trade. According to Sutherland, "Tutelage by professional thieves is essential for the development of skills, attitudes, codes, and connections, which are required in professional theft."[12]

In *The Professional Thief,* Sutherland likened the learning of crime to the learning of any other "group way of life." In 1939, he combined this emphasis on learning with his previous concerns relating to differential group organization. In this first formal statement of the theory of differential association, Sutherland proposed that while "systematic criminal behavior is determined in a process of association with those who commit crimes, cultural conflict is the underlying cause of this differential association."[13] By this formulation, Sutherland tried to address both the specific causes of criminal behavior as well as variations in the rates of crime between groups exposed to the forces of differential social organization. The theory generated considerable comment, debate, and criticism. Was it necessary for persons to directly associate with criminals in order to learn criminal behavior? Although Sutherland had indicated that "the chance that a person will participate in systematic criminal behavior is determined roughly by the frequency and consistency of his contacts with the patterns of criminal behavior," critics such as Richard Korn and Lloyd McCorkle claimed that Sutherland's 1939 theory represented little more than a thesis proposing "contamination by exposure, without specifically delineating the learning process by which certain frequencies and consistencies of exposure lead to actual criminal behavior."[14]

Responding both to criticism and to the evolving nature of his own concerns, Sutherland thoroughly reformulated the theory of differential association in preparation for the 1947 edition of *Principles of Criminology*. The 1947 version has remained essentially unchanged in subsequent editions of the text authored by Sutherland and his student and colleague, Donald Cressey. The 1947 presentation of the theory is important both because it is more specific about the dynamics of the criminal learning process and because it separates Sutherland's model of the social-psychological causes of deviance from his social-structural account of variations in the crime rate. In other words, it separates the theory of differential association from that of differential social organization. These two theories were related but operated at different levels of analysis. As Sutherland and Cressey state the matter, "Differential social organization . . . should explain the crime rate, while 'differential association' should explain the criminal behavior of a person. The two explanations must be consistent with each other."[15]

The theory of differential association, as formulated in 1947, was intended as a comprehensive explanation of criminal behavior. It is considered applicable to a wide range of noncriminal deviance as well. The theory is based upon two core assumptions: (1) that deviance occurs when people define a certain human situation as the appropriate occasion for violating social norms or criminal laws, and (2) that definitions of the situation are acquired through an individual's history of past experience, particularly in terms of past associations with others. As such, the theory emphasizes the social-psychological processes whereby people produce subjective definitions of their situation in life. It deemphasizes social-structural factors which operate as objective constraints upon the types of associations which an individual is most likely to encounter. This is not to say that Sutherland was unconcerned with structural factors. Throughout his career he maintained a consistent interest in the manner in which the structural outgrowths of differential social organization exposed different groups of people to different associational ties. The point is simply that Sutherland argued that in considering the social-psychological processes which cause individual deviance, "it is not necessary . . . to explain why a person has the associations he has."[16] What is necessary is to examine the normal learning process whereby a person comes to define a particular social situation as more or less appropriate for deviant behavior.

Learning deviance involves learning to (1) define certain situations as the appropriate occasions for deviant behavior, (2) master the techniques of successful deviant activity, and (3) acquire motives, drives, attitudes, and rationalizations which justify violations of norms and/or laws. According to the theory of differential association, these three things are learned principally in the process of communicative interaction with others, within intimate personal groups. The crucial step in learning deviance occurs when people acquire an excess of definitions favorable to deviance over definitions unfavorable to deviance. Acting deviant then becomes probable. This is the essence of differential association: an imbalance in the interactional forces for and against favoring the path of nonconformity. When what one learns from others about deviating or conforming is weighted in the direction of deviating, it is probable that one will engage in deviant behavior. But how probable? The answer is said to depend on the frequency, duration, priority, and intensity of one's associations with those who define deviance positively or negatively. Each of these things is mentioned by Sutherland, who developed the following nine propositions to summarize his theory:

1 Criminal [deviant] behavior is learned.

2 Criminal [deviant] behavior is learned in interaction with other persons in a process of communication.

3 The principal part of the learning of criminal [deviant] behavior occurs within intimate personal groups.

4 When criminal [deviant] behavior is learned, the learning includes (a) techniques of committing the crime, which are sometimes very complicated, sometimes very simple; (b) the specific direction of motives, drives, rationalizations, and attitudes.

5 The specific direction of motives and drives is learned from definitions of the legal codes [conventional norms] as favorable or unfavorable.

6 A person becomes delinquent because of an excess of definitions favorable to violation of law [conventional norms] over definitions unfavorable to violation of law [unconventional norms].

7 Differential associations may vary in frequency, duration, priority and intensity.

8 The process of learning criminal [deviant] behavior by association with criminal and anti-criminal [deviant and anti-deviant] patterns involves all of the mechanisms that are involved in any other learning.

9 While criminal [deviant] behavior is an expression of general needs and values, it is not explained by those general needs and values since non-criminal [non-deviant] behavior is an expression of the same needs and values.[17]

The frequency, duration, priority, and intensity of prodeviant and antideviant associations are difficult to measure. Ideally, each of these factors could be converted into a precise mathematical formula. The likelihood of deviant behavior could then be determined by calculating the difference between favorable and unfavorable associations. Yet, as Sutherland recognized, "The development of such a formula would be extremely difficult." One short but highly intense involvement with a very high priority prodeviant friend might overshadow hundreds of long-term but less significant antideviant associations. How can such things as priority and intensity be adequately measured? What is commonplace for the widely experienced person may be extraordinarily intense for the naive person. Although the importance of associations is obviously influenced by such factors, the factors themselves are difficult to reliably measure in any standardized fashion.

The Legacy of Differential Association Sutherland's theory of differential association normalized our understanding of deviance. It allowed us to imagine that, given an exposure to strong interpersonal forces favoring nonconformity, we could be as deviant as any of our fellow human beings. The differential association idea contributed to the notion that deviants were normal people overly exposed to a learning process which equated being normal with what others saw as being deviant. Its image of deviance as learned behavior has become the most widely accepted modern perspective on deviance.

Sutherland's theory prompted a number of research efforts aimed at testing key elements of the process of differential association. In 1957, James Short reported on a study of adolescents (126 boys and 50 girls) housed in a training school for youths. After obtaining self-reported measures of delinquency (e.g., asking youths about whether they had stolen things of small, medium, and large value, driven without a license, used narcotics, defied parental authority, etc.), Short attempted to obtain information on the frequency, duration, priority, and intensity of their prodelinquent associations. To obtain a measure of frequency, Short asked the following question: "Think of friends you have associated with most often. Were (or are) any of them juvenile delinquents?" Similar questions were asked regarding friends known for the longest time (duration), the first friends remembered (priority), and best friends (intensity). Although Short acknowledged that his research represented an "extremely limited application of a very broadly conceived concept,"[18] his data suggest a moderately strong relationship between exposure to delinquents and delinquent behavior.

Of related concern was a study of Albert J. Reiss, Jr., and A. Lewis Rhodes.[19] Short had used youth assessments of other youths as his measure of the delinquency of one's associates. Reiss and Rhodes obtained measures of the actual delinquent behavior of 299 boys and each boy's two best friends. These researchers discovered that close friendships were "closely correlated with delinquency," but less so with specific patterns of delinquency of the same type as those of one's friends. Reiss and Rhodes also concluded that correlations with the same type of delinquent patterns, although greater than chance, "were well below what one expected from the learning hypothesis in differential association theory." Nor were the correlations independent of social class. Thus, the work of Reiss and Rhodes provides a general but qualified support for differential association theory as a whole. Their findings are similar to a variety of other studies[20] which, as summarized by social-learning theorist Ronald Akers, suggest that "while not all research directed toward testing the theory has supported it, on balance, the empirical evidence accumulated thus far supports the importance in deviant behavior of associations in primary groups such as families and peers.[21]

Despite its generally favorable reception, differential association theory has not lacked its critics. For instance, Sheldon Glueck has charged that Sutherland's original theory was too vague to be adequately tested, since it is practically impossible to quantitatively assess the enormous number of prodeviant and antideviant definitions to which someone is exposed.[22] Glueck also argued that differential association was inapplicable to certain forms of deviance which persons learn to perform on their own (e.g., lying, taking things that belong to another, fighting, and sex play) and that Sutherland's theory ignored the role of various physiological or psychological factors which allegedly predispose one to define things in a prodeviant way. Another critic, David Matza, has commented upon the "overly deterministic" imagery in Sutherland's formulation. Matza contends that the theory of differential associations ignores the role of human choice in human action. According to Matza, "Sutherland nearly made his subject a captive of the milieu . . . a creature of affiliational circumstances. . . . Sutherland's subject was a creature, but he was half a man.[23] Other critics have raised questions about the necessity of first-hand, intimate associations with prodeviant people.[24] Is direct contact a necessary stage in the learning of deviance?

Criticism has indicated the need for caution but has not curtailed the importance of the differential association theme. After a thorough review of the logical structure and empirical testability of the theory, Melvin DeFleur and Richard Quinney[25] conclude that while all but one of the theory's propositions are logically consistent,[26] its high level of abstraction makes it nearly impossible to test the theory as a whole in a strictly empirical fashion. Nonetheless, DeFleur and Quinney observe that the theory has generated a large number of more specific hypotheses capable of being operationally measured and empirically examined.

Modifying the Image of Differential Association

The theory of differential association has also generated several important modifications which extend and strengthen the applicability of the learning perspective. Major modifications include Glaser's principle of differential identification, Sykes and Matza's and later Douglas's consideration of the problem of neutralizing conventional morality, and Burgess and Akers's reformulation according to the operant principles of modern social-learning theory.

Differential Identification Is direct intimate contact with prodeviant people necessary for deviant learning? This question has been raised since the initial exposition of the theory of differential association. Certainly people are socialized indirectly by the media and more distant reference groups. Daniel Glaser had this in mind when he suggested reformulating the idea of differential association in terms of differential identification.[27] We may identify with Clint Eastwood, James Bond, or "the Fonz" without ever associating directly with any of these real or fictitious characters. That identification may affect us, our definitions about the world, and our actions within it. According to Glaser this identification, rather than interpersonal association per se, is at the heart of deviant learning.

Learning Techniques of Neutralization This modification of differential association picks up on Sutherland's suggestion that one of the things learned in learning deviance is a set of rationalizations which protect one against the moral claims of the conventional world. Sykes and Matza's contribution to the learning perspective is also less deterministic than most. It recognizes that deviants live in, and often in-between, worlds of conformity and nonconformity. Deviants are affected by both. They are not strictly determined by either. What Sykes and Matza refer to as techniques of neutralization are verbal or linguistic strategies "chosen" by deviants to reconcile one world to the other.

Neutralizing rhetorics or vocabularies are developed by deviants who together use them to ward off the normative attacks of the social world, to make the constraints of conventional social control inoperative, and to free-up the deviant for further deviant action. Sykes and Matza list five such typical neutralizing techniques.[28] These include:

1 *Denial of Responsibility*. With this technique the deviant declares, "I didn't mean it!" The social scientist's view of what causes deviance is applied to and by oneself. What one ends up with is a "billiard ball" concept of the self, pushed and pulled by uncontrolled social forces. One here imagines the delinquents in the play *West Side Story* humorously singing about how they are unfortunate products of society. In many ways, this is a modern expression of "the devil made me do it" theme.

2 *Denial of Injury*. "I didn't hurt anybody." With this neutralization, deviants admit that they chose to do something, but not something which was really harmful. Car theft becomes simply an act of borrowing. Stealing probably helps those who have insurance.

3 *Denial of Victim*. "They had it coming!" Here, deviants accept responsibility for the act and for the resultant harm, but suggest that the victims are really the rightful targets for retaliation or retribution. They are not really victims. Often this neutralization has a Robin Hood flavor. "We ripped off the store. But everybody knows that the store itself is a 'rip-off.'" "The minority group kids we beat up had no right to be in our neighborhood." "The homosexuals we frightened on the train had it coming." Language games of this kind contribute to the rationalization of deviant action.

4 *Condemning the Condemners*. "Everybody's picking on me!" With this verbal defense, deviants attack those who would point their finger at them. "Everyone knows the police are corrupt." "The government is more violent than we are." "Teachers are biased and unfair." "Parents are hypocrites." Agents of social control are ridiculed, their moral power undermined.

5 *Appeal to Higher Loyalties*. "I didn't do it for myself!" Deviance is admitted, but its motive is unselfish. The act was done in order to help one's friends, family, gang, holy and/or political causes. Higher loyalties excuse lower acts.

Sykes and Matza's work is important because it reminds us that deviants must regularly deal with moral challenges from members of the straight world. Yet for sociologists such as Jack Douglas, the positing of rhetorical vocabularies of denial may be seen as too rationalistic or too cognitive. While not denying the value of such cognitive constructs, Douglas argues that in everyday social life, feelings often operate independently of and even more powerfully than thoughts.[29] Verbal rationalizations may commonly be used to connect rule-breakers with the world of conventional people. Nevertheless, their value dissipates greatly when deviants are confronted with the feeling that their comforting cognitive fictions are not shared by members of the straight world. When this happens, the clever vocabularies of neutralization may do little to cover a deviant's deep feeling of shame.[30] Something else is needed. Successful deviants need to learn strategies of self-deception or self-seduction in order to master their feelings of shame. If such feelings cannot be hidden or evaded, then at least they may be managed through such emotionally charged protection strategies as "aggressive countermoralism" or "counterpride displays." In this sense, Douglas's discussion of the deviant's self-deceptive or manipulative management of feelings represents an important counterpoint to the cognitive defense strategies outlined by Sykes and Matza. Both represent useful extensions of key components of Sutherland's original theory.

Modern Social-Learning Theory: The Principle of Differential Reinforcement

What makes one association or identification more influential (e.g., of higher priority or more intensity) than others? This question has been recurrently raised by critics of Sutherland's theory of differential association. This criticism has arisen, in part, because of the open-ended nature of Sutherland's own conception of learning. Recall that in his 1947 formulation, Sutherland stated only that "the process of learning criminal behavior . . . involves all of the mechanisms that are involved in any other learning." In certain ways, the vagueness of Sutherland's statement was an advantage. Since its initial formulation, major advances have occurred in the social and psychological study of learning. By the early 1960s, these advances led Donald Cressey to suggest that critics should stop complaining about the vagueness of Sutherland's propositions and get on with the business of completing the differential association project by drawing upon developments in modern social-learning theory. In Cressey's words, "It is one thing to criticize the theory for failure to specify the learning process accurately and another to specify which aspects of the learning process should be included and in what ways."[31]

In the mid-1960s, sociological students of crime and deviance responded to Cressey's challenge by suggesting ways in which Sutherland's theory could be enhanced by insights derived from contemporary studies on learning, particularly those which made use of the principles of behavioral or operant psychology. In 1965 C. Ray Jeffery outlined the basis for such a revision of Sutherland's work.[32] A thorough behaviorist reformulation of differential association would, however, await the 1966 publication of Robert Burgess and Ronald Akers's article "A Differential Association: Reinforcement Theory of Criminal Behavior."[33]

Burgess and Akers begin their reformulation of Sutherland's theory with an explanation of the basic principles of operant psychology. They point to an important difference between operant psychology and respondent psychology. Respondent psychology is associated with the work of the Russian psychologist Pavlov and is commonly formulated in terms of a stimulus-response model of learning. The hungry dog is presented with an image of food (stimulus) and salivates (response). The sound of a bell is paired with the sight of food; it gradually takes on the salivation-producing effects of the food itself. It becomes a conditioned stimulus, such that the bell itself may bring about the behavioral response even without the presence of food. The stimulus-response model of respondent psychology is not used by Burgess and Akers. They look, instead, to the principles of operant psychology. Operant psychology, the study of operant behaviors, was originally associated with the learning theories of B. F. Skinner. It may be thought of as a response-stimulus-response, or r-s-r, model of learning. According to the operant model, behavior at one point in time (the initial response) produces an environment effect or consequence (stimulus), which influences the likelihood of similar behavior in the future (the subsequent response).

The basic principles of operant learning theory are relatively simple. They are used to explain the behavior of human as well as nonhuman organisms. All behaviors, whether mental, emotional, or physical, are said to be shaped or governed by the consequences they produce. Some acts lead to consequences (stimuli) which humans experience as positive, pleasurable, or desirable. These acts are reinforced and are thus likely to be repeated in a similar fashion. This happens in one of two ways: by *positive reinforcement,* in which something good happens as a result of one's actions (e.g., one is given praise, a kiss, or a piece of cake), or by *negative reinforcement,* in which something bad is removed or avoided (e.g., one is spared the anticipated scolding or let out of the boring class early). Other acts produce negative, painful, or undesirable consequences. These acts are punished and are thus not likely to be repeated in a similar fashion. Once again, this happens in one of two ways: by *positive punishment,* in which something bad happens (e.g., one is spanked, reprimanded, or humiliated), or by *negative punishment,* in which something good is taken away (e.g., one is denied the affection of a valued person, prohibited from watching a favorite television show, or whatever). In abbreviated form, this is the essence of operant theory. We repeat behaviors which have in the past produced reinforcement. We shy away from behaviors which have produced punishment.

When applied to the learning of deviant behavior, operant theory transforms the concepts of differential association into a sequence of differentially reinforced and punished social experiences. Why is it that we associate more or with greater intensity with prodeviant others? Why do we define and rationalize certain occasions in terms of a preference for deviance instead of conformity? According to Burgess and Akers's operant reformulation, it is because either (1) those behaviors have been reinforced in the past or (2) they have come to be associated with certain discriminative stimuli which provide cues that reinforcement is forthcoming (e.g., the teacher's smile, which the student associates with a good grade). Following the logic of these operant principles, Ronald Akers has recently presented the following statement of his and Burgess's reformulation of differential association in terms of differential reinforcement.

1 Deviant behavior is learned according to the principles of operant conditioning.

2 Deviant behavior is learned both in nonsocial situations that are reinforcing or discriminating and through that social interaction in which the behavior of other persons is reinforcing or discriminating for such behavior.

3 The principal part of the learning of deviant behavior occurs in those groups which comprise or control the individual's major source of reinforcements.

4 The learning of deviant behavior occurs in those groups which comprise or control the individual's major source of reinforcements.

5 The learning of deviant behavior, including specific techniques, attitudes, and avoidance procedures, is a function of the effective and available reinforcers and the existing reinforcement centerpieces.

6 The probability that a person will commit deviant behavior is increased in the presence of normative statements, definitions, and verbalizations which, in the process of differential reinforcement of such behavior over conforming behavior, have acquired discriminative value.

7 The strength of deviant behavior is a direct function of the amount, frequency, and probability of its reinforcement. The modalities of association with deviant patterns are important, insofar, as they affect the source, amount, and scheduling of reinforcement.[34]

Burgess and Akers's perspective offers a way of measuring the balance between the prodeviant and antideviant forces of learning. Akers's recent text *Deviant Behavior: A Social Learning Approach* creatively applies this rather simple perspective to an entire range of deviant behaviors from murder to homosexuality to white-collar crime. In each instance, he outlines a general pattern of social reinforcement which provides the basis for involvement in deviant behavior. Undoubtedly, there is a great deal of merit to this approach. Who would doubt that our future definitions, feelings, and actions are influenced by the consequences of our present actions? If my students respond positively to the way that I explain the theory of differential association, surely I will be likely to explain it in a similar fashion in the future. The same goes for punching my spouse, picking your pocket, creating an artificial gas shortage, or forging a check.

Another advantage of Burgess and Akers's differential-reinforcement perspective is its interdisciplinary focus. Burgess and Akers present a social-psychological framework which bridges the fields of sociology and psychology. Social psychology refers to the study of individuals in a social context. Social psychologists trained within departments of sociology are likely to have been exposed to the tenets of a perspective known as symbolic interactionism. Psychologically trained social psychologists are more likely to have been influenced by some version of operant behaviorism or modern social-learning theory. Following the lead of social philosopher George Herbert Mead, symbolic interactionism emphasizes the dynamic adjustment of humans acting together in anticipation of the reactions of others. For symbolic interactionists, the way we define ourselves, our world, and appropriate lines of action in the world depends upon our grasp of the viewpoint of others toward ourselves. The process by which people imagine and adjust the viewpoint of others is referred to as "taking the role of others." Through this process of interpretive interaction, particularly with those significant others who are closest and/or most important to us, we come to define social reality in a particular way.

Given these assumptions about the nature of social life, it is easy to see why many sociologists saw the imagery of symbolic interaction as highly compatible with Sutherland's theory of differential association.

Key components of Sutherland's formulation are clearly amenable to an interactionist framework, i.e., that people will define situations in a prodeviant manner if the balance of their frequent, high-priority, intense, and long-term interactional associations provide definitions favoring deviance. These interpretive or "mentalistic" components of Sutherland's theory are rejected by strict behaviorists. According to hardcore behavioral psychologists, the scientific analysis of behavior must confine itself to the relationship between overt behavioral responses and directly observable external stimuli. Such rigid behaviorism is an extremely limited framework which unfortunately ignores the rich and important terrain of the human mind and heart.

To Burgess and Akers's credit, their behaviorist reformulation of the idea of differential association is not of the rigid Skinnerian variety described above. Burgess and Akers's work is more closely associated with the "soft behaviorism" of psychologists such as Julian Rotter,[35] Albert Bandura and Richard Walters,[36] Leonard Ullmann and Leonard Krasner,[37] and Arthur and Carolyn Staats.[38] These theorists emphasize the importance of reinforcement and punishment, while also recognizing the role of cognitive processes (e.g., self-reinforcement, anticipations of reinforcement, and vicarious or imitative reinforcement). If raising one's arm is amenable to behavioral analysis, why shouldn't raising one's expectations be studyable as well? If being painfully punished for acting in a certain way is likely to affect my future actions, why shouldn't watching another being painfully punished have a similar effect? If the electric light bulb on the stove acts as a discriminative stimulus that touching the burner will hurt, why shouldn't the conceptual light bulb in my mind be afforded the same respect? For Burgess and Akers these things are both permitted and important for a thorough social-learning-theory analysis. This applies even to the imaginative self's conversation about the anticipated reaction of others that is so central to the symbolic interactionist framework. This conversation, its form and content, this process of defining social reality in interaction with others, can be viewed as a set of behaviors (albeit less observable than arm or leg movements) governed by the same reinforcement contingencies affecting any other set of behaviors. This is the crux of Burgess and Akers's interdisciplinary focus. It joins key sociological concepts with concepts employed by less rigid versions of psychological behaviorism. Akers points out that the concept of verbalization in his and Burgess's differential-reinforcement model "is taken more from the meaning of *definition* in the original Sutherland theory than from the way verbal behavior is treated in . . . [rigid] behavior theory. . . . Insofar as it is implied that one may apply these definitions to his own behavior in a sort of conversation with himself or to protect his self concept, it is congruent with . . . symbolic interactionism."[39]

Burgess and Akers's reformulation promises greater researchable precision and the strengths of an interdisciplinary focus. Nonetheless, the theory of differential reinforcement does not escape other problems associated with the learning perspective. Reinforcements and punishments may seem more amenable to tight measurement than such vague concepts as intensity and priority. But how exactly does one measure the quantity of reinforcement provided by a lifetime of complex prodeviant and antideviant associations? In actuality, differential reinforcement may offer little more than a new set of hard-to-measure imagery. With this in mind, let us examine the various research strategies employed by advocates of the learning perspective.

IDENTIFYING LEARNED DEVIANCE

From a learning perspective, it is not enough to isolate deviants in terms of some individualistic legal infraction (the classical approach) or abnormal characteristic (the pathological approach). Nor is it sufficient to aggregate deviants in terms of some abstract social condition (the disorganizational, functionalist, and anomic approaches). To study deviance one must identify the deviant as a person with a specific biographical history of social experiences and interpersonal associations and a favoring engagement in unconventional or rule-breaking behavior. As Ronald Akers suggests, the goal of this approach is "to spell out a typical process or processes through which the person progresses from conforming to deviant behavior—a 'natural history' of becoming a homosexual, an addict, an alcoholic, and so on."[40]

Official statistics do not provide the biographical and associative information necessary to identify factors related to the learning of deviance. As a result, learning theorists have relied on in-depth interviews, observations, and self-reports to describe and analyze the deviant learning process. From these multiple sources of data, learning theorists generally develop a profile of the deviant behavior system.

Sutherland provided a model for this behavior-systems approach in his 1937 study *The Professional Thief*. In-depth interviews with "Chic Conwell" provided information on the biographical or career stages involved in learning highly skilled criminality, the network of associations through which thieves learn the techniques, deviance-confirming attitudes, and rationalizations of their trade, and the social context which affects the success and duration of their work.

The behavioral system of the thief is not the same as that of the violent criminal, the corporate defrauder, or the prostitute. Learning theorists have provided behavioral-system descriptions of these and numerous other deviant types. Recurrent differences and/or similarities have been observed between the biographical or career stages, associative patterns, and social-psychological contexts of varying deviant activities. In general, learning theorists have examined the comparative differences and similarities between various deviant behavior systems by using one or more of the following analytic techniques: (1) typological classification, (2) analytic induction, and (3) reinforcement contingency analysis.

Typological Classification

Typologies are means of classifying differences and similarities between comparable analytic units. By categorically arranging factors associated with the learned acquisition of deviance, deviant-systems typologies permit an understanding of the social development of nonconforming behavior. The biographical road to one type of deviance can be cataloged and compared with the avenue to another type and to the path of conformity as well. According to Don Gibbons, an early proponent of the typological approach to the study of criminal behavior, typologies are "a way of gaining a more detailed and accurate group of causal processes."[41] Gibbons used a "role-career" typology to classify the biographical backgrounds of criminal offenders into four broad categories: social-class origins, family-background patterns, peer-group associations, and contacts with defining or control agencies. Another typology, proposed by Daniel Glaser, relates crime and criminals by intersecting "offense descriptive factors," such as those which separate personal from property crime and predatory from nonpredatory offenses, with "career commitment factors" associated with such things as repeat offending and criminal-group contacts.[42] Yet another typology, developed by Marshall Clinard and Richard Quinney, examined criminal-behavior systems according to four additional dimensions: (1) the career stages of the offender, (2) group or associative support for criminal activity, (3) the correspondence between criminal and legitimate behavior patterns, and (4) the social reaction to criminality.[43] These factors were used to analyze the recurrent, regular, or typical behavioral system associated with nine different kinds of crime. These include violent personal crime (murder, assault, rape, etc.), occasional property crime (shoplifting, check forgery, vandalism, etc.), occupational crime (embezzlement, fraud, false advertising, fee-splitting, etc.), conventional property crime (burglary and larceny), political crime (treason, espionage, sabotage, terrorism, etc.), public-order crime (prostitution, gambling, drug addiction, homosexuality, etc.), organized crime (racketeering, organized drug traffic, gambling, prostitution, etc.), and professional crime (confidence games, professional thievery, pickpocketing, etc.).

For the student of learned deviance, typologies offer a convenient mechanism for sorting out and examining factors related to the development of prodeviant behaviors, attitudes, and rationalizations. Typological analysis has also been viewed as a first step toward a sociologically informed policy of social control. As Nanette Davis points out, "the typological approach attempted to identify homogeneous patterns of deviant conduct. The notion was that once behavior was sociologically ordered, causal, diagnostic, and treatment propositions could follow."[44] The central problem with typological analysis, however, is that there is little one-to-one correspondence between the abstract types proposed by sociologists and the complexities of real-life deviant behavior. This is recognized by Don Gibbons, whose recent survey of the behavioral and role-career diversity of criminal offenders suggests that while "some lawbreakers closely resemble the sketches of 'naive check forgers,' 'semi-professional property criminals,' or 'aggressive rapists' that appear in offender typologies . . . a much larger number . . . defy classification in some distinct type category."[45] Thus, while typological analysis has been used extensively by students of crime and deviance, it is today recognized as an oversimplified categorization of the complex world of deviant learning, unlearning, and relearning.

Analytic Induction

Most typological analyses begin with a listing of general factors which sociologists believe to be related to the learned development of deviant behavior. Individual cases are then examined in terms of their relationship to these general factors. Analytic induction reverses the process. It constructs a theory of deviant learning from the ground up. As such, analytic induction involves two steps: (1) the detailed study of individual cases in order to produce generalizations applicable to all cases, and (2) the use of negative cases (those which don't fit the typically proposed pattern) to modify or reject generalizations.

The most well-known example of the analytic-induction strategy is, perhaps, Alfred Lindesmith's study of opiate addiction.[46] Lindesmith was forced to revise his original thesis suggesting that addiction was produced by a self-conscious use of drugs to the point where physical withdrawal symptoms would occur in their absence. The basis for his revision was a negative case involving one nonaddicted physician who had knowingly taken opiates to the withdrawal level. Lindesmith ended up by suggesting that the self-conscious use of drugs to eliminate withdrawal was the crucial factor in addiction. This proposition was again subsequently modified by data providing a wider description of the biography, associations, and context of the street addict than originally available to Lindesmith. Analytic induction is extremely rigorous. Most researchers rely more on a general-tendency typology. Analytic induction provides a detailed analysis of the developmental stages, interactional patterns, and environmental contingencies which constitute the core of the learning perspective.

Reinforcement Contingency Analysis

This research strategy is associated with modern social-learning theory. It examines the specific arrangements of reinforcing and punishing stimuli by which operant theorists explain the development and maintenance of deviant behavior. Ideally, this approach requires an experimental framework to sort out the differential impacts of varying forms of reinforcement and punishment. Indeed, all of the basic principles of operant psychology were derived from tightly controlled laboratory experiments. Most of these studied the behavioral learning processes of nonhuman animals.

Some studies of deviance have attempted to transport an experimental model from the psychologist's laboratory to the lab of everyday learning. Examples are found in the social-psychological study of aggressive behavior. In Brown and Elliot's study of the behavioral control of aggression in nursery school, teachers were instructed to ignore all examples of aggressive behavior and simultaneously to reward cooperative behavior with generous doses of praise and attention.[47] Researchers made behavioral notations of classroom behavior for a period of two weeks. A significant decrease in the level of classroom aggression was observed. In another experiment by Parke, Ewall, and Slaby, increased aggressive behavioral displays were associated with increases in the social reinforcement of aggressive verbalizations.[48] Male college students were differentially reinforced for saying words that were aggressive, neutral, or helpful. The same students were subsequently presented with the opportunity to deliver electric shocks to other individuals. Those who had been previously reinforced for aggressive talk delivered the strongest shocks. Those who had been reinforced for neutral verbalization administered intermediate levels of shock, while those reinforced for helpful talk provided the lowest levels of shock.

Experiments such as those described above aid social psychologists in understanding basic processes through which deviant behaviors may be acquired. More difficult is an operant behavioral analysis of complex patterns of deviance which have been learned over many years. How are operant theorists to retrospectively reconstruct this intricate patterning of reinforcement and punishment? The solution to this problem is neither easy nor clear. Research typically begins with data collected for some other purpose. Behavioral researchers then retrospectively examine this existing data for indirect evidence of patterns of differential reinforcement.

Examples of this retrospective approach to the study of differential reinforcement include Linda Anderson's analysis of the learning of marijuana use,[49] and Rand Conger's study of peer and parental reinforcement for delinquency.[50] These studies reconstructed operant patterns from a behaviorist reading of available interview and questionnaire data. Anderson concluded that both formal and informal sanctions impact on the likelihood of marijuana use. Those most apt to smoke were those who perceived little legal risk, whose friends approved of and/or smoked marijuana themselves, and whose parents did not show active disapproval. Along similar lines, Conger found evidence suggesting that those who report the highest involvement in delinquency are those who experience both positive reinforcement for such behavior and low social support for behaving conventionally.

The frequent use of retrospective reconstructions has produced criticism regarding the tautological or circular nature of operant theorizing. Behavioral sociologists Burgess and Akers admit that this criticism would be valid if learning formulations asserted simply that a certain stimulus strengthens deviant behavior *because* it is reinforcing. According to Burgess and Akers, careful operant analysis avoids such a circular statement. It awaits the results of a direct test of whether or not something is reinforcing: "Observe the frequency of a selected behavior, then make a stimulus event contingent upon it and observe any change in frequency. If there is a change in frequency, we may classify the stimulus as reinforcing to the individual under the stated conditions."[51]

The nontautological test proposed by Burgess and Akers is, unfortunately, more applicable to the tightly controlled experiment than to a retrospective reading of reinforcement contingencies into past biographical reports. In the 1977 revision of *Deviant Behavior: A Social Learning Approach,* Akers recognizes this problem. He recognizes that, for nonexperimental analyses, the solution that he and Burgess originally proposed "may not be satisfactory."[52] Akers instructs researchers to precisely describe and document the "sources, content and impact of differential reinforcement, . . . imitation, and other behavioral processes," so as to construct "a typical learning history . . . which shows how a person first emerges in the behavior and then progresses to more habitual or stable patterns."[53]

SOCIAL CONTROL OF LEARNED DEVIANCE

According to the learning perspective, deviance may be controlled either by the *preventive learning* of proconventional attitudes and behaviors or by the *corrective unlearning* of unconventionality. Preventive learning is a broad concept that includes the entirety of a person's social experience. It encompasses all that is referred to by the term *socialization*. It involves all our direct interpersonal contacts with others (i.e., the way we are influenced by parents, peers, teachers, and others) and even indirect contacts with those who enter our lives through the television and other forms of mass mediation. When religious organizations or parent groups present demands for less violence on TV, they are advocating a strategy of preventive learning. Proponents of summer employment or supervised recreation programs for youths may also have a preventive learning concept in mind. By giving youths something constructive to do it is often hoped that they will learn the values of responsible citizenship and shun deviant involvements.

Corrective learning strategies are ordinarily more focused. Corrective learning control programs attempt to influence the imitation process by providing positive, or antideviant, role models, alter the differentiation association process by surrounding a deviant with a group of persons who define deviance in an unfavorable way, or shape the operant learning process by the use of behavior-modification strategies. Each of these approaches is briefly described below.

Imitative Control: Providing Models of Conventionality

Social workers, counselors, and other "helping professionals" often express satisfaction when they feel that they have been an influential positive role model for but a single client. Youth-serving programs such as the Big Brothers and Big Sisters are based on a belief in the efficacy of the imitative power of the influential adult. Control programs which employ detached youth or gang workers to reach out to kids in trouble operate with a similar philosophy. Youth workers are commonly selected because they embody a number of positive, prosocial, or conventional characteristics and are believed to be people with whom troubled youths will easily identify.

Despite their commonsensical appeal, there is little evidence that role-model control programs actually reduce deviance. Gene Kassebaum has reviewed programs of this type in the area of juvenile delinquency.[54] Drawing upon the evaluative research of Malcolm Klein and others, Kassebaum contends that such programs may inadvertently encourage more deviance than they prevent. A 1979 report by the Federal Office of Juvenile Justice and Delinquency Prevention arrives at a similar conclusion. According to the authors of the report, "From the standpoint of differential association theory, workers' efforts to introduce 'definitions unfavorable to violation of the law' had the unintended side effects of increasing the frequency and intensity of interaction within the gang."[55]

This unanticipated prodeviant learning effect is illustrated by a role-model youth-worker program which operated in the city of Boston between 1954 and 1957. The program involved extensive contact between youth workers and gang members. Yet, when compared to a control-group sample of gangs not exposed to this treatment, youth-worker gangs showed a greater increase in the recorded incidence of serious criminal offenses.[56] Why? According to Kassebaum, the attention afforded gang members by role-model youth workers increased the gang's sense of group cohesion and resulted in increased interaction among gang members. This may have resulted both in increased group pressure to deviate and in a greater visibility of the gang to the suspicious eye of law enforcers. Thus, a program originally intended to reduce delinquency may have had the opposite effect. This points to the difficulty of trying to reduce deviance through an overly simple imitative-learning approach. Imitation may affect the unlearning of deviance, but its impact is always complicated and sometimes confounded by other factors related to learning.

Group Unlearning: Altering Differential Association

A second form of corrective unlearning involves exposing deviants to strong group pressures toward conventionality. Sometimes this is done by professional agents of rehabilitative control. Most typically this involves removing offenders from previous prodeviant associations and providing them with a new source of group support for going straight. As Walter Reckless points out, "most knowledgeable probation workers, parole workers, and institutional staff are . . . helping the juvenile or adult offender . . . internalize new models of behavior [and] working on social ties, anchors, supportive relationships, limits and alternative opportunities."[57]

Professional control agents may use residential settings or intensive group therapy to develop proconventional differential associations. Similar control strategies have been employed by self-help groups of deviants who wish to aid one another in returning to conventionality. Alcoholics Anonymous (AA), Recovery Inc. (a support group for persons confronted with mental problems), and Synanon (a self-help drug-addiction rehabilitation organization) are examples of such groups. Members of AA receive strong group support in exchange for testimonial-like admissions to being alcoholics. The typical AA meeting is a weekly event. It begins when one member stands up and declares that he or she is an alcoholic. After telling a personal story of being "down and out," the confessed alcohlic then proceeds to delineate the wonders of AA and the benefits of the supportive understanding that only alcoholics can provide for each other if they are to avoid future deviation. Members exhort one another to stay in each other's company as often as possible and to regularly check in with members struggling to stay off the bottle.

All of this suggests that the principle of reverse differential association is a key part of the strategy of AA. In essence, AA provides the deviant drinker with a new set of associations, the intensity, duration, frequency, and priority of which are intended to aid in the unlearning of unconventional behavior. A similar concept is advanced by Recovery Inc., a group founded by Dr. Abraham Law to aid persons afflicted with mental problems to develop the will to be well. According to Law, members were encouraged to "meet frequently and regularly in classes and at parties; they get together in family gatherings and consort socially; they form sewing clubs, bowling parties, and dancing teams; many of them spend evenings or Sundays together, dining or visiting theaters and amusement places.[58]

In recent years Law has somewhat reversed himself about the benefits of Recovery Inc. members spending an inordinate amount of time in each other's presence. Concerned that members would learn to "normally" interact only with one another, Law sought to limit the time that participants shared together.[59] Synanon does somewhat the opposite.

Unlike AA and Recovery Inc., Synanon is a total learning environment. Within its self-contained boundaries, drug addicts are taught to kick their habits. Synanon is a nearly complete, if unintended, application of the differential association perspective. Members initially share a common residence in which everyone lives, eats, works, plays, and participates in daily group discussions together. In subsequent stages of the Synanon program, members obtain employment outside the house and eventually graduate to life on the outside. According to Rita Volkman and Donald Cressey, Synanon is structured upon (1) the addicts' willingness to suppress individual desires in order to become completely assimilated into a group dedicated to "hating" drug addiction, (2) maximization of family-styled cohesion of members engaged in continuously joint activity, (3) an exchange of valuable social status for staying off drugs and developing anti-drug-use attitudes, and (4) emphasis on total dissociation from former drug- and criminal-culture acquaintances.[60]

The most dramatic part of Synanon may be its daily group sessions in which members attempt to trigger raw feelings and thereby produce a cathartic release from drugs. Such sessions often involve what is referred to as the "haircut," a method of attack therapy in which members are challenged to tell the truth, the whole truth, and nothing but the truth. In actuality, such therapy is aimed at altering a member's truth by altering his or her direct interpersonal associations. People are pushed to renounce the former truths of drug addiction and to accept the present truth of a drug-free existence. Each person "must be willing to give up all ambitions, desires and social interactions that might prevent the group from assimilating him completely."[61] Those who resist are subjected to intense ridicule, emotional denunciations, and tests of organizational loyalty, such as having one's hair shaved off, giving up all one's money, or severing all ties to one's family.

How successful are Synanon's strident efforts to alter the differential associations of its members? Volkman and Cressey sought to answer this question by obtaining information on 372 members. Twenty-nine percent were classified as being off drugs. More significantly, of 215 members who had participated for at least one month, the drug-free percentage rose to 48. For those in Synanon for three months, 66 percent were off drugs, while 86 percent of those in the program for seven months were similarly nonusers. This suggests that the longer one is exposed to intense, frequent, and high-priority antidrug associations, the more likely she or he will learn to kick the drug habit. On the other hand, it should be remembered that Synanon is a highly selective program. It accepts only those willing to make a total commitment to the group process. It has a very high rate of attrition by members during the first few months of involvement. According to Volkman and Cressey, of 263 members admitted during a three-year period, 72 percent dropped out, with 90 percent of the dropouts occurring during the first three months. For this reason, Synanon's success with long-term members may reflect more about the power of strong motivational investment than about the general benefits of proconventional group learning. Nonetheless, Synanon stands as an important example of the practical use of differential-association-like thinking in the area of planned correctional unlearning.

Behavior Modification: Modern Social Learning Theory as Social Control

Operant psychology is commonly presented as a theory of how learning occurs. According to sociologist Richard Emerson, it is more correct to view operant psychology as a theory of behavior control.[62] This is nowhere more evident that in the correctional uses of operant psychology to modify deviant behaviors in the direction of conformity.

As opposed to more traditional forms of psychotherapeutic intervention, behavior modification does not concern itself with a person's inner thoughts or feelings or with such things as helping someone gain insight into the deep but hidden causes of deviance. Behavior modification is instead directed toward manipulating the various ways in which socially organized reinforcements and punishments exercise control over an individual's actions.

In the late 1950s and early 1960s, operant psychologists paved the way for the widespread use of behavior-modification techniques by reporting upon a number of successful cases in which manipulations of the learning environment resulted in dramatic reductions in deviant behavior.[63] In 1960, for instance, Isaacs, Thomas, and Goldiamond reported that they had drastically improved the behavior of a 40-year-old male who was diagnosed as a catatonic schizophrenic.[64] The modification technique they used is referred to as *successive approximation*. Existing behavior is reshaped by successively reinforcing elements which are in the desired direction and extinguishing those which are not. In the case of the catatonic schizophrenic, psychologists were working with someone who had remained mute and relatively motionless throughout the course of his nineteen-year hospitalization. He had been all but abandoned as an uncurable case. Behavior-modification specialists observed, however, that the sight of a stick of gum produced eye movement on the part of the patient. Using gum as a reinforcer, they carefully introduced a succession of learned responses which began with the eyes and in stages included facial movement, the mouth, lips, vocalizations, word utterances, and eventually, the restoration of verbal behavior.

In the first two weeks of their work, the behavioral psychologists held a stick of gum before the patient's face. They waited until the patient moved his eyes toward the gum. When this happened, he was given the gum. By the end of the second week, the patient's eyes moved toward the gum as soon as it was presented. During the third and fourth weeks the psychologists waited for the patient's lips to move before reinforcing him with the gum. During the fifth and sixth weeks, they waited until he actually said, "Say gum, gum." Giving the gum was made contingent upon the patient's increased vocalizations. Eventually he began to talk.

Other dramatic breakthroughs in the control of deviant behaviors were reported at approximately the same time. Walton presented data on the use of behavioral techniques to eliminate compulsive scratching. Williams published findings suggesting the progressive reduction of childhood tantrums.[65] Allyon and Michael discussed techniques used to "extinguish" violent outbursts and to promote positive behaviors, such as patient self-feeding.[66] Each case was different, but the general approaches were similar: systematically evaluate the contingencies of reinforcement and punishment in order to manipulatively produce successive approximations of the desired response. This is illustrated in the following excerpt from the instructions given by behavioral psychologists Allyon and Michael to a nurse attempting to treat a psychotic patient. The patient's eating habits had so deteriorated that she had to be spoon-fed in bed each day. Note the behavioral prescriptions set forth in the modification plan:

> Continue spoon feeding the patient; but from now on, do it in such a careless way that the patient will have a few drops of food fall on her dress. . . . As the patient likes having her clothes clean, she will have to choose between feeding herself and keeping her clothes on her, or being fed by others and risk getting her clothes soiled. Whenever she eats on her own, be sure to stay with her for a while . . . talking to her, or simply being seated with her. We do this to reinforce eating on her own.[67]

The number of clinical cases reporting the successful use of behavior-modification techniques grew steadily during the 1960s. Many of these are presented or reviewed in such volumes as H. J. Eysenck's *Experiments in Behavior Therapy,*[68] L. P. Ullmann and L. Krasner's *Case Studies in Behavior Modification,*[69] J. A. Wolpe, A. Salter, and L. J. Regina's *The Conditioning Therapies,*[70] and A. Bandura's *Principles of Behavior Modification.*[71] Although these early studies often involved but a single case, many dealt with serious disorders unable to be treated by other intervention strategies. In 1969, behavioral researchers Ullman and Krasner posed the following question, "If what has been done with a smile, a head nod, and a grunt is fact, what can be done with stronger and continuing reinforcing stimuli?"[72] The therapeutic and/or control possibilities of behavior modification loomed large. By the 1970s, a great number of behavior-modification programs were being used in mental health, mental retardation, and correctional facilities and in nonresidential programs concerned with the treatment of various forms of sexual deviance, alcohol and drug abuse, and other forms of nonconventionality. Two prominent examples of such control efforts include the use of *token economies* and *aversive conditioning.*

Token Economies A common application of behavior modification in the fields of mental health and criminal justice involves the use of token economies. In such programs, persons who demonstrate compliance with the rules or goals of a particular institution are reinforced by being given a token which can be exchanged for certain institutional privileges (e.g., smoking, a pass to leave the premises, the opportunity to attend a movie, etc.), or commodities (e.g., candy, an extra soda, a pack of cigarettes, etc.). Inmates typically receive tokens when they do such things as be on time, be courteous, be cooperative, be well groomed and, most particularly, be obedient. When they fail to do such things they may be penalized or punished by having a certain amount of tokens taken away.

Examples of token economies include programs implemented at the Walter Reed Hospital in Washington, D.C., the Draper Correctional Center in Elmora, Alabama, the Medical Center for Federal Prisoners in Springfield, Missouri, and the Patuxent Institution in Jessup, Maryland.[73] At the Walter Reed Hospital, soldiers with character or behavior disorders were provided with token points for such nondeviant activities as fulfillment of military assignments, attendance at educational classes, dressing in appropriate attire, etc.[74] Points could be exchanged for such privileges as obtaining a semiprivate room, free coffee, or access to recreational activities. At the Draper prison, points were deposited to inmate "token checking accounts." Checks could be written for television watching, being away from the cellblock, or purchases at the prison commissary. Points were awarded when inmates contributed to the custodial management of the prison—e.g., making their beds, getting out of bed on time, being physically presentable, cleaning their living area, etc.[75]

The START program in Missouri was considerably more controversial. This Special Treatment and Rehabilitative Training Program required inmates to pass through eight distinct levels of behavioral competence. Designed for hardcore and hard-to-manage inmates, the various levels of the START program were arranged so that graduation to each successive level meant both higher levels of behavioral control and higher levels of available reinforcing privileges. Critics, however, argued that the participants in the START program were selected because they were among the handful of inmates who had managed to maintain a sense of individuality, leadership, and independence, and that the real goals of START were to force strong-willed inmate leaders into submission. The behavioral goals reinforced by the START system included such things as performing assignments "without needing persuasion" and accepting assignments "without bickering." Representatives of the American Civil Liberties Union and other observers have charged that START was little more than a program of coerced compliance, designed to eliminate dissent and cloaked in the guise of scientifically proven behavioral therapy.[76]

The Patuxent Institution in Maryland was the home for another highly controversial behavior-modification program. There, inmates diagnosed as compulsively criminal or dangerously antisocial were given an indeterminate sentence. They were held within one of the institution's four-level behavioral-incentive systems until they were assessed to be under proper behavioral control and thereby cured. Like the START program, Patuxent's incentive levels involved the progressive attainment of greater personal autonomy and privileges in exchange for increased behavioral compliance. Inmates could also be demoted in level for a number of vaguely defined behavioral infractions, such as displays of inappropriate attitudes. Each demotion was viewed as a negative reinforcer. One such negative reinforcer involved confinement in the "hole" (an isolated, bare, and dark segregation cell). The behaviorally minded staff referred to this as a "negative reinforcement unit." In 1971, a federal judge outlawed Patuxent's ill-governed use of this behavior-modification technique.

Token economy programs treat the deviant like a rat in a psychologist's box. Like the rat who finds its way through the maze, the captured deviant is reinforced when she or he acts in conformity with an established regime of social control. When the deviant fails or refuses to conform, punishment is delivered. Candy, cigarettes, or television privileges are denied. Extra work assignments or time in isolation may be meted out. The objective is to reshape the behavior of nonconformers toward compliance.

Despite their popularity, token economy programs share a common conceptual and practical flaw. They fail to realize that outside the walls of a particular social-control institution, candy bars and television privileges may not be very powerful reinforcements. Indeed, there is virtually no evidence documenting a long-term pattern of conformity following a behaviorally modified deviant's graduation from a token economy program. In part, this may be because very little sound evaluative research has been conducted about the effects of such programs. As psychologist Michael Nietzel points out, "Evaluations of institutional behavior modification have yet to reveal a single instance in which an adequate non-treatment control group has been included.[77] On the other hand, there are good social and psychological reasons to suspect that such programs will, at best, have a very short-term impact on a deviant's life. Once released from a token economy, a person may be reexposed to the reinforcers and punishers that gave shape to his or her deviation in the first place. Thus, most token economies represent little more than systematic efforts to instill order among deviants during the term of their containment. Other behavior-modification programs make claims that are more powerful. Of particular concern are various programs of aversive therapy.

Aversive Therapy Programs Those who have read Anthony Burgess's novel *A Clockwork Orange* or who have seen Stanley Kubrick's film version of this story of futuristic deviance and social control will undoubtedly recall the behavioral reconditioning of "young Alex." Alex, whose escapades of sexual violence had led him to incarceration, was offered a way out. He would be released if he first agreed to undergo a program of reconditioning. Strapped to a chair, Alex was presented with a mixture of violent and sexual stimuli, each paired with excruciating electrical shocks and physical pain. Thereafter, Alex avoided all violent and sexual urges. When confronted with violent or sexual stimuli, he would convulse with pain.

The reconditioning depicted in *A Clockwork Orange* is not distant fiction. It is but a dramatic example of certain forms of aversive therapy that are today used to reshape the behavior of deviants. Some of these therapies have been directed toward drug addicts. Electric shocks and nausea-inducing chemicals are used to convert the experience of drug use from one of pleasure to one of pain. Several related techniques have been applied to the behavior control of sexual deviants. Most of these control strategies have been used on voluntary subjects whose sexual offense was of a nonviolent nature (e.g., public exhibitionism, voyeurism or "peeping Tomism," and fetishes associated with arousal toward socially inappropriate objects for sexual attraction). In recent years aversive techniques have also been used to alter the behavior of violent offenders, such as rapists.

Aversive therapy directed at sexual deviants typically attempts to reduce sexual arousal associated with deviant stimuli by pairing the presentation of such stimuli with electrical shock or chemically induced pain. An offender may be shown sexually stimulating films or pictures. The person is encouraged to masturbate. Sometimes offenders are simply asked to fantasize or imagine deviant sexual acts. Subsequent presentations of the prohibited act are accompanied by painful punishments. This continues until arousal levels associated with deviant stimuli are significantly reduced.

Many programs using such aversive techniques attempt to simultaneously recondition arousal to more appropriate sexual objects through similar procedures which induce masturbatory pleasure rather than pain. In 1976, for instance, Forgione reported upon the aversive reconditioning of two pedophiles (persons who engage in sexual activities with children). Photos were taken of the two clients engaging in sex with two life-size child mannequins. These images, which produced high levels of arousal on the part of the patients to whom they were shown, were subsequently paired with painful aversive stimuli. Sexually explicit photos of heterosexual couples and provocative adult females were interspersed with the deviant photographic images. The clients were able to avoid shocks by verbally rejecting the deviant photos within three seconds of their initial display. After thorough exposure to this program of behavior modification, the two patients were followed up for periods of two and three years respectively. According to Forgione, this follow-up revealed a total absence of their previous child-molesting behaviors as well as general improvement in the areas of interpersonal and adult heterosexual communication.

Most information on the use of aversive therapy comes from a small number of successful case studies with nonresidentially treated deviants. Aversive techniques have also been used upon persons involuntarily confined within state institutions. In 1970, Reimringer, Morgan, and Bramwell reported upon the use of a chemically based aversion technique to alter the behavior of troublesome patients at California's Atascadero State Hospital.[78] This "therapy" was used upon ninety patients described by staff as manifesting "persistent physical or verbal violence, deviant sexual behavior and lack of cooperation and involvement with the individual treatment prescribed by the patient's ward team."[79] In order to quell uncooperative behavior, staff injected intravenous doses of succinylcholine, a chemical producing paralysis of the diaphragm and suppression of breathing. The experience is terrifying. Those who receive such injections feel as if they are drawing their last breath. Overcome by this fearful physical sensation, patients were admonished to discontinue their unacceptable behaviors and to act more constructively.

As measured by frequency of "acting out" over the next three months, the Atascadero program was declared a success. Sixty-eight percent of the patients were classified as having improved. Nonetheless, professional and ethical criticism of this program resulted in its eventual termination. Its proponents argued that it was helpful in treating patients unresponsive to more traditional forms of hospital therapy (e.g., restraint, isolation, and the use of tranquilizing drugs). Opponents argued that it resembled torture more than treatment, and that practitioners had failed to obtain the informed consent of those whom they allegedly were helping to unlearn deviance.[80]

The Atascadero project is not an isolated example of the use of aversive therapy within institutions. In recent years, reports have described the deployment of aversive procedures at Vacaville, a California medical-correctional institution, the California Institute for Women, the Wisconsin State Penitentiary, the Iowa Security Medical Facility, the Connecticut Correctional Institution, and several branches of the Ontario Regional Penitentiaries.[81] Unlike the Atascadero project, several of these programs made greater efforts to obtain permission from those who were subjected to rigorous aversive regimes of behavior modification. Yet, like the Atascadero project, they represent vivid examples of the dramatic conversion of the learning perspective from paper to practice. Ralph Schwitzgebel, an expert on the use of behavior modification, has recently alluded to the control potential of what he calls "behavioral engineering" or "behavioral instrumentation." In describing the use of various electronic devices used to modify behavior, Schwitzgebel cites studies in which animals have been reconditioned to alter their heart rates, intestinal and stomach contractions, brain waves, and even urine formation. The potential for control over human behavior is both staggering and frightening. Schwitzgebel himself has suggested the use of electronic surveillance apparatus as an alternative to incarceration. Wired with specialized monitoring devices, deviants could be watched and then shockingly jolted should their actions depart from those programmed by "hi-tech" specialists in behavior modification.[82]

From minor to major forms of behavior modification, the learning perspective is associated with a posture of practical social control. New technologies for altering behavior raise the potential for such control. They also raise the frightening specter of mass behavioral manipulation. Indeed, the power of the state to socially control deviants has increased dramatically with recent advances within the learning perspective.

THE LEARNING PERSPECTIVE TODAY

The learning perspective is today a major perspective on deviant behavior. Its importance is reflected in the diversity of its contemporary research applications. These are too numerous to list in their entirety. Instead, I shall review four general themes addressed by these projects and provide illustrative examples of each. These include analyses of the *stages, content, modes,* and *social context* of learned deviance.

The Stages of Learned Deviance

Learning theorists often use the metaphor of a career to depict the development of deviant behavior. Just as career development entails various stages, so too do people pass through a sequence of steps on the road to becoming deviant. As Paul Higgins and Richard Butler point out, "One does not go from being square to being hip overnight. Instead, there is likely to be a gradual progression from one activity to another."[83]

Barbara Sherman Heyl's recent study of the stages of becoming a professional madam is a good illustration.[84] A madam is a combined business manager and hostess for a house of prostitution. According to Heyl, a woman passes through four distinct stages en route to this deviant role. Learning at each stage is analyzed according to five dimensions: (1) an assessment of interactional partners (the relative balance between a woman's "square" and "in the racket" associates); (2) employment (the world in which a woman works—straight or deviant); (3) perception of prostitution (a woman's cognitive and ethical images of this oldest of professions); (4) normative conceptions of sexuality (a woman's sense of the dos and don'ts of permissible sexual expression); and (5) the timing of the sexual encounters (the frequency and degree of predictability of a woman's actual sexual behavior).

As the future madam passes through successive stages of involvement in prostitution, Heyl notes, there are changes in the several dimensions of the learning process.

The initial stage is that of "willing to try." It is typically associated with three influential subjective predispositions. The first of these involves a strong feeling of dissatisfaction or tension regarding one's present situation in life. Perhaps a woman feels trapped in a boring, low-paying job, is experiencing great stress in her domestic life, or is alone and isolated in a strange city. The second concerns a woman's gradual perception that prostitution represents a way out of her personal and/or economic malaise. The third occurs when a woman comes to view herself as capable of providing men with the sexual satisfaction required by prostitution. These things are nurtured by and nurture her associations with persons "in the racket" until she is "willing to try." At that point a woman may advance to the novice stage. Novices have continued contacts with persons already in the racket. Through such people they are presented with the opportunity to "turn tricks." After such initial experiences the fledgling prostitute is provided with assistance in learning to interpret her work positively, i.e., in beginning to reformulate her own sense of sexuality and realize that she can make good money in the business.

The third and fourth stages of becoming a madam involve processes of additional learning. In the stage in which a woman graduates from novice to professional she receives additional training in the behavioral skills, attitudes, and rationalizations appropriate to the business of exchanging sex for money. She is also encouraged to compartmentalize her sex life, to separate nonemotional or impersonal sex on the job from personal sex with her pimp or lover. In a final stage of learning the professional becomes a madam. Heyl describes the sponsorship and learning of administrative skills required by this phase of an entrepreneurial prostitute's career. In essence the prostitute learns to advance from a line staff position to one of management. Only then does she become madam of the house.

Another example of the sequential development of learned deviance is Lawrence Sherman's analysis of the six stages of the "moral career of the corrupt policeman."[85] Sherman describes the process through which a new police officer becomes a "grafter" (someone who accepts bribes). The key determinant of the strength of this process is the extent to which grafting is already a routine part of normal police work. Where grafting is a regular feature of daily work, there is great peer pressure to accept small favors, or "perks." These usually involve little more than free coffee and meals from restaurants along an officer's beat. Yet in accepting perks the officer also learns to make minor adjustments in his or her on-the-job morality. Receiving perks is the initial step along a career continuum of corruption. According to Sherman it is but the first step "up a ladder of increasing self-perceived social harm . . . , neutralizing any moral objections to the (crime-specific) graft at each rung of the ladder—each stage of the moral career."[86]

The officer who accepts a perk soon enters a second stage in the grafting career. Here the officer is confronted with a bar owner operating after hours who offers a drink. The decision to drink while ignoring the clock once again "redefines the policeman's self."[87]

The officer learns to adjust self-concepts and moral notions to justify his or her actual behavior. Subsequent steps in learning to be corrupted include accepting the *regulatory bribe* (the $5 handed over along with the license of a stopped motorist, or the $10 forked over by the construction contractor for overlooking materials illegally obstructing a sidewalk), the *gambling payoff* (for passing over local betting operations), *prostitution graft*, and eventually *narcotics money* (earned for inattention to drug dealing). Like Heyl's description of the career phases of becoming a madam. Sherman's analysis of the sequential development of police corruption exemplifies the cumulative nature of the stages of deviant learning. Each stage prepares the emerging deviant for continued and deeper involvement in the underworld of rule-breaking.

The Content of Learning

This second theme in contemporary studies of learned deviance elaborates Sutherland's notion that the development of deviant behavior involves the acquisition of prodeviant attitudes and guilt-neutralizing rationalizations as well as the "how-to-do-it" techniques of the deviant trade or activity. Howard Becker's study of learning to become a marijuana smoker during the 1950s represents a classic example of this approach.[88] During the 1950s marijuana smoking was considerably more of an underground phenomenon than it is today. In many ways, however, Becker's learning model is still applicable to the process through which new users are exposed to the ritualized pleasures of "getting high." According to Becker a person must first overcome any previous feelings about the negative effects or the immoral images of smoking. This is typically done in association with good friends or positively perceived associates who help the novice learn that smoking can be fun, that nothing bad will happen, that one is not likely to get caught, that people do not become slaves to the drug, and that it is possible to manage or fake the appearance of normality even when high. Equally important is learning the proper techniques of smoking and to perceive and enjoy the effect of pot. This, contends Becker, is no automatic process. His research points out that careful observation, imitation, and direct instruction are often necessary for the new user to cue into the proper techniques of smoking and to sense and enjoy the physical effects of the drug in a pleasurable manner.

Another important study related to the content of learned deviance is Gilbert Geis's examination of the corporate criminality of electrical equipment company officials involved in the price-fixing and price-rigging conspiracy of 1961.[89] The conspirators were forty-five reputable executives from twenty-nine major companies, including General Electric, Westinghouse, Allis-Chalmers, ITE, and Federal Pacific. They engaged in an elaborate plot to eliminate the competitive nature of open bidding for lucrative government contracts. The means used by these supposedly respectable executives appeared to have been borrowed from the scenario of a gangster film or some far-out spy movie. They developed a specialized language (their own peculiar argot) and a set of secret operating procedures designed to outwit government inspectors and deceive the public. Attendance at conspiratorial meetings was recorded by means of "Christmas card lists," while the meetings themselves were code-named "choir practices."

How was it that top business officials came to act in a manner more commonly associated with the slick criminal or the sleazy con-artist? According to Geis external business and control conditions were an important factor. When market conditions were unstable and the policies of government enforcers weak, business price-fixing flourished. These factors in themselves do not explain the development of shrewd criminal activity by those within the corporate world.[90] In search of a more specific explanation, Geis follows the lead of Edwin Sutherland's own 1949 pioneer investigation, *White Collar Crime,* in pointing to "learning and associational patterns as important elements in the genesis of the violations."[91] In the complex of informal associations within the corporation, executives learned that significant personal and professional rewards were available for those willing to risk breaking the law.

According to Geis the offenders also learned to neutralize or rationalize their behavior in a manner in keeping with their image as "law-abiding, decent, respectable persons."[92] This was accomplished by a process of informal learning in which executives arrived at self-definitions of their behavior as not really criminal. Consider the following statement of one corporate official as reported by Geis.

> Illegal? Yes, but not criminal. I didn't find that out until I read the indictment. . . . I assumed that criminal action meant damaging someone, and we did not do that. . . . I thought that we were more or less working on a survival basis in order to keep our plant and our employees.[93]

Modes of Learning Deviance

Studies of socially acquired deviance have also focused on different modes in which the techniques, attitudes, and rationalizations of rule-breaking are acquired. While certain forms of deviance are acquired through direct, almost formal instruction or coaching, others are more loosely picked up by hanging around a deviant scene. Still others are learned through indirect imitation.

Formal Instruction Examples of the formal-instruction route to deviance include David Maurer's description of learning to become a professional thief[94] and separate analyses by James H. Bryan[95] and Barbara Sherman Heyl[96] of the formal apprenticeship provided for novice prostitutes. Maurer's work resembles Sutherland's earlier analysis of the tutelage of thieves by thieves. Maurer describes the complicated and often lengthy period of instruction and testing used by such diverse professionals as con-artists, pickpockets, and safecracking specialists in introducing a select few new members into their ranks.

Bryan and Heyl report upon formal procedures used to instruct novice prostitutes about the tricks of their trade. Heyl describes one "house" in which a madam specializes in "turning out" new professionals. Novices are instructed in the physical, verbal, and business skills necessary for the successful management of a deviant career. Physical training includes instruction in various sexual positions, specialized or kinky tricks, and techniques of self-defense. More difficult is the teaching of proper techniques of hustling. As Heyl points out, a new "girl" must be taught to "be mentally alert and sensitive to the client's response" and to "maintain a steady pattern of verbal coaxing, during which her tone of voice may be more important than her actual words."[97]

Informal Learning This second mode is exemplified by Robert Prus and C. R. D. Sharper's depiction of learning the trade of road hustling.[98] Professional road hustlers are masters of the deceptive card or dice game. Like other professional deviants they occasionally take on apprentices. Novice hustlers are taught techniques of larceny, strategies for interacting with coworkers in a nonexploitive manner, and ways to "make the nut," hints for minimizing expenses on the road.

While hustling requires such learning, it does not usually involve formal instruction. Experienced professionals tend to select novices familiar with the general attitudes and techniques required in the trade. Crews do not see the tutelage of newcomers as a central responsibility. Thus, "much of the learning comes about either . . . by 'hanging around' practicing hustlers, or through being criticized in post-facto 'coaching.'"[99]

Indirect-Imitative Learning Other forms of deviance may be learned by imitating behavior presented in the media or in some other type of indirect communication. This is the case for embezzlers, employees who steal secretly from their companies. Donald Cressey describes the typical embezzler as a person in a position of financial trust who views a secret trust violation as a way out of a financial problem that cannot be shared with others.[100] The embezzler develops a "vocabulary of adjustment" to rationalize theft in such terms as: "I am just borrowing the money; I will pay it back soon," or "It is only fair that I get something more. I'm certainly not getting paid what I'm worth."

How do people learn to become self-justified embezzlers? Unlike corporate criminals, who conspire to fix prices or deceive the public, embezzlers do not ordinarily share associative ties with fellow deviants. This is not to say that their deviance is unlearned. Cressey points to indirect sources by which embezzlers learn their "secret solution" and its accompanying rationalizations. People learn of the practical potential of embezzlement in the mass media, from company folklore about employee dishonesty, and from a company's policy of bonding its "trusted" employees.[101] Business culture is, moreover, filled with rationalizations for illicit action. As Cressey points out, employees do not invent new rationalizations for each trust violation, but depend instead upon a "culture" in which such verbalizations are present.[102]

Additional evidence for the indirect learning of deviance is found in studies on the impact of televised violence. In 1972 a report of a special commission of the surgeon general of the United States reviewed all existing correlational, laboratory-experimental, and field-experimental research on this topic.[103] The vast majority of these studies found consistent, if not always strong, evidence that watching aggression on television or in films is positively associated with the likelihood of acting aggressively.

Context of Learning Research has also produced knowledge regarding the varying social contexts in which deviant behaviors may be acquired. Some contexts openly encourage deviance. The prototype of such manifestly supportive contexts is the so-called deviant subculture. Subcultural theories have been advanced as accounting for a wide range of deviance, including such divergent activities as violent behavior, illegal drug use, public nudity, homosexuality, and juvenile delinquency.

One illuminating account of the role of subcultures in fostering deviance is Martin

Weinberg's study of the management of moral respectability by the managers and members of a nudist camp.[104] Weinberg observes that to become a nudist one must relearn moral meanings associated with public heterosexual nudity. In addition to learning about the positive healthful benefits of nudity, nudists must also learn that nudity and sexuality are unrelated, and that there is nothing shameful about public nakedness. These new moral meanings violate widely held social beliefs. Hence, the nudist subculture involves a careful process of adult resocialization in which members learn to protect themselves from the moral accusations of others.

Weinberg's research combines participatory field work with data gathered from interviews and questionnaires. It describes strategies used by the nudist subculture to reeducate its members into nudist morality. One important strategy involves precautions regarding who can enter a nudist camp. Most camps prohibit or discourage "singles." Another typical screening device involves an elaborate procedure for certifying the respectability of prospective members. Some camps require letters of reference regarding an applicant's moral character. Equally important are in-the-camp norms of interpersonal conduct. These include such prohibitions as no staring, no sex talk, no body contact, no alcoholic beverages, no unauthorized photo taking, no accentuation of the body, and no "unnatural" attempts at covering the body. These strictly enforced rules aid the nudist subculture in resocializing members into its "new system of moral meanings."[105]

Other group-learning contexts are not as manifest. Lewis Yablonsky uses the term *near-group* to describe associative contexts where deviance may be encouraged but not in the explicit manner of an all-encompassing subculture.[106] Yablonski describes juvenile gangs as near-groups. In such loose contexts deviant social learning is characterized by diffuse role definitions, limited cohesion, impermanence, minimal consensus about norms, shifting membership, disturbed leadership, and a limited definition of membership expectations. The near-group concept is applicable to a variety of other deviant learning contexts.[107] Think of the informal association of people who occasionally "toot" cocaine together. Deviant learning may occur, but probably not in the elaborate manner suggested by the term *subculture*.

At the other extreme of the learning continuum are contexts where interactional associations may latently encourage deviance. This may happen independently of the intent or awareness of the parties involved. Two examples come to mind. The first is Ronald Akers's description of the social reinforcement of self-destructive behavior.[108] Akers reviews a variety of studies of extremely self-injurious behavior on the part of emotionally disturbed and/or retarded children.[109] He concludes that "*social attention* commonly follows and subsequently reinforces the self-mutilating behavior."[110]

Another example of latent social support for deviance is found in the in-depth case studies of severe schizophrenia by psychiatrist R. D. Laing and his associates.[111] Laing discovered that the immediate "communicative nexus" of the schizophrenic (his or her network of significant social relationships) contains strong but contradictory social forces, pulling the person in different directions at the same time. The schizophrenic is trapped within what anthropologist Gregory Bateson describes as the "double bind" of intimate interpersonal communications.[112] If the person acts one way, he or she is rewarded by one of the conflicting parties but punished by the other. If the person acts in a manner pleasing to the other party, the opposite occurs. How can one escape this double bind? One way, suggests Laing, is to learn the language of madness, to act in a fashion that will get one classified as a schizophrenic. For Laing, the term *mental illness* unfortunately disguises the fact that schizophrenic behavior may be a rationally learned response to a contradictory and excruciatingly painful social situation. By acting in a schizophrenic manner, by existentially leaping into the dark reality of madness, one escapes the contradictory demands of the double bind. One cannot, after all, be held responsible if one is sick. Thus schizophrenics may be said to escape the dilemma of contradictory social expectations by learning to sleep under the safe covers of sickness.

THE ADEQUACY OF THE LEARNING PERSPECTIVE

From its early inception in Tarde's three laws of imitation, the learning perspective has exerted an enormous impact on the study of deviance and social control. The learning perspective normalizes our images of deviance. It presents the deviant as a fellow human being. Deviance is no longer far away. It is neither an abnormal condition nor the product of abstract social forces. It is concrete. It is the product of learning to be in the world in a particular way, learning with and from others about how to define, feel, and act within a world which we create together.

Despite its widespread appeal, not all versions of the learning perspective have gained equal acceptance. This is evident when one compares Sutherland's theory of differential association with Burgess and Akers's subsequent reformulation. According to Clinard and Meir, "In spite of its shortcomings, no other theory of deviance has generated such a favorable long-term acceptance as . . . differential association theory."[113] On the other hand, Rand Conger has commented upon the relative neglect of Burgess and Akers's work in sociological circles.

According to Conger several things account for sociologists' general disregard of Burgess and Akers's operant social-learning model.[114] Many of Burgess and Akers's propositions are borrowed from another discipline—psychology. This may have retarded the acceptance of the differential-reinforcement framework. Of greater importance, may be the highly abstract nature of early operant formulations.

Another factor related to the lack of interest in reinforcement theory was the rise of the societal-reaction perspective. As Conger points out, at the time when Burgess and Akers's work was first introduced, many sociologists had begun to shift their attention from the study of causation to an analysis of the deviant labeling process. The social-historical reasons for this will be discussed in the following chapter. For now it is enough to note that in the 1980s, interest in causal explanations has returned to center stage. Basic causation research is again a top priority for government funding. Liberal reforms associated with the societal-reaction perspective were intended to reduce harsh and ineffective control policies. Such reforms, however, did little to alter the basic social conditions out of which deviance arises. In the economically bad times of the 1980s liberal efforts aimed at humanizing control policies are being replaced by conservative rhetoric and policies again directed at deterring, containing, or rehabilitating the deviant. This new conservative mood has rekindled interest in the learning perspective. Indeed, in a recent speech on priorities for criminal justice policy, Warren Burger, Chief Justice of the United States Supreme Court, called for a renewed emphasis on rehabilitative strategies which would teach convicted criminals "respect for self, respect for others, accountability for conduct, appreciation of the value of work, of thought, of family," and for a program by which offenders would literally "learn the way out of prison."[115]

Concluding Comments: Two Reservations about the Scope and Uses of the Learning Perspective

Renewed interest in the learning perspective leads me to conclude this section with two general reservations. These focus on its tendency to be overly deterministic and its relative neglect of questions related to the social origins of deviant categories. Neither counters the advantages of incorporating some form of learning model in any comprehensive analysis of deviance. Each simply cautions against an overemphasis on learning.

Overly Deterministic Learning Critics such as Ian Taylor, Paul Walton, and Jock Young argue that "human choice is not adequately stressed and the resulting behavior appears to be totally determined."[116] A similar conclusion is arrived at in Short and Strodtbeck's study of delinquent gangs. Short and Strodtbeck suggest that youths are neither blindly driven nor irrationally lured into subcultures of deviance. Potential deviants enter into subcultural associations only after assessing the gains and losses, benefits and risks. Deviants, in other words, understand the risks entailed by nonconformity.

Short and Strodtbeck argue that youths enter delinquent subcultures believing that the advantages of achieving high status within the deviant group outweigh the disadvantages of getting caught.[117] Their assessment of risks is aleatory. It is dependent upon unforeseen contingencies. Much can go wrong. There is no way of assuring successful deviance, of reaping its benefits without paying the price of social control. For this reason Short and Strodtbeck describe their theory as one of aleatory risks.

Once someone is involved in the delinquent gang, the subculture may reinforce his or her confidence in the rationality of the choice for deviance. Short and Strodtbeck's theory thus modifies rather than rejects the central tenets of the learning perspective. Subcultures are said to reinforce deviant options in two ways: by emphasizing the low probability of unforeseen negative sanctions, and by promising high status to those who remain members. Again the emphasis is on rational choice. Persons choose to enter and remain within deviant subcultures because these are perceived as efficient avenues for obtaining status, respect, and relative success.

Short and Strodtbeck's work inserts the concept of rational choice into the learning perspective. David Matza takes the issue one step further. He suggests that deviance, like any other human behavior, can best be understood as partly chosen and partly determined. Matza's work has been referred to as "soft determination." Matza's image of the deviant is of a person who drifts in and out of conventional society.[118] Matza's image of drift suggests that persons do not once and for all enter into a deviant subculture, but, rather, join loosely together in a process of mutual support. Neutralization techniques arise as verbal strategies which provide distance from the hold of conventional norms and values. The drift towards deviance is supported, moreover, by a "subterranean" American tradition favoring excitement, risk, and adventure. Matza suggests that below the surface of conventional life is a set of attitudes and values favoring nonconventionality. Thematized in literature, art, and the mass media, this desire for adventuresome risk-taking is a present, if ordinarily suppressed, element of American life. When deviants tap into this subterranean tradition they are revealing another face of the dominant culture. Deviants are thus less unconventional than they may seem. The realization of this reinforces the drift into deviance.

Matza offers an open-ended rather than deterministic vision of the deviant learning process. Through interaction with others someone prepares for rule-breaking by learning to neutralize guilt and explore the realm of subterranean value convergence, thus becoming a potential deviant. Then this person is hit by an unforeseen crisis. Things seem desperate. He or she is beset by a mood of fatalism and the sense that things are out of control. In an attempt to regain control, he or she may experiment with deviance. The whole process is described by Matza as a drift toward deviance. If the experiment with deviant action proves successful, i.e., if it helps the person regain a sense of control, then he or she is likely to continue to choose to deviate. This is Matza's image of how deviance is learned. It involves a combination of choice and determination, of being desirous and being socially propelled.

Matza's alternative to an overly deterministic learning theory is elaborated by Edwin Pfuhl.[119] Pfuhl stresses the importance of *biographical affinity* for becoming deviant. This refers to a constellation of prodeviant associations, rationalizations, opportunities, meanings, and self-concept. Nonetheless, Pfuhl contends that even a very strong biographical affinity is but a general condition favoring deviance. Biographical affinities encourage but do not determine deviant action. In the final analysis, deviance remains a choice, an act of human willingness.

Willingness, however, is not to be confused with free will. Willingness is an openness to deviance. It exists only in a situated context of immediate social experience. In such contexts the assessment of alternative courses of action is partially shaped by a history of prior learning. Thus, for Pfuhl, as for Matza, and for Short and Strodtbeck, while it may be technically incorrect to state that deviance is learned, it is correct to state that people learn that deviance is possible, permissible, rationalizable, and even valued within a particular social context.

Relative Inattention to the Social Learning of Deviant Categories The learning perspective does little to clarify why it is that certain types of behavior are thought of as deviant. In this sense, the general acceptance given to Sutherland's theory of differential association submerged or buried the more critical elements of his previous differential-organization ideas. The learning perspective is largely social-psychological. It ignores or downplays the role of conflicting social interests in producing a particular order of conformity (favoring those with greatest power) and controlling the nonconformity of those (relatively powerless individuals and groups) with little stake in that order. Sutherland's early observations concerning the relationship between law and cultural conflict become lost in the flurry of attention generated by his model of the mechanisms of deviant learning.

Why has Sutherland's learning theory received far greater attention than the more critical focus of his earlier thought? The answer may lie in the fact that most men and women who have studied deviance have shared, at least implicitly, the official governmental position as to what acts and which people were really deviant.

In the years following World War II social scientists came to play an increasingly important role in the social control process. Accepting governmental money for research, researchers commonly accepted the government's definition of deviance as well.

In abstract terms questions raised by the government about deviance were different than those asked by social scientists. The government wanted to know what caused people to deviate so that deviance could be stopped. Social scientists wanted to know such things as whether differential-association theory was testable. In concrete terms, however, the questions were the same. Social science research provided information on how to best control deviants. The ultimate test of social science explanations was whether they offered workable programs of social control. Herein lies the preference for the learning perspective. The government could use it in an attempt to change deviants into conformists. All that had to be done was to alter the learning environment of the nonconformist.

Had social scientists placed an equal emphasis on differential organization, the task of providing social control solutions would be more complex and more precarious. The structural environment of societal interests, rather than the learning environment of particular deviants, would have to be changed. Social scientists would be asking the government itself to change. Unfortunately such recommendations have little payoff in government-sponsored research contracts. The proposals of learning theorists fared much better. Perhaps this was because such theorists offered little challenge to society's official position on deviance.

Compliance with official definitions of deviance may be less of an inherent problem with the learning perspective than a problem with the way the perspective has been used in practice. This point is made by Conger. He argues that the same learning principles that are used to explain deviance might be used to account for particular policies of control.[120] While this is undoubtedly true, there has been little systematic use of the perspective toward this end. Maybe most theorists and researchers have simply learned to see deviance in the same way that it is seen by those charged with its control. Social scientists are, after all, generally middle-class, generally white, generally male, generally sheltered from social indignities. Perhaps these advantages provide social scientists with a biographical affinity for identifying the problem of deviance in the same way as those who pay them—the government and their universities.

Like the deviants they study, researchers may also learn to associate themselves with the path of greatest reinforcement. In any event, until the emergence of the societal reaction and conflict perspectives during the 1960s, social science research did little to challenge and a lot to support official definitions of deviance. Deviance remained a problem of deviants. The nearly exclusively social-psychological focus of the learning perspective guaranteed that this would happen.

NOTES

1 Gabriel Tarde, *Penal Philosophy,* Little, Brown, Boston, 1912, p. 322.
2 Edwin H. Sutherland and Donald R. Cressey, *Principles of Criminology,* 10th ed., Lippincott, Philadelphia, 1978, p. 81.
3 Jack Henry Abbott, *In the Belly of the Beast: Letters from Prison,* Vintage, New York, 1981.
4 Tarde, *Penal Philosophy.*
5 Ibid., p. 340.
6 Edwin H. Sutherland, *Principles of Criminology,* Lippincott, Philadelphia, 1934, p. 51.
7 Thorsten Sellin, *Culture Conflict and Crime,* Social Science Research Council, 1938. According to Don C. Gibbons, Sutherland worked with Sellin on this monograph even though he did not share in its authorship. See Don C. Gibbons, *The Criminological Enterprise,* Prentice-Hall, Englewood Cliffs, N.J., 1979, pp. 47–48.
8 Albert Cohen, Alfred Lindesmith, and Karl Schuessler (eds.), *The Sutherland Papers,* Indiana University Press, Bloomington, 1956, p. 103.
9 Edwin H. Sutherland, "Development of the Theory," in Cohen, Lindesmith, and Schuessler, *The Sutherland Papers,* pp. 14–15.
10 Ibid., p. 19.
11 Edwin H. Sutherland, *The Professional Thief,* University of Chicago Press, Chicago, 1937.
12 Ibid., pp. v–vi.
13 Edwin H. Sutherland, *Principles of Criminology,* 3d ed., Lippincott, Philadelphia, 1939, pp. 4, 7. This edition of *Principles of Criminology* was subsequently reprinted as a War Department Educational Manual (EM 266) by the United States Armed Forces Institute. Its practical utility to the government is suggested by Sutherland who states that "criminology is concerned with the immediate application of knowledge to programs of social control of crime. . . . If practical programs wait until theoretical knowledge is complete, they will wait for eternity, for theoretical knowledge is increased most significantly in the efforts at social control." (pp. 1–2)
14 Richard R. Korn and Lloyd W. McCorkle, *Criminology and Penology,* Holt, Rinehart & Winston, New York, 1959, pp. 298–301.
15 Edwin H. Sutherland and Donald R. Cressey, *Principles of Criminology,* 10th ed., p. 83.
16 Ibid., p. 82.
17 Ibid., pp. 80–82.
18 James F. Short, Jr., "Differential Association as a Hypothesis: Problems of Empirical Testing," *Social Problems,* vol. 8, Summer 1960, pp. 14–25.
19 Albert J. Reiss and A. Lewis Rhodes, "An Empirical Test of Differential Association Theory," *Journal of Research in Crime and Delinquency,* vol. 1, January 1964, pp. 5–18.
20 See also Donald Cressey, *Other People's Money,* Free Press, Glencoe, Ill., 1953; John C. Ball, "Delinquent and Non-Delinquent Attitudes Toward the Prevalence of Stealing," *Journal of Criminal Law, Criminology and Police Science,* vol. 48, September–October 1957, pp. 259–74; Harwin Voss, "Differential Association and Reported Delinquent Be-

havior: A Replication," *Social Problems,* vol. 12, Summer 1964, pp. 28–85; Marvin D. Krohn, "An Investigation of the Effect of Parental and Peer Association on Marijuana Use: An Empirical Test of Differential Association Theory," in Marc Riedel and Terrence P. Thornbery (eds.), *Crime and Delinquency: Dimensions of Deviance,* Praeger, New York, 1979, pp. 75–89; Gary F. Jensen, "Parents, Peers and Delinquent Action: A Test of the Differential Association Perspective," *American Journal of Sociology,* vol. 78, November 1972, pp. 63–72; Steven Burkett and Eric L. Jensen, "Conventional Ties, Peer Influence, and the Fear of Apprehension: A Study of Adolescent Marijuana Use," *Sociological Quarterly,* vol. 16, Autumn 1975, pp. 522–533.

21 Ronald L. Akers, *Deviant Behavior: A Social Learning Approach,* 2d ed., Wadsworth, Belmont, Calif., 1977, p. 56.

22 Sheldon Glueck, "Theory and Fact in Criminology: A Criticism of Differential Association," *British Journal of Delinquency,* vol. 7, October 1956, pp. 92–109.

23 David Matza, *Becoming Deviant,* Prentice-Hall, Englewood Cliffs, N.J., 1969, p. 107.

24 Daniel Glaser, "Criminality Theories and Behavioral Images," *American Journal of Sociology,* vol. 61, March 1956, pp. 433–444.

25 Melvin L. DeFleur and Richard Quinney, "A Reformulation of Sutherland's Differential Association Theory and a Strategy of Empirical Verification," *Journal of Research in Crime and Delinquency,* vol. 3, January 1966, pp. 1–22.

26 Ibid. The authors reformulate Sutherland's sixth proposition regarding an excess of procriminal or prodeviant definition to read as follows: "Overt criminal behavior has as its necessary and sufficient conditions a set of criminal motivations, attitudes, and techniques, the learning of which takes place when there is exposure to criminal norms in excess of exposure to corresponding anti-criminal norms during symbolic interaction in primary groups."

27 Glaser, "Criminality Theories and Behavioral Images," pp. 433–444.

28 Gresham M. Sykes and David Matza, "Techniques of Neutralization: A Theory of Delinquency," *American Sociological Review,* vol. 22, December 1957, pp. 664–670.

29 Jack D. Douglas, "Existential Sociology," in Jack D. Douglas and John M. Johnson, *Existential Sociology,* Cambridge University Press, Cambridge, 1977, p. 27.

30 Jack D. Douglas, "Shame and Deceit in Creative Deviance," in Edward Sagarin (ed.), *Deviance and Social Change,* Sage, Beverly Hills, Calif., 1977, pp. 59–86.

31 Donald R. Cressey, "Epidemiology and Individual Conduct: A Case from Criminology," *Pacific Sociological Review,* vol. 3, Fall 1960, p. 54.

32 C. Ray Jeffery, "Criminal Behavioral and Learning Theory," *Journal of Criminal Law, Criminology and Police Science,* vol. 56, September 1965, pp. 294–300.

33 Robert L. Burgess and Ronald L. Akers, "A Differential Association: Reinforcement Theory of Criminal Behavior," *Social Problems,* vol. 14, no. 2, Fall 1966, pp. 128–147.

34 Akers, *Deviant Behavior,* pp. 42–43.

35 Julian Rotter, *Social Learning and Clinical Psychology,* Prentice-Hall, Englewood Cliffs, N.J., 1954.

36 Albert Bandura and Richard H. Walters, *Social Learning and Personality Development,* Holt, Rinehart & Winston, New York, 1963.

37 Leonard P. Ullman and Leonard Krasner, *A Psychological Approach to Abnormal Behavior,* Prentice-Hall, Englewood Cliffs, N.J.: 1969.

38 Arthur W. Staats and Carolyn K. Staats, *Complex Human Behavior: A Systematic Extension of Learning Principles,* Holt, Rinehart & Winston, New York, 1963.

39 Akers, *Deviant Behavior,* p. 62.

40 Ibid., p. 60.

41 Don C. Gibbons, *Society, Crime and Criminal Behavior,* 4th ed. Prentice-Hall, Englewood Cliffs, N.J., 1982, p. 233.
42 Daniel Glaser, *Adult Crime and Social Policy,* Prentice-Hall, Englewood Cliffs, N.J., 1972.
43 Marshall B. Clinard and Richard Quinney, *Criminal Behavior Systems,* 2d ed., Holt, Rinehart & Winston, 1973.
44 Nanette Davis, *Sociological Construction of Deviance,* Brown, Dubuque, 1980, p. 171.
45 Gibbons, *Society, Crime and Criminal Behavior,* p. 232.
46 Alfred R. Lindesmith, "A Sociological Theory of Drug Addiction," *American Journal of Sociology,* vol. 43, January 1938, pp. 593–613.
47 P. Brown and R. Elliot, "Control of Aggression in Nursery School Class," *Journal of Experimental Child Psychology,* vol. 2, 1965, pp. 103–107.
48 R. Parke, W. Ewall, and R. Slaby, "Hostile and Helpful Verbalization as Regulators of Non-Verbal Aggression," *Journal of Personality and Social Psychology,* vol. 23, 1972, pp. 243–248.
49 Linda S. Anderson, "The Impact of Formal and Informal Sanctions on Marijuana Use," M.A. thesis, Florida State University, as described in Akers, *Deviant Behavior,* pp. 56–57.
50 Rand Conger, "Social Control and Social Learning Models of Delinquency: A Synthesis," *Criminology,* vol. 14, May 1976, pp. 17–40.
51 Robert L. Burgess and Ronald L. Akers, "A Differential Association-Reinforcement Theory of Criminal Behavior," in Robert L. Burgess and Don Bushell, Jr. (eds.), *Behavioral Sociology: The Experimental Analysis of Social Process,* Columbia, New York, 1969, p. 299.
52 Akers, *Deviant Behavior,* p. 55.
53 Ibid., pp. 58, 60.
54 Gene Kassebaum, *Delinquency and Social Policy,* Prentice-Hall, Englewood Cliffs, N.J., 1974.
55 Grant Johnson, Tom Bird, and Judith Warren Little, *Delinquency Prevention: Theories and Strategies,* prepared for the Office of Juvenile Justice and Delinquency Prevention, Department of Justice, Washington, D.C., April 1979, p. 28.
56 Ibid., p. 78.
57 Walter Reckless, *The Crime Problem,* 5th ed., Appleton-Century-Crofts, New York, 1973, p. 57.
58 Abraham A. Law, *Mental Health Through Will-Training,* Christopher, Boston, 1950, p. 15.
59 John Lofland, *Deviance and Identity,* Prentice-Hall, Englewood Cliffs, N.J., 1969, p. 238.
60 Rita Volkman and Donald R. Cressey, "Differential Association and the Rehabilitation of Drug Addicts," *American Journal of Sociology,* vol. 69, 1963, pp. 129–142.
61 Ibid., p. 132.
62 Richard M. Emerson, "Operant Psychology and Exchange Theory," in Robert L. Burgess and Don Bushell, Jr. (eds.), *Behavioral Sociology: The Experimental Analysis of Social Process,* Columbia, New York, 1969, p. 386.
63 For an extended discussion of pioneering efforts in behavior modification, see Staats and Staats, *Complex Human Behavior,* pp. 488–511.
64 W. Isaacs, J. Thomas, and I. Goldiamond, "Application of Operant Conditioning to Reinstate Verbal Behavior in Psychotics," *Journal of Speech and Hearing Disorders,* vol. 25, 1960, pp. 8–12.
65 C. D. Williams, "The Elimination of Tantrum Behavior by Extinction Procedures," *Journal of Abnormal and Social Psychology,* vol. 59, 1959, p. 269.
66 T. Allyon and J. Michael, "The Psychiatric Nurse as Behavioral Engineer," *Journal of Experimental Analysis of Behavior,* vol. 29, 1959, pp. 323–334.

67 Ibid., pp. 330–331.

68 J. J. Eysenck (ed.), *Experiments in Behavior Therapy: Reading in Modern Methods of Treatment of Mental Disorders Derived from Learning Theory,* Macmillan, Pergamon, New York, 1964.

69 Leonard P. Ullmann and Leonard Krasner (eds.), *Case Studies in Behavior Modification,* Holt, Rinehart & Winston, New York, 1965. See also Leonard Krasner and Leonard Ullmann (eds), *Research in Behavior Modification,* Holt, Rinehart & Winston, New York, 1965.

70 Joseph A. Wolpe, Andrew Salter, and L. J. Regina (eds.), *The Conditioning Therapies,* Holt, Rinehart & Winston, New York, 1964.

71 Albert Bandura, *Principles of Behavior Modification,* Holt, Rinehart & Winston, New York, 1969.

72 Ullmann and Krasner, *A Psychological Approach to Abnormal Behavior,* p. 408.

73 For a comprehensive review and analysis of these programs, see Michael T. Nietzel, *Crime and Its Modification: A Social Learning Perspective,* Pergamon, New York, 1979, pp. 121–141.

74 J. J. Boren and A. D. Colman, "Some Experiments on Reinforcement Principles Within a Psychiatric Ward for Delinquent Soldiers," *Journal of Applied Behavioral Analysis,* vol. 3, 1979, pp. 29–38.

75 M. A. Milan and J. M. McKee, "Behavior Modification: Principles and Applications in Corrections," in Daniel Glaser (ed.), *Handbook of Criminology,* Rand McNally, Chicago, 1974.

76 R. E. Kennedy, "Behavioral Modification in Prisons," in W. E. Craighead, A. E. Kazden, and M. H. Mahoney (eds), *Behavior Modification: Principles, Issues and Applications,* Houghton-Mifflin, Boston, 1976.

77 Nietzel, *Crime and Its Modification,* p. 228.

78 M. J. Reimringer, S. Morgan, and P. Bramwell, "Succinylcholine as a Modifier of Acting and Behavior," *Clinical Medicine,* July 1970, pp. 28–29.

79 Ibid.

80 R. Space, "Conditioning and Other Technologies Used to 'Treat?' 'Rehabilitate?' 'Demolish?' Prisoners and Mental Patients," *Southern California Law Review,* vol. 85, 1972, pp. 616–684.

81 Nietzel, *Crime and Its Modification,* pp. 141–146.

82 R. K. Schwitzgebel, "Electronic Alternatives to Prison," *Lex et Science,* vol. 5, no. 3, 1968, pp. 99–104.

83 Paul C. Higgins and Richard R. Butler, *Understanding Deviance,* McGraw-Hill, New York, 1982, p. 182.

84 Barbara Sherman Heyl, *The Madam as Entrepreneur: Career Management in House Prostitution,* Transaction, New Brunswick, N.J., 1979.

85 Lawrence Sherman, *Police Corruption,* Doubleday, New York, 1974.

86 Lawrence Sherman, "The Subculture of Police Corruption," in Earl Rubington and Martin S. Weinberg (eds.), *Deviance: The Interactionist Perspective,* 4th ed., Macmillan, New York, 1981, p. 323.

87 Ibid.

88 Howard S. Becker, *Outsiders: Studies in the Sociology of Deviance,* Free Press, New York, 1963, pp. 41–58.

89 Gilbert Geis, "White Collar Crime: The Heavy Electrical Equipment Anti-Trust Cases of 1961," in Gilbert Geis and Robert F. Meir (eds.), *White Collar Crime,* rev. ed., Free Press, New York, 1977.

90 Edwin H. Sutherland, *White Collar Crime,* Holt, Rinehart & Winston, New York, 1949.

91 Gilbert Geis, "White Collar Crime," The Heavy Electrical Equipment Anti-Trust Cases of 1961," in Marshall B. Clinard and Richard Quinney (eds.), *Criminal Behavior Systems: A Typology*. Holt, Rinehart & Winston, New York, 1967, p. 150.
92 Ibid.
93 Ibid., p. 144.
94 David W. Maurer, *Whiz Mob: A Correlation of the Technical Argot of Pick-Pockets with Their Behavior,* College and University Press, New Haven, Conn., 1964.
95 James H. Bryan. "Apprentices in Prostitution," *Social Problems,* vol. 12, Winter 1965, pp. 287–299.
96 Barbara Sherman Heyl, "The Madam as Teacher: The Training of House Prostitutes," in Delos H. Kelly (ed.), *Deviant Behavior: Readings in the Sociology of Deviance,* St. Martin's, New York, 1979.
97 Ibid., p. 514.
98 Robert C. Prus and C. R. D. Sharper, *Road Hustler,* Lexington Books, Heath, Lexington, Mass., 1977.
99 Robert C. Prus and C. R. D. Sharper. "Road Hustlers," in Earl Rubington and Martin S. Weinberg (eds.), *Deviance: The Interactionist Perspective,* 4th ed., Macmillan, New York, 1981, p. 327.
100 Donald R. Cressey, *Other People's Money: A Study in the Social Psychology of Embezzlement,* Free Press, New York, 1953.
101 For an extended discussion of these adjustive vocabulary practices, see ibid., pp. 93–138.
102 Ibid., p. 137.
103 Surgeon General's Scientific Advisory Committee on Television and Social Behavior, *Television and Growing Up: The Impact of Televised Violence,* Department of Health, Education and Welfare, Washington, D.C., 1972.
104 Martin S. Weinberg, "The Nudist Management of Respectability," in Earl Rubington and Martin S. Weinberg (eds.), *Deviance: The Interactionist Perspective,* 4th ed., Macmillan, New York, 1981, pp. 336–345. See also Martin S. Weinberg, "Becoming a Nudist," *Psychiatry,* vol. 29, February 1966, pp. 15–24.
105 Weinberg, "The Nudist Management of Respectability," p. 345.
106 Lewis Yablonsky, "The Delinquent Gang as a Near-Group," *Social Problems,* vol. 7, no. 2, Fall 1959, pp. 108–117.
107 J. L. Simmons, *Deviants,* Boyd & Fraser, San Francisco, 1969, p. 115.
108 Akers, *Deviant Behavior,* pp. 297–304.
109 See, for instance, B. G. Tate and G. S. Baroff, "Aversive Control of Self-Injurious Behavior in a Psychotic Boy," *Behavior Research and Therapy,* vol. 4, 1966, pp. 281–287; I. O. Lovaas and J. Q. Simmons, "Manipulation of Self-Destruction in Three Retarded Children," *Journal of Applied Behavioral Analysis,* vol. 2, Fall 1969, pp. 143–157; and I. O. Lovaas, G. Freitag, V. Gold, and I. Kassorla, "Experimental Studies in Childhood Schizophrenia, I: Analysis of Self-Destructive Behavior," *Journal of Experimental Child Psychology,* vol. 2, 1968, pp. 67–84.
110 Akers, *Deviant Behavior,* pp. 298–299.
111 See R. D. Laing, *The Divided Self,* Penguin, Baltimore, 1965 (originally published in 1960); and R. D. Laing and A. Esterson, *Sanity, Madness and the Family,* Basic Books, New York, 1964.
112 G. Bateson, D. D. Jackson, J. Haley, and J. Weakland, "Toward a Theory of Schizophrenia," *Behavioral Science,* vol 1, 1956, pp. 251–264.
113 Marshall B. Clinard and Robert F. Meir, *Sociology of Deviant Behavior,* 5th ed., Holt, Rinehart and Winston, New York, 1979, p. 92.

114 Rand D. Conger, "From Social Learning to Criminal Behavior," in Marvin D. Krohn and Ronald L. Akers (eds.), *Crime, Law and Sanctions: Theoretical Perspectives,* Sage, Beverly Hills, Calif. 1978, pp. 91–104.

115 Warren Burger, "The Perspective of the Chief Justice of the U.S. Supreme Court," speech given at the annual conference of the American Bar Association, February 8, 1981, Houston, Texas, as printed in *Crime and Social Justice,* vol. 15, Summer 1981, p. 46.

116 Ian Taylor, Paul Walton, and Jock Young, *The New Criminology: For a Theory of Deviance,* Harper & Row, New York, 1973, p. 132.

117 James F. Short and Fred L. Strodtbeck, *Group Process and Gang Delinquency,* University of Chicago Press, Chicago, 1965.

118 Matza, *Becoming Deviant.*

119 Edwin H. Pfuhl, Jr., *The Deviance Process,* Van Nostrand, New York, 1980, pp. 55–79.

120 Rand Conger, "From Social Learning to Criminal Behavior," pp. 91–104.

Behind the Words By Joseph LaMantia and Stephen Pfohl

CHAPTER **9**

THE SOCIETAL REACTION PERSPECTIVE: *Labeling and the Work of Social Control Agents*

Deviance, like beauty, is in the eyes of the beholder. There is nothing inherently deviant in any human act, something is deviant only because some people have been successful in labelling it so.

J. L. Simmons[1]

INTRODUCTION

Deviance does not exist independent of the negative reaction of those who condemn it. Behaviors are never weird, bad, sick, or deviant in themselves. They are deviant only because someone or some group responds to them in this fashion. This is the essence of the societal reaction perspective. In the words of reaction theorist Howard S. Becker, "Deviance is not a quality of the act the person commits, but rather a consequence of the application of rules and sanctions to an 'offender.' The deviant is one to whom the label has successfully been applied; deviant behavior is behavior that people so label."[2]

Throughout the course of my graduate studies in sociology I became familiar with the major theoretical concerns of the societal reaction perspective. It made great sense to me that the study of social deviance should include an analysis of the processes by which certain types of behavior become viewed as unacceptable and by which certain types of people are made subject to corrective or rehabilitative machinery of social control. During the oral portion of my Ph.D. examination I was challenged to defend this perspective. One of my examiners asked whether the theoretical claims of the societal reaction viewpoint were not somewhat exaggerated. I was asked about the existence of certain types of behavior which were naturally deviant in any society.

What about homicide? Isn't homicide deviant regardless of how anybody reacts to it? My answer was no.

Homicide is a way of categorizing the act of killing, such that taking another's life is viewed as totally reprehensible and devoid of any redeeming social justification. Some types of killing are categorized as homicide. Others are not. What differs is not the behavior but the manner in which reactions to that behavior are socially organized. The behavior is essentially the same: killing a police officer or killing by a police officer; stabbing an old lady in the back or stabbing the unsuspecting wartime enemy; a black slave shooting a white master or a white master lynching a black slave; being run over by a drunken driver or slowly dying of a painful cancer caused by a polluting factory. Each is a type of killing. Some are labeled homicide. Others are excused, justified, or viewed, as in the case of dangerous industrial pollution, as environmental risks, necessary for the health of our economy, if not our bodies. The form and content of what is seen as homicide thus varies with social context and circumstance. This is hardly the characteristic of something which can be considered to be naturally or universally deviant.

"Well," continued the examining professor, "what about hyperkinesis? Certainly the problems caused by hyperkinetic children cause a universal disturbance in any culture." Again I disagreed. I suggested that the professor's perspective was colored by the way that our society views unruly and hyperactive children. I asked that he consider how similar behaviors are interpreted by the inhabitants of several South Sea island communities. There, behaviors which we associate with hyperkinesis are revered with a categorical halo of religious sanctity. As the examiner paused to consider my answer for an infinitely long second, I felt the panic of skating on the thin ice of a potentially deviant intellectual response. I awaited the examining committee's reaction. To my relief, a second examiner, an anthropologist who had studied island communities, agreed with my interpretation. He cited other examples of things which we may consider naturally deviant but which peoples in other places or other times would not.

"All right," replied the original examiner, "Is there anything that is universal about deviance?" I answered that what is universal is not a matter of content or substance but of process—the process by which definitions of acts and persons as deviant are socially generated and applied. A concern with the dynamics of this process differentiates the societal reaction perspective from other theoretical vantage points on deviance. This point is made by John Kituse, who states that "the distinctive character of the societal reaction perspective . . . leads . . . to a consideration of how deviants come to be differentiated by imputations made about them by others, how these imputations activate systems of social control, and how these control activities become legitimated as institution responses to deviance."[3]

THEORETICAL IMAGES

The theoretical study of societal reactions to deviance has been carried out under different names—labeling theory, the interactionist perspective, and the social constructionist perspective. In general, societal-reaction theorists have pursued three interrelated concerns: (1) the social-historical development of deviant labels; (2) the application of labels to certain types of people in specific times and places; and (3) the symbolic and practical consequences of the labeling process.

Although it was not until the 1960s that the societal-reaction perspective emerged as a major theoretical tradition, its intellectual origins may be traced to a 1918 essay by social philosopher George Herbert Mead. In "The Psychology of Punitive Justice," Mead likened the majesty of criminal labeling to "that of the angel with the fiery sword at the gate who can cut one off from the world to which he belongs."[4] The labeling process, in other words, sets boundaries between those who are acceptable and those who are condemned, between insiders and outsiders, between conventional people and deviants. Mead's essay points to the positive contributions of labeling in awakening the consciences of law-abiding citizens and in strengthening the cohesiveness of society as a whole. In this sense, Mead's ideas resemble those of the functionalist theorists discussed in Chapter 5. Yet, unlike the functionalists, Mead was less concerned with the systemic consequences of deviance than with the interactional ritual through which labels were applied. In 1938 Frank Tannenbaum used the term *tagging* to describe a similar process.[5] According to Tannenbaum, the stigma accompanying the deviant label may drive people deeply into the realm of nonconformity.

The Emergence of the Societal Reaction Perspective During the 1960s

The early ideas of Mead and Tannenbaum were elaborated by Edwin Lemert in his 1951 book *Social Pathology*.[6] Lemert's book took issue with the way that deviance was defined by theorists working within the pathological, disorganizational, functionalist, anomie, and learning traditions. These perspectives took the existence of deviance for granted. For Lemert this was a mistake. The other perspectives failed to consider how something or some people came to be defined as deviant in the first place. So also did they fail to examine the impact of labeling on persons processed as deviants. Rather than accepting conventional definitions of deviance, Lemert argued that deviance should be seen as "behavior which is effectively disapproved of in social interaction."[7] The social dynamics and consequences of such disapproval were presented as important topics for sociological investigation.

Lemert's ideas waited a full decade before blossoming into a major new sociological perspective. During the early 1960s this perspective "took off" in the writings of Howard S. Becker, John Kituse, Erving Goffman, Kai Erikson, and others. In the fall of 1962 a series of articles using the societal reaction framework first appeared in a special issue of the journal *Social Problems*. A year later many of the same papers were reissued in the pages of *The Other Side,* a book edited by Howard Becker. The importance of Becker's contribution cannot be overstated. As Don Gibbons points out, while "Lemert's book was a dozen years ahead of its time . . . Becker's volume quickly became one of the critical works to which many others paid homage."[8]

What was it about the early 1960s that made American sociologists particularly ripe for the societal reaction viewpoint? The answer to this question involves some reference to the massive social and political struggles which rocked college campuses nationwide. During the late fifties and early sixties, college students (and even some of their professors) had begun to join with black civil rights advocates and later with anti–Vietnamese war activists in demanding a more humane and just social order. This brought the label of deviance closer to home. Sociologists soon found their students, children, friends, spouses, and even themselves being tear-gassed, arrested, spied upon, stigmatized, and bullied around like "common deviants." The target of social control had shifted from burglars and dope addicts to political activists and disenchanted young people.

Riots in the ghettos of urban America. Imprisonment for those who refused to participate in what they believed was an unjust war. Criminal status for those who preferred the use of marijuana to alcoholic beverages. These things contributed, not only to the development of a youthful counterculture and the rise of political militancy, but to a new viewpoint on social deviance. Understanding deviance meant first to understand why people react against certain forms of behavior. It required that one study the activities of social control agents as well as the behavior of labeled deviants.

When the police broke into the Chicago apartment of members of the Black Panther party and opened fire on its residents, violent death was referred to as justifiable homicide. When an angry black youth returned fire it was murder. When a skilled politician talked of an everpresent Communist conspiracy he was considered realistic. Political activists who alleged that their phones were being tapped were labeled paranoid. Men who drove tailor-suited bodies into heart attacks, ulcers, and high blood pressure were viewed as dedicated. Women who wanted equal pay for equal work were pictured as psychological misfits. Awareness of such contradictions led reaction theorists to question the relationship between the labelers and those who are labeled as deviant.

With the societal reaction perspective came what Howard Becker referred to as an "unconventional sentimentality." Becker noted the tendency of reaction theorists to "fall into deep sympathy with the people we are studying, so that while the rest of society views them as unfit . . . , we believe that they are at least as good as anyone else, more sinned against than sinning."[9] By challenging conventional stereotypes about deviance and laying the blame for much of the deviance problem upon the doorstep of respectable control agents, societal reaction theorists participated in the growing mood of rebellion and social critique which was gathering momentum during the early 1960s. According to Nanette Davis this liberal response resembled that of an earlier generation of social turmoil. "Like some intellectuals in the 1930s who identified with the oppressed working class, labelers took on the deviant's plight as their own."[10] A similar point is made by Edwin Lemert, who traces the development of the societal reaction perspective to a growing awareness of the "powerlessness of individuals" before the ever-widening control machinery of the "welfare state," the "administrative state," the "garrison state," and the "military industrial combine."[11]

Spatial Influences on the Societal Reaction Viewpoint

The societal-reaction perspective was a product, not only of the times, but of particular places. Two places are of importance: the University of Chicago and the west coast. "The vast majority of the [early] labelling proponents received their graduate training" in the sociology department of the University of Chicago.[12] There they were exposed to the so-called Chicago school of symbolic interaction, a sociological theory stressing the importance of the real or imagined reactions of others upon how we act and how we conceive of ourselves. This perspective would play a critical role in early formulations of reaction perspective.

At Chicago societal-reaction theorists were also trained in the methods of participatory field research. Under the guidance of Everett Hughes they came in direct contact with deviants and control agents. As a result, their research was not mediated by the official viewpoint of government statistics. Through contact with those whom they studied they achieved a certain empathy and often sympathy for people who otherwise might have remained little more than another number on a long sheet of anonymously coded computerized data. Such field work was often accompanied by an interest in liberal social reform. According to Everett Hughes, it was undertaken by people "who believed that social facts well presented would point the way to reform."[13] During the 1960s such field work also nurtured what Alvin Gouldner once referred to as the hip style of early reaction theorists and their attraction to the deviant underlife of American cities. According to Gouldner, "This group of Chicagoans finds itself at home in the world of the hip [and] prefers the off beat to the familiar, the vivid ethnographic detail to the dull taxonomy, the seriously expressive to dry analysis, naturalistic observation to formal questionnaires."[14]

The other place which proved particularly fertile for societal-reaction theorizing was America's west coast. In California, a host of Chicago-trained sociologists of deviance found academic jobs. For this reason early reaction theorists were for a time referred to both as Neo-Chicagoans and as the west coast school. These designations served to contrast their studies of deviance with the etiological, or causal, research of the so-called eastern establishment. According to Edwin Lemert, "The western-looking deviance sociologists . . . focused their work on the consequences of the moral order and social control, seeking to show how categories of deviance are invoked and applied to individuals and groups."[15]

What was it about California universities which encouraged the development of the societal reaction viewpoint? Of foremost importance was the fact that during the early 1960s the California university and state college system was rapidly expanding. In response to major increases in population, resulting from westward migration and the postwar baby boom, California's colleges hired many new faculty. This provided room for new young scholars with fresh ideas. Also important was the fact that higher education in California was by and large public education. It was cheap and attracted an array of students from far more widely varying backgrounds than those accepted within the costly gates of elite eastern universities. This meant that California professors would more quickly be confronted with students of varied class and color, students whose concerns would not easily be addressed by more traditional theoretical and research frameworks. Also important was the failure of conservative functionalist theorizing to dominate west coast sociology. The dominance of functionalism in eastern sociology was discussed in Chapter 6. Suffice it to say that the zenith of functionalism was passing just as California sociology was expanding during the early 1960s. This permitted a plurality of new ways of envisioning the social world to rise up more quickly in the west than in the east.

Another factor contributing to the westward rise of reaction theorizing was the political turmoil which beset California campuses throughout the 1960s. Just as expansion opened the gates of the university to new and sometimes radical viewpoints, the state government was being captured by conservatives led by a former movie star and spokesperson for the General Electric Company. When Ronald Reagan assumed the governorship in Sacramento he immediately set about fulfilling one of his most important campaign promises—to stem the spread of unorthodox and radical thinking at state universities. Assisted by a notoriously conservative board of regents Reagan delivered on many of his promises. California campuses soon became hotbeds of conflict and controversy. Students claimed that they were denied the rights to freely think, speak, and act. Professors charged that a "correct" political viewpoint had subtly become a criterion for tenure. New conservative policies of academic social control had come to campus, and with them a new breed of deviants. Teachers and students were targeted for public labeling and harsh sanctions. Thus, for many sociologists on the west coast the societal reaction perspective was born as much out of personal as intellectual concern. As social unrest spread nationwide so did this new perspective.

Theoretical Foundations of the Societal Reaction Perspective: The Influence of Interpretive Sociology

Societal reaction theorists work within the interpretive sociological tradition. Following the lead of the classical German sociologist Max Weber, interpretive sociology emphasizes the importance of *subjective meaning* in the social organization of everyday life.[16] Three variants of interpretive sociology were particularly influential: symbolic interactionism, phenomenological sociology, and ethnomethodology.

Symbolic Interactionism This perspective traces its origins to the writings of University of Chicago philosopher George Herbert Mead. Mead's work emphasized the interpretive adjustment of humans to the real or imagined reactions of others. The phrase *symbolic interaction* was coined by Mead's student, Herbert Blumer. According to Blumer, "The term 'symbolic interaction' refers to the fact that human beings interpret or 'define' each other's actions instead of merely reacting to each other's actions."[17]

For symbolic interactionists society is processual—a dynamic alignment of people, each acting in relation to how they interpret the actions of others. Interactionists also view the self in processual terms. The self is described as a "moving communication process," a dynamic series of "self-indications" by which people interpretively take the viewpoint of others toward themselves. Of particular influence is the viewpoint of significant others, people whose importance contributes greatly to the way we define ourselves and decide upon appropriate lines of action.

The definitional and processual emphasis of symbolic interactionism permeates the societal reaction perspective. Their influence is particularly evident in the way in which reaction theorists conceive of such matters as *labeling*, the *sequential model of deviance, master status, secondary deviance,* and *stigma*.

Labeling: Interactional and Historical Concerns Labeling refers "to the process by which deviants are defined by the rest of society."[18] Reaction theorists such as

Howard Becker contend that we cannot assume a given act to be deviant "simply because it is commonly regarded as so. Instead, we look to the process by which the common definition arises . . . the process of labeling."[19]

Becker's concerns with the labeling process are pitched at two levels: (1) the concrete interaction between the labelers and potential targets for labeling, and (2) the historical construction of labels themselves. The first level concerns what goes on between control agents and others such that deviant labels are applied, withheld, or avoided. Becker's work questions the adequacy of official definitions of deviance. Some people act in a manner which is defined as deviant, get caught, and are labeled. Others may not act in such a fashion but are falsely labeled anyway. Still others may do it and get away with it unlabeled. Becker refers to such persons as "secret deviants." These several types of interactional possibilities are displayed in Table 9-1.

The labeling process may be either formal or informal. In formal terms, imagine a police officer late at night on a darkened street. She has just received word that a burglar is nearby. She turns the corner and sees a figure in an alley. Will she apprehend the person? Will a formal deviant label be applied? Think of all the social contingencies which might affect the officer's actions: the person's gender, size, color, age, mode of dress, way of walking, manner of speech. Also of importance might be pressures from the department to make more arrests, the presence of witnesses, or the kind of neighborhood and whether the suspect is perceived as the type of person who would normally be found in such a place. The interaction of all these factors is important to an analysis of the formal labeling process.

Similar factors are applicable to informal labeling. This is illustrated in an early societal-reaction study in which John Kituse examined how college students label others as homosexual.[20] Kituse discovered that imputations of homosexuality reveal as much about informal labelers as about those being labeled. People who acted similarly were reacted to differently by different labelers under different circumstances. Labeling occurred, in other words, independent of the actual speech, interest, dating patterns, or sexual relations of those categorized as homosexual.

But why has something like homosexuality acquired the label of deviance in the first place? Where in history do deviant labels come from? This is the second set of questions raised by Becker. In *The Other Side* he suggests that deviant labels arise as the result of the efforts of powerful "moral entrepreneurs." Moral entrepreneurs are persons or groups who lobby for the deviantization of certain types of behavior. One classic study of moral entrepreneurship is Becker's analysis of the origins of the Marijuana Stamp Tax Act of 1937, legislation which made it a criminal offense to

TABLE 9-1
TYPES OF DEVIANT BEHAVIOR

	Obedient behavior	**Rule-breaking behavior**
Perceived as deviant	Falsely accused	Pure deviant
Not perceived as deviant	Conforming	Secret deviant

Source: Adapted from Howard S. Becker, *Outsiders*, 1963, p. 20.

smoke pot. The specific details of Becker's study are discussed later. At present it is enough to note that a concern with the historical development of deviant categories is an important aspect of the societal-reaction perspective.

A Sequential Model of Deviance Deviance unfolds in time. The factors which influence its development do not operate at the same time. Some factors may be more important in encouraging a person to experiment with nonconformity. Others are more influential in sustaining existing patterns of rule-breaking. For these reasons Becker proposes a sequential model of deviance—"a model which takes into account the fact that patterns of behavior develop in orderly sequence."[21] Becker illustrates the importance of such a sequential model by pointing to the progressive stages involved in becoming a deviant drug user. Factors which may be significantly associated with drug use may affect some persons and not others. Why? The answer lies in the fact that unaffected persons may not (yet) have reached a stage in the development of deviance where such factors really count. According to Becker, variables such as personal alienation "will only produce drug use in people who are in a position to experiment because they participate in groups in which drugs are available; alienated people who do not have drugs available to them cannot begin experimentation and they cannot become users, no matter how alienated they are."[22]

Becker employs the metaphor of career development to explicate progressive stages in deviant involvement. Other societal reaction theorists, such as J. L. Simmons, analyze the sequential unfolding of deviance in terms of such phases as (1) initial recruitment, (2) role imprisonment, and (3) entrance into sustaining deviant subcultures.[23] At each stage in the process potential deviants face a wide range of pushes and pulls, and choose (although not freely) to continue or discontinue their advance into nonconformity. According to John Lofland, such choices are influenced by a variety of situational factors (whom one associates with, one's immediate sociogeographical environment, the availability of the "hardware," or physical props, necessary for certain forms of deviant action, and individual capacities, such as self-esteem, technical skill, and self-concept), and by the more generic cultural and social-institution setting in which one is located.[24]

Sequential "career contingencies" include both objective facts of social structure and changes in the perspective, motivations, and desires of the individual.[25] Of particular importance are the reactions of others to deviant labeling. Other people may come to think and act toward the labeled deviant in a manner different than before. The life chances of a deviant may thus be drastically altered. He or she may be locked up, denied employment, or forced to hide. All of this may lead to a new identity organized around the awareness of one's status as an outsider.

Even if one is not caught, the fear of being discovered might significantly change a person's life. Rule-breakers must constantly be on their guard: classifying others as potential threats, controlling the kinds of communications they have about their activities, hiding traces of the deviant act.[26] Think of the teenager who smokes marijuana behind his or her parents' backs. Such people must be cautious about whom they associate with, and what they say about what they were doing or whom they were with last night. In hiding the physical traces of their deviant act they may go so far as to light incense, use an eyewash to remove redness, or even to splash alcohol on their faces in order to provide a more acceptable cover for being high. In any event the threat of being labeled is an important variable in the sequential development of deviance.

Deviance as a Master Status Almost everybody occupies multiple social positions or statuses. Such things as age, gender, occupation, race or ethnicity, educational background, religious preference, class, political affiliation, and even physical appearance tell us about who people are and how we can expect them to act. Some statuses may be more central than others. Race is a good example. Somebody may be tall, wealthy, personable, a Harvard graduate, married, the parent of three children, a successful lawyer, and also black. Yet, in a racially stratified society such as the United States, one status may stand out above all others—being black. "I met a black lawyer at the party." According to Everett Hughes, a status like race may operate as a *master status,* one which overshadows all others.[27]

Deviance may also operate as a master status. According to Hughes's student Howard Becker, "Possession of one deviant trait may have a generalized symbolic value, so that people automatically assume that its bearer possess other undesirable traits allegedly associated with it."[28] Being gay has virtually nothing to do with being a teacher or a banker. Nonetheless, as long as homosexuality continues to be labeled as deviant, it is likely that it, like race, will function as a master status. "I met a gay banker at the party." When deviance operates as a master status, labeled deviants may encounter severe interactional troubles in dealing with other people. They may even identify with the primacy of the deviant label in defining themselves. This can be troublesome.

Secondary Deviance People may initially deviate for any number of reasons—biological, psychological, or sociological. Nonetheless, once one is caught and labeled, the reaction to deviance may itself cause further deviance. Labeling may amplify deviance. This point is made by Edwin Lemert, who differentiates between primary and secondary deviation. The former may be caused by anything; the latter by an individual's reactions to others' reactions. According to Lemert, "When a person begins to employ his deviant behavior or a role based upon it as a means of defense, attack, or adjustment to the overt and covert problems created by the consequent societal reaction to him, his deviation is secondary."[29]

Stigma The writings of Erving Goffman liken social interaction to the performance of theatrical roles.[30] Like actors on a stage, people are said to carefully manage social cues which enable them to create and sustain an impression of who they are and what they are up to. Some people, however, are cast into roles which constrain their abilities to manage positive impressions of themselves. Such persons are stigmatized, the bearers of what Goffman describes as a "spoiled identity."[31]

Goffman parallels the stigmatized problems of labeled deviants to the plight of physically or mentally handicapped persons. He extends the scope of the societal-reaction perspective to those who are negatively labeled for how they appear in addition to how they may act. The threat of stigmatization does not, however, eliminate a person's capacity for impression management. Stigmatized persons who are "wise" to their precarious social conditions may restrict themselves to the company of other stigmatized persons or to those sympathetic to their condition. In this way they restrict the flow of information about themselves to those whom they can trust. Whether or not one is successful in managing stigma, labeled deviants are confronted with social problems not faced by the straight world. This underscores a central theme of the societal reaction perspective—that a full sociological understanding of deviance requires attention to the interactive dynamics between those who condemn nonconformity and those who are condemned.

Phenomenological Sociology Phenomenological sociology is the study of society as it appears within the consciousness of its members. Phenomenological sociologists suspend judgment as to the objective reality of social life in order to describe social reality as it is constructed in the minds of those who experience it.[32] Many phenomenological sociologists trace their concerns to the writings of Alfred Schutz.[33] Schutz depicted the experience of everyday life as filtered through a set of categorical definitions or typifications about what the world is and how one should act within it. This stock of typical meanings and recipes for action provides people with a common sense about the nature of social reality, with a sense that the everyday social world can be taken for granted, that it exists independently of our immediate experience of it, and that, for all practical purposes, others experience it in similar fashion.

Schutz's work provides a description of the structure of the everyday-life world as it is typically experienced by those who live within it. Where does this structure come from? How do we commonsensically come to know that a "real man" should act in certain fashion, while a "real woman" should not? How do we know what is normal? How do we know what is deviant? One answer is presented by Schutz's students Peter Berger and Thomas Luckmann in their book *The Social Construction of Reality*.[34] Berger and Luckman contend that, unlike other species of animals, we humans are not instinctually provided with a fixed and stable sense of social order. We must rely, instead, on our ability to use language to symbolically create an artificial world order. Once this occurs, the names we affix to things begin to take on a life of their own. We are trapped in the reality of our own words. We become prisoners of the symbols we create. We are in a position not unlike Victor Frankenstein in Mary Shelley's terrifying novel. The creature has come to rule the creator.

The process whereby humanly created symbols are experientially transformed into externally given social realities is described by Berger and Luckmann as *objectification*. Through socialization the reality of these symbols is brought within. They come to rule not by external force but by the internal constraints of conscience. They come to be experienced as natural realities. Forgotten is the fact these symbols were once nothing but an arbitrary way of naming something, derivatives of prior symbolic *externalization*. As institutionalized versions of social reality they operate as controls over what we experience as real. To deny their reality is to defy common sense and run the risk of being labeled deviant.

Ethnomethodology Ethnomethodology extends the phenomenological perspective to the study of everyday social interaction. It is concerned with the methods which people use to accomplish a reasonable account of what is happening in social interaction and to provide a structure for the interaction itself. Unlike symbolic interactionists, ethnomethodologists do not assume that people actually share common symbolic meanings.[35] What they share is a ceaseless body of interpretive work which enables them to convince themselves and others that they share common meanings. Ethnomethodologists also differ from phenomenological sociologists who emphasize the manner in which people are socialized into a particular version of reality. For ethnomethodologists social reality is far more fragile. It is organized, not by an internalized stock of meanings, but by the moment-to-moment creation and re-creation of the social world in interaction with others.[36]

More important are the differences between ethnomethodology and theoretical perspectives which assume the independent existence of social structure. For ethnomethodologists, social structure is never independent of the consciousness of the actors who experience its force. The sense that social life is governed by a predefined structure of meanings, roles, and rules is just that—a sense, a common sense. This makes social structure no less important. It simply relocates it within, rather than outside, the world of human thinking and doing, talking and acting, working and playing. Social structure, in other words, is viewed as a practical accomplishment rather than a determinant of our daily social existence. From the ethnomethodological vantage point, the structures of everyday life experience are never fully independent of the interpretive work which people do in order to make sense of a particular moment or place in social life. For this reason ethnomethodologists attend to the small, detailed, practical features of interpretive social interactions as keys to deeper mysteries of social structure and life in general.

Given its concern with the processes by which people construct believable, acceptable, or defendable accounts of what social life "really" is, it is not surprising that ethnomethodology has paid particular attention to the problems of deviance and social control. By categorizing certain behaviors as deviant we dramatize the recognizably "real" boundaries of social life itself. By interpretively "recognizing" that certain people are outside the accepted rules of society we pay homage to the reality of these rules and the social structure which we assume to be behind them. Ethnomethodology addresses these matters by focusing on the practical interpretive work of people in constructing imputations about what is deviant and what is normal. Its theoretical contribution to the societal-reaction perspective can best be understood by examining what are considered to be the three interrelated features of all practical interpretive work: indexicality, reflexivity, and documentary interpretation.

Indexicality The term *indexicality* refers to the fact that all human interpretive work is bound to the context in which it occurs. The "reality" of deviance will be conceived very differently, depending on whether it is viewed from a police patrol car or from the backseat of a vehicle full of partying teenagers. The importance of indexicality to the labeling of deviance is suggested by David Sudnow's study of public defenders.[37] Sudnow describes an overcrowded court context in which public attorneys are pressured toward using commonsense stereotypes about who is and who isn't the "normal" criminal and who should be provided with a certain type of defense or plea bargaining. The stereotypical identification of "normal crimes" is linked to the practical demands of an overworked and understaffed public defender's office. Such contextual or indexical demands significantly influence the shape of societal reactions. Their importance is also observed in other ethnomethodological studies, including Aaron Cicourel's examination of juvenile justice decison-making,[38] Richard McCleary's consideration of career contingencies affecting parole officers' production of "bad records for good reasons,"[39] and Arlene Kaplan Daniel's research into the use of psychiatry in the military.[40]

Reflexivity Ethnomethodologists use the term *reflexivity* to express that paradoxical characteristic of human existence whereby objects exist only in relation to the interpretive meaning they have for the people who behold them. In other words, for all practical purposes, who you are is never independent of the way in which I construct and express my understanding of you. The key phrase here is "for all practical purposes." For some abstract philosophical purposes I may speculate about such things as your universal metaphysical essence. Ethnomethodologists care little about such abstract speculations. They are concerned with the mundane, practical ways in which people arrive at knowledge about things of this world. In this very practical sense, what I know about you as an object is always shaped by how I, as a subject, reflexively envision you. There is no pure objectivity, or for that matter pure subjectivity. Everything is impure. Everything is contaminated by everything else. Everything is in relationship to everything else. By the principle of indexicality I understand my interpretations of you to be bound by the social and material context in which we are related. Thus my grasp of you is never purely subjective. Yet, since I must make interpretive use of our context to arrive at a certain knowledge of you, it is also impossible for my knowledge to be purely objective. It is always the product of my own context-bound interpretive work. This I understand by the principle of reflexivity.

Reflexivity and indexicality are forever interrelated phenomena. Each conditions the other. What is reflexively constructed in one moment becomes indexically part of the context of my experience in the next. They are as altering moments in the hour that is life. The bright interpretive activities of reflexivity fold into the dark shadows of indexicality just as the day folds into dark, just as the experience of creating a world folds into the experience of being created by a world that is fixed and prestructured. Ethnomethodologists Hugh Mehan and Houston Wood liken the difference between reflexivity and indexicality to that between dawn and dusk.[41] At dawn I awaken; my eyes (reflexively) putting all things in their place. At dusk I doze; my eyes (indexically) put into context as things among other things, each in its own place.

What does all of this talk about indexicality and reflexivity have to do with the labeling of deviants? The answer is plenty. The principles of indexicality and reflexivity constitute the interpretive core of the labeling process. They are present at each step of the labeling process, yet often pass unnoticed by most participants. The unnoticeable character of interpretive work is particularly evident in the production of deviant labels. The end-product of successful imputational work is paradoxically to forget (or at least be inattentive to) the fact that such interpretive work was even involved. This reflexive disguising of the created character of deviance is observed by Melvin Pollner, who notes that "while a community creates deviance, it may simultaneously mask its creative work from itself."[42]

A good example of the unnoticed character of reflexive interpretive work is Lawrence Weider's study of the inmate code of the halfway house.[43] This code operates not as an abstract set of rules but as an interactionally generated solution to specific instances of tension. It permits inmates to call one another into question. The code is invoked to order a disorderly situation. According to Weider this code is reflexively invoked only when strategically useful. This is rarely noticed. The reflexive use of rules to give a sense of structure to life in the halfway house fades into its indexical shadows as soon as its work is complete.

The paradoxical character of unnoticed interpretive work is further illustrated in Harold Garfinkel's study of jury decision-making.[44] Garfinkel notes that jurors commonly provide retrospective justifications for decisions which they have already made. They look backward in producing a quasi-legal rereading of the available evidence after having already decided upon a person's guilt or innocence. Once this is done jurors appear oblivious to the fact that they have engaged in such retrospective interpretation. They reorder their understandings so as to suggest that "fair deliberations" were guided by the same sound logic from the beginning—logic which was, in fact, after the fact. A similar hiding of the reflexive nature of the labeling process is shown in Sacks's analysis of the reality of suicide threats discovered during hot-line crisis conversations[45] and in Douglas's examination of official descriptions of suicide as cause of death.[46]

Documentary Interpretation Harold Garfinkel, the central figure in the development of ethnomethodology, uses the term *documentary interpretation* to refer to the way in which people infer meaningful action patterns from the appearance of simple behavioral stimuli. Appearances are treated as documents of something deeper, as expressions of underlying patterns or structures. According to Garfinkel, "Not only is the underlying pattern derived from its individual documentary evidences, but the individual documentary evidences, in their turn, are interpreted on the basis of 'what is known' about the underlying pattern. Each is used to elaborate the other."[47]

The method of documentary interpretation is used by people to make sense of other people. By documentary interpretation we know that the politician who shakes our hand outside the supermarket is doing what is expected and not exercising a hand fetish. But would we think the same of someone who was not a politician? Probably not. We see the politician as acting normally because we pair the appearance of handshaking with patterned expectations we have come to associate with the person's position (e.g., what you're supposed to do if you're a politician). Taken-for-grantedly we assume that appearances document something deeper, that they tell us about who the person is and why the person is doing what he or she is doing. How shocked I would be if I discovered that the little man in the cafeteria with the mushrooming white cap and the apron was stirring mud rather than vegetables into my soup. Why? Because by his appearance I had documentarily interpreted him as a cook. Now I know him as a jokester or as a deviant in need of control.

The study of documentary interpretive practices has contributed much to the theoretical scope of the societal reaction perspective. Examples include Egon Bittner's description of the interpretive work employed by police officers in documenting the presence of "real" troublemakers,[48] Robert Emerson's analysis of how juvenile court personnel use a few pieces of surface information to construct elaborate biographical profiles of troublesome youths,[49] and Jacqueline Wiseman's consideration of the way control agents size up persons charged with public drunkenness.[50] Wiseman describes the manner in which such things as physical appearance, past performance, and social position are taken as indicators of the kind of person a particular offender is and how his or her case should be handled.

In each of the studies described above, the interpretive work of social control agents reduces complex and often contradictory social, political, and economic realities into a neatly packaged stereotype of the offender as a deviant individual. Similar findings were reported in my own ethnomethodological analyis of the way in which psychiatric professionals arrived at judgments regarding the potential dangerousness of patients confined within a hospital for the criminally insane.[51] Of particular importance was the way in which clinicians used past records to construct a theoretical view of a patient's problems in the present, the manner in which the conversational structure of clinical interviews was selectively managed in keeping with what diagnosticians already knew about their clients, and the influence of such things as the anticipation of the legal consequences of a particular diagnosis in shaping the form and substance of what was clinically said about patients. Also important was the omnipresent influence of power struggles between members of a diagnostic team and the strategies for diagnosticians to come off as a certain kind of expert professional, a "tough-minded shrink," a "humanitarian reformer," a "good guy," or whatever. Although none of these things were elements pertinent to the case of a patient being diagnosed, each contributed significantly to the interpretive imputation of a deviant label.

Societal Reactions and Power: A Note on Driving Force

Whether working within the theoretical traditions of symbolic interactionism, phenomenological sociology, or ethnomethodology, one concern remains constant for students of the societal reaction perspective—a concern with power as a driving force behind the labeling process. Differences in power translate into differences in the ability to label. In the words of Howard Becker, "The groups whose social position gives them weapons and power are best able to enforce their rules. Distinctions of age, sex, ethnicity, and class are all related to differences in power, which accounts for differences in the degree to which groups, so distinguished can make rules for others."[52]

Although a concern with power is a central feature of the societal-reaction perspective, this concern has sometimes been more implicit than explicit. For a time, many students of societal reaction were distracted from issues of power by a preoccupation with the interpretive microdynamics of the labeling process.[53] Some, however, were never so distracted. One example, is John Lofland, who defines deviance as a "conflict game in which individuals or loosely organized small groups with little power are strongly feared by a well-organized, sizable minority or majority who have a large amount of power."[54] Another is Edwin M. Schur, whose recent book *The Politics of Deviance* is subtitled *Stigma Contests and the Uses of Power*.[55] Similar ideas are presented by Erich Goode, who likens labeling to a form of "linguistic armament,"[56] and by Peter Conrad and Joseph Schneider, who contend that the proper designation of deviance is "a political question . . . decided frequently through political contact."[57]

With this in mind let us consider the manner in which reaction theorists study the problem of deviance.

IDENTIFYING SOCIETAL REACTION DEVIANCE

The societal reaction perspective has contributed significantly to the methods of deviance research. Its influence is particularly evident regarding (1) the critique of official statistics, (2) the definition of what should be considered deviant, and (3) the reflexive nature of the research process.

The Critique of Official Statistics

Much research on deviance involves an uncritical acceptance of official statistics on rule breakers and what they do. The societal reaction perspective questions the validity of research which relies exclusively on such official data. It suggests that the social production of official statistics may tell us more about the organizational concerns of control agencies than about the actions of deviants.[58] According to Edwin Schur, this means "that official statistics should be considered an object of investigation to be explained in their own right. Our primary interest should not be in what they might tell us about the causation of deviance, but rather in exploring the causation of the rates themselves."[59]

The societal reaction perspective encourages us to study the social construction of official statistics. Many students of societal reaction have done just that. The results of their research suggest that official accounts of deviance are influenced by such things as the perceptual biases of control agents, the situational dynamics of the labeling process, the differential visibility of potential deviant populations, the organizational characteristics of control bureaucracies, and the politicality of official data.

Perceptual Bias of Control Agents The production and perpetuation of stereotypical perceptions of race, ethnicity, gender, social class, age, religion, and even physical appearance influence one's chances of being caught and officially labeled as a deviant. The influence of stereotypical perceptions is noted in such research as Aaron Cicourel's *The Social Organization of Juvenile Justice*. Cicourel spent two years as a participant-observer in police and probation agencies in two cities. Cicourel's detailed description of the manner in which control agents employ stereotypical notions of who is deviant unmasks the myth of objectivity surrounding official statistics. Boys whose deviant behavior may be relatively harmless, but whose social characteristics are stereotypically associated with serious criminality, are often labeled more harshly than youths whose acts are more harmful, but whose social backgrounds are more respectable. The case of Smithfield is a good example. Smithfield was a young black male from a socioeconomic environment alien to that of the white middle-class control agents who sought to help him. According to Cicourel, "It is difficult for white, middle-income teachers, probation officers, policemen, therapists, students, and the like, to view . . . Smithfield in clinical terms, and make clinical imputations about the cause of his 'deviant' behavior, because [his] appearance . . . is itself a frightening experience for all of them."[60] Similar observations are made by Arnold S. Linsky, William Rushing, and William Wilde, each of whom presents data suggesting class and social-attribute bias in the official diagnosis of mental illness.[61]

Other studies documenting the influence of stereotypical perceptions in the construction of official data on deviance include Chambliss and Nagasawa's comparison between the official arrest rates of white, black, and Japanese-American youths in Seattle, Washington.[62] Chambliss and Nagasawa conclude that ethnic stereotypes lead police to overestimate the criminal involvement of blacks and underestimate the involvement of Japanese-Americans. With regard to shoplifting, Mary Cameron also discovered a significant difference between the treatment of blacks and nonblacks who were caught and subsequently charged with larceny.[63] Approximately 11 percent of nonblacks were charged, compared to 58 percent of those apprehended who were black. Along similar lines Jack Douglas notes that factors such as religious background, the presence or absence of supportive social relations, and the social status of the deceased impact upon whether a coroner perceives a death as a suicide.[64] Such biases distort the public record regarding the true population of typical deviants.

Situational Dynamics of Labeling Whether something is officially recorded as deviance also depends upon the dynamics of the situation in which labeling occurs. Irving Piliavin and Scott Brian, for instance, underscore the importance of demeanor in determining whether juvenile suspects will be apprehended by police.[65] Of youths who displayed a posture of polite cooperation, only two of forty-five were arrested. Of youths with a noncooperative demeanor, fourteen of twenty-one were apprehended. Noncooperative youths were those whose body movements, dress, facial expressions, and manner of talking suggested to police that they were "punks." They acted nonchalantly, wore leather jackets and/or soiled jeans, and displayed little remorse. Regardless of the seriousness of their actual behaviors they were far more likely to be officially categorized as deviant.

In *The Police and the Public* Albert Reiss points to another situational contingency affecting the likelihood of official labeling—the presence of a citizen complainant who demands that an arrest be made.[66] Police typically defer to such demands. Moreover, black citizens made such demands more commonly than whites. Hence, official arrest statistics were systematically distorted by a situational factor independent of the behavior of those labeled. A related distortion is noted by Temerlin regarding psychiatric labeling.[67] Temerlin presented the same videotape of a patient to different groups of diagnosticians. What differed was how the case was clinically explained. Some diagnosticians were provided with clinically favorable information; others with the opposite. This apparently made all the difference. Presented with exactly the same tape different groups literally saw very different things. Those with a positive preview noted positive attributes. Those with prior negative information saw negative symptoms everywhere. Such are the situational dynamics of labeling—dynamics which when converted into official statistics distort and confuse the nature and extent of the deviance problem.

Differential Visibility This is another limit to the accuracy of official statistics. Some populations of people are more visible than others to the watchful eyes of control agents. "This is particularly the case for persons on welfare, ADC mothers, and others whose lives, as part of the price of obtaining public assistance, are subject to sometimes microscopic scrutiny."[68] The relative visibility of lower-class persons is just one aspect of the problem. Alienation generated by differential surveillance may also limit what lower-class persons voluntarily report about deviance. Lower-class citizens, and particularly lower-class black citizens, are, for instance, less likely to make such reports.

At the upper end of the social ladder people may be more protected from deviant labels. It is big news when the child of a wealthy family is arrested. Bigger news still are a variety of poorly controlled deviant behaviors which only the privileged have a chance to commit. Corporate and so-called white-collar crimes cannot be committed by just anyone. Offenders must be in positions of trust or power to deviate in such "high-brow" fashion. Such crimes are, moreover, among the least reported, prosecuted, or punished. Thus, public knowledge about the extent of said deviance is distorted by the relative invisibility of the crimes of the privileged.

Organizational Characteristics Official statistics on deviance are produced by bureaucratic organizations. They are influenced by the way work is organized and by internal and external sources of pressure. Consider James Q. Wilson's analysis of the organizational styles of police work in two cities.[69] In Western City the police department was organized around a highly centralized and legalistic enforcement of the law. The laws were enforced in an impersonal and professional manner by officers who were more middle-class, more educated, and more likely to follow universal standards than their Eastern City counterparts. Eastern City police were more decentralized and personal in their work. Locals themselves, they knew people in the areas they patrolled and were organized more to contain trouble than to make arrests. The opposite was true in Western City. Pressurized by bureaucratic demands for conformity, "some [Western City] officers felt that their 'productivity' was being measured—number of arrests made, citations written, field contact reports filed, and suspicious persons checked."[70] As a result, Western City officers were more likely to handle such matters as juvenile crime in a more formal fashion. In the more bureaucratically pressurized Western City, officers were more likely to check IDs and question juveniles. This resulted in higher rates of officially recorded deviance—not because there was more deviance but because there was greater organizational demand to record deviance.

Sometimes the pressure to officially record deviance is differentially distributed within the same control bureaucracy. Thus, the "peace-keeping" work of officers patrolling skid row varies greatly from the arrest-producing activities of the narcotics squad.[71] While the former try to prevent trouble without burdening the department with the arrest of unsavory drunks, the latter depend upon arrest records as a measure of organizational performance. The same is true for detectives. Under pressure to clear unsolved crimes, such officers are often willing to make the "big case" by accepting the confession of a suspect for many offenses which in all likelihood he or she never committed. In this way police clear their books and fend off organizational pressure.

In exchange, the big-case confessor is promised an easy time with the charges that can be proved. This, of course, distorts the construction of official records. Yet, as Jerome Skolnick observes, "If clearances are valued, then criminality becomes a commodity for exchange. Thus it is possible that in some cases defendants who confess to large numbers of crimes will tend to be shown more leniency."[72]

The Politicality of Official Statistics Official statistics are not produced in a politically neutral context. They are produced by agencies with a stake in showing that they are doing a good job. The officials of such agencies are ordinarily responsible to elected politicians who campaign with promises to fight deviance. This may affect the social production of crime rates. As Richard Quinney points out, "Crime rates are . . . used to justify or instigate a multitude of political (including social and economic) interests. High crime rates are used by the police to rationalize the need for more personnel and equipment. . . . The police have an interest in maintaining both a high and a low rate of crime."[73]

Political pressure to show both high and low rates of crime was particularly acute during the Nixon administration's "war on crime" during the late 1960s. This encouraged police to invent a new statistic—one showing that crime was increasing but at a decreasing rate. Law-enforcement officials could thus have it both ways: they could show that they were making good use of the resources they had (the rate decreased) and that they needed new resources (crimes were still going up). Sometimes the distortion of official crime rates was more deliberate.[74] As Charles McCaghy has noted, "Departments may encourage police to deliberately downgrade for record purposes the seriousness of some offenses. Aggravated assault becomes simple assault; robbery becomes larceny. By such manipulations, departments can prove to the public that they are 'doing something' about crime."[75]

Defining Deviance

A second methodological contribution of the societal reaction perspective concerns the issue of what is to be considered deviant. Students of deviance have long argued over this issue. Some contend that deviance should be limited to those acts which are legally prohibited. Others maintain that deviance should be equated with behaviors which are normatively prohibited. Still others wish to define deviance as things which ought to be prohibited, even if they are not. The societal reaction position is clear. Do not start with any preconceived definition. Rely, instead, on definitions used by real people in particular historical contexts. This follows from the reaction perspective's assumption that deviance never exists independent of the interpretive work of the control agents who see it. If this be true, then the way that everyday people define deviance should be the starting point for sociologically informed research.

This concern with how everyday people define deviance has prompted many societal reaction researchers to employ field methods to study the labeling process. Whether being a participant-observer in a mental hospital, riding in the back seat of a police car, or hanging out in a gay bar, the researchers who have produced many of the most notable studies of societal reaction have used naturalistic field strategies. Yet, regardless of methodological strategy, societal reaction researchers share a common investigative edict—*begin with the interpretive perspective of those being studied.*

The Reflexive Nature of Societal Reaction Research

Societal reaction researchers, like anyone else, are bound to the social context in which their studies occur. In interpreting the interpretations of others, researchers must rely on the same interpretive practices as everyday people. How, then, can they claim objectivity for their analyses?

The answer is not found by retreating to the scientific haven of survey analysis or fixed-choice questionnaires. These methods may be useful, but they also depend upon interpretive inferences and context-bound judgments about what is or isn't a meaningful answer to a prepackaged question. In constructing surveys or questionnaires, researchers must rely on essentially the same interpretive practices as field researchers. The difference is simply that they do all their interpreting before coming in contact with the people they study. Unfortunately, this means that many respondents are unable to "get into" or hear questions in the same way as those who made them up. This is because respondents, when asked to choose an answer, are likely to be involved in an entirely different set of interpretive relevancies than researchers. Maybe their dog died or they won the lottery or were robbed. These things, which might be noted by the field researcher, will unfortunately be missed by those conducting a survey. The use of such allegedly objective research instruments may thus present as many interpretive problems as those raised in the course of field work. The societal reaction perspective's answer is twofold. It acknowledges that objectivity is partial, at best. The task of the disciplined researcher is to approximate objectivity while providing a detailed account of the "natural history" of his or her research—a description of the social context and context-bound interpretive decisions that are an inherent feature of the research process. Two things help researchers to approximate objectivity. The first involves attempts to partially replicate a particular study. No two research projects are ever identical. But what happens if one tries to repeat a particular investigation in some other context? Does one find something similar? If not, why not? By approaching research in such a comparative fashion, one may better understand and thus transcend the social factors which limit objectivity. This helps us to become more objective.

A second strategy used by reaction theorists to maximize objectivity is to display the verbal or nonverbal actions of those being studied. The use of verbatim audio or visual transcripts permits the audience to partially join the researcher in interpreting the scene being analyzed. It provides data by which others may reject, modify, or accept a particular interpretive account. The advantages of such procedures are summarized by Aaron Cicourel, who advocates the "examination of verbatim materials to show how the researcher makes sense of the subject's remarks, while also involving features of the action scenes or past scenes felt to be relevant to the subject and the observer in deciding what is happening."[77]

SOCIAL CONTROL OF SOCIETAL REACTIONS TO DEVIANCE

Many societal reaction studies document the differential nature of social control. Control agents often discriminate between individuals of varying race, sex, age, ethnicity, gender, and social class. Indeed much of the societal reaction literature may be read as an "expose" of inequalities of control as dished out by official state agents and others. Because of this, reaction theorists are generally supportive of reforms which limit the discretionary power of control agents and guarantee the basic civil rights of all accused deviants. Two other programs of reform are supported as well: decriminalizing victimless crimes and deploying "least restrictive" control options.

Decriminalization of Victimless Crimes

The term *victimless crime* refers to a wide range of consensual social exchanges punished by the criminal law: abortion, gambling, deviance, drug use, selling sex, choosing alternative sexual orientations.[78] Although the term is used extensively in the literature of the societal reaction perspective, *victimless* may not best define this category of deviance. Indeed, some people see victimization as resulting from each of these moral offenses. Others do not.

Consider the issue of abortion. Today there is widespread disagreement as to whether abortion violates the rights of an unborn fetus or whether its prohibition violates the rights of a woman to control her own body. Is there a true victim in the choice of a woman, unready, unable, or unwilling to assume the responsibilities of parenthood, to terminate pregnancy after two months? What about after three months or five? The answer varies with the person you ask. Even if one believes that there is a violation of rights, is the criminalization of abortion the best way to control against its occurrence?

Similar ambiguity exists with regard to other "moral," or "public order," offenses. Gambling and illegal drug use are said to detract from the industriousness of society, corrupt youths, and provide escapes from necessary social responsibilities. Other critics point to the way in which such deviance destabilizes lower-class and minority communities.[79] The same is said of prostitution and pornographic businesses. Antiprostitution forces also argue that areas dominated by "sex for sale" soon become havens for more predatory forms of crime, such as robbery or pickpocketing. Straight businesses and real estate values may be damaged by the porn movie house, street hookers, or massage parlors down the block. Feminist groups stress the manner in which sexist and often violent pornography contributes to the victimization of women. The harm of alternative forms of sexual expression, such as homosexuality, is more difficult to document. Nonetheless, zealous religious groups commonly depict sexual relations between members of the same gender as a demonically inspired assault upon the kingdom of God on earth.

Regardless of whether such "moral offenses" have documentable victims, another question must be asked: Does making them illegal contribute to the good of society? The societal reaction perspective's answer to this question is an unambiguous no. It contends that the legal prohibition of consensual deviant exchanges amplifies rather than decreases the negative consequences of nonconformity. The negative effects of criminalization are seen as far worse than any possible positive gains. In support of this position, reaction theorists raise the following issues.[80]

Laws prohibiting consensual deviant exchanges are essentially unenforceable.

Abortion does not cease to exist when it is made illegal. It is simply more costly and dangerous as women are forced to obtain illegal abortions without the guarantee of medical safeguards. The same goes for gambling, illegal drug use, the sale of sex, and alternative forms of sexual relations. Unlike such predatory crimes as burglary, fraud, or assault, there are no unwilling participants in such deviant activities. Moreover, since these exchanges generally occur in private, there is little that society can do to enforce prohibitions against such behavior, short of a policy of total surveillance, undercover espionage, and a thorough disregard for the sanctity of private life. There are, of course, self-proclaimed moralists who believe that the protection of their own versions of morality justify tactics of total control. Societal reaction theorists refuse to be counted among their number.

Laws prohibiting consensual deviant exchanges lead to discriminatory enforcement patterns.

Some persons' private lives are less private than others. The wealthy woman who desires to terminate a pregnancy will not have to rely upon the services of a known underground abortionist. She is able to afford the discreet services of a less visible respectable physician. When a crackdown comes her ability to obtain an abortion is not likely to be jeopardized in the same manner as that of her less privileged lower-class sister. The same holds for the lower-class junkie when compared to the rich and famous addict, or for the lower-class street hooker when compared to the high-priced and low-profile call girl, whose "favors" are purchased by the wealthy executive. Thus the criminalization of consensual deviance invariably produces a pattern of discriminatory enforcement.

Laws prohibiting consensual deviant exchanges encourage deviant behavior on the part of social control agents.

This is true regarding two aspects of the law enforcement: the likelihood that control agents will (1) use illegal means to obtain evidence, and (2) be corrupted by those who do business in the market of desired but prohibited goods and services. In the first instance, control agents may find themselves under strong organizational pressures to bend the rules of proper legal procedure in order to enforce laws which are essentially unenforceable. Undercover agents may beat up on a lower-class junkie in order to obtain evidence on "Mr. Big." Police officers may physically harass homosexuals. Vice squad members may entrap or even assault prostitutes. To whom are such persons to complain? Who would believe them if they did? The illegal nature of their personal activities makes them relatively vulnerable to equally illegal activities of law-enforcers.

Corruption is also a problem for the controllers of consensual deviance. Unseen by anyone but the deviants with whom they do business, police officials, judges, and politicians may find it very easy to line their wallets with funds obtained by looking the other way. Given public ambivalence about such matters, it is easy for corrupt officials to rationalize their behaviors. According to the highly publicized 1972 report of New York City's Knapp Commission, laws against gambling, narcotics, and prostitution were themselves major contributors to police corruption.[81]

Laws prohibiting consensual deviant exchanges may increase secondary deviance. The illegal status of heroin makes it extremely expensive to purchase. As such, the addict may have to resort to other illegal activities simply to obtain enough money to fight off the pains of withdrawal. In this sense, the criminalization of consensual deviance may lead to secondary deviance—deviance resulting from the labeling process itself. The addict may become a burglar or robber. So too may certain consensual deviants become victims of blackmail. Blackmail has historically represented a problem for many homosexuals, forced to pay large sums of money in order to prevent someone from making public the nature of their private sexual preference.

Laws prohibiting consensual deviant exchanges are extremely costly to enforce. The public pays an enormous economic price for attempts to enforce the prohibition of consensual deviance. Law-enforcement officials estimate that approximately 22 percent of all arrests during a given year are for moral offenses such as those being discussed.[82] The dollar total for the control work which produces those arrests is fantastic. The amount of money spent on marijuana busts alone is staggering. In California during 1972 the average arrest cost taxpayers approximately $1,340.[83] During 1977, 457,600 such arrests occurred nationwide.[84] At a figure of only $1,000 per arrest, that would drain the public of almost $500 million per annum.[85] Once California changed its drug laws by decriminalizing the possession of less than one ounce of marijuana, the state treasury saved more than $25 million per year.[86]

Laws prohibiting consensual deviant exchanges support organized crime. Many criminal organizations are staked by profits reaped from the black-market sale of illegal goods and services. Revenues from gambling, prostitution, pornography, and the sale of illegal drugs constitute the economic backbone of organized criminal activity.

Laws prohibiting consensual deviant exchanges damage the public's respect for law.

Efforts to enforce laws over which there is great public disagreement and little chance of success may instill a spirit of public cynicism toward law in general. How common it is to hear young people disdainfully comment upon a system of law which permits their parents to get high on booze but threatens to imprison them for smoking a joint.

Least Restrictive Control

A central theme in the societal reaction perspective is that social control can turn back upon itself when it is too severe. Severely labeled deviants may be propelled by circumstances or an altered self-concept toward further deviance. They may become imprisoned or encapsulated within a deviant role. This is particularly the case for deviants closed-in by the walls of the "total institution"—the prison, mental hospital, or some other environment of total control. According to Erving Goffman such extreme settings of social control have four distinctive characteristics:

1 Everything in the life of an inmate takes place within the same place and under the everwatchful eye of a centralized institutional authority.

2 Everything that an inmate does is carried out in the immediate company of a large batch of other people, each of whom are treated alike and forced to enact the same routines.

3 All of an inmate's time is tightly scheduled by a body of rules and administrative order imposed by those in charge.

4 The entire system of enforced activities, time and space control, is purportedly organized around an overall rational plan of institutional goals—in the case of deviance, the goals of correction and/or treatment.[87]

In *Asylums* Goffman reports upon his research as a participant-observer on the staff of St. Elizabeth's mental hospital in Washington, D.C. Rather than rehabilitating deviants, this total institution contributed to the self-mortification and stigmatization of patients, reducing their chances of returning to the normal world. During the late 1960s and early 1970s the research of Goffman and other reaction theorists was used to support reform movements advocating deinstitutionalization and least restrictive policies of social control. Reformers hoped to curtail the stigmatizing and amplification of deviance by limiting the use of total institutions to those who were severely disturbed and dangerous.

Related policy developments were supported by societal reaction theorists in the fields of criminal justice and delinquency prevention. Works such as Edwin Schur's important *Radical Non-Intervention* is a case in point.[88] In 1967 the Presidential Commission on Law Enforcement and the Administration of Justice echoed the concerns of many labeling theorists by calling for efforts to divert offenders from the stigmatization of the courtroom. Youthful offenders, for instance, were targeted for counseling or community work rather than a formal hearing or trial. Such programs were far less costly than formal adjudication and possible incarceration. Estimates suggest that the cost of diversion is a tenth of that entailed by formal prosecution, and that the public might save as much as $1.5 billion per year by implementing such lesser-restrictive-option alternatives for minor offenses.

In sociological terms the results are less clear. Although some research suggests that diverted offenders may perceive themselves as less stigmatized, there is little evidence that such programs actually reduce future crime. Unfortunately most studies of this matter have been poorly constructed, using very small samples and less than ideal matches between persons assigned to diversion and those subject to more traditional crime-control measures. Nonetheless, the financial and perceptual advantages of diversion are significant enough to justify continued experimentation with efforts to control deviance in the least restrictive manner possible.

THE SOCIETAL REACTION PERSPECTIVE TODAY

The societal reaction perspective today exerts an enormous influence on the field of deviance and social control. Guided by an omnipresent concern for the relationship between control agents and those who are labeled deviant, societal reaction researchers have pursued three general areas of inquiry: (1) the historical development of deviant labels, (2) the process by which labels are applied, and (3) the consequences of being labeled.

The Historical Development of Deviant Labels

The social history of deviant labels involves what Malcolm Spector and John Kituse refer to as the study of "claims-making" activity on the part of various groups within society. Groups with sufficient power are able to stake and defend their claims regarding what should be considered deviant. In the words of Spector and Kituse, "The theoretical problem is to account for how categories of deviance are produced, and how methods of social control and treatment are institutionally established."[89]

Numerous historical studies fall within the general historical concerns of the societal reaction perspective. Classic studies in this tradition include Joseph Gusfield's analysis of the class and cultural politics of the Women's Christian Temperance Union and its crusade to prohibit the sale of alcoholic beverages,[90] Kai Erikson's analysis of the construction and control of crime in the Massachusetts Bay Colony,[91] Anthony Platt's study of the "invention of delinquency" and the founding of the first juvenile court,[92] William Chambliss's investigations into the origins and use of vagrancy laws,[93] and Elliot Currie's examination of the social control of witches in Europe and Great Britain.[94] More recent studies include Joseph Schneider's analysis of the development of the medicalized concept of alcoholism,[95] Peter Conrad's account of the discovery of hyperkinesis,[96] Kathleen Tierney's consideration of the origins of the spouse-abuse movement, and Gerald Markle and Ronald Troyer's examination of the antismoking movement.[97] These are just a few of the growing number of sociological investigations into the developmental history of deviant labels.

In order to provide a familiarity with the kinds of historical questions raised by reaction research, I have selected two examples for further elaboration. The first is Howard Becker's classic analysis of the origins of the Marijuana Tax Act of 1937.[98] The description of Becker's research is accompanied by a discussion of related inquiries into the origins of U.S. drug laws in general. The second study considered in this section is my own analysis of the discovery of child abuse as a form of labeled deviance.[99] Both studies illustrate a central theme in the reaction perspective—that deviance never exists independently in the eyes of those who have a powerful interest in not seeing it.

The Marijuana Tax Act of 1937: U.S. Drug Laws and the Control Work of a Bureaucratic Agency To appreciate the historical origins of the antimarijuana laws of the 1930s one needs to first consider the criminalization of opiate use some twenty years earlier. The antiopiate and antimarijuana laws are connected by an important historical thread—the bureaucratic politics of the Federal Bureau of Narcotics and its predecessor, the Narcotics Division of the U.S. Treasury Department.

During the nineteenth century opiate use was permitted without legal sanction. The typical morphine addict was a white middle-class housewife. There was little interest in developing formal legal controls against the use of opiates by such persons. By the early twentieth century things had changed. Of particular importance was the growing fear of competition from Chinese laborers, a population equated in the public mind with opium use. This fostered a new view of opiate use as a social problem. Following an international conference on this problem, U.S. officials pledged tight legislative controls restricting the distribution of opiates to authorized medical prescriptions, which would be registered with federal authorities and for which a tax would be collected. These terms were set forth in the 1914 Harrison Stamp Act. The Narcotics Division of the U.S. Treasury was established to oversee its proper administration.

What happened next is the story of a social control agency redefining its mission and expanding its bureacratic scope and power.[100] Once in existence the Narcotics Division reached beyond the law in efforts to criminalize rather than regulate the use of opiates (including morphine and the recently synthesized heroin). Medical prescriptions to kill pain would be permitted, but the medical maintenance of addicts would not. Through a series of administrative decisions, accompanied by a well-orchestrated campaign against the moral depravity of addiction, the Narcotics Division effectively curtailed the ability of doctors to treat outpatient addicts by administering safe and regular doses of the drug. When doctors balked at this legal interference, they were harassed and arrested. In 1925 the aggressive control policies of the Narcotics Division were challenged in the case of *Lindner v. United States*. The position of doctors was technically and temporarily vindicated. The Supreme Court ruled that medical practitioners had the right to treat addicts as they deemed best.

The *Lindner* ruling did little to change the Narcotics Division's policies or politics. The division continued to harass physicians and arrest addicts. The powerful American Medical Association fell into line. In 1925 it passed a resolution condemning the ambulatory, or outpatient, maintenance of addicts. The Narcotics Division had won. Without technically changing the law it had effectively created a new category of deviance—persons who possessed opiates.

Through its successful campaign against opiate use the Narcotics Division had expanded its function from tax collector to police officer. So also had it enlarged its bureaucratic scope, prestige, and power. In 1930 it separated from the Treasury Department to become an independent agency, the Federal Bureau of Narcotics. It is here that Becker begins his analysis of the Marijuana Tax Act of 1937. Once again we see a federal agency generating a campaign to condemn and control a form of deviant drug use—marijuana smoking. Led by Commissioner Harry J. Anslinger, the bureau launched a campaign which involved "cooperating in the development of state legislation affecting the use of marijuana, and providing facts and figures for journalistic accounts of the problem."[101]

The facts and figures presented by the bureau may today seem highly unscientific, even laughable. Despite many years and millions of dollars of research there is no reliable empirical evidence that marijuana endangers a person's health or welfare. Such are the findings of the recent National Commission on Marijuana and Drug Abuse, which concluded that "from what is now known about the effects of marijuana, its use at the present level does not constitute a major threat to public health."[102] The facts alleged by the Bureau of Narcotics during the 1930s were considerably more "creative." Using pseudo-scientific language the bureau suggested that marijuana led to everything from madness to murder. Sexual immorality, crime, and physical deterioration were all said to be common side-effects. The 1937 film *Reefer Madness* was an outgrowth of this period of moral crusading. So were articles such as the one published in the *American Magazine* in which Commission Anslinger told the following tragic story of pot smoking.

> An entire family was murdered by a youthful [marijuana] addict in Florida. When officers arrived at the home they found the youth staggering about in a human slaughterhouse. With an ax he had killed his father, mother and two brothers, and a sister. He seemed to be in a daze. . . . He had no recollection of having committed the multiple crime. The officers knew him ordinarily as a sane, rather quiet young man; now he was pitifully crazed. They sought the reason. The boy said he had been in the habit of smoking something which youthful friends called "muggles," a childish name for marijuana.[103]

The propaganda campaign engineered by the Bureau of Narcotics inspired a rash of antimarijuana warnings everywhere. Illustrated posters in public trains and buses read: "BEWARE! This marijuana cigarette may be handed to you by the *friendly stranger*. It contains the Killer Drug Marijuana in which lurks MURDER! INSANITY! DEATH!"[104] A scientific-sounding pamphlet distributed by the International Narcotics Education Association referred to marijuana as a "narcotic poison," a "killer drug," the habitual use of which "always causes a very marked mental deterioration and sometimes causes insanity," and which "sometimes gives man the lust to kill unreasonably and without motive."[105]

The Federal Bureau of Narcotics supported antimarijuana legislation at both the federal and state levels. Such legislation was passed with ease. The 1937 Marijuana Federal Tax Act sailed through the halls of Congress virtually unopposed. As Becker points out, "Marijuana smokers, powerless, unorganized, and lacking publicly legitimate grounds for attack, sent no representatives to the hearings and their point of view found no place in the record. . . . The [moral] enterprise of the Bureau had produced new rules, whose subsequent enforcement would help to create a new class of outsiders—marijuana users."[106]

Becker's analysis of the entrepreneurial campaigning of the Federal Bureau of Narcotics was supplemented by subsequent research within the societal reaction tradition. Donald Dickson, for instance, has argued that the bureau's motives may have been more budgetary than moral; that cutbacks in the agency's funding prompted it to search for a new "dangerous" drug to fight so that it could preserve or expand its bureaucratic position.[107] Another interpretation is offered by David Musto, who points to a popular association between marijuana use and the unrestricted flow of Mexican migrant laborers into the American southwest.[108] This stereotypical link between Mexican immigrants and marijuana made the southwest particularly susceptible to horror stories about the evils of pot. There tales of marijuana-induced rape, mayhem, and murder fed into economic anxieties and hateful ethnic stereotypes. Still another interpretation, by John Galliher and Allynn Walker, suggests that marijuana legislation was prompted by concerns which were more symbolic than practical; that the legislation provided symbolic assurance of the values of order and orderliness in a period of social and economic disorder.[109] This interpretation has much contemporary relevance. Given the rather large body of evidence suggesting that pot smoking is relatively harmless, why today is such behavior still labeled deviant? Perhaps its prohibition is more symbolic than practical. In any event the continued deviantization of marijuana use presents a challenge to students inspired by Becker's early formulation of the problem.

Discovering Child Abuse: The Professional Politics of Control Recent work on the origins of child-abuse laws (by Stephen Pfohl of all people) has also contributed to an understanding of professional social control work and the creation of deviant categories.[110] It is startling to learn that there were no laws which prohibited child abuse until the early 1960s. Then in a few short years all fifty states "discovered" the problem and hurriedly passed legislation calling for its control. Why then? Violence against children is as old as the earliest of our nation's legal statutes. In actuality there were several attempts to draw attention to this problem during the nineteenth and early twentieth centuries. None, however, had the backing of groups powerful enough to break the legal hold that parents held over children. Rather than deviantize violent parents, early efforts to fight child abuse generally resulted in institutionalizing beaten children.

Medical professionals, who would seemingly be the most logical people to see and report the ravages of parental violence, were actually unaware of the problem until they were dragged into the arena by one of medicine's subspecialities, pediatric radiology. At last a group of medical professionals were rewarded for seeing what other doctors had failed to see. Other medical professionals, even those who treated children directly, had simply not seen or perceived child abuse before it was "discovered" in the x-rays of the pediatric radiology researchers.

There were strong professional reasons why doctors had not seen violence against children. Medicine as a profession was dominated by a concern for totally controlling the consequences of its professional activities. To see something like child abuse was likely to subordinate medicine to the working interests of another profession—the law. Doctors would have to leave the hospitals they controlled to become accessories in the courtroom domain of lawyers. Furthermore, doctors perceived parents as their real clients. Parents, not children, paid the bills. Seeing abuse might create conflict for those hypothetically protected by the shadows of professional medical confidence. Likewise, child abuse was not something doctors had been trained to diagnose. Up until its discovery by the pediatric radiologists, doctors, most of whom were parents themselves, bypassed the psychological horror of child abuse and saw instead a wide range of unusual yet physiological problems. Where they could have seen evidence of deliberate beatings they saw unexplained bruisings and bone fractures. Their failure to see child abuse for what it was involved not bad motives but a socially organized lack of perception; a lack of perception that kept them from coming into conflict with their organized professional interests.

Pediatric radiologists broke through the perceptual barriers impeding doctors from seeing child abuse, not because they were more heroic, but because they had more to professionally gain than lose. Radiologists were near the bottom of the prestige rankings within medicine, but the discovery of child abuse allowed them to participate in the higher-status, life-or-death work of their more clinically oriented colleagues. Moreover, their indirect technical investigations and research mission to uncover new diagnoses may have freed radiologists from the restraints of psychological denial and confidentiality which inhibited the diagnostic vision of other medical professionals.

In a similar manner, the radiologists avoided the subordination of medical to legal interests by discovering, not a new form of criminal behavior, but a medical "syndrome." Following this medical model child abuse would generally be treated rather than punished. Perpetrators would be viewed as sick rather than bad. Parents would be referred to medically styled clinics rather than legally structured prisons.

The lesson to be learned from all the medical maneuvering behind the discovery of child abuse is nothing less than a lesson in the omnipresent relationship between social control and social conflict. The discovery and control of something that today seems as consensually deviant as anything we can imagine awaited a moment in history in which it would be advanced with the professional interests of a group that (1) had the power to make deviant labels stick and (2) had something to gain by doing so. This is not to impute bad or cynical motives to the medical authorities who acted as agents of social control. Good or bad motives are not a central feature of the conflict perspective. What is central is the fact that control efforts arise when social interests are provided with an opportunity for advance or confronted with the need for defense. In the case of child abuse, social control advanced with the advance of powerful and defensible medical interests.

Application of Deviant Labels

This second body of societal reaction research concerns such matters as the conditions under which control agents successfully label others, as well as the social contingencies under which potential deviants resist or escape the labeling process.[111] Of the many studies on the social dynamics of the labeling process, none is more systematic than Thomas Scheff's work on the societal reaction to mental illness.[112] A detailed discussion of Scheff's work will permit us to appreciate the empirical character of one of the most important studies within the societal reaction tradition.

A Labeling Theory of Mental Illness: The Work of Thomas J. Scheff Scheff defines mental illness as a type of *residual deviance,* a catchall category for a variety of behaviors which violate the rules of everyday social interaction. Such violations include inappropriate gestures and postures, and inappropriate ways of looking, talking, or positioning one's body in relation to other people. People who act in such a fashion may be thought of as odd. They may even be labeled as mentally ill, but not always. What determines whether this will happen? Scheff formulates nine propositions which guide the labeling process. The core of Scheff's theory is that without labeling most residual rule-breaking will be ignored or denied and pass away as a matter of transitory significance. It is labeling that fixes a residual rule-breaker into a stereotypical career as a mentally ill person. This is underscored in Scheff's ninth proposition, which states that "labeling is the single most important cause of careers in residual deviance."[113]

But what causes labeling? According to Scheff seven factors are important: the degree of rule-breaking, the amount of rule-breaking, the visibility of rule-breaking, the power of the rule-breaker, the social distance between the rule-breaker and control agents, the tolerance level of a particular community, and the availability of alternative nondeviant roles. The first two variables, degree and amount of rule-breaking, are characteristics of the individual being labeled. The last five are social factors which exist independently of an act of rule-breaking. The logic of Scheff's thesis is this—that labeling may be regarded as the single most important cause of a career in residual deviance if the last five variables outweigh the influence of the first two. Social contingencies, in other words, are said to be more important than the bizarre behavior of the deviant.

Scheff tested his labeling theory in a two-phase study of psychiatric decision-making. The initial phase (obtaining independent psychiatric ratings of candidates for involuntary commitment to a mental hospital) uncovered high levels of clinical uncertainty regarding the mental state of patients examined. Despite such uncertainty, Scheff observed 196 consecutive cases in which patients were committed anyway. From this Scheff inferred that there was a presumption of illness behind the work of psychiatric labelers.

Why do psychiatric examiners presume illness on the part of patients being considered for involuntary commitment? David Mechanic attributes this predisposition for medical labeling to the professional socialization of psychiatrists as physicians and to the pressing time constraints of hospital work.[114] Scheff identifies three additional factors—financial, ideological, and political. Paid on a per case basis, psychiatrists have a financial incentive to process cases quickly. Ideologically, several features of the so-called medical model reinforce the tendency to see illness. One is the belief that, like other diseases, mental illness will get progressively worse unless detected and treated. Another assumes that a finding of illness is not irreversible and that the results of a little treatment will be neutral at worst. Political considerations also encourage psychiatrists to be "safe rather than sorry." Of major concern is the fear of public censure for releasing patients who later act violently. Visions of newspaper headlines reading "Psychiatrist Released KILLER" must undoubtedly pass through a clinician's mind.

Each of the above factors contributed to labeling that was rapid and perfunctory. The formal court commitment hearings lasted an average of only 1.6 minutes. The consequence was that persons from marginal social backgrounds, who were subject to social isolation or family conflict, were placed in mental hospitals for a period of ninety days. According to Scheff, the reasons were typically more social than medical, influenced more by organizational contingencies surrounding labeling than by the behavior of those labeled.[115] Other studies of psychiatric labeling arrive at similar conclusions. Controlling for patient behavior such things as the preference of family members,[116] socioeconomic status,[117] whether or not a lawyer is present,[118] how patients rank on a host of nonclinical social attributes,[119] and diagnosticians' knowledge of prior labels have all been determined to have an impact.[120]

One particularly vivid example of the impact of prior labels is found in the work of psychologist David Rosenhan.[121] Rosenhan placed eight sane people (pseudo patients) in twelve different mental hospitals. To gain admission each reported a phony symptom of schizophrenia (hearing voices) during the course of a diagnostic interview. Thereafter the pseudo patients were instructed to act as they would in normal, everyday life. The pseudo patients were a varied group. Among them were three psychologists, a painter, a pediatrician, a housewife, and a psychiatrist. What did not vary was the reaction of hospital staff. Despite the fact that they acted normal, the pseudo patients remained hospitalized for an average of nineteen days. Their length of hospitalization ranged from seven to fifty-two days.

During the course of confinement the pseudo patients soon discovered that behaviors which might be ordinarily seen as normal were now interpreted by staff members in accordance with the manner in which they had been labeled. Routine frictions in interpersonal relationships were seen as deep-seated signs of personal instability. Boredom was interpreted as nervousness. A review of the nursing records for three of the pseudo patients revealed that even the writing of research notes was laden with negative clinical meaning. Notetaking was recast in a pathological framework, as but a symptom of some deeper disturbance.

Interestingly enough other patients did not read the behaviors of the pseudo patients in such a negative fashion. It was common for real patients to detect the pseudo patients or to suspect them of being undercover journalists or covert researchers. Caught on the other side of the official labeling process, staff members perceived no such thing. Even when eventually discharged, all but one of the pseudo patients retained the diagnosis of being schizophrenic, although their symptoms were said to be "in remission." Thus, as Rosenhan points out, "the data speak to the massive role of labeling in psychiatric assessment. Having once been labeled schizophrenic, there is nothing the pseudo patient can do to overcome the tag."[122]

The Consequences of Being Labeled

Societal reaction researchers follow the lead of Edwin Lemert in examining how labeling may amplify deviance or produce secondary deviation. Also of importance is Harold Garfinkel's depiction of the labeling process as a ceremony of social degradation, a process whereby a person's social identity is literally reconstituted as a lesser form of human being.[123]

One need not be publicly labeled to experience the identity transformation suggested by Garfinkel. Carol Warren and John Johnson suggest that groups such as homosexuals may engage in *symbolic labeling,* a process whereby people adopt culturally disseminated deviant stereotypes without actually being caught up in a cycle of public condemnation.[124] Warren's research within the gay community indicates that members commonly "defined themselves as essentially being homosexual, and tend to organize their lives around the fact of possessing this symbolic stigma."[125]

Whether one is labeled by others or by oneself, the consequences of labeling may be profound. In his study of the social control of public drunks, James Spradley reports upon drastic identity changes for persons labeled as "bums." Such persons are "cut off from former roles and identities, treated as objects to be manipulated, and coerced into being acutely aware of the new definitions of social interaction, space, time and identity which are part of the jail."[126] Related findings were presented by Robert Scott in analyzing the stigma of physical blindness[127] and by Charles Frazier in considering the case of "Ken," a young man from a small town who was "branded" a criminal.

Following the degradation ceremony of a public trial, virtually all of Ken's life was retrospectively read as indicative of deviance. Rejected by previous friends and associates Ken began to reformulate his own definitions about life. "What the hell," states Ken in Frazier's narrative, "if I'm going to be named a criminal I might as well be one."

Sometimes the stigma of labeling extends to a person's close friends, associates, or relatives. Erving Goffman uses the term *courtesy stigma* to describe this phenomenon.[129] Merle Miller notes this with regard to the families of both convicted felons and gays.[130] Research by Yarrow, Schwartz, Murphy, and Deasy discovered something similar with reference to the spouses and offspring of hospitalized mental patients.[131] Birnbaum notes its effect on the families of the retarded.[132]

Quasi-Experimental Assessments of Labeling Consequences Other researchers have used quasi-experimental measures to assess the consequences of labeling. Derek Phillips collected information on the likelihood that people will reject persons labeled as having a mental problem.[133] Phillips presented a set of hypothetical cases about people with behavioral problems to a sample of 300 married white females in a southern New England town. Each respondent was presented with exactly the same behavioral descriptions. What varied was whether people in the hypothetical cases sought no help or utilized the services of a member of the clergy, a physician, a psychiatrist, or a mental hospital. The more someone was perceived as obtaining help from an official mental health (labeling) source, the more likely he or she was rejected by the respondents.

Another study, by Loman and Larkin, presented college students with videotapes of a counseling session depicting another student's poor academic progress.[134] In one version of the tape, the student's problems were attributable to the impersonality of the school atmosphere. In another the student was labeled mentally ill. Characteristics of the client's behavior and his own self-accounts were also manipulated. Measures were taken to discover which factors were most influential in determining an audience's assessment of the troubled student's "social competence." What counted most was whether the person being observed was labeled as mentally ill. When this occurred viewers were significantly more likely to provide low assessments of the student's social competence.

Other research documents the *self-fulfilling* nature of certain deviant labels. An example is Delos Kelly's study of the consequences of having been labeled a "remedial type" student in school.[135] Kelly combined a variety of data sources (observation, interviewing, the results of educational testing, etc.) to determine the basis for high school teachers' nomination of certain students for placement in a remedial-reading track. He discovered that a students' current performance and actual test scores were less important than the stigma of prior labels. Thus, "the label *remedial reader* can effectively be viewed as a *master status* such that, instead of considering present academic performance, some teachers appear to look, retrospectively, to a student's past history, and if the student has been involved with remedial reading, then such involvement increases his or her chances of being selected again."[136]

Labeling also affects a person's material life chances. This is demonstrated in a study by Schwartz and Skolnick of the impact of a criminal record on employment. Introducing themselves as representatives of the employment agency, researchers presented prospective employers with the employment credentials of fictitious job applicants. The applicant credentials were identical except for one factor—whether or not the applicant had a past criminal record. Twenty-five prospective employers were exposed to each of the following conditions: (1) information that the applicant had been sentenced for assault; (2) information that the applicant had been tried for assault but acquitted; (3) information that the applicant had been tried and acquitted, along with a letter from the judge affirming the person's innocence; and (4) no reference at all to past criminal involvement. Schwartz and Skolnick discovered that labeling made a difference in the likelihood that candidates would be considered for a job. For employers in the no-criminal-record condition, 36 percent indicated that they might use the person. Thereafter the percentage of positive responses shrunk in proportion to the severity of labeling. Twenty-four percent in condition 3, 12 percent in condition 2, and only 4 percent in condition 1 gave an affirmative answer. Similar findings were presented by W. Buikhuisen and P. H. Dijksterhuis, who presented companies in the Netherlands with employment applications varying only by reference to convictions for theft, drunk driving, or no criminality.[138] Findings revealed that 52 percent of the noncriminal group were reviewed positively, in comparison to 32 percent of the theft group and 26 percent of the drunk-driving group.

Labelers and the Expansion of the Deviance Problem: The Ironies of Social Control

To this point we have been considering the possibility that labeling may amplify the problems of deviance for those labeled—that it may alter their self-concepts and position in the material world, and may stabilize their careers in deviance. Labeling may also have unintended negative consequences for society as a whole. In a recent article entitled "The Ironies of Social Control," Gary Marx makes this point by suggesting that through escalation, nonenforcement, and covert facilitation, control agents may create as much deviance as they curtail.[139]

Escalation Marx uses this term to describe how control work may generate new forms of deviation. Police intervention into domestic disputes may, for instance,"up the ante" in family quarrels. It may make a big issue out of what was once a small disturbance. Police overreactions to collective disturbances may have a similar effect. History is filled with cases in which police intervention has fueled the fire of minor outbreaks into major riots. Another is the high-speed chase in which dramatic police action raises the risk that someone, even innocent bystanders, may be hurt. What starts out as a traffic problem may escalate into a bloody incident of a much more serious nature.

Nonenforcement This is a common by-product of control work. In order to be successful, police must frequently negotiate with underworld informants, trading information for the tacit permission to deviate. At other times police may look the other way so as not to see the illegal activities of vigilante-type groups whose general objectives mirror their own. In other instances, legal authorities may actually make use of the deviant skills of persons whose activities they supposedly oppose. Consider the symbiotic relationship between the CIA and members of organized-crime syndicates who combined forces to develop "executive action programs" directed at "eliminating the effectiveness" of certain foreign leaders. It is public record that the U.S. government contracted Mafia "hit men" to help murder Cuban President Fidel Castro and Congo President Lumumba. Also important are instances where authorities fail to take action to stop a crime until after the whole episode is complete. According to Marx, "This permits arrest quotas to be met and can lead to heavier charges, greater leverage in negotiations, better evidence, and a higher level of offender arrest."[140]

Covert Facilitation By using deceptive law-enforcement tactics, control agents may intentionally encourage rule-breaking. Critics of Operation ABSCAM (an undercover FBI program in which agents posing as Arab sheikhs offered bribes to government officials, including members of Congress) contend that it is an example of zealous legal authorities going "beyond the law" to encourage others to break the law. Officials caught "holding the money" in this so-called sting operation argued that they had been lured into deviance by undercover control agents and that they never would have committed such crimes on their own. Regardless of the merits of such claims, covert facilitation has for years been an element of control policies aimed at exposing the deviance of drug dealers, prostitutes, homosexuals, and political activists. The use of decoys, undercover infiltrators, and agents provocateurs (secret police agents who urge others to take the step into deviance) has long been recognized by less respectable rule-breakers who are the common targets of such authorized deviousness. Public concern about this issue has appeared only after a few respectable officials have been caught in the web of such covert control work. Along with escalation and nonenforcement, covert facilitation may expand the problem which control work is supposed to solve. As suggested by Marx, "Each involves the possibility of deviance amplification and illustrates—from the labeling perspective . . . —the ironic insight that authorities often contribute to the deviance they set out to control."[141]

Collective Responses of Deviants to Deviant Labels

This final consequence of the labeling process generally takes one of two forms. The first involves the organization of deviant subcultures in which labeled or potentially labelable rule-breakers find support or positive recognition for their nonconformity. Since deviant subcultures were discussed in Chapter 8, we shall here briefly examine a second form of collective reaction to labeling—the development of voluntary associations of deviants aimed at restoring respectability to those stigmatized. According to Edward Sagarin, author of *Odd Man In,*[142] a study of societies organized to promote a positive image of labeled deviants, voluntary associations of deviants are today on the rise. Their proliferation may be the result of several factors: the permissive anonymity of contemporary urban life, the civil rights movement and its concern for alleviating the problems of oppressed minorities, the 1960s counterculture, with its challenge to the desirability of conventional standards and call for a greater tolerance of human diversity. Even the growth of a medical (or pathological) model of deviance, with its emphasis on helping rather than punishing deviants, may have contributed.

Not all voluntary associations of deviants have the same goals or operate in the same fashion. Some may seek to show that the moral meaning of certain forms of deviance is compatible with the existing social order. Others may seek to change the social order. Following the lead of Stanford Lyman one might classify the goals of the first of these two types as *conformative* and the second as *alienative*.[143] The means selected by deviants to achieve these goals may likewise be divided into two analytic types: *expressive* and *instrumental*. Expressive groups tend to focus on the social, emotional, or recreational needs of their members, while instrumental groups are more practical in their efforts to restructure the shape of societal reactions. In combination these characteristics reflect the following types of voluntary deviant associations.

Conformative-Instrumental Groups This type of deviant association includes groups which campaign to be included within the existing social order. The Gay Activist Alliance is a good example. Founded in 1969 this organization is dedicated to working within the system so that gay people can be made part of the system. Through public information, political lobbying, and organized protest, the GAA endeavors to eliminate discrimination against gay people in such areas as employment and housing and to present a positive image of gays as respectable citizens.[144]

COYOTE represents another example of a conformative-instrumental group. Its objective is to decriminalize prostitution. An acronym for the slogan "call-off-your-old-tired-ethics," COYOTE claims a membership of over 3,500, publishes a newsletter, *Coyote Howls,* and together with several affiliate chapters, such as PONY (Prostitutes of New York) and ASP (Associated Seattle Prostitutes), promotes legislation permitting prostitutes to utilize the services of public defenders, fights discriminatory laws, and advocates prostitution as a legitimate business.[145] The National Organization for the Reform of Marijuana Laws (NORMAL) employs similar strategies in hopes of decriminalizing the possession and sale of pot. So does the National Stuttering Project, whose goals involve an end to employment discrimination against stutterers.

Conformative-Expressive Groups Groups such as Weight Watchers and Alcoholics Anonymous fit within this second type. They encourage their members to see themselves not as deviants but as people with a problem that can be overcome. By attending weekly meetings and keeping in close contact, members assist each other in fitting back into the existing social order. Other conformative-expressive groups, such as Little People of America (a group of dwarfs and others of diminutive height), circulate information geared toward helping stigmatized persons develop normal competencies as well as helping normal people to feel at ease with people bearing a particular deviant stigma.

Alienative-Instrumental Groups This type of association uses practical political means to change the system. One example is the Gay Liberation Front. Founded about a month after the "Stonewall Rebellion" of 1969, GLF is a self-consciously militant and politically radical organization. The Stonewall Inn was a small but well-known gay bar in Greenwich Village. Such places had long been subject to police harassment and intimidation—ritualized ceremonies of public humiliation. On June 27, 1969, things became different. Patrons of the Stonewall Inn fought back, hurling rocks and bottles and shouting "Gay Power": a new, aggressive, politically aware gay community was born. Unlike straightforward gay rights groups, such as the Gay Activist Alliance, the GLF was organized to liberate, not just homosexuals, but oppressed peoples the world over.[146]

Certain radical feminist organizations might also be classified as alienative-instrumental. Groups such as Redstockings demand more than a bigger slice of the pie of the existing social order. Viewing women as an oppressed class, the Redstockings and WITCH (Women's International Terrorist Conspiracy from Hell) seek to uproot the entire sexist order of things.

Alienative-Expressive Groups Certain deviant religious groups and "cults" of various sorts fall into this category. Rather than seeking to change the world, such groups offer their participants a change of worlds. They commonly attract and often consciously recruit people whose personal lives are in great disarray, people experiencing great trauma, confusion, or isolation, people who may feel deviant. Membership in groups such as the Unification Church (the "Moonies") or the People's Temple (the group led to its ceremonial death in Jonestown by Rev. Jim Jones) has great appeal to people who see themselves as outsiders. Membership in a more traditional religious group might serve a similar purpose, providing expressive support for the alienative notion that the things of this world are meant to pass away.

Some voluntary associations of deviants do not fit clearly into any of the above types. Examples include groups of ex–mental patients and prisoners' rights organizations. These associations may be both instrumental and expressive, trying to change public policy while at the same time offering emotional and/or material support for persons released from public institutions. In any event, the study of voluntary associations is yet another part of the wider picture of deviance painted by scholars of the societal reaction perspective.

THE ADEQUACY OF THE SOCIETAL REACTION PERSPECTIVE

The societal reaction perspective is one of the most important approaches to the study of deviance and social control. Substantively it reminds us that the study of deviance can never be fully detached from the study of social control work. It contends that behaviors are never deviant in themselves. Things are deviant only because they are viewed that way by people with enough power to make deviant labels stick. The tribal leader who hallucinates is viewed as a sacred visionary. The contemporary urban dweller who hallucinates is viewed as a psychotic. One is normal. The other is deviant. The behavior is the same. Its social meaning is different.

Methodologically, the societal reaction perspective offers an important lesson as well. Treat official statistics as a topic for research rather than as reliable data on deviance. Who gets classified as deviant? Why are classifications done the way they are? Who is missing from official classifications of deviants? Why? The societal reaction perspective makes the official production and recording of deviance as much a topic for investigation as the distribution of deviance within the population.

Despite its important substantive and methodological contributions, the societal reaction perspective has been the target of a number of criticisms. These fall into four general categories: (1) the causal critique, (2) the normative critique, (3) the empirical critique, and (4) the structural critique.

The Causal Critique

Since its inception critics have taken issue with the perspective's alleged theory that labeling is the true cause of deviant behavior. I use the term "alleged" because this criticism clearly misunderstands the theoretical thrust of the perspective itself. As presented by reaction theorist Howard Becker, the perspective is not intended as a causative theory per se, but as a "way of looking at a general area of human activity," a way of looking which expands the traditional scope of deviance research, so as to include a focus on the processes of social control and thereby undermine the "hidden power" of those who define nonconformity and attempt to contain nonconformists.[147]

Not all reaction theorists state the matter as succinctly as Becker. Perhaps unclarity on the part of some proponents has confused critics as to the general intentions of this perspective. In actuality, the societal reaction perspective seeks to supplement, rather than replace, the causal insights of other theoretical frameworks. Why have so many critics missed this point? One reason is offered by Travis Hirschi. According to Hirschi:

> It is not easy for a traditional student . . . to approach labeling theory with an open mind. Labelling theorists are not kind to the traditional approach: they typically begin with a flat denial of the validity of most of the research the traditional approach has produced. Further, and perhaps worst of all, labelling theorists often appear with little effort to have won the battle. Students are enthralled: the journals begin to bulge with "critiques," "tests," "appreciative reviews," and all the other perquisites of theoretical victory.[148]

The major exception to the reaction perspective's disinterest in causative theories of deviance concerns the issue of secondary deviance. Even here, reaction theorists have not so much argued that labeling invariably causes further deviance as that labeling must always be considered a potential factor in the causation of subsequent deviance. In this sense, the societal reaction perspective is something which sensitizes us to issues ignored by other theories. Being labeled may indeed affect the future lives of deviants. Exactly how is an empirical question. Sometimes being labeled may box one into a deviant career. But not always. What are consequences of labeling? Sensitization to this issue, rather than an assumption as to its causal significance, is the real strength of this perspective.

The Normative Critique

This critique is set forth by Jack Gibbs, who attempts to interject clarity at points where the idea of labeling stumbles into conceptual confusion.[149] One such point involves the topic of secret deviance, Becker's category for unlabeled acts which were nonetheless deviant. How did Becker know they were deviant if they were not labeled? According to Gibbs, Becker must have been using some set of normative standards. Norms thus precede labels. Hence, norms, not labels, should be the focus for a truly sociological study of deviance.

Gibbs uses two examples to buttress his argument. In the first he asks the reader to imagine two persons on the street. One is naked. The other is not. Need one wait to see how each is reacted to in order to decide which is the deviant? After all, won't one be immediately seen as violating a rather clear set of societal norms? In his second example, Gibbs criticizes Becker's interpretation of a Trobriand marital dispute (reported by the anthropologist Malinowski) as an instance of the ambiguity of labeling theory. Becker suggests that although a man who has sexual relations with his mother's sister does something which is generally disapproved, his act does not become deviant until the woman's discarded lover returns and accuses (or labels) the violator. Why wait to focus on the accusal or labeling process, asks Gibbs. Hasn't the act already been evaluated as violating normative expectations? Implicitly, Malinowski, Becker, the discarded lover, and everyone else must have recognized that a norm was broken. If not, how did they recognize the accusal as an accusal? Preceding the labeling process there must have been a judgment that a norm was violated.

Gibbs's criticisms are helpful in delineating inconsistencies in the societal reaction perspective. Yet, his own formulation is no easy solution to the study of deviance. His preference for defining deviance by reference to norms confronts him with the problem of identifying the rules which spell out the dos and don'ts of normative behavior. The sociologist addressing this problem has but two solutions: to survey members of a social group as to their expectations of others or to infer rules from observations of how members actually behave.

As solutions these two alternatives present further problems. Verbal statements offer no assurance that people actually do what they say they do. Moreover, such "statements may not even be 'normative' in the sense that they urge that persons *ought* to behave as their statements specify, but simply represent what is said when people are asked about conduct in certain circumstances, an expression of an ideal that prescribes no sanctions when the norm is violated, set aside, or otherwise ignored."[150]

Inferring norms from behavior may be even more complicated. Many inferences may be drawn from any one observation. The sociologist is thus confronted with the task of constructing valid rules of inference. The problem is to decide upon a set of operational definitions which best represent the normative world as it really exists. This is no simple matter. Adequate and pertinent definitions entail a high degree of specificity regarding the questions of what conduct is prescribed or proscribed, by whom, for whom, in what situations, under what circumstances, assuming what degree of mental and social competence, etc. To date sociologists have not been very successful in specifying all these variables for all or even most situations. Instead, "the common practice is for the sociologist to gloss over the methodological problems by relying, as a (presumed) member of the system being studied, on his or her own implicit and tacitly held understanding of the social norms."[151]

Such sociological glossing is troubling for two reasons. First, it ignores the fact that their own social backgrounds, training, and political ideologies hardly qualify sociologists as typical members of a cultural system being studied. As John Kituse points out, "Sociologists may find that members ignore, dismiss, and even applaud those acts that sociologists classify as unambiguously clear violations of the norm."[152] The second problem with sociological glossing is that it ignores the situated character of deviance. For instance, "the naked person on the street" example offered by Gibbs takes on an entirely different meaning when we realize that the street in question is in the middle of a nudist camp. Gibbs's question (Won't one be immediately seen as in violation of a rather clear set of societal norms or rules?) is presented in a different light. The evaluation of normativity becomes less immediate and more problematic. It is preceded by a process of definitional or interpretive work (i.e., by the work of societal reaction). It is this situated construction of deviance which is at the heart of societal reaction theorizing.

If norm violations are the products of actors' interpretive work and not mere behaviors, then to appreciate fully the problem of deviance the sociologist must attend not to a catalog of norms, but to the context-bound cataloging of actors themselves. This frees sociologists from the dilemma of trying to decide whether their definitions or those of the people they study are more appropriate operationalizations of norm violations. As Kituse points out, it is this focus on members' accounting practices, on the interactional, context-bound process of deviant attribution, which is offered as something *distinctive* or *new* by the societal reaction perspective.

The Empirical Critique

Empirical critiques of the societal reaction perspective have, for the most part, focused on two questions: (1) Do social variables account for a higher proportion of deviant labeling than behavioral variables? and (2) Are labeled persons more likely than nonlabeled persons to deviate more often or with greater seriousness in the future? In general, critics have either ignored or accepted the empirical insights of the perspective regarding the historical origins of deviant categories and the social dynamics of the labeling process. At issue are questions of a more quantitative nature: Do social factors account for more than half of all deviant labels? Do more than half of all labeled deviants deviate more after labeling?

The use of such questions as a definitive test of the societal reaction thesis does violence to the central theoretical concerns of the perspective as a whole. As suggested previously, the main contribution of reaction theorizing is to direct attention to the social dynamics and consequences of labeling, not to propose that more than half of something causes more than half of something else. When critics such as Charles R. Tittle state that "general studies of recidivism do not confirm labeling expectations that more than half [of those labeled] will be recidivists," it is not clear which reaction theorists are being rebuked.[153] Such critics present propositions which misrepresent the basic concerns of the reaction framework, discover that these propositions are not supported by quantitative data (taken mostly from official statistics), and thereby condemn the perspective for failing to prove what it never promised to prove in the first place. As Don Gibbons points out, it is as if straw men were set up and then attacked.[154]

An example of the "straw man" critique is Tittle's often-cited paper "Labelling and

Crime: An Empirical Evaluation." Tittle provides an excellent guide to the methodological problems involved in testing the reaction perspective. With few exceptions, reaction research fails to meet such rigorous methodological standards as (1) holding constant actual rule-breaking while measuring the relationship between labeling and social factors influencing labeling, and (2) comparing the magnitude of that relationship with that measured when social factors are held constant and the levels of actual rule-breaking and labeling are associated. Nonetheless, when proposing his own test, Tittle is far less careful. He proposes a test which is alien to the perspective itself—a test of whether "the probability of being officially classified as a deviant is more heavily influenced by other variables, particularly social disadvantages, than by actual rule-breaking."[155]

Despite the inadequacy of Tittle's empirical standard, his review of the literature uncovers numerous studies which support the general reaction thesis. Thirteen out of seventeen studies suggest that social disadvantage has *some* effect on labeling. A similar pattern is noted for studies which assess the impact of labeling on future deviation. Thus, the vast majority of labeling studies suggest "that social disadvantage may have some effect on labeling and that labeling may have some influence in producing criminal behavior."[156]

A similar conclusion may be drawn regarding the labeling of mental illness. In response to critics such as Walter Gove,[157] reaction theorist Scheff reviews eighteen studies measuring the impact of social contingencies on labeling.[158] Thirteen present evidence favorable to the societal reaction perspective. Evidence favoring secondary deviation is somewhat weaker. Yet, as Ronald Farrell and Victoria Swigert point out, nearly all studies of stigma are weakened by a disregard for the role of *reference groups* in mediating the impact of labeling.[159] One exception is Farrell and James Nelson's study of gays confronted with the label of homosexuality.[160] Here reference groups were seen to have a decisive impact in determining the positive or negative effects of labeling. Had similar measures been included in studies of psychiatric labeling, we would today have a clearer empirical grasp of this type of societal reaction.

The Structural Critique

This important criticism suggests that while reaction theorists have spent much time studying (micro) interactions between labeling and deviants, less time has been devoted to examining the relationship between control work and (macro) structural features of society as a whole. "It is not," as Taylor, Walton, and Young point out, "that structural analysis . . . is precluded in the social reaction perspective, but rather that it remains consistently under-applied."[161] A similar point is made by Alex Liazos, who suggests that reaction theory has been guided by a misplaced emphasis on lower- and middle-level agents of control to the exclusion of more basic questions related to the structural organization of power at the top of the social ladder.[162]

Why this misplaced emphasis, this relative inattention to structural questions? Some critics suggest that reaction theorists were unduly constrained by the microlevel theoretical insights of interpretive sociology. Others, such as Alvin Gouldner, suggest that reaction theory was hampered by "a liberal conception . . . that wins sympathy and tolerance for the deviant [but which] does not see deviance as deriving from the specific master institutions of this larger society, or as expressing an active opposition to them."[163] In recent years societal reaction theorists have begun to take this structural critique to heart. In increasing numbers, reaction theorists today reach beyond micro-level studies of labeling in order to explore the relationships between labeling and the social, political, and economic organization of society as a whole. As this happens, the concerns of the societal reaction perspective become more critical. With this in mind, we turn to our final theoretical image of deviance—an image of deviance as a power-reflexive feature of the struggle for such control.

NOTES

1 J. L. Simmons, *Deviants,* Boyd & Fraser, San Francisco, 1969, p. 4.

2 Howard S. Becker, *Outsiders: Studies in the Sociology of Deviance,* Free Press, New York, 1963, p. 9.

3 John Kituse, "The 'New Conception of Deviance and Its Critics," in Walter Gove (ed.), *The Labeling of Deviance: Evaluating a Perspective,* Halstead, New York, 1975, p. 274.

4 George Herbert Mead, "The Psychology of Primitive Justice," *American Journal of Sociology,* vol. 23, 1918, pp. 577–602.

5 Frank Tannenbaum, *Crime and Community,* Ginn, New York, 1938, pp. 19–21.

6 Edwin M. Lemert, *Social Pathology,* McGraw-Hill, New York, 1951.

7 Ibid., p. 449.

8 Don C. Gibbons, *The Criminological Enterprise: Theories and Perspectives,* Prentice-Hall, Englewood Cliffs, N.J., 1979, p. 148.

9 Howard S. Becker, "Whose Side Are We On?", *Social Problems,* vol. 14, Winter 1967, p. 240.

10 Nanette J. Davis, *Sociological Constructions of Deviance,* Brown, Dubuque, Iowa, 1980, p. 200.

11 Edwin M. Lemert, *Human Deviance, Social Problems and Social Control,* 2 ed., Prentice-Hall, Englewood Cliffs, N.J., 1972, pp. 16–17.

12 Joseph A. Kotarba, "Labelling Theory and Everyday Deviance," in Jack Douglas et al. (eds.), *Introduction to the Sociologies of Everyday Life,* Allyn & Bacon, Boston, 1980, p. 87.

13 Everett C. Hughes, "Introduction," in Richard Wright, *Black Metropolis: A Study of Negro Life in a Northern City,* Harcourt Brace, New York, 1962, p. xxxvii.

14 Alvin W. Gouldner, "Anti-Minotaur: The Myth of Value Free Sociology," *Social Problems,* vol. 9, 1962, p. 209.

15 Lemert, *Human Deviance, Social Problems and Social Control,* p. 15.

16 Max Weber, *The Methodology of the Social Sciences,* Free Press, New York, 1949.

17 Herbert Blumer, *Symbolic Interactivism,* Prentice-Hall, Englewood Cliffs, N.J., 1966, p. 148.

18 Howard S. Becker, ed., *The Other Side: Perspectives on Deviance,* Free Press, New York, 1964, p. 2.

19 Ibid., pp. 2–3.

20 John Kituse, "Societal Reaction to Deviant Behavior," *Social Problems,* vol. 9, no. 3, Winter 1962, pp. 247–256.

21 Becker, *Outsiders,* p. 23.

22 Ibid., pp. 23–24.

23 Simmons, *Deviants,* pp. 50–102.
24 John Lofland, *Deviance and Identity,* Prentice-Hall, Englewood Cliffs, N.J., 1969, pp. 30–31.
25 Becker, *Outsiders,* p. 24.
26 Simmons, *Deviants,* pp. 64–84.
27 Everett C. Hughes, "Dilemmas and Contradictions of Status," *American Journal of Sociology,* Vol. 50, March 1975, pp. 353–359.
28 Becker, *Outsiders,* p. 33.
29 Edwin Lemert, *Social Pathology,* as excerpted in Stuart H. Traub and Craig B. Little, *Theories of Deviance,* Peacock, Itasca, Ill., 1975, p. 120.
30 Erving Goffman, *The Presentation of Self in Everyday Life,* Doubleday, Garden City, N.Y., 1959.
31 Erving Goffman, *Stigma: Notes on the Management of Spoiled Identity,* Prentice-Hall, Englewood Cliffs, N.J., 1963.
32 Following the lead of philosopher Edmund Husserl, phenomenological theorists refer to this suspension of judgment as "bracketing" or *epoche*. See, for instance, Edmund Husserl, "Phenomenology," in *Encyclopaedia Britannica,* 14th ed., Chicago, 1946, vol. 17, pp. 699–702.
33 Alfred Schutz, *Collective Papers I: The Problems of Social Reality,* Maurice Natanson (ed.), Nijhoff, The Hague, 1962. Schutz's work represents a synthesis of the phenomenological concerns of philosopher Edmund Husserl and interpretive sociologist Max Weber.
34 Peter Berger and Thomas Luckmann, *The Social Construction of Reality,* Anchor Books, Doubleday, Garden City, N.Y., 1967.
35 For a comparison between ethnomethodology and symbolic interactions, see Don H. Zimmerman and D. Lawrence Weider, "Ethnomethodology and the Problem of Order: Comment on Denzin," in Jack Douglas (ed.), *Understanding Everyday Life,* Aldine, Chicago, 1970, pp. 285–298; see also Stephen J. Pfohl, "Social Role Analysis: The Ethnomethodological Critique," *Sociology and Social Research,* vol. 29, no. 3, April 1975, pp. 243–265.
36 For an ethnomethodological discussion of socialization in the development of interpretive competence, see Peter K. Manning, "Talking and Becoming: A World View of Organizational Socialization," in Jack Douglas (ed.), *Understanding Everyday Life,* Aldine, Chicago, 1970, pp. 239–256.
37 David Sudnow, "Normal Crimes," *Social Problems,* vol. 12, Winter 1965, pp. 255–270.
38 Aaron V. Cicourel, *The Social Organization of Juvenile Justice,* Wiley, New York, 1969.
39 Richard McCleary, "How Parole Officers Use Records," *Social Problems,* vol. 24, June 1977, pp. 576–589.
40 Arlene Kaplan Daniels, "The Social Construction of Psychiatric Diagnosis," in H. P. Dreitzel (ed.), *New Sociology No. 2,* Macmillan, New York, 1970, pp. 182–205.
41 Hugh Mehan and Houston Wood, *The Reality of Ethnomethodology,* Wiley, New York, 1975.
42 Melvin Pollner, "Sociological and Commonsense Models of the Labeling Process," in Roy Turner (ed.), *Ethnomethodology,* Penguin, Middlesex, England, 1974, p. 39.
43 D. Lawrence Weider, "Telling the Code," in Roy Turner (ed.), *Ethnomethodology,* Penguin, Middlesex, England, 1974, pp. 144–172.
44 Harold Garfinkel, *Studies in Ethnomethodology,* Prentice-Hall, Englewood Cliffs, N.J., 1967, pp. 104–115.
45 Harvey Sacks, "On Initial Investigation of the Usability of Conversational Data for Doing Sociology," in David Sudnow (ed.), *Studies in Social Interaction,* Free Press, New York, 1972.

46 Jack D. Douglas, *The Social Meanings of Suicide,* Princeton University Press, Princeton, N.J., 1967.
47 Garfinkel, *Studies in Ethnomethodology,* p. 78.
48 Egon Bittner, "The Police on Skid-Row: A Study of Peace Keeping," *American Sociological Review,* vol. 32, 1969, pp. 669–715.
49 Robert M. Emerson, *Judging Delinquents: Context and Process in Juvenile Justice,* Aldine, Chicago, 1969.
50 Jacqueline P. Wiseman, *Stations of the Lost: The Treatment of Skid Row Alcoholics,* Prentice-Hall, Englewood Cliffs, N.J., 1970.
51 Stephen J. Pfohl, *Predicting Dangerousness: The Social Construction of Psychiatric Reality,* Lexington Books, Heath, Lexington, Mass., 1978.
52 Becker, *Outsiders,* p. 18.
53 Edwin M. Lemert, "Beyond Mead: The Societal Reduction to Deviance," *Social Problems,* vol. 21, April 1974, pp. 457–468.
54 Lofland, *Deviance and Identity,* p. 14.
55 Edwin M. Schur, *The Politics of Deviance: Stigma Contests and the Uses of Power,* Prentice-Hall, Englewood Cliffs, N.J., 1980.
56 Erich Goode, "Marijuana and the Politics of Reality," *Journal of Health and Social Behavior,* vol. 10, September 1969, pp. 83–94.
57 Peter Conrad and Joseph W. Schneider, *Deviance and Medicalization: From Badness to Sickness,* Mosby, St. Louis, 1980, p. 26.
58 See, for instance, Garfinkel, *Studies in Ethnomethodology,* pp. 186–207; and John I. Kituse and Aaron V. Cicourel, "A Note on the Use of Official Statistics," *Social Problems,* vol. 11, Fall 1963, pp. 131–139.
59 Edwin M. Schur, *Interpreting Deviance: A Sociological Approach,* Harper & Row, New York, 1979, p. 363.
60 Cicourel, *The Social Organization of Juvenile Justice,* p. 207.
61 Arnold S. Linsky, "Community Homogeneity and the Exclusion of the Mentally Ill: Rejection v. Consensus about Deviance," *Journal of Health and Social Behavior,* vol. 14, December 1970, pp. 304–311; William A. Rushing, "Legitimate, Transitional and Illegitimate Mental Patients in a Midwestern State," *American Journal of Sociology,* vol. 77, November 1971, pp. 511–526; William Wilde, "Decision-making in a Psychiatric Screening Agency," *Journal of Health and Social Behavior,* vol. 9, September 1968, pp. 215–221; and Arnold S. Linsky, "Who Shall Be Excluded: The Influence of Personal Attributes in Community Reactions to the Mentally Ill," *Social Psychiatry,* vol. 5, July 1970, pp. 166–171.
62 William J. Chambliss and Richard H. Nagasawa, "On the Validity of Official Statistics: A Comparative Study of White, Black, and Japanese High-School Boys," *Journal of Research in Crime and Delinquency,* vol. 6, January 1969, pp. 71–77.
63 Mary O. Cameron, *The Booster and the Snitch: Department Store Shoplifting,* Free Press, New York, 1964, p. 136.
64 Douglas, *The Social Meanings of Suicide.*
65 Irving Piliavan and Scott Brian, "Police Encounters with Juveniles," *American Journal of Sociology,* vol. 70, 1964, pp. 206–214.
66 Albert Reiss, *The Police and the Public,* Yale, New Haven, 1971.
67 Maurice Temerlin, "Suggestion Effects in Psychiatric Diagnosis," *Journal of Mental Disease,* vol. 147, April 1968, pp. 349–353.
68 Edwin Pfuhl, *The Deviance Process,* Van Nostrand, New York, 1980, pp. 110–111.

69 James Q. Wilson, "Police Work in Two Cities," in E. Rubington and M. S. Weinberg (eds.), *Deviance: The Interactionist Perspective,* 4th ed., Macmillan, New York, pp. 169–177.

70 Ibid., p. 174.

71 Bittner, "The Police on Skid-Row."

72 Jerome Skolnick, *Justice Without Trial,* 2 ed., Wiley, New York, 1975, pp. 176, 179–180.

73 Richard Quinney, *Criminology: Analysis and Critique of Crime in America,* Little, Brown, Boston, 1975, p. 23.

74 Michael E. Milakovich and Kurt Weis, "Politics and Measures of Success in the War on Crime," *Crime and Delinquency,* vol. 21, January 1975, pp. 1–10.

75 Charles H. McCaghy, *Crime in American Society,* Macmillan, New York, 1980, p. 38.

76 See, for instance, Michael Phillipson, *Understanding Crime and Deviance: A Sociological Introduction,* Aldine, Chicago, 1974.

77 Cicourel, *The Social Organization of Juvenile Justice,* p. 15.

78 See, for instance, Edwin M. Schur, *Crimes Without Victims: Deviant Behavior and Public Policy,* Prentice-Hall, Englewood Cliffs, N.J., 1965.

79 John Helmer, *Drugs and Minority Oppression,* Seabury, New York, 1975.

80 For a more detailed discussion of these problems, see McCaghy, *Crime in American Society,* pp. 318–357.

81 *The Knapp Commission Report on Police Corruption,* Braziller, New York, 1972.

82 *Crime in the United States, Uniform Crime Reports, 1977,* Department of Justice, Washington, D.C., 1978, p. 172.

83 *Marijuana: A Study of State Policies and Penalties,* report prepared for the National Governors' Conference Center for Policy Research and Analysis, National Institute of Law Enforcement and Criminal Justice, Washington, D.C., 1977.

84 *Uniform Crime Reports, 1977,* p. 172.

85 McCaghy, *Crime in American Society,* p. 346.

86 *Marijuana: A Study of State Policies and Penalties,* p. 140.

87 Erving Goffman, *Asylums,* Anchor Books, Doubleday, New York, 1961.

88 Edwin Schur, *Radical Non-Intervention,* Prentice-Hall, Englewood Cliffs, N.J., 1973.

89 Malcolm Spector and John Kituse, *Constructing Social Problems,* Benjamin/Cummings, Menlo Park, Calif., 1977, p. 72.

90 Joseph R. Gusfield, *Symbolic Crusade,* University of Illinois Press, Urbana, 1963.

91 Kai Erikson, *Wayward Puritans,* Wiley, New York, 1966.

92 Anthony Platt, *The Child-Savers,* University of Chicago Press, Chicago, 1969.

93 William Chambliss, "A Sociological Analysis of the Law of Vagrancy," *Social Problems,* vol. 12, Summer 1964, pp. 46–47.

94 Elliot Currie, "Crime Without Criminals: Witchcraft and Its Control in Renaissance Europe," *Law and Society Review,* vol. 3, August 1968, pp. 7–32.

95 Joseph Schneider, "Deviant Drinking as Disease: Alcoholism as a Social Accomplishment," *Social Problems,* vol. 25, April 1978, pp. 361–372.

96 Peter Conrad, *Identifying Hyperactive Children: The Medicalization of Deviant Behavior,* Heath, Lexington, Mass., 1976.

97 Kathleen Tierney, "The Battered Women Movement and the Creation of the Wife Beating Problem," *Social Problems,* vol. 29, February 1982, pp. 207–220; Gerald E. Markle and Ronald J. Troyer, "Smoke Gets in Your Eyes: Cigarette Smoking as Deviant Behavior," *Social Problems,"* vol. 26, June 1979, pp. 611–625; and Ronald J. Troyer and Gerald E. Markle, *Cigarettes: The Battle Over Smoking,* Rutgers, New Brunswick, N.J., 1983.

98 Becker, *Outsiders.*

99 Stephen J. Pfohl, "The 'Discovery' of Child Abuse," *Social Problems,* vol. 24, February 1977, pp. 310–323.

100 For a sociohistorical account of this organized shift in social control policy, see Alfred R. Lindesmith, *The Addict and the Law,* Indiana University Press, Bloomington, 1965; Charles E. Reasons, "The Politics of Drugs: An Inquiry into the Sociology of Social Problems," *Sociological Quarterly,* vol. 15, Summer 1974, pp. 381–404; and David F. Musto, *The American Disease: Origins of Narcotic Control,* Yale, New Haven, 1973.

101 Becker, *Outsiders,* p. 138.

102 *Marijuana: A Signal of Misunderstanding,* First Report of the National Commission on Marijuana and Drug Abuse, GPO, Washington, D.C., 1972, p. 90. See Also *Drug Use in America: Problem in Perspective,* Second Report of the National Commission on Marijuana and Drug Abuse, GPO, Washington, D.C., 1972; *Marijuana and Health,* Report to Congress from the Department of Health, Education and Welfare, GPO, Washington, D.C., 1976; and Lester Grinspoon, *Marijuana Reconsidered,* Harvard, Cambridge, Mass., 1971.

103 This July 1937 article is cited in Becker, *Outsiders,* p. 142.

104 Cited in Charles H. McCaghy, *Deviant Behavior: Crime, Conflict and Interest Groups,* Macmillan, New York, 1976, p. 299.

105 Allen Gellen and Maxwell Boas, *The Drug Beat,* McGraw-Hill, New York, 1969, pp. 24–26.

106 Becker, *Outsiders,* p. 145.

107 Donald T. Dickson, "Bureaucracy and Morality: An Organizational Perspective on a Moral Crusade," *Social Problems,* vol. 16, Fall 1968, pp. 143–156. See also Charles E. Reasons, "The 'Dope' on the Bureau of Narcotics in Maintaining the Criminal Approach to the Drug Problem," in Charles E. Reasons (ed.), *The Criminologist: Crime and the Criminal,* Goodyear, Pacific Palisades, Calif., 1974, pp. 144–155.

108 Musto, *The American Disease.*

109 John F. Galliher and Allynn Walker, "The Puzzle of the Social Origins of the Marijuana Tax Act of 1937," *Social Problems,* vol. 24, February 1977, pp. 366–376.

110 Pfohl, "The 'Discovery' of Child Abuse."

111 See, for instance, Robert C. Prus, "Resisting Desynations: An Extension of Attribution Theory into a Negotiated Context," *Sociological Inquiry,* vol. 45, 1974, pp. 3–14, and "Labelling Theory: A Reconceptualization and a Propositional Statement on Typing," *Sociological Focus,* vol. 8, January 1975, pp. 79–96.

112 Thomas Scheff, *Being Mentally, Ill: A Sociological Theory,* Aldine, Chicago, 1966.

113 Ibid., pp. 92–93.

114 David Mechanic, "Some Factors in Identifying and Defining Mental Illness," in S. Spitzer and N. Denzin (eds.), *The Mental Patient: Studies in the Sociology of Deviance,* McGraw-Hill, New York, 1968, pp. 197–198.

115 Of related concern is Richard Hawkins and Gary Tiedman's ethnomethodological description of the manner in which organizational demands for efficiency, self-perpetuation, and accountability contribute to the style and content of labeling. See Richard Hawkins and Gary Tiedman, *The Creation of Deviance,* Merrill, Columbus, Ohio, 1975.

116 James R. Greenley, "The Psychiatric Patient's Family and the Length of Hospitalization," *Journal of Health and Social Behavior,* vol. 13, March 1972, pp. 25–37.

117 Linsky, "Community Homogeneity and the Exclusion of the Mentally Ill"; William Rushing, "Legitimate, Transitional and Illegitimate Mental Patients in a Midwestern State," *American Journal of Sociology,* vol. 77, November 1971, pp. 511–526.

118 Dennis R. Wegner and C. Richard Fletcher, "The Effect of Legal Counsel on Admissions to a State Mental Hospital: A Confrontation of Professions," *Journal of Health and Social Behavior,* vol. 10, June 1969, pp. 349–353.

119 William A. Wilde, "Decision-making in a Psychiatric Screening Agency," *Journal of Health and Social Behavior,* vol. 9, September 1968, pp. 215–221.

120 Maurice K. Temerlin, "Suggestion Effects in Psychiatric Diagnosis," *Journal of Nervous and Mental Disease,* vol. 147, April 1968, pp. 349–353.

121 David L. Rosenhan, "On Being Sane in Insane Places," *Science,* vol. 179, January 1973, pp. 205–258.

122 Ibid., as reprinted in E. Rubington and M. S. Weinberg (eds.), *Deviance: The Interactionist Perspective,* 4th ed., Macmillan, New York, 1981, p. 230.

123 Harold Garfinkel, "Conditions of Successful Degradation Ceremonies," *American Journal of Sociology,* vol. 61, February 1956, pp. 420–424.

124 Carol Warren and John Johnson, "A Critique of Labeling Theory from the Phenomenological Perspective," in J. D. Douglas and R. Scott (eds.), *Theoretical Perspectives on Deviance,* Basic Books, New York, 1973.

125 Ibid., p. 77.

126 James P. Spradley, *You Owe Yourself a Drink: An Ethnography of Urban Nomads,* Little, Brown, Boston, 1979, p. 254.

127 Robert A. Scott, *The Making of Blind Men,* Russell Sage, New York, 1969.

128 Charles Frazier, *Theoretical Approaches to Deviance: An Evaluation,* Merrill, Columbus, Ohio, 1976.

129 Erving Goffman, *Stigma.*

130 Merle Miller, "What It Means to be Homosexual," *New York Times Magazine,* January 17, 1971, pp. 9 ff.

131 Marion Yarrow, Charlotte Schwartz, Harriet Murphy, and Leila Deasy, "The Psychological Meaning of Mental Illness in the Family," *Journal of Social Issues,* vol. 11, 1955, pp. 12–24.

132 Arnold Birnbaum, "On Managing Courtesy Stigma," *Journal of Health and Social Behavior,* vol. 11, September 1970, pp. 196–206.

133 Derek Phillips, "Rejection: A Possible Consequence of Seeking Help for Mental Disorders," *American Sociological Review,* vol. 28, December 1963, pp. 963–973.

134 Anthony L. Loman and William E. Larkin, "Rejection of the Mentally Ill: An Experiment in Labelling," *Sociological Quarterly,* vol. 17, Autumn 1976, pp. 555–560.

135 Delos H. Kelly, "The Role of Teachers' Nominations in the Perpetuation of Deviant Adolescent Careers," in Delos H. Kelly (ed.), *Deviant Behavior,* St. Martin's, New York, 1979, pp. 322–333.

136 Ibid., p. 332.

137 Richard D. Schwartz and Jerome H. Skolnick, "Two Studies of Legal Stigma," in Becker, *The Other Side,* pp. 103–117.

138 W. Buikhuisen and P. H. Dijksterhuis, "Delinquency and Stigmatization," *British Journal of Criminology,* vol. 11, April 1971, p. 186.

139 Gary T. Marx, "Ironies of Social Control: Authorities as Contributors to Deviance Through Escalation, Non-enforcement, and Covert Facilitation," *Social Problems,* vol. 28, February 1981, pp. 221–246.

140 Ibid., pp. 230–231.

141 Ibid., p. 221.

142 Edward Sagarin, *Odd Man In: Societies of Deviants in America,* Quadrangle, Chicago, 1969.

143 Stanford Lyman, *The Asian in the West,* Western Studies Center, Desert Research Center, Reno/Las Vegas, Nev. 1970, p. 37.
144 D. Teal, *The Gay Militants,* Stein & Day, New York, 1971.
145 See, for instance, Maurica Anderson, "Hookers, Arise!", *Human Behavior,* January 1975, pp. 40–42.
146 For a more detailed discussion of these matters, see Conrad and Schneider, *Deviance and Medicalization,* pp. 199–204.
147 Howard S. Becker, "Labelling Theory Reconsidered," Howard S. Becker, *Outsiders: Studies in the Sociology of Deviance,* rev. ed., Free Press, New York, 1973, pp. 177–208.
148 Travis Hirschi, "Labelling Theory and Juvenile Delinquency: An Assessment of the Evidence," in Walter Gove (ed.), *The Labeling of Deviance: Evaluating a Perspective,* Halstead, New York, 1975, p. 181.
149 Jack Gibbs, "Issues in Defining Deviant Behavior," in R. A. Scott and J. D. Douglas (ed.), *Theoretical Perspectives on Deviance,* Basic Books, New York, pp. 56–64.
150 John Kituse, "The 'New Conception of Deviance' and Its Critics," in Walter Gove (ed.), *The Labeling of Deviance: Evaluating a Perspective,* Halstead, New York, 1975, p. 277.
151 Ibid.
152 Ibid., p. 278.
153 Charles R. Tittle, "Labelling and Crime: An Empirical Evaluation," in W. Gove (ed.) *The Labeling of Deviance,* Halstead, New York, 1975, pp. 157–179.
154 Gibbons, *The Criminological Enterprise,* pp. 151–152.
155 Charles R. Tittle, "Labelling and Crime: An Empirical Evaluation," in W. Gove (ed.), *The Labeling of Deviance,* Halstead, New York, 1975, pp. 157–179.
156 Ibid., p. 175.
157 Walter Gove, "Societal Reaction Theory as an Explanation of Mental Illness: An Evaluation," *American Sociological Review,* 35, October 1970, pp. 873–874.
158 Thomas J. Scheff, "The Labelling Theory of Mental Illness," *American Sociological Review,* vol. 30, June 1974, pp. 444–452.
159 Ronald A. Farrell and Victoria L. Swigert, *Deviance and Social Control,* Scott, Foresman, Glenview, Ill. 1982, pp. 115–122.
160 Ronald A. Farrell and James F. Nelson, "A Causal Model of Secondary Deviance: The Case of Homosexuality," *Sociological Quarterly,* vol. 17, Winter 1976, pp. 109–120.
161 Ian Taylor, Paul Walton, and Jock Young, *The New Criminology: For a Social Theory of Deviance,* Routledge & Kegan Paul, London, 1973, p. 167.
162 Alexander Liazos, "The Poverty of the Sociology of Deviance: Nuts, Sluts, and Preverts," *Social Problems,* vol. 20, Summer 1972, pp. 103–120.
163 Alvin W. Gouldner, "The Sociologist as Partisan: Sociology and the Welfare State," *American Sociologist,* May 1968, p. 107.

Make-Over   By Joseph LaMantia and Stephen Pfohl

CHAPTER **10**

THE CRITICAL PERSPECTIVE: *Toward a Power-Reflexive Understanding of Deviance and Social Control*

The Judge said five-to-ten but I say double that again,
I'm not working for the Clampdown,
No man born with a living soul,
Can be working for the Clampdown.
Kick over the wall, cause governments to fall
How can you refuse it?
Let Fury have the hour, anger can be power
D'you know that you can use it?

Joe Strummer and Mick Jones[1]

Without critical thought we are bound to the only form of social life we know—that which currently exists. We are unable to choose a better life; our only activity is in further support of the system in which we are enslaved.

Richard Quinney[2]

INTRODUCTION

The word *power* is derived from the Latin verb *potere,* meaning "to be able." To experience power is to be able to make things happen. It is to be able to transform things according to one's will. It is to impact upon or exercise control in relation to things and people. The experience of power is a fundamental human experience. According to psychologist Rollo May, to experience power is to experience "Being" itself. It is to experience a basic feature of our human nature—the ability to create or procreate, the ability to exercise one's being in relation to others.

In his book *Power and Innocence,* May examines what happens when something blocks the experience of power, when something suppresses our "power to be."[3] When this occurs we tend to search for alternative means by which to affirm, assert, or even aggressively realize the experience of power. Sometimes even these alternative avenues of power are denied us. When this is the case we may resort to violence. Violence is thus a power-play, a final and dramatic gesture to assert control over a world which appears to escape our grasp.

May's perspective on the relationship between power, powerlessness, and violence helps us to understand the social meaning of violence in a world in which power is unevenly distributed. People in positions of great power regularly use violence or threats of violence to defend their ability to transform the world according to their will. Powerful governments such as those of the United States and the Soviet Union willfully unleash violence against others who resist less forceful efforts to make things happen politically or economically. In the 1980s we witness such acts of powerful violence in the U.S. policy of providing economic and military assistance to repressive Central American political regimes such as those in El Salvador and Guatemala. Similar violence aimed at enhancing a position of power may be observed in the U.S.S.R.'s invasion of Afghanistan and in its support of the suppression of independent trade unions in Poland. By using or supporting violence, both the United States and the Soviet Union endeavor to defend against threats to their own exercise of power.

May's conception of the relationship between power and violence is applicable as well to violence by the relatively powerless. Consider the case of people who find few experiences of power in the public world of social, economic, and political life. The people I have in mind are people who may be unemployed or work in jobs which provide very low income and even less prestige. Experiencing little control over their public destinies, such people may concentrate their search for power in the private sphere. There, in relation to spouses, lovers, children, or other intimate acquaintances, people who are relatively powerless in public life may concentrate their efforts to make things happen. This may be placing too many eggs in the same basket. The problem is exacerbated by the fact that powerlessness in the public sphere generates additional stress in private life. Such things as crowded living spaces, inadequate health care, and limited provisions for recreation or other sources of tension-release may narrow the publicly impoverished family's options for private power. Small interpersonal tensions or relatively minor disagreements can quickly escalate into big challenges to one's sense of power. This is a structural liability of persons whose search for power is concentrated in the sphere of private, interpersonal relationships. These relationships become overstressed or overburdened with power. The result may be higher rates of interpersonal and family violence. This is the image of private or family violence suggested by contemporary research. As Richard Gelles reports in his eight-family study, *The Violent Home,* violence is more likely to occur in families located on the lower rungs of the [public] social ladder."[4]

So far we have been discussing May's ideas about power as they relate to violence.

His thesis leads us to suggest that where we find the smoke of violence we are also likely to find the fires of a power struggle. But what about the more general categories of deviance and social control? Are these related to power in a similar way? Such is certainly the case with social control. After all, what is social control but the ability to make things happen in a certain way? Social control is always an exercise of power. Does this mean that social control is always an exercise of power by some people over others—a hierarchical exercise of power such that some have more at the expense of those who have less? If this be the case, then deviance is always a power struggle too, an effort to reassert or regain power in relation to controllers who limit one's access to power in the first place.

When conceived in this fashion deviance appears as a strategy of resistance, a way of asserting lost power, a mode of reestablishing the ability to make things happen, to transform things according to one's will. Social control is the opposite. It is the labor of the powerful to keep the powerless in positions of relative disadvantage. Deviance and social control are thus the twin blades of a power struggle, each like a razor slashing into the other's ability to transform the world in its own image and likeness. Moreover, just as with other power struggles, the trump card of both sides in the battle of deviance and social control is violence—the use of violent force to curtail the behavior of those who trespass upon the other's claim to power!

This is a fairly dramatic way of looking at deviance and social control. Are power struggles really so central to an understanding of deviance? Is social control truly to be conceived as a struggle to deviantize people whose thoughts, feelings, or actions challenge those in positions of greater power? These are troubling questions. If Rollo May is correct that power is a basic feature of all human action, then to answer such questions we must critically examine the very core of our human social existence. In struggling with others over power, we must ask whether it is inevitable that one side must triumph while the other is branded deviant. Or is it possible to exert power without exerting restrictive control over the power of others? Is it possible, in other words, to socially structure power such that power relations are more reciprocal than hierarchical, such that power struggles might be resolved by reconciliation rather than conquest, such that power may be collectively shared instead of institutionally stratified? An inquiry into such possibilities marks the beginning of the critical perspective on deviance and social control.

THEORETICAL IMAGE

The critical perspective combines a theoretical concern with deviance and social control as interrelated aspects of the human struggle for power in history with a practical concern for the realization of social justice. It examines the relationship between power, social control, and actions which resist control. It is concerned with the way in which social control affects the human rights, dignity, and material well-being of all people. Does it do so justly and with respect for the interests of each person, or does it favor the interests of some over others?

The general concerns of the critical perspective should, at least implicitly, be relatively familiar to you the reader. They have been with us for much of this book. In Chapter 1 deviance and social control were said to tell a story of the battle to define the "normal" organization of social life. In each subsequent chapter we have explored the diverse ways in which theoretical images of deviance arise out of and feed back upon the social organization of power at different moments in history. In this final chapter these concerns will be made more explicit.

Power Hierarchies and the Control of Deviance

The critical perspective proposes that, in a society stratified by a hierarchical structuring of power, the social control of deviance will be shaped by the interests of those in positions of established power. The categorization of certain acts of deviance is one way to suppress the resistance of those who threaten existing arrangements of power.

The categorization of people as deviant is an important tool in the production and reproduction of social inequality. If the "haves" had to constantly use force to keep an upper hand over the "have-nots," life would be little more than an ongoing war between opposing interests. But what if the haves successfully produce the impression that many of the have-nots are to blame for their own problems? If this were the case, then a systemic control over the resistive behaviors of the have-nots would appear natural or necessary. The likelihood of an overt state of war would be reduced. This, of course, is exactly what happens when power-resistive people or groups of people are categorized as deviant. The label of deviance depoliticalizes the process whereby the powerful maintain control over the organization's life.

The societal stereotype of deviance, implying as it does a class of troubled or defective persons, can both hide and advance the interests of those in positions of power. As George Jackson, the militant black prison writer, stated, shortly before his own murder behind the harsh bars of California's Soledad Prison, "The textbooks on criminology like to advance the idea that prisoners are mentally defective. There is only the merest suggestion that the system is at fault."[5] Jackson's life within an American society "stamped unalterably" by racism and by rigid structural divisions between those with and those without the privileges of power led him to realize that the simple categorization of certain acts and people as deviant is, in actuality, a complex political act—an act located within a particular framework of social, economic, and political power relations. Jackson's analysis prompts us to see deviance as structurally related to the production and reproduction of power reflections. This is the vision of the critical perspective, a vision its theorists hope will contribute to the destructuring of unequal arrangements of power and a restructuring of a more just and reciprocal social order.

Historical Background: Questioning the Powers That Be

Which laws get enforced depends on who is in power. . . . The police do on the domestic level what the armed forces do on the international level: protect the way of life for those in power.

Eldridge Cleaver[6]

The occurrence of crime is inevitable in a society in which wealth is distributed unequally. . . . [C]rime is at once a protest against society and a desire to partake in its exploitive content.

Angela Davis[7]

The critical perspective did not merely emerge. It exploded against the conflictual social landscape of America and western Europe during the late 1960s and early 1970s. Although intellectually nurtured by the development of the societal reaction perspective and its efforts to demystify the process by which certain behaviors and people are labeled deviant,[8] the central impetus for critical theorizing was far more concrete. Ivory towers of university scholarship were rapidly transformed into intellectual battlegrounds for discerning the nature of a widespread and deeply felt political crisis.[9]

In America the crisis erupted both internally and externally. Internally it reflected a lengthy history of racial and economic oppression, the ignition of a long-smoldering fire set by those who were promised a piece of the American pie but were blocked in its consumption at every street corner and discriminatory workplace. In the years following the Second World War the struggles of black Americans for social equality were intensified by the combined experience of rising expectations and relative deprivations. During the war many blacks ventured for the first time into social terrain previously the domain of whites. In so doing they expanded their visions of who they were and what they could become. Whether in military service or in migration to the booming wartime economy of the industrial north, many blacks were exposed for the first time since the years following slavery to a wide range of new hopes and aspirations. They were encouraged to believe that they too could earn an honored place in the American dream.

In the years following the war the optimism of black Americans was quickly squashed. During the war the income of Afro-American workers had taken a significant step forward. From 1939 to 1947 the wages of blacks grew from 41.4 percent to 54.3 percent of the wages of whites. There, however, the advance halted. Modest gains in the postwar years were soon reversed as white males reassumed their positions in the peacetime economy. When we measure for both men and women and examine median family income, the position of blacks was no better in 1959 than it was in 1947.[10] During that same time period the rapidly growing electronic mass media were beaming images of a happy and prosperous American family life nationwide. For the impoverished family of color this added insult to injury. There was little in the well-to-do lives of Ozzie and Harriet, June and Ward Cleaver, and the rest of the American television's early first families that resembled the actual experiences of struggling black families. There was much, however, to be envied.

Fueled by a combination of wartime optimism and the relative deprivations of postwar existence, American blacks began their conflictual march toward social equality. By the mid-1960s modest gains in terms of formal legal equality (e.g., hard-fought victories on such issues as the right to vote, ride buses, and urinate in integrated public restrooms) left many young blacks with an angry sense of how far they still had to go. The noted Afro-American leader Malcolm X spoke for many young blacks when he stated that "in the ghettoes the white man has built for us, he has forced us to riot to aspire to greater things, but to view everyday life as survival."[11] The anger associated with this awareness was like tinder awaiting a match. During the mid-1960s that match was lit by a series of glaring acts of police brutality.[12] The result was an outpouring of violent protest and rioting in the black ghettos of the nation's largest cities. Following the 1968 murder of civil rights leader Martin Luther King, violent protests erupted no farther than ten blocks from the White House. For nearly a week federal troops occupied the nation's capital. Street corners were patrolled by faceless soldiers wearing gasmasks and firing rifles at rebellious citizens. The image of these events as broadcast worldwide was of a nation divided against itself, a serious crisis in the organization of power in America.

This image was enlarged by a subsequent wave of political protest from behind the bars of America's prisons. Impoverished inmates who had entered prison as legally defined victimizers soon came to radically redefine themselves as victims of a larger order of social oppression. They became reflective theorists of their subordinate position within a hierarchically organized power structure, read widely, and organized themselves to challenge that structure from within its deepest confines. Their actions resulted in a renewed wave of repressive control practices. They became "victims of politically inspired actions against them by the prison administrators and the parole boards . . . victims of politically inspired frame-ups within the prison."[13] Others involved in the struggle for prisoner rights met untimely deaths at the hands of state control agents. These included the over forty inmates and guards slaughtered by state police in quelling the rebellion at New York's Attica State Prison. Why were these politicized prisoners so feared by those in positions of power? This answer is simple. They had broken with the official interpretations of themselves as individual bad guys. They had connected their crimes and criminality to a struggle for power within society as a whole.[14]

The political struggles of blacks and prisoners were a major internal impetus for the development of a critical perspective on deviance and social control. The importance of these internal crises was compounded by the external resistance of various "third world," or underdeveloped, countries to exploitive domination by "first world" nations. For the United States this resistance was embodied in the struggles of the Vietnamese and Indo-Chinese peoples against America's claim to control the political and economic destiny of southeast Asia. During the early 1960s attention to the growing U.S. involvement in Vietnam was prompted by Buddhists who sacrificially set themselves on fire before television cameras in order to protest what they saw as the imperialist actions of the American state. Disregarding these protests the American government escalated its military involvement, so that by the late 1960s hundreds of thousands of young American men had been drafted to fight a ground war in defense of a corrupt and unpopular but allegedly democratic regime in South Vietnam.

The result was intensified fighting abroad and the generation of a dramatic war of protest and resistance at home. In increasingly large numbers, Americans began to say no. Resistance to the war affected nearly all aspects of American life—the family, the workplace, schools, and religious institutions. Cadres of young Americans went to jail as draft resisters or fled the country to avoid the compulsory command to fight a war they considered both unnecessary and unjust. Against them the mechanisms of official justice cranked out prison sentences and a nationwide campaign of illegal surveillance on citizens suspected of encouraging others to resist.

All of this resulted in increased political turmoil, particularly on college campuses, where students were at once privileged with temporary deferments from the draft and presented with an opportunity to reflectively ask questions about the power structure that their advanced education was preparing them to answer. Students were also confronted, often for the first time, by blacks and others from disadvantaged backgrounds who challenged them with questions about racism and such matters as affirmative action or reparation for past injustices. Other aspects of campus life reminded them of the war which awaited them after graduation—the presence of ROTC (officer training), on-campus recruiting for the military and government intelligence agencies, and knowledge of university research involvement in producing the weapons of war. All of this disrupted "business as usual" at America's leading colleges and universities and prompted scholars to seek new answers to the urgent questions that troubled students and divided the nation as a whole.

Struggles over racial equality and the Vietnamese war deeply affected the organization of daily life and thought in America's institutions of higher education. The nation's universities, like the country as a whole, were plunged into a state of crisis. Old theories about the nature of social order no longer seemed as applicable. Fresh new ways of envisioning social life were demanded. Out of such demands grew what we today refer to as the critical perspective. One additional factor contributing to the birth of this perspective was the significant on-campus influence of what may be loosely described as a counterculture of middle-class youths. Like the black civil rights movement, the origins of this highly publicized challenge to the style and content of dominant American values may be traced to social, political, and economic developments in the years following World War II. The postwar baby boom and the return to economic prosperity created the material basis for the youthful counterculture. Middle-class young people remained in school longer, postponing the economic commitments of adulthood while becoming the target of a massive advertising campaign aimed at making them an independent class of consumers, purchasers of the symbols of youthful style (clothing, cars, rock music, and the like) with money extracted from their parents' newly found and quickly mortgaged affluence.[15] The emergence of an educated and leisurely youth culture meant that an unprecedented number of middle-class youths remained, for an extended period of time, uncommitted to the practical experiences of the American economic and political system.[16] At the same time, this new generation was bombarded in an equally unprecedented fashion by the dominant sociological message of the 1950s—that America was the land of the free and the home of the brave, any one of whom could make it to the top by fair play and hard work. This, after all, was the first truly mass-mediaized generation, the children of the early years of television, rock music, and extended adolescent consumerism. And the more they consumed the more they were told how blessed they were to be born into a plentitude of Coca-Cola, disposable plastic containers, good cars, record players, and sexy makeup, and to be spared the cruel injustices which awaited those living on the other side of the awful "iron curtain."

Encouraged to believe both in the profitable pursuit of their generation's uniqueness and in the validity of the American dream, the 1960s youth culture was ripe for disillusionment and rebellion. It was deeply affected by the jarring images of racial discrimination and the violent and imperialist nature of the U.S. war effort in Vietnam. These images violated the more noble image of a good and generous America that had been presented to youth since birth. Large segments of youth disengaged themselves stylistically from the mainstream of American culture, sprouting long hair and disavowing the discipline of the adult work ethic and the war which symbolized its established truths. In search of another truth, perhaps that of resembling the innocence contained in previously cherished images of "America the Beautiful," members of the youth culture experimented with consciousness-expanding and pleasure-inducing drugs, explored new avenues of sexual expression, and pursued the spiritual insights of a variety of eastern religious outlooks. More than occasionally they also challenged what they took as the irrelevant or politically untenable theories of their teachers. Indeed many college classrooms, particularly those involving the social sciences, became hotbeds of dissent and disagreement. In dramatic instances students would shout out in class, seize university offices, or walk out in protest.

For many instructors this was a time of profound confusion, disillusionment, and retreat. For others it was a time of radicalization. While some struck back at students with power, verbal rebukes, or punitive grading policies, others struck out into new conceptual terrain. This was the case for an emerging generation of critical sociologists. For such scholars, U.S. miliary action in Indochina and riots in the ghettos of urban America no longer appeared unrelated. The huge cadres of young black and poor whites who were drafted to fight and die in Asia shared a single attribute with their brothers and cousins overcrowding the cells of American prisons. They were outside the power structure of America. So were the nearly thirty members of the militant Black Panther party laid to rest by police bullets. So were the thousands of political dissidents brought to trial for protesting the injustices of America's military-industrial political elite. The political struggles of such groups prompted sociological students of deviance to begin relating theoretical discourse to the discourse of social justice. Their initial message was simple—that deviance and its control must be studied as a political phenomenon, the meaning of which can be understood only by reference to the organization of power in society as a whole.

Within a short time these early lessons of critical thought were manifestly observable on campuses themselves. Radical professors and students were singled out for surveillance and control. Many were spied upon. Many were beaten by police. Some were denied tenure. For others control was more lethal. In 1970 students at Jackson State College in Mississippi and Kent State University in Ohio were gunned down while protesting.

With the eventual withdrawal of U.S. troops from Vietnam a relative calm returned to the campuses. The war, it seemed, was the primary catalyst for intense university politicalization. For while the deprivation of blacks and other minorities remained a major problem, it was swept beneath the rug of the late 1970s economic crisis which the war had, in part, precipitated. Unlike previous wars, America's Vietnam involvement was not followed by a postwar boom. A defeated America had dissipated many resources in nontransferable military spending. At the same time its industrial allies in Japan and West Germany had been tooling up for a new technological assault on the world's marketplace. The slumping American economy was caught off guard. It was surprised as well by the rising economic power of the oil-producing nations. Unable to command Asia by military force, the United States was now also limited in its exertion of economic power. Resulting cycles of spiraling inflation, recession, and high unemployment remained with America through the mid-1980s. With these came a new conservative mood, a period of retrenchment during which many Americans forgot the lessons of our most recent history. Searching nostalgically for bygone dreams of American omnipotence, many Americans ignored the plight of those whose race, ethnicity, gender, or age had excluded them from this dream in the first place. For many young people the romantic dreams of the counterculture were exchanged for practical anxieties about how to economically make it in a perceivably less prosperous world. Many who had participated in the struggles for social justice a decade earlier were said to have grown up with a "big chill," to have traded in idealism for the more confined realities of a career and conventional family life.

This trade-off was not made by a growing number of scholars whose critical theoretical orientations have matured during the last decade. Stimulated by the events of the 1960s, the development of a critical perspective has more recently been influenced by contemporary feminism, the continued struggles of third world peoples, and an increased awareness of the systemic nature of corporate and governmental deviance.

The influence of feminism is particularly important. While the struggles of women for social equality have long been a part of American history, several factors have escalated their impact in recent years. These include the mass introduction of middle-class women to the realities of nonhousehold labor during the Second World War, increased education for women in the postwar years, and the significant involvement of women in the civil rights, antiwar, and countercultural movements of the 1960s. The first two of these factors provided women with a combination of increased independence, elevated aspirations, and realistic knowledge of unjust discrimination related to gender. The third informed women that, even in supposed movements of liberation, male leadership and female followership remained an unwritten rule of the game. Out of such experiences the contemporary women's movement was born. Throughout the 1970s and into the 1980s it has grown as a strong force favoring reciprocal relations of power between all people.

The women's movement has propelled critical theorists to recognize that the second-class citizenship of women in society is mirrored in the marginalization of woman in social science theory and research. According to Dorothy Smith, the male-oriented theoretical structure of social science had led to a "conceptual imperialism," by which images of women were mediated through men's eyes.[17] In the words of Marçia Millman and Rosabeth Kanter, "Feminist critiques have shown us how social science has been divided by models representing a world dominated by white males, and so our studies . . . have been limited by the particular interests, perspectives, and experiences of that one group."[18] Sociological studies of crime, deviance, and social control were no exception. As Eileen Leonard suggests, "Theoretical criminology was constructed by men, about men. It is simply not up to the analytic task of explaining female patterns of crime [or deviance]."[19]

Yet another catalyst for the critical perspective came from outside the boundaries of western society. The 1970s was a decade marked by power struggles between less developed nations and their imperalist counterparts in the third world. In Africa the people of Mozambique, Angola, and Guinea-Bissau freed themselves from the blood-stained grip of Portuguese colonial rule. Revolution resulted in independence for Zimbabwe and began in Namibia, while South Africa became an armed camp, the last outpost of a tyrannical white minority in southern Africa. In the middle east oil-producing nations leaped to power in the international marketplace, while the countries of Indochina struggled to redefine themselves in the wake of the U.S. defeat in Vietnam. South and Central America were also ablaze with the dream of liberation. While a U.S.-backed coup overthrew the democratic reforms of the duly elected Chilean socialist president, Salvadore Allende, Sandinista freedom fighters in Nicaragua overcame nearly a half-century of harsh dictatorial rule by the brutal Somoza family. In El Salvador prominent officials of the Roman Catholic Church supported the efforts of rebels to establish a just society, free of class and foreign domination. Some, such as the beloved Archbishop of San Salvador, Oscar Romero, paid with their lives, as the U.S. government spent millions of dollars to reinforce the existing Salvadoran regime with its vicious death squads and friendly attitude toward American business. All of this raised critical questions for serious students of social control. No longer could theorists sleep easily in the comforting bed of perspectives which ignored the relationship between control and the struggle for power.[20]

Also influential was the growing struggle of gay men and women against the deviantization of physical intimacy between people of the same gender. So too was the critical perspective nurtured by increased attention to deviance by the powerful. The annual economic cost of corporate crime in America alone totals over $40 billion.[21] In addition to the economic costs of corporate collusion, price-fixing, and fraud consider the enormous physical costs of unsafe or unhealthy working conditions and those incurred as a result of faulty or poorly tested production practices and industrial pollution. The human toll of such deviance is astronomical. Yet when compared to the social control of other, "less respectable" types of deviance, efforts to curtail such crimes are minimal. Laws are weak. Enforcement is rare, and penalties are minor when compared to corporate gains. Quite simply, crimes by powerful corporations have not been a priority for most public law-enforcement officials in their mission of social control. Indeed, on the same day in 1981 that President Ronald Reagan pledged an all-out fight against "street criminals," the *Wall Street Journal* reported the quiet dismantling of virtually all federal programs aimed at corporate, or white-collar, deviance.

This relative inattention to corporate wrongdoing is not surprising to critical theorists. During the 1960s and 1970s critical theorists became well versed in the crimes of government itself: public corruption, domestic spying upon citizens, police violence, military torture and warfare against civilians, and even collaboration with gangland criminals in the planned assassination of foreign leaders. The Watergate scandal was only the tip of an iceberg of governmental deviance. Yet, just as with business crime, the illegal activities of the "controllers" were seldom subject to control. According to critical sociologist C. Wright Mills, deviance by the powerful seemed shrouded by a veil of "high morality."[22]

During the early 1960s Mills's provocative essays on the privileged position of America's "power elite" inspired the development of the critical perspective. Mills argued that power in America was controlled by an interlocking network of economic, political, and military interests. But just as power was hierarchically structured, so was it subtly deployed; so subtly, in fact, that many or most people failed to realize that in our formally democratic society, they were routinely subjugated by the rule of the most powerful. In Mills's words, "those who hold power have often come to exercise it in hidden ways: they have moved and are moving from authority to manipulation."[23] Mills vehemently attacked his sociological colleagues for not attending to the implications of this unequal and often unnoticed exercise of hierarchical power. In 1962 Mills's struggle to develop a critical perspective was cut short when he died of a heart condition at the age of 46. His call for a thorough study of the injustices perpetrated by those in positions of power would not be answered by sociologists of deviance until a decade later. Why? The answer was posed by Alex Liazos in 1972. Sociologists had become inordinately distracted by "a fascination with 'nuts, sluts, and preverts,' " As a result they paid "little attention . . . to the unethical, illegal, and destructive actions of powerful individuals, groups and institutions,"[24] With the development of the critical perspective all of this was to change.

Pluralistic Conflict Theory: A Step in the Direction of a Critical Perspective

From the conflict perspective, those who are in positions of power have the ability to determine what . . . and . . . who shall be identified and processed as deviant, criminal or delinquent.

C. Ronald Huff[25]

The critical perspective was not produced overnight. Prior to the emergence of a theoretical image relating deviance and its control to the power structures of society as a whole, numerous sociologists viewed deviantization as the result of pluralistic conflict. Pluralistic conflict theory assumes an ongoing struggle between a variety of social, religious, political, ethnic, and economic factions. To the winner go the spoils of criminal law, the power to decide on what is deviant and legally prohibited. The classic statement of this position is provided in George Vold's 1958 theory of group conflict.[26] Vold likened legislatively defined criminals to a minority group, losers in a social struggle for power. "On the surface, the offenses [of groups struggling for power] may seem to be the ordinary common-law ones involving persons and property, but on closer examination they often are revealed as the acts of good soldiers fighting for a cause and against the threat of enemy encroachment."[27]

Vold's pluralistic thesis complemented the early culture-conflict theories of Lewis

Wirth and Thorsten Sellin. Wirth and Sellin described the process by which dominant groups impose a vision of cultural reality upon weaker groups, deviantizing the behaviors of those with less power. Particular attention was paid to the delinquency of second-generation immigrants caught in a struggle between two cultures. According to Wirth, "One of the most convincing bits of evidence for the importance of the role played by culture conflict . . . is the frequency with which delinquents, far from exhibiting a sense of guilt, made the charge of hypocrisy toward official representatives of the social order such as teachers, judges, newspapers, and social workers with whom they came in contact."[28]

Sellin extended culture conflict to include struggles which occur as societies become more complex, conflicts between different cultural groups sharing a proximate geographic border, and groups which impose cultural realities through colonization.[29] By imposing cultural standards, imperialist powers are better able to exploit the aspirations and efforts of colonized subjects. Think, for instance, of the imposition of western law upon the indigenous cultures of Africa and Asia. Religious practices, family structures, and tribal rituals that did not fit the "civilized" outlook of European colonizers were overnight declared illegal and subject to harsh, punitive control measures.

The Social Reality of Crime: Law, Order, and Power Prefigured in the writings of Vold, Wirth, and Sellin, a full realization of the pluralist conflict thesis awaited the 1970 publication of Richard Quinney's influential *The Social Reality of Crime*.[30] For Quinney, the enactment and enforcement of criminal law was more than a legal victory. It was a victory in the struggle to control social reality. According to Quinney: "We end up with some realities rather than others for good reason—because someone has something to protect. . . . Realities are then, the most subtle and insidious of our forms of social control. . . . The reality of crime that is constructed for all of us by those in a position of power is the reality we tend to accept as our own. . . . *This is the politics of reality*."[31]

Pluralistic conflict theory is particularly attentive to the law as a tool of power. Nowhere is this more evident than in the 1971 publication of William Chambliss and Robert Seidman's *Law, Order and Power,* a detailed study of the impact of power differentials upon the daily work of lawmakers, the police, prosecutors, defense attorneys, criminal and appellate court judges, and other members of the legal bureaucracy.[32] Chambliss and Seidman review a great number of studies on the law in action. They conclude that the conflict model provides the most useful framework for understanding the actual operation of legal institutions in a complex, stratified, and bureaucratic society. As such, "the law represents an institutionalized tool of those in power which functions to provide them with superior moral as well as coercive power in conflict."[33] The distinction between moral and coercive power is important. It is not brute force but a subtle organization of "normative pressures" which guides the career decisions of legal actors in accordance with the interests of the most powerful. Conflict may thus be both present and disguised. It may operate in the form of structurally routinized pressure as well as overt struggle.

Universal Conflict over Authority A final theory of pluralistic conflict is presented in Austin Turk's 1969 *Criminality and the Legal Order*.[34] Turk argues that conflict is the inevitable result of universal divisions between those in authority and those subject to authority. Turk builds upon the general conflict theory of sociologist Ralf Dahrendorf, which proposes that "societies . . . are held together not by consensus but by constraint, not by universal agreement but by coercion of some by others."[35] Coercion, however, is not the most stable form of organizational control. Total coercion requires that those in authority constantly expend their resources. A more stable order necessitates a balance between consensus and coercion. Thus, those in authority would be able to "condition" their subjects to accept and live with existing authority relations, if not to actually celebrate their existence.

Despite efforts to condition subjects, authority relations are always in a state of dynamic tension. One strategy which those in authority may use to keep an upper hand is their ability to deviantize or criminalize resistive subjects. Turk's theory attempts to specify the conditions under which this strategy is likely to be employed. Such variables as the organizational sophistication of conflicting parties, degrees of agreement between upper-level and lower-level authorities, and the differential effectiveness, or "realism," of certain "conflict moves" are all said to impact upon the use of criminal law as a tool of power.

The Limitations of Pluralistic Conflict Theories Pluralistic conflict theories were extremely influential and paved the way for a more historically and structurally informed critical perspective.[36] In particular, the conflict approach played a major role in the demystification of what had been the more generally accepted view that law was consensually created and implemented with "value-neutrality."

Despite its advantages, pluralistic theory fails to adequately examine the historically based structural context in which power struggles occur. This limitation has been recognized by several of its most important proponents. In 1973 Richard Quinney stated that his own *The Social Reality of Crime* was "merely another bourgeois academic exercise" which failed to realize the structural "dynamics and contradictions of concrete historical conditions and processes."[37] In search of a more thoroughly critical understanding, Quinney adopts the standpoint of Marxist social theory. A similar change is evident in the 1982 revision of William Chambliss and Robert Seidman's *Law, Order and Power*.[38]

Pluralistic conflict theory implies that the human struggle for power inevitably results in the universal triumph of the mighty and the perpetual deviantization of the powerless. This is nowhere more evident than in the writings of Austin Turk. Unlike Quinney, Chambliss, and Seidman, Turk has remained within the theoretical confines of a pluralist model. This is not to say that Turk's theorizing has remained static. His more recent pronouncements are more structurally informed than his earlier instrumentalist ideas.[39] Turk's structuralism, however, is highly abstract and ahistorical. Structures that separate superordinates from subordinates are pictured as invariant features of the human condition. While "new authorities can be expected to replace old ones," hierarchical structures remain a timeless feature of all social life.[40] "The assumption here is that there are limits to the human capacity to include others as 'we.' "[41] Turk regards all suggestions to the contrary as little more than "metaphysical hopes for some tremendous breakthrough to a utopian state of universal love."[42] The most we can hope for is a more mutually beneficial way of "containing, redirecting, deescalating, transforming or otherwise handling"[43] losses incurred in the inevitable conflict between those within and those without authorized positions of hierarchically structured power.

Despite its analytic utility, Turk's theory is little more than a description of the way in which contemporary social life is hierarchically structured. Turk falsely equates the way things are with the way things naturally have to be. He fails to realize that social structures are historical creations. Structures do not exist naturally. They exist only as they are produced and reproduced by the concrete struggles of people in history. This awareness separates the critical perspective from the more limited confines of conflict theory. Critical theorists realize that under certain historically structured conditions, power relations can be relations of reciprocity rather than relations of hierarchical domination.

The Vision of the Critical Perspective: The Reciprocal Structuring of Power in History

Reciprocal power relations are those in which each party gains, in which each experiences the ability to transform things or make things happen, although not always or necessarily in the same fashion. Under conditions of reciprocal power, social control need not be a battle with winners and losers. Social control can be participatory rather than imposed. It can reconcile conflicting parties by dissolving the troubles which separate them rather than by restricting the options of those with least power. Thus, while deviance may always represent a power struggle, its control need not represent a process of one-sided domination, a division between winners and losers, a structural differentiation between powerful insiders and powerless outsiders.

Unfortunately the conditions which foster reciprocal power relations are generally absent from the world in which we currently live. Most elements of contemporary society promote hierarchy rather than reciprocity: hierarchies which position owners and managers over workers, citizens in developed nations over those in third world countries, men over women, whites over people of other colors, and the old (but not too old) over the young. These hierarchical divisions are so deeply rooted in our culture that they are often taken for granted or seen as natural. Critical theorists, however, see nothing natural about such hierarchies. They see them as nothing but the legacy of the differential exercise of power in history.

This historical structuring of hierarchical power is of great concern to the critical theorist. So is the manner in which such structures are reproduced in the often unnoticed rituals of everyday social life. It is in these rituals that we locate ourselves within history, that we reproduce the hierarchical structures which have surrounded us since birth, that we create the impression that the way things are is the way they naturally have to be, and by which we creatively disguise the forces which control us.

As long as this ritualistic reproduction of power hierarchies continues, there is little chance that deviance and social control will be more than an endlessly conflictual battle over who will control whom. We will remain trapped in a history which seemingly creates us more than we create it. It is possible to find a way out? It is possible to begin to create history in a different way, in a way which permits a greater reciprocity in power relations, in a way which allows social control to be participatory rather than imposed? These are among the essential questions posed by the critical perspective. In addressing these issues critical theorists draw extensively upon two interrelated theoretical traditions: Marxist and anarchist social theory.

A Political Economy of Deviance and Control: The Marxist Tradition

The fathers of the present working-class were chastised for their enforced transformation into vagabonds and paupers. Legislation treated them as "voluntary" criminals, and . . . depended on their own good will to go on working under . . . old conditions that no longer existed.

Karl Marx[44]

The clearest indication of the unbounded contempt of the workers for the existing social order is the wholesale manner in which they break its laws. If the demoralization of the worker passes beyond a certain point then it is just as natural that he will turn into a criminal—as inevitably as water turns into steam at boiling point.

Friedrich Engels[45]

Marxist social theory is rooted in the writing and practical political activities of Karl Marx. Marx's life was spent on the unjust margins of social life as organized in nineteenth-century Europe. Born on May 5, 1818, into a family of German Jews, Marx experienced first-hand the alienation of those who were structurally denied the power to shape their own economic, political, and social destinies. Although both of Marx's parents came from families with a long line of rabbis, his father, Heinrich, "conveniently" converted to Lutheranism in the year before his birth, to escape the stigma of anti-Semitism and thereby make an uneasy compromise with the hierarchical arrangment of power in his country. For the young Marx such compromise was increasingly uneasy. His native Germany was covered by a blanket of repression from top to bottom. The 1830s and 1840s were periods of great intellectual and political despair. Marx lived in the European aftermath of the French Revolution, when the "Holy Alliance, established by the powers that had defeated Napoleon in order to repress the forces of libertarian revolution, of radicalism and the rights of man, seemed forever able to stifle even faintly liberal stirrings."[46] The Germany of Marx's young adulthood was particularly stifling. Prussian officials promised strict control over all dangerous ideas, surveillance of political agitators, and a close monitoring of life at the universities. Lacking a representative parliament and the rights of free speech, assembly, and even trial by jury, the German state also instituted censorship over all publications.

Efforts to critically understand and alter the repressive character of hierarchically imposed social structures were of importance to Marx from a young age. As part of his secondary-school examinations, the adolescent Marx wrote an essay entitled "Reflections of a Young Man on Choosing a Career." In that essay Marx articulated a principle which would guide his intellectual and practical activities for a lifetime. Simply stated: to fully realize the power of one's own being, one must encourage the reciprocal expression of power by others as well. In the words of the young Marx:

> The central principle which must guide us in the selection of a vocation is the welfare of humanity, our own perfection. One should not think that these two interests combat each other, that one must destroy the other. Rather, man's nature makes it possible for him to reach his fulfillment only by working for the perfection and welfare of his society. . . . History calls those the greatest men who ennobled themselves by working for the universal.[47]

Marx's concern with understanding and changing the social organization of unequal and unjust social relations led him beyond the boundaries of existing social theory. In particular it led him to confront both the idealist philosophy of thinkers such as Georg Hegel and the materialist interpretation of life espoused by theorists such as Ludwig Feuerbach. Hegel viewed human life as but a moment in the ceaseless unfolding of Absolute Spirit. Human history was nothing but the evolutionary movement of all things toward increasing rationality, toward a state of perfect reason. For Hegel the contradictions of history served as catalysts which (dialectically) advanced the self-realization of Absolute Spirit in its totality. The materialists, such as Feuerbach, opposed the view of human life as part of a progressive unfolding of rational spirit. Feuerbach viewed all things, including the things of Hegelian philosophy, as nothing but a reflection of the human struggle for material existence. What Hegel saw as Absolute Spirit Feuerbach saw as an illusion projected by the concrete organization of material forces. Stated simply, Feuerbach argued that spirit or thought proceeds from concrete material being, not being from thought.[48]

Marx borrowed extensively from both Hegel and Feuerbach in developing his own social theory. From Hegel he took the notion that human history proceeds according to a dialectical movement in which contradictions generate structural strains toward change or social transformation. Yet, unlike Hegel, Marx rejected the view that dialectical contradictions or structural strains originated in the realm of spirit, rational ideas, or thought. Here Marx is indebted to Feuerbach. Feuerbach's theories about the origins of all things in the concreteness of material existence aided Marx in turning Hegelian thought upside down. Synthesizing the insights of Hegel and Feuerbach, Marx produced a new theoretical viewpoint, arguing that the primary moving force behind history was the social production of concrete material relations, relations by which humans secured their material existence in the world, relations which thereby permeated all other aspects of human social life.

Marx's attempt to locate the historical relations between people within the socially generated confines of material production has been of great practical and theoretical importance. Practically Marx spent the remainder of his life working toward a transformation of what he perceived as the unequal material relations of the capitalist economic system. Theoretically he endeavored to demonstrate the material basis for systemic inequalities in history and to describe the historical contradictions which (dialectically) gave birth to capitalism and those he envisioned as ultimately destroying the exploitive cojoining of social and economic forces. Marx died in 1883, long before the full realization of either his practical or his theoretical objectives. Nonetheless, Marx's work continues to inspire critical thought and action. The rudimentary features of the Marxist image of deviance and social control are outlined below.

The Marxist Image of Deviance and Social Control

The Marxist image of deviance suggests that the social organization of material existence is a primary factor in determining the style and content of social control. Following Marx this perspective asserts that the foremost task of any society is to secure the conditions of its own material survival. To do this society must have adequate physical or material resources, a sufficient population of workers, and a capable technology. All of these things are necessary for the survival of the human group. They are not, however, in themselves sufficient. Material resources, human population, and technological know-how must be socially organized if they are to provide for a stable economic environment. Economic production is a social art. It is structured by organized social relations. The way this structuring occurs is what Marx referred to as the "mode of production." Central as it is to the very survival of the social group, the mode of production is said to influence all other social relations, be they legal, religious, formal, or whatever. How the mode of production influences the relations of social control is central to the critical understanding of social deviance.

The Marxist interpretation of history stresses the impact of unequal economic relations on the entirety of social life. In the earliest forms of known economic life, all capable workers were required to work together, to contribute a maximum of their economic productivity, just so that the group as a whole could survive. In this sense all of society's members were equal workers. Each contributed as much as she or he could. Each shared equally in the productivity of the group as a whole. These simple, survival-oriented societies existed in what Marx called a state of "primitive communism." The trouble that any member presented for others was genuinely trouble for the group as a whole. In this sense, the burden of deviance and the activities of social control were truly a collective matter. All members lost and gained in proportion to the collective action of the group as a whole.

This equalitarian structuring of economic relations changed as more efficient technologies evolved. These freed the time of some to administer and live off the labor of others. Once this happened, once one class of persons gained the upper hand in controlling society's economic mode, the course of history would no longer be that of collectively shared fate. Nor would social control arise from the needs of all and contribute to the good of all. Some, by virtue of greater structural control over the production and distribution processes, would benefit more by social controls which preserved the existing and unequal economic mode. From this unequally distributed need the state, or the institutions of centralized authority, arose to ensure a stability no longer guaranteed by equal distribution of the benefits of socially structured work. The economy became politicalized. Political and economic institutions merged. Through them one class maintained control over another.

From Marx's perspective the regularization of an unequal mode of production affected the entire network of human social relations. The division between those who controlled and those who were subject to the dominant economic mode drove a wedge through the experience of collective cooperation. People were placed in structured positions of competition, in positions to either benefit from or lose by the maintenance of existing unequal economic relations. This did not mean that people always consciously experienced this competitive conflict. In fact, according to Marx, social institutions such as religion and education produced theological and philosophical systems of thought which justified or at least blunted the experience of structured conflict. In this sense, Marx argued that knowledge itself, dominant modes of thought, and conceptions of truth were subtly shaped by the economic mode of a particular historical period. So were definitions of human trouble and deviance. Acts which threatened to disrupt patterns of social relations associated with the dominant economic mode were those that provoked the strongest forces of social control. What became defined and controlled against as deviant was, in other words, directly related to the needs of that class of citizens benefiting most from structured economic inequality.

In their work *The German Ideology,* Karl Marx and his collaborator Friedrich Engels traced the development and societal influence of the dominant economic mode through slave, feudal, and capitalist economies.[49] Each of these unequal economic modes created a structural division between those who controlled economic activity and those who served it. In slavery, through the total domination of the time and space of productive human activity; in feudalism, through the control of subsistence determined by the amount of production remaining after taxation levied on serfs by lords; in capitalism, through the control of wages in accordance with the principle of optimal profit, an upper class was structurally differentiated from a class of workers with little or no control over their economic destinies. Dominant ideas about deviance and the practice of social control were structured in a similar fashion. According to the Marxist perspective, it is no accident that feudal law was primarily concerned with issues of land and tenure, while law in capitalist society is primarily concerned with protecting the rights of those who own property. The central targets for the control of deviance are those who resist, disrupt, or symbolize the inequities inherent in the smooth functioning of the dominant economic mode. To understand why something is considered deviant and in need of social control, one must first locate that something in the overall system of economic relations. This is the primary task of the Marxist model of deviance, a model which locates the battle over deviance within the larger conflictual structures of the political economy. In the words of British theorists Taylor, Walton, and Young:

> A full-blown Marxist theory of deviance . . . would be concerned to develop explanations of the ways in which particular historical periods, characterized by particular sets of social relationships and means of production give rise to attempts by the economically and politically powerful to order society in particular ways. It would ask . . . who makes the rules and why?[50]

Marx himself did little in the way of any formal analysis of deviance or crime as such. What writing he did do on these matters suggests that the criminal and the laws that control the criminal are both inextricably bound to the larger political-economic order with which people struggle. According to Marx, "Crime, i.e., the struggle of the isolated individual against the prevailing conditions, is not the result of pure arbitrariness. On the contrary, it depends on the same conditions as that of rule."[51] This is not to suggest that Marx romanticized criminals as self-conscious rebels against the existing order. A close examination of Marx's view of the lower-class *lumpen-*

proletariat criminals of his own day suggests that he often viewed them as a demoralized and unproductive lot. At other places in his writings, Marx ironically pictured the criminal as a contributor to social productivity by creating jobs for the police and other social control agents as well as by stimulating the invention of such property-protecting devices as the lock and the investigative microscope. Thus, according to Marx, "The criminal produces not only crime but also criminal law; he produces the professor who delivers lectures on this criminal law, and even the inevitable text-book in which the professor presents his lectures as a commodity for sale in the market. . . . The criminal therefore appears as one of those natural 'equilibrating forces' which open up a whole perspective of 'useful' operations."[52]

It is evident, even in this biting use of irony, that for Marx crime and deviance were inseparable from the problems of the political economy. To solve the problem of deviance one must first erase the historical reproduction of structural inequality. This was Marx's vision of the move toward socialism—the creation of a democratic economy in which the interests of all, rather than the demands of a few, would guide the mode of production. This vision serves as a guide for the critical perspective. As Taylor, Walton, and Young point out, "the abolition of crime is synonymous with the abolition of a criminogenic system of domination and control."[53]

Applications of Marxist Imagery One of the first systematic attempts to apply Marxist theory to the problems of deviance and crime is found in the work of the Dutch criminologist Willem Bonger (1876–1940).[54] Bonger was particularly concerned with crime and its relationship to an exploitive capitalist political economy. Capitalism was viewed as related to criminality in two ways. In the first instance crime was seen as engendered by the miserable conditions forced upon the underclasses in the emergence of industrial capitalism. In the second, the economic logic of capitalism itself was viewed as promoting an endless greed, or "egoism," that fostered crime. In these two ways Bonger sought to explain both the crimes of the underclasses and the crimes of the controlling classes pushed on by a socially structured egoism.

Although generally the best-known, Bonger was not the only European theorist to explain crime as shaped by the unequal economic relations of capitalism. K. G. Rakowsky, Filippo Turati, Bruno Battaglia, Napoleone Colezanni, Achille Loria, Alfred Niceforo, August Bebel, Paul Lafargue, and Joseph Van Kan each also employed a Marxist framework in interpreting crime or criminal justice. It was not, however, until the early 1970s that a Marxist approach was systematically developed within American sociology and criminology. Seminal to the emergence of an American Marxist tradition were the writings of Richard Quinney[55] and the publication of *Crime and Social Justice,* a journal of radical criminology edited by Tony Platt, Paul Takagi, and others. Also important were Herman and Julia Schwendinger's analysis of the relationship between social justice and a definition of crime,[56] Paul Takagi's historical study of the illusionary nature of bourgeois penal reforms and the founding of the Walnut Street Jail in Philadelphia,[57] Jerome Hall's examination of the political-economic context for the modern legal concept of larceny or theft,[58] Raymond Michalowski and Edward Bohlander's analysis of the relationship between ruling-class repression, commonsensical definitions of crime, and criminal justice in America,[59] Anthony

Platt's study of the political and economic origins of the juvenile justice movement and his early call for the development of radical criminology,[60] and William Chambliss's exploration of the economic basis and political consequences of vagrancy laws and the 1975 appearance of Chambliss's important theoretical article "Toward a Political-Economy of Crime."[61]

Within a short time the influence of Marxist thought had become evident in a number of other notable studies. The Marxist approach was, however, nowhere more evident than in the work of Quinney. According to this most prolific Marxist criminologist of the 1970s, "The basic question in the Marxist analysis of crime is this: What is the meaning of crime in the development of capitalism?"[62]

Quinney's Marxist formulations begin in 1973 with the publication of two important essays: "Crime Control in Capitalist Society" and "There's a Lot of Us Folks Grateful to the Lone Ranger."[63] In the latter work Quinney traces his own biographical movement away from the naive mentality of the heroic individual "do-gooder." For Quinney, the Lone Ranger myth, as an aspect of capitalist folklore, prevents us from recognizing the structural barriers which deny most people control over the historical conditions of their own existence. Marxist theory demands that such myths be abandoned in order to prepare for a more power-reciprocal form of social order. Toward this end Quinney produced a variety of Marxist critiques of crime, criminology, and crime control. The most succinct of these is the 1977 *Class, State and Crime*. In this work, Quinney not only connects the organization of state crime control apparatus to the economic structures of capitalism, but views the crimes of both the powerful and the powerless as reflections of a ceaseless struggle for advantages within the contradictory structural confines of capitalism itself.

A more comprehensive Marxist model is presented by Steven Spitzer.[64] Spitzer suggests that potentially deviant "problem populations" arise from within the capitalist political economy in two ways: (1) through the fundamental contradictions of the capitalist economic modes (e.g., the creation of a surplus worker population, whose lack of stake in the system increases the likelihood of social tensions) and (2) through the indirect contradictions produced by social control institutions (e.g., the rising expectations, critical awareness, or alienating disenchantments produced by mandatory public schooling). Spitzer also identifies factors which increase the likelihood that troublesome populations will be officially controlled as deviants. These include such things as the extensiveness and intensity of existing state control apparatus, the size and level of the threat presented by the "problem population," the effectiveness of informal civil controls as opposed to formal state controls (e.g., controls through family, church, the media, etc.), the availability and effectiveness of alternative types of official processing, other than deviant processing (e.g., the draft or public works projects, etc.), the availability and effectiveness of parallel control structures (e.g., vigilante groups or private police agencies), and the social utility of problem populations (e.g., as tension drains, scapegoats, etc.).

In conclusion, the Marxist approach locates deviance and control in the fundamental and recurrent struggles to control material existence. It is, moreover, a mode of critical thought that is associated with critical action. As Quinney points out, "the solutions proposed by Marxism are predicated on transforming society, on constructing socialist political and economic institutions."[65]

The Hierarchical Structuring of Authority: The Anarchist Tradition

Any rule is tyranny. The duty of the individual is to accept no rule, to be the initiator of his own acts, to be responsible. Only if he does so will the society live, and change, and adapt, and survive. We are not subjects of a State founded upon law, but members of a society. . . . We are responsible to you and you to us.

Ursula K. LeGuin[66]

The social stratification of material resources undoubtedly affects the control of deviance. Those in hierarchical positions of material advantage are structurally pitted against those whose unequally rewarded labor makes this advantage possible. This is a basic Marxist thesis. Anarchist theory goes one step further. Anarchist theorists are concerned, not only with structured differences in material advantage, but with any structures that legitimize, "naturalize," or authorize some people to hierarchically exercise power over others. Anarchists, in other words, are critical of the centralization of authority and the manner in which centralized authority cuts people away from a direct, reciprocal experience of power in relation to their own lives and the lives of others.

Hierarchical State Authority: A Structural Obstacle to Reciprocity State societies are those that authorize rulers to command and correct the behavior of everyone else. In Chapter 2 we discussed the transition from headless, or acephalous, social groups to early states organized around centralized religious authority. Anthropologists distinguish these early *protostates,* with their relatively simple technology and division of labor, from *civil states* constructed around centralized administrative bureaucracies. In the west, the study of what we call "ancient history" is marked by the birth of civil states in the societies of Persia, Greece, and Rome. With the fall of the Roman empire the full rule of the centralized state was for a period submerged, only to reappear in its modern form as the interrelated forces of capitalist economic development, bureaucratic social organization, and secular political ideology joined together in transforming the social landscape of post-fifteenth-century Europe.

We are here less concerned with a precise history of state society than with the implications of this mode of social organization for the control of troublesome deviance.[67] In state societies, the ritualistic control of deviance is removed from the hands of those who are most directly involved in a situation of trouble. It is invested, instead, in the office of some lawfully ordained authority. The consequences of this change are far-reaching. It displaces strategies of interpersonal reconciliation with impersonal rituals whereby those in positions of authority lawfully exclude the deviant. The problem of deviance is thus focused almost exclusively on a deviant person or group. Structural tensions which may have produced or intensified deviant divisions between people tend to be systematically disguised or ignored. Why? The answer is found in the fact that state societies, unlike their acephalous antecedents, are themselves structurally oriented toward the production of trouble. From their inception state societies are stratified according to a hierarchy of authorized political control of social and economic activity.[68] This division between those who legitimately control and those who are subject to control drives a wedge through the experience of the collective cooperation which was so prominent a feature of acephalous societies.

In state societies we are placed in structured positions of competition against one another. We are positioned so as to either benefit or lose by the reproduction of existing and unequal political-economic relations. This competitive positioning is an essential feature of state society. So too is it a recurrent source of trouble—a structural inducement to deviate from one's present position in life in order to advance beyond others in an ever-elusive struggle for privileged hierarchical position. In other words, the core social structure of state society promotes the very competitive conflict and deviance which its lawful controls are designed to solve. As such the central policies of state societies are doomed to endless failure. They create deviance in the actions they take to contain it.

The contradictory nature of social control within centralized state societies may not be consciously recognized by many or even most of their citizens. People are not kept in positions of hierarchical advantage and disadvantage by coercion alone. The stable patterning of stratified state power requires that structured differences in the ability to control one's destiny be justified, legitimized, or authorized by the social production of a "common sense" that things are the way they "naturally" have to and should be. This means that the hierarchical structuring of power in state societies is as much a state of mind and experience as a reflection of the more visible institutions of centralized governmental coercion. This is recognized by the Italian critical theorist Antonio Gramsci.[69] Gramsci used the term *hegemony* to describe the dynamic process whereby the hierarchical structuring of power penetrates the consciousness of those subject to its rule. This penetration is often as subtle as it is deep. According to British theorist Stuart Hall, those occupying legitimate positions of hierarchical control exercise "total social authority" over their subjects, not only by the threat of coercion, but by "winning and shaping consent so the power of the dominant classes appears both legitimate and natural."[70]

The hegemonic dimension of control in state society makes life inherently complex and fragile. The structured social inequality is the historical product of the way that life is organized in the image and likeness of centralized authority. This reality, however, must be constantly disguised by the appearance that all this is a natural state of affairs. If such inequities are to be reproduced without major outbreaks of trouble or resistive deviance, a variety of everyday control rituals must be enacted so as to connect people to a common sense that things could be no different. In the daily routines of family life and in schooling, television watching, job hunting, dressing stylishly, and making ourselves up to look and feel attractive, we citizens of the state society ritualistically contribute to the reproduction of the very structures which imprison us; structures which authoritatively position us according to a naturalized hierarchy of power.

One type of ritual which often contributes to the naturalization of hierarchical control is religion. This need not be the case. In Chapter 2 we noted that religion can both awaken and dull people's sense of the social structuring of injustice. When the latter happens, religious ritual can be an important ally of hierarchical oppression. This led Marx to comment on the opiatelike quality of certain forms of religious ritual. A similar view is taken by Andrew Gill and Jon King of the political art/rock group Gang of

Four. In the lyrics of the song "Muscle for Brains" we hear the following critique of religion as a ritual of hierarchical control:

Don't help me, I can save myself
If I'm incomplete don't fill the gaps.
Save me from the people who would save me from my sin
They got muscle for brains.

For reasons that are not mysterious
The weak are sent to the wall
They have reservations in heaven
Down there they are not so fashionable

For reasons that are not so mysterious
Morality's used as a tool
The poor are told to be contented
But in this life they've no chance at all.[71]

The fragility of hegemonic control rituals and the structural strains inherent in the hierarchical positioning of people in state societies mean that state societies must rely heavily upon reactive (rather than reconciliatory) strategies of control. This is because state societies are founded upon the structural bedrock of nonreciprocal power. Reconciliation requires action to defuse or destructure trouble. This cannot truly happen under the rule of a centralized state. To reconcile is to bring conflictually separated people back together. The hierarchical separation of people is, however, a central element of the social structure of state societies. A true process of reconciliation would require a thorough destructuring of the authority, an end to the hierarchy of the centralized state.

Rather than change the structures by which they are legitimately empowered, state rulers have acted historically to delegitimate nonconformers, to isolate and exclude the deviant. When accomplished in a "lawlike" manner, this exclusion creates the impression that deviants are the primary source of the trouble in which they find themselves. This is the importance of formal law in state society. As it legally excludes the deviant it produces the appearance (or collective representation) that troublesome persons rather than troublesome social structures are at fault. This mystifies the social roots of trouble in a society that is structurally unequal. A critique of this mystification constitutes the core of anarchist theory.

The Anarchist Vision: A Restoration of Reciprocity

Anarchism alone makes non-authoritarian organization of common interest possible, since it abolishes the existing antagonism between individuals and classes.

Emma Goldman and Max Baginsky[72]

Anarchist theorists such as Larry Tifft and Dennis Sullivan, authors of *The Struggle to Be Human: Crime, Criminology and Anarchism,* offer a vision of human order without law, without the state.[73] This is a vision of return, not to the past but to the possibility of reciprocal relations in the immediate present. Under the domination of the state, humans are said to progressively lose their ability to act directly in mutual aid and support, resistance, and reconciliation. In state society direct action is replaced by the mediation of rules, personal responsibility by the actions of rulers. The immediacy of natural struggles with one another is supplanted by rituals of indirect mediation "in the interests of the ruling few, to maintain hegemony, hierarchy and authority."[74]

For anarchist theorists there is nothing natural about this hierarchical mediation of human experience. Contemporary anarchist writings on crime, social control, and social deviance by Tifft, Sullivan, and Harold Pepinsky,[75] among others, suggest that reciprocal cooperation was a natural human possibility and that such cooperation was torn asunder, not by a collection of individual deviants but by the unnaturally repressive institutions of centralized authority and state law.

But what is the alternative posed by anarchism? The answer is suggested by Emma Goldman, the brilliant Russian immigrant whose dedication to anarchist theory and the struggle for social justice led her to be denounced as a dangerous criminal and madwoman by no less lofty a representative of the American state than President Theodore Roosevelt. In her memoirs *Living My Life,* Goldman presents us with a succinct summary of the critical vision of anarchist theory.

> Anarchism asserts the possibility of an organization without discipline, fear, or punishment and without the pressure of poverty: a new social organism, which will make an end to the struggle for the means of existence—the savage struggle which undermines the finest qualities of man and ever widens the social abyss. In short, anarchism strives toward a social organization which will establish well-being for all.[76]

METHOD OF THE CRITICAL PERSPECTIVE

There is no one method for studying deviance and social control as matters of social struggle. Some critical theorists use historical methods to uncover past connections between the social organization of power and the control of people who threaten existing power relations. Others use participant observation and related field methods to pull back the covers of the bed where power and control lie in intercourse with each other. Others examine the way in which symbolic rituals justify or naturalize certain forms of social domination. Still others employ such established social science techniques as the quantitative measurement of social class in pursuing the relationship between social control and social power.

Critical Theory and Positivism: A Question of Ideology

Despite its diverse methods, critics argue that the critical perspective is ideologically biased and thereby unable to provide a truthful picture of the world.[77] Such critics argue that by emphasizing a conjuncture of theory and practice, and by concerning themselves with questions of social justice, critical theorists distort the factual nature of the scientific enterprise. Critical theory, it is said, depends less upon empirical proof than upon political belief.

Critics who chastise the critical perspective for confusing the scientific study of facts with the political pursuit of value generally adhere to a positivist approach to knowledge. They assume that the social world is knowably independent of the subjective vantage point of any particular researcher. Positivists search for objective research methods which will enable them to see the social facts as they really are. By such methods they hope to master the natural laws of the social universe. Ideology is seen as an obstacle to the realization of this goal. Ideology is said to distort objective knowledge by a filter of value. To counter such ideological distortion positivists opt for a "value-free" methodology, a methodology which permits the scientist to distinguish things as they are from things as they might be, to separate fact from value. Under the banner of this value-free approach, positivists condemn the critical perspective as scientifically inadequate and ideologically tainted.

How do critical theorists respond to such charges? Some try to turn the tables back upon their critics, arguing that positivism is itself ideological, that it is rooted in an ideology of rational technocratic control over the world and its people. This critique is made salient by the historical affinity between the development of positivistic human science and the calculative demands for rational, efficient, and masterful control over human labor, occasioned first by the development of modern capitalism, and subsequently by the "scientific socialism" of certain hierarchical state-socialist societies.

The affinity between capitalism, totalitarian state-socialism, and positivism's promise of rational social control was discussed previously in Chapter 4. There, we noted that the positivist human sciences were born in the economic transition from feudalism to capitalism and in the political transition from sacred to secular authority. By offering an image of society as governed by natural laws and a method for rationally controlling these laws, positivism helped provide legitimacy for both of these interrelated historical developments. For secular capitalist society, positivism provided a strategy for obtaining causal knowledge about the basis for order and disorder, conformity and nonconformity. This knowledge promised to be of great use to a society which had set itself free from the rule of God and was now organized around the calculative rationality of the competitive marketplace. The same was true for the authorities who issued rational orders from the centralized command posts of the state-socialist bureaucracy. To rulers in both of these hierarchical types of society, positivism pledged to provide knowledge useful to those on top.

In the case of secular capitalism, positivism promised instrumentally useful knowledge about how to efficiently manipulate human labor, while cost-effectively managing problems generated by such manipulations—the problems of classes of people denied equal structural access to the capitalist marketplace and the problems of madmen, madwomen, and other "deviants" suffering from a systemic absence of the power to meaningfully control their own material and spiritual destinies. In the case of centralized state-socialism, positivism pledged instrumental knowledge which could be used to administratively plan for the rational interests of all the people, while simultaneously curbing the dissent of hooligans, "mental misfits," and others who labor under the deviant delusion that the demise of the oppressive capitalist order meant increases in participatory control over the workplace and freedom to equally celebrate the diverse artistry of human solidarity.

The historical affinity between positivism and the instrumentalist control over people is traced by Jurgen Habermas in *Knowledge and Human Interests*.[78] A similar conclusion is reached by David Held, who observes that "the methods which positivism considers scientific and therefore rational are those which allow for the gathering of knowledge useful for prediction and feedback-control operations. Theoretical knowledge and questions of scientific inquiry are, as a result, made co-extensive with technically useful knowledge."[79]

A more playful critique of the instrumental character of positivism is found in the following prose-poem by Joseph Stephens. The title, "Regress toward the Mean," plays upon a common statistical technique used by many positivistic social scientists—regression analysis. Later in the poem we encounter the term *survival model*. This also is a quantitative strategy used by positivists to reduce the complexities of social life to a series of neat formulas. Such mathematical formulations promise increased instrumental control over people and their actions. Stephens's poetic critique of the control promise of positivism was written while he was "squirming in the sociology classroom" of a prestigious Ivy League university.

Regress toward the Mean

By Joseph Stephens, December 1981

I was sitting in the sociology classroom.
The professor said, "Think wildly for a moment!
Imagine that a man tried to strangle me but
didn't succeed. He succeeded only in interfering
with the oxygen supply to my brain. Put in
a home for the retarded I was victimized again."

Amused by his own laughter, the professor
opened his mouth. Out came a model—
a survival model. We could use it,
he explained, to explain victimization.
We could use it, he explained, to explain.

I was squirming in the sociology classroom.
The professor said, "Think wildly for a moment."
We could use it, he explained, to explain survival
between the time to and the time to the time
after the time to and thereby control the
time to that time too!

We could use it, I thought wildly for a moment,
until the last light bulb burnt out,
and then we could go home.

In addition to promising instrumental control over those who fail or refuse to conform to a particular social order, positivism distracts attention from the way in which hierarchical forms of social order generate deviance in the first place. Thus, from its onset, positivism has been value-oriented. It is and always has been ideological. Its value-free posture is little more than a cloak disguising the basic value commitments which are at its core.

This is the central paradox of positivistic social science. Positivism is trapped within the contradiction of its own logic. It claims to be free of ideology, able to objectively explain the lawlike development of social facts. But how can it explain its own development? It cannot without referring to the historically laid "laws" of the value framework upon which it is erected. It cannot without exposing its own relationship to power, in particular to the instrumental power associated with secular capitalism and totalitarian state-socialism. In the words of Richard Quinney, "The intellectual failure of positivism is that it is not reflective. . . . Positivists do not question the established order, just as they do not examine scientific assumptions."[80]

In summary, although positivists condemn critical theory for being ideological, positivism is itself ideological. Positivism is ideological because it is deeply committed to the values of instrumental rationality. It is linked to a powerful belief system which values knowledge as a means for efficient control over people. This belief system has become so firmly entrenched in the common sense of western society that it is hard to see it as anything but natural. In the preceding pages I have suggested that this is not the case. To view instrumental rationality as a natural state of affairs and to accept positivism as a naturally superior method of knowledge is to ignore history. It is to ignore the historical affinity between this form of knowledge and the powers it serves—the hierarchical powers of secular capitalism and totalitarian state-socialism. Such ignorance is systematically nurtured in most western thinking. It is for this reason that it is so hard for positivists to conceive of their commitment to the rational-instrumentalist value framework as ideological.

The Power-Reflexive Methodology of Critical Theory: Toward a Nonideological Way of Knowledge

To recognize that positivism is ideological is not to spare critical theory from the charge of also being ideological. Indeed certain types of theorizing which claim to march under the banner of the critical perspective are no more free of ideological bias than positivism. Orthodox Marxists claim that knowledge of the deterministic laws of material existence is needed to achieve rational control over the stages of human history. This commitment to instrumental rationality makes orthodox Marxism as ideological as positivism. Orthodox Marxists are no more able to reflectively account for the superiority of their knowledge claims than positivists. If the social world is determined by fixed economic laws, how is it that orthodox Marxists are able objectively to master such laws? Orthodox Marxism's commitment to instrumental knowledge makes it ideology under yet another name.

This leads us to wonder whether any nonideological knowledge is possible? The critical perspective suggests that nonideological knowledge is possible, but only in conjunction with a power-reflexive methodology. Unlike positivism, orthodox Marxism, and other forms of ideology, a power-reflexive methodology never claims an objective vantage point from which to rationally master the laws of the social universe.

A power-reflexive approach breaks from the ideological trap of instrumental rationality by declaring that knowledge is never free of value and that no types of knowledge are ever disentangled from power relations. A power-reflexive methodology does not seek knowledge which is detached from value or free of power. Such value-free knowledge is an impossibility. To know something is to evaluate that thing within a context of power. Knowledge, in other words, is never neutral. To know is to exercise power. To know is to delimit, to affix a certain value or meaning. It is to designate a particular object, now no longer anything but a special value-laden something. Thus when we know someone as a woman or as a black person we constrain who it is that another is allowed to be for us at a particular moment in time. We exert power. When we know someone as a "chick" or a "nigger" we also exert power, this time in perhaps a more controlling manner. To know someone is thus to objectize them, to constrain their subjective possibility, to entrap them in a name, to make them into an "it." This is the case always. Power and knowledge are inseparable. Where one travels, so journeys the other. A power-reflexive methodology recognizes this conjuncture of power and knowledge as a basic feature of our human condition. Rather than feign a false posture of value-freedom, it seeks to expose the power-base of knowledge and to lay bare the values attached to all knowledge claims.

The inseparability of power and knowledge is a fundamental assumption of a power-reflexive methodology. As expressed by Michel Foucault, "power and knowledge directly imply one another. . . . [T]here is no power relation without the correlative constitution of a field of knowledge, nor any knowledge that does not presuppose and constitute at the same time power relations."[81]

The inseparability of power and knowledge is rooted in a critical understanding of the nature of human nature. It understands humans as a particularly precarious species of animals. Like other species, we humans must establish a certain measure of power in relation to our environment simply to survive. Yet, unlike other species, we do not find the necessary technologies of this power within our own bodies. We lack an innate, instinctual, or biologically imprinted technology for survival. Our bodies do not possess the internal apparatus necessary to secure stable relations with our natural environment. The power to do so, the power to survive, must be found in a technology external to the human body itself. Fortunately, our bodies carry within them the possibilities of such an external technology of power. By virtue of a highly developed central nervous system, our bodies permit us to create externally, through signs and symbols, a power in relation to our environment that is not found in our biology itself. Bodily survival is thus dependent upon the creation of a symbolic order, upon knowledge. As such, knowledge is essentially an exercise of power. Power and knowledge are at all times interconnected. One is never present except in the shadow of the other.

By linking power and knowledge to the problems of species survival, a power-reflexive methodology offers a somewhat materialist interpretation of their interconnection. It recognizes that we are essentially embodied beings. We are, as it were, spirits in a material world. Our struggles for bodily existence engender modes of knowledge by which we establish power in relation to our environment, and thereby secure the conditions of our material survival. Knowledge, however, is no simple servant of power. As it secures environmental stability, it becomes power. It exerts itself. Knowledge is an externalization. It rises out of the subjective experience of human bodiliness. Once this happens, once knowledge operates to constrain or control elements of the environment, it takes on a kind of life of its own. It constrains the very human bodies from which it arose in the first place. Hence while power constitutes knowledge, it is simultaneously constituted by the same knowledge.

A power-reflexive methodology begins by acknowledging that everything which humans know to be true is conditioned by power. With this in mind a power-reflexive approach must begin with a process of critical self-scrutiny. Power-reflexive researchers must lay bare the linkages between what they see theoretically and the power-filled social relations which are both conditions and consequences of this way of seeing. This is no easy task. In the preceding chapter we noted how societal reaction theorists often use verbatim displays of data to permit readers to learn as much as possible about the practical social context in which they conducted their research. Power-reflexive theorists must do the same, only they must make additional displays of the manner in which power relations condition and are conditioned by the way they conceive of their subject matter. They must, in other words, endeavor to examine and expose the politics of their own theoretical vision.

How can this be done? How are power-reflexive researchers able to expose the power-bases of their own knowledge claims? The task confronting power-reflexive theorists is not one of simply trying to separate the facts of science from the biases of ideology. As Michel Foucault suggests, "It is necessary to think . . . not in terms of 'science' and 'ideology,' but in terms of 'truth' and 'power.' "[82] The promise of a power-reflexive method is to make more explicit the actual power context in which knowledge is generated and thereby to increase the objective character of a research project by granting readers greater access to the concrete conditions under which its ideas were produced.

Assuming an intrinsic link between power and knowledge, critical theorists employing a power-reflexive methodology must ask themselves three basic questions. These questions are to be addressed regardless of the particular methods (e.g., field, statistical, historical, etc.) employed in a specific study. First, researchers must inquire as to how biographical relations of power may shape the questions they ask and the way they ask questions. A power-reflexive approach assumes that such things as my own class, gender, ethnic, and age relations influence my approach to truth and the truths I am capable of seeing. To examine such matters in the course of my research is to reflexively locate my own biography within social history. It is to realize that critical research is an expression of my relationship to other people and not simply a matter of studying others as one might study shells on the seashore or rats in a maze.

The second question posed by a power-reflexive methodology concerns what the finding of any particular study suggests about power relations in the society as a whole. Whether I'm studying corporate price-fixing, prostitution, or the medical labeling of madness, a power-reflexive approach asks that I relate my particular topic to how power is organized in society in general. What do the everyday pressures of corporate competition say about the balance between deviance and social control in a capitalist society? Would the reality of price-fixing be different in some other type of political-economic system? How is prostitution related to the long history of socially sanctioned power differences between men and women? Would prostitution exist, or exist in the same way, if women had greater power to affect their own economic destinies? What about mental illness? Does the medicalization of deeply felt emotional problems distract from an understanding of madness as a socially generated response to feelings of human powerlessness? To ask such questions is to begin to think critically. It is to search for the wider social and political meaning of otherwise isolated events and behaviors. It is a step toward integrating what we study with how we live.

For critical theorists a power-reflexive methodology poses a third question. Having examined my research topic in terms of both biographical and systemic power relations, I now ask whether I have learned anything which may help transform society in the direction of social justice. This question need not be asked at a huge, global level. Perhaps my project has sensitized me to some small aspect of my own behavior which could be changed. Perhaps I have learned something which will help me and those I live or work with to begin to break down some of the petty obstacles to establishing truly reciprocal power relations. On the other hand, maybe I have identified some bigger obstacles which affect us all. How best can I communicate about such matters? How can my research be a step toward social justice? By confronting such questions, a power-reflexive methodology attempts to integrate theory with life. If knowledge is always related to power, the final task of a power-reflexive methodology is to guide knowledge toward a greater reciprocity of power. In so doing a power-reflexive approach seeks to replace old hierarchical links between power and knowledge with new modes of self-critical knowledge production. This might enable us to knowledgeably find power together, rather than powerfully use knowledge to dominate one another. This vision of a power-reflexive knowledge is suggested by Foucault, who comments:

> The essential political problem . . . is not to criticize the ideological contents supposedly linked to science, or to ensure that . . . scientific practice is accompanied by a correct ideology, but that of ascertaining the possibility of constituting a new politics of truth. The problem is not changing people's consciousness . . . but . . . the production of truth.
>
> It's not a matter of emancipating truth from every system of power (which would be a chimera, for truth is already power) but of detaching the power of truth from the forms of hegemony, social, economic and cultural, within which it operates at the present time.[83]

SOCIAL CONTROL FROM A CRITICAL PERSPECTIVE

A fundamental transformation. . . . is needed if we are to effectively deal with the problems of crime and deviance.

Sheila Balken, Ronald J. Berger and Janet Schmidt[84]

In order to eliminate deviantization as a tool of hierarchical domination it is necessary to radically alter the unequal organization of social, political, and economic resources. Existing power hierarchies must be overturned in order to permit the development of more power-reciprocal social relations. This is the vision of social control offered by the critical perspective. For critical theorists social control is synonymous with a thorough restructuring of society.

The structural changes proposed by the critical perspective reach far beyond the liberal reforms suggested by other sociological theories. Liberal perspectives, such as anomie, societal reaction, and pluralistic conflict theory, advocate changing existing control mechanisms so as to treat all people more fairly. For critical theorists this is not enough. For insomuch as existing control mechanisms are seen as structurally connected to the hierarchical organization of social power, the whole of society must be changed if significant and long-lasting solutions to deviance are to be discovered. Critical theorists seek a full realization of social justice for all people. Without a thorough restructuring of power relations, they contend that attempts to control deviance will be no more effective than placing a patch on a bursting balloon. This may help in the short run, but eventually the patch will explode along with the balloon it reinforces.

But What About Liberal Reform?

In the past, critical theorists tended to view liberal reform as little more than an effort to bandage broken parts of a system which should, in its entirety, be abandoned.

Today this one-sided opposition to partial reform may be changing. Critical theorists are learning that it is possible both to modestly support and to provide a constructive critique of reformist efforts. Modest support may be provided for three reasons. First, concrete opposition to unnecessary human suffering should be supported by anyone who claims to care for social justice. Second, by engaging in reform activity, liberals often learn first-hand about the structural resistances which permeate our current control systems. Nothing that one learns in a course or thesis about the critical perspective matches the radicalizing effects of the frustrations of co-opted reform work. Third, reform can itself stress or stretch the structural mechanisms of an unjust power hierarchy by exaggerating and exposing contradictions to which it cannot respond.

In addition to providing modest support, critical theorists need also to remind liberal change agents of the dangers of being absorbed by the parts and thus losing sight of the wider structural terrain upon which reformers walk. They must offer a constructive critique along with their partial support. As Ron Kramer points out, most liberal students of deviance and social control "may simply not know what specifically they can do to bring about structural change."[85] Although often sympathetic with the general goals of the critical perspective, liberals may lack a sense of practical strategy about how to connect piecemeal reforms to a larger program of structural change. In recent years critical theorists have become increasingly concerned with assisting change agents in making these connections. Kramer cites two examples which his own students have found helpful: the epilogue to David Simon and Stanley Eitzen's book *Elite Deviance*, and Elliot Currie's proposals on reducing traditional crime while increasing movement toward structural change.[86] Harold Pepinsky's 1980 book *Crime Control Strategies* reads as another critical contribution to the same project.[87] Everyone, conservative, liberal, or critical, is a victim of crimes generated by the existing social order. According to Pepinsky, the challenge for those with a critical perspective is "to promote social justice without sacrificing gains in crime control."[88]

Social Control and Critical Praxis: Realizing a Union of Critical Thought and Action

What specifically is the nature of the structural changes advocated by the critical perspective? How are such changes to occur? For critical theorists the answer is found in critical praxis. The term *praxis* suggests that we are self-creating beings, that we depend upon our practical action together in history to secure the material and ideational conditions for our survival. Praxis is thus a union of practical activity and thought. Just as thought grows out of practical experience, so is practical activity organized in relation to how we think. Thought and practice, theory and action—these are endlessly interwoven in human praxis, in the daily production and reproduction of our lives together.

Critical praxis is action informed by a critical theoretical perspective. It struggles to realize a union of social control and social justice. Such a union requires that control be expressed in terms of reciprocal relations of power; only then will social order be produced in such a fashion as to enhance rather than constrict the life chances of all people. This happens only as a critical praxis is based on the realization of several aspects of our lives together.

Realization of Cooperation As social animals, it is necessary for us to cooperate with each other to secure the conditions of our life as a species. We are dependent upon mutually coordinated actions for everything from the production and reproduction of material existence to the construction of selves with self-awareness. From economic to sexual to spiritual to a host of other thoroughly social relationships, we must coordinate our activities if we are to realize the minimum stability necessary for us to practically adjust to the ever-changing times and places of our naturally social environment. One way of achieving such coordinated stability is to institutionalize or mythologize relatively arbitrary ways of doing things. This provides a type of natural, or commonsensical, character to certain modes of human action. Once institutionalized or mythologized, these actions appear, not just as a way of doing something, but at *the* way of doing something. Myths or social institutions are thus an essential aspect of our human social existence.

Realization of Our Ability to Demythologize Social Institutions The many institutionalized ways in which we human animals coordinate our actions are nothing more than the products of our prior actions together in history. Despite their mythic weight and their commonsensical character, there is nothing natural about all the norms and taken-for-granted senses of social reality which enclose our daily lives. We are the ones who have bestowed these things with a sense of closure, with a sense of being how things really are and how things really should be. In realizing this we realize the ability to open them up again; to claim them as our products, rather than to be produced by the claims they exercise over us. All of these "things," as powerful as they may seem, have a life of their own only because we have ritually provided them with life. Thus their life can be denaturalized or demythologized and their power destructured. This we can make happen once we realize that it is within our power to do so.

Realization of Human Diversity We humans have much in common. We are members of the same species of animals. At the same time we have much that makes each of us unique. None of us lives within the same body, or within the same biography as anyone else. We have different vantage points in time and space. This makes it likely that we may wish to act differently about different things at different times; about the ways we experience such things as sex, food, color, texture, mood, sound, temperature or temperament, style, or even the kinds of social relations we desire at a particular place or moment in life.

Realization That Expressions of Diversity Can Produce Trouble Most differences can be expressed without harming the well-being of others. Nonetheless, certain expressions of diversity may produce troublesome social situations in which people deviate from one another's ideas about what actions should (or shouldn't) be permitted.

Realization That When Power Is Reciprocally Structured, Most Trouble Can Be Dissolved Through Some Form of Ritualized Reconciliation Ours is a society which rarely reconciles parties in situations of trouble or conflict. In our society one party is usually declared correct or normal, while the other is labeled incorrect or deviant. Rituals which divide normal people from deviants are the stuff of social control in hierarchically organized societies. Such control rituals are exclusionary. They practically and symbolically remove deviants from the normal organization of life.

Exclusionary control rituals have little place in a society organized by a critical praxis, in a society which structures power reciprocally. In such a society people troubled by each other's actions will ordinarily create rituals of reconciliation, rituals which produce an agreement to act in a certain way for a certain time, even if that course of action is not most desired by some or all parties. Reconciliatory rituals are likely to be the ordinary mechanism for handling trouble in power-reciprocal societies because no parties are structurally empowered to enforce their will upon others; no parties are hierarchically authorized to command the actions of others; no parties are legitimately empowered to trespass upon the power of others. To solve trouble in power-reciprocal societies members must be willing to give and take and thereby dissolve their situation of conflict. Under all conditions but one, no parties in conflict are structurally permitted to exclude the other party as deviant.

The one exception concerns that situation where the actions of some person or group are demonstrably harmful to the well-being of others and such offenders, for whatever reason, refuse or fail to achieve reconciliation with their victims. Even then, the social control efforts directed at offenders by members of a power-reciprocal society are likely to be quite different from those that deviantize people in the society in which we currently live. The general nature of such responses will be discussed later. For the present it is important to realize that responses to harm are likely to be needed far less often in power-reciprocal societies than in power-hierarchical societies. Why? The answer is suggested in the theoretical imagery of the critical perspective. The organizational structures of hierarchical societies systematically encourage harmful deviance and control strategies. The structures of a power-reciprocal society do not. This is not to say that harmful social behaviors or violent impositions of power will not occur within power-reciprocal societies. Greed, disease, fear, and the like, may still prod humans to act in an evil fashion. It is simply to say that, without structural pressures toward violence, pressures generated by the hierarchical arrangement of power itself, harmful social acts are likely to occur less frequently.

Realization That the Reciprocal Structuring of Power Is a Present Possibility Critical theorists realize that it is today possible to socially organize power in a reciprocal manner and simultaneously to secure the material well-being and dignity of all people. At present we realize this is possible by virtue of our highly developed technological knowledge. It is within the realm of science, not simply science fiction, for us to generate the resources for each person to experience the safety and pleasures of a secure material environment, as well as the ability to express a great and potentially creative diversity of action. The material conditions for the good life can realistically be secured for all without denying any the dignity of pursuing diverse and imaginative courses of action, so long as these do not infringe upon the power of others to do the same. The economic basis for this awareness is outlined by Murray Bookchin.[89] Bookchin points to the development of a wide range of mega and medium technological capabilities which make it possible to secure material to survive in a more personalized, diversified, and decentralized fashion. The dissemination and implementation of such technologies may enhance our ability to realize the development of a power-reciprocal society. This is because such humanly scaled technologies create the conditions for a postscarcity material existence, and thereby eliminate the age-old need to secure one's own survival by keeping the upper hand over others.

The possibilities of a postscarcity technology are not now being realized. This is not because they are impossible. They are within the realm of our know-how. We need only to begin to implement them. The fact is they are not currently realized because of the relatively intransigent power structures of our current hierarchical society. These structures have fostered desires which make us endlessly dissatisfied with the present, and tirelessly protective of whatever big or small positions of advantage we have in relation to others. Although such desires may seem natural, critical theorists realize that there is nothing natural about a longing to possess more than we can produce together in a fashion which enables us to secure a stable and pleasurable material well-being, and a diversity of human action. The seeming naturalness of such desire is mythologized, just like any other social institution, by its relationship to the existing system of power.

In basic anthropological terms our supposedly natural desires to be in a better place or position than others and to endlessly have more tomorrow than we do today are fundamentally unnatural. Such desires contradict the fundamental spatial and temporal conditions of our life as a species of social animals inhabiting the same planet. We have only so much space in which to arrange our lives together and only so much time before we die. Yet, rather than permit us to live in the space which is there for all and the time which is here in our present, hierarchical power relations push or pull us into positioning ourselves so as to maintain a spatial advantage over others and into living for a future which never comes. Such is the perpetual discontent of hierarchical society. Forever unable to live in space and time that are shareable, we endlessly desire what is not here and now. This separates us from the possibility of structuring life reciprocally, even if this is possible technically and within our reach. Critical theorists realize that this estranged state of human affairs is not natural but historically of our own doing. This they seek to change via critical praxis.

Power-Reciprocal Control: Where to Go from Here

A realization of the historical character of the social structures in which we find ourselves is a first step toward a critical praxis. To begin to change history is the next step. For most critical theorists this means restructuring society according to the principles of democratic socialism. As summarized by critical theorists Sheila Balkan, Ronald Berger, and Janet Schmidt, this "means that the central economic institutions of the society will become subject to democratic control and self-management by the working class."[90]

The emergence of a truly democratic socialism involves much more than economic change. It is not enough that greedy capitalist institutions be abolished. These must be replaced by what Paul Sweezy refers to as an ongoing process of "revolutionizing practice."[91] Otherwise some new centralized class of state bureaucratic managers may come to occupy the seats of hierarchical power in much the same manner as the capitalists they ousted. This unfortunately is exactly what has happened in such supposedly socialist countries as the Soviet Union.

Pressed by the material strains of a technologically underdeveloped and economically impoverished homeland, and threatened by the advance of foreign aggressors, Soviet socialists soon abandoned the transformative strategies of revolutionizing practice for the centralized management of economic reforms. The result was the reconstitution of class rule, this time by a class of state bureaucrats. Workers who had been promised full socialist control over their own productive activities were once again atomized, repressed, and divided; "deprived of all means of self expression, and terrorized by an omnipresent secret police."[92]

The lack of democratic participation in economic life is mirrored in other aspects of Soviet social control. The long shadow of hierarchical party power casts itself upon the entirety of the Russian landscape. In the U.S.S.R., as in capitalist countries, the experience of relative powerlessness and lack of control contributes to such forms of deviance as property crimes, youth delinquency, and alcoholism. Such activities are seen by party officials as individual pathology or as a remnant of presocialist consciousness. Rarely are the social problems seen as a reflection of systemic contradictions in the Soviet system itself. Soviet social scientists reflect the same party line. "Like their American counterparts, Soviet social scientists attribute the course of crime and deviance to the individuals rather than to the social system."[93]

Individuals who express dissenting opinions are likely to be censured or dealt with repressively. Many Soviet dissidents are declared mentally ill and institutionalized.[94] The overt political use of psychiatry presents a dilemma for medical practitioners. As Sidney Bloch and Peter Reddaway point out: "The Soviet psychiatrist is part of the Soviet system. He cannot say, 'I find no symptoms of illness in this person . . .' He cannot regard dissent as a normal phenomenon generated by the realities of Soviet experience; if he did, he would be a dissenter himself."[95]

Less-discouraging experiences with socialist social control have been observed in Yugoslavia, China, and Cuba. In the 1950s socialists in Yugoslavia broke from the Soviet model of centralized state bureaucratic planning.[96] Economic decision-making became decentralized, providing for the development of worker-owned industries and a competitive market. In the economic sphere, Yugoslavia took long steps toward dismantling the totalitarian rule of the socialist state without returning to the hierarchical ownership structures of capitalism. These changes altered the scope of the social control problem in Yugoslavia. In the years immediately following World War II, when Yugoslavian socialism was organized according to the Soviet mode, such crimes as embezzlement, fraud, forgery, and the theft of collectively owned state property increased dramatically. Likewise, peasants, who were legally required to pay a portion of their agricultural surplus to the socialist state, often refused; opting instead for the higher prices provided by the capitalist black market. Why should this happen? Under socialism, property is collectively owned by everyone. Why should people steal from themselves?

The answer is that under totalitarian state socialism, while property may theoretically be owned by everyone, practically it is controlled by an elite few. Once Yugoslavia effectively decentralized its economic activities, the pattern of deviance again changed. According to Yugoslavian criminologist Dragomir Davidovic, black market profiteering and individualistic crimes against property decreased "because individuals identified more with their enterprises than if they had been owned by some abstract collectivity . . . the state."[97]

This is not to say that Yugoslavia has eliminated the structural basis of its social deviance. Yugoslavian society is much more democratic in the economic workplace than in other areas of social life. Major political decisions remain within the hierarchy of the centralized state bureaucracy. According to Jon Gross, this creates significant problems for the administration of social control.[98] Gross points out that bureaucratic control structures, since they are typically the only public power game in town, may systematically encourage the corruption of public officials and the abuse of state-authorized power for personal gain.

The development of strategies of "popular justice" in China and Cuba represents something of a counterpoint to this top-heavy mode of state socialist control. With regard to China, James Brady notes that "the 'popular' model is tied to the radical ideals of continuing revolution. . . . Justice professionals are expected to work closely with citizen activists and to maintain procedures which are informal and open to popular participation."[99]

Mental health controls in China are also highly communal. Rather than being removed from their communities for institutionalized care, emotionally disturbed citizens are more commonly reconciled to and within the community in which they experience their disturbances. Some of this participatory or communal social control may be changing today as party officials declare that the needs of greater industrialization and modernization demand a more centralized legal control structure. As Brady comments, "It remains to be seen what [the new legal order now under construction in China] owes to the masses of Chinese working people as opposed to the looming power of an elitist 'new class.' "[100]

In Cuba, experiments in popular justice have also been widespread. Although state courts still preside over major criminal cases and military tribunals try cases of alleged counterrevolutionary activity, "popular tribunals" have arisen nationwide to handle an increasingly wide range of criminal and civil control matters. These "people's courts" are overseen by nonlawyer magistrates elected by the citizens of a certain district or neighborhood. Well-attended sessions meet in the evenings to solve troublesome disputes and disturbances and may employ such diverse controls as imprisonment, mandatory agricultural labor, school attendance, and psychiatric therapy. Most commonly the tribunals resort to the ritualistic admonition of offenders. Such innovative Cuban experiments represent "an effort to rely as little as possible upon rigid structures and forms, and to continue to carry out revolutionary aims."[101]

As innovative as the control policies in Yugoslavia, China, or Cuba may seem in comparison to those in the Soviet Union, these societies are still largely state-ruled and not truly participatory in the manner envisioned by democratic socialists. Historically the most power-reciprocal expressions of socialism have been short-term experiments in participatory economic democracy. In virtually all instances these experiments were halted by the hierarchical forces of either capitalism or some repressive state-socialist regime. Examples include the revolutionary Paris Commune, a form of direct worker democracy which existed only from March to May of 1871; the Soviet communes and democratic factory committees organized during the early years of the Russian Revolution; the Hungarian revolts of 1919 and 1956; the Italian factory councils in the early part of the 1920s; the efforts of Spanish revolutionaries in 1936 and anarchists at several periods of time.[102] More recent examples include the brief flourishing of democratic socialism in Czechoslovakia before a Russian invasion toppled the reform government headed by Alexander Dubcek in 1968, and in Chile, before a fascist coup, supported clandestinely by corporate capitalist interests and by the U.S. government, murdered the democratically elected socialist president, Dr. Salvador Allende, and smashed his program of social, political, and economic reforms.

In the 1980s the hierarchically structured battle against the power-reciprocal possibilities of democratic socialism continues in such socialist countries as Nicaragua and Poland. In Nicaragua initial promises of extensive participatory economic and political reforms by revolutionary Sandinista leaders during the 1970s are today being rescinded. Nicaragua today tilts further in the direction of centralized state control. The reason has much to do with external threats to Nicaragua's autonomy by the aggressive and subversive actions of the United States. Fearful of the spread of socialism in the western hemisphere, the Reagan administration instituted a costly secret war to destabilize Nicaragua and to isolate it from its Central American neighbors. The extensive nature of this subversive secret war against democratic socialist development has been documented in cover stories by such politically moderate magazines as *Newsweek.* In Poland attempts to realize democratic socialism through the development of independent trade unions, such as Solidarity, are being quashed, not by capitalist power hierarchies but by their hierarchical state-socialist cousins in Russia and eastern Europe. Thus, from both sides, from capitalist and socialist hierarchies, power is applied to quell efforts to implement democratic socialist policies.

Traditionally, state-socialist regimes have based their opposition to democratization on the grounds that their countries are poorly industrialized or composed of relatively illiterate peoples for whom a full participation in democratic socialism is premature. Today such justifications make less and less sense. As stated by the editors of *In These Times,* America's foremost democratic socialist newspaper, "Today the Soviet Union and the East European nations are industrialized. They have literate and even well-educated populations. They have modern means of communication. But they still act as if only the Communist Party, and within that only a small elite, can be trusted to run society."[103]

The conditions for realizing a democratic socialism are today perhaps greatest in western Europe and in the United States. Free both of the preindustrial concerns of many developing nations and of the deeply entrenched socialist state power hierarchies that dominate eastern Europe, the transformative possibilities of democratic socialism are currently being explored in such countries as France, Italy, Greece, and Spain. Under the banner of "Eurocommunism" democratic socialists in these countries have forged coalitions around such interrelated concerns as worker self-management, democratic trade unions, women's rights, tenants' rights, ecological safety, energy conservation, and debate about nuclear disarmament. It is in the United States, however, with its long tradition of formal democracy, high aggregate standard of living, and advanced technology, that the possibilities for developing a truly democratic socialism may be the greatest.

Power-Reciprocal Control: How Do We Get There from Here?

What can be done today to begin realizing the power-reciprocal vision of critical praxis? The old hierarchical order is not about to throw out its power and die. What can be done to introduce a new order of democratic socialism or some other form of direct, participatory, nonauthoritarian social control? Antonio Gramsci put the question this way: "How to weld the present to the future, satisfying the urgent necessities of the one and working effectively to create and integrate the other?"[104] According to anarchists Larry Tifft and Dennis Sullivan, we must start by changing our own lives and consciousness. We must begin to realize the principles of critical praxis in the way we think and act toward others in the here and now. Thus, "If authority, hierarchical, external and rational, is to be replaced, it must happen by the very process in which persons acquire power over their own lives, in which persons 'discover' themselves, their natural relationships to others through mutual aid, and in which they experience the power to be present to self and others in the context of community."[105]

Michael Albert and Robin Hahnel are more specific about how this might happen. They propose the development of local revolutionary councils as vehicles for a critical praxis. These councils would be thoroughly democratic associations, participatory organizations struggling to unite theory and practice, open to the thoughts, feelings, and passions of all members and organized so as to begin the long journey toward practically realizing a vision of reciprocally organized social power. According to Albert and Hahnel: "The Councils are the institutions of revolutionary counter-hegemony. They are the vehicle through which we the people prepare ourselves mentally and socially to administer our own lives and to overcome all obstacles to such self-management."[106]

As vehicles of critical praxis such revolutionary councils would have no room for old, hierarchical ways of doing things. They must be ongoingly self-critical, rooting out elitism, such that leadership is expressed without "followership" becoming institutionalized. They must, in other words, reciprocally structure power by continually destructuring the positioning of power. This requires great fluidity, patience, tolerance, and generosity. More experienced or more theoretically sophisticated members must struggle to share rather than impose or dictate their concerns. All members must learn how to organize their lives differently and how to collectively resist structuring action so as to authorize some people to organize the lives of others.

The direct, participatory, and radically democratic councils are envisioned as incubators of critical praxis. By generating a struggle for reciprocal power relations at many levels and in many forms, the federated actions of such councils might eventually transform the basic mode in which human relations are controlled in society as a whole. This is the hopeful future of social control set forth by democratic socialists.

THE CRITICAL PERSPECTIVE TODAY

A fully mature critical [perspective] . . . has yet to emerge; however a blending of radical criminology and critical sociology . . . would be a significant advance and would contribute to the modification and eventual elimination of those structures that render human freedom and growth subservient to the vested interests of privileged classes.

Raymond Michalowski[107]

Since its inception in the early 1970s, the development of the critical perspective has significantly altered the way in which many sociologists view crime, deviance, and social control. By 1973 the impact of this new way of looking at deviance was so widespread as to prompt William Chambliss to observe that "the prevailing consensus that has characterized the past 30 years of sociological and criminological inquiry in theoretical models has been shattered."[108] In a related observation Charles Reasons points to "a growing realization" among sociologically informed criminologists and other students of deviance "that criminology deals with an inherently political phenomenon which should be viewed in the context of power, conflict, and interests groups in our society."[109] In 1978 William Pelfry sought to empirically assess the adequacy of such claims by surveying a sample of 761 members of four well-known professional organizations dedicated to the social-scientific study of crime and deviance.[110] This sample included a cross-section of members of the criminology section of the American Sociological Association, the American Society of Criminology, the Academy of Criminal Justice Sciences, and the criminal justice section of the American Society of Public Administration. Of 384 respondents over 57 percent indicated that a critical perspective, the so-called new criminology, was "a viable alternative" to the more traditional approach.[111] This and related responses led Pelfry to conclude that contemporary students of crime and deviance "were inclined towards a critical approach as a perspective with definite potential and one which is seen to be capable of transposing traditional criminology."[112]

Critical Studies of Deviance and Social Control

Increased interest in the critical perspective is also reflected in a growing number of theoretical and empirical studies. Many of these locate the origins of criminal deviance in the stratified or hierarchical organization of social life. One recent example is Jeffrey Reiman's "pyrrhic-defeat" theory of crime control.[113] Reiman documents the structural roots of crime in a highly competitive economic system which "refuses to guarantee its members a decent living" and thereby "places pressures on all members to enhance their economic positions by whatever means available."[114] This systemic structuring of "economic pressures work[s] with particular harshness on the poor, since their condition of extreme need and their relative lack of access to opportunity for lawful economic advancement vastly intensify for them the pressures toward crime that exist at all levels of our society."[115] Nonetheless, just as the dominant economic system induces crime, so does it generate a host of unworkable crime controls (individual arrests, trials, punishment, rehabilitation, etc.). These individualistic responses to crime are at once doomed to fail and destined to (ideologically) disguise the systemic origins of the criminality.

This is the essence of Reiman's pyrrhic-defeat theory, "that the criminal justice system fails to reduce crime while making it look like crime is the work of the poor."[116] To be more successful the criminal justice system would have to overturn the systemic pressures and inequalities within the wider economic system in which it is structurally located. But this strategy of fighting crime through radical social change would bring criminal justice officials into open confrontation with the richest and most powerful sectors of society. Structural pressures to avoid such confrontation constrain the vision of state crime-control agents, who "create a particular crime: the image that it is a threat from the poor." Guided by this image control agents fight crime, but never in a way which is "enough to reduce or eliminate crime."[117] In this manner Reiman's pyrrhic-defeat theory depicts current crime control strategies as systematically reproducing the crime they claim to fight.

Other notable critical analyses of crime include David Greenberg's location of delinquency in terms of the contradictory and structurally blocked aspirations of youths subordinated by the compound power hierarchies of age, class, and race;[118] Lynn Curtis's analysis of the "contraculture" of urban ghetto violence generated by racial and socioeconomic barriers to power;[119] William Chambliss and Frank Pearce's studies of the systemic relationship between organized crime and legitimate political and economic organizations within capitalist societies;[120] and Jim Brady's provocative investigation of the relationship between profitable capitalist banking and insurance practices, the red-lining of certain "high-risk" (i.e., lower-class and/or racially segregated) urban neighborhoods, and the structural encouragement of "arson for profit."[121]

Another important critical study of crime is Don Wallace and Drew Humphries's analysis, "Urban Crime and Capitalist Accumulation."[122] Wallace and Humphries use multiple-regression analysis to analyze the impact of capitalist accumulation (the production of higher rates of profit or surplus value when compared to the wage value of labor returned to workers) on rates of urban crime. Controlling for such other independent variables as region of the country, population density, and size of police force, Wallace and Humphries discovered that "in cities that matured as centers of industrial accumulation, high rates of some types of property crime and violence have their origins in individualized and destructive aspects of class struggle. . . . Central city hardship reflects the near colonial status of marginalized groups concentrated in ghettos and subjected to racial oppression."[123]

In addition to the critical criminological studies mentioned above, other areas of deviance subject to recent critical inquiry include madness, rape, and the crimes of the "respectable" business and governmental classes. Critical research on each of these topics is reviewed below.

Madness and Powerlessness Critical researchers locate the origins of serious mental disturbances within a social context of imbalanced power relations. Since the 1958 appearance of Augustus Hollingshead and Frederich Redlich's *Social Class and Mental Illness,*[124] sociologists have repeatedly uncovered significant relationships between one's position in the socioeconomic hierarchy and the likelihood of being diagnosed and treated for a serious mental health problem. Hollingshead and Redlich's survey of persons treated for mental disorders in New Haven, Connecticut, suggested that low-class persons were far more likely to be diagnosed as having serious psychiatric disorders. Relatively powerless patients are also more likely to be subject to the least intensive and most debilitating treatments, such as shock therapy, psychosurgery, and chemical sedation. This means that, once diagnosed, powerless people may be made even more powerless. The harsh realities of this form of double victimization are documented by Robert Perrucci's *Circle of Madness,* an observational study of institutional treatment in an Indiana state mental hospital.[125]

Psychiatric intervention may exaggerate powerlessness, but is the experience of powerlessness itself a cause of mental disorders? Psychiatrist R. D. Laing suggests that this is the case.[126] In a series of in-depth case studies of the significant family and interpersonal relationships of severely disturbed schizophrenics, Laing found consistent evidence that so-called mentally ill persons were victims of a powerful and oppressively distorted communications network.[127] Patients were caught in a powerplay of conflicting expectations between people in positions of significant interpersonal influence, authority, or control. When acting to meet the expectations of one party they were punished by the other. Anthropologist Gregory Bateson describes this phenomenon as a double-bind of contradictory interpersonal relations.[128] In such oppressive situations people may escape into the "crazy" confines of madness. Thus, Laing reads madness as somewhat of a rational response to an irrational situation. In a complex, disguised manner, madness may be one way of removing ourselves from the painful oppression of those who deny us the experience of reciprocal control over our own lives. In this sense madness may be viewed as a distorted statement about the unequal structuring of social power.

Critical psychiatric theorists, such as Laing, decode the political meaning of madness. In *The Politics of Experience,* Laing connects the personal pain of madness to the political-economic conditions of our age.[129] The importance of such a connection is documented by researcher Harvey Brenner.[130] Brenner's analysis of 127 years of U.S. economic cycles suggests that rises in unemployment have been consistently associated with rises in hospitalization for serious mental disturbances. "Loss of employment seems to be the most pervasive source of emotionally destructive pressure within the capitalist economic structure."[131]

Rape and the Political Economy of Gender Recent studies of sex and gender hierarchies have also contributed significantly to the development of the critical perspective. Nowhere is this more evident that in the study of sexual violence against women. Feminist theorists have described the deeply rooted mechanisms of gender stratification which have long distorted our society's understanding of rape. According to Susan Brownmiller, rape or the threat of rape has been used throughout history to keep women in their place and to reinforce the belief that women are legitimately the property of men.[132] In an article entitled "Rape: The All-American Crime," Susan Griffin connects contemporary violence against women to a culture of male domination in which "eroticism is wedded to power" and rape operates as "a form of mass terrorism."[133] This inhibits a woman's ability to move freely throughout society, and perpetuates an unsupported mythology of "victim instigation" in which "propagandists for male supremacy broadcast that it is women who cause rape by being unchaste or in the wrong place at the wrong time."

Empirical studies of rape have uncovered virtually no evidence of the pernicious mythology of victim instigation.[134] Nor does the victimization of women end with the violent act of rape itself. As documented by Lynda Lytle Holmstrom and Ann Wolbert Burgess, the rape victim is victimized a second time by the legal and medical institutions which are supposedly designed to assist her and control her offender.[135] The reality is starkly the opposite. As Dorie Klein and June Kress point out, the social control of rape has historically functioned to safeguard the rights of men to lawful access to the bodies of "their women," rather than to ensure the right of women to control their own bodies.[136]

Researchers such as Kurt Weiss and Sandra S. Borges have also connected sexual violence against women to the sexist socialization of both men and women in our society.[137] In a related analysis, Stuart Hills attributes the encouragement of "normal" rape to the traditional imprisonment of males within a mystique of machismo and control over women.[138] Such analyses challenge the stereotype of the rapist as a lone, psychopathic, disturbed offender. To the extent that rape mirrors a deeper pattern of hierarchically structured power differences between men and women, its solution must involve more than the punishment or treatment of the rarely convicted offender. As Weiss and Borges point out, "Only liberation from the confines of usual sex-specific role behavior and expectations will lead to less exploitation, less misunderstanding, less hostility, and eventually less rape. For effective social change, it would be necessary to alter the cultural conception of woman as a sexual object and completely change her economic position as an article of male property. . . . Only then will it be possible to free the woman from the status of legitimate victim."[139]

Several recent analyses of the political economy of rape take this analysis one step further. Julia and Herman Schwendinger, for instance, connect the problem of rape in contemporary capitalist societies to the hierarchical inequalities of capitalism.[140] The point here is not that capitalism causes rape, but rather that capitalist production of a viewpoint of people as exchangeable commodities encourages a "fetishism of violence" whereby the male who experiences an absence of control in the economic marketplace may turn to the marketplace of sexual relations to express a coercive assertion of what he blindly equates as the "natural" control prerogatives of his falsely objectified manhood.[141]

Respectable Crime: Corporate and Governmental Deviance

Crimes by corporations reflect the underlying political economy. . . . Not only is the economy determined by corporate power, but the state itself increasingly serves the corporate economy. Crimes of exploitation inevitably flow from this system of domination and expansion.

Richard Quinney[142]

They are coming amongst and in between us. Tapping
our phones—you can be sure they've seen us.
Are you working for or with the state. . . .
They are closing down—communications
They've taken control—of our situations
The forces of control are gathering around
our heads

Au Pairs[143]

The study of crime and deviance on the part of the so-called respectable social classes is often traced to Edwin Sutherland's 1939 presidential address to the American Sociological Association.[144] Sutherland's speech, entitled "White-Collar Criminality," was a discussion of the criminal activities of some of America's largest corporations. Sutherland's ideas generated an initial flurry of sociological interest in the crimes of business people. Notable early studies, each reflecting the influence of Sutherland, include Marshall Clinard's 1952 *Black Market,* Robert Lane's 1953 "Why Businessmen Violate the Law," and Richard Quinney's 1963 "Occupational Structure and Criminal Behavior: Prescription Violation by Retail Pharmacists."[145]

For the most part, early studies of white-collar criminality paid more attention to the process of differential association, whereby respectable citizens learned to violate the legitimate rules of business, than to the social or political-economic structures in which deviance by powerful persons and groups operates as a normal feature of the competitive capitalist marketplace. Quinney's concern with the manner in which the organizational structure of the pharmaceutical business fostered differential orientations to lawbreaking and Vilhelm Aubert's 1952 consideration of socially structured contradictions between the norms of lawful citizenry and the profit-oriented values of competitive business were exceptions to the rule.[146] Yet, even these works did little to explicate the general structural environment of respectable crime. As Diane Vaughan points out, "Although the work of Aubert, Quinney, and others began to point to the relation between structure and illegal behavior, the . . . classic period of inquiry offered nothing further in elaborated theory."[147]

By the early 1960s this period of white-collar crime research had died and was buried by a new generation of professional sociologists eager to cash in upon the promise of functionalism, learning theory, and the anomie perspective by obtaining corporate and governmental grants to study the causes and controls of lower-class deviance. Not unsurprisingly, little corporate or governmental money was available to study crimes of business or deviance by powerful state agencies. What resulted was "a nearly ten-year hiatus, during which inquiry was practically abandoned."[148] This hiatus was broken during the 1970s as a new generation of more structurally informed researchers was confronted by the Watergate scandal, evidence of corruption, business fraud, illegal campaign contributions, and deals between government officials, corporate leaders, and organized criminals to interfere with the domestic activities of foreign governments. Also shocking were revelations that government agencies were illegally tapping into the private lives of citizens suspected of actively disagreeing with official state policies.

As foreshadowed in the 1974 publication of Harold Pepinsky's influential "From White-Collar Crime to Exploitation,"[149] crimes of the powerful have become increasingly important to researchers concerned with the relationship between deviance, social control, and social justice. For critical theorists such as Richard Quinney, the crimes of corporations and governments are to be viewed as natural products of a capitalist political economy.[150] A similar point is made by Ronald Kramer, who suggests that a variety of liberal reforms aimed at restricting corporate deviance will prove unworkable unless measures are simultaneously taken to alter the criminogenic structures of the capitalist marketplace.[151] A related analysis is developed by Vaughan, who identifies the structural strains of competition within a marketplace of scarce resources as inducement for high levels of "innovative" corporate wrongdoing.[152] Vaughan also points to the structural interdependence of corporate and governmental control agencies, each providing resources needed by the other. This interdependence impedes effective social control of corporate deviance. As noted by Quinney, "Crime as an economic enterprise depends on the symbiotic alliance between politics and business, which in turn enhances all three realms."[153]

Frank Pearce takes the symbiotic relationship between business and government one step further. In his 1976 *Crimes of the Powerful,* Pearce documents the collusion of big business, government control agencies, and organized crime syndicates on mutually beneficial projects, such as union busting and Communist fighting.[154] Pearce reviews evidence of CIA sponsorship of international heroin traffic in exchange for Mafia help in "removing" striking Communist workers from the docks of Marseille, France, in 1950; joint plans to assassinate Fidel Castro, whose antiracketeering policies angered gangsters, just as his pro-Soviet initiatives angered government officials; and the maintenance of an anti-Communist vigilance among opium farmers in southeast Asia during the Vietnamese war.

The studies mentioned above are only a few of an increasing number of critical inquiries into the deviance of those in hierarchically structured positions of power. Other researchers have documented the relationship between stratified political and economic power and the differential organization of social control. Of particular importance was the rediscovery during the 1970s of Georg Rusche and Otto Kirchheimer's 1939 *Punishment and Social Structure,* a historical study suggesting that changes in penal practice are shaped, to a significant degree, by changes in the political economy of society at large.[155] Also important were a variety of studies that indicated that the severity of control practices (police violence, length of prison sentence, and the like) was shaped by variables related to race and socioeconomic status (such that disadvantaged offenders were dealt with most severely)[156] and by the general level of inequality within a particular legal jurisdiction (such that areas with greater social inequality were characterized by more severe forms of social control).[157] These and other recent critical inquiries suggest that a comprehensive understanding of crime, deviance, and social control must locate them as struggles within the unequal confines of hierarchical society as a whole.

ASSESSING THE CRITICAL PERSPECTIVE

The chief had assured her the officer would be punished if I would identify him. . . . I refused. . . . I told Katherine, much to her disappointment, that the dismissal of her officer would not restore my tooth; neither would it do away with police brutality. "It is the system I am fighting, my dear Katherine, not the particular offender."

Emma Goldman[158]

At the core of the critical perspective is an awareness that the systemic structuring of power shapes the diverse ways in which our lives are socially controlled, and by which some people deviantly resist the control of others. The critical perspective recognizes that each of our thoughts and actions is laden with power. Each has the potential to make things happen in a certain fashion and thereby affect the potential of others to similarly exercise power in a world we inhabit together. In this sense the struggle between deviance and social control is a natural struggle, an aspect of our interdependent human condition, a product of our precarious historical existence as a species of social animals who must continuously produce a common sense of collective action simply to secure the conditions of our material survival.

What is not natural is the way in which the hierarchical structuring of power shapes control processes so as to systemically favor the social, political, or economic interests of some over others. When this happens social control ceases to be a matter of reciprocal struggle. It becomes, instead, a mode of social domination, a form of oppression or tyranny. Critical theorists see nothing natural about such hierarchical structurings of control. They are the products of the way in which some people in history have manipulated physical and symbolic expressions of power to secure a structural advantage over others; to systematically exclude others from experiencing the power of a reciprocal control over their own human destinies. Nor do critical theorists see anything natural in the deviance which arises in resistance to such domination. Such forms of deviance and social control are the unnecessary products, not only of particular individuals, but of an unequal and unjust system of social institutions. Thus the critical perspective might well borrow from the words of Emma Goldman in declaring, "It is the system we are fighting, not the particular offender."

Critical theorists employ a power-reflexive methodology to explore the relationship between their own ideas and the social contexts of power in which all human knowledge arises. A power-reflexive methodology enables us to better approximate objectivity by accounting for the manner in which our own relations to power give shape to what we see and how we act. This provides an advantage over other perspectives which, despite lip service to objectivity, remain subjected to relations of power which are never made explicit.

This is not to say that the critical perspective explains all there is to explain about deviance. Think, for instance, of the process through which one learns to become a prostitute or explodes in a violent rage against one's spouse. To understand such behavior one must examine factors which, on the surface, have little to do with the hierarchical structuring of power. Nonetheless, the critical perspective probes beneath the surface of social life in order to connect deviance and control to wider historical contexts. The actions of the prostitute are taken beyond a limited consideration of self-concept, family background, and previous sexual experience and planted in a landscape reflecting the long history of unequal cultural and economic relationships between men and women. The violent spouse is likewise understood as harvesting centuries of structurally denied public power through an explosive personal search for physical power over another's body.

Self-concepts, family background, and the like, may indeed be involved. But they are not involved independently of the wider structural questions raised by the critical perspective. The critical perspective makes the study of deviance somewhat more complex, more uneasy. Recall our discussion of the two senses of uneasiness in Chapter 1. To view social life within a historically generated context of structured power makes the task of studying deviance considerably complex. This is the first dimension of uneasiness promoted by the critical perspective. Self-concepts and family backgrounds may be simpler and easier to grasp than the complexity of relationships between self, family, and the ever-changing power structures of social, political, and economic life. The critical perspective requires that we enrich our understanding of deviance by exploring such complexities.

The second sense of uneasiness also enriches our understanding, but at the price of the comfortable disengagement that is typical of most detached professional social science. This type of uneasiness was displayed in a jazz-arts Good Friday liturgy which I once attended at Boston's Emmanuel Church. The combination of soaring, sorrowful music and dance was entitled "A Preface to Uneasiness." It told a story of deviance and social control. The deviant was tried and put to death by crucifixion. The message in this liturgy was one of uneasiness. Good Friday was being reenacted in a world which regularly crucifies those who threaten the domain of hierarchical power. And where do we stand in all of this? This was the question raised by the Good Friday service. Participants were not given an easy out. Unlike Pilate, they were not allowed to wash their hands of life's inequities.

The critical perspective offers a similar sense of unease. Unlike perspectives which create the impression that deviants exist in a world totally different from our own, the critical perspective suggests that we are structurally connected to deviance and its control, just as we are connected to all other expressions of power. Where do we stand in relation to structures of unequal power? Where could we stand? How can we get to a more reciprocal place together? These uneasy questions are part of the richness of the critical perspective. Yet, this richness comes with a price—the price of detached comfort. Like the Good Friday service, a critical perspective asks us to reexamine our own lives and to participate in preparing for a resurrection from the socially structured inequalities which lie beneath most current approaches to deviance and its control.

Despite its strengths, the critical theory occasionally fails to realize the full potential of a power-reflexive analysis. In closing, I have outlined several common conceptual problems encountered in critical theorizing. It is hoped that an awareness of these issues will be of assistance to those concerned with furthering the development of the critical perspective.

Confusing Structural Affinity and Dialectical Tension with Instrumentalist State Control and Conspiratorial Motives

Critical theorists contend that hierarchical power differences give shape to deviance and social control. This is not to say that those in positions of power self-consciously or conspiratorially act to secure power. To say this is to fall prey to an overly simplistic instrumentalist theory of social control. The social reproduction of hierarchical power structures is a far more complex matter.

Consider the work of therapeutic control specialists. As suggested in Chapter 4, the power of medicalized control strategies is aligned with the structural demands of capitalist and totalitarian state-socialist societies for individualistic solutions to problems generated by contradictions in hierarchical organization within such societies themselves. It is almost *as if* therapeutic professionals conspired with other powerful individuals in an effort to pressure the legitimacy of the existing order of social inequality. But did they? There is no evidence that this is the case. Studies of rehabilitative control agents suggest concern with accomplishing cures and advancing careers, but little self-conscious awareness of the political consequences of therapeutic work for the organization of power in society as a whole.

The issue then is not conspiracy but affinity. How is it that certain structural conditions have an affinity with certain social control practices? The answer lies in the complex chain of subtle and often unnoticed incentives and counterincentives which shape control practices in relation to the hierarchical organization of social power. Sometimes conspiracies may be involved. There is evidence, for instance, that during the 1960s the FBI self-consciously sought to deviantize Dr. Martin Luther King and that it waged a secret, illegal, and often violent war against members of the Black Panther party.[159] But even in such instances it is not altogether correct to say that federal agents were operating as self-conscious agents of class and racial oppression.

Isn't it more likely that such things as seductive professional rewards, subtle bureaucratic pressures, and the unavailability of alternative frameworks for thinking may blind many control agents to the structural consequences of their actions? Everett Hughes once suggested that structural inducements get good people to do bad things.[160] This is an important insight. If reduced to the instrumentalist logic of good guys versus bad guys, the critical perspective loses the conceptual richness that is its strength. The motives of control agents cannot be inferred from the bad or oppressive consequences of their work. Thus, the critical perspective must avoid the mere ascription of bad motives, and set itself upon the much more difficult and complex task of tracing the path of power as it crosses the practice of social control.

Unfortunately, critical theorists have not always avoided the pitfalls of instrumentalist theorizing. Instrumentalism was a conceptual weakness in the early Marxist writings of Quinney and Chambliss.[161] In recent years, critical research has demonstrated a more careful grasp of the relationship between power, control, and historical context.[162] Important studies such as E. P. Thompson's *Whigs and Hunters,*[163] Tigar and Levy's *Law and the Rise of Capitalism,*[164] and Andrew Scull's *Decarceration*[165] shun instrumentalist theory in favor of concrete historical analysis. Scull's work, for instance, examines the relationship between the fiscal crisis of the contemporary capitalist state and the deinstitutionalization of mental patients, prisoners, and delinquents during the early 1970s. Other critical studies which demonstrate a concern for structural consequences rather than conspiratorial inferences include Jim Thomas's study of domestic surveillance,[166] Stuart Hall and his associates' analysis of the political meaning of mugging in racially and economically troubled Britain,[167] and Phil Cohen's "Policing the Working-Class City."[168]

Theoretically a strong case against instrumentalist theorizing is made by Steven Spitzer.[169] Spitzer criticizes instrumentalism for failing to account for the conflictual divisions between state agents, as well as between control agents and the powerful class they serve. By contrast, Spitzer directs attention to the complex ways in which contradictory structural arrangements generate dialectical tensions and spawn conflicts within and between the controlling classes. It is the historical resolution of these contradictions, rather than an assumed unity of class interest, that represents the proper empirical concern of the critical perspective.[170] Of related concern is the recent work of William Chambliss which proposes a dialectic approach as an alternative to instrumental Marxist theory.[171] Chambliss underscores the complex and often contradictory relationship between *historical structuring* and *systemic structuration;* between the concrete historical activities of people who create structures and the structures which, once established, both systemically constrain and induce new patterns of action. We shall return to the distinction between structuring and structuration in the final section of this chapter.

Consensus, Hegemony, and Common Sense

A frequent objection to the critical perspective is brought by those who argue that social control originates, not in struggles for power, but in a normative consensus. This issue is raised, for instance, by Graeme Newman in his 1976 study *Comparative*

Deviance: Perception and Law in Six Cultures.[172] After surveying respondents in six different cultures, Newman reported consistently high levels of condemnation regarding such traditional crimes as robbery. He did not find the same "universal" condemnation for nontraditional forms of deviance, such as factory pollution. From this Newman concluded that, while a conflict or critical model may be helpful in explaining control strategies related to nontraditional deviance, the more universally condemned traditional crimes are to be understood by a consensus model.

Do high levels of consensus really mean that there is no room for a critical interpretation? Five of Newman's six cultures revealed a consensus (ranging from 70 percent to 95 percent agreement) that robbery should be reported to the police. Does this mean that there is a natural or universal moral condemnation of robbery (except in Sardinia, where a 50 percent reporting rate is explained away by the atypical presence of what Newman calls a dominant "criminal subculture")?

There are two basic problems with this consensus-by-survey argument. First, it is historically uninformed. A consensus may exist, but this does not mean that it has always existed. The category of robbery implies an acceptance of the concept of private property. Recall our discussion of social control in relatively reciprocal acephalous societies. Our concept of robbery would be relatively meaningless for our acephalous ancestors. Acephalous peoples, after all, had no notion of private property. It was by a long process of political-economic struggle that the capitalist west arrived at its current view of the supposed naturalness of private ownership. Contemporary measures of consensus thus disguise the historical process which has given shape to that which we currently construe as taken for granted, commonsensically true, or self-evident.

A related problem with the assertion of consensus is that it asks no questions about how that consensus came about. People are not born with consensus. What they agree about is a learned agreement. How is that learning accomplished? Does everybody have an equal chance to influence this learning, or is the social organization of common sense mediated more by the structured power of some than of others? Does each of us have an equal opportunity to structure school curriculums, to organize the news, or to shape the electronic images which bombard us daily with "facts"? Are we truly in reciprocal control of the communicative tools out of which consensus is produced?

The answer, of course, is no! Society does not start with consensus. What consensus exists is systematically nurtured. It is structured by the mediating communications of institutions which are themselves responsive to the demands of power. Much of what goes on in school, for instance, subtly shapes student adjustment to the existing order of political-economic inequality.[173] The same can be said of the way in which corporately controlled mass media produce the news and other collective representations of what life is and should be.[174]

Institutions such as schools, news agencies, and television networks are powerful mediators of knowledge and experience. Out of such institutions a relative consensus about the commonsensical nature of deviance and social control may emerge. The social reality of such consensus does not contradict the central theoretical tenets of the critical perspective. In asking questions about the origins and consequences of this supposedly universal consensus, one is again confronted with the historical realities of power. Consensus doesn't spring spontaneously from the souls of the citizenry. It is manufactured or produced. How is this production achieved? Who guides it? Who benefits and who loses from the social production of particular images of deviance and social control?

In recent years, an increasing number of critical theorists have come to view the creation of consensus more in terms of the structural consequences of certain forms of social positioning rather than conscious intentions of people occupying positions within an existing order of power. Such theorists have been influenced by the writings of the Italian Marxist theorist Antonio Gramsci[175] and by developments in the critical theory of semiotics, as pioneered in the work of French theorist Roland Barthes.[176]

Gramsci employs the term *hegemony* to describe the social production of an apparent consensus, or the "moving equilibrium" which legitimizes a stratified positioning of power. Unlike orthodox Marxist thinkers, who theorize about how repressive ideologies are forced from above upon the "falsely conscious" lower classes, Gramsci contends that the production of hegemonic power paradoxically involves the active input of the dominated. How does this happen? How do people buy into a set of commonsense (ideological) assumptions which keeps them in place? Barthes's semiotics attempts to decode the ideological character of popular culture. His work is grounded in the tradition of French structuralism,[177] an approach to the study of sign systems related to the early analysis of primitive classification by Émile Durkheim and Marcel Mauss, the linguistic theories of Ferdinand Saussure, and the anthropology of Claude Lévi-Strauss. His studies of the ideological language of film, fashion, and other aspects of the popular culture resemble the approach of French Marxist theorist Louis Althusser. For Althusser, ideology was an intrinsic part of the social production and reproduction of the material world. Embodied in such diverse ritual practices as schooling, church attendance, and participation in a public sporting event, ideology is said to represent the "imaginary relationship of individuals to their real [material] conditions of existence."[178]

Barthes's semiotics seeks to decode or recover the subtle and often hidden manner in which *signs* forge a relationship between the material medium of communication, a *signifier* (such as a spoken word, visual image, or musical sound pattern), and that which is *signified* (the content or meaning of a message). In the sign material and meaning are joined, each mediated by the way they are connected by the social organization of sign systems. For humans, in other words, there are no purely material or purely meaningful things. There is only a mediated relationship between matter and meaning in the world of signs. It is for this reason that Barthes seeks an answer to the riddle of (hegemonically) controlled consciousness in the world of signs. For it is within a system of signs that people find acceptable *signified* meanings for their *signified* material positions in the political-economic order.

We need not here concern ourselves with the technical complexities of Barthes's critical semiotics to appraise the sociological thrust of his project. His aim was to decode the mythic sign system of contemporary capitalist culture. Myth, contends Barthes, is a second-order sign system in which ordinary signs are transformatively given an extraordinary meaning so as to naturalize, dehistoricize, and thereby ideologically justify an existing social order. Barthes reads numerous features of the capitalist bourgeois culture as part of a mythological system which naturalizes the hierarchical relations of its structurally unequal political-economics. The rituals of culture, in other words, give things a commonsensical character. By enacting these symbolic rituals we transform the historical exigencies of capitalist society into something that seems to have a natural life of its own. The power of capitalism is thus no longer outside us. It becomes a self-evident part of our lived relation to a world which is at once (materially) real and (symbolically) imaginary. How this happens is a story of power. Its result is a naturalization of the "things" which constitute capitalist power—surrounding us with the subtle imageries of sexism, racism, classism, and imperialism. In Barthes's words, "Myth has the task of giving a historical intention a natural justification, and making contingency appear eternal. . . . What the world supplies to myth is a historical reality, and what myth gives in return is a *natural* image of this reality."[179]

A critical semiotics follows the lead of Barthes in examining the way in which power guides everyday language systems in naturalizing, or making hegemonic common sense out of, that which results from specific political-economic relations in history. The challenge is one of decoding, demythologizing, or rehistoricizing the commonsensical structures of everyday language, and thereby exposing the power relations which underlie the collective representations of control. Recent empirical responses to this challenge include such studies as *Resistance Through Rituals,* an analysis of British working-class youth cultures by Stuart Hall and his colleagues at the Birmingham Centre for Contemporary Culture Studies,[180] and Dick Hebdige's 1979 *Subcultures: The Meaning of Style*.[181] On the surface Hebdige's book is a study of the emergence of the punk subculture in Britain. Yet, concealed within the surface signs of punk style, Hebdige reads a coded refusal to locate oneself within the normal representational system of the existing power hierarchy. Hebdige describes the outrageous disfigurement of commonsensical images of aesthetics and beauty and the abrasive, destructive codes of punk style. These are aesthetic inversions of the normal, or consensus-producing, rituals of the dominant culture's style. Thus, in the representational deviance of punks Hebdige discovers "a fundamental tension between those in power and those condemned to subordinate positions and second-class lives."[182]

Other efforts to decode symbolically disguised power relations include Julia Kristeva's studies of the control consequences of "signifying practices"[183] and the program of "critical deconstruction" undertaken by Gayatri Chakravorty Spivak and the Texas school of cultural analysis.[184] Also of note are Williamson's *Decoding Advertisements*[185] and Janet Wolff's *The Social Production of Art*.[186] Williamson's is a critical study of the process through which we become symbolically lodged in and controlled by the system of signs in which senses of ourselves are marketed, bought, and sold as so many capitalist commodities. Wolff's study is of interest because it suggests that, while artists and art audiences are constrained by a complex aesthetic consensus, or power code, they are also partially free to reformulate or recode a new collective aesthetic. The hope here is that critical theorists will do the same, that they will decode and thereby transformatively recode their concrete historical relationship to power. By drawing upon the tools of critical semiotics, deconstruction, and related modes of inquiry, critical theorists are thus today reconstructing the study of cultural consensus as it relates to the historical reality of structured power differentials.

Conceptual Links to Other Theoretical Perspectives

In recent years it has been intellectually fashionable for critical theorists to expose, demystify, or debunk the shortcomings of other perspectives. Many critical theorists, for instance, have tirelessly criticized what they believe to be the uncritically liberal assumptions of societal reaction theorizing. The argument here is that, while societal reaction theorists often generate a kind of sympathy for the deviant underdog, reaction theory as a whole fails to come to terms with the larger social structuring of power.

The trouble with such critiques is not that they are incorrect. Indeed, the labeling of deviants always reflects a structural affinity with the complex and often contradictory organization of social power. Nonetheless, critical studies have often been weakest at precisely those points where the societal reaction perspective is strongest—in making sense of the diverse ways in which control agents routinely come to "know" and label deviants. Hence, a more comprehensive critical analysis would seemingly build rather than erase conceptual links to the reaction theory.[187] This is just beginning to happen today. The research of sociologists such as Carol Warren is a good example. In studying the labeling of persons as mentally ill, Warren observes that "social control policies in operation at any given historical period are easily in part shaped by conceptions of madness, since they are also highly dependent upon economic and other material factors."[188] Another attempt to bridge societal reaction and critical theorizing is H. Laurence Ross's 1981-edited volume *Law and Deviance*. According to Ross, the papers collected in this work "demonstrate the power and promise of a viewpoint premised on an emerging synthesis of these positions."[189]

Thus, although a variety of other theoretical perspectives might be faulted for not attending to matters of structured social power, this is an insufficient reason for ignoring the contributions of other "ways of seeing." More promising are efforts to build theoretical links between critical thought and other analytic frameworks. Isn't it possible to construct a critically informed or power-reflexive learning theory? Couldn't the parameters of the anomic perspective be enlarged to include a consideration of structural contradictions "of the system," not just "within the system"? Such conceptual links are necessary for a truly comprehensive understanding of deviance and social control.

Structural Determination versus Free Will: A Question of Agency

Structure is both medium *and* outcome *of the reproduction of practices. Structure enters simultaneously into the constitution of the agent and social practices, and "exists" in the generating moments of this constitution.*

Anthony Giddens[190]

Critical theorists view deviance and control within the confines of socially structured power. Does this suggest an overly deterministic view of human life? Where is the human agent who makes choices in history? In certain early expressions of critical theorizing, the role of agency was indeed neglected. This was the case in many versions of dogmatic or orthodox Marxism. In such theories, human consciousness and the role of historically situated actors or agents deciding to pursue particular avenues of action were more or less neglected in favor of sweeping generalizations about the determining influence of invisible political-economic forces. A more recent generation of critical scholars is less deterministic. As Drew Humphries and David Greenberg point out, the crucial question for a critical Marxism is not to explain social change by reference to invariantly deterministic laws, but to "locate agents of change 'structurally' within the confines of specific historical situations, such that particular courses of action come to be viewed as 'desirable' and 'able or unable' to be achieved."[191]

This chapter has taken a similar position. I have argued that while the social control of deviance is never strictly determined by the social structuring of power, neither is it ever free of the systemic influence of power as structured at particular moments in history. The same goes for us as actors or agents in a world which is only partly of our making. In the ritualized activity of our everyday lives we are at once structuring and structured by our relations to power.

Marx argued both that people create history and that history creates people. This is a fundamental paradox of human life as we know it. In our expressions of social, political, and economic power we are, at once, creative or self-structuring subjects and created or structurally subjected selves. We are "decentered subjects"; subjects who actively assess our situations and make historical choices, while experiencing our choices as limited by the objective possibilities available within the structural confines of our position in history.[192]

A long and darkly shrouded history of hierarchical power arrangements has given shape to what we today commonsensically consider normal and what we control against as deviant. By demythologizing and thereby destructuring the oppressive bondage of this common sense, we are able to partially recover our freedom of thought and action. This is the power-reflexive potential of the critical perspective—to cast light upon the dimly lit hallways of our own lost history. This light may enable us to better see the shackles of past social, political, and economic injustices and their impact on our present conceptions of deviance and social control. By this increased sight we are somewhat freed from the darkness of structures which create us more than we create them. We are provided with a clearer awareness of the historical landscape on which we walk. The "truth" of the critical perspective may not set us free. It may, however, increase our potential for freedom and act as an incentive for us to further free ourselves.

NOTES

1 Joe Strummer and Mick Jones, "The Clampdown," from the album *London Calling* by the Clash, Epic Records, CBS, New York, 1979.

2 Richard Quinney, *Criminal Justice in America: A Critical Understanding,* Little, Brown, Boston, 1974, p. 16.

3 Rollo May, *Power and Innocence: A Search for the Source of Violence,* Norton, New York, 1972.

4 Richard Gelles, *The Violent Home,* Sage, Beverly Hills, Calif., 1974, p. 188.

5 George Jackson, *Soledad Brother: The Prison Letters of George Jackson,* Coward, McCann & Geoghegan, 1970, as excerpted in Barry Krisberg, (ed.), *Crime and Privilege,* Prentice-Hall, Englewood Cliffs, N.J., 1975.

6 Eldridge Cleaver, *Soul on Ice,* McGraw-Hill, New York, 1968, as excerpted in Barry Krisberg (ed.), *Crime and Privilege,* Prentice-Hall, Englewood Cliffs, N.J., 1975, p. 119.
7 Angela Y. Davis, "Political Prisoners, Prisons and Black Liberation," in Barry Krisberg (ed.), *Crime and Privilege,* Prentice-Hall, Englewood Cliffs, N.J., 1975, p. 94.
8 Raymond Michalowski, "Conflict, Radical, and Critical Approaches to Criminology," in Israel Barak-Glantz and C. Ronald Huff (eds.), *The Mod, the Bad, and the Different,* Heath, Lexington, Mass., 1981, p. 40.
9 See David O. Friedrichs, "Radical Criminology in the United States: An Interpretive Understanding," in James A. Inciardi (ed.), *Radical Criminology: The Coming Crisis,* Sage, Beverly Hills, Calif., 1980, pp. 35–36; Gresham M. Sykes, "The Rise of Critical Criminology," *Journal of Criminal Law and Criminology,* vol. 65, no. 2, June 1974, pp. 206–213; Anthony Platt, "Prospects for a Radical Criminology in the United States," *Crime and Social Justice,* vol. 1, Spring–Summer 1974, pp. 2–10.
10 U.S. Department of Labor statistics, as analyzed in Michael Harrington, *The Other America: Poverty in the United States,* Penguin, Baltimore, 1963, p. 74.
11 Malcolm X, *The Autobiography of Malcolm X,* Grove Press, New York, 1966, p. 90.
12 See, for instance, *The National Advisory Commission on Civil Disorders Report,* GPO, Washington, D.C., 1968.
13 Bettina Aptheker, "The Social Functions of Prisons in the United States," in Angela Davis (ed.), *If They Came in the Morning,* New American Library, Signet, New York, 1971, pp. 58–59.
14 See also Isaac Balbus, *The Dialectics of Legal Repression,* Russell Sage, New York, 1973.
15 For an analysis of the relationship between the emergence of the youth counterculture and economically manufactured youthful leisure, see Simon Frith, *Sound Effects Youth, Leisure and the Politics of Rock and Roll,* Pantheon, New York, 1981.
16 See, for instance, Kenneth Kenniston, *The Uncommitted,* Bell, New York, 1965.
17 Dorothy Smith, "Women's Perspective as a Radical Critique of Sociology," *Sociological Inquiry,* vol. 44, no. 1, 1973, pp. 7–13.
18 Marcia Millman and Rosabeth Moss Kanter, *Another Voice: Feminist Perspectives on Social Life and Social Science,* Doubleday, New York, 1975, p. viii.
19 Eileen B. Leonard, *Women, Crime and Society: A Critique of Criminological Theory,* Longman, New York, 1982, pp. xi–xii.
20 See William Chambliss and Robert Seidman, *Law, Order and Power,* 2d ed., Addison-Wesley, Reading, Mass., 1982, pp. 303–305.
21 John E. Conklin, *Illegal But Not Criminal: Business Crime in America,* Prentice-Hall, Englewood Cliffs, N.J., 1977.
22 C. Wright Mills, *The Power Elite,* Oxford University Press, New York, 1959, p. 343.
23 C. Wright Mills, *White Collar: The American Middle Classes,* Oxford University Press, New York, 1951, p. 110.
24 Alexander Liazos, "The Poverty of the Sociology of Deviance: Nuts, Sluts, and Preverts," *Social Problems,* vol. 20, Summer 1972, p. 111.
25 C. Ronald Huff, "Conflict Theory in Criminology," in James A. Inciardi (ed.), *Radical Criminology: The Coming Crisis,* Sage, Beverly Hills, Calif., 1980, p. 75.
26 George Vold, *Theoretical Criminology,* Oxford University Press, New York, 1958.
27 George Vold, *Theoretical Criminology,* 2d ed., prepared by Thomas J. Bernard, Oxford University Press, New York, 1979, p. 242.
28 Lewis Wirth, "Culture, Conflict and Misconduct," *Social Forces,* June 1931, reprinted in R. Farrell and V. Swigert (eds.), *Social Deviance,* 2d ed., Lippincott, Philadelphia, 1978, p. 304.

29 Thorsten Sellin, *Culture, Conflict and Crime,* Bulletin 41, Social Science Research Council, Washington, D.C., 1938.
30 Richard Quinney, *The Social Reality of Crime,* Little, Brown, Boston, 1970.
31 Ibid., p. 304.
32 William Chambliss and Robert Seidman, *Law, Power and Order,* Addison-Wesley, Reading, Mass., 1971.
33 Ibid., p. 504.
34 Austin Turk, *Criminality and the Legal Order,* Rand McNally, Chicago, 1969.
35 Ralf Dahrendorf, "Out of Utopia: Toward a Reorientation of Sociological Analysis," *American Journal of Sociology,* vol. 64, September 1958, p. 127.
36 The influence of pluralistic conflict theory is evident in such texts as Stuart C. Hills, *Crime, Power and Morality,* Chandler, Scranton, Pa., 1971; Clayton A. Hartjen, *Crime and Criminalization,* Praeger, New York, 1974; Charles H. McCaghy, *Deviant Behavior: Crime, Conflict and Interest Groups,* Macmillan, New York, 1976; Alex Thio, *Deviant Behavior,* Houghton Mifflin, Boston, 1978. Works which attempt to combine societal-reaction and pluralistic conflict models include John Lofland, *Deviance and Identity,* Prentice-Hall, Englewood Cliffs, N.J., 1969, and Edwin M. Schur *The Politics of Deviance: Stigma Contests and the Uses of Power,* Prentice-Hall, Englewood Cliffs, N.J., 1980.
37 Richard Quinney, "Feature Review Symposium on the New Criminology," *Sociological Quarterly,* vol. 14, Autumn 1973, pp. 589, 595.
38 Chambliss and Seidman, *Law, Order and Power,* 2d ed., p. x.
39 See, for instance, Austin T. Turk and Ruth-Ellen Grimes, "Legal and Social Scientific Views of Law and Deviance," in H. Lawrence Ross (ed.), *Law and Deviance,* Sage, Beverly Hills, Calif., 1981, pp. 266–267.
40 Austin T. Turk, "Conceptions of the Demise of Law," in P. J. Brautigham and J. M. Kress (eds.), *Structure, Law and Power,* Sage, Beverly Hills, Calif., 1979, p. 24.
41 Austin T. Turk, "Analyzing Official Crime: For Nonpartisan Conflict Analyses in Criminology," in James A. Inciardi (ed.), *Radical Criminology: The Coming Crisis,* Sage, Beverly Hills, Calif., 1980, p. 84.
42 Ibid.
43 Ibid.
44 Karl Marx, *Capital: A Critique of Political Economy,* vol. 1, Friedrich Engels (ed.), Samuel Moore and Edward Aveling (trans.), Swan Sonnenscheen, Lowry, London, 1887, as excerpted in David F. Greenberg (ed.), *Crime and Capitalism,* Mayfield, Palo Alto, Calif., 1981, p. 48.
45 Friedrich Engels *The Condition of the Working Class in England,* W. O. Henderson and W. H. Chaloner, (ed. and trans.), Basil Blackwell, Oxford, 1968, as excerpted in David F. Greenberg (ed.), *Crime and Capitalism,* Mayfield, Palo Alto, Calif., 1981, p. 48.
46 Lewis Coser, *Masters of Sociological Thought,* Harcourt Brace Jovanovich, New York, 1971, p. 76.
47 Karl Marx, from Lloyd D. Easton and Kurt H. Goddat (eds.), *The Writings of the Young Karl Marx on Philosophy and Society,* as excerpted in Anthony Giddens, *Capitalism of Modern Social Theory,* Cambridge University Press, London, 1971, p. 1.
48 For a discussion of Feuerbach's 1841 *Essence of Christianity,* see Sidney Hook, *From Hegel to Marx* Reynal & Hitchcock, New York, 1936, p. 221.
49 Karl Marx and Friedrich Engels, *The German Ideology,* Lawrence & Wishart, London, 1965.
50 Ian Taylor, Paul Walton, and Jock Young, *The New Criminology: For a Social Theory of Deviance,* Harper, Colophon, New York, 1973, p. 220.

51 Marx and Engels, *The German Ideology*, p. 367.
52 Karl Marx, "Theories of Surplus Value," in David F. Greenberg (ed.), *Crime and Capitalism*, Mayfield, Palo Alto, Calif., 1981, pp. 52–53.
53 Taylor, Walton, and Young, *The New Criminology*, p. 214.
54 Willem Bonger, *Criminality and Economic Conditions*, Little, Brown, Boston, 1916.
55 Richard Quinney's Marxist criminological writings include *Critique of Legal Order*, Little, Brown, Boston, 1973; *Criminal Justice in America: A Critical Understanding*, Little, Brown, Boston, 1974; with John Wildeman, *The Problem of Crime*, 2d ed., Harper & Row, New York, 1977; *Class, State and Crime: On the Theory and Practice of Criminal Justice*, McKay, New York, 1977; and *Criminology*, 2d ed., Little, Brown, Boston, 1979.
56 Herman Schwendinger and Julia Schwendinger, "Social Class and the Definition of Crime," *Crime and Social Justice*, vol. 7, Spring–Summer 1977, pp. 4–13.
57 Paul Takagi, "The Walnut Street Jail: A Penal Reform to Centralize the Powers of the State," *Federal Probation*, vol. 39, December 1975, pp. 18–25.
58 Jerome Hall, *Theft, Law and Society*, Bobbs-Merrill, Indianapolis, 1952.
59 Raymond Michalowski and Edward Bolander, "Repression and Criminal Justice in America," *Sociological Inquiry*, vol. 46, 2, 1976, p. 99.
60 Anthony Platt, *The Child Savers*, University of Chicago Press, Chicago, 1969, and "Prospects for Radical Criminology in the United States," *Crime and Social Justice*, No. 1, Spring–Summer 1974, pp. 2–3.
61 William J. Chambliss, "A Sociological Analysis of the Law of Vagrancy," *Social Problems*, vol. 12, Summer 1964, pp. 46–67, and "Toward a Political Economy of Crime," *Theory and Society*, vol. 2, Summer 1975, pp. 150–170.
62 Quinney, *Criminology*, 2d ed., p. 399.
63 Richard Quinney, "Crime Control in Capitalist Society: A Critical Philosophy of Legal Order," *Issues in Criminology*, vol. 8, Spring 1973, pp. 75–95; and "There's a Lot of Us Folks Grateful to the Lone Ranger: Some Notes on the Rise and Fall of American Criminology," *Insurgent Sociologist*, vol. 4, Fall 1973, pp. 56–64.
64 Steven Spitzer, "Toward a Marxian Theory of Deviance," *Social Problems*, vol. 22, June 1975, pp. 641–651.
65 Quinney, *Criminology*, 2d ed., p. 26.
66 Ursula K. LeGuin, *The Dispossessed*, Avon, New York, 1974, pp. 288–310.
67 For an elaboration of this thesis, see Stephen J. Pfohl, "Labeling Criminals," in H. Laurence Ross (ed.), *Law and Deviance*, Sage, Beverly Hills, Calif., 1981, pp. 65–97.
68 See, for instance, Marvin Harris, *Culture, People, Nature*, Cromwell, New York, 1975.
69 Antonio Gramsci, *Selections from the Prison Notebooks*, International Publishers, New York, 1971.
70 Stuart Hall, "Culture, the Media and the Ideological Effect," in J. Curran et al. (eds.), *Mass Communications and Society*, Arnold, London, 1977, pp. 332–333.
71 Andrew Gill and Jon King, "Muscle for Brains," from the album *Songs of the Free* by Gang of Four.
72 Emma Goldman and Max Baginski, "The Relation of Anarchism to Organization," *Mother Earth*, vol. II, October 1907, as quoted in Richard Drinnan, *Rebel in Paradise: A Biography of Emma Goldman*, Harper Colophon, New York, 1961, p. 106.
73 Larry Tifft and Dennis Sullivan, *The Struggle to Be Human: Crime, Criminology and Anarchism*, Cienfuegos, Orkney, Scotland, 1980. See also Larry Tifft, "The Coming Redefinition of Crime: An Anarchist Perspective," *Social Problems*, vol. 26, April 1979, pp. 392–402.

74 Tifft and Sullivan, *The Struggle to Be Human,* p. 83.

75 Harold Pepinsky, "Communist Anarchism as an Alternative to the Rule of Criminal Law," *Contemporary Crisis,* vol. 2, 1978, pp. 315–334. See also George Woodcock, *Anarchism: A History of Libertarian Ideas and Movements,* New American Library, New York, 1962.

76 Emma Goldman, *Living My Life,* Dover, New York, 1970, vol. 1, p. 403.

77 See, for instance, Marshall B. Clinard and Robert F. Meir, *Sociology of Deviant Behavior,* Holt, Rinehart & Winston, New York, 1979, p. 88.

78 Jurgen Habermas, *Knowledge and Human Interests,* Jeremy Shapiro (trans.) Beacon, Boston, 1970; see also Jurgen Habermas, "A Positivistically Bisected Rationalism," in Anthony Giddens (ed.), *Positivism and Sociology,* Heinemann, London, 1974.

79 David Held, *Introduction to Critical Theory: Horkheimer to Habermas,* University of California Press, Berkeley, 1980, p. 306.

80 Quinney, *Criminology,* 2d ed., p. 13.

81 Michel Foucault, *Discipline and Punish: The Birth of the Prison,* A. Sheridan (trans.), Vintage Books, New York, 1979, p. 27.

82 Michel Foucault, *Power/Knowledge: Selected Interviews and Other Writings, 1972–1977,* Colin Gordon (ed.), Pantheon, New York, 1980, p. 132.

83 Ibid., p. 133.

84 Sheila Balkan, Ronald J. Berger, and Janet Schmidt, *Crime and Deviance in America: A Critical Approach,* Wadsworth, Belmont, Calif., 1980, p. 316.

85 Ronald C. Kramer, "Teaching Critical Criminology to Criminal Justice Students," paper presented at annual meeting of American Society of Criminology, Toronto, Nov. 4, 1982, p. 11.

86 David R. Simon and D. Stanley Eitzen, *Elite Deviance,* Allyn & Bacon, Boston, Mass., 1982; Elliott Currie, "Fighting Crime," in *Working Papers,* vol. 9, July–August 1982, pp. 16–25.

87 Harold E. Pepinsky, *Crime Control Strategies,* Oxford, New York, 1980.

88 Harold E. Pepinsky, "A Radical Alternative to Radical Criminology," in James A. Inciardi (ed.), *Radical Criminology: The Coming Crisis,* Sage, Beverly Hills, Calif., 1980, p. 310.

89 Murray Bookchin, *Post-Scarcity Anarchism,* Ramparts, San Francisco, 1971. For a related discussion of Bookchin's thesis, see Jerome Judson, *Families of Eden's Communes and the New Anarchism,* Seabury, New York, 1974, and Tifft and Sullivan, *The Struggle to Be Human,* pp. 175–177.

90 Sheila Balkan, Ronald J. Berger, and Janet Schmidt, *Crime and Deviance in America: A Critical Approach,* Wadsworth, Belmont, Calif., 1980, pp. 316–317.

91 Paul M. Sweezy, "The Transition to Socialism," in Richard Quinney (ed.), *Capitalist Society: Readings for a Critical Sociology,* Dorsey, Homewood, Ill., 1979.

92 Ibid., p. 412.

93 Balkan, Berger, and Schmidt, *Crime and Deviance in America.*

94 Zhores Medvedev and Roy Medvedev, *A Question of Madness,* Knopf, New York, 1971.

95 Sidney Bloch and Peter Reddaway, *Psychiatric Terror: How Soviet Psychiatry Is Used to Suppress Dissent,* Basic Books, New York, 1977.

96 Frank Parkin, *Class Inequality and Political Order: Social Stratification in Capitalist and Communist Societies,* Praeger, New York, 1974.

97 Davidovic's unpublished 1978 paper, "Some Significant Changes in the Phenomenology of Crime in Yugoslavia During Recent Decades," is summarized in Balkan, Berger, and Schmidt, *Crime and Deviance in America,* p. 327.

98 Jon Gross, *Polish Society Under German Occupation,* Princeton University Press, Princeton, N.J. 1979.

99 James P. Brady, "A Season of Startling Alliance: Chinese Law and Justice in the New Order," in Piers Beirne and Richard Quinney (eds.), *Marxism and Law,* Wiley, New York, 1982, p. 350.
100 Ibid., p. 360.
101 Balkan, Berger, and Schmidt, *Crime and Deviance in America,* p. 330.
102 Michael Albert and Robin Hahnel, *Unorthodox Marxism,* South End Press, Boston, 1978, pp. 253–254.
103 Editorial "Socialism Means Trusting People," *In These Times,* vol. 7, no. 6, December 27–January 11, 1983, p. 14.
104 Antonio Gramsci, quoted in Albert and Hahnel, *Unorthodox Marxism,* p. 329.
105 Tifft and Sullivan, *The Struggle to Be Human,* p. 168.
106 Albert and Hahnel, *Unorthodox Marxism,* p. 329.
107 Michalowski, "Conflict, Radical, and Critical Approaches to Criminology," p. 49.
108 William Chambliss, "Functional and Conflict Theories of Crime," *MSS. Modular Publications,* vol. 17, 1973, p. 1. Reprinted in W. J. Chambliss and M. Mankoff (eds.), *Whose Law? What Order?* Wiley, New York, 1976.
109 Charles Reasons, *Criminology: Crime and the Criminologist,* Goodyear, Santa Monica, Calif., 1974, p. 5.
110 William V. Pelfry, "The New Criminology: Acceptance Within Academe," in James A. Inciardi (ed.), *Radical Criminology: The Coming Crisis,* Sage, Beverly Hills, Calif., 1980, pp. 233–244.
111 Ibid., p. 238.
112 Ibid., p. 241.
113 Jeffrey H. Reiman, *The Rich Get Richer and the Poor Get Prison,* Wiley, New York, 1979, p. 7.
114 Ibid.
115 Ibid.
116 Ibid., pp. 5–6.
117 Ibid., p. 6.
118 David F. Greenberg, "Delinquency and the Age Structure of Society," *Contemporary Crisis,* vol. 1, April 1977, pp. 189–223.
119 Lynn Curtis, *Violence, Race and Culture,* Heath, Lexington, Mass., 1975.
120 William Chambliss, "Vice, Corruption, Bureaucracy, and Power," *Wisconsin Law Review,* vol. 4, 1971, pp. 1130–1155; Frank Pearce, "Organized Crime and Class Politics," in David F. Greenberg (ed.), *Crime and Capitalism,* Mayfield, Palo Alto, Calif., 1981, pp. 157–181.
121 James Brady, "Arson, Urban Economy, and Organized Crime: The Case of Boston," *Social Problems,* vol. 31, no. 1, October 1983, pp. 1–23.
122 Don Wallace and Drew Humphries, "Urban Crime and Capitalist Accumulation: 1950–71," in David F. Greenberg (ed.), *Crime and Capitalism,* Mayfield, Palo Alto, Calif., 1981, pp. 140–156.
123 Ibid., p. 150.
124 Augustus Hollingshead and Frederich Redlich, *Social Class and Mental Illness,* Wiley, New York, 1958.
125 Robert Perrucci, *Circle of Madness: On Being Insane and Institutionalized,* Prentice-Hall, Englewood Cliffs, N.J., 1974.
126 R. D. Laing, *The Divided Self,* Penguin, Baltimore, 1967.
127 R. D. Laing and A. Esterson, *Sanity, Madness and the Family,* Basic Books, New York, 1964.

128 Gregory Bateson, D. D. Jackson, J. Haley, and J. Weakland, "Toward a Theory of Schizophrenia," *Behavioral Science,* vol. 1, 1956, pp. 251–264.

129 R. D. Laing *The Politics of Experience,* Penguin, Baltimore, 1967.

130 Harvey Brenner, *Mental Illness and the Economy,* Harvard, Cambridge, Mass., 1973.

131 Balkan, Berger, and Schmidt, *Crime and Deviance in America,* p. 289. See also D. D. Braginsky and B. M. Braginsky, "Surplus People: The Lost Faith in Self and System," *Psychology Today,* vol. 9, no. 3, August 1975, pp. 68–76.

132 Susan Brownmiller, *Against Our Will: Men, Women, and Rape,* Bantam, New York, 1975. For a related discussion by black women, of the experience of rape, see Angela Davis, *Women, Class and Race,* Vintage, New York, 1983, pp. 172–201.

133 Susan Griffin, "Rape: The All-American Crime," *Ramparts,* vol. 10, September 1971, pp. 28, 35; see also Susan Griffin, *Rape: The Power of Consciousness,* Harper & Row, New York, 1979.

134 For an analysis of police data on the social circumstances surrounding rape in seventeen major cities, see Lynn Curtis, *Crimes of Violence,* Heath, Lexington, Mass., 1974.

135 Lynda Lytle Holmstrom and Ann Wolbert Burgess, *The Victim of Rape: Institutional Reactions,* Wiley, New York, 1979; See also Lynda Lytle Holmstrom and Ann Wolbert Burgess, "Rape: The Victim and the Criminal Justice System," *International Journal of Criminology and Penology,* vol. 3, 1975, pp. 101–110.

136 Dorie Klein and June Kress, "Any Woman's Blues," *Crime and Social Justice,* vol. 5, Spring–Summer 1976; see also Camile E. Le Grand, "Rape and Rape Laws: Sexism in Society and Law," *California Law Review* vol. 6, no. 3, 1973, pp. 919–941.

137 Kurt Weiss and Sandra S. Borges, "Victimology and Rape: The Case of the Legitimate Victim," *Issues in Criminology,* vol. 8, no. 2, 1973, pp. 71–115.

138 Stuart L. Hills, "Rape and the Male Mystique," in *Demystifying Social Deviance,* McGraw-Hill, New York, 1980, pp. 57–77.

139 Weiss and Borges, "Victimology and Rape," p. 110.

140 Julia Schwendinger and Herman Schwendinger, "Rape, Sexual Inequality and Levels of Violence," *Crime and Social Justice,* vol. 16, Winter 1981, pp. 3–31.

141 Ibid., p. 19.

142 Quinney, *Criminology,* 2d ed., p. 197.

143 Au Pairs, lyrics of "Headache for Michelle," from the album *Playing with a Different Sex,* Human Records/Ideal Home Noise, United Kingdom, 1981.

144 Edwin H. Sutherland, "White-Collar Criminality," *American Sociological Review,* vol. 5, February 1940, pp. 1–12; see also Edwin H. Sutherland, *White Collar Crime,* Dryden, New York, 1949.

145 Marshall B. Clinard, *The Black Market,* Rinehart, New York, 1952; Robert A. Lane, "Why Businessmen Violate the Law," *Journal of Criminal Law and Criminology,* vol. 44, 1953, pp. 151–165; Earl R. Quinney, "Occupational Structure and Criminal Behavior: Prescription Violation by Retail Pharmacists," *Social Problems,* vol. 11, 1963, pp. 179–185.

146 Quinney, "Occupational Structure and Criminal Behavior," and Vilhelm Aubert, "White Collar Crime and Social Structure," *American Journal of Sociology,* vol. 58, 1952, pp. 263–271.

147 Diane Vaughan, "Recent Developments in White-Collar Crime Theory and Research," in Israel L. Barak-Glantz and C. Ronald Huff (eds.), *The Mad, the Bad, and the Different,* Heath, Lexington, Mass, 1981, p. 136.

148 Ibid., p. 137.

149 Harold Pepinsky, "From White Collar Crime to Exploitation: Redefinition of a Field," *Journal of Criminal Law and Criminology,* vol. 65, June 1974, pp. 225–233.

150 Quinney, *Criminology,* 2d ed., pp. 141–215.

151 Ronald Kramer, "Corporate Crime: An Organizational Perspective," paper presented at Conference on Trends and Problems in Research and Policy Dealing with Economic Crime, State University of New York at Potsdam, Feb. 7–9, 1980.

152 Diane Vaughan, *Controlling Unlawful Organizational Behavior,* University of Chicago Press, Chicago, 1983.

153 Quinney, *Criminology,* 2d ed., p. 210.

154 Frank Pearce, *Crimes of the Powerful,* Pluto, London, 1976; see also Morton Halpern et al., *The Lawless State: The Crimes of the U.S. Intelligence Agencies,* Penguin, Middlesex, 1976; David R. Simon and D. Stanley Eitzen, *Elite Deviance,* Allyn & Bacon, Boston, 1982; and M. David Erman and Richard J. Lundman, *Corporate and Governmental Deviance,* Oxford, New York, 1982.

155 Georg Rusche and Otto Kirchheimer, *Punishment and Social Structure,* Columbia, New York, 1939. For related analysis see Dario Melossi, "Punishment and Social Structure," in Tony Platt and Paul Takagi (eds.), *Punishment and Penal Discipline,* Crime and Social Justice Associates, Berkeley, Calif., 1980, pp. 17–27; Michael Ignatieff, *A Just Measure of Pain: The Penitentiary System in the Industrial Revolution, 1750–1850,* Pantheon, New York, 1978; Russell Hogg, "Imprisonment and Society Under Early British Capitalism," in Platt and Takagi, *Punishment and Penal Discipline,* pp. 57–70; Ivan Jankovic, "Labor Market and Imprisonment," in Platt and Takagi, *Punishment and Penal Discipline* pp. 93–104; Don Wallace, "The Political Economy at Incarceration Trends in Late U.S. Capitalism: 1971–1977," *Insurgent Sociologist,* vol. X, no. 4–vol. XI, no. 1, Summer–Fall 1981, pp. 59–65; Drew Humphries and David Greenberg "The Dialectics of Crime Control," in David F. Greenberg (ed.), *Crime and Capitalism,* Mayfield, Palo Alto, Calif., 1981, pp. 209–254.

156 Ivan Jankovic, "Social Class and Criminal Sentencing," *Crime and Social Justice,* vol. 10, Fall–Winter, 1978, pp. 9–16; Alan J. Lizotte, "Extra-Legal Factors in Chicago's Criminal Courts: Testing the Conflict Model of Criminal Justice," *Social Problems,* vol. 25, no. 5, June 1978, pp. 564–580; John Hagan, "The Social and Legal Construction of Criminal Justice: A Study of the Presenting Process," *Social Problems,* vol. 22, 1975, pp. 620–637; Marvin Wolfgang and Marc Riedel, "Race, Judicial Discretion and the Death Penalty," in William Chambliss (ed.), *Criminal Law in Action,* Hamilton, Santa Barbara, Calif., 1975, pp. 365–375.

157 David Jacobs, "Inequality and the Legal Order: An Ecological Test of the Conflict Model," *Social Problems,* vol. 25, no. 5, June 1978, pp. 515–535; David Jacobs and David Britt, "Inequality and Police Use of Deadly Force: An Empirical Assessment of a Conflict Hypothesis," *Social Problems,* vol. 26, no. 4, April 1979, pp. 403–412; Kirk R. Williams and Michael Timberlake, "Structured Inequality, Conflict and Control: A Cross-National Test of the Threat Hypothesis," *Social Forces,* 1984, in press; Michael Timberlake and Kirk R. Williams, "Dependence, Political Exclusion and Governmental Repression," *American Sociological Review,* 1984, in press.

158 Goldman, *Living My Life,* vol. 1, p. 308.

159 David J. Garrow, *The FBI and Martin Luther King Jr.,* Penguin, Middlesex, 1981.

160 Everett Hughes, "Good People and Dirty Work," *Social Problems,* vol. 10, Summer, 1962, pp. 3–11.

161 For a review of this problem, see Dragan Milovanovic, "Ideology and Law: Structuralist and Instrumentalist Accounts of Law," *Insurgent Sociologist,* vol. X, no, 4–vol. XI, no. 1, Summer–Fall 1981, pp. 93–98.

162 For a review of other noninstrumentalist Marxist historical research, see Pat O'Malley, "Historical Practice and the Production of Marxist Legal Theory," *Crime and Social Justice*, vol. 19, Winter 1982, pp. 53–61.

163 E. P. Thompson, *Whigs and Hunters: The Origin of the Black Act*, Allen Lane, London, 1975.

164 M. Tigar and M. Levy, *Law and the Rise of Capitalism*, Monthly Review Press, New York, 1979.

165 Andrew Scull, *Decarceration: Community Treatment and the Deviant*, Prentice-Hall, Englewood Cliffs, N.J., 1977.

166 Jim Thomas, "Class, State and Political Surveillance: Liberal Democracy and Structural Contradictions," *Insurgent Sociologist*, vol. X, no. 4–vol. XI, no. 1, Summer–Fall 1981, pp. 47–58.

167 Stuart Hall, Chas Critcher, Tony Jefferson, John Clarke, and Brian Roberts, *Policing the Crisis: Mugging, the State, and Law and Order*, Macmillan, London, 1978.

168 Phil Cohen, "Policing the Working Class City," in B. Fine et al. (eds.), *Capitalism and the Rule of Law: From Deviancy Theory to Marxism*, Hutchinson, London, 1979, pp. 118–136.

169 Steven Spitzer, " 'Left-Wing' Criminology—An Infantile Disorder?" in James A. Inciardi (ed.), *Radical Criminology: The Coming Crisis*, Sage, Beverly Hills, Calif., 1980, pp. 169–189. For an empirical application of this noninstrumentalist approach, see Steven Spitzer and Andrew T. Scull, "Social Control in Historical Perspective: From Private to Public Responses to Crime," in Piers Beirne and Richard Quinney (eds.), *Marxism and Law*, Wiley, New York, 1982, pp. 236–251.

170 For related critiques of instrumentalism, see Peter K. Manning, "Deviance and Dogma," *British Journal of Criminology*, vol. 15, January 1975, Piers Beirne, "Empiricism and the Critique of Marxism on Law and Crime," *Social Problems*, vol. 26, no. 4, April 1979, pp. 373–385; Isaac Balbus, "Commodity Form and Legal Form: An Essay on the Relative Autonomy of Law," *Law and Society Review*, vol —, Winter 1977, pp. 571–587; and David F. Greenberg, "On One Dimensional Criminology," *Theory and Society*, vol. 3, 1976, pp. 610–621.

171 William J. Chambliss, "The Criminalization of Conduct," in H. Lawrence Ross (ed.), *Law and Deviance*, Sage, Beverly Hills, Calif., 1981, p. 52.

172 Graeme Newman, *Comparative Deviance: Perception and Law in Six Cultures*, Elsevier, New York, 1976.

173 See, for instance, Samuel Bowles and Herbert Gintis, *Schooling in Capitalist America: Educational Reforms and the Contradictions of Economic Life*, Basic Books, New York, 1976; and Paul Willis, *Learning to Labor: How Working Class Kids Get Working Class Jobs*, Columbia, New York, 1977.

174 See, for instance, Stuart Hall, Dorothy Hobson, Andrew Lowe, and Paul Willis, *Culture, Media, Language*, Hutchinson, London, 1980; Howard Davis and Paul Walton (eds.), *Language, Image, Media*, St. Martins, New York, 1983; Gay Tuchman, *The Social Construction of News*, Free Press, New York, 1978; Todd Gitlin, *The Whole World's Watching*, University of California Press, Berkeley, 1980; and Michael Gurevitch, Tony Bennett, James Curren, and Janet Woolacutt, *Culture, Society and the Media*, Methuen, London, 1982.

175 Gramsci, *Selections from the Prison Notebooks*

176 Roland Barthes, *Mythologies*, Paladin, London, 1973; See also Susan Sontag (ed.), *A Barthes Reader*, Hill & Wang, New York, 1982.

177 For an overview of these theoretical developments, see Rosiland Coward and John Ellis, *Language and Materialism: Developments in Semiology and the Theory of the Subject,* Routledge & Kegan Paul, Boston, 1977.

178 Louis Althusser, "Ideology and Ideological State Apparatuses" in *Lenin and Philosophy and Other Essays,* Ben Brewster (trans.) Monthly Review Press, New York, 1971, p. 162.

179 Barthes, "Myth Today," in Sontag, *A Barthes Reader,* p. 131.

180 Stuart Hall and Tony Jefferson (eds.), *Resistance Through Rituals,* Hutchinson, London, 1976.

181 Dick Hebdige, *Subcultures: The Meaning of Style,* Methuen, New York, 1981.

182 Ibid., p. 132.

183 Julia Kristeva, *Desire in Language: A Semiotic Approach to Literature and Art,* Columbia, New York, 1980.

184 See Gayatri Chakravorty Spivak, "Revolutions That As Yet Have No Model: Derrida's 'Limited Inc.,'" *Diacritics,* vol. 10, no. 4, Winter 1980, and "Translator's Preface" to Jacque Derrida, *Of Grammatology,* Johns Hopkins, Baltimore, 1976; and for a presentation of critical cultural analysis by one of Spivak's students, Michael Ryan, *Marxism and Deconstruction,* Johns Hopkins, Baltimore, 1982. My own knowledge of Spivak's analytic approach is rooted in my participation in her seminar "The Production of the Colonial Subject in Discourse: A Marxist-Feminist Reading," University of Illinois, Teaching Institute in Marxism and the Interpretation of Culture, June–July 1983.

185 Judith Williamson, *Decoding Advertisements: Ideology and Meaning in Advertisement,* Marion Boyars, London, 1978.

186 Janet Wolff *The Social Production of Art,* St. Martins, New York, 1981.

187 For an elaboration of this argument and an attempt to relate labeling rituals to social structure, see Stephen J. Pfohl, "Labeling Criminals," in H. Laurence Ross (ed.), *Law and Deviance,* Sage, Beverly Hills, Calif., 1981, pp. 65–97.

188 Carol A. B. Warren "Labeling the Mentally Ill," in H. Laurence Ross (ed.), *Law and Deviance,* Sage, Beverly Hills, Calif., 1981, p. 180.

189 Ross, *Law and Deviance,* p. 10.

190 Anthony Giddens, *Central Problems in Social Theory,* University of California Press, Berkeley, Calif., 1980, p. 5.

191 Greenberg and Humphries, "The Dialectics of Crime Control," p. 213.

192 For a discussion of the term *decentered subject* in recent "poststructuralist" analysis, see Coward and Ellis, *Language and Materialism.*

INDEX

WESTMAR COLLEGE LIBRARY